Ex Libris

EXECUTIVE
MANAGEMENT
PROGRAM

THE PENNSYLVANIA STATE UNIVERSITY
University Park, Pennsylania

July, 79

THE PROCESS OF MANAGEMENT

Prentice-Hall, Inc., Englewood Cliffs, N.J. 07632

THE PROCESS OF MANAGEMENT
Concepts, Behavior, and Practice

William H. Newman Samuel Bronfman Professor of Democratic
Business Enterprise, Graduate School of Business, Columbia University

E. Kirby Warren Professor of Management
Graduate School of Business, Columbia University

Fourth Edition

Library of Congress Cataloging in Publication Data

Newman, William Herman
    The process of management.

    Includes bibliographies and index.
    1. Industrial management. I. Warren, E. Kirby,
joint author. II. Title.
HD31.N484 1976   658.4   76–25060
ISBN 0–13–723429–5

Cover design by Felix Cooper.

THE PROCESS OF MANAGEMENT   Concepts, Behavior, and Practice.   Fourth edition.
by William H. Newman and E. Kirby Warren.
© 1977, 1972, 1967, 1961 by Prentice-Hall, Inc., Englewood Cliffs, New Jersey   07632.
Printed in the United States of America.

10 9 8 7 6 5 4 3

PRENTICE-HALL INTERNATIONAL, INC., London
PRENTICE-HALL OF AUSTRALIA, PTY. LIMITED, Sydney
PRENTICE-HALL OF CANADA, LTD., Toronto
PRENTICE-HALL OF INDIA PRIVATE LIMITED, New Delhi
PRENTICE-HALL OF JAPAN, INC. Tokyo
PRENTICE-HALL OF SOUTHEAST ASIA PTE. LTD., Singapore
WHITEHALL BOOKS LIMITED, Wellington, New Zealand

Contents

Preface

Concern with improving the quality of management continues to accelerate —worldwide. New pressures such as inflation, energy shortages, changes in life-styles, equal opportunity, personal accountability—along with expectations of rising supplies of goods and services—keep managers in a central role in our society. And more attention to not-for-profit ventures helps single out managing as a distinct social process.

Fortunately, we are also learning more about the process of managing. Significant research is underway on behavior of people in managerial situations, and actual practice is being scrutinized with a variety of analytical techniques. This research provides insight, sometimes confirming widely held beliefs, sometimes pointing to a needed shift in emphasis. Especially important, it helps us adapt basic concepts to new situations and to an increasing diversity of joint ventures.

The professional manager, the person who must apply these managerial concepts and insights to specific situations, needs a way of thinking about his total task. Of necessity, he is primarily interested in achieving results. And for this purpose the manager wants the concepts stated in an integrated framework directly applicable to his concerns.

The *process* approach provides this practical framework for thinking about managing. It is by far the approach most widely used by business executives. Foreign enterprises and not-for-profit ventures also find the process viewpoint suited to their managerial tasks. An added virtue is that specific techniques such as management-by-objectives, strategy formulation, organization development, cybernetic control, and the like can be quickly placed in a broader context.

In focusing on the *process of managing,* as we do in this book, we are therefore dealing with concepts that have direct usefulness to persons in managerial positions. Moreover, we are developing an underlying framework that is a basic prerequisite to many advanced techniques and to sensing the relevance of most of the behavioral research in the field.

New features in this edition of *The Process of Management* include:

Activating. An innovative, action-oriented way of looking at the whole spectrum of power, motivation, and leadership is presented in Part VI. Starting from a manager's task of putting plans into action, the new Part presents an operational framework that a manager can use in the vital step of activating. The contingencies covered range from employee opposition, through indifference, to self-directed commitment.

Not-for-profit management. Each Part of the fourth edition has a Note showing how concepts covered in that Part apply to managing not-for-profit enterprises. These Notes will be particularly helpful to instructors who wish to have their course deal with both profit-seeking and not-for-profit enterprises.

Intraorganization politics. Building on political scientist Graham Allison's three models of decision making, a political dimension is added to the more familiar rational and bureaucratic viewpoints. Frankly examining politics, a new chapter confronts a set of issues that today's students know exist. It also invites greater use of political-science concepts in business-management courses. We are aware that for some people politics has a sordid connotation. In a broader sense, however, politics is as inevitable as informal organization, and a competent manager needs to know how to harness political forces.

A fresh array of cases. These include new cases from "service" industries and manufacturing, small firms and large ones, public and private enterprises, as well as two classics from earlier editions. Because each one is multifaceted, these cases can be used in several ways: case discussion first, followed by study of concepts; text analysis interwoven with cases; concentration on text and outside readings, with the cases being used for review and application. The optimum arrangement will depend on the educational objectives, the time available, and the background that readers bring to the endeavor.

The entire text has been updated, including substantial revision of chapters on organization and growth and on different modes of control. Most of the suggestions for further reading list newly published material. The questions for class discussion have been revised to keep them relevant to current events and issues.

The introduction of *activating* as a key concept called for a change in sequence of Parts of the book. We now build a clearer link between planning and controlling by turning to control in Part V, immediately following our exploration of the planning process. Then Part VI deals with activating based on the total design of organization–planning–control.

The sequence of chapters and Parts, however, is primarily for convenience in exposition. In real life, the phases of managing are closely interrelated. A total, integrated management structure must be developed for each specific company, as we stress frequently throughout the book. But because all aspects of a complex subject cannot be discussed at the same time, we start our analysis with the structure of work and then weave in additional elements. Once the elements are understood, they can be fitted together into harmonious designs suited to unique company requirements.

Two associated books are available for expanded study of *The Process of Management,* and both have been revised to tie into the fourth edition. A new *Study Guide* has been written by J. E. Schnee, and a new edition of the readings book, *The Progress of Management,* is being published concurrently. The availability of these related books creates wide flexibility in the way this fourth edition of *The Process of Management* can be used.

It is impractical to acknowledge all the helpful comments and suggestions coming from users of the previous edition, literally from every continent of the world. Nevertheless, we do want to note several specific contributions: Harvey W. Wallender III, Director of Research, Council of the Americas, made substantial contributions to the Not-for-Profit Notes; Edmond H. Curcuru of the University of Connecticut wrote the Delaware Corporation case; Jerome E. Schnee of Rutgers University carried primary responsibility for coordinating the related publications with this book. We also benefited from thoughtful reviews by Professor James E. Gates, Department of Management, College of Business Administration, The University of Georgia; Dr. James Gatza, Director of Management Education, American Institute for Property and Liability Underwriters, Malvern, Pennsylvania; Professor Paul D. Miller, Institute of Middle Management, University of Miami, Coral Gables, Florida; and Professor Sherman Tingey, College of Business Administration, Arizona State University, Tempe, Arizona. Our secretary, Camilla C. Koch, has ably and cheerfully shepherded the entire revision process from illegible notes, through bewildering sets of manuscripts, to final page proofs. For all this help we are very grateful.

The Samuel Bronfman Foundation, through its sustaining grant to the Graduate School of Business, has made possible a wide array of our management studies, many of which are reflected in this book. In the terminology of Part VI, close congruence exists between the aims of the Foundation and our interests, and we hope the Foundation trustees are as enthusiastic as we are about this latest aid to management education.

WILLIAM H. NEWMAN
E. KIRBY WARREN

Introduction: Social Role of Managers

THE MISSION OF MANAGEMENT

Modern mankind's aims and aspirations call for unprecedented cooperative effort. Our capacity to rebuild the slums, to eliminate pollution, to give individuals an opportunity for self-expression, to raise the standard of living, and to achieve our many other social and personal objectives rests on joint activity. If individuals or even whole tribes attempt to be self-sufficient—producing their own food, clothing, and shelter—subsistence is meager at best. But when people join together in various enterprises, pooling their resources and exchanging their outputs with many other persons or enterprises, they grasp the means to flourish.

Management seeks to make such cooperative enterprises work smoothly. Managers are needed to convert disorganized resources of people, machines, and money into a useful enterprise. They conceive of the service an enterprise can render, mobilize the required means of production, coordinate activities both within the enterprise and with the outside world, and inspire people associated with the enterprise to work toward common objectives. Managers are the activating element.

In the past, management concepts have been vigorously applied in private firms, but the need for effective managers is just as pressing in nonprofit enterprises, such as hospitals, training centers, space agencies, urban transport, and wildlife refuges. In today's world of increasing specialization, complexity, size, and multinational dependence, the task of achieving coordinated action has been intensified.

To understand the significance of managing, let us take a closer look at the role managers play in our society.

Multiple Integration

One key facet of management is integration. The successful firm must be integrated externally with its environment and internally among its departments.

External integration. Every enterprise, be it a university or a steel mill, requires continuing give-and-take relationships with an array of contributors. Consumers provide markets, suppliers provide materials and equipment, investors provide capital, local governments provide functioning communities, and so on. Typically, the relationship with each contributor extends over an indefinite period, and benefits flow both ways—to the contributor and to the firm.

Each of these relationships is dynamic. For instance, the amount, specifications, and delivery schedule that a company desires for its raw materials will change as it adjusts to shifting consumer desires. Likewise, a supplier faces his own shifts in costs, other demands, and capacity. Consequently, continuing mediation is needed to maintain a mutually acceptable flow. Even though the give-and-take between an enterprise and its community or its financial advisor involves intangibles, the need for a sustained exchange of benefits is no less vital.

Management is concerned with more than maintaining good relations with each contributing group separately. In addition, it must make sure that the "price" for cooperation desired by one contributor is compatible with the requirements of *all* the others. For example, before a manufacturer can promise a customer goods of a certain quality at a specific price for delivery on a given date, he must be sure that the supplier of raw materials will not insist on condi-

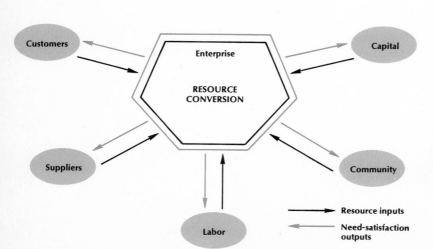

Figure 1–1 A manager must integrate 1) the flow of resources from the environment to his unit and 2) the conversion of these resources within the unit.

tions that hinder him from keeping his promises.[1] Another issue of integration arises when the college administrator is trying to induce alumni to support the kind of education that appeals to students and at the same time to attract students to the kind of education the alumni are supporting.

Employees pose a dual integration problem for management: 1) They, like other contributors, must find the satisfactions derived from their association with the enterprise sufficiently attractive to "take the job." At the same time, the inducements provided by the company (such as steady employment, suitable pay, interesting work) must be compatible with necessary inducements to other contributors. 2) In addition, while they are on the job, employees are a volatile element of internal integration—as we shall see in many parts of this book.

Integrating the enterprise externally with its key contributors is a never-ending task. Much more than price negotiations is involved. Dependability, agreement on timing, numerous intangible benefits and inconveniences, adaptability to needs of either party—all enter the picture. Fortunately, many aspects of these relationships are covered by custom or even by legal regulation; without some such stability, the cooperative action of diverse groups would be impossible. But change is sure to be occurring somewhere in the total system, and adjustments to meet this change are likely to impinge on existing arrangements with other contributors.

Internal integration. If an enterprise is going to fulfill its side of all agreements with contributors, internal operations must be astutely managed. Here, also, integration is vital. The actions of various departments must be synchronized—people must be hired and trained so that they are available when needed, and the like. Balance in allocating resources and in setting priorities must be adjusted in terms of external demands. While such regulating is being pursued, management must also cultivate enthusiasm for achieving the multifold mission of the enterprise.

A vital part of management's task is integrating the efforts of employees, each of whom has his own values and aspirations, into a company program. The program itself reflects the pressures of synchronization and of balancing claims for limited resources (all of which is restrained and shaped by arrangements necessary to keep contributors contributing).

Innovation as Well as Adaptation

For many years a manager was widely regarded as a person who merely adapted to his situation. If demand for his products fell off, he cut back his production; if a new source of low-cost raw materials opened up, he switched

---

[1] The English language at times compels the use of the masculine gender for pronouns in the third person singular. Throughout this book, therefore, the use of "he" and "his" should be interpreted as meaning "he or she" and "his or hers," and as referring to women as well as men.

suppliers; if labor became scarce, he raised his wage rates to get the workers he needed. According to this conception, a manager performed an essential function—responding to changing conditions—but his actions were dictated by forces beyond his control. The early economists clearly held this view. Consequently, they gave scant attention to the problems of management; in fact, their attitude still permeates much of economic literature.

Actually, a modern manager goes well beyond adapting; he exercises a positive influence to make things happen. When he anticipates that the need for his product will drop off, the manager seeks new products or services so as to maintain employment of the resources he has mobilized; he takes the initiative in looking for cheaper sources of energy and promotes their development; he sponsors research for more economical methods of production; he tries to anticipate his manpower needs and trains people to fill them. In short, he is a dynamic, innovating force.

This self-confident, aggressive attitude reflects a deep-seated sense of obligation, or mission. He is not complete master of his activities, of course; indeed, he must be highly sensitive to a wide range of pressures and restrictions. But a manager does more than simply adjust passively. He *initiates* changes in his operating situation and *follows through* with action that, to some extent, makes dreams come true.

Society's Changing Needs

During the past hundred years, management attention has been directed primarily to increasing the output of goods and services desired by a growing population. The unprecedented size of our gross national product attests to the success of these efforts.

National priorities are shifting. Now management must deal with new emphases, including:

1) *Individual self-expression.* The rising generation of both men and women wants meaningful jobs—as well as the fruits of high productivity.
2) *Racial and urban problems.* Society must make racial equality meaningful; interwoven with this is urban renewal.
3) *Pollution control.* Our material achievements are fast overtaking the finite capacity of our natural environment, as is painfully evident in the energy crisis and in air and water pollution.
4) *Health, education, and welfare.* An ever-increasing share of our natural resources is being directed into such things as medical care, education, public recreation, pensions.
5) *Guns and butter.* Our combined space and military expenditures are already on a scale that challenges our ability to have both guns and butter.

These new priorities affect the managerial task in various ways. Points 4 and 5 emphasize the high value attached to increasing the output of goods and services. Their major effect will be a sharp rise in the role of nonprofit enterprises; and this emphasizes the urgency of extending our best managerial practice beyond the business corporation.

The racial and pollution issues pose dual tasks for management. Tremendous allocations of resources will be necessary, so the pressure for high productivity continues. In addition, significant adjustments of internal operating practices must be made to provide job opportunities and to preserve our natural resources.

Individual self-expression is even more a matter of devising new arrangements for internal operations. Job structure, decentralization, freedom versus regulation, and similar issues (which we examine in later chapters) are involved.

Clearly, these new national priorities, and others that will undoubtedly arise, create additional management problems of internal and external integration. They add to the challenge. The task of maintaining workable balances among all the diverse forces calls for a high order of ingenuity; and in contributing to solutions, a manager is dealing with social reform at the level of concrete action.

A single executive rarely performs all the managerial tasks we have been discussing (except in a small "single-person" business). Instead, delegation and use of staff allow the total managerial job to be divided among a variety of people (as we shall see in Chapters 3 and 4). Nevertheless, the concepts of external and internal integration are useful in understanding the job of a department manager or a first-line supervisor. Such managers have to integrate "externally" with other departments and service units of their company, and they have an internal-integration problem within their own unit.

IMPROVING MANAGERIAL EFFECTIVENESS

Asserting, as we do, that management is one of the most vital and exciting activities flags a career opportunity. But knowing of an opportunity and being prepared to grasp it are quite different. This book is directed toward the latter —toward helping present and potential managers improve their ability to manage.

We shall explore the managerial process and subprocesses, which can be applied to all sorts of enterprises—small and large, profit-seeking and not-for-profit. However, before embarking on this analysis, which focuses on the modern *process* of managing, several different ways of viewing management should be identified. Each of these viewpoints helps us understand what managers do. It will be useful to know in advance how such insights are woven into the basic approach adopted in this book.

The ancient story of blind men describing an elephant fits here. One felt the elephant's leg and spoke of a tree; another took hold of the tail and thought it like a rope; a third compared the elephant's side to a wall, while a fourth judged the ear to be a huge leaf. Each man had part of the truth, but over-emphasized his particular observation. All the following views of managing give us helpful insights, but we have to combine them to comprehend the full task of a manager. Our specific interest is what each viewpoint can contribute to improving managerial effectiveness.

The Productivity Approach

The oldest theories of management, indeed the mainstream of ideas, concern productivity. Attention in this approach centers on learning how to *produce in abundance*.

Two supporting ideas are implied when we speak of productivity: (1) A productive operation yields *results*—results in terms of the goods and services sought by the manager. Here we take a tough and pragmatic stand about whether a specific practice actually produces desired results. (2) A productive operation is *efficient*. The ratio of outputs to inputs is high.

Scientific Management. The first systematic study of management in the United States was made by production engineers. Frederick W. Taylor and his associates shifted an interest in production bonuses to a focus on management, and thus launched what became known in 1910 as *Scientific Management*.

Before bonuses could be set, Taylor insisted, the best conditions and manner of doing a job must be determined. To ensure that machines operated properly, he insisted on preventive maintenance and on keeping tools properly sharpened in a central toolroom. For these methods to work, raw materials could not vary, so he set up raw-material specifications and quality-control checks. Also, to prevent delays due to time lost in giving workers new assignments, careful production scheduling, dispatching, and internal-transport systems were established. Finally, workers suited to the newly designed jobs had to be selected and trained. Only when all of these conditions were met was Taylor ready to use time study to determine a standard day's work.

This sort of approach creates a minor revolution in a shop or hospital that has operated in a haphazard, traditional manner—a revolution in the method of work, in planning and control by management, and in productivity. Nevertheless, these basic concepts, nurtured in a machine shop, have been adapted to all sorts of production operations in plants throughout the world.

The founders of Scientific Management made two great contributions: (1) They invented and developed an array of techniques that vastly improve productivity. The United States could never have grown into the world's leading industrial nation without their concepts; and developing nations must master these techniques if their output aspirations are to become realities.(2) More important, they fundamentally altered the way we think about management problems. Instead of relying on tradition and intuition, we now believe any management problem should be subjected to the same kind of critical analysis, inventive experiment, and objective evaluation that Taylor applied in his machine shop.

Extensions of the productivity approach. The analytical productivity approach soon moved beyond the plant to all divisions of an enterprise. Notable improvements arose, for example, from systematic arrangements for recruiting, training, promoting, compensating, and providing a variety of fringe benefits to *personnel*. Financial *budgeting* and cost analysis, originally control mechanisms but soon used for planning as well, are now applied to all areas of any kind of enterprise. A steady flow of *mechanization* and automation has transferred from workers to machines a wide array of tasks that can be standardized.

Best known for their use in industrial firms, all these productivity techniques can easily be adapted to nonprofit enterprises that perform large volumes of similar activities.

Many of our modern concepts of planning and control are derived from the productivity approach. Its direct tie between desired results and management methods avoids the abstractions that tend to clutter other approaches. To be sure, we have expanded its scope and time horizon and have added ways to gain flexibility; and especially we have tempered its mechanistic assumptions with insights from behavioral science.

The Behavioral Approach

The behavioral approach to management is oriented to *research,* rather than to the successful practice emphasized in the productivity approach. Some research does have practical application, but the behavioral scientist is primarily interested in describing and explaining. Consequently, in seeking guides for management practice, we must select those theories and ideas that relate directly to management and then convert them into operational terms.

From 1927 to 1932, Elton Mayo and Fritz Roethlisberger made a landmark study of the Western Electric Company. In their conclusions they stressed that workers respond to their *total* work situation and that attitudes toward their work and their social relations constitute an important part of this total. A corollary of such a conclusion is that the early writers on Scientific Management and many people in personnel management had acted on an inadequate notion of worker motivation.

Controlled management experiments in real-life settings, such as those at Western Electric, are rare. We do try many new arrangements, but typically these are tests of feasibility; we pick what we think is the best idea and then we see whether it works. To experiment with all opportunities—both good and bad—under carefully controlled operating conditions, as is done in a laboratory, is far too complex and expensive for most management problems; often, indeed, it is impossible.

Social psychologists, however, experiment with small bits of human behavior in laboratory conditions, and often their findings throw light on some management issue. For instance, we have learned a lot about small-group behavior from such experiments. Also, an array of psychological studies on individual perception, motivation, learning, and other responses help greatly in designing jobs and methods.

Sociologists rely primarily on field studies. Here, the classic is Max Weber's insightful observation of *bureaucracy* in government, churches, and political parties. For him, pure bureaucracy includes (1) a division of labor with each job clearly defined and filled by a technically qualified person, (2) a well-established hierarchy with clear lines of authority and appropriate staffs and salary for those at each level, and (3) a systematic set of aims and regulations so that actions can be impersonal and coordinated.

Even though many of the ideas need more supporting research, managers can learn a great deal from behavioral science, which often supplies solid verification of intuitive judgments. More important, new ways of thinking about a problem are often suggested.

Concepts and insights from the behavioral sciences take up a substantial part of this book. Parts, chapters, and sections focus predominantly on human behavior; in fact, the entire management process can be seen as conditioning behavior. However, except for Weber, behavioral scientists offer no comprehensive management systems; their chief aim is research, not devising managerial tools. Consequently, we have to use behavioral insights primarily as important supplements and restraints on formal mechanisms. Since our goal is to improve managerial effectiveness, and not just to summarize research data, we have built the book around an operational framework and woven behavioral-science findings into that.

The Decision-Making Emphasis

A third view of management deals only with the way executives make decisions. A political scientist, Graham Allison, and his associates have recently developed the most comprehensive framework available for analyzing managerial decisions. They suggest that to understand why a company decides to open an office in Singapore or to fire its president, three kinds of analyses are necessary. The three analyses—or models—are labeled: the rational-individual, bureaucratic, and political.

The rational-individual model presumes that decisions are based on thorough analysis, careful weighing of evidence, and logical choice reflecting clear criteria. Here, concepts from microeconomics and mathematic formulae from *operations research* provide refined logical propositions. Although many managerial problems are not specific enough or lack the data needed for such neat quantitative solutions, a formal approach to decision-making does force managers to think more sharply.

The bureaucratic model looks at how decisions are made within an established organization. For major problems, no single person can do all the analysis prescribed for a fully rational choice, so the task is divided into pieces

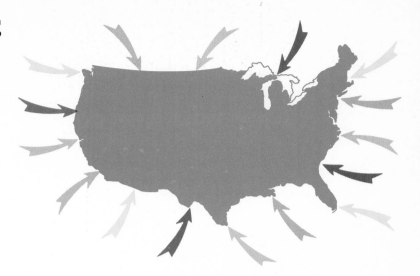

Figure 1–2 As immigrants from many nations have contributed to our national heritage, so have several approaches formed our modern concepts of managerial processes.

and dispersed throughout the organization. Also it is spread over time. This dispersion and the mechanisms necessary to handle the bits and pieces profoundly change the answers that emerge. Obviously for managers who must rely on the help and decisions of their subordinates, this second view of decision-making is very illuminating.

A political view of decision-making is even further removed from individual rationality than the bureaucratic model. For some people, politics is immoral and therefore they deny its existence. Realists recognize political behavior but have difficulty predicting the decisions that arise from political pressures. Nevertheless, no manager can afford to overlook the way politics conditions the choices that are made.

All three views of decision-making help us design planning mechanisms for a company. When combined, they are far more powerful than the single approaches to decision-making we previously relied upon. Nevertheless, they deal with only part of a manager's job. Making wise choices is obviously important—but motivating, controlling, and coordinating are also essential.

In Parts Three and Four we shall examine ways each of these decision-making models can be used by managers. The focus there is twofold—first to relate the concepts to realistic operating situations faced by managers, and second to place decision-making within the total managerial process so that the decisions themselves are better and their execution is more effective.

The Systems Approach

The total is greater than the sum of its parts—especially when we are thinking about a total system. Just as a TV set differs from a collection of parts, managing is more than an assembly of plans and reports. The pieces must fit together into a workable system.

Starting from the way a medical doctor must think of the total body, or a telephone engineer must think of all the parts of a communications system, a theory about systems in general has been developed. This theory applies to many complex situations, ranging from space exploration to nursery schools.

Managing a company can be viewed as a system. The various moves that executives make—borrowing capital, controlling quality, hiring black executives—do indeed interact. By relating all these moves in terms of an overall system, we can develop a much stronger, coordinated force.

In this book we repeatedly stress the benefit of thinking about managing as a total system. Thus, plans create the need for resources and organization; control reports provide the basis for new plans; and so forth. We enthusiastically embrace the system viewpoint. But a systems view is only one dimension. Before we can consider interaction, we must know the nature of the pieces, what purposes they serve, the conditions in which they work well, and their cost. Also we need to know about the resources and requirements of the environment. Conceiving the total system is an essential but insufficient step in good management design.

The Contingency Viewpoint

The "contingency" viewpoint is a currently fashionable expression for a simple, fundamental idea. There is no single best way to manage in all circumstances; instead, what should be done in any particular situation is contingent upon the needs of that situation. Only a quack doctor prescribes the same medicine to all his patients. The professional first makes a diagnosis; then drawing upon his knowledge of alternative actions and their likely effect, he prescribes for the individual case.

Likewise in management. In our studies—and in this book—we can describe likely issues, suggest alternatives that have worked well in some companies, identify the pros and cons of these alternatives, and propose ways to develop a good fit for a selected alternative. But always the particular course drawn from this background should be carefully fitted to the unique local situation. Managing is too complex, dynamic, and uncertain for pat solutions. Its contingent quality, nevertheless, makes it challenging and rewarding.

Need for an Operational Framework

All the streams of thought summarized in this section contribute to the emerging profession of management. Each is making a distinctive contribution, and we shall draw freely on their ideas throughout this book.[2] Our quick review

---

[2] The *process* view of managing developed in this book provides a broad base for study of more specialized subjects such as the five approaches noted above, and fields like operations research, organization theory, budgetary control, personnel management, behavioral research, systems engineering, and the like. Such subjects will become more meaningful and useful when they are seen in relation to the total management process.

noted, however, that none of these approaches gives us a full picture of managing. So we face the task of relating valuable ideas within a workable scheme (and of translating special jargon into simple, understandable terms).

For dealing with this array of ideas, thinking of management as a process has great advantages. Focusing on the process of managing is 1) *operational*, because it expresses ideas in terms of actions a manager must take; 2) *comprehensive*, embracing the major tasks of managing; 3) *universal*, in that all managers should give some attention to each part of the process; 4) and a key for harnessing executive action to the "mission of managers," as discussed in the beginning of this chapter.

Since the process of management serves as the framework of this book, we should take a close look at its nature and components.

THE MANAGEMENT PROCESS

Social processes, of which management is one, are common in civilized society. We worship together, play group games, stand in line while we wait for buses, negotiate contracts, and try people for murder. In each case, because we have an established pattern of what we should do and what we expect others to do, we can achieve a result that would not otherwise be feasible. The particulars of a process may, of course, be changed from time to time. A major college football game has rituals for spectators and players that are quite different from those of the old-fashioned jousting match, and a modern murder trial has changed considerably from legal procedures in the days of Henry VIII. But to understand what is happening in any social activity—including the management of an enterprise—and, especially, to ensure that what we want to happen does happen, we need a keen appreciation of the social process involved.

Management, like education or government, is a *continuing* process. There are always new mouths to feed, fresh minds to stimulate, and more people to govern. And satisfying today's needs invites higher aspirations for tomorrow. Thus new problems crop up as old ones are solved. For purposes of analysis, of course, we may focus on a single problem, or just one series of actions that lead to a specific end; but in practice, a manager must learn to deal simultaneously with a wide range of problems, each in a different stage of resolution.

Managing is so complex that our minds cannot consider all its facets at the same moment. We need to divide the whole activity into parts in order to grasp the full significance of each, just as we get a clear picture of a company by looking separately at its financial statements, its key personnel, its reputation, its facilities, its policies and organization, its traditions and social structure. Then we can fit the different aspects into a total system.

The total task of management can be divided into four elements: organizing, planning, controlling, and activating. Although all are closely interrelated, each of these elements can be analyzed as a subprocess. Each is vital to the success of managers at all levels—from first-line supervisors to presidents. And these four elements are present in managing every kind of enterprise—small and large, manufacturing and selling, partnership and corporation, profit and nonprofit. While looking briefly at these four processes, we shall point out the plan of this book.

Organizing

Once the work of an enterprise grows beyond what a single craftsman can do, organization becomes necessary. We have to assign the various tasks to different people and to coordinate their efforts. As the enterprise expands, this process leads to departments and divisions, each of which has its particular mission. One way to think about the resulting organization is as a complex machine—say, an airplane designed for transatlantic passenger service. Each part of a plane performs a necessary function—supplying power, pressure, heat, steering, communication, and so forth; *and* the different parts are so carefully balanced and fitted together that changing any one of them often calls for an adjustment in several others.

A manager must also view organization as a social arrangement, because it is composed of people rather than physical objects. The people who are assigned tasks are independent, self-respecting individuals with a variety of motives; informal groups influence the way persons respond to managerial action; and the attitudes of all these people are continually shifting and evolving. In organizing, then, we must seek ways of getting the necessary work done at the same time we build a social structure that helps meet the needs of people doing the work. The technical and behavioral aspects of organizing will be examined in Parts One and Two respectively.

Planning

A key activity of all managers is planning the work under their direction. Working with each other and with the people who will carry out the plans, they clarify objectives and set goals for each subdivision; establish policies and standard methods to guide those who do the work; and develop programs, strategies, and schedules to keep the work moving toward the objectives. Most of these plans they will have to readjust periodically in light of new information and changes in operating conditions. And time and again, managers will face questions about how detailed the plans should be, who should participate in formulating them, and how much freedom of action should be given to subordinates.

The process of planning can best be understood if we first examine the basic stages in making a decision rationally: diagnosing the problem, finding good alternative solutions, projecting the results of each alternative, and, finally, selecting the one course of action to be followed. We shall analyze these elements of rational decision-making in detail in Part Three.

Decision-making, however, is not the act of an isolated individual; it takes place in the organization we have established. In fact, many different persons may contribute to the formulation and final selection of a major plan. Consequently, since we need to know how the organization can be used most effectively in this decision-making (or planning) process, we explore in Part Four the topic of decision-making in a formal or "bureaucratic" organization. Also in Part Four, we consider internal political aspects of planning.

Measuring and Controlling

For a ship to reach its destination without sailing far off course, the captain regularly "takes his bearings." A manager, likewise, must measure his progress if he is to reach his objectives. And when he discovers that operations are not proceeding according to plan, he takes corrective action to get back on course or, if this is not feasible, readjust his plans. This process of measuring progress, comparing it with plans, and taking corrective action is called *control*. In practice, as our analysis in Part Five will show, control is not so simple as it sounds. Measuring intangibles, such as customer goodwill or executive morale, poses difficulties, and devising corrective action that both overcomes an immediate difficulty and creates a favorable climate for future performance often calls for ingenuity. Moreover, the dispersal of activities that result from organization creates problems of just who should control what.

Activating

To these three processes—organizing, planning, and controlling—we must add a final step, putting the plans into action. All our preparation and systems come to naught unless people throughout the organization actually execute our carefully drawn decisions. This fourth phase of managing we call *activating*.

More than simply giving instructions is involved. A wise manager first predicts how his subordinates will respond to his request. And if that predicted response is inadequate, he takes steps to shift the response. He may use his power to coerce people to fulfill his requests; or he may cultivate voluntary, though indifferent, compliance; or compromise and bargain to gain compliance; or perhaps he will be able to establish genuine commitment. As we shall see in Part Six, considerable skill is required to select an activating mode best suited

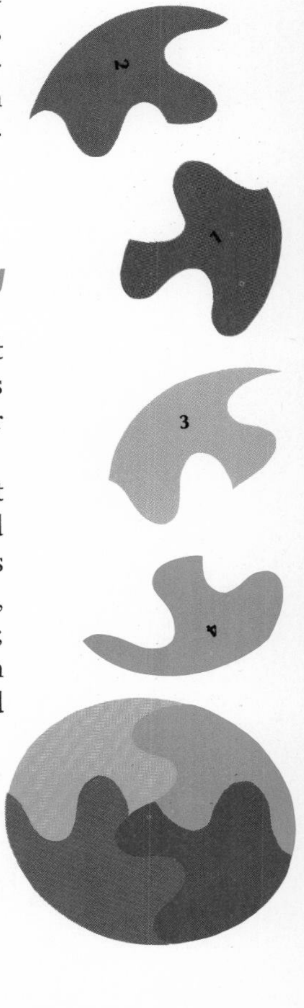

Figure 1–3 Managing is so complicated that a separate examination of its subprocesses is necessary for a full understanding. But we should never lose sight of the way the processes fit together to form the whole.

to the situation that confronts a manager at the moment he wishes to "put the show on the road."

FRAMEWORK RATHER THAN PROCEDURE

In the following chapters, then, we shall examine each of these four elements—organizing, planning, controlling, and activating—in some detail, and we shall divide these major aspects of the overall management process into even narrower subprocesses. Such a systematic view of management provides a convenient device 1) for diagnosing complex management problems and 2) for working on improvements at one stage without losing sight of other stages.

But a framework that helps us think in an orderly fashion is not necessarily a step-by-step procedure that we must follow. Actually, when we deal with a concrete management problem, the available information is not neatly classified and labeled; instead, a great array of facts hits us at once, while some data remains stubbornly hidden. In response to such confusion, our thoughts tend to flit first to one subject and then to another. So the chief purpose of a conceptual framework, such as the systematic examination of the management process in this book, is to help us quickly to place diverse ideas in a useful order.

The framework is more than a series of pigeonholes to tuck ideas in, however; for among the pigeonholes there is a rational relationship that we know in advance. Thus, when we mentally classify a new bit of information as bearing on the long-range objectives of department-A, we can immediately relate it to a host of other ideas we have stored in our mind; and, in this relation, the piece of information takes on meaning because it contributes to our comprehension of the total situation. Mankind has advanced from a primitive state largely by developing orderly ways of thinking about problems; in proposing a systematic approach to management, then, we are simply following this time-proved method.

There are, of course, many ways to think about so complicated a subject as management. The approach presented in this book has proved very useful for both practical and theoretical analyses of a wide variety of management situations. So while we should be alert for improvements, we can proceed with confidence that this approach has practical value for anyone in a managerial or staff position or for the researcher who is trying to understand how managers get things done.

One further introductory note: Because people with diverse backgrounds talk about management, words are used in different ways. Since this is so, we should clarify our terminology. For ease of discussion, we shall use "manager," "executive," and "administrator" as synonyms. And when we deal with person-to-person relationships, we may use "supervisor" or even "boss" to designate the manager who sits *immediately* above his "subordinate" in the organization hierarchy. For these terms, we are simply following common usage. Other words, which have more precise meanings, will be defined as we encounter them.

Design of This Book

This book contains two kinds of aids for improving managerial ability: text and cases. The text discussion assists in analyzing the numerous facets of managing and in finding ways to proceed. It provides help in recognizing problems, seeing their interrelationships, conceiving of possible solutions, and developing sensitivity to the advantages and limitations of alternative solutions. Mastery of the "mental framework" provides a foundation for developing skill.

At the end of each Part, we briefly explore difficulties that may arise in applying to not-for-profit enterprises the management concepts drawn from experience in profit-seeking companies.

Cases then offer an opportunity to start applying the general concepts to specific situations; and a discussion of proposed solutions with other persons will give some check on how well the concepts are being applied. At best, these cases can offer only a beginning in the practice that is necessary for developing managerial proficiency. But this beginning is quite important, for it *builds a bridge* between general concepts and concrete situations; and we hope it will establish a pattern for going on to the use of concepts in real life.

Careful study of the cases serves three other purposes:

1) They help us overcome the unreal separations that are inevitable in any analytical treatment of an interdependent phenomenon. For example, we shall discuss organizing, planning, and activating, separately. But in actual problems, the plans and policies of a company (Part Four) are partly determined by the organization structure (Parts One and Two), and vice versa. And the activating mode of an executive (Part Six) is influenced somewhat by the organization structure. So, in actuality a manager must solve planning and activating problems *along with* organization problems. Most of our cases present a whole situation; that is, they do not merely illustrate the issues in any one chapter. Instead, they provide a way of seeing the interrelated application of various concepts from all chapters in a realistic, whole-problem sense. They provide a sense of the *system,* while the chapters enable us to concentrate on the parts.

2) They make the ideas in the chapters more *meaningful.* Sometimes we shall find that an idea appears rather simple—even obvious—as explained in the text, but only when we apply it to a real problem will its full and complex meaning begin to unfold. Applying concepts helps to clarify and reinforce their meaning.

3) They help show that we do not always have facts and concepts that cover all aspects of a complex management problem. As in medicine, management problems often include variables that theory does not explain; there are unique elements in each specific situation. At times, then, all the answers needed to solve a case *neatly* will not be found in the book. This can be very frustrating. Nevertheless, it is a difficulty faced by leaders down through the ages. Actually, it is precisely this need to blend general concepts with the stubborn facts of a practical situation that makes management challenging and fascinating.

CONCLUSION

Two broad developments have made the study of management timely. (1) In a world where hopes and aspirations are mounting, managers play a crucial role in fulfilling these new goals—and we expect it of them. They initiate growth as well as adapt to dynamic forces. (2) Fortunately, we are learning more about how this important task can be performed effectively. The recognition of management as a distinct social process has led to many studies by researchers and by executives themselves. And from this study has emerged a whole array of insights and precepts that can be put to practical use.

Treating management as a *process* puts our ideas about managing into *operational* terms—that is, in terms that directly relate to executive decisions and actions. And a further division into the subprocesses of organizing, planning, controlling, and activating provides an analytical framework that has proved useful in all kinds of businesses and nonprofit enterprises.

We can improve our management skill by first learning about these elements of managing, and then by deliberately applying them to concrete situations. Each chapter helps us to learn about managing, and the cases give opportunities to apply the basic concepts.

FOR CLASS DISCUSSION

1) A well-known management consultant wrote a book several years ago entitled *Every Employee a Manager.* Based on the concept of management presented in this chapter, is it possible for *every* employee to be a manager? Which management tasks might be left for "official" managers if every employee were a "manager"?

2) In this chapter, the authors indicate that a manager must innovate as well as adapt and must be "a dynamic, innovating force." If this is indeed a requirement for all managers, does this mean that any person who has subordinates reporting to him must be a dynamic, innovating force?

3) Many otherwise dissimilar groups find agreement in their common tendency to place the blame for many of our current problems on "the system." The system or systems they criticize, run by "managers," are considered impersonal, bureaucratic, inflexible institutions that have not only failed to anticipate or shape change, but have even failed to adapt to it. To what degree do you feel business, as part of "the system," is guilty of these charges? How does your response fit with the material on the mission of management presented in this chapter?

4) Frederick Taylor began most of his pioneer work on management more than 70 years ago. In what ways have social, political, and economic changes in the U.S. affected the basic assumptions on which the productivity approach to management is based?

5) "At the same time that a manager's job is becoming more complicated, society expects management to provide higher pay, stable employment, and attractive jobs." Why should such vital things as wages and employment levels be left to the discretion of individual managers? If they should act in their own interest, rather than in the public interest, what would result?

6) The "system thinker" argues that we must first study the system, to see how it works as an integrated whole. Only after we understand the whole can we begin to take it apart and look at its elements. How does this perspective differ from the one taken in this book? How do you reconcile such differences?

7) In what ways do you feel that the "process of managing" a large private corporation 1) differs from and 2) is similar to the process of managing equally large or larger public or nonprofit organizations, such as hospitals, universities, or government agencies?

Cases

For cases involving issues covered in this chapter, see especially the following. Particularly relevant questions are listed after each case.

Merchantville School System (p. 217), 2, 4, 18
Family Service of Gotham (p. 532), 5, 6, 14, 19
Central Telephone and Electronics (p. 527), 13
Southeast Textiles (p. 620), 6, 8, 16

FOR FURTHER READING

Anshen, M., ed., *Managing the Socially Responsible Corporation.* New York: The Macmillan Company, 1974.

A series of lectures on the problems of companies putting "social-responsibility" programs into action.

Hart, D. K. and W. G. Scott, "The Organization Imperative." *Administration & Society,* November 1975.

A provocative statement about the critical importance of modern organizations as social institutions, and the impact of such organizations on personal values.

Jacoby, N. H., *Corporate Power and Social Responsibility.* New York: The Macmillan Company, 1973.

Develops a social–environment model of the forces to which corporations must adjust in a constructive, dynamic manner.

McFeely, W. M., "The Manager of the Future." *Columbia Journal of World Business,* May 1969.

Knowledge and skill required of future managers.

Paluszek, J. L., *Business and Society: 1976–2000.* New York: AMACOM, 1976.

Business executives' views on where corporate social responsibility is heading. What form will social responsibility of private corporations take in last quarter of the 20th century?

Steiner, G. A., "Social Policies for Business." *California Management Review,* Winter 1972.

Reviews the irresistible pressure for a revised "social contract" for business firms, and suggests that business managers should take initiative in helping to shape this revision.

PART **I** ――――――――――――――

The process of managing can be viewed by a dilettante as an interesting bit of human behavior along with, say, mountain climbing or playing in string quartets. Or we may be concerned with managing as a source of personal income and status. Both views are valid, and the study of management can be both intriguing and rewarding. But the really compelling force underlying the serious study of management is its profound social value.

If we desire to increase our skill in performing this crucial social process, we must examine each of the subprocesses involved. Managing is too complex to comprehend all at once, so we shall probe—in separate parts of the book— four essential aspects: organizing, planning, controlling, and activating. All these subprocesses are interrelated; in life they take place concurrently. We turn first to organizing, merely because it is easiest to perceive.

Organizing helps a manager unite the work of different people in order to achieve goals. Whether the number of people be only a few or thousands, their effective cooperation requires organization. Two elements are invariably present in organizing: dividing the work into jobs and, simultaneously, ensuring that these separate clusters of work are linked together into a team effort. We can see these two elements in a football team, in a hospital, or in a government bureau, as well as in business firms. The success of any of these enterprises depends significantly upon how skillfully their managers assign individual tasks so that they combine into integrated, purposeful action. This basic process— organizing—will be discussed in the following chapters.

Chapter 2—Designing Operating Units. Here we focus on merging simple operating tasks into jobs; linking such jobs into work groups; and then combining work groups into major operating departments and service divisions of the enterprise. The aim is to find those combinations that will bring forth the most effective cooperative effort.

Organizing:

Structural Design

Chapter 3—Designing the Hierarchy: Delegating and Decentralizing. The work of managing must also be allocated. This involves delegating and redelegating to successively lower levels of supervision. In this chapter, we shall see that the scope and degree of decentralization are critical features in this dispersing of authority.

Chapter 4—Use of Staff. As enterprises grow, the task of managing them becomes more complex; thus, we explore the ways staff can lighten the burden of key executives.

Chapter 5—Effect of Growth on Structure. The overall structure of a company must be adjusted as the firm expands. In this chapter, we see how organizations can be adapted to four stages of development: single entrepreneur, departmentalized company, multiple-mission company, and conglomerate.

Chapter 6—New Approaches to Structural Design. Here we look at five frontiers where social and technological pressures are leading to new organizational forms. The modifications of structure take the form of matrix organizations; external, independent staff; a president's office; provision for special-interest groups; and adjustments for use of computers. These are refinements of, not replacements for, the basic organizational elements discussed in preceding chapters.

All these chapters deal with "formal" organization—"formal" in that the patterns of division of work and of personal relationships are deliberately set up and are clearly recognized and discussed by those concerned. The primary interest is to achieve goals of the enterprise; thus the analysis is based largely on the "productivity approach." The more informal aspects of organization, which arise out of social and personal relationships, will be examined in Part Two.

2 Designing
Operating Units

HARNESSING SPECIALIZED EFFORT

Organizing starts with creating operating jobs. Basic operations—such as the actual baking of bread or teaching a class—are assigned to different individuals. Then, to aid in coordinating this work, several of these jobs are combined into sections, sections into departments, and so on until all operations of our enterprise are covered. We may choose to add a variety of advisors and helpers, but it is the operating work that generates the actual flow of services to consumers.

This grouping of operating activities into jobs, sections, and departments —"departmentation" in technical jargon—should be done carefully.[1] For example, the kind of service customers get in a department store or medical office depends greatly on how work is divided. Or to cite production examples, the effectiveness of textile mills in India and electronic plants in the United States has been sharply improved by changing the basis for *combining* operations into sections and departments.

Also, the way work is structured affects the kinds of people who are qualified to be hired and promoted. And after a job is established, employees often guard their roles jealously; in fact, companies and even whole industries (e.g., airlines) have been shut down by jurisdictional disputes.

---

[1] Because the design is deliberately created and explicit, some scholars call it "formal" organization, without any implications of how ceremonial or informal personal relationships may be.

To emphasize the significance of first-level operations, this chapter focuses first on the combining of operating tasks into individual *jobs*. Next we consider grouping jobs into effective *work groups*. Only then do we treat the consolidation of work groups into *departments*.[2] By starting with the simplest units and moving to more complex ones, we can keep the beguiling issues of grand design for an entire enterprise in proper perspective.

SCOPE OF INDIVIDUAL JOBS

How many different tasks can a single person perform well? In practice we find jobs ranging from the nut-tightener on an assembly line to a cabinet-maker who does everything from selecting his raw wood to polishing his finished product. These are extremes. Let us examine several other examples for keys to how much division of labor is desirable.

How Much Division of Labor?

Flying a small plane in Alaska, a bush pilot fuels, loads, navigates, communicates with the ground, calms his passengers, and makes minor repairs. In the operation of a 747 jet, however, these tasks are divided among dozens of persons, each of whom has a limited number of clearly specified things to do. Why the difference?

The explanation lies partly in the large volume of work required to operate a 747. But also we want each person to be highly skilled in his particular tasks, and we want to be sure that adequate attention is given to a task when it is needed. Moreover, the larger payload can support the expense of a multiple crew; so this example suggests that a greater division of labor is desirable if it can be afforded.

In the medical field, general practitioners are now hard to find. Increasingly, doctors are specialists, and the patient spends a lot of time reaching the particular doctor who treats his specific ailment. The reason, as in the 747 crew, is the benefit from a high degree of skill and knowledge. But when we extend this approach to insurance sales representatives, doubts begin to arise. Should we specialize our sales force—one for annuities, another for estate planning, separate people for fire and liability insurance? And the more recent issue, should another specialist sell mutual funds? Several companies have concluded that such specialization is unwarranted. Instead, they argue that a single rela-

---

[2] The departmentation concept can be extended beyond the enterprise into structure of an "industry." The work of the total industry has to be distributed among firms. Although this division is determined by competition, similar issues arise: specialization, coordination, optimum size, maintenance of suitable cost levels, ability to adapt to new kinds of work, and the way firms relate to each other.

tionship with each customer provides a coordinated service and is less expensive, and that these benefits offset gains from high specialization.

The design of jobs in a filling station illustrates another consideration. One worker might only pump gasoline, a second grease cars, and a third serve as cashier. The catch here is providing enough work to keep each person busy. The volume of work fluctuates; also, some jobs take longer than others. So specialization is eliminated in order to ensure full-time jobs.

College teaching is one area in which high division of labor along functional lines has been resisted. The tasks of course design, instruction, and testing could be allocated to separate specialists. However, most college professors resent any interference with "their" courses. In fact, professors are urged to do research and still perform the whole gamut of teaching tasks. The rationale for such a broad job scope includes the ease of coordinating the various phases of teaching and a belief that a man cannot be good at one teaching task without being proficient in all the others. Students themselves undoubtedly have an opinion about the effectiveness of this arrangement!

The question of job *scope*—how many different tasks one is expected to carry out—arises in every walk of life. Because of the way jobs are structured, people quit jobs, professions are built, unions call jurisdictional strikes, psychological security is found or lost, and companies prosper or languish.

Striking a Balance

As the preceding examples show, effective job structure requires a careful assessment of what the physical circumstances permit and of the primary benefits sought. Factors that usually deserve attention include the following.

Benefits of functional specialization. By narrowing the scope of a job, full utilization can be made of any distinctive skill an individual possesses. As a person concentrates on a limited range of duties, he can learn these very well and give them full attention. Wage economies may also arise; instead of paying a premium for a versatile "triple-threat man" for all positions, the more routine tasks can often be assigned to less experienced and less expensive employees.[3]

Need for coordination. Often several tasks should be closely synchronized or coordinated—as in labor negotiations—and one person can do this more easily than several. When information about a specific situation has to be pooled in a single spot, the difficulty of communicating bits of information from person to person may more than offset benefits of specialization. Relevant here is the rule that tasks should be separated only where there is a "clean break," as between lunch and dinner but not during a meal.

---

[3] Whenever a sufficient volume of routine work is isolated, mechanization becomes a possibility; for example, use of computers for office work.

Morale of the operator. How the operator feels about the scope of his job may be vital. The employee's pride in his work and work suited to professional dignity can be positive factors. On the other hand, monotony is depressing for most people. Sometimes monotony can be partially relieved by rotating people from job to job or by allowing the worker to deviate from his set routine. In fact, if a *wide variety* of choices must be made, some operators feel that the job is unreasonably complex. This broad area of human response to organization is explored more fully in Part Two.

Rarely will any single job design be all good or all bad. Some potential benefits of specialization may have to be sacrificed for better coordination and employee morale, or vice versa. That choice depends primarily on values derived from what we call, in Chapter 16, the "master strategy of the enterprise."

Two restraints on designing individual jobs should not be overlooked: (1) The volume of work always places a limit on the division of labor. We do not want a specialist to sit around most of the day waiting to do his part. Also, it takes effort not only to design a sophisticated system of work but also to have the workers adopt it as a normal way of doing things. Such investment is warranted only when the system will have repeated use. (2) One technology may be so superior for some kinds of work that we have little choice in job design. Operating a taxicab, playing first violin in a symphony orchestra, and removing bark by means of a hydraulic machine in a lumber mill are situations of this type.

EFFECTIVE WORK GROUPS

To have well-designed jobs is not enough. The complexities of modern production require the combined efforts of a variety of people. So, after tasks are grouped into jobs, the next step is to combine jobs into work groups. By work groups we mean a set of people who see each other on the job almost daily, whose work is usually interdependent in some respects, and whose output is viewed by outsiders as a single achievement. Of course, it is possible to have a work group composed entirely of managers and staff persons, but for the present we shall concentrate on people doing *operating* work. Social psychologists and others have devoted a lot of attention to behavior within such groups; here, however, we shall consider a more basic issue: How should these groups be formed?

Whenever several similar jobs exist, they can be put in the same section, as suggested in the upper part of Fig. 2–1. For example, selling and computing can each be combined. On the other hand, when several different skills are needed to complete a block of work, jobs can be grouped as indicated in the lower part of the diagram. For example, a salesman, repairman, and bookkeeper could be placed together in a branch office of an office-equipment company. The former grouping we call "functional," the latter "compound."

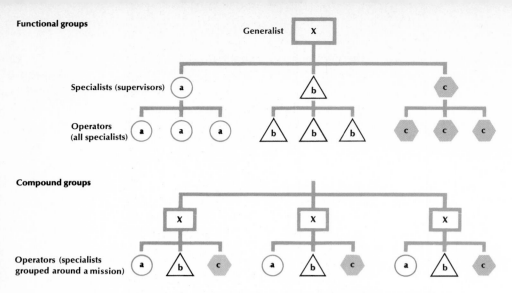

Functional groups

Generalist

Specialists (supervisors)

Operators (all specialists)

Compound groups

Operators (specialists grouped around a mission)

Figure 2–1   In functional groups, operators perform the same kind of work, and their supervisor is a specialist in that field. In compound groups, operators perform different but related work, and their supervisor is more of a generalist concerned with coordination.

Benefits of Compound Groups

Under some circumstances, the use of compound groups permits us to take advantage of a combination of several benefits that are sought in the design of jobs. Individual members of the group can be specialists in different fields, and coordination is achieved by interaction within the group. Furthermore, close personal relations and a sense of group achievement contribute to morale. Small branches of a bank, a 747 airplane crew, and other geographically separated units often have these characteristics. Compound work groups may also be formed around a product or service, such as a maternity ward in a hospital.

A crew of workers operating a highly automated chemical plant or power station is usually a compound group of specialists. In fact the operators on a single assembly line can be viewed as a compound group, although here the design and pace of the equipment carry most of the burden of coordination.

Compound groups should be used especially when local coordination is vital. An industrial-equipment company, for instance, might combine sales, repair service, and parts warehousing in each of its local offices in an effort to provide distinctive customer service. Local coordination is even more vital for a surgical team composed of a surgeon, assisting doctor, anesthetist, and nurses. Here, as in all the previous examples, a clear-cut block of work calls for the efforts of several specialists.

Reasons for Functional Grouping

Attractive though compound groups may be, functional grouping of operations is actually more prevalent. Why so?

Functional grouping usually makes full-time jobs easier to arrange. While a compound group may consist of six sales representatives, two repairmen, and one accountant, it cannot readily be made up of six sales representatives, one and two-thirds repairmen, and five-sixths of an accountant. With the latter workload the spare time of the repairman and the accountant is usually lost. Also the need for different specialists in any one compound group may be high today and low tomorrow. Functional grouping, with interchangeable people in the same group, allows a manager to balance these partial and irregular workloads more efficiently.

When each specialist requires high-cost equipment, the expenses of idle time are even greater. The operator of a multimillion-dollar wind tunnel used in aircraft engineering is an extreme example, but even the office space and company car of a field investigator can be expensive.

Technical supervision is often desirable. Unless the operators themselves possess high professional competence, their manager will normally need substantial technical knowledge. Even when plans are made centrally, the supervisor must interpret policies, resolve on-the-spot problems, coach new employees, and relay to his bosses the information they need. This kind of supervisory work can be done with greater expertise within a functional group. A supervisor need not be the only source of technical guidance, as we shall see in Chapter 4, "Use of Staff," but often his expert understanding of the work being done is essential.

Compatibility within a group and with the supervisor is more likely to

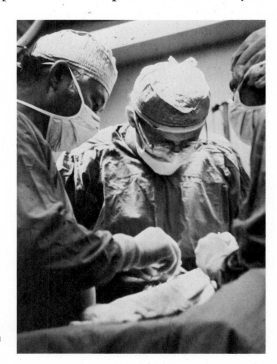

Figure 2–2 A surgical team illustrates 1) clear division of labor within the group and 2) responsive interaction of the group to achieve a coordinated result.

exist in a functional group than in a compound group. Our feeling of compatibility with fellow workers rests heavily on similar attitudes and values—for example, attitudes toward risk-taking, meeting deadlines, short-run versus long-run achievements, and the importance of people versus things. In these terms we can achieve greater compatibility by putting, say, caseworkers together, researchers together, accountants together, and so forth. It is true that such a group tends to reinforce one another's biases and as a result may be less cooperative with other functional groups. But the social satisfactions they derive from their work will also be enhanced.

The design of work groups, then, involves at least broadly a set of considerations that are similar to those used in the formation of individual jobs: benefits of specialization, need for coordination, effect on operators' morale, and expense repeatedly claim attention.

As we shall see in Part Two, work groups tend to become close-knit social groups. Once jelled, they tend to resist change. They can be a great source of strength for an enterprise or a seriously retarding influence. So we should compose these groups with care.

SHAPING MAJOR DEPARTMENTS

To achieve unified action, work groups must be combined into departments. At this level, we as organization designers shift our attention from an array of very specific operations to a broad grouping of these activities that will facilitate central management. The work groups become building blocks. We seek to arrange these blocks so that the major missions of the enterprise receive proper emphasis, while the various operating groups are supported in performing their respective tasks. But as the enterprise adjusts to its changing environment, we may of course have to alter the shape of these major departments.

An enterprise should usually establish as a separate, major department those activities that are most likely to affect its success. The heads of these departments should normally report directly to the chief executive so that he can be in close touch with crucial activities.

What work is emphasized will depend on the nature of the industry and the way a particular firm seeks to be distinctive. Some discount stores, for example, believe that advertising is a primary key to success, so they set up a separate advertising department that reports directly to the president. On the other hand, a computer company—where advertising is much less important—will probably make the advertising department a service division within its sales department. Developing new products is vital to the success of any manufacturer of industrial equipment, so engineering is usually a major department. In contrast, a company that is principally concerned with processing established products—such as a dairy or a textile mill—almost always relegates engineering to a subordinate role in the production department.

Adapting to Change

Growth forced a small manufacturer of instruments to recast his basic organization structure. A resourceful instrument maker and a chemistry instructor had teamed up to make high-quality instruments for laboratories, and the business grew around specially designed equipment. The organization consisted of a production shop, a sales manager, and an office that handled all finance and clerical work. Then the company designed a machine for testing water pollution and found a potential market for hundreds of identical instruments. Sales jumped, and the shop was swamped with work.

The new business called for a major reorganization. Selling a standard item to governments and to utilities differed sharply from selling special designs to laboratories, and repetitive production was a sharp change from making one-of-a-kind instruments. So, instead of merely expanding the three existing departments, the company departmentalized by product line, each of which has its own production and selling subdivisions. A single office department still serves both product departments. Overhead expense is higher in the new setup, but the prospect for preserving the strength of a close-knit, responsive laboratory-instrument business while opening the way for unfettered growth in the pollution-control field offsets this extra cost.

The decline of "central-city" shopping, to cite another reorganization, is causing Schrader's Department Store to scramble for survival. For years Schrader's followed the usual department-store organization and divided itself into product departments—women's wear, jewelry, furniture, and so on—with each doing its own buying, merchandising, and selling. Now Schrader's has pursued its customers to the suburbs by opening four branch stores. Unhappily, the old organization no longer fits. Each branch manager feels responsible for the success of his branch. At the same time, product department heads try to supervise merchandising and selling in the branches as they have been doing in the main store. This conflict has recently been mitigated by placing branch selling clearly under the control of branch managers, but the next logical step of putting a person in charge of all selling at the main store has not yet been taken. If and when this move is made, product department heads will concentrate on buying and merchandising, while selling will be supervised by five "regional" managers. Under the new setup, coordination of buying and selling will be more difficult, but department heads will have more time for product specialization, and selling will receive closer, local supervision.

Note that in this latter example the change is away from product grouping toward a functional split, whereas in the instrument company the shift was from function to products. The choice of departmentation depended on where coordination and specialized attention were most needed and on the impact of technology.

Adjusting major departments to new needs is not always easy. Consider African studies in a university. We accept the premise that the whole history of black people and their current problems warrant more attention. Should the added attention be incorporated into existing courses, or should new African-studies courses be added? Should African-studies courses be given by a separate department with its own faculty? Should such a department admit students and set its own degree requirements? Should the department have its own library, scholarships, and research funds, and otherwise have the status of a separate school? Instances of positive and of negative answers to each of these questions can be found somewhere on the American educational scene. Positive answers inevitably lead to further questions. If African studies are to be a part of the university, what will be their relationship with existing departments in history, sociology, economics, education, law, urban planning, and so on, and with service departments such as admissions, library, registrar, fund raising, and the like?

The crux of this problem from an organization point of view is that the new "product" is unlikely to receive *adequate attention* under the existing structure, yet organizational separation leads to overlap and duplication. Comparable departmentation problems often arise when a new but relatively small product or service is added. Here are some examples: a public library adds phonograph records to its services; a commercial airline begins carrying freight; a leading metal ski manufacturer decides to market ski clothing; a predominantly domestic company opens an international division.

In all these instances the fledgling activity is too small to justify revamping the entire organization. But it is also so small, new, and different that it is apt to be undernourished if it is merely appended to the activities of large existing departments; and so we often give the new activity independent status. The independence may mean merely that the new activity is a separate section in one or two existing departments, but if potentialities for growth are great enough the new venture may warrant the creation of a new department.

Each time, however, that we grant an activity a separate status that cuts across existing departments we are inviting trouble. The existing departments will resent exceptions to company policy, and jurisdictional squabbles are likely. We speak here not of new activities having no connection with existing operations but rather of new types of business that seek to build on some company strengths while enjoying independence in some other respects. Experience indicates that minor deviations from the major departmentation can be tolerated but that large overlappings create so much confusion that they need very strong justification.

As the preceding discussion of pressures to create new overlapping departments suggests, the major departmentation of an enterprise is continually open to challenge. Every job design embodies preference to some factors—local coordination, functional specialization, and so on—and the reasons for that preference change over time. Growth, new opportunities for service, the occurrence of wars or riots, shifting competition, newly discovered technology, and other shifts may make a formerly good design obsolete. We will further examine this need for readjustment in Chapters 5, 6, and 29. This dynamic character of departmentation, however, makes discriminating design even more valuable.

ADDING AUXILIARY UNITS

Designing individual jobs, combining jobs into work groups, and forming major departments of these building blocks establish the main framework of an organization. But further refining is necessary. One such refinement is creating *auxiliary*, or service, units. The Buildings and Grounds section of a hospital, for example, is clearly a unit serving the basic medical-care departments. The existence of such auxiliary divisions is justified only when operating departments work more economically or effectively as a result.

Potentialities of Service Units

A large variety of such service units is possible. For instance in a manufacturing concern we may establish a traffic division so that the production and marketing departments will not have to be concerned with moving goods to and from the plant. In financial establishments, the purchasing division typically functions as an auxiliary service for all other departments. A legal division can be set up to handle the bulk of corporate legal problems and to work with outside legal counsel on special issues. These are technical matters that the operating departments are rarely qualified to handle.

The principal reasons for separating auxiliary activities from primary operating activities are these: to secure adequate attention for all phases of an operation, to ensure that all work is assigned to technically competent employees, and to relieve busy executives of subsidiary duties.

There is another, and perhaps more fundamental, reason for distinguishing between primary and auxiliary divisions. Auxiliary divisions tend to grow uncontrollably, and it is difficult to tell how much of their service is economically justified. In his zeal for doing a good job, a manager of a service department is likely to magnify its importance. But if in our departmentation we clearly identify service work, we shall be in a good position to maintain a proper balance between services and primary operating units.

Hazards in Separating Services

The reasons for *not* separating service activity from primary operating activity usually center around problems of coordination and of overhead ex-

A. Organization with no service division; each operating section performs its own service activities

Figure 2–3 Alternative locations of service units. In the diagrams, the darker color indicates service activities.

B. Organization with service units in each operating department

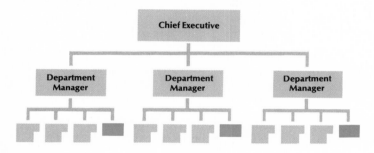

C. Organization with separate service division

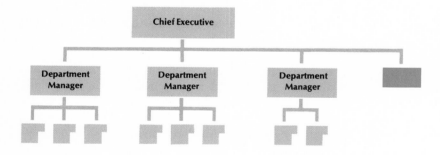

D. Organization with multiple service units

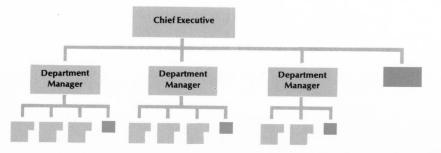

pense. If separated from basic operations, *some* auxiliary tasks, such as janitor service, warehousing, and traffic, present no particular difficulties of coordination. However, statistical computations, internal transportation, legal review of activities, and a large part of personnel work typically are closely related to day-to-day operations. The performance of such work by separate divisions generates additional problems. Where there is frequent need for synchronized action, we may be wiser to sacrifice some skill in performance to secure greater harmony.

In this connection, one danger of functional specialization, such as is found in most auxiliary units, is that it leads to provincial thinking. The functional specialist—for example, lawyer, purchasing agent, or accountant—permits his sophistication in one area to delude him into a misconception of, and lack of interest in, other areas. In his zeal to perform his particular specialty well, he becomes careless about the effect of his action or inaction on related activities.

Service divisions cost money in terms of salaries, office space, and the like. They often produce substantial economies that offset this expense by a comfortable margin, but this is not always the case. Such divisions tend to be a fixed-overhead item that is not reduced with a drop in volume of operations. Likewise, a division that originally served a useful purpose may be continued long after its usefulness has passed.

Establishment of service units, then, requires careful examination in each particular situation. Most enterprises of moderate size have several such units, but the desirability of a particular type of service unit should rarely be taken as a foregone conclusion, and the extent of the service is almost always a topic calling for considerable judgment. At least one generalization should be borne in mind when dealing with this issue: The burden of proof should always rest on the separation of service from basic operations. Every step in this direction increases to some extent the complexity of the organization; therefore, unless a strong case can be made for separation, we should leave the activity as an integral part of the operation.

CONCLUSION

The designing of jobs or work groups can rarely be done well without also thinking about departments and service units. Contrariwise, the scope of departments depends partly on what makes good work groups, and so forth. That is, design choices are interdependent, so we hold back final decision at one level until we have thought through the impact elsewhere in the structure. Two kinds of considerations are valuable when we review our preliminary framework—the match with technology and key factors in departmentation.

Think First of Technology

Technology in a very broad sense means the methods used to convert inputs (materials, ideas, labor) into more valuable goods and services. In addition to physical processes for converting raw materials into finished products (crude oil into gasoline), technology includes techniques for the following: converting truckloads of groceries into consumer food purchases; creating medical services in a hospital; providing transportation across the Atlantic; training unemployables to be craftsmen; handling the buy-and-sell transactions on the New York Stock Exchange.

Technology in this general sense is always a consideration when we design an organization. Technology fashions the work to be done; organization merely combines the work into jobs, sections, and so on.[4]

Where physical processes are concerned, the need to match technology and organization is clear. For instance, Hawaiian pineapples are processed in highly mechanized plants by equipment that peels, cores, slices, or crushes the pineapples. The nature of the process largely determines duties of individual jobs and also the scope of work groups. Similarly, modern retail technology has virtually eliminated personal selling in food supermarkets. Even the selling of fresh meats, once the domain of a skilled butcher, is now done by placing packaged meat in showcases. This latter change led many supermarket chains to modify their field organizations significantly. Instead of having separate departments for meats, produce, and groceries—which ran from the main office down to the retail stores—they switched to an area organization in which store and district managers supervised all products, aided by central buying of meat. As the selling technology changed, so did the organization.

Of course, the choice of technology is not always clear-cut. Volume of work, for instance, affects the degree to which standardization and mechanization are feasible; and such mechanization may affect not only departmentation but also other aspects of management (see Chapters 5 and 29). Also, in research laboratories, consulting firms, and to some extent classrooms, operators have wide discretion on how they will do their work; where such freedom exists, technology drops to a minor influence on departmentation. We stress looking at technology early because it so often places limits on the forms of organization that are worthy of careful study and because an ingenious matching of technology and organization can yield outstanding results. Solutions to some of our most pressing urban problems in education, government, and transportation, for instance, undoubtedly require innovation in technology and organization.

---

[4] We are treating technology here as an *intervening variable* between strategy (discussed in Chapter 16) and departmentation. That is, selection of a strategy leads to—perhaps even dictates—the technology to be used; then the technology determines the operating work to be done and is a major factor in the way this work is grouped into jobs, small units, and departments. The effect of technology on the total management design is explored in Chapter 29.

Several key factors are found in almost every departmentation problem, regardless of level. So we typically seek an optimum arrangement of the various factors instead of relying on a single consideration. The following paragraphs provide a useful summary of factors already noted and add new dimensions to several of them.

Take advantage of specialization. We should always at least consider a division of labor that permits persons to become specialists in certain kinds of work. Such concentration enables people to become experts and, assuming appropriate placement of personnel, allows a company to make full use of the distinctive abilities of its operators.

Usually we think of specialization by functions, but we should not overlook the possibility that an employee may become an expert on a product or on a particular type of customer. In other words, "What is the focus on the person's specialty?" The question forces us to consider whether a particular body of knowledge and skills is important for getting a job done. The more crucial such knowledge and skills are to the success of the enterprise, the stronger will be the pull on us to set up a division or a job built on that specialty.

Aid coordination. Even though certain activities are dissimilar, we may put them under a single executive because they need close coordination. Buying and selling women's dresses in a department store, for example, may be the responsibility of a single executive because he can sense style trends and customer reactions and can time changes accordingly.

A clearly recognized *common objective* is important in securing coordination. The type of decentralization stressed by duPont, General Electric, and many other companies splits up engineering, production, and selling among product divisions. This arrangement enables the management of each division to coordinate these diverse functions because the dominant objective of each unit is to make a success of its particular product line.

Coordination may be a factor when we decide where to place miscellaneous activities, as well as when we group major functions. In any organization, there are a number of "orphan operations"—receptionists, chauffeurs, telephone operators—and no compelling reason may exist for putting them in a particular place. We can decide to assign such employees to the department that makes the *most use* of their work. This solution at least simplifies coordination between a service and its major user.

Facilitate control. The way activities are apportioned has a marked effect on control in an organization. Clearly, if one activity is to serve as an *independent check* on another—as accounting on disbursement of cash or inspection on quality of production—these activities should be separated.

Departmentation, which makes it easier for management to measure performance and to hold people accountable for results, is a real aid to control. Thus it is desirable to make a *clean break* between the duties of one department and those of another. Oil companies, for example, often place all the work done by a refinery under a single manager because the line between what is inside and what is outside the refinery is a fairly clear one and also because all work within the refinery is so interrelated that a neat separation into two or more divisions would be difficult to establish.

Those companies whose volume and technology justify two or more operating units may use the *deadly parallel* as an aid to control. This means that operating units are made as nearly identical as possible so that their respective expenses and productivity can be directly compared. Chain stores, telephone companies, government bureaus, and even schools find that the deadly parallel provides performance standards that bring inefficient operations into sharp focus.

Control of actual operations is always simplified if an *immediate supervisor is on the spot* where he can see what goes on and can talk to workers

Figure 2–4   Basic factors in departmentation.

When Grouping and Reassigning Activities into Administrative Units, Seek the Optimum Combination of the Following Benefits:

1. Take advantage of specialization
   Functional specialists
   Other kinds of specialists
   Special equipment

2. Aid in coordination
   Interrelated activities
   Common objectives
   Most-use criterion

3. Facilitate control
   Independent check
   Deadly parallel
   Clean break
   Ease of supervision

4. Secure adequate attention

5. Reduce expenses

6. Recognize human considerations
   Available personnel
   Informal groups
   Full-time jobs

The importance of each point must be determined for the specific situation at the given time.

frequently during the day. For this reason, a firm may place final assembly operations in a branch warehouse under the control of the sales department, even though the work seems logically part of production.

Secure adequate attention. A principal reason for separating auxiliary services from primary operations, as we have already pointed out, is to ensure adequate attention for all phases of work that should be done. Also, we may place an activity high up in an organization structure to ensure that this operation receives full consideration from top administrators.

"Adequate attention," however, is a difficult guide to use in departmentation. If an executive pays heed to all demands for attention, he may be inclined to break up an otherwise neat pattern that works well most of the time. Therefore an executive must decide not only how important an activity is at a given moment but also how important it will be in the future.

Reduce expenses. The pattern of departmentation may directly affect expenses in two ways. First, a new unit—say, a purchasing department or a central training service—may require additional executives. These new executives will add to salaries, traveling expenses, secretarial work, telephone and other services. In addition to these identifiable costs, the people in a new unit inevitably use up some of the time of other executives by talking with them and writing memoranda that have to be read and answered. Perhaps the addition of a single person will make no marked difference, but if an array of specialists all press for attention from busy line managers, the total burden on the line managers can become quite heavy.

A second expense consideration is the rate of pay needed for different kinds of jobs. An industrial sales department, for instance, might require that all sales representatives have engineering training plus five years experience with company products. But another organization might reserve such high-paid positions only for special assignments, using lower-paid people for routine sales work. Obviously, no company will want to incur additional payroll expense unless by doing so it will benefit significantly from improved effectiveness.

Recognize human considerations. In Part Two we shall give careful attention to the human-relations aspects of organization structure. There are a number of reasons why we may have to modify the coldly logical and emotionally detached organization plans we are discussing here in Part One. Among the reasons are availability of personnel, the existence of informal groups, traditions within an enterprise, and prevailing attitudes toward different forms of organization. We mention these points here simply as a reminder that we must bring human factors into consideration before we reach a final decision.

Frequency of Change

Organization structure should contribute to the stability of working relations. It enables each person to know the particular part he is expected to play in the total activities of his company. And from it he also learns what he can expect others to do. For these reasons, we should not shuffle duties among people each time a new idea strikes us. On the other hand, dynamic pressures in society and within a company require the modern manager to be constantly alert to the need for readjusting the way he has divided work among his subordinates. In enterprises generally, *thoughtful* changes in departmentation are made too infrequently rather than too often.

FOR CLASS DISCUSSION

1) "Setting up a formal organization structure is only a starting point from which *people* take over. After all the organization charts are drawn and job descriptions are written, people move in to get the work done. As they do, they create their own organizational relationships and job breakdowns. If you want to study how the work in a company is accomplished, don't waste your time on the formal descriptions, but seek to understand the informal organization which evolves." This statement was made by a critic of formal organization planning. Do you agree with the statement? Explain. How can it be reconciled with the content of this chapter?

2) Change in the grouping of activities may be made necessary by a variety of changes in the environment. Such changes in grouping can be disruptive and take years to become as efficient as the earlier grouping. What steps can managers take to reduce the negative impact of changes in groupings? How can overlapping patterns ease such shifts?

3) What factors determine whether it will be easier or more difficult to fix responsibility for the success or failure of a functional group than of a compound group?

4) "My greatest concern with service or auxiliary units is that they forget that they were set up to provide *service* to basic operating units. They soon become so concerned with the requirements of their specialized activities that they behave like a tail trying to wag a dog." What does this statement, made by a plant superintendent, mean to you? Can you give an example of this from your experience? How might we deal with the concerns he is expressing?

5) "We used to have a great safety record in this plant," said a firstline foreman. "That is," he went on, "until we set up a separate safety department in the plant personnel office. In the year and a half since this group was set up, accidents have gone up almost 20 percent." How would you explain this phenomenon?

6) In what ways do you suppose the technology available at the time of the building of the pyramids influenced the determination of 1) the grouping of operating tasks into individual tasks, 2) the combining of jobs into work groups, and 3) the combining of work groups into departments? What other factors probably supported these forms of organization design?

7) Discuss the relationships between key factors in departmentation and the three factors to be considered when seeking to strike a balance in the design of individual jobs.

8) Arrangements have just been completed to transfer the franchise of a minor-league baseball team to your hometown. A ballpark is being built to seat 12,000, and the owners of the team have offered you the job of organizing

and managing the refreshments concession. They will provide any capital and facilities you may require.

1) Describe the operating work that would have to be carried out in running the concession.

2) What alternative means of organizing this work are plausible? What factors influence the desirability of each alternative?

3) In dividing the operating work, did you use the "top-down" or "bottom-up" approach, or did you trace the steps of the operation? What are the arguments for each of these approaches?

Cases

For cases involving issues covered in this chapter, see especially the following. Particularly relevant questions are listed after each case.

The Delaware Corporation (p. 113), 1, 3
Milano Enterprises (p. 124), 2, 5
Atlas Chemical Company (p. 321), 2
Graham, Smith, & Bendel, Inc. (p. 445), 1, 2
Monroe Wire and Cable (p. 436), 1
Household Products Company (p. 627), 3

FOR FURTHER READING

Anderson, J. W., "The Impact of Technology on Job Enrichment." *Personnel,* September 1970.

Technology and the feasibility of changing job content.

Filley, A. C., R. J. House, and S. Kerr, *Managerial Process and Organizational Behavior,* 2nd ed. Glenview, Ill.: Scott Foresman and Company, 1976, Chapters 15 and 16.

Summarizes research evidence on behavioral effects of division of labor, and on product vs. functional departmentation.

Gulick, L., "Notes on the Theory of Organization," in *Papers on the Science of Administration,* ed. L. Gulick and L. Urwick. New York: Institute of Public Administration, Columbia University, 1937, pp. 3–45.

A classic that is fully applicable today.

Litterer, J. A., *The Analysis of Organizations,* 2nd ed. New York: John Wiley & Sons, 1973, Chapters 15 and 16.

Good discussion of elements involved in division of work at operating level.

Newman, W. H., *Administrative Action,* 2nd ed. Englewood Cliffs, N.J.: Prentice-Hall, Inc., 1963, Chapters 9, 10, 15, 16, 17.

Explores in greater depth the issues discussed in this chapter, especially the total structure of an enterprise.

Widing, J. W., "Reorganizing Your Worldwide Business." *Harvard Business Review,* May 1973.

Briefly discusses alternative ways to organize multinational operations, and explores reasons for lag in adjusting an organization to suit new requrements.

3 Designing the Hierarchy:
Delegating and Decentralizing

DIVIDING MANAGERIAL WORK

Growth invariably leads to a management hierarchy. As a firm becomes larger, we need more levels of managers to ensure coordinated planning, direction, and control. Centralization–decentralization—the focus of this chapter—concerns the vertical allocation of management action along this hierarchy, whereas departmentation—discussed in the previous chapter—involves a horizontal allocation of operating work.[1]

Persistence of the Problem

The question of how much work the chief executive should do himself and how much he should reassign to his subordinates has bothered administrators for centuries. One of the earliest references to the problem is found in the Book of Exodus, where there is a report of Moses' experience with this dilemma:

[1] *Operating* work, as noted in Chapter 2, embraces the basic activities necessary to create goods and services—the selling, machine-running, bookkeeping, and engineering in a manufacturing plant; the copywriting, art work, media selection, and campaign scheduling in an advertising agency; or the arranging for temporary care of children, locating foster homes, making actual placements, raising funds, and keeping records in a child-placement agency. *Managerial* work refers to the guidance of other people, and includes the activities of all levels of supervisors from first-line foreman to president.

Moses sat to judge the people; and the people stood about Moses from the morning unto the evening. And when Moses' father-in-law saw all that he did . . . he said unto him: "The thing that thou doest is not good. Thou wilt surely wear away, both thou and this people with thee; for the thing is too heavy for thee—thou are not able to perform it thyself alone.

"Hearken now unto my voice. . . . Be thou for the people Godward, and bring thou the causes unto God. [Then] thou shalt teach [the people] the statutes and the laws, and shalt show them the way wherein they must walk, and the work that they must do.

"Moreover thou shalt provide out of all the people able men, such as fear God, men of truth, hating unjust gain; and place such over them, to be rulers of thousands, rulers of hundreds, rulers of fifties, and rulers of tens; and let them judge the people at all seasons. And it shall be that every great matter they shall bring unto thee, but every small matter they shall judge themselves. So shall it be easier for thyself, and they shall bear the burden with thee."

The fundamental problem Moses faced is still with us. The burden on executives is especially acute in enterprises that are changing and growing. As product lines are diversified and new employees added, executives find that they can no longer give proper attention to all the management problems that cross their desks. Unless they decentralize, they find that they, like Moses, are unable to cope with the job by themselves.

The allocation of managerial work is one of the most subtle aspects of the organizing process. The degree of decentralization may vary from department to department within a single company. The sales department, for example, may be highly decentralized. But the controller may retain direction over a great deal of the planning, organizing, and motivating of the operations under his direction.

For insight into this web of relationships we shall first examine the delegation process and then consider factors determining the degree of decentralization that is desirable in a specific situation. The chapter closes with a penetrating look at profit-decentralization—an organizational arrangement well suited to a dynamic society.

THREE INEVITABLE FEATURES OF DELEGATING

Delegation is familiar to anyone in a supervisory position; it simply means entrusting part of the work of operations or management to others. A filling station owner delegates car greasing to Bill and pump tending to Charlie. The president of Republic Aircraft Corporation entrusts financial matters to Ms. MacGregor, the treasurer. Such delegations give rise to what we commonly call a boss–subordinate relationship.

Every time a manager delegates work to a subordinate—say, a president to a foreign manager, or a first-line supervisor to an operator—three actions are either expressed or implied:

1) The manager assigns *duties.* The person who is delegating indicates what work the subordinate is to do.

2) He grants *authority.* Along with permission to proceed with the assigned work, he will probably transfer to the subordinate certain rights, such as the right to spend money, to direct the work of others, to use raw materials, to represent the company to outsiders, or to take other steps necessary to fulfill the new duties.

3) He creates an *obligation.* In accepting an assignment, a subordinate takes on an obligation to his boss to complete his job.

These attributes of delegation are like a three-legged stool; each depends on the others for support, and no two can stand alone.

Duties

Duties can be described in two ways. First, we can think of them in terms of an activity. For instance, we may say that Turner's duties are either to run a turret lathe, to sell in Oshkosh, to direct an employment office, to discover and analyze facts about the money market and trends in interest rates, or to measure distribution costs. According to this view, delegating is the process by which we assign activities to individuals.

Second, we can describe duties in terms of the results we want to achieve. Following this approach, we would say that in the first two examples, Turner's duties are to turn on his lathe a certain number of pieces per day according to engineering specifications, or to build customer goodwill and secure a prescribed number of orders in the Oshkosh territory. Here we are talking about objectives. We define the duties not just in terms of "going through certain motions," but also in terms of accomplishment.

Because of differences in jobs, we may state such goals as either long-run or short-run results. They may represent overoptimism or realistic expectation. Nevertheless, if we phrase the delegation of duties in terms of goals, a subordinate is likely to get psychological satisfaction from his work, and he will have advance notice of the criteria on which his performance will be judged. A

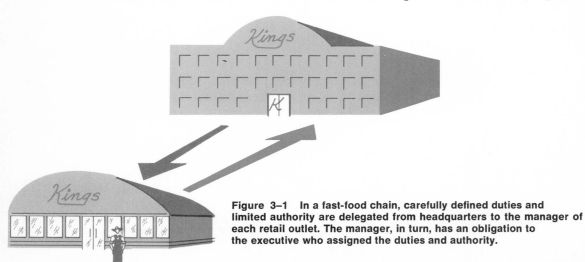

Figure 3–1   In a fast-food chain, carefully defined duties and limited authority are delegated from headquarters to the manager of each retail outlet. The manager, in turn, has an obligation to the executive who assigned the duties and authority.

person's duties will be clear to him only if he knows what activities he must undertake *and* what missions he must fulfill.

Authority

If we assign a person duties to perform, is it not obvious that we must give him all necessary authority to carry them out? An advertising manager needs authority to buy space, hire a copywriter, and take other necessary steps if he is to gain his assigned objective of building customer demand for company products.

Unfortunately, assigning authority is not simple. We should understand exactly what kind of authority is within the power of a manager to grant; typically, several restrictions fence in the authority a manager has at his disposal.

Administrative authority consists of certain permissions or rights: the right to act for the company in specified areas (to buy raw material, accept orders from customers, issue press releases, admit people into a plant); the right as spokesman for the company to request other employees to perform activities of various kinds; and the right to impose sanctions and discipline if a subordinate disregards his instructions. These rights are vested in the head of an enterprise by law and custom, and they are supported by the moral approval of society. They stem partly from concepts of private-property rights, partly from acknowledged authority of the political state, and particularly from the long-established human habit of looking to hierarchical leadership in cooperative undertakings. Because of this background, employees and, in fact, our whole society accept the idea that the head of an enterprise—whoever he may be—has certain rights of authority and that he may reassign these rights.

When an employee takes a job, he also 1) expects to take orders from someone designated by the company; 2) looks to management for permission to use company property or to act as an official representative of the enterprise; and 3) expects a superior to review his work and bring pressure on him to improve if it is unsatisfactory. Such socially accepted rights constitute formal authority, and management can assign these rights when it erects a formal organization.

Authority is an essential element of any modern enterprise, but we must not confuse it with unlimited power. No company president or section manager can grant someone of lower rank the power to change the physical laws of the universe, the power to force customers to sign orders or suppliers to sell raw materials, or the power to compel the *enthusiastic* cooperation of associates and subordinates. The rights that an administrator may transfer are more akin to authorization than they are to power.

In addition to inherent limitations on the authority that an executive can delegate, virtually every company imposes limitations of its own. Typically, an executive is permitted to act strictly "within company policy" and "in accordance with established procedures." A manager may in theory have formal authority to hire and fire people in his division, but in fact he must adhere to a myriad of restrictive procedures that require him, for example, to refer job descriptions to the planning department before he can fill a new position, to satisfy the personnel department that no capable person is available within the company before he can hire an outsider, to set salaries within an established range for each job classification, and to refrain from discharging anyone without two prior warnings at least a month apart. Another department head may have to endure comparable restrictions surrounding purchases of raw materials and, especially, of new equipment.

Because of these various limitations on authority, when we delegate a task we must be sure to specify what rights are associated with it.

Obligation

By obligation—the third inevitable feature of delegation—we mean the moral compulsion felt by a subordinate to accomplish his assigned duties. When duties are delegated to him, a subordinate is not free either to do the work or leave it as may happen to suit his convenience. For instance, a price checker is derelict in his duty if on Friday afternoon he mails out a batch of unaudited bids to customers merely because his "work had piled up and salesmen were anxious to get the bids to their customers." Similarly, a clerk assigned to unlock the office in the morning fails in his obligation when he shows up two hours late and gives the excuse that his brother had unexpectedly stopped overnight for a visit.

Although agreement is usually implied rather than expressed, when a subordinate accepts an assignment he in effect gives his promise to do his best in carrying out his duties. Having taken a job, he is morally bound to try to complete it and can be held accountable for results. A sense of obligation, then, is primarily an attitude of the person to whom duties are delegated. Dependability rests on the sense of obligation, and without dependability our cooperative business enterprises would collapse.[2]

APPLYING CONCEPTS OF DELEGATION

Should Duties and Obligations Extend beyond Authority?

A common saying in popular management literature declares that "authority and accountability should always be equal." Behind this statement lies the

[2] In delineating the chief features of delegating, we have avoided using the word "responsibility" because it means different things to different people. Some use it as a synonym for duty, whereas others think its meaning is identical with obligation. To avoid this confusion, we will shy away from the word. From time to time, however, we shall use accountability as a synonym for obligation.

conviction that if we assign a person duties, we ought to furnish him with enough authority—no more and no less—to carry them out; and if we give him authority, we certainly expect from him a corresponding obligation to use it wisely. Although there are elements of truth in this contention, it is unfortunately an oversimplification. Let us see why.

The first difficulty is the word "equal." Duties are concerned with objectives and activities, authority with rights, and obligation with attitudes. Although these three concepts are indeed related, it is hard to find a common denominator for measuring equality among them. Also, as we have seen in our discussion of formal authority, there are only certain kinds of rights that an enterprise can pass along to its managers, and there are usually very substantial restrictions on how even these rights may be used. To permit anyone to charge into action without constraints would lead to chaos. Frequently a person must try to achieve objectives with authority far short of his desires.[3]

It is more nearly accurate, though not so pat, to say to the boss—the person doing the delegating—"Duties, authority, and obligation depend on each other and you should therefore correlate them thoughtfully"; and to the subordinate—the person receiving the delegation—"You are obligated to fulfill your duties to the maximum extent that is feasible in light of your authority and the conditions under which you have to work."

An Obligation Cannot Be Delegated

What happens when duties and authority are redelegated? Does this redelegation relieve the executive who makes it of *his* obligations? Suppose the treasurer of the Omaha Chemical Company delegates to the chief accountant the task of maintaining an accounts-payable ledger. The chief accountant, being too busy to maintain the records himself, assigns the job to a clerk.

The redelegation of the job by the chief accountant to the clerk does not at all change the initial relationship between the treasurer and the chief accountant. The chief accountant still has the same duties and as much authority, and even though he has turned over the major parts of these to the clerk, he can reclaim them if he wishes. More importantly, the chief accountant still has the same obligations to the treasurer. The additional obligation between the clerk and the chief accountant in no way relieves the chief accountant of his obligation. It is as though the treasurer lent ten dollars to the chief accountant, and the chief accountant in turn lent the money to the clerk; the chief accountant cannot satisfy his obligation to the controller by giving him the clerk's IOU.

If we were to abandon this principle that a man cannot delegate obligation, there would be no way of knowing who was accountable for what.

---

[3] *Legal* authority is not dealt with here. Such authority is principally concerned with the enterprise's relationships with outsiders. In business firms, executives typically have far-ranging legal authority but are restrained by internal limitations on its use.

Dual Subordination

An issue we face over and over in delegating is whether each person should have only one boss. On this point, formal organization theory is clear. A worker—operator or manager—may have relations with many people, but he needs one supervisor whose guidance can be regarded as final. What are the reasons supporting this concept of a single chain of command?

All executives and all subordinate employees respond to a variety of influences, not just to those emanating from their line bosses. Nevertheless, the evidence indicates that as important as other people may be in influencing the behavior of an employee, the line boss is usually far more significant. Reasons for the overriding influence of the line boss are not hard to find. Normally the boss trains and directs an employee and explains what he should do; the boss authorizes what the subordinate may do; he assists in getting necessary materials and tools and often represents "his" people throughout the organization; he checks results and initiates corrective action when necessary; he praises, blames, disciplines, promotes, recommends changes in pay, and otherwise motivates his subordinates. These activities are closely interrelated, and if they are to have their greatest impact, they should spring, integrated, from one source.

When two bosses try to share the fundamental role of immediate supervisor, their actions are likely to be inconsistent. One may praise, whereas the other may suggest improvements; the first may urge speed and initiative, whereas the second may withhold authority; they may make assignments that conflict. People can and do get along with two bosses, just as a child accepts guidance from two teachers; but unless the two bosses have a very close working relationship, they may find many opportunities for maneuvering for advantage and may tend to be unjust to the subordinate. When there is one boss, the likelihood of a consistent pattern of supervision is greatly increased. The experience of managers over the years indicates that we are wise to have one supervisor who resolves conflicting demands and has final say on priorities.

Duties Include Interactions

Clear-cut duties and authorities do not imply that everyone should work in his own isolated corner. Instead, in most delegations, managers make it very clear that a subordinate should consult with others and keep them informed as he proceeds with his own duties.

Furthermore, a few assignments are specifically joint undertakings. Some companies emphasize their concern with cooperation by saying that a person is accountable for both work and teamwork, and they are dissatisfied with the person's performance unless he measures up well on both counts. Cooperation is definitely part of a job and should be as clear as other duties.

Relations between supervisors and subordinates are subject to continual readjustment. We should modify delegations as the work to be done and the people who do it change. Nevertheless, the vast number of relationships are stable—at least for some period of time. This stability is important. A worker learns what to expect of his boss; the boss learns how much he can depend on each of his subordinates; people doing related work learn how to deal with an established hierarchy. Such patterns of expectations are essential if we are to get day-by-day work done smoothly and quickly. If the delegating has not been done well, and if boss–subordinate relationships are unclear and become sources of friction, then the company unity we seek will be lacking.

HOW MUCH DECENTRALIZATION?

The preceding discussion centered on the process of delegating. Now we turn to the extent and content of such delegations.

Focus on Planning

Experience has shown that *planning*—that is, identifying problems and deciding what action to take—is usually the most crucial element in thinking about decentralization. Organizing, leading, and controlling are also important, but assigning those activities to various executives typically depends on how we have allocated planning duties. When we look more closely later on at leadership and control, we shall trace the interplay of these phases of management with decisions concerning decentralization.

There are several ways to divide the work of planning among executives, and these are important for describing varying degrees of decentralization.

By subject. This is the simplest way to divide planning. An executive normally makes decisions only for the operations that he also directs. However, when an operation affects several related departments, as does pricing or inven-

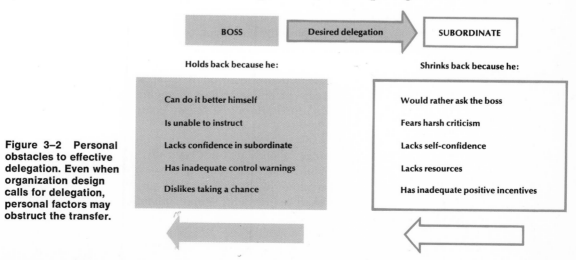

Figure 3–2 Personal obstacles to effective delegation. Even when organization design calls for delegation, personal factors may obstruct the transfer.

BOSS → Desired delegation → SUBORDINATE

Holds back because he:

Can do it better himself

Is unable to instruct

Lacks confidence in subordinate

Has inadequate control warnings

Dislikes taking a chance

Shrinks back because he:

Would rather ask the boss

Fears harsh criticism

Lacks self-confidence

Lacks resources

Has inadequate positive incentives

tory control, we may stipulate that certain other persons are to be consulted before binding decisions are made.

Dividing planning by subject is especially useful in situations where there is a senior executive and a lower executive who reports to him. A chief accountant, for example, might say to his office manager: "I'll decide what accounts to keep and where different types of items should be charged—that is, I'll set up the accounting system. But I want you to schedule the flow of work through the office, determine the number and types of people we need, and figure out whether it would pay us to get more automatic equipment." Or the vice-president in charge of sales might select the markets to be cultivated and then assign to his sales manager the detailed planning of direct-mail publicity, personal contacts, and other activities designed to secure orders from the customers within these markets. Note that in each of these examples certain subjects are decided by the senior man and other subjects by his subordinate.

By type of plan. Often a sharp division of administrative work by subject is not feasible. A senior executive may want some say in the way a particular type of situation is handled, and yet lack time to make daily decisions on individual problems. This partial involvement can be accomplished by the use of *objectives* and *policies*, which set the direction and limits of action. Subordinates can then make decisions on specific cases within this guiding framework. For instance, the president of a telephone company can say, "No employee with more than two years of service is to be discharged as a result of the installation of automatic-dialing equipment." The managers of local branches must act within this limit and plan for the transfer or retraining of any displaced workers with a two-year service record.

Sometimes a senior executive wishes to be more specific. If so, he can lay out a step-by-step *procedure* to be followed, or a *schedule* of dates by which specific action is to be completed. Thus an advertising manager often sets deadlines for drawings, magazine copy, radio scripts, and other parts of his promotion campaign. His subordinates are free to make detailed schedules for their own work provided the master schedule is met.

In still other situations an executive may announce that certain *premises* are to be adopted when plans are made for the future. For example, he tells the production manager to prepare his budget on the assumption that there will be a twenty percent increase in sales volume during the following year.

From the point of view of decentralization, the questions are *to what extent* these different types of plan should be used and *who* should set them up. Clearly, the more management circumscribes or regiments work by means of objectives, policies, and so forth, the more highly centralized the organization will be.

By phase of planning. Planning is not typically an isolated activity performed by a single person insulated from his associates. In fact, the more important the plan, the more likely that several people will participate in formulating it. As we shall see in Part Three, planning consists of several identifiable phases: diagnosing and identifying a problem, finding possible solutions to the problem, gathering facts, projecting the results of each alternative, and, finally, choosing one alternative as the course of action to be followed. In practice, the work of each of these phases may be performed by different persons.

Except for final decision-making, none of these phases need be regarded as the exclusive domain of a particular person. Anyone who spots a trouble area that needs to be cleaned up or has evidence that will contribute to the sound analysis of a problem should be encouraged to volunteer his ideas. Eliciting such voluntary assistance, however, is not enough in itself. Someone must still be responsible for ensuring that each phase of the planning process is properly performed.

Just how these phases are actually handled depends a great deal on the atmosphere that prevails within each company. In one company it might be presumptuous for a first-line supervisor to suggest a change in personnel policies, whereas in another company the supervisor might get fired if he failed to spot potential trouble and recommend a plan for avoiding it. When a possible change is being studied, some companies expect a lower-level supervisor to provide only the information he is asked for, whereas others expect him to speak his mind on anything he believes pertinent and, perhaps, to come up with counterproposals. These are all examples of how the burden of planning may be allocated in terms of phases or steps in the planning process.

Summary. To decide who should do what about planning, we need to ask ourselves these questions:

1) What is the subject?
2) Is a *single* problem being decided, or is a *general* guide being established— such as an objective, policy, procedure, schedule, or premise?
3) Do we want several executives to participate in the decision? If so, which phase of the decision-making process is each expected to take on?

Decentralization is concerned with how much of this complex planning activity should be assigned to each executive, from the president down to first-line supervisors.

Degrees of Decentralization

How are these concepts put into practice? The following two examples help answer this question. To make it easier to compare the degrees of decentralization, both examples concern sales activities.

Decentralized planning. A company that manufactures materials-handling equipment has a field force of twenty-four representatives. Six are branch managers, and each has one to four sales representatives. The branch managers spend at least half their time in actual selling. Because industrial equipment is purchased at irregular intervals, the sales people have to follow new sales leads; they cannot depend on a regular flow of repeat business from established customers.

The management of this company thinks it has a highly decentralized sales operation. However, two important areas are definitely centralized: products and prices.

Product-planning is handled by the engineering department in the main office. A variety of standard equipment is described in a product book, and sales representatives sell this equipment whenever it is suited to the customer's needs. If special equipment is required, the sales representatives simply gather the operating data and submit these facts to the home office. The engineering department then decides what to recommend to the customer and prepares the necessary sketches.

The setting of prices is also centralized. Prices of standard items and special orders are set by the sales manager. In making these decisions, the sales manager draws on field information on customers, cost figures from the estimating department, and his knowledge of the competitive situation.

Except for product-planning and price-setting, people in the field have almost complete freedom. Which customers to call on, what selling methods to use, which conventions and trade association meetings to attend, when a long-distance phone call is worth its cost—all are determined locally. The branch manager is the key person in many of these decisions, but he may rely on an experienced sales representative to do his own planning.

The home office provides a variety of descriptive circulars, prospect lists, technical advice, and other services. Nevertheless, it is up to the branch manager and the sales representatives to decide what use, if any, they will make of these services.

Notice that the planning of sales is rather sharply divided by subject. The chief engineer decides what products will be sold, the sales manager sets the prices, the branch managers select the customers. Only limited use is made of policies and standing procedures. There is considerable cooperation in the planning process, particularly through the exchange of ideas and information. This exchange has not been formalized, however, to a point where the executive making the decision feels relieved of the preliminary phases of planning (except for the preparation of cost estimates used in pricing).

Not everyone in the company is convinced that the present method of dividing up the sales-planning work is the best. One manager advocates much more centralized planning and direction; he insists that sales quotas should be established, that sales representatives should be directed to specific prospects, and that direct-mail advertising should be tied in closely with sales calls. However, most executives believe that the local people can judge what will produce on-the-spot results better than anyone sitting in the home office.

Centralized planning. A quite different way of dividing sales-planning work is followed by a successful Midwestern oil company. Each of the forty-two branch managers has a fuel-oil and industrial-sales manager, a gasoline sales manager who concentrates on sales through filling stations, and a branch

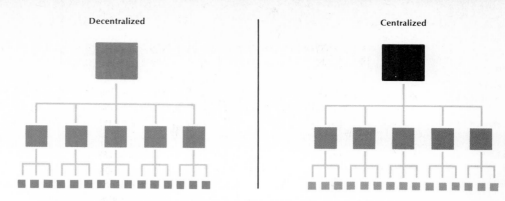

Decentralized

Centralized

Figure 3–3 Centralized versus decentralized planning. The intensity of black suggests the degree of regulation; the intensity of color suggests the degree of autonomy.

engineer who leases, staffs, builds, and exercises financial control over company-owned filling stations.

Most sales-planning is done in the main office. The marketing vice-president sets general prices and establishes policies covering any price reduction to meet local competition. Advertising is planned and executed at headquarters. Sales promotion, keyed in with the advertising program, is planned in detail at the home office and includes decisions on the color stations are to be painted and on the design of signs. A variety of training aids for station operators are also planned centrally: instructions for waiting on customers, care of washrooms, methods of car greasing, and the like.

The branch managers, then, are primarily concerned with carrying out plans that have already been made. They hire, train, pay, direct, and motivate the key people in the branch office—all in accordance with company policy and other plans. If a price war breaks out, they adjust local prices in accordance with policy or, if necessary, request the home office to adjust them. They take care of the innumerable little problems that inevitably arise in the sale of a substantial dollar-volume of product. Often they pass new ideas for sales promotion along to the main office. Their principal duty, however, is to carry out the sales program as effectively as possible rather than to propose new ideas. The executives of this oil company would strongly resist any proposal to give branch managers the freedom in planning permitted by the manufacturer described above.

These two examples illustrate not only the general difference between a centralized and decentralized department, but also the need to think specifically about each type of problem (for instance, pricing in the industrial-equipment company) even though a general pattern has been established. In practice, an endless variation in degrees of delegation exists, and properly so. Each company operates in its own unique circumstances of size, reputation, competitive strategy, existing equipment, abilities of key executives, and similar factors. Each manager must figure out what allocation of executive duties best fits his needs. We can, however, identify certain factors that will help a manager make that allocation wisely.

Guides to "How Much Decentralization?"

We should carefully weigh the following seven factors when choosing the best place in the executive hierarchy for each category of decision-making.

1) *Who knows the facts on which the decision will be based, or who can get them together most readily?*

Sometimes a single individual—salesman, caseworker, advertising manager, foreign-plant director, purchasing agent—is in constant command, through the normal course of his work, of all the facts needed to make a given type of decision. Such a person alone is naturally best equipped for decision-making on the issue. Many decisions, however, require information from several different sources—a decision whether or not to buy a new machine, for example, requires data on production methods, plant layout, future volume, availability of capital, workers' attitudes, and so forth. Channels of communication must be established to funnel all this information to a single point; the question, then, is whether it will be easier to pass general information down the line or specific information up the line. This raises considerations of the accuracy, time, and cost of such communication.

2) *Who has the capacity to make sound decisions?*

Clearly, if people at lower levels—engineers, foremen, office supervisors, branch managers—lack the ability and experience needed to make a wise decision, there is a compelling reason to withhold decision-making authority from them. Such capacity, however, is usually a relative matter. Perhaps the president can make a very wise decision about granting credit, but the branch manager can make one that is almost as effective. Since we want to save the president's energies for more important matters, and the branch manager's judgment on this subject is satisfactory, we should lodge the planning for extending credit with the branch manager.

3) *Must speedy, on-the-spot decisions be made to meet local conditions?*

The repair of railroad breakdowns or the buying of fruit at wholesale auctions obviously requires that someone with authority be at the scene of action. A similar, though less dramatic, need for prompt action occurs in negotiating contracts, employing personnel to meet unexpected work loads, or adjusting the complaints of irate customers.

4) *Must the local activity be carefully coordinated with other activities?*

Sometimes *uniformity* of action is so important that all decisions must be made centrally—for example, ensuring that all customers in a single area are charged the same prices or determining the length of vacation for all employees in the same plant. Other decisions, such as determining a weekly production schedule or laying out a national sales-promotion program, require that activities in several areas be closely *synchronized;* here, at least some central planning is called for.

5) *How significant is the decision?*

A relatively minor decision—one that will increase or decrease profits only by a dollar or two, for example—clearly should be left to a junior executive or operator. The expense of communication up and down the channel of command and of the time required for the senior executive to handle the problem, would be far greater than any savings that might result from his judgment. On the other hand, any decision that will have a major effect on the total operation —either a single transaction or a basic policy—should be approved at least by a senior executive.

6) *How busy are the executives who might be assigned planning tasks?*

In dividing up work among executives, overloads must be avoided. A top executive may already have so many duties that he will have to shirk additional responsibility for planning; or a plant superintendent may lack the time for careful analysis and thoughtful decision. If a busy executive has a distinctive contribution that only he can make, perhaps he can be brought in on one phase of the planning, while the rest of the chore is assigned to someone else.

7) *Will initiative and morale be significantly improved by decentralization?*
Decentralization typically builds initiative and good morale in lower-level executives. We should be sure, however, that such feelings will be generated, and that they are desirable, in each specific situation. Companies that are faced with frequent shifts in consumer demand, in technology, or in the competitive situation must actively promote adaptability and initiative among their workers. In other enterprises, such as many public utilities, where the rate of change is slower, too much originality and initiative among junior executives may actually create discontent and lower morale. Similar sharp differences in the need for initiative are also found in various departments of a single company.

In using these factors as guides to the degree of decentralization that is appropriate in a specific situation, we have to determine how much weight to attach to each. Often the factors pull in opposite directions—the need for speed may suggest greater decentralization, while the desire for coordination may dictate greater centralization. Clearly, each factor must be carefully balanced against the others. Allowance must also be made both for traditional behavior and for growth in the abilities of individuals. So we see again that the managerial task of organizing calls for a high order of judgment.

PROFIT DECENTRALIZATION

There is one form of decentralization that is highly important to larger companies: profit decentralization. Under this plan, we split a company into product or regional divisions, each of which is responsible for its own profit or loss.

Self-sufficient, Semiautonomous Units

Two characteristics lie at the heart of the plan: 1) All the major operations necessary to make a profit are grouped under the manager of a *self-sufficient* unit. This, of course, is a matter of departmentation (discussed in Chapter 2). Typically, several such self-sufficient, self-contained units are established in a company. 2) The management of these units is so highly decentralized that each of them becomes *semiautonomous*. In effect, we have a series of little businesses operating within the parent company. The manager of each unit has virtually the same resources and the freedom of action that he would enjoy if he were president of an independent company, and he is expected to take whatever steps are necessary to ensure that his "little business" will make a profit.

Though profit decentralization is the key concept in organizing large concerns like General Motors Corporation, it is by no means confined to industrial giants. Smaller companies such as Johnson & Johnson and Abex Corporation have found it admirably suited to their needs.

Ordinarily the operating units are built around product lines, and the engineering, production, and sales of each line are placed within the decentralized division. The same idea, however, has been applied by department-store chains, which place all their operations in each *region* on a profit-decentralization basis. In fact, this form of organization has become so successful and popular that most diversified companies use it in at least a modified form.

Benefits

A major advantage of profit decentralization is its stimulating effect on the *morale* of the key men in each of these self-sufficient, semiautonomous divisions. Executives are able to see the results of their own methods, to take the action they believe best, and to feel that they are playing an important role. The resulting enthusiasm and devotion to the success of their division tend to spread to employees at all levels in the division.

Because operating units established under profit decentralization are of a *manageable size,* fewer people have to exchange information, and they can communicate with one another swiftly and effectively. Thus, executives find it easier to comprehend the information that is funneled to them.

Situations requiring administrative action are more likely to receive *adequate attention* under profit decentralization. In a large-scale enterprise, it is all too easy to neglect a product or an operation that contributes only a minor part to the total sales volume. In a smaller division, however, such problems become relatively more important, and executives are much more likely to take the necessary corrective action.

The smaller size of the operating units and the heightened ease of communication also lead to improved *coordination,* particularly in the critically important areas of serving customers, matching production and sales, and keeping costs in line with income. Bureaucratic attitudes are less likely to interfere with voluntary cooperation.

By making both measurement and accountability more clear cut, profit decentralization promotes more effective *control.* The profit-and-loss statement of each operating division provides a significant measure of results, and there is less need to make an arbitrary allocation of costs. Moreover, because a self-sufficient division is also semiautonomous, its manager can be held accountable for resulting profit or loss. If the results are poor, he can be required to take corrective action; if they are good, he can be, and often is, generously rewarded.

Limitations and Difficulties

If profit decentralization contributes all these impressive advantages, why is it that all large enterprises are not organized in this fashion? Unfortunately, certain distinct limitations and problems are inherent in its use.

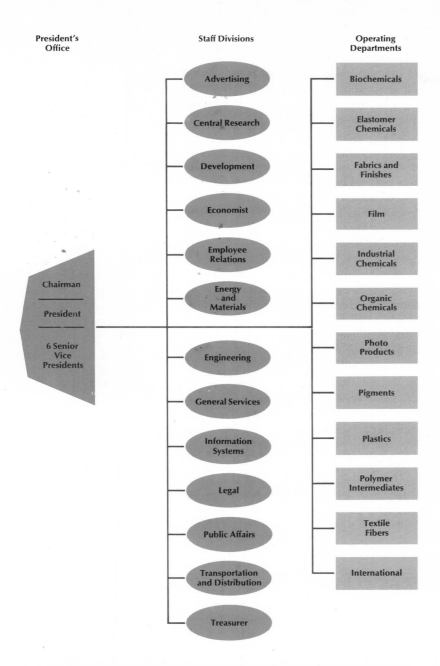

Figure 3–4 Organization of the Du Pont Company. Each operating unit is a self-contained business with its own engineering, production, marketing, and finance activities. The staff divisions provide services to the departments and to the president's office.

For one thing, not all companies can be *divided neatly* into self-contained operating divisions. Technology may make it impossible for a large operation to be broken up into several smaller ones. A steel mill, for example, cannot be split down the middle. On the other hand, in operations such as wholesaling or retailing, which involve a large number of products, sales volume of any one product may be insufficient to support the expense of a separate management and staff of specialists. One of the limitations of profit decentralization, then, is that the operations of the company must lend themselves to being divided into self-sufficient units of manageable size.

A related problem springs from the auxiliary-service activities that the company must perform for the operating divisions. Will a single, central *service unit,* such as purchasing or plant engineering, be really *responsive* to the needs of each of several operating divisions? Will the operating divisions be required to use the service divisions? If so, what happens to their presumed autonomy and accountability for profits? These are not insurmountable problems, but they do emphasize that profit decentralization brings in its wake a series of potentially troublesome issues.

Although we have referred to this type of organization as profit decentralization, we must remember that profits, though important, may be an *inadequate measure* of the performance of a division, at least in the short run. A division may decide, with the full approval of top management, to spend money on advertising to improve its market position; for two or three years it may spend large sums developing a new product. In other words, the division may be achieving its objectives even though it is showing a relatively small profit. Conversely, by keeping down expenses for nonrecurring or deferable items, a division may make a good profit showing even though it is slipping in customer goodwill or development of potential executives. This means that the use of profit for purposes of control is valid only if it is interpreted with a full understanding of what is happening within the division.

Perhaps the greatest difficulty in the use of profit decentralization is to find executives with the *capacity and willingness* to work effectively within the system. The division managers must be prepared to take the initiative on any matter that affects the long-run success of their units. They must be aware of the direct and indirect results of their own actions, instead of relying on someone in the home office to keep them out of trouble. In other words, they must act as responsible stewards of the resources put under their direction.

Top administrative officials in the company, in turn, must accept their obligation to maintain a "hands-off" attitude toward the decentralized divisions. As the president of a successfully decentralized company put it, "This calls for confidence in the capabilities of other people, a belief in teaching rather than telling, patience while others are learning—perhaps through their own mistakes —and a willingness to let others stand out in the public eye."

And yet we must remember that many executives of operating divisions have been trained to concentrate on a particular specialty rather than to take an overall view of an integrated business unit and that the top executives of many corporations have achieved their position through positive, aggressive action. This experience makes the behavior described in the two preceding paragraphs difficult to achieve in practice. The key managers in a company that adopts profit decentralization must have a realistic understanding of their new roles and must be flexible enough to adjust their behavior accordingly.

Restrictions on Autonomy

Clearly, there are many areas in which operating divisions are *not* autonomous. Everyone agrees that top management should retain some influence over the operating divisions. In consultation with the division managers, top management should 1) set long-range objectives and annual goals, 2) establish the broad policies within which the divisions are to operate, 3) approve the selection of key executives within the division, 4) approve major capital expenditures (which in effect means approving any major expansion), and 5) review any single transaction that might entail a major change in the profit or loss of the division. In addition, the headquarters office might want 6) to establish certain procedures for accounting, personnel, or purchasing to ensure consistent action throughout the company. Furthermore, top management can interpret all these limitations so broadly that it may retain the right to interfere with the division operations almost anywhere it wants to.

The use of policies, procedures, programs, and other types of plans will be examined later in this book, as will means for securing motivation and control. The point here is that the manner in which these processes are performed can either support or vitiate the underlying concept of profit decentralization. Therefore, if we organize along profit-decentralization lines, we must also plan, control, and activate in a manner compatible with profit decentralization.

CONCLUSION

In this chapter, we discussed first the process of delegating and then related this to the allocation of managerial work, especially its assignment to executives at different levels, from first-line supervisors to the president. Planning—that is, making decisions about actions to be taken—stands out as the crucial activity in managerial decentralization; once we decide who should do what planning, then other aspects of managerial work can be adjusted to fit into the pattern. Each manager has to allocate planning work among his subordinates, and we have identified several factors that can help him design a pattern of decentralization suited to the particular conditions he faces.

One special type of allocation, especially appealing to diversified companies, is "profit decentralization." Analysis of profit decentralization highlights the intimate connection between the way we departmentalize a company and the forms of decentralization that are desirable. We shall return to this interrelationship in the chapters on overall organization structure. But first we need to consider, in the next chapter, how staff men can be fitted into the total allocation of managerial work.

FOR CLASS DISCUSSION

1) In what ways will decisions on departmentation—particularly the choice between functional and compound groupings—affect decisions on how much and what kind of duties to delegate?

2) In what ways may a manager's experience in lower-level jobs (jobs that now fall under his supervision) positively and negatively affect his decision on how much he should decentralize?

3) "When I delegate a portion of my job, I inevitably *add to* rather than reduce my duties and obligations." How do you interpret this statement made by a department head?

4) The chief accountant of the Chicago division of a company reports to the general manager of that division. Accounting forms, regulations, and procedures, however, are designed by the corporate controller and must be followed by the division chief accountant. 1) Who is the chief accountant's boss? 2) What is the nature of his obligation to the division general manager? To the corporate controller? 3) How, by wise delegation, might potential friction be avoided? 4) How does this situation relate to bypassed supervision?

5) A great scholar once observed, "A fundamental pillar of freedom is the willingness of those who seek it to limit its application through the acceptance of just authority." Do you agree? Discuss in the context of the three inevitable features of delegation.

6) The seven guides to decentralization are based on key questions whose answers will vary from situation to situation. Nonetheless, the basic degree of decentralization will be relatively fixed in the short run. How can we deal with situations in which answers to "How much decentralization?" lead to a different conclusion from those drawn when establishing the basic degree of decentralization?

7) In what ways would you expect the degree and type of decentralization in a conglomerate with sales of $200 million to differ from the degree and type practiced by an equally large farm-equipment producer?

8) The warehouse manager of a plumbing-supplies company receives a phone call from a company sales person requesting him to get a rush order out to an important customer. At one P.M., the warehouse manager assigns the job of preparing the shipment to three warehouse workers and stresses that they have to get the job done by four P.M. so that the shipment can get to the customer's plant an hour later. Although three hours is ample time to get the shipment ready, at four P.M. the three men are not finished with their task. 1) Who is accountable if the order does not get to the customer by five P.M.?

2) Who had the obligation for getting the shipment loaded? 3) Discuss these forms of obligation in light of the authority that was granted. 4) How might better delegation have been achieved in this situation? 5) If three hours had not been ample time, how would this affect your answers to 1) through 4)?

Cases

For cases involving issues covered in this chapter, see especially the following. Particularly relevant questions are listed after each case.

The Delaware Corporation (p. 113), 2
Petersen Electronics (p. 211), 3
Merchantville School System (p. 217), 1
Central Telephone and Electronics (p. 527), 1
Southeast Textiles (p. 620), 1, 3
Household Products Company (p. 627), 1, 2

FOR FURTHER READING

Brooke, M. Z. and H. L. Remmers, *The Strategy of Multinational Enterprise.* New York: American Elsevier Publishing Company, 1970, Chapters 2–4.

Description of various relationships between head offices and national operating units. The different degrees of decentralization are strongly influenced by the global strategy the company is pursuing.

Dubin, R., *Human Relations in Administration,* 4th ed. Englewood Cliffs, N.J.: Prentice-Hall, Inc., 1974, Chapters 12–14.

Excellent synthesis of ideas on power, authority, and status.

Greenwood, R. G., *Managerial Decentralization.* New York: D. C. Heath and Company, 1974.

Description of General Electric Company's move to a highly decentralized organization.

Stewart, R., *The Reality of Organizations: A Guide for Managers.* London: The Macmillan Company, 1970, Chapters 5–8.

A useful short statement, written for managers, on delegation and other relationships within organizations.

Weisse, P. D., "What A Chief- or Group-Executive Cannot Delegate." *Management Review,* May 1975.

A senior executive of a Stage III company explains the kind of issues that he feels he cannot turn over to divisional managers.

4   Use
of Staff

THE CONCEPT OF STAFF

Staff is a key device managers can use to cope with pressures from our increasingly complex world. It is a special way of sharing the total managerial load—a device that supplements decentralization.

Definition of Staff

Staff work is that part of managerial work that an executive assigns to someone outside the chain of command. If an executive wants to relieve himself of some of his administrative burden, he may assign it to a staff assistant instead of delegating it to subordinates who would also be accountable for operations.

As we explained in Chapter 3, a manager always reserves some of the duties of planning, motivating, and controlling when he delegates operating duties to a line subordinate. If he uses staff help, he simply assigns part of this reserved administration to a third person.

A president or the head of a large department may use several staff people for different phases of his total management task. Some of these staff assistants may even have several subordinates of their own who form a staff section. Whatever the number and size of staff sections, the aim of staff work remains the same—to help an executive manage.

The concept of staff comes from military organization, but the business world uses the term more broadly and loosely. Practices vary widely from company to company and from job to job, with the result that we find widespread confusion about what a staff person is supposed to do. Because there is no single pattern, we as managers must design each staff position individually, as we do other jobs, deciding what activities we can advantageously assign to each position. Three examples will indicate the range of possibilities.

Specialized staff. Market research illustrates *specialized* staff work. A typical market-research unit gathers a wide variety of information about consumer habits, economic trends, competitors' actions, and marketing practices. The unit carefully analyzes this information and gives operating executives advice on marketing problems. For example, market researchers can suggest sales potentials to use in setting quotas for individual salespeople, and can test customer response to product changes. Operating executives do not have time to gather such information themselves, and they hesitate to ask their sales force to do the work for several reasons: Specialized skills are required, objectivity is essential, and sales people should spend their time getting orders from customers.

An industrial engineer is a good illustration of a staff person in the production area. Typically he not only gathers information but also goes further than the market researcher in preparing specific plans. Layout of plant equipment, production methods, operating standards based on time studies, incentive plans, systems for production scheduling, quality-control techniques, preventive maintenance—these are among the problems an industrial engineer often tackles. Solution of such problems requires concentrated attention and may involve technical knowledge a production manager is not familiar with.

When management asks an industrial engineer to make a study, it expects him to draw on all ideas that operating people can suggest and discuss with these people the practicability of any tentative plans. After a production manager has approved the final recommendations, an industrial engineer may be asked to assist in putting them into effect. He interprets the approved plans, assists supervisors in adjusting to them, explains their advantages and otherwise helps sell them to operators, and checks on results to determine whether operations are proceeding as he anticipated, or whether he must recommend further adjustments. Throughout this work, everyone understands that the industrial engineer functions as an agent of the production manager.

An internal auditor is also specialized staff, predominantly concerned with control. He checks the accuracy of accounting records, and may also check on how well employees comply with procedures and company regulations. Here again, operating executives could conceivably do this auditing, but companies often feel that it is more economical to assign the task to a full-time specialist.

General staff.   Not all staff people concentrate on a specific type of work. Sometimes a manager wants an assistant to whom he can turn over a wide variety of problems. The assistant's duties can vary all the way from functioning as a first-class secretary to serving as an *alter ego* to the boss in delicate negotiations. The staff person with such unspecified duties is often called "assistant to the _____."

On different days, we might find an assistant to a president gathering information on the national economic outlook, editing a statement for the president to make before a Congressional committee, investigating a complaint about company service, meeting with a group of long-service employees who urge the company to advance the compulsory retirement age to seventy, or coaching a new office boy on how to please the boss.

Corporate services.   Very large companies sometimes attach to the central headquarters staff units that work primarily as consultants to operating divisions. In the General Electric Company, for instance, one corporate "service" unit focuses on community relations, another on operations research, and so on. Each "service" is charged with anticipating external developments, advancing the state of the art in its particular field, organizing training courses to pass these advanced techniques on to executives and staff people in the operating departments, and being available as consultants on the invitation of the operating departments. Service is stressed. And to encourage operating people to use this service, senior executives at General Electric do *not* use these units for evaluation and control.

In all these examples of staff and in the many others that will appear from time to time in this book, we find a delegation of managerial work to people who do not supervise operations. These delegations, like all delegations, carry with them duties, authority, and obligation. But the duties do not entail direct supervision over executives or operators.

SCOPE OF STAFF WORK

Clarifying Assigned Duties

We can define the work of a staff person in terms of both the subjects or problems he covers and what he does about them. Unless a staff person, his boss, and everyone he works with understands the scope of his work, his efforts may cause more trouble than help. It is not enough, for example, to say that a personnel director should handle staff services in the field of personnel relations. Rather it is more constructive to list the types of problems in the field and then decide how far we expect a staff person to go in dealing with the problem. Figure 4–1 indicates this general approach.

Activities	Subjects							
	Recruiting	Selecting Employees	Training	Com-pensation	Benefit Plans	Health and Recreation	Union Relations	Employee Records
1. OPERATING WORK								
Supervises service operations	■				■	■		■
2. STAFF WORK								
Influences actions outside own department; to do so, he:								
A. Advises boss								
1. Identifies areas that need improvement				■			■	
2. Finds likely solutions				■			■	
3. Gathers and analyzes data bearing on choice of solution				■			■	
4. Gets concurrence or objections of people affected				■			■	
5. Recommends tentative solution			■	■			■	
B. Advises associates (mostly operating executives under his boss)								
1. Identifies areas that need improvement			■				■	
2. Finds likely solutions		■	■				■	
3. Gathers and analyzes data bearing on choice of solution		■	■				■	
4. Gets concurrence or objections of people affected			■				■	
5. Recommends tentative solution		■	■				■	
C. Prepares documents putting plans into effect		■		■			■	
D. Interprets and sells established plans	■							
E. Reports compliance to associates			■	■				
F. Reports compliance to boss			■					
G. Concurs on specific acts		■		■				
H. Sets policies and systems			■					

Figure 4–1   **Chart for analyzing the duties of a personnel director.**

This chart reveals that the role of a personnel director may differ in various areas. In dealing with unions, for example, he is likely to serve principally as an advisor. On the other hand, it is not an uncommon practice that no appointment to vacancies can be made without the concurrence of the personnel director.

The chart also suggests that for some activities, such as recruiting employees, handling pension plans, or sponsoring company athletic teams, a firm may grant its personnel director operating authority; in these areas he ceases to be staff and becomes a supervisor of auxiliary services.

Each check mark on a chart such as this represents careful thought about the functions of a particular staff person in a specific company. The chart is of course only a summary. For many duties under the heading of Subjects, we must think through several subtopics. "Training," for instance, includes by implication considerations of what should be done for executive personnel, orientation of new employees, training on the job, personal-development plans, and so forth. All this detail cannot be shown on a single chart, but the same kind of analysis applies to each subdivision.

The same approach should be followed when we determine the duties of each staff position. The principal task of the market researcher is to gather and analyze data for his boss and other operating executives—A.3 and B.3 on the chart. The industrial engineer, on the other hand, is likely to undertake all duties listed under A to F on the chart. An internal auditor is predominantly concerned simply with reporting compliance to his associates and his boss—items E and F on the chart. If we analyze duties in this manner, we will go a long way toward eliminating misunderstandings about the use of staff.

Completed Staff Work

Some people feel that the ideal staff arrangement results in "completed staff work," a concept that General Archer H. Lerch has described as follows:

Completed Staff Work is the study of a problem, and presentation of a solution, by a staff officer, in such form that all that remains to be done on the part of the head of the staff division, or the commander, is to indicate his approval or disapproval of the completed action. The words "completed action" are emphasized because the more difficult the problem is, the more the tendency is to present the problem to the chief in piecemeal fashion. It is your duty as a staff officer to work out the details. You should not consult your chief in the determination of these details, no matter how perplexing they may be. You may and should consult other staff officers. The product, whether it involves the pronouncement of a new policy or affects an established one, should, when presented to the chief for approval or disapproval, be worked out in finished form.

. . . It is your job to advise your chief what he ought to do, not to ask him what you ought to do. He needs answers, not questions. Your job is to study, write, restudy and rewrite until you have evolved a single proposed action—the best one of all you have considered. Your chief merely approves or disapproves.

Do not worry your chief with long explanations and memoranda. . . . In most instances, completed staff work results in a single document, prepared for the signature of the chief without accompanying comment. If the proper result is reached, the chief will usually recognize it at once. If he wants comment or explanation, he will ask for it.

The theory of completed staff work does not preclude a "rough draft" but the rough draft must not be a half-baked idea. It must be complete in every respect except that it lacks the requisite number of copies and need not be neat. . . .

The completed staff work theory may result in more work for the staff officer, but it results in more freedom for the chief. This is as it should be. Further, it accomplishes two things:

1) The chief is protected from half-baked ideas, voluminous memoranda, and immature oral presentations.
2) The staff officer who has a real idea to sell is enabled more readily to find a market.

When you have finished your "completed staff work" the final test is this: If you were the chief would you be willing to sign the paper you have prepared, and stake your professional reputation on its being right? If the answer is in the negative, take it back and work it over, because it is not yet completed staff work.

Although there is room for argument about some details of this proposal, such as the heavy use of written documents and the infrequency of personal discussions between a staff person and his boss, the central theme has much to recommend it. All too often, a staff person is willing to toss in ideas or information without thinking a matter through to a practical conclusion.

Useful as completed staff work may be, it is not ideal for all situations. It is expensive in terms of both the quality and the number of staff people needed. An additional expense is the interference with busy supervisors and operators involved in preparing a completed recommendation. Not many management posts warrant such extensive assistance.

Still another drawback in some companies is the tendency for a strong staff to undermine decentralization. A staff person may initially emphasize help to managers in lower echelons, but if cooperation is not immediately forthcoming, he then turns to completed staff work and urges the big boss to issue an order. If the boss does so, of course, the center of decision-making moves higher in the chain of command.

In view of these possible objections, we may find ourselves saying, "It's a good idea when used in the right place." To return to our previous examples, we can conclude that completed staff work would be an approach well suited to an industrial engineer but not to a market-researcher or an internal auditor.

RELATIONSHIPS BETWEEN STAFF AND MANAGERS

Normal Staff Relationships

The relationship between a staff member and the operating executive with whom he works depends in part on the staff duties we discussed on the preceding pages. A person who only gathers facts or only checks on performance, for instance, will have relations with his superior that differ from those of an assistant who has concurring authority. Nevertheless, we can identify several features that characterize almost all successful staff relationships:

1) A staff person is primarily a representative of his boss. He does things that the boss would do if he had the necessary time and ability. He is an extension of the boss's personality—advising, investigating, imagining, encouraging, following up on matters in his particular sphere. A staff person's position gives him stature and imposes an obligation *not to misrepresent* the boss. If occasionally he declares his own views, which may be at variance with those of his boss, he should be careful to make the distinction clear, for people normally presume that a staff representative is sufficiently close to his boss to be able to reflect accurately the thinking of his superior. Let us note in passing that a boss has an obligation to spend enough time with each of his staff assistants so that they can, in fact, establish a mutual and consistent point of view.

2) A staff person must *rely largely on persuasion* to get his ideas put into effect. Lacking the power of command, he must build confidence in his opinions and must be sufficiently sensitive to the problems of those he would influence to win their acceptance of his proposals. The staff person who cannot accomplish all, or at least most of, the things he wants done by winning voluntary cooperation had better look for another job.

3) A staff person must be prepared to *submerge his own personality* and his own desire for glory. He must be an ardent teamworker, recognizing that his boss or some other operating executive will get credit for carrying the ball. To achieve improved results, he must be prepared to see others receive recognition for ideas that he may have subtly planted several months earlier.

These three characteristics of staff work, when consistently maintained, go far in overcoming the inevitable friction that arises when a third party is interposed in what is naturally a close, two-person relationship between a line supervisor and his subordinate.

We usually speak as though a staff person performed his job by himself. But in larger companies he may in fact have several assistants. Multiplication of people does not, however, change the relationship between staff and operating executives. *Within* a staff unit, there are of course the usual subordinate–boss, or "line," relationships. Just as any boss delegates—setting up duties, authority, and obligation—so the head of a staff unit builds a series of line relationships between himself and others within his group. We call these people "staff"

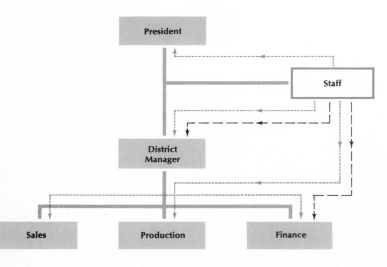

Figure 4–2 Typical relationships of central finance staff with managers in the regular line of command. The dotted line (color) indicates advice and assistance. The dashed line indicates functional authority.

because of their work, not because they are in any way absolved from the customary subordinate–boss relationship.

Staff Influence within the Chain of Command

A staff person charged with bringing about improvements in a particular area has two courses of action open to him: He may make a recommendation to an operating executive who is directly or indirectly his boss and then rely on the executive to issue the necessary orders to put the plan into effect, *or* he may try to secure voluntary acceptance of his ideas without the support of formal orders transmitted down the chain of command. The second, or voluntary, approach is very common, because a top operating executive is either too busy to bother with an issue, or he does not want to upset a pattern of decentralization.

In such circumstances, how does a staff person accomplish a mission? Let us say a senior operating executive has delegated a task to his West Coast superintendent; he has assigned duties and granted authority, and the superintendent has a sense of obligation to him. Because of the direct relationship with the senior executive, the superintendent is free (except as we will note below) to accept or reject the counsel of a staff person. Why then can a staff person expect to exert any significant influence?

For one reason, people are inclined to accept the advice of a staff person because they regard him as a *technical expert*. Engineer, statistician, repair mechanic, or lawyer—each has a specialized field in which his word is likely to be taken as authoritative.

For a second reason, when a staff person has an impressive title, reports high up in the organization hierarchy, and has an office that exhibits the symbols of importance, he enjoys exalted *status*. His views will be taken seriously by reason of his status alone.

Skill in presenting ideas, as we mentioned earlier, is still another reason why staff people are likely to be influential.

A perhaps more subtle source of influence is *potential backing* by a senior operating executive. If people down the line believe that advice they have rejected is bound to return as a command, they often conclude that it is wiser to take the advice in the first place. (Conversely, a staff person soon learns when and how far he can push a particular point.)

Finally, if a staff person's views may significantly *influence* an employee's salary increases or promotions, that employee will probably accord the staff person's recommendations more than just polite acknowledgment. This inclination is especially strong for employees away from the seat of a company—for example, a branch personnel officer or a branch accountant who aspires to transfer within his functional field, perhaps to the home office.

In summary, then, even though a staff person may have no command authority whatsoever, he may still get his recommendations accepted if he is intelligent, persuasive, impressive, and influential. Obviously, the potency of influence depends on each individual and each situation.

Compulsory Staff Consultation

Despite all the influence he can muster, a staff person may find himself on the sidelines watching the real action taking place without his participation. In a healthy organization, operating executives are strong-minded, vigorous individuals. Not infrequently, such executives welcome staff assistance only on highly technical matters or when it suits their convenience. To counteract this tendency, some companies follow a practice of compulsory staff consultation. Under this arrangement, a staff person *must* be consulted before action is taken. For example, department heads cannot confront a personnel manager with salary increases already promised or promotions already made; they must instead consult with him before they act. In other cases, a lawyer must have a chance to read a contract before a vice-president signs it. Under this plan an operating executive is not blocked from proceeding as he thinks best, but he is required to stop and listen to advice from another point of view.

Compulsory consultation supplements a more general requirement for successful staff work, the requirement that a staff should have access to any information that relates to its field of interest. No mere directive, of course, can ensure that a staff person will gain access to underlying motives that are often important for complete understanding of a problem; he can obtain such information only when he shares with others mutual respect and confidence. Nevertheless, it is helpful for management to make clear to employees that they are to keep the staff fully informed.

A related practice that some firms follow is to require each staff unit to make a semiannual or annual report on any weak spots it has uncovered in its field. This requirement may put a staff person in the delicate position of revealing a weakness that an operating executive at a low level wants to conceal from senior administrators. The staff person finds himself playing detective and risks not being welcomed back later. On the other hand, the inevitability of the report may prod the operating executive into taking corrective measures, presumably with the help of staff, so that the latter can mention constructive steps along with unfavorable conditions. Fundamentally, what each company needs is a climate that nourishes bold statements of fact to anyone concerned, coupled with sympathetic and constructive efforts to help improve deteriorated conditions. Covering up facts because of fear of criticism is not healthy. Managers and staff people can count on a free flow of pertinent information on troublesome situations only if operating personnel are confident that they will receive constructive help in return.

Concurring Authority

Under some circumstances, a manager may desire to further strengthen the hand of his staff. If control over certain operations is very important, staff may be granted concurring authority so that no action can be taken until a designated staff person agrees to it. Such concurring authority is probably most familiar in quality control, where an inspector usually must pass on raw materials or semifinished parts before they move to the next stage of production. Other examples include required legal approval before signing a contract, or the personnel manager's o.k. before making a promotion.

Whenever we grant concurring authority to staff, we realize that a senior administrator wants to ensure that the staff viewpoint is incorporated into operating decisions. It is a "safe" arrangement, because operating executives cannot take heedless action. On the other hand, it slows down action, for if the staff and operating people do not agree, someone must appeal up the administrative line, perhaps even to a senior executive who is boss of all operations and staff. In addition, although management can hold both a staff and an operating person accountable for any actions they *do* take, both have plenty of opportunity for passing the buck when they do *not* take action.

These considerations suggest that we should grant concurring authority only when the point of view represented by a staff person is particularly important, and when possible delay in action, while agreement is being ironed out, will not be serious.

Even when these conditions are met, it is important that we carefully define the grounds on which a staff may withhold its approval of a proposal. For instance, it is one thing for a controller to block a capital expenditure because of lack of funds, and quite another if he blocks it because of his personal disapproval of a plan. An inspector may delay a shipment of goods because they do not come up to standard, but his company should not permit him to take over the engineer's function of deciding how a product should be redesigned. Dynamic action would be difficult under such a system.

Functional Authority

The most extreme formal technique for extending staff influence is the granting of functional authority. This means that a staff person can give direct orders to operating personnel in his own name instead of making recommendations to his boss or to other operating executives. His instructions then have the same force as those that come down the channel of command. As in direct-line relationships, a staff person probably consults with whomever he instructs; and the person receiving the instructions may point out difficulties in execution to the staff and to the line boss. But until orders are rescinded or revised, the company expects the worker to carry them out.

Naturally, we give a staff functional authority only over those areas in which its technical competence is recognized and its opinion would probably be accepted anyway. Thus a chief accountant may have functional authority over accounting forms and systems, a medical officer over physical examinations, and a legal counsel over responses to any legal suits against the company. On such matters, the word of a staff officer will be followed in at least 99 percent of the cases; it is simpler to have it clearly understood that his word is final.

The trouble with functional authority is that it is tempting. It is beguiling in its apparent simplicity. For example, it is too easy merely to say that a personnel director will have functional authority over all personnel matters, a sales promotion director over sales promotion activities, and a controller over all expenses. Such sweeping assignments can wreak havoc in an organization. For if the personnel director can issue instructions that cover the selection, training, and motivation of all employees, he is virtually in a position to dominate all operations. And since expenses are fundamental to nearly every company decision, the controller with functional authority over such matters becomes tantamount to a general manager. In addition, wide use of functional authority may burden operating managers with conflicting orders; it tends to undermine the status of supervisors, and it complicates accountability. These difficulties arise from the indiscriminate use of a delicate arrangement.

What then are the circumstances in which we may use functional authority? The following three conditions are desirable, and at least two should always be present before we grant a staff person such authority:

1) *Only a minor aspect of the total operating job is covered.* Accounting forms and Blue Cross contracts, for instance, are only incidental to most operating jobs. Although these matters should receive the thoughtful attention of somebody, the plans adopted do not substantially affect the bulk of operations.

2) *Technical or specialized knowledge of a type not possessed by operating executives is needed.* If a sales manager or a production superintendent is going to accept the advice of, say, a tax expert or a medical director anyway, we can simplify decision-making by granting functional authority to such specialists.

3) *Uniformity, or at least consistency, of action in several operating units is essential.* For instance, pension rights of employees who are transferred among several divisions of a company should be treated consistently, as should credit terms extended to customers. A staff unit with functional authority is more likely to deal consistently with such matters than the divisions acting separately.

A Composite Pattern

Of the various means we have considered for strengthening the influence of staff, functional authority moves farthest from the purely assisting and counseling relationship first described. Compulsory consultation and concurring authority are intermediate positions. For reasons already noted, we should move cautiously from establishing an easy, simply helpful relationship toward insisting that a staff person must be heeded. Briefly stated, as staff is made more powerful, its scope should be confined.

In practice we often provide a different kind of relationship for different duties of a single position. A company attorney, for instance, might cover the whole range: On most matters he just *gives advice;* but in one or two areas *consultation* is compulsory; for a limited group of decisions his *concurrence* is required; and possibly over a few technical matters he has *functional authority.* But such a composite set of relationships is apt to be confusing. We will court the least trouble by keeping staff people in *advisory roles.*

We have just implied many difficulties that arise in connection with staff. Nevertheless, a summary of four common areas of trouble may be helpful to those who will either use staff or serve in staff positions.

Vague Definition of Duties and Authority

Time and again, we find friction between operating executives and staff people simply because the role of staff is misunderstood. The word "staff" provides no formula for resolving questions of what the duties should be. Some people within an enterprise may assume that a staff person is merely a fact-gatherer or, at most, an advisor to his own boss. A boss may want a staff assistant to make suggestions to people throughout the organization; and the staff person himself may be so zealous about his areas that he believes he should control as well as plan. With three such disparate views in competition, sooner or later we can expect a clash and perhaps hard feeling.

A common source of confusion is strengthening the influence of staff to meet a specific problem—through either required consultation, concurring authority, or functional authority—but failure to delineate the scope of this additional authority. For instance, during an energy shortage the chief engineer may be given "concurring authority over new uses of power." Trouble will arise unless everyone concerned recognizes that the new authority extends only to adding power-consuming equipment.

What we need to overcome these problems is mutual understanding by all principal parties of the duties and authority of each staff person and, even more importantly, a working relationship built out of experience that translates the general understanding into smooth work habits and attitudes.

Figure 4–3 Staff often serves as coach. But as in athletics, the distinction between advice and command is difficult to determine.

Scarcity of Good Staff

All too often, we can trace a staff failure back to a selection of wrong individuals for staff positions. A staff person needs both competence in his specialty and skill in staff work. Without technical competence, of course, he is hardly worth the nuisance he is to other executives. But technical competence alone is not enough. He must be affable, sensitive, discreet, and honest so that he may earn the confidence of other people; he must be articulate and persuasive so that he may win genuine acceptance of his proposals; he must be patient but persistent (rather than resort to commands) in his efforts to get results; he must find satisfaction in good team results rather than in personal glory; he must have a high sense of loyalty to his boss and of obligation to duty, even in the face of the frustration of highly circumscribed authority. Unfortunately, we do not often find a person with this combination of abilities and attitudes coupled with technical competence.

Sometimes a company uses a staff job as a training post for future operating executives, but also occasionally as a dumping ground or pasture for an unwanted operating executive. If such a man is a misfit in his staff position, the company creates a new problem in trying to solve an old one. Staff work, by its very nature, creates delicate relationships, and if a company has only unqualified people available, it had better sharply curtail staff jobs in scope or eliminate them entirely.

Mixing Staff and Operating Duties

It is not always practical to completely separate staff duties and operating duties to different jobs. We noted, for example, that a controller typically supervises corporate accounting directly and also has staff duties in connection with budgets and analysis of expenses of other departments.

Small companies that can afford only a limited number of executives may ask a single individual to fill two positions. For instance, a sales-promotion manager may also supervise selling in one district. Or a company with one large plant and two or three small assembly plants may have its production superintendent run the main plant and also maintain an undefined staff relationship with the assembly plants.

Still a third type of mixture of staff and operating duties—one which we find in both large and small companies—is to have senior operating executives serve as staff to the president on companywide problems. A large operating department may follow a comparable arrangement by having key executives wear two hats: one when they run their own divisions and another when they act as advisors on whatever problems face the whole department.

Theoretically, such a combination of duties should cause no difficulty so long as the executive and the people he works with understand which role he is playing at any one time. The practical difficulty is that this distinction is hard to maintain. The executive himself may be unable to shift gears from being a hard-driving operating executive to being a reflective staff counselor. Even when it is clear in his own mind, he may fail to tell others which role he is playing. When we compound this difficulty by failing to clearly define duties and authority in each kind of work, we wind up with a "staff" that has a vague assignment to dabble in other people's problems.

The remedy lies in real understanding of what staff work is, agreement on what each person should do, and care in assigning individuals who are both technically and temperamentally qualified.

Disregard of Staff by the Boss Himself

A fourth source of staff difficulties may be the very manager who has created staff positions in the first place. He undoubtedly finds his total administrative burdens more than he himself can carry and sets up one or more staff positions to relieve him of part of the load. But if he falsely assumes that he has solved his difficulties and can forget about them, he is certainly sowing seeds for future woe.

A boss must maintain close enough and frequent enough contact with a staff person to enable the latter to serve effectively as an extension of the eyes, ears, and mind of his superior. It is by no means necessary for a specialized staff person to see his boss daily. What is essential is that the two maintain sufficient contact to ensure their general accord on approaches and values.[1]

Even more devastating to confidence than lack of contact is the willingness of some executives to make decisions in an area assigned to a staff person without ever consulting him. Suppose a senior executive specifically charges his budget director with preparing capital-expenditure budgets. But later, when an operating subordinate presses him, the senior executive approves a large expenditure without first talking to the budget director. The next time the operating executive needs capital, he will probably again bypass the budget director and go directly to the senior executive. Soon the budget director will be a useless adjunct.

In contrast, the budget director will have greater status if the senior executive insists that his operating executives talk through all matters of capital expenditure with the budget director before bringing any request to him. Soon the operating people will learn that to get approval for capital expenditures, they must work with the budget director. In short, when an executive creates a staff position, he must be prepared to discipline *himself* to use the staff if he expects others to do so.

---

[1] In the Army, a Chief of Staff plays an important part in ensuring full communication between the commanding officer and the technical staff. This device has found little application in business; however, occasionally a much more junior "Assistant to the ————" may be sufficiently intimate with the boss to assist in this important communication to the staff.

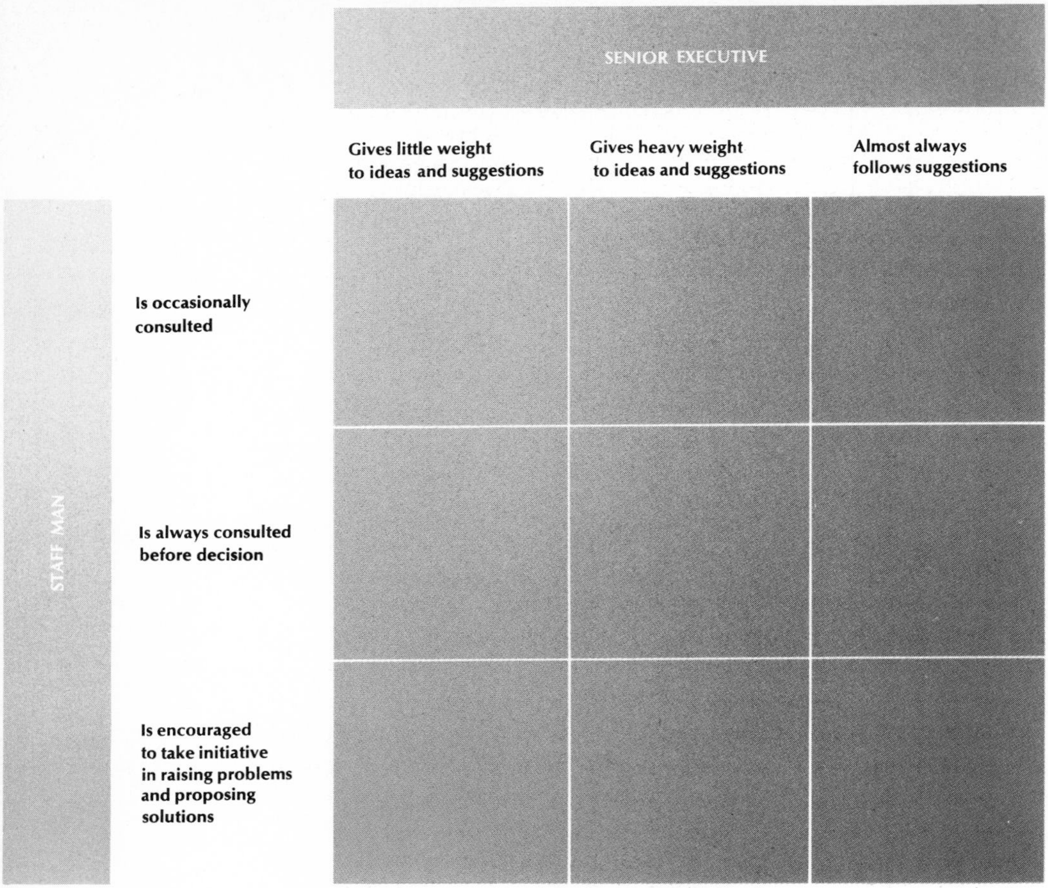

Figure 4–4 A senior executive, by his treatment of suggestions, strongly affects the influence of staff throughout the organization. In this chart, the color shading represents degrees of the staff person's participation; the black shading represents degrees of the senior executive's response.

CONCLUSION

The concept of staff is appealing, for it permits an executive to extend his capacity. The staff assistant performs managerial work that the executive is too busy to do or for which he may lack technical competence. However, the arrangement is easily abused. Unless mutual understanding exists regarding the subjects covered and the action expected of the staff, relations between supervisors and subordinates may become confused.

Moreover, anything as delicate as staff relationships rarely continues on an even keel. Somebody will undoubtedly become too aggressive, one person will step on another's toes, people will observe consultations in the letter rather than in the spirit, jealousies will creep in. To keep emotional flare-ups at a minimum and to maintain relationships between staff and operators as he desires, a manager must take time to provide continuing coordination and guidance. He must know whether his staff has become autocratic or lazy, whether their assistance is constructive, whether they are persuasive of their viewpoint, and whether operating people are too submissive or too independent.

In other words, by creating a staff an executive may facilitate his total job, but he also imposes upon himself new burdens: contact with staff, supervision of relations between staff and operating executives, and self-restraint to the point where he too uses the staff according to his prescription.

FOR CLASS DISCUSSION

1) The line superintendent of a production department receives information on the optimum combination of materials to be used in producing a new product in his department. The information comes from a staff group that uses computer programs to work out such optimum combinations. This staff group gets information from the line superintendent, industrial engineering, purchasing, and the product-development engineer who has developed the production specifications. After three months of production, the line superintendent learns that, though the new product he has been producing has passed his inspection, it has been returned in large quantities as "too brittle."

   Who are the various people who might be held accountable for this failure? Who should carry what degrees of obligation?

2) If a corporate line officer has staff assistants who perform their functions in the manner prescribed by General Lerch, then what is the line officer's function? How does the functional area in which the staff man works affect his ability to do "completed staff work"?

3) "Staff people are worse than college professors," said an experienced plant manager. "Since they don't have to face the day-to-day problems, they have all kinds of time to develop theories about how we should get our work done. But instead of writing books on their theories like the professors, they write reports to the president and cause us no end of problems. I wish my boss's staff would go to some university. I'd rather deal with the professors." 1) What do you make of this person's comment? 2) Would a good college (business school) professor be a likely candidate for a staff position in industry? Discuss.

4) Consider the following two statements:

   a) The more heterogeneous a company's products, markets, and technologies, the less the potential for effective functional staff groups at the corporate level.

   b) The more heterogeneous a company's products, markets, and technologies, the greater the need for effective functional staff groups at the corporate level.

   How do you reconcile these two statements?

5) Assume that a staff man takes serious objection to an action recommended by a line manager who reports to the same vice president as the staff man. Their common boss, the vice president, hears both parties out and cannot see a clear advantage to either position. 1) What should the vice president do? 2) If the vice president supports his line subordinate, what impact has the former had on the duties, authority, and obligation of the disagreeing staff subordinate?

6) What should be the major differences between the work of a corporate staff group in marketing, research, and the like and divisional counterpart staff groups? How will their work (corporate and divisional staffs) complement each other? How may they conflict?

7) In contrast to the advocacy of filling corporate staff positions with younger men, in some companies high-level staff groups are made up of seasoned line officers who are taken out of line management positions as they near retirement age. This is done so that the company "can use their years of experience even after they have passed their peak as line officers." Comment on the wisdom and potential pitfalls of this approach.

8) "The key requirements for a good staff person are the same as those for a good diplomat. They both should be bright, articulate, self-effacing, willing and able to compromise, and be independently wealthy." What do you think of this comment by the president of a West Coast bank?

Cases

For cases involving issues covered in this chapter, see especially the following. Particularly relevant questions are listed after each case.

The Delaware Corporation (p. 113), 1(d)
Milano Enterprises (p. 124), 1
Merchantville School System (p. 217), 2, 3
Family Service of Gotham (p. 532), 1
Central Telephone and Electronics (p. 527), 2
Southeast Textiles (p. 620), 2

FOR FURTHER READING

Allen, L. A., "The Line–Staff Relationship," in M.D. Richards and W. A. Nielander, eds., *Readings in Management,* 4th ed. Cincinnati: South-Western Publishing Co., 1974, pp. 543–54.

Sound advice to managers, based on extensive field study.

Atchison, T. J., "The Fragmentation of Authority." *Personnel,* July 1970.

Effect of staff expertise on authority and accountability.

Dubin, R., *Human Relations in Administration,* 4th ed. Englewood Cliffs, N.J.: Prentice-Hall, Inc., 1974, Chapter 10.

Behavioral views on the role of staff specialist.

Litterer, J. A., *Analysis of Organizations,* 2nd ed. New York: John Wiley & Sons, 1973, Chapters 23 and 24.

Clear review of various roles of staff in business, and of line–staff relationships in business organizations.

Rhenman, E., L. Stromberg, and G. Westerlund, *Conflict and Cooperation in Business Organizations.* New York: John Wiley & Sons, 1970.

Penetrating analysis of difficulties with traditional line–staff concepts, as revealed in Swedish companies.

Effect of Growth

on Structure

5

This chapter has a dual purpose—1) to examine overall organization structure and 2) to explore the effect of a company's size and complexity on the overall structure best suited to its needs.

Designing a Total Structure

Departmentation, decentralization, and staff can be analyzed as separate issues—as we have done in the three preceding chapters. In an active firm, however, they are closely interrelated. Just as in the design of an airplane, the relative size and weight of each component and the ways the components are related to one another affect the performance capabilities, so it is with the structure of an enterprise. The components must be melded together.

Typically we give close attention to this integration into an overall structure when a company adopts a new strategy. If we neglect to change the structure to fit the new strategy, tensions and bottlenecks will force us to make tardy adjustments.

A constructive approach to this recasting of the total structure is to:

1) Identify key operating departments that fit the new mission.
2) Decide on the level at which operating decisions can be made most effectively.
3) Consider the nature and location of auxiliary and staff units that are needed.
4) Adjust the parts to secure balance, optimum spans of supervision, and parallel designs where feasible.

We have already examined the major elements; now we can focus on balancing and designing a workable whole.

Stages in Growth

The best organization design for any company is strongly influenced by its size and complexity. Smaller firms with simple activities operate very well with an elementary organization. But as a firm grows in size and its activities become more diversified, a more elaborate structure is necessary.

Four stages in organization development highlight this effect of size and complexity. Although the transition from one stage to the next may be gradual —and many firms may never be forced to move into the complicated forms— recognition of the different features of each stage is helpful. Strategy and structure can be more quickly matched. The four broad stages are: single entrepreneur, departmentalized firm, multiple-mission company, and conglomerate.[1]

I SINGLE ENTREPRENEUR

The simplest form of organization is one key individual with a group of helpers. The central figure is aware of the details of what is happening and personally gives instructions to the helpers. Of course, the assistants learn the routines of repetitive activities and can proceed with minimum guidance. And they may become specialized in their normal assignments—for example, accounting, dealing with customers, or making repairs. But changes from customary patterns and initiatives toward moving in new directions rest with the boss.

Basically, the division of labor among the operators depends upon the type and volume of work. Delegation is simple. There is no formal staff, although experienced personnel often guide newcomers; and when several people do similar work one of them may become the informal leader.

A typical single-leader organization is the diner and twenty-room motel run by G. P. Olsen in eastern Minnesota. The diner was Olsen's first venture, and recently he added an adjoining motel unit. Olsen continues to be very active in the daily operation of both the diner and the motel, and he closely supervises the work of persons indicated in Figure 5–1.

Many other small businesses—dress shops, drugstores, filling stations—are operated in this fashion, often with remarkable success. The key individual normally has high energy and skill, doing part of the work himself as necessary.

---

[1] The following discussion draws freely on Chapter 16 of W. H. Newman and J. P. Logan, *Strategy, Policy, and Central Management,* 7th ed. (Cincinnati: South-Western Publishing Co., 1976).

Figure 5–1   Organization of Olsen's diner and motel.

Even though the business may be legally a corporation, action pivots around the moving spirit.

The limitation of this simple organization form is the capacity of the single entrepreneur (or two individuals if it is run as a partnership). He can add helpers as the business grows, but each new subordinate requires some supervision. Sooner or later the coordinating head can no longer keep track of what each person is doing; motivation and control slip; and planning lacks careful backup investigation. Especially when the business involves nonroutine activities and frequent emergencies, the manager must find some way to free himself from normal day-to-day operations.

II   DEPARTMENTALIZED COMPANY

A shift in organization from the single-leader form to a departmentalized structure opens up opportunity for great expansion. First, a change must take place in the way the senior executive sees his role. This is crucial. Next we can establish a *series* of departments, each organized to suit its growing needs. As the total volume increases, staff positions may also be added. Having escaped from the restraint of the supervisory capacity of a single person, the company can multiply its activities many fold, as our discussion will indicate.

Reliance on Functional Departments

Delegation to strong department managers provides relief for the overburdened entrepreneur. Typically a manager is appointed for each major function—sales, production, finance, and the like. These people (or *their* helpers), take charge of day-to-day operations: they schedule, expedite, and watch inputs and outputs. And because they focus on a narrower span of work than the entrepreneur, they become more sensitive to particular needs and opportunities.

With such help, the behavior of the senior executive should differ sharply from that of the single entrepreneur in a Stage I organization. The senior executive must be willing to delegate. This means that he no longer knows what is happening day by day and accepts decisions that are not quite the way he would have made them. A cardinal purpose of creating functional departments is to give the senior executive time to focus on interdepartmental coordination and on policy and strategy issues. Many executives whose success as Stage I managers makes possible a Stage II organization find this required change in their personal behavior very difficult and sometimes impossible.

The contrast between an entrepreneur who runs the show single-handed and a departmentalized setup is indicated in a comparison of Figures 5–1 and 5–2. The organization for a three-hundred-room motel shown in Figure 5–2 leaves the general manager free to coordinate, deal with emergencies, be active in community relations, and give more attention to long-range planning. His job differs sharply from that of G. P. Olsen.

Most Stage II companies focus on a single product/market objective. For such firms, dividing operations into major functions is usually the best method of primary departmentation. For example, firms concentrating on automobile insurance usually have departments for sales, underwriting, claims, finance, investment, and legal. Similarly, a hi-fi-equipment manufacturer will probably have research-and-development (R&D), production, marketing, and finance as basic departments. As we noted in Chapter 2, such functional departments become expert in their particular area, give adequate attention to an activity that otherwise might receive hurried treatment, and act in a consistent fashion on such matters as price concessions.

Organization within Departments

Once the critical transition from the personal, closely supervised organization of Stage I to a series of departments in Stage II has been made, a whole array of possibilities are available for further expansion. Each department can organize for its own growth.

A small functional department can be organized on the one-dominant-individual basis, but soon its own size and need for systematic relations with other departments call for orderly grouping of internal activities. One form is, of course, the assignment of work by subfunctions. There are other options:

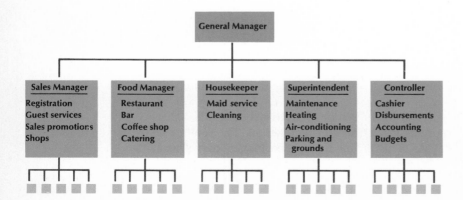

Figure 5–2 Organization of a large motel.

Products. The work of a purchasing department is often divided by products—permitting each buyer to become expert in his dealings with certain supplying industries and companies. Likewise, with department-store merchandising, specialized knowledge about product lines, such as hosiery, jewelry, furniture, and men's suits, is essential in selecting goods to sell, pricing, and sales promotion. Product subunits are often introduced within an engineering department to aid in acquiring detailed knowledge about the diverse aspects of a product.

We use such product subdivisions when the products handled differ significantly from each other, and when those differences are important in gaining a relative advantage over competitors.

Processes. Manufacturers—and government offices—often perform several distinct processes that may serve as the basis for organization within a production department. For example, in steel production we usually find separate shops for coke ovens, blast furnaces, open-hearth furnaces, hot-rolling mills, cold-rolling mills, and the like. Each process is performed in a separate location and involves a distinct technology.

The grouping of activities by process tends to promote efficiency through specialization. All the key people in each unit become expert in dealing with their aspect of the business. On the other hand, process classification increases problems of coordination. For one thing, scheduling the movement of work from unit to unit becomes somewhat complex. Also, since no unit has full responsibility for a customer's order, a process unit may not be as diligent in meeting time requirements and other specifications as a group of people who think in terms of the total finished product and their customers.

The conflict between the desire to increase skill in performance through specialization and mechanization, and the need for coordination to secure balanced efforts, recurs time and again in organization studies. Insurance companies, hospitals, and even consulting firms face the same issue.

Territories. Companies with salespeople who travel over a large area almost always use territorial organization within their sales departments. Large companies will have several regions, each subdivided into districts, with a further breakdown of territories for individual sales representatives. Airlines, finance companies with local offices, and motel chains all by their very nature have widely dispersed activities and consequently use territorial organization to some degree.

The primary issues with territorial organization are three:

1) What related activity should be physically dispersed along with those which by their nature are local? For example, should a company with a national sales-force also have local warehousing, assembling, advertising, credit and accounting, and personnel? And how far should the dispersion occur—to the regional level or to the district level? Typically, whenever such related activities are dispersed, they are all combined into a territorial organization unit.

2) How much authority to make decisions should be decentralized to these various territorial units? In other words, how much of the planning and control work should go along with the actual performance?

3) What will be the relations between the home-office service and staff units and these various territorial divisions?

The major advantage of territorial organization is that it provides supervision near the point of performance. Local conditions vary and emergencies do arise. Persons distantly located will have difficulty grasping the true nature of the situation, and valuable time is often lost before an adjustment can be made. Consequently, when adjustment to local conditions and quick decisions are important, territorial organization is desirable. On the other hand, if many local units are established, some of the benefits of a large-scale operation may be lost. The local unit will probably be comparatively small; consequently the degree of specialization and mechanization will likewise be limited.

Customers. A company that sells to customers of distinctly different types may establish a separate unit of organization for selling to and serving each. A manufacturer of men's shoes, for instance, sells to both independent retail stores and chain stores. The chain-store buyers are very sophisticated and may prepare their own specifications; consequently, any salespeople calling on them must have an intimate knowledge of shoe construction and of the capacity of their company's plant. In contrast, sales representatives who call on retailers must be able to think in terms of retailing problems and be able to show how their products will fit into the customer's business. Few sales representatives can work effectively with both large chain-store and independent-retail customers; thus, the shoe manufacturer has a separate division in its sales organization for each group.

Commercial banks, to cite another example, often have different lending officers for types of customers—railroads, manufacturing concerns, stock-brokers, consumer loans, and the like. These people recognize the needs of their own group of customers, and they also are in a good position to appraise their credit worthiness.

Ordinarily, customer groups include only selling and direct-service activities. Anyone who has been shunted around to five or six offices trying to get an adjustment on a bill or a promise on a delivery will appreciate the satisfaction of dealing with a single individual who understands the problem and knows how to get action within the company. On the other hand, this form of organization may be expensive, and a customer-oriented employee may commit the company to actions that other departments find hard to carry out.

Summary. This short review of product, process, territory, and customer departmentation indicates the many variations that are possible in organizing within a major department. Further refinements, and the factors involved in their selection, have been discussed in Chapter 2. A by-product of this review is to mention alternatives to functional departments. In special circumstances we may decide that, say, an international department or a government-contract department fits a company strategy better than a functional department.

This elaboration of a Stage II organization aids expansion but it does not change the basic process. We start with a sharply focused product/market mission, and then we establish specialized departments, each of which has a different though important contribution to make to that mission. The work of these departments is interdependent, so the entire operation has to be managed as an integrated whole. The role of the general manager of such an organization is to find department managers who will be responsible for day-to-day operations while he concentrates on coordination and longer-run strategy and policy issues.

Addition of Staff

A successful Stage II company may become quite large. Some such firms —for example, in the life-insurance, paper, and pharmaceutical industries— have sales or assets of several hundred million dollars. By the time companies reach this size—and much sooner if their activities become complex—staff assistants will probably be added under the general manager and under major department managers (e.g., Colonial Chemical Company, Figure 5–3).

Staff complicates the organization, as we noted in Chapter 4. So the need for staff assistants should be examined with care. Generally speaking, a manager *can* justify assigning duties to staff when he is overburdened or lacks the necessary skill, and when, for any of the following reasons, he hesitates to delegate more of his managerial work to his operating subordinates.

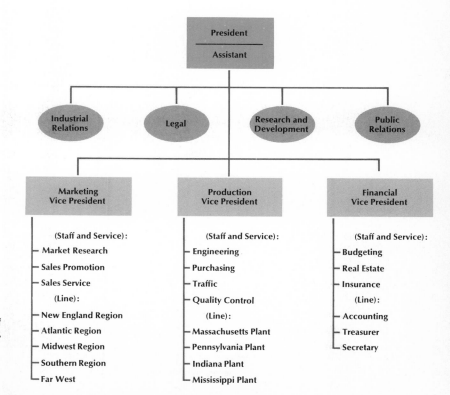

Figure 5–3   Organization of Colonial Chemical Company.

1) *Operating subordinates would not give an activity adequate attention.* For instance, a vice president of personnel may be appointed if department managers are skeptical of modern techniques and central management fears they will slight this activity.

2) *The work requires an expert.* Most managers, for instance, lack knowledge of real estate and the law, so staff assistants may be provided in these areas.

3) *The company needs coordinated and consistent action among several operating units.* The need for consistency in fair-employment practices or in pricing may prompt a staff appointment. Or, coordination of a national advertising campaign with local sales promotion may need concentrated attention.

4) *The chief executive wants help in controlling the operating departments.* Keeping track of local operations is especially difficult when activities are dispersed in many geographical locations.

5) *Top management seeks aid in analyzing problems.* Any manager may become so busy with pressing short-run problems that he needs an assistant who can help him think through basic questions.

All these reasons have been factors in adding staff to the organization of the Colonial Chemical Company.

Span of Supervision

A recurring issue in overall organization design, especially as a firm grows, is the workload of each executive. How many immediate subordinates should each executive have? This topic has been the subject of much debate, particularly since behavioral scientists discovered what every practical manager knows: No single number is the correct answer in all cases.

Very real limits do exist on any person's capacity to supervise. His time and energy are limited, and if he has too many subordinates he cannot provide good personal leadership to all. It takes time to assign tasks, to answer questions, to motivate subordinates, to mediate arguments, to coordinate work within the unit and with other departments, to make sure that necessary supplies are on hand, and to perform the many other duties of a supervisor.

The question of limits on the span of supervision is important in designing

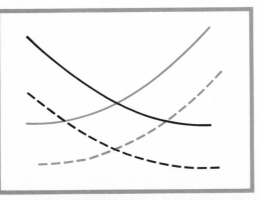

Degree
of centralization

Instability
of activities

Amount
of staff assistance

Ability
of subordinates

Figure 5–4 The optimum span of supervision is not fixed. Rather, it depends on several variables that should be weighed in each situation.

Optimum number of subordinates increases ⟶

an organization structure, for it directly affects the number of executives needed. The narrower the average span, the more supervisors needed, and that adds to payroll expense. Another drawback is that additional layers of supervisors complicate communications from the chief executive down to operators and back up the line.

The personal energy of an executive influences to some extent the number of people he can supervise effectively. The following factors also affect what spans are feasible in a specific situation:

1) *Time devoted to supervision.* All supervisors spend part of their time personally doing operations. Foremen serve as relief men; sales managers call on important customers; company presidents testify before Congressional committees. In addition, nearly all executives participate in company planning, serve on company committees, and plead for new personnel and equipment. Both types of work reduce the time an executive can devote to supervision.

2) *Variety and importance of activities being supervised.* A manager who is confronted with complex issues needs more time to dispose of them than an executive who deals with routine, one-person problems.

3) *Repetitiveness of activities.* New and different problems take more time to handle than those we have faced many times before.

4) *Ability of subordinates.* Green, inexperienced help takes more of a supervisor's time than well-trained persons who have good judgment and initiative.

5) *Degree of decentralization.* An executive who personally makes many decisions is able to supervise fewer people than one who must merely provide occasional coaching and encouragement.

6) *Staff assistants provided.* When subordinates get from staff people much of their guidance on methods, schedules, personnel problems, quality standards, and perhaps other aspects of their work, they need less contact with their line supervisor.

For these reasons we should tailor the span of supervision to each executive position. And such optimum spans relate directly to the number of departments and divisions we can place under each executive. Span of supervision, then, is another interdependent factor to be included in the balancing of an overall structure. When growth strains a span of supervision, we must seek relief: increase decentralization, add a supervisory layer, increase staff, simplify activities—or perhaps move to a Stage III design.

III MULTIPLE-MISSION COMPANY

Successful enterprises outgrow a Stage II departmental organization. They become too large or too diversified. Ordinarily, as a Stage II company grows from fewer than a hundred to over a thousand employees, communications become more formal, standard procedures prevent quick adjustments, the convenience of each department receives more consideration than company goals, and people feel insignificant in terms of total results. Careful management can diminish these tendencies, but sooner or later sheer size saps vigor and effectiveness.

In addition, successful companies take advantage of opportunities to diversify product lines, to develop new sources of materials, and to provide new services in response to changing social needs. This adds complexity. But large functional departments often give secondary attention to such opportunities; they are too busy doing their established tasks well. So the new developments fail to receive the attention and the coordinated effort they deserve.

Unless a company makes a deliberate strategic decision to stay relatively small and clearly focused on a particular mission—a strategic option few American companies elect—a shift in organization becomes necessary.

Semi-independent Divisions

The basic remedy for oversize is to split up into several Stage I or Stage II divisions. A series of small businesses are created within the larger company.

Ordinarily these divisions are built around product lines. The part of marketing that deals with a particular product is transferred from the marketing department to the product division. And likewise with production, engineering, and perhaps other functions. Ideally each division has within it all the key activities necessary to run independently—it is *self-sufficient*. Moreover, the management of the newly created division is given a high degree of authority, making the division *semiautonomous*. The general manager of such a division then has virtually the same resources and freedom of action as the president of an independent company, and is expected to take the necessary steps to make the "little business" successful.

This form of organization we called "profit decentralization" in Chapter 3 —stressing the need for initiative and a feeling of full accountability by division managers, matched with loose-rein supervision by central managers.

Even when it is practical to place within a division all of its own marketing and production activities, some central services are retained. Obtaining capital, exploratory research, and staff assistance on labor relations, law, and market research, for example, usually can be performed more economically in one place for all divisions of the company. Such central assistance gives operating divisions an advantage over fully independent companies.

Typically, self-contained divisions are based on separate product lines. A company may have anywhere from two to (for the General Electric Company) a hundred such product divisions. The same idea, however, has been applied by department-store chains on a territorial basis. Also, large metal fabricators place their mining and transportation activities ("process" units) in self-contained divisions.

The main advantages of setting up such self-contained divisions are ease in management, better morale, adequate attention, faster coordination, and sharper control—as explained in Chapter 3, under "Profit Decentralization."

The drawbacks are of two types. Overhead expenses are increased because of the larger number of high-ranking executives and associated costs of more headquarters offices. Unless a reasonably large and sustained volume of business can be developed for each division, this increased expense may even offset the benefits. The second kind of limitation is technological: Can the major departments be split up and still remain relatively efficient? We need to take a closer look at this second issue.

Difficulties with Optimum Size

When shifting an organization to small, self-contained divisions, we soon discover that functional departments often cannot be neatly divided. Technology and other forces dictate an *optimum size* for various activities. For instance, an oil refinery to serve Salt Lake City alone would be much too small to be efficient. On the other hand, the task of increasing employment of minorities can readily be handled within separate product or territorial divisions.

The optimum-size issue is complicated because a desirable volume for one function may be undesirable for another. A men's-clothing firm, for instance, found that plants with two to three hundred employees could achieve virtually all economies of scale in production and that larger plants caused more personnel problems. However, the output of one such plant would be far too small for marketing purposes. National advertising and promotion were the key to the firm's marketing success, and the sales volume needed to support national distribution was six times the output of a single plant.

Figure 5–5   The optimum size for marketing a company's products may be much larger—perhaps national—than the optimum size of a plant producing those products. Such imbalance makes it expensive to create semi-independent regions, each with its own marketing and production functions. In some industries, the balance tilts the other way: markets would be best served on a regional (or product) basis, whereas efficient production requires a plant large enough to make products for the whole nation. So, if we choose to organize a company into several self-contained divisions, we often must sacrifice efficiency in at least one function.

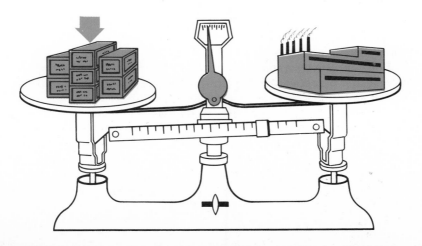

These differences in optimum size affect the number of self-contained divisions we establish. In an aluminum company, for instance, marketing considerations call for a dozen separate divisions, each focused on a product/market-type target. Production technology, however, dictates that almost all end-products come out of a few large plants. These plants cannot be split up by product lines. So twelve self-contained product divisions are impractical.

A review of self-contained divisions in a wide variety of industries indicates that most of them have a volume of work that is below the optimum size for one or two functions and above the optimum size for other functions. The aim, of course, is to build divisions that are optimum in size for critically important functions, even though this results in some diseconomies in other areas.

Compromise Arrangements

Companies often try to get most of the benefits of self-contained divisions and also keep functional operations at optimum levels. For example, one paper company leaves production in a single functional department, but it breaks product engineering and marketing down into strong product divisions. The division managers are expected to act like "independent businessmen," except that they must contract for their supply of products from the production division.

A comparable arrangement is used by a food processor, except that here it is selling rather than production that is centralized in one department. Each product division does its own product design, engineering, buying, production, merchandising, and pricing, but it utilizes the sales department to contact customers. The rationale here is that a single field organization can cover the country more effectively for all divisions than each could do separately.

Whenever a product division has to rely on an outside department for a key activity, problems of adequate attention, coordination, and control become more difficult. Occasions for bickering jump dramatically. Central management has to judge whether the harm done by restricting self-sufficiency is offset by the benefits of the larger-scale activities in the functional department.

The compromises just discussed all presume that self-contained product or regional divisions will be the primary organizational form of a company, with an exception being made for some one functional department. Another variation—matrix organization—retains the functional departments of a Stage II organization, but injects project managers who temporarily act much like a division manager in a Stage III organization. This special variation is discussed in the next chapter.

The concept of a series of self-sufficient, semiautonomous divisions is an appealing answer to the problems of growth. It is particularly suited to those increases in volume that are based on diverse markets or additions of related products. However, designing such divisions that are of optimal size is not a simple task.

Conglomerate organization differs from that of a Stage III multiple-mission company primarily in the absence at headquarters of service and staff units and in the limited attempt to secure synergistic benefits among its components. Typically, conglomerates are built of previously independent companies, each with its own traditions and a full complement of central services. Moreover, these companies are not expected to contribute to each other's business. So there is little to be gained from "coordination" and from overall service units. A conglomerate is truly a collection of disassociated businesses.

Focus on Financing

The primary activity at the headquarters of a conglomerate is financing—raising and allocating capital. This may be done by public issue of securities or by an ingenious array of mergers, spin-offs, and subsidiary financing. However, the number of employees directly involved is small. "Corporate planning" in the majority of conglomerates consists entirely of looking for attractive acquisitions and does not deal with businesses already in the fold. The presumption is that each operating unit will do its own strategic planning—except for major questions on sources and uses of capital.

Since the interactions between the central office and the operating companies in a conglomerate are largely limited to finance, the basic organization structure can be simple. The chief executive in each operating company reports to the president or a group vice-president in the central office. In addition, there will be the usual transfer of funds and upward flow of financial reports. This is all that's needed.

Of course, each operating company has its own organization; this may be a Stage I, II, or III organization or any variation that best suits the needs of each member company. Incidentally, the legal status of the operating company is not significant from the viewpoint of managerial organization. Each operating unit will be treated as a separate company even though its corporate identity may be washed out for financial reasons.

Strengthening Subsidiary Boards of Directors

In addition to financing, conglomerates can perform a significant role in directing and controlling their subsidiaries. The relationship should be that of an "outside" member of the subsidiary's board of directors.

Every company needs objective senior counsel to its chief executives. Presumably this independent counseling is the main job of an outside member of the board of directors. Unfortunately, all corporations face severe difficulties in attracting to their boards of directors individuals who are 1) wise, courageous, and well informed, and also 2) sufficiently concerned to devote energy and initiative to the affairs of the company they represent. Obtaining good outside directors is a chronic and serious problem.

A conglomerate, however, can overcome this difficulty. It has sufficient stake in the success of its operating companies to locate and employ individuals who are fully qualified to be good "outside directors." Such a person should devote full time to serving as a member or head of the board of, perhaps, half a dozen operating companies. By ensuring that major decisions are wisely made, insisting that unpleasant action be taken promptly, and providing counsel on future possibilities, a strong director can stimulate operating executives.

Thus, by aiding with finance and by providing able outside directors, conglomerates help strengthen their operating companies. Most of the central-management functions, however, should be left to the fully staffed operating companies.

CONCLUSION

As a company succeeds and grows, it must change its organization. Four quite distinct stages are clear. Stage I represents the small, budding enterprise in which *one dominant individual* does both long-range planning and day-to-day managing. Sooner or later the business exceeds the capacity of even the most energetic single manager. At this point a shift must be made to Stage II, in which day-to-day operations are delegated to *functional departments*. Then, as the firm expands and diversifies, the functional departments become too large and bureaucratic, so a further shift is necessary. In Stage III an organization is composed of *self-contained product or regional divisions*. Finally, though not necessarily, a collection of independent companies may be combined into a Stage IV *conglomerate organization*.

Many variations and compromises are essential to fit the organization to the specific technology, optimum size, resources, and other features of a specific firm. A cardinal aim in making such variations should be to strengthen the company in those areas in which it has chosen to build a strategic distinction. In this way the organization gives potency to the unique services the company wants to provide.

In each of these diverse overall structures, the elements of organization examined in Chapters 2, 3, and 4—departmentation, decentralization, and staff —are the bricks and mortar. The way they are combined and interwoven differ. But the underlying processes of combining activities into operating and managerial jobs, of mapping relationships between these jobs, and of adding supplementary services reappear over and over again. Although these four stages of growth suggest ways of adjusting to size and complexity, the structure for each specific company must be a unique application of the elementary organizing concepts. The opportunity, indeed the necessity, for creative adaptation arises in every structural design.

Several variations in design that deal with emerging management issues are examined in the next chapter.

FOR CLASS DISCUSSION

1) How would you respond to G. P. Olson (see Figure 5–1) if he said: "I can grow much bigger without shifting to a departmental structure. I can probably supervise 20 or 30 people as long as I can hire good people. If I tell them what I expect and make sure they are trained, then I just watch results and get rid of those who don't perform. I don't need any fancy organization, just good people and the willingness to give them the freedom to do their jobs"?

2) To what extent may serious organization problems arise as a company grows and shifts its strategy from skimming new products and markets to servicing more mature products and markets? How might these problems be dealt with?

3) If your college or business school were to be organized on a process basis, what would be the key departments? What might be the strengths and weaknesses of such a structure?

4) Can you give an example of an organization you have worked in or know firsthand that is organized on a product, process, *and* territory basis?

5) "If a chief executive decides to use staff to help him control operating departments, he must be careful not to have the same staff actively involved in planning his subordinates' programs." What do you think of this comment by a divisional manager?

6) Why do few companies elect to stay relatively small and clearly focused on a single mission, since to do so would probably make organization simpler and more efficient?

7) In what ways might longer-range planning assist central management in dealing with design changes arising from changes in strategy?

8) Is it desirable to have one or more major divisions operate as semiautonomous units in a company that is otherwise highly centralized? Explain. Under what conditions would such an arrangement be necessary?

Cases

For cases involving issues covered in this chapter, see especially the following. Particularly relevant questions are listed after each case.

The Delaware Corporation (p. 113), 1(c)
Milano Enterprises (p. 124), 2, 5
Atlas Chemical Company (p. 321), 1
Marten Fabricators (p. 316), 2
Graham, Smith, & Bendel, Inc. (p. 445), 2
Family Service of Gotham (p. 532), 2

FOR FURTHER READING

Bower, J. L., "Plannng and Control: Bottom Up or Top Down?" *Journal of General Management,* Spring 1974.

Explores the relationship between stages of growth—especially Stages III and IV—and the location of initiative in resource-allocation decisions.

Katz, R. L., *Cases and Concepts in Corporate Strategy.* Englewood Cliffs, N.J.: Prentice-Hall, Inc., 1970, pp. 501–16.

Ties stages of growth and organizational form to strategy choice being pursued by a firm.

Salter, M. S., "Stages of Corporate Development." *Journal of Business Policy,* Autumn 1970.

Insightful analysis of the concept of stages of growth—in terms of both organization and product/market relationship.

Widing, J. W., "Reorganizing Your Worldwide Business." *Harvard Business Review,* May 1973.

Problems in fitting a Stage III organization to multinational operations.

New Approaches
to Structural Design

6

NOVEL NEEDS, NOVEL SOLUTIONS

Organization is an instrument—a powerful tool—designed to fill specific needs. As the needs change, we naturally seek new ways to organize that are suited to the new conditions. In this chapter we look at five frontiers on which social and technological pressures are leading to new organizational designs:

1) Rapid technological change and complexity are fostering *matrix organizations.*
2) The magnitude of some corporate commitments is leading to *external, independent staff.*
3) Increasing involvement in social issues accentuates the need for an *office of the president.*
4) Current success of organized pressure groups raises the question of how to deal with *interest representation.*
5) Fascination with electronic computers calls for examination of the *impact of computers on organization.*

These five developments, of course, are not the only forces calling for new approaches in design. They illustrate the way environmental change impinges on an organization and show how a basic social institution such as managerial organization is adapted rather than scrapped.

MATRIX ORGANIZATION

Landing a man on the moon was largely a scientific achievement. It also required *managing* a huge, highly complex, interrelated, and uncertain development and production undertaking. Matrix organization was used in this effort, and part of the "fall-out" of the space program has been more careful analysis of this organizational form. Actually, matrix organization did not originate in the space program, and it has applications in a wide variety of enterprises.

Need for Coordinated, Focused Action

A drawback of the typical organization with its functional departments is that unusual, complex projects often get shunted about, progress slowly, and are the cause of endless meetings of key departmental executives. The more innovative and complicated the project, the more likely is fumbling to occur.

Matrix organization strives to 1) ensure the coordinated, focused attention that such projects require and 2) retain at the same time the benefits of specialized expertise and capabilities that only functional departments can provide. For example, the production of reactors for nuclear power plants calls for unusual engineering, materials and parts with heat-resistance far beyond any previously fabricated, scientific knowledge concerning reactor design, a special and very large assembly operation, and a whole array of new inspection techniques. Production is complicated by high uncertainty about how to achieve required quality and safety margins, by a desire to keep costs low enough to allow nuclear power to compete with coal- and oil-generating stations, and by the pressure to complete such units in time to overcome national electric-power shortages.

Companies making nuclear reactors do have departments that are expert in science, engineering, purchasing, fabrication, and inspection, but each of these departments has twenty to a hundred different orders to work on at one time. Also, they do not have standard answers for dealing with nuclear reactors, and do not know what related decisions other departments may make for a specific order. Many conferences within and between departments become necessary. Disagreement on design or manufacture is likely to arise. Production falls behind schedule, and costs rise. To overcome these typical difficulties on an important piece of business, some mechanism is needed to channel part of the company's store of talent into the specific project and to ensure open communications on interrelated issues and prompt agreement on action to be taken.

This kind of situation is not peculiar to heavy-equipment manufacturers. An advertising agency, to pick an example far removed from physical hardware, is in the same predicament. It has departments staffed with experts in market research, copywriting, art work, television shows, media selection, and other functions—all useful to various clients. Client-A wants a specific advertising mission accomplished, one suited to its particular situation. The organization problem is how to draw on the outstanding capabilities of the functional departments and at the same time get an imaginative, tailored program for client-A when he needs it. Comparable situations in management-consulting firms and in large building-construction firms are easy to visualize.

Project Managers
of Cross-functional Teams

93

CHAPTER 6
New Approaches
to Structural
Design

The matrix-organization answer to the problems just posed is to appoint a project manager for each clear-cut mission and then to assign from each of the functional departments the talent needed to complete the mission. Figure 6–1 indicates the arrangement for the nuclear-reactor order.

During the time a functional specialist is working on the project, he looks to the project manager for direction; he is "out on loan." When the project is finished, or when he is no longer needed, each specialist returns to his functional department for assignment to other duties. The project manager must rely heavily on these assigned people for counsel and decisions in their respective areas. If the team is small, its members will have frequent contact with one another and will be fully informed of the current status of the project. In these circumstances most of the coordination will be voluntary. From time to time, tough, trade-off decisions (sacrificing in one place to gain in another) may be necessary, and these will be made by the project manager.

The personal relations within a project team are delicate. Although the project manager is the nominal boss, each member of his team is on temporary assignment and will return to his functional department, where his long-run career is primarily determined. To draw the best from his group, the project manager must therefore rely on both the challenge of the job and on his per-

Figure 6–1   Matrix organization. Each project manager is boss for his project, borrowing the talent he needs temporarily from the functional departments. The heads of functional departments develop capable people—and perhaps other services—but do not supervise them while they are assigned to the project team.

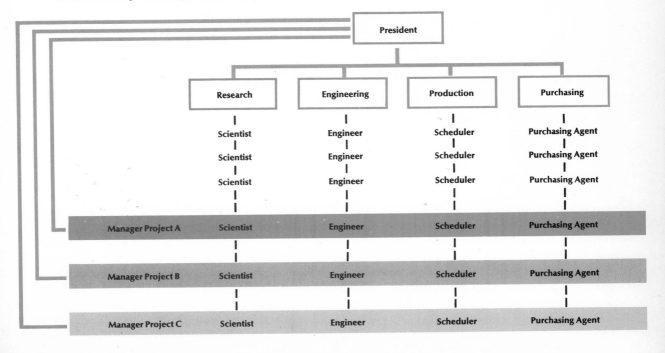

sonal leadership. Because of this heavy reliance on voluntary cooperation, project teams work best on projects for which the quality of the finished product or service, its deadline, and its costs are clearly specified.

Service Role of Functional Departments

Usually a functional department does more than supply the project team with its members. It also provides backup service. The project engineer may want drafting help and advice on technical matters; and perhaps at some stages a whole crew of additional engineers will be needed. Similarly, the market-research man calls on personnel in his home department when he needs specialized assistance. When actual production is begun, the work will be done in the company shops (or subcontractors' shops), which are supervised by the department head. Only in the case of large projects lasting several years, or when work is performed on a remote site (as in construction), are the people who do this backup work transferred to the project. Instead, the functional department performs backup work according to requests from the project team in the same way an outside subcontractor might take on a specified task.

Thus, the project manager calls each move, watches progress, and decides on the next moves. His success, however, depends largely on the capabilities that the functional departments place at his disposal. In the short run, the project manager supplies the initiative; then he and his team provide the co-ordinated, positive direction that is hard to obtain in a purely functional setup. In the long run, however, the quality and training of the specialists, and the operating capabilities of the functional departments, determine the kind and volume of projects a company can handle effectively.

Obviously this kind of interdependence is hard to keep in balance. Members of the project team, in their push to get specific results, tend to take over line supervision and stir up the resentment of those who are being pushed around. Furthermore, the service that a functional department can provide is rarely performed as fully, as well, or as quickly as project managers would like. Especially when progress is poor, tension arises over who is failing to do all that he should.

In the construction and space industries, and occasionally in other situations suited to matrix organization, the job we have been describing for a functional department may be performed by a subcontractor. For instance, an advertising agency may use an outside creator of television commercials rather than maintain a department for this purpose within its own firm. This increases the negotiating aspects of the project manager's job, but basically the respective roles are not altered by the multiplication of legal entities.[1]

---

[1] Project managers and teams can also be used for special, one-time, cross-organizational changes, such as moving to a new location, absorbing a small company, or opening a foreign plant. Here the arrangement is clearly temporary and does not create any continuing modifications in organization design.

The strong position we have given project managers creates difficulties in scheduling work within functional departments. Each project has its own time-table. Also, not all projects will use any one service to the same extent. The resulting irregular call for service is likely to conflict with the requirements of other projects, and each project manager will think that his work should have priority. Even when an advanced plan for all services is neatly dovetailed, the inherent uncertainties connected with such projects results in some being late and in others wanting greater use of needed specialists or facilities than was originally requested. The manager of a late project naturally feels it is important to catch up, and the manager who has struggled to stay on target strenuously objects to being penalized for another project's tardiness. Someone must decide who gets served first.

The head of a functional department is rarely the right man to set priorities. He naturally wants an even flow of work, and what is convenient for him is not necessarily best for the overall enterprise. Incidentally, periods of peak demand are often followed by little or no work, and the functional head is then seeking business to justify retaining his trained personnel. Perhaps a bottleneck can be relieved by working overtime, but who decides when the overtime premium is warranted and which project is assessed the additional cost? Priority squabbles are eventually resolved, partly by give-and-take and partly by improved scheduling methods (as we will note in Chapter 19). But a residual set of priority and trade-off decisions will have to be made by a senior executive who can attach weights in light of total company values.

Because a **matrix** organization is both delicate and complicated, we should use it only when simpler organization designs are inadequate to cope with the dynamic nature of the work to be done.

Product Managers

Matrix organizations should be distinguished from the use of product managers. Theoretically, a company organized on a functional basis but with several different products could have a manager for each product. Each product manager would work very much like the project managers we have just discussed, and would shepherd his product through the functional departments from research to customer delivery. But there is a difference between projects and products. We expect a product to generate repetitive sales and become "part of the line." Most of the activities relating to it become a normal part of operations. Only occasionally, or in limited areas such as seasonal sales promotions or competitive pricing, does the product need more attention than the functional departments provide.

Therefore, a product manager typically needs less power than a project manager. He serves in a *staff* capacity, making sure that his product does not get lost, calling attention to unexpected opportunities, bringing together people from two or more departments when agreement on coordinated action is needed, suggesting ways to improve results, and the like. Usually the final decisions about the product are made by departmental executives, although in the case of highly competitive consumer goods a product manager sometimes decides on pricing, sales promotion, and inventory. Primarily, however, the product manager aids and stimulates the functional departments to do their jobs well, whereas the project manager carries the initiative and accountability while departments act in a service capacity.

Both project and product managers are organizational members who secure alert, responsive action in a milieu of rapid change. At the same time, both rely on the technical competence and efficient operations of functional departments. All sorts of variations are possible. Personal relationships are delicate; conflicts can be sharp. But we have here the possibilities for flexible, sophisticated action.

EXTERNAL, INDEPENDENT STAFF

Sheer magnitude poses new burdens on managers. Our larger enterprises often require staggering commitments of resources—people, materials, capital. Urban renewal, oil from Alaska, new automobile engines, atomic power, and many other developments call for inputs equivalent to the entire gross national product of several United Nations members.

A few large companies use a special type of staff to double-check such major decisions. In contrast to our description of staff in Chapter 4, this external group is not expected to collaborate with operating managers in the initial preparation of plans. Instead they provide an independent check.

Six significant features stand out in this design for staff work as it has been developed by a large computer manufacturer:

1) Each operating division has its own highly competent staff that provides technical and coordinating assistance in the usual fashion. The external staff is not regarded as a substitute for this kind of help. Nevertheless, top management does want assurance that the multimillion-dollar decisions embraced in operating plans are wise, and that no major opportunities for improvement are overlooked. The magnitude of commitments and the uncertainties faced by this company call for extraordinary efforts to ensure that the right action is taken.

2) The external staff is judged on the basis of the success of the operating divisions. If results are good, previous staff work is considered to be good even though the external staff did no more than endorse operating-division proposals. However, when divisional results do not come up to par, the external staff person who approved the plans may be in deep trouble along with executives of the division. Clear evidence of bungled execution reduces staff accountability somewhat. But the basic doctrine is: "If the patient is well, the doctor gets a good fee. If the patient gets sick, the doctor may find himself even sicker." This means that both the external staff and the operating divisions are evaluated by the same standard—good results.

To make this accountability stick, the cause of any large difficulty is traced back to major decisions, and the staff person is penalized if he concurred with an error made perhaps two to five years earlier.

3) The external staff reviews the annual and five-year plans of the operating divisions, before central management's endorsement. If the staff believes the plans are good it concurs in writing. The plan may, and often does, involve substantial risks, but these risks should be fully explored and potential losses minimized.

4) When the staff does not concur, it must develop an alternative proposal. Mere "viewing with alarm" is not enough. The external staff must seek, and the operating division must provide, data that permits the staff to formulate a positive plan to eliminate its objections to the operating division's proposals. The staff has to be realistic and prepared to defend its alternative.

5) Often differences between the proposals of the operating division and the staff are ironed out voluntarily. One group convinces the other, or an even better third plan emerges. Both parties, however, are committed. Pressure from either side is no excuse. When sincere differences in judgment arise, these are presented to one or more senior executives to "umpire" the decision. Such umpiring is necessary to get on with the game—to prevent positive, aggressive action from being stalled.

6) To ensure that staff focuses on major issues and to prevent the entire planning mechanism from being bogged down with nonconcurrences, the size of the external staff is limited. With only a few people to investigate and to prepare alternative plans, the external staff must be very selective in the issues it tackles.

The external-staff concept has strong supporters. The chief benefit is an independent check on major planning decisions. Alfred Sloan sought a similar independent judgment throughout General Motors through his "finance" men, but he placed them inside each division; they were internal rather than external staff.

In thinking about when to use external, independent staff, one should also recognize some limitations. A comprehensive, explicit, forward-looking procedure must be in use if the external staff is to grow with the plans and exercise a constructive influence. The scheme is expensive in terms of both talented personnel and the energies of many executives involved in the duplicate planning effort. The vital accountability concept requires careful evaluations delving back several years and a willingness to censure an executive for his actions that far in the past. Attitudes about external interference with planning have to be modified to tolerate two or more competitive proposals. In addition, but by no means least important, a new type of resilient, farsighted staff has to be located and trained; unless such individuals have practical wisdom about the industry they serve, the entire procedure is only an added burden.

A satisfactory way to carry this external, independent-staff concept over to major government decisions has not yet been worked out. Numerous clearances and checks exist in the government, to be sure, but neither the key aspect of continuing accountability nor a provision for prompt resolution of differences in judgment are evident in government-planning procedures.

The modern chief executive of every large enterprise is under severe pressure. The demands placed on his time by external and internal problems, by nonbusiness as well as business affairs, by both long-range and short-range planning cannot possibly be met by one human being. Relief must be found.

The intensity of the pressure is growing, but the problem is not new. For years chief executives have had a few personal assistants to relieve them of minor tasks and to expedite their numerous conferences, public appearances, and problem analyses. In a relatively stable situation, a whole array of corporate staff units may be created. Although these staff units normally provide service to their associates and to others throughout the organization, they are also available to assist the chief executive directly.

Decentralization, especially profit decentralization, is a second way to relieve the harried chief executive. As we have seen, a variety of factors affect the wisdom of decentralizing, and so this alternative may not be attractive. Furthermore, even after decentralizing the remaining tasks for central management are very heavy.

A third alternative, practiced by a few companies including du Pont and Exxon Corporation, is to have some (though not necessarily all) full-time members of the board of directors. Such board members are full-time employees who have been relieved of supervision of their part of the enterprise. They devote their full energies to central-management tasks.[2] Some allocation of work among the board members is made, and channels of communication are established. However, all regular board members are available to give undivided attention to new problems and future opportunities. Two drawbacks make this arrangement unattractive to most enterprises. First, a full-time board of highly successful executives is expensive; few companies can afford it. Second, the benefits of an independent, objective check on company actions by outside directors, who are not judging their own decisions, are lost.

Recently the concept of a "president's office" is becoming more widely used and, as is the case with the office of President in our federal government, the president's office is viewed as a distinct unit of the organization. It has its own internal structure as well as its relations with other separate units and departments. Various staff aides and communication flows are part of the design, but the key feature is a team of two to five senior executives who share the central-management tasks.

The division of duties among the senior men depends on their own capabilities and the currently pressing problems. One man might deal with external relations—with customer groups, governmental bodies, industry associations, and the like—while another might concentrate on internal operations. Three other executives might normally handle technological questions, legal matters,

---

[2] Recently a few outside board members, who devote only part of their time to serving on the board, have been added. The basic pattern of a full-time board continues, however.

and finance. But the essence of the concept is synthesized action rather than specialization along any line. Regardless of how the work is shared, an intimate and frequent interchange is essential so that the office functions like a close-knit partnership. The office is expected to respond to numerous external and internal integration needs (discussed in Chapter 1) in a way that provides a consistent and unified posture for the company.

The success of this arrangement rests predominantly on the personalities of the executives involved. At the top level they are sure to be strong individuals; yet a president's office requires a high degree of sharing and mutual support. Not all strong people are willing to play the game this way. Other features of organization design may depend on the characteristics of persons in key positions, but this dependency is never so great as in the case of the president's office.

We should note in passing that the concept of a manager's "office" might also be applied to the head of any large, complex unit. Certainly dual executives are not unique. In this case a manager typically has an alter ego who shares with him the duties of the position. For this arrangement to be effective there must be a proper blending of personalities, and the managers must have experience in working together. The senior person must have complete confidence in his associate because, as in a legal partnership, either partner can usually speak for the office. The relationship is so highly personal and unstable, that it should be avoided if some other provision is practical.

REPRESENTATION OF SPECIAL INTERESTS

"Our group should have a voice in management" is a claim often heard from women, unions, blacks, neighborhood councils, investors, and others whose own well-being can be significantly affected by operations of the enterprise. Official representation—on policy boards or even in management positions—is becoming more popular as a method of "reform."

Managers of business firms, hospitals, and other enterprises usually have some experience with interest representation. Labor unions and suppliers of capital have often taken strong positions on how an enterprise should be run. Interference by a major customer (for example, the Air Force) or a major supplier (auto manufacturers) is not unknown. But too often the reaction to such interference has been based solely on traditional "prerogatives." A more constructive approach divides the response to a representation request into two parts.

First there is a board of directors composed of "watchdogs" appointed to advocate the views of particular interest groups. But such a board will rarely perform their essential functions adequately. The board *should* do all of the following: provide an objective check on the strategy and programs devised by

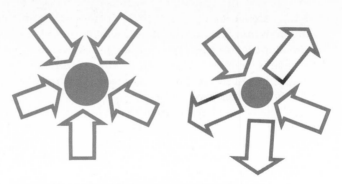

Figure 6–2 Impact of watchdog members on the effectiveness of a board of directors. If the primary interest of some members is directed away from the organization, the area of the board's usefulness shrinks.

the management group; share in the prediction of critical developments; evaluate results; select the top executives; and give personal advice informally. It supplements, stimulates, and checks the judgment of central management. To fill this role, each board member should treat the long-run interests of the enterprise as paramount. Even one or two directors who are grinding their own ax will prevent a candid, wholesome review of company problems.

This divided-loyalty objection applies also to the appointment of persons to key jobs because they are selected by an interest group. We do not imply that persons from diverse backgrounds, especially in areas where problems of heritage or sex arise, should be unwelcome. The point is that if they are to serve the enterprise—to be on "the team"—they should not try to serve the conflicting interests of two masters.

This means that neither labor unions nor bankers should be entitled to select directors or executives who represent their interests. It also means that an effective governing body of a university should not be composed of members elected by students, faculty, or employees. To run an enterprise we prefer professional management to politics.

Second, effective two-way communication between the enterprise and each interest group must be maintained. Formalities are not enough. The enterprise needs to know the aspirations, beliefs, values, and alternatives facing each group contributing to the enterprise system. Also, each interest group should be advised in advance of proposed actions significantly affecting it so that counterproposals can be made. The interest group should have ample opportunity to recommend action to the enterprise, so as to lay the basis for constructive joint action.

Such a communication arrangement, if conducted in good faith, allows the interest group to influence the decision-making body even though the interest group is not actually represented on the body. The opportunity for mutually beneficial action is retained, even though change is made in the underlying bargaining power of the various parties. On the other hand, managing of the enterprise as an independent social institution is not hamstrung by ineffective boards or executives—as would be the case if every interest group were permitted to have a member on every decision-making body.

IMPACT OF COMPUTERS
ON ORGANIZATION

Dazzling advances in the capabilities of electronic computers have been accompanied by comparable predictions of their effect on managerial organization. Science fiction pictures worlds in which managers no longer exist, and learned articles compare executive decision-making with machines playing chess. Actually the serious organization designer needs to consider the impact of computers largely in three areas: 1) mechanization of clerical activities; 2) possibilities of *either* more *or* less decentralization; and 3) shrinking of middle management.

Mechanization of Clerical Activities

By far the greatest use of computers to date, and their chief effect on organization, has been in performing clerical operations. Millions of man-hours have been saved by machines that sort, calculate, and record. Life-insurance companies, banks, internal-revenue offices, social-security offices, to name just a few, are experiencing a technological revolution in their routine activities. In businesses whose clerical operations are a relatively minor part of the total technology, the payroll, accounting, and billing units are usually affected most.

Note that the change just described does not alter the results; basically the *same* work is now being done by machines—faster, probably more cheaply, and perhaps better. It is mechanization pure and simple. Obviously the units being mechanized are drastically affected, and as with most mechanization a variety of peripheral efforts must be devoted to match the incoming work to the capacity of the machines. The magnitude of the details involved is staggering. Nevertheless, neither the primary functions of the enterprise nor its basic organization has been changed. The effect on overall organization design is minimal.

One familiar problem does appear. The computer-processing unit, because of its large capacity and its high expense, is usually set up as a new auxiliary service. As we noted in Chapter 2, the organization designer must decide how many separate service units should be established and where to attach them to the total structure. More than physical processing and hardware are involved. Especially during the introductory stage, learning how to use the computer— the "software"—is an essential part of the service.

The location of computer service units is usually resolved by the criterion of "most use." If the engineering department is the chief user of the computing center, the center will probably be placed in that department. The final resolution of location, however, is very unsettled because of continuing changes in the size and capabilities of computers. Perhaps many small computers will meet the needs of an enterprise most economically; if so, small computer units can be located throughout the organization. The dominant consideration, as with any auxiliary service, is providing effective service when and where needed; the second factor is performing the activity at low cost.

Possibilities of More or Less Decentralization

Computers, coupled with vastly improved communications equipment, can affect decentralization design. Objective data can now be transmitted, analyzed, and retransmitted very rapidly. This new technical capacity changes the answer to questions of who can readily get what information; and we know from our examination of decentralization in Chapter 3 that availability of pertinent, current information is one of the considerations in deciding where to center decision-making.

But the effect may be either *more* or *less* decentralization. Background data can be fed to the field, or local data can be fed to headquarters. A few companies are systematically sending information on industry production, competitive prices, and economic indicators to their local sales offices so that these units can move promptly in making contracts with customers. A more common response has been rapid assembly of local information at a centralized point. Commercial banks, for instance, can now centralize both activities and some decision-making formerly done at local branches. Improved air travel allows higher-level executives to make more firsthand observation trips. This along with computerized sources of local data contributes to centralization of decision-making.

The impact of computers on decentralization, however, can easily be exaggerated. For instance, the scheduling of the arrival of material at very large construction projects is being carried out more and more by a central purchasing office rather than by the site manager; computers are often used, but the major impetus comes from adoption of new planning and control techniques.[3]

---

[3] The most widely used of these new techniques, PERT, is described in Chapter 22.

Also computers affect only one of the factors we have to consider when deciding whether to centralize or decentralize. They make objective data available very quickly, but they are not adept at handling subjective impressions, intensity of feelings, shades of values, and other nonquantified information. Computers affect neither the ability and availability of executives at various points in the organization nor the morale benefits of decentralization (see Chapter 3, under "Guides to 'How Much Decentralization?'"). Consequently, in designing an organization we should recognize that computers reduce the importance of who has the data but leave untouched the intangible aspects of decentralization.

Shrinking of Middle Management

The elimination of a large number of middle-management positions is conceivably the greatest impact of computers on organization. A few conspicuous examples are cited by proponents of this development. Oil-refinery output is being scheduled by computers, and engineering specifications for special-purpose transformers are being prepared by electronic means. These achievements have reduced the number of staff planners.

The prediction that a whole layer of middle management can be discarded is based on the premise that most of what these managers do can be automated. In thinking about the validity of this assumption, we should first note several requirements for automation. The computer must 1) identify the need for action; 2) possess a suitable array of programmed actions that might be taken; 3) draw upon available data for cues to which alternative is best; and 4) issue instructions in a way that will lead to the desired action. In highly standardized operations where future difficulties can be foreseen and the alternative actions are limited, perhaps the "judgment" of a manager can be duplicated by a computer. Clearly in designing an organization this possibility should be recognized.

A review of the work of virtually all managers will reveal, however, that only a small proportion of managerial decisions can be recast to conform with the four requirements listed above. Furthermore, most middle- and first-line managers devote a large part of their energy to mobilizing resources, directing, leading, controlling, and to other tasks beyond decision-making in the narrow sense. Computers have been programmed to play chess, but a chess game is a grossly simplified concept of the managerial role. Moreover, change is the order of the day. We design organizations to deal with tomorrow's problems, and as fast as some types of problems can be routinized and automated, new problems arising from social or technological change will press for attention.

In summary, we should carefully appraise the impact of computers on the operating and managerial work to be done. However, we need not anticipate a new type of social arrangement. The issues and key factors discussed in previous chapters will continue to be the major concern in designing future organizations.

CONCLUSION: INTEGRATING ORGANIZATION WITH OTHER PHASES OF MANAGEMENT

The examples of new emphases in organization discussed in this chapter illustrate again how organization design needs to be adapted to the technological, economic, and social environment in which the enterprise operates. The basic elements of managerial organization have persisted over the centuries, but designing the specific structure is a never-ending task of adjusting to current opportunities.[4]

Before leaving our discussion of formal organization, we should emphasize again the close relationship between organization and other phases of management. Especially when we consider changes in organization structure, we should try to evaluate repercussions in planning, controlling, and activating. Rarely can major changes be made in one area without at least some adjustment in others.

The Lerner Shops serve as an example of the need for consistency in management. This operating company sells women's clothes in many small outlets throughout the country. Compared with the apparel industry in general, it does a high-volume business in the low-priced range. To be successful, it must place popular-style dresses on the market quickly and continue to make them available during a season; yet the stores must have a minimum inventory on hand at the *end* of each season, for what is left is almost a total loss.

Conceivably, the shop managers could be free to buy the dresses that they believed would sell in their localities. If the managers were given such freedom, headquarters in New York would then serve as buying agent and general counsel for the local stores. Instead, the organization is in fact highly centralized. People in headquarters select, purchase, and price the dresses and distribute them to the outlets. Each local store makes daily reports on the styles, colors, and sizes of dresses it sells. If a particular styles does not move in one locality or if the inventory in a store is unbalanced, headquarters issues instructions to trade inventory with a store in another town. The chief purpose of a local store is simply to display and sell the dresses. Selecting, training, and supervising salespeople are, of course, largely local matters, and suggestions for new merchandise or advertising are welcome. But virtually all merchandising decisions are made in headquarters.

This manner of operation means that, in addition to formulating policies, the top-management level of the business must prepare detailed schedules and methods. On the lower level, little initiative is expected. The people selected to manage shops in a company like Lerner's need not be merchants. In fact, a person who bubbles over with new ideas or has highly creative and artistic

---

[4] This long-recognized need to fit organizations to the particular activities of each enterprise has recently been labeled the "contingency approach," as noted in Chapter 1.

sensibilities would probably make a poor manager in such a chain. A local manager should be someone who enjoys dealing with people, selling merchandise fast, and keeping a neat and efficient store. Frequent and detailed control reports are required, and regional directors insist on close adherence to company procedures and regulations. Thus all aspects of management—the planning process, the organization, the kinds of executives selected, the type of supervision, and the methods of control—fit together into a consistent pattern for this particular business.

When organization changes are not matched by consistent modifications in other areas of management, the move will probably be ineffective or even harmful. To cite a specific case, a steel company, which for years had operated with almost as tight and centralized an administration as that of the Lerner Shops, decided to decentralize and made much to-do about pushing authority down the line. But the company did not make corresponding adjustments in other areas of management. For example, heat reports on each open-hearth furnace had to be submitted up the line, and staff assistants in the chief engineer's office insisted on explanations of a heat that varied far from normal. Everyone from the vice-president down continued to "keep right on top of the situation." Because management did not adjust its planning, supervisory, and control practices to the announced changes in organization, no real change occurred. Staff expenses were higher than they should have been, and morale was harmed by building up expectations that failed to materialize.

Organizing must be recognized, then, as only a part of the total management task. We have separated organization issues from the whole maze of management problems for convenience of analysis. Nevertheless, organization never actually exists alone, any more than a person's nervous system can exist apart from his whole body. The result of organizing comes to life only in association with other acts of management—planning, controlling, and activating—and in an assembly of real people. Consequently, if our plans for organization are to be carried out, they must be meshed with other forces in the specific situation.

FOR CLASS DISCUSSION

1) How does the use of a matrix approach affect the span of supervision possible for a functional department?

2) Consider a highly trained group of professionals "working" around a patient during delicate open-heart surgery. 1) In what ways is this group similar and dissimilar to a matrix organization? 2) How does the organizational approach used in the operating room differ from that used to care for patients in their rooms or wards? How would you account for these differences, and what is their probable effect on patient needs?

3) What criteria should be used to decide whether to coordinate design, produc-

tion, pricing, promotion, and other facets of a key product through a matrix-type project manager or through a product manager?

4) If external staff does not concur with a division proposal and, after much debate, no basis for agreement can be found, what elements should be contained in the *review, decision,* and *follow-up* that will be taken by higher-level line umpires?

5) If special-interest-group representatives are included on organization boards or in decision-making groups, what dangers do you see to the interest-group representatives?

6) What organizational guides can you offer to increase the likelihood that the "service" contribution of computers to line organizations includes the kinds of services most useful to the line organization? Consider, in your answer, the problems raised because line men often fail to understand what the computer can offer, while computer men often fail to understand the kinds of services most needed by line managers.

7) As computers mechanize, if not automate, more lower-level jobs, do you see any changes other than shrinkage that may affect middle-management jobs? Discuss.

8) How may the participation of special-interest groups in decision-making affect the job of the line manager responsible for making and activating those decisions? Consider the three inescapable features of delegation discussed in Chapter 3.

Cases

For cases involving issues covered in this chapter, see especially the following. Particularly relevant questions are listed after each case.

The Delaware Corporation (p. 113), 4
Merchantville School System (p. 217), 4
Graham, Smith, Bendel, Inc. (p. 445), 3
Monroe Wire and Cable (p. 436), 2

FOR FURTHER READING

Brink, V. Z., *Computers and Management.* Englewood Cliffs, N.J.: Prentice-Hall, Inc., 1971.
Organizational and personnel problems associated with computer use.

Cleland, D. I. and W. R. King, eds., *Systems Analysis and Project Management,* 2nd ed. New York: McGraw-Hill Book Company, 1975, Chapters 9–11.
Good discussions of project management and matrix organization.

Corey, E. R. and S. H. Star, *Organization Strategy: A Marketing Approach.* Boston: Harvard Business School, 1971, Chapters 1–5.
These summary chapters highlight the natural conflict between product/market program management and "resource" management.

Galbraith, J., "Matrix Organization Designs: How to Combine Functional and Project Forms," in M. D. Richards and W. A. Nielander, eds., *Readings in Management,* 4th ed. Cincinnati: South-Western Publishing Co., 1974, pp. 530–42.

Good review of the underlying concept of matrix organization.

Groggin, W. C., "How the Multidimensional Structure Works at Dow Corning." *Harvard Business Review,* January 1974.

Description of a four-dimension matrix organization that has executives focusing on product lines, cost centers, areas, and functions.

Jones, K. A. and D. L. Wilemon, "Emerging Patterns in New-Venture Management." *Research Management,* November 1972.

Describes special provisions being made for managing new ventures in companies dominated by established operations.

Means, D. E., "The Task Force at Work—The New Ad-Hocracy." *Columbia Journal of World Business,* November 1970.

Describes the use of task forces by I.B.E.C. to assess and plan its foreign development projects.

Newman, W. H., *Administrative Action,* 2nd ed. Englewood Cliffs, N.J.: Prentice-Hall, Inc., 1963, Chapter 18.

Developing effective relationships with interest groups.

Not-for-Profit Note

for Part I

ORGANIZING NOT-FOR-PROFIT ENTERPRISES

Managing not-for-profit ventures is very similar to managing profit-seeking enterprises. Most modern management concepts apply equally well to the not-for-profit group—even though the concepts evolved primarily in business firms.

Nevertheless, as we shall point out repeatedly, each enterprise has its distinctive characteristics, and basic management concepts must be fitted to the particular needs of that firm. In Part One we have just considered how organization structure can be designed for a specific firm, and the following Parts extend this adaptive approach to planning, controlling, and activating. Not-for-profit enterprises need the same sort of tailor-made management.

The purpose of these Notes on not-for-profit enterprises (there is such a Note at the end of each Part of the book) is to suggest very briefly certain features of not-for-profit ventures that may call for special tailoring.

WIDE ARRAY OF "INDUSTRIES"

Thousands of different kinds of nonprofit organizations perform a bewildering range of services. Major groups include those in the table opposite:

Clearly, no single management design will fit such diverse operations. As with business firms, we need an analytical approach that helps us identify key issues and suggests possible solutions. Our discussion in these Notes will focus

Services Performed	Some Organizations Involved	Services Performed	Some Organizations Involved
HEALTH SERVICES	Hospitals Nursing Homes Clinics	OTHER PRIVATE	Religions Scientific Research Associations Clubs
EDUCATION	Universities Schools Trade Institutes	OTHER GOVERNMENT	Unions Uniformed: Military
SOCIAL SERVICES	Welfare Child-Care Family Counseling		Police Fire Civilian: Regulatory
ARTS AND CULTURE	Orchestras Libraries Museums		Fiscal Justice
COOPERATIVES	Insurance Savings Banks Utilities Marketing		

primarily on the first four groups listed above; and within these "industries," we will be concerned with self-contained, self-administered operating units— which we call "enterprises." [1]

CHARACTERISTICS REQUIRING SPECIAL TREATMENT

The organizing, planning, controlling, and activating approach—outlined in this book—can be readily applied to not-for-profit enterprises. These basic management processes relate to all sorts of purposeful group endeavors. What will be helpful, *in addition,* is to single out those frequent characteristics of

[1] Profit-seeking enterprises can be found in health, education, and social-service industries as well as in fields where cooperatives flourish. The basic management problems are much the same for proprietary and public hospitals, for mutual and stock insurance companies, for public and private nursery schools, and so on. From a management viewpoint, the profit versus not-for-profit distinction by itself appears to be less significant than the characteristics listed in the next section.

not-for-profit enterprises that call for special treatment. When these characteristics are strong, management design should be adjusted to reflect them.

Six characteristics to watch for are these:

1) *Service is intangible,* and hard to measure; this difficulty is often compounded by the existence of *multiple* service objectives.

2) *Customer influence may be weak;* often the enterprise has a local monopoly, and payments by customers may be a secondary source of funds.

3) Strong *employee* commitment to *professions* or a cause may undermine their allegiance to the enterprise.

4) *Intrusion of resource contributors* into internal management—notably fund contributors and government agencies.

5) *Restraints on the use of rewards and punishments,* as a result of 1), 3), and 4) above.

6) Importance of a *charismatic leader* and/or a "mystique" of the enterprise as means of resolving conflict in objectives and overcoming restraints.

These characteristics do not exist in all not-for-profit enterprises (and they may be present in some profit enterprises). But when they are strong, and especially when found in combinations, we know that typical profit management techniques will have to be modified. Examples of the impact of these characteristics on effective management practices will be given in the Notes for each Part.

The Note for each Part, then, presents modifications of concepts presented in that Part—modifications that may be required to reflect one or more of the characteristics of not-for-profit enterprises.

IMPACT ON ORGANIZING

Decentralization should be given special attention in not-for-profit enterprises. If employees have strong professional training and standards—as do most medical doctors and teachers—then decisions about work embraced within the professional code can be safely decentralized. In fact, the professionals will probably insist that they make their own local decisions.

In contrast, for intangible, hard-to-measure services not covered by clear professional standards—ranging from art selection to zoo-keeping—important decisions must be centralized. For such matters, senior executives have difficulty communicating to subordinates the meaning of enterprise objectives, and consequently do not dare make broad delegations. Moreover, full delegation may be obstructed by two other characteristics often present in not-for-profit enterprises:

1) Because judgment about good or poor performance is necessarily subjective, the use of rewards and punishments tends to be restricted. Sales and produc-

tivity bonuses—or their equivalent—are simply not feasible. Instead, promotion, discharges, and the like are traditionally made on the basis of external training or seniority. This separation of rewards from performance of assigned tasks weakens the influence of managers on subordinates, and—lacking confidence that their instructions will be carried out—the managers are reluctant to delegate.

2) Private donors, government agencies, and other suppliers of resources to not-for-profit enterprises often impose special conditions on their continuing support. Senior managers must always be alert to how action of the enterprise will be viewed by these outside interest groups. This leads to "defensive centralization": managers retain decision-making authority so that they can avoid actions that outside interest groups find objectionable.

When deciding how much decentralization is appropriate in a specific not-for-profit enterprise, clearly these factors of professionalization, clarity and measurability of objectives, traditions of rewards and punishments, and vulnerability to outside criticism should be considered—in addition to the more general factors discussed in Chapter 3.

A second distinctive issue in organizing not-for-profit enterprises is providing links with contributors of funds and other resources. Often special jobs or sections for this purpose must be created. Quite obvious is the need for a donation-raising organization in a venture heavily dependent on private contributions, or for a government contract unit in a venture supported by public grants. The critical task, however, is integration. The interests and values of contributors may differ sharply from those of scientists, prima donnas, and doctors who actually create the services of the enterprise. As Paul Lawrence and Jay Lorsch point out, the orientation of such special groups makes even communication between them difficult.[2] Consequently, we need people to fill buffer roles, who can relate to both inside and outside groups and can promote agreement on actions to be taken. This integrating task is especially difficult in those not-for-profit enterprises in which the service is intangible and objectives are multiple and shifting. A good organization will recognize this need.

A third and more general aspect of organizing not-for-profit enterprises is the care required in shifting from a Stage-I to Stage-II structure. Most small not-for-profit organizations have a strong "mystique" about the importance of their service mission and the unique contribution being made by their enterprise. These beliefs encourage informal relationships, flexible work assignments, and widespread commitment to enterprise goals. But when growth leads to a Stage II organization, with more specialized jobs and layers of supervision, worker reaction is likely to be much more negative than in similar transition in a profitmaking concern. The mystique loses its charm for all but élite occupations, and entrenched executives neither recognize a need nor have skills for managing in a more formal manner. Recent alienation and unionization of hospital workers and stagehands illustrate this problem. Whenever possible,

[2] See Chapter 1 of their *Studies in Organization Design* (Homewood, Illinois: Richard D. Irwin, Inc., 1970) for a brief statement of this proposition.

then, a move to a Stage-II organization should be gradual and accompanied by planning, training, measuring, and rewarding on a sophisticated basis.

These suggestions regarding decentralization, liaison with resource groups, and transition to a Stage II structure illustrate the approach we recommend for managing a not-for-profit enterprise:

1) Use basic management concepts, since in large measure they apply to both profit-seeking and not-for-profit ventures.
2) Do not assume that all not-for-profit enterprises are alike—they differ even more than profit-seeking companies.
3) Instead, when shaping a structure for a particular enterprise, be alert for the six characteristics above, and adjust for these in the tailoring that must occur in each specific management design.

This approach to managing not-for-profit enterprises will be amplified in Notes following each of the next five Parts of the book.

Case Studies

for Part I

The Delaware Corporation is a large graphic arts firm doing a diversified business in printing, advertising, artistic preparations, and business magazines. Its head offices are in Wilmington, with regional offices located in many of the larger cities throughout the United States. The corporation has done exceptionally well in recent years and is in an excess cash position; as a result, the board of directors has recently decided to expand the corporation's varied enterprises. The board has turned to the Business Publications Division for its first expansionary effort, although this division comprises only five percent of the corporation's assets.

Operating as an almost autonomous unit in an industrial section of North Philadelphia, the division grosses approximately $3,000,000 annually (net before taxes about $540,000) while employing 33 persons and publishing the following monthly magazines:

Motor Guide—60,000 circulation, sold to gargages, automotive-sales and repair services, and individual subscribers; serves the reader through describing new repair techniques and equipment as developed and advertised by spare-parts manufacturers.

Industrial and Home Oils—9,000 circulation, sold to independent fuel-oil and heating-equipment distributors; describes new equipment, techniques of servicing industrial- and home-oil burner equipment, and promotional ideas for increasing use of oil over coal in the local community. The advertisers are oil companies and manufacturers of heating equipment.

Architectural Engineering—16,000 circulation, sold to architects and architectural-engineering firms in both the home- and industrial-construction fields; advertisers are large construction firms and manufacturers and suppliers of building materials.

The magazine publishing industry reports that for magazines such as these, approximately 90 percent of income is derived from advertising, with ten percent from circulation revenues. As a result, some publishers have noted that it costs less to give magazines free to readers than to sell subscriptions. However, Delaware believes that circulation revenue is an important addition to current and future income. Consequently, a circulation department is maintained to obtain more paid subscriptions, which will in turn increase the opportunity of expanding the advertising revenues.

The company recently completed arrangements to purchase the Perlman Publishing Company of Philadelphia, a sole proprietorship owned by Alvin A. Perlman, who has been in the publishing business for almost 40 years. Perlman gained control of the company as a young man and currently publishes three very successful monthly magazines with 32 personnel and the following annual circulation:

Mechanical Farm Journal—600,000 circulation on a nationwide basis; sold to farm-equipment dealers, who distribute copies free to farmers to encourage more complete farm mechanization and care of equipment by farmers.

Chemical Engineer—10,000 circulation to chemists, chemical engineers, and industrial-chemical manufacturers; serves as a scientific journal in the field of chemistry. Advertisers are chemical manufacturers.

Municipal Engineer—8,000 circulation, sold to city managers and engineers; describes new improvements for construction and maintenance of city water plants, equipment, and sewage systems.

The executive vice president of Delaware has informed the manager of the Business Publications Division of the completion of arrangements through the following letter:

Mr. John Wordsworth
General Manager, Business Publications Division
The Delaware Corporation
Philadelphia, Penna.

Dear John:

This will confirm our telephone conversation of May 19th, in which I discussed these matters at length with you. As you well know, we have been working with Mr. Alvin Perlman for several weeks, attempting to close the deal for purchase of the Perlman Publishing Company. With the formal agreements that were signed two days ago and with our acquisition of the stock, the company is now 100 percent owned by Delaware. I know you will be pleased to hear that we have given you full sway over the operations of all six magazines.

Since beginning your employment with the company about ten years ago as advertising director of *Motor Guide,* after your successful decade as editor of the Harrisburg *Times Herald,* you have shown determination, initiative, and foresight in your operations. Three years ago, *Industrial and Home Oils* was acquired through your prospecting efforts, as was *Architectural Engineering* last year. Your preliminary prospecting arrangements with Mr. Perlman certainly paved the way for the approval by the board of the merger and your promotion to general manager.

Recognizing that this acquisition doubles your operations, I presume that you have a blueprint in mind for the new organization and integration of the Perlman Publishing Company into your division. I would appreciate your stopping by to discuss this with me early next week.

Again, congratulations for a job well done.

Sincerely,

Crowell James
Executive Vice President

John Wordsworth immediately prepared the following letter, in which he outlined his proposal to Crowell James:

Dear Crowell:

Your confirmation letter was most welcome, and I want to express my appreciation for your recommending my promotion and your kind comments concerning my operations. Since I will be at an advertising convention in Chicago for the next few days, I am enclosing my proposals for taking over the Perlman Company. I feel that a swift and complete "clean-break" type of acquisition and a move to the Delaware Building here in North Philadelphia will integrate the Perlman Company quickly and more easily than if we delay. As you know, that is the policy I followed with each of the other acquisitions. I think this can be completed within a month or six weeks and should be done, since Perlman's annual lease is up for rewriting on July 1st.

I will stop by next week after you have had a chance to review this so that we can begin the new operations as soon as possible.

Sincerely,

John Wordsworth
General Manager

Encl: Proposal

PROPOSAL FOR INTEGRATION OF PERLMAN COMPANY

1) *Purpose of the Merger*
   As I see it, the purpose in combining operations is making greater profits for the corporation. These can be accomplished because of

   a) Horizontal growth through acquisition of a similar type of business
   b) New business—all six magazines, old and new, are currently profitable, but the margins should be doubled with more efficient operations, improved promotional efforts, and, thus, greatly increased advertising revenues, all of which are important
   c) Acquisition of some good people for use in our expanded operations. This is cheaper and faster than proselyting existing publishers and establishing new service publications

d) Economies through centralization of publishing services, circulation activities, and long-range editorial planning—with specialization, uniformity of operations, and budgetary control being the key factors in my new operations

2) *Detailed Operations*—current:

As you know, the production of a typical issue in our operations follows these specialization lines:

a) A magazine editor plans the issues and makes long-term assignment of stories to associate editors. This is where the high-level thought and pulse-taking is quartered within each magazine's editorial policy.

b) When completed, the stories are turned over to the managing editor, who serves as chief clerk, seeing that the galleys for all magazines are prepared and forwarded to a presentation editor on schedule.

c) The presentation editor puts the magazine together in terms of layout, art work, photography, etc., and then sends it to the contract printing press, where the copies are produced and circulation completed.

3) Our circulation sales personnel serve all three magazines alike, and the same is true for advertising sales. The latter work closely with the editors and presentation editors for advertising space and presentation techniques.

4) The current organization chart is as follows:

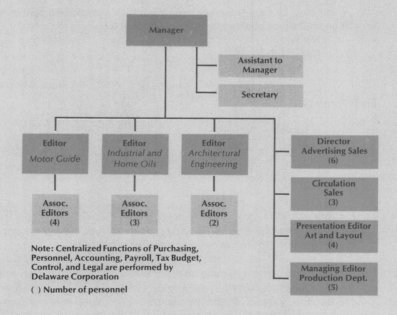

Note: Centralized Functions of Purchasing, Personnel, Accounting, Payroll, Tax Budget, Control, and Legal are performed by Delaware Corporation

( ) Number of personnel

5) My present thinking on what the organization will look like a year from now is as follows:

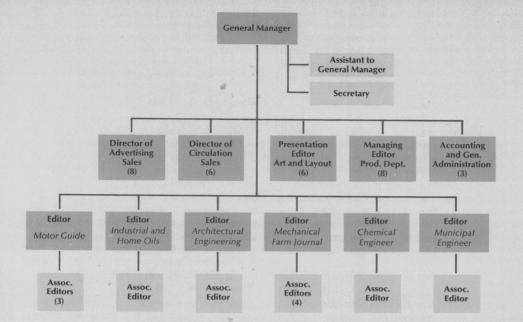

The accounting and general-administrative section is a facilitating unit to handle coordination with centralized purchasing, personnel, accounting, payroll, and so on.

The basic reason the staff and service type of organization has been recommended is my desire to maintain uniformity and standardization of all six magazines. This will permit great economies in purchasing, production, and layout work, which will, of course, lead to increased profits. An example of where this can be done is in magazine format. If I may say so, I feel that the formats of the Perlman publications are old, classical, and stuffy. They need to be streamlined, utilizing the same modern format and popular grade of paper as we are using. This will save many thousands of dollars in addition to volume discounts, as anticipated by the doubling of our purchases.

An additional area of savings is in such mechanical costs as printing, wrapping, postage, etc. With this centralized staff service to watch these areas, we should be able to have cost figures about as follows with our increased production:

Cost Per 1,000 Copy Page

Average Press Runs	Postage	Paper and Printing	Wrapping	Total
Up to 10,000 copies	$0.44	$7.20	$1.80	$9.44
10,000 to 15,000 copies	.40	4.60	1.50	6.50
15,000 to 20,000 copies	.40	4.40	1.40	6.20
20,000 to 30,000 copies	.39	3.20	1.30	4.89
Over 30,000 copies	.38	3.00	1.20	4.58

As you can plainly see, the reduction of these costs is all important and can be squeezed down if you have the proper organization and operating methods to get these economies.

My desire to continue on a more detailed monthly budgetary program requires closer control by staff and service sections over the editorial components of the division. This is needed because of the increasing size of the division.

6) In terms of the actual integration, I would like to complete the move by July 1, with their organization moving into our quarters. We will make room by doubling up for the time being, but I am sure that the details can be worked out as we go along. I don't plan to discharge anyone immediately, but would like three to six months to look over their people to see which ones will fit into our long-run organizational scheme of things. Of course, there will be a few personnel adjustments to make. For example, I would like to keep Mr. Sams, who is 63 years old and is their advertising director, for about six months until we can assure the advertisers that Perlman is essentially the same old organization with the same personal service that they received in the past. I am grooming young Ed Johnson to take over that position, and I think eventually he'll make a cracker-jack of an advertising director. He's tough, virile, dynamic, and really gets the business. He's our boy!

7) Also Mr. Perlman will be kept as editor of *Mechanical Farm Journal* for a five-year maximum period per our agreement, but this can be terminated at the end of any year by mutual consent, as you know.

We'll consult Perlman and his key people regarding these changes, but I think you can rest assured, Crowell, that they will comply with our terms.

These are my recommendations, Crowell. I'll stop by next week to discuss them with you so we can get under full steam as soon as possible.

John

DISCUSSION WITH PERLMAN

Crowell James, after reading John Wordsworth's recommendations, called Alvin Perlman over to his office. The conversation which took place was substantially as follows:

"Hello, Al, how are you?"

"Fine, thanks Crowell. I'm happy we were able to swing the deal, and from now on I should probably call you *Mr.* James rather than Crowell."

"On the contrary, Al, our personal relationship will remain the same. Al, I enjoyed working out the details on the financial side; that is, from the legal, tax, and purchase-agreement considerations. Now that the deal's closed, let's talk about you, your background, current methods of operation, and your personnel."

"Okay, where do we start?"

"Well, let's start at the beginning."

"Guess that's the best place, Crowell. Well, I saw the light of day in Brooklyn and lived a pretty normal life until graduating from high school and joining the advertising firm of 'Old and Rubaiyat' in New York City. Was a messenger boy but finally managed to get into production and layout work on the mechanical-equipment accounts that were being put into the farm magazines. Then the war came along and I enlisted. As I look back, it probably was one of the wisest decisions of my life."

"Why was that, Al?"

"Well, from the time I enlisted everyone said, 'What a fool. He had one of the brightest futures that the advertising game has seen in a long time.' But somehow, Crowell, I have always felt it was the best policy for me to do the harder right instead of the easier wrong, and it would have been wrong if I couldn't have done my share. You see, that basic concept of service has become our motto.

"When I finally got home I decided to get into publishing rather than advertising-agency work. I joined *Mechanical Farm Journal,* which was then just getting started, as advertising director in Philadelphia. This was the opportunity I needed—no restrictions, the field wide open, and a real opportunity to prove myself. Four years later circulation was up to 60,000 which was good for our field. John Price, the owner and editor, died that year and the estate offered to sell the magazine to me. I bought it with reservations, since I had never had professional management or editorial experience; and I now had 12 full-time employees to look after, a magazine to publish, and advertising contracts to keep in force.

"Within a few more years we were up to 100,000 circulation, and the duties of one man wearing three hats became too burdensome. Joe Sams, who joined the organization after I did, was promoted to advertising director, and I appointed Jim Maxwell as circulation and business manager a little later, while I retained the title of president and editor. Practically, we operated as associates, although I was owner of the business. Then the opportunity to acquire *Chemical Engineer* and *Municipal Engineer* arose. We bought them out, retained their complete staffs and editors, and after several years merged their operations with ours. Actually, we were completely satisfied with our *Mechanical Farm Journal* operation and only bought them when we learned that their owners were reluctant to sell to a large magazine-publishing house. They apparently liked our personal method of operation, thought we would continue our good service to the reader, and would allow a small family-type of operation. This we did and actually picked up the magazines at a reduced price."

"Al, how old are the editors of *Chemical Engineer* and *Municipal Engineer*?"

"Well, let's see. I'm 60; Joe Sams, Advertising Director, is 63; and Jim Maxwell is 67. John Brennan is 62—he's with *Chemical Engineer*—and Sam Levine, editor of *Municipal Engineer,* is 69."

"Do you have any associate editors or managing assistants that you have trained? Also, how did you operate?"

"No, Crowell, you see we really didn't have any need for training associate editors because each of us operated pretty much independently, although the spirit of cooperation certainly was one of our most valuable assets.

"Before I describe our organization and operations, Crowell, I'd like to say that it has always been our objective that the reader came first. Good technological information printed in a respectable style gained an editorial reputation that we felt was the cornerstone of our existence. This was hard to do because the advertisers were always pushing us to change our style, or paper, or something. We refused, and perhaps lost some money. But in the long run we have thought that advertising was the by-product and readership education was paramount. Of course, about 85 percent of our income comes from advertising revenues, but our main effort is editorial.

"You know, Crowell, James McGraw of McGraw-Hill always felt it was better to get out a publication for the benefit of the reader even though it took greater courage than giving in to the wishes of the advertisers. That about expresses our philosophy, too, Crowell, and I think helps to account for the phenomenal growth of *Mechanical Farm Journal.*"

"Al, how many associate editors do you now have in your organization?"

"None, Crowell. You see we believe in letting each editor determine his own employment needs. Thus far the editors have done their jobs without having to hire any associate editors. We're a small, family type of outfit, and each editor knows what he has to do and can keep it in his own shop."

"Well, Al, how about an organization chart?"

"Never had one! You see, each magazine editor is independent and puts his own magazine together. He obtains stories from outside sources, edits them, works with his layout and production people, approves, disapproves, and, finally, arranges for the completed product to go to the printer. He's in charge of a total operation, which permits a complete package to be handled closely, personally, and efficiently. Everyone knows what his job is and can fill in for others in case of illness or vacation. Each editorial group understands the personality of the reader that the magazine serves, and there is no confusion or red tape.

"The advertising director works with each editor to determine the number of pages and types of ads needed. He actually operates like the old country retailer who knows his customers well. He very seldom has to go into the field, and places most of his business by telephone. He knows his companies inside and out because many of the advertising directors of the advertisers he used to contact 25 years ago are now presidents or high officers in their companies. They tell Joe to call them direct rather than go through the advertising departments. Joe tells me he gets more business than he needs.

"Jim Maxwell, the circulation and business director, services all three magazines for purchasing and administrative purposes. For example, if John Brennan's shop wanted a steel desk or Sam Levine wanted an oak desk, Jim's office would merely assist in placing the order and arranging for delivery. Jim also helps the editors with circulation administration, but our job is simplified by having each editor concern himself with circulation and promotion problems peculiar to his field."

"Well, Al, from what you say this is my impression of what your organization chart looks like." [Perlman adds the number of employees.]:

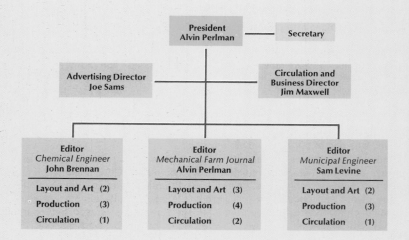

"Now, Crowell, you know that looks pretty cold and unreal. But I guess that's the general way we operate. If you had to chart it, I guess that would do it."

"Well, Al, why haven't you ever had a chart before?"

"Heck, Crowell, it's not the chart that counts. I feel that in this business it's the intangibles that are important. Without them this business is lost, for it's the personality of the publisher and the people that make or break a magazine. Look at Hearst, Henry Luce, James H. McGraw. As a result, a major area where we have concerned ourselves is that of personnel. We feel that we have a high level of clerical, artistic and production personnel. Our turnover is nil and our personal and job contacts are very close. We operate as a family group. We have Christmas parties, birthday parties, and if we want an extra holiday coupled with a long weekend or the Fourth of July, I usually give them an extra day. We still made plenty of money, Crowell, as you know.

"Our location is ideal in that we have a nice cool building with plenty of space. We're also close to train and bus stops, with good restaurants, and the better downtown retail stores around the corner for the girls to do their noontime shopping. Of course we have staggered hours for those people who live far away to avoid the rush crowds if they would like to.

"As I said before, we aren't overly organized, but the work always gets done because we have always tried to preserve the identity of the employee and cooperate with each other."

"Tell me, Al, what about budgets?"

"Well, Crowell, we never had a budget because I didn't think they were necessary. At the beginning of the year I always tried to forecast the revenues from advertising and circulation and compare them with the costs. If it looked like we were going to be short on revenue, Joe Sams would get on the phone and would sign up a few more contracts. We always came out with a handsome profit, however, and each Christmas paid a bonus. Even in the lean years of the depression, we paid our employees $100 bonuses, and now the melon averages $1,000 per employee. The editors and directors get considerably more, of course."

"Well, Al, you know Delaware doesn't pay bonuses except to its executive personnel."

"Yes, I understand that, and I think it may be a difficult time next Christmas. That's one of the reasons I agreed to serve for the next five years—to assist in making the merger as smooth and comfortable as possible. Crowell, my main reason for selling at this time was because we had no plan for succession in our company. We're not getting any younger, and I knew that the inheritance-tax problems would be considerable should I pass away in the immediate future. I have discussed this with my key people, and they knew the problem I had.

"Their main concern, however, was what effect this would have on the workers. The main resistance appeared to be that the employees did not necessarily desire to be acquired by a large company and lose their identity and distinctiveness after all these years of comparative independence. They don't want this cooperative spirit to get lost in the shuffle."

"Well, Al, you know that the Business Publications Division operates as a completely independent unit both physically and operationally."

"Yes, Crowell, I know that; but this concept of the giant, like an ogre ready to count their last heartbeats and footsteps, still pervades their fears."

"Well, Al, what about your people? Don't you think they can work for us as well as anyone else? After all, they'll still be taking home the same paychecks, benefits, and security."

"Crowell, I had a real loyal bunch, but maybe I can show you what I mean better this way. Here's a letter from Sam Levine. He's the editor of *Municipal Engineer* and he sent the letter while on vacation early this month.

Dear Al:

I certainly appreciated your telling me last month about your problem of having to sell the business. At first I was very upset, but after spending a couple of weeks on vacation things begin to shape up. Al, as long as you stay with the outfit, I'll stick with you. As a matter of fact, I think that goes for the rest of the boys, too.

We've been with you a long time, and we've made good money. We're not wealthy but have lived a prosperous life and enjoyed our work. That's the thing that stands out. We liked your methods of operation, and the boys have "put out" for the company.

You said you weren't going to quit, even though for financial reasons you sold the ownership, and that is reassuring. It's been a pleasant 22 years, and I hope it continues. Good luck in your selling problem.

See you next week.

Sam

"Well, there it is, Crowell."

"Al, I know that you wouldn't be happy unless you got the whole load off your chest. So let's have it: what are your recommendations?"

"Thanks, Crowell! With your indulgence I'd like to recommend the following plan of action as it concerns our operations:

"1) Leave the physical operations just as they are now, in the same location with the same personnel for at least a year and possibly two.

"2) Permit me to remain in charge of Perlman Publications, making it a separate division reporting to you in a parallel with John Wordsworth's division. I can then work with John during the next few years in determining what is the best method of operation for our publications and arrive at a definite, clearcut plan of action. Also, this will permit our employees to become acquainted with the Delaware Corporation and should make the merger more pleasant for them over a period of time.

"3) Keep our present editors, advertising director, and circulation and business director for at least as long as I am with the Delaware Corporation, in order to continue the same operation and contacts with our readers and advertisers. As I have said before, this is important in our business."

"Well, Crowell, there it is. I've done all the talking. What do you think about it?"

"Al, I'm just not sure yet. I've got the complete picture now and we'll let you know next week before we make the announcement to your employees and the press. I certainly will call you in before then, or have Wordsworth and you get together. Thanks a lot for spending this afternoon with me."

"Crowell, I think this will be a pleasant association and, again, thanks for the opportunity of letting me air my views."

Following his discussion with Perlman, Crowell James discussed this matter with his management adviser, Carl Denis, giving him full information on what had transpired to date. In the course of this conversation, James indicated he was looking to Wordsworth to handle the merger of the two operations.

However, James did ask Denis to look into the situation from the management point of view and to make his recommendations to Wordsworth.

FOR DISCUSSION AND REPORT-WRITING

Organizing: Structural Design

1) Assume that Perlman's suggestions for integrating his company within the Delaware Corporation were accepted for a two-year period:

a) Do you believe the differences in structural design between Perlman and the Business Publications Division can be reconciled by James? How?

b) Would the two "divisions" (Perlman and Business Publications) offer any "deadly parallels" to facilitate comparison and control?

c) What steps would you recommend that James take to facilitate a shift after two years to a structure more like the one Wordsworth has in mind?

d) What staff assistance and/or auxiliary units could James use to help him integrate Perlman over the first two years?

2) Which of the criteria considered and "how much decentralization" should be given heaviest weight in James's decision on how much autonomy to grant Alvin Perlman?

3) Assuming that there were no personal or personnel problems involved in implementing Wordsworth's recommendations, what do you think of the basic design?

4) (Summary Report Question: Part One) Considering the difficulties involved in implementing either Perlman's or Wordsworth's proposals, what alternative organization designs might work for at least the first two years? Which do you recommend from among these alternatives and those of Perlman and Wordsworth? Why?

Human Factors in Organizing

5) Clearly, there will be very different customs within the two units (Perlman and Business Publications). What steps might be taken to deal with these differences and the informal groups that likely exist? Who should take these steps?

6) There is strong likelihood of conflict if anything approaching Wordsworth's plan were to be approved. *a)* What are the most likely sources of conflict? *b)* What are the most desirable methods of dealing with each source?

7) How can the management of Delaware "adjust for individual differences" in the personnel available and the needs of the merged organization?

Planning: Elements of Rational Decision-Making

8) What do you feel to be the impact of Wordsworth's implied style of managing on the creativity of key people in his *present* division?

9) How might James rationally decide how much Perlman's philosophy of management might "cost" Delaware if he supports his philosophy rather than Wordsworth's?

Planning: Decision-Making in an Enterprise

10) How might James's current problems with Perlman Publishing Company have been reduced if the former had done a better job of planning before the acquisition? Be specific about what James could realistically have done and how.

11) Develop a detailed plan for reducing the combined work force of Perlman and Business Publications. Assume whatever organization structure and timetable you feel best, and then prepare a staff-reduction plan consistent with your decisions on structure and timing.

12)   What numbers and types of standing plans will be needed if Wordsworth's recommendations are accepted by James?

Controlling

13)   Which of the two proposed organization designs (Perlman's or Wordsworth's) is more likely to facilitate control at James's level?

14)   How will the differences between Perlman's and Wordsworth's philosophy of management affect the development of standards and measurements if Wordsworth's structural design is approved by James and Perlman does not resign?

Activating

15)   We may easily forecast Perlman's response to Wordsworth's plan. If James wishes to approve an organizational plan that is much closer to Wordsworth's than to Perlman's:

a)   What activating mode should he choose?

b)   What energizing force(s) should he employ?

c)   How should he communicate his decisions to both Perlman and Wordsworth?

16)   If Wordsworth's plan is approved and Perlman stays on, what use, if any, should be made of Perlman in activating the necessary changes within Perlman's current personnel?

Summary Question for Solution of the Case as a Whole

17)   Develop detailed recommendations for Denis to provide to James. Be specific about *a)* the immediate steps to be taken (or not taken), *b)* who would take them, *c)* how they would be implemented, and *d)* how potential problems arising from the recommendations would be dealt with. Indicate why you make these recommendations.

CASE 1-2
MILANO ENTERPRISES

Mr. Milano is concerned about the long-run future of the group of enterprises he has personally built into a flourishing establishment. Located in a Latin American country, Milano Enterprises is recognized as a dynamic factor in the private sector of the nation. In fact, the success of the business complicates its continuation.

Mr. Milano, son of Italian immigrants, started in business 45 years ago in a small but growing city. He anticipated a building boom and left the family grocery store to enter the building-supply business. Several of Mr. Milano's present companies are a direct outgrowth of this early start. He still owns two regional wholesale companies dealing in building supplies. A separate company imports specialty plumbing items; and another is the national representative of a worldwide electric-elevator manufacturer—selling, installing, and servicing elevators for apartment buildings, offices, and warehouses. Currently, the largest company in the building field is a plant manufacturing boilers and other heating equipment. Also, another plant manufactures electric fixtures.

Mr. Milano's activities in other fields followed a somewhat similar pattern. Foreseeing needs arising out of urbanization and industrialization, he sought to become the import representative for products serving these needs. And, as imports were sharply restricted for economic and political reasons, he undertook the manufacture of selected items. For example, in the automotive field he has been the Ford representative for many years. One company does the importing of Ford cars, trucks, and parts. In addition, Milano Enterprises owns a controlling interest in several large dealerships. It also represents the British and German Ford affiliates. Both quotas and tariffs place severe restrictions on the number of vehicles that can be imported, and local legislation encourages manufacture. Consequently, a separate company has been established for truck assembly and body manufacture. Also in the automotive area, Milano Enterprises owns a chain of modern filling stations.

In the office-equipment area, Milano Enterprises has separate companies for the importation of duplicating equipment and typewriters. In addition, there is a substantial and growing unit manufacturing metal furniture for offices.

About ten years ago, a new company was established to manufacture electric refrigerators locally. Compressors are imported but the cabinets are manufactured in a plant adjacent to the furniture plant. Other units include a large textile plant, which weaves and finishes cotton fabrics, a prominent hotel, a soft-drink bottling company, and a small mining-exploration venture.

In total, there are 25 active operating companies ranging in size from 20 to 500 employees. The textile plant and the boiler plant are the largest units in terms of employment. Milano Enterprises owns all or at least a majority of the stock in each of these operating companies. In several instances, the manager of a company owns a minority interest, but he is under contract to Milano Enterprises to sell back his stock at current book value when he retires.

Obviously, the man who can put together such an array of companies possesses unusual ability. Part of Mr. Milano's success arises from working in growth areas. Within these areas, he has been willing to invest risk capital, but has also been unusually adept at picking particular spots where growth was strong and at adjusting his operations as the economic environment shifted. Also, once an investment was made, it has been carefully nurtured and controlled. Mr. Milano is modest in manner, eagerly seeks advice wherever he can find it, and works hard in a well-disciplined manner. His personal integrity is widely respected throughout the business community. He is a religious man and highly devoted to his family.

PRESENT ORGANIZATION

Each of the 25 companies has its manager and, with minor exceptions, its own offices and other facilities. As might be expected, the central organization reflects its evolutionary background and is not sharply defined. Six people, in addition to Mr. Milano, share in the general direction of Milano Enterprises.

Mr. Lopez has been closely associated with Mr. Milano during most of his business career. Both men are the same age and, like Mr. Milano, Mr. Lopez has had only elementary-school education. In general, Mr. Lopez is more concerned with the operation of existing enterprises than with starting new ones. He acts as troubleshooter for Mr. Milano, takes care of labor problems when any arise, and represents the enterprises at various public functions. Managers of the various companies often find that Mr. Lopez is available for consultation when Mr. Milano is concentrating on some new negotiations.

Mr. Peche has been chief accountant for Milano Enterprises for over 20 years. He has an intimate knowledge of the accounting system of each company, even though great variation exists in the way records are kept. Mr. Peche keeps a close eye on the profits, liquidity, expense ratios, and other key figures for each of the companies, and calls Mr. Milano's attention to any significant deviations. He works up estimated projections for Mr. Milano's use in negotiations and in arranging financing, and he takes care of tax matters.

Mr. Gaffney has been Mr. Milano's chief associate in the automotive end of the business, although he is 12 years younger. Mr. Gaffney serves as manager of the automobile-import company and exercises supervision over European imports, all distributors, and the filling stations. He spends about two-thirds of his time with this group of companies but is available for general consultation on other matters. In several new ventures, Mr. Milano has asked Mr. Gaffney to make the preliminary investigation.

Mr. Bolivar is the official representative of Milano Enterprises to the government. He obtains import licenses, which often involves protracted negotiation. Numerous changes in regulations, often without much warning, require Milano Enterprises to maintain an able representative in close contact with administrative and legislative personnel. Also involved is a certain amount of "lobbying" when new legislation is being discussed. Mr. Bolivar devotes his full time to this government work and does not get involved in operating problems of the companies.

Juan Milano is the 32-year-old son of the company's founder. He has been educated abroad, and now works with his father and Mr. Lopez on special projects. He has worked on several consumer studies (for the hotel, bottling company, gasoline filling stations, and electric-refrigerator company) and because of his education often meets with foreign visitors.

Mrs. Rodriques, who has an M. B. A. from a leading American university, serves a dual role. She is a personal assistant to and interpreter for Mr. Milano, who has a keen interest in the latest developments and management thought of companies abroad. In this capacity, she not only presents the ideas but also discusses with Mr. Milano the way they might be related to the enterprises. Mrs. Rodriques' more formal assignment deals with executive and technical personnel. A few general conferences have been held, but thus far most of the work in the senior personnel field is still in the planning stage. Competent executives are very scarce, and even though Milano Enterprises has an excellent reputation, executive selection and development has been more opportunistic than programmed.

All of these people are very busy, and there is rarely a time when two or three of them are not working on some pressing current problem. The board of directors is composed of Mr. Milano, his wife, Juan Milano, Mr. Lopez, and Mr. Gaffney. Since most of these people are in frequent informal contact, formal meetings of the board are held only when some official business must be transacted.

CONCERN FOR THE FUTURE

Even though Milano Enterprises has been successful and is highly regarded in business circles, Mr. Milano is concerned about the future. For one thing, he recognizes that the central organization lacks system and is too dependent upon him personally. He says, "I'm not proud of our organization. All I can say is that thus far it has proved adequate."

More pressing is what will happen after Mr. Milano's death. At 65 he is in good health, but he wishes to take steps for the perpetuation of the enterprises. He would like any reorganization to provide for three objectives:

1) Modern, effective management that will be flexible enough to meet changing conditions as he has had to do over his lifetime

2) Continuing contribution to the national economy, particularly with respect to the initiative and adaptability that free enterprise can provide better than government bureaus

3) Continuing family ownership of a controlling block of the stock. This does not mean that some of the stock may not be sold publicly, as local capital markets develop, nor that family members will always hold top executive positions, unless they are fully qualified to do so.

A banker with whom Mr. Milano has thoroughly discussed this matter urges "decentralization." "No one," he says, "can keep track of all of your companies the way you have, because only you have the background that comes from founding and working with these companies and their executives over a long period. Consequently, you should follow the practice of the leading U. S. companies by appointing able people as the chief executive of each of your operating units and then decentralizing authority to each of them. You already have this general form, but too many decisions are made in the central office. You should immediately decentralize and find out which of your managers are competent and which ones have to be replaced. The sooner you start, the better, because it will be some time before all 25 of the companies can stand on their own feet."

The idea of strong managers in each operating company appeals to Mr. Milano, but he is dubious about the long-run effect of such a decentralization. He fears that Milano Enterprises will become primarily a passive holder of investments, and this certainly has not been the key to success in his personal experience. He anticipates that local managements will continue to do well what they are now doing. But he is worried about their adaptability to changing conditions, the incentive to seek out new opportunities, and some kind of control that spots difficulties early and ensures vigorous remedial action.

Since so much is at stake, Mr. Milano decided to call in an international management consultant. On the basis of advice from companies with whom Milano Enterprises does business and of several personal interviews, Mr. Eberhardt Stempel was selected to make a thorough organization study of the Milano Enterprises. Mr. Stempel presented his recommendations orally and then wrote the following summary report.

INTERNATIONAL CONSULTANTS, INC.
New York–London–Frankfurt–Caracas

Dear Mr. Milano:

You have asked that we briefly summarize the recommendations we discussed in your office a week ago. In the original assignment, you requested that we focus on the central management of the Milano Enterprises; and our investigation confirms your diagnosis that major problems of the future lie in this area.

No report on Milano Enterprises can be made without first recognizing past achievements. Milano Enterprises occupies a unique position in the national economy. Highly respected for its growth, financial strength, willingess to back new ventures, and alertness of management—this group of companies has become a recognized leader in the private business sector. The Milano name carries a high and well-deserved prestige throughout the business community.

The crucial question now facing Milano Enterprises is not immediate. Instead, it is how to prepare for the time when you, Mr. Milano, can no longer serve as the guiding force of the combined group. Note, the problem is greater than the continuing direction of present enterprises. In addition, the future management of Milano Enterprises must have wisdom and courage to expand or contract in various lines as economic opportunities change. Any true perpetuation of your leadership must be dynamic, not static.

We believe the best way to perpetuate Milano Enterprises is to build a strong central organization. The present organization is able to cope with the problems it faces only because of long experience in the field and the exceptional talents of the senior executives. To maintain your present success and to provide for growth, a variety of high-grade specialists should be added to the central organization so that expert talent is readily available to help each of the operating companies meet its problems. The organization that we believe will best meet future needs is shown on the accompanying chart. This organization is patterned after several of the most successful companies in the world, and it embraces features we have found helpful to many of our other clients.

After you have had an opportunity to study this organization carefully, we will be glad to prepare job descriptions and manpower specifications for each of the positions shown on the chart. Before doing so, however, you should be clear in your own mind that this is the direction you wish to follow. We would like to stress again the advantages of this form of organization to Milano Enterprises:

1) A strong central office is provided, including experts in marketing, production, and finance. Every company, large or small, must perform these basic functions well. Consequently, you should have strength to deal with the problems in these areas.

2) Provision is made for current effectiveness. Subsections are provided for industrial engineering, purchasing, marketing methods, accounting, finance, legal advice, and government representation. When these sections are properly staffed, the central office will have talent to help streamline the operations of any existing and newly acquired operating company.

3) In addition, provision is made for growth. The sections on market research, new-product development, financial analysis, and public relations will be primarily concerned with finding opportunities for expansion.

4) Senior executives of Milano Enterprises are given titles and recognition commensurate with the important roles they will play in the group itself and in the nation. Here is the aforementioned chart:

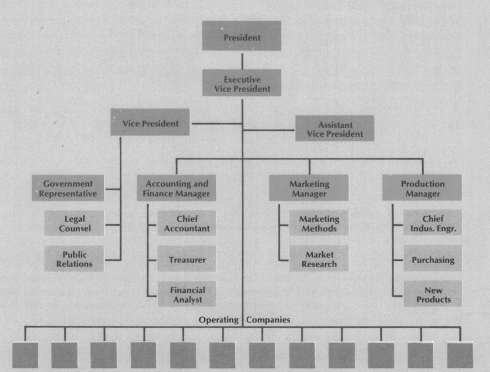

We fully recognize that time will be required to find the proper individuals to fill these posts and to get the entire group working together effectively as a team. We believe that you can best serve Milano Enterprises by devoting most of your time toward this end. You should anticipate that it may take three or four years before the transition can be completed. It is important that the change be made while you are still able to give it your personal attention and endorsement.

It has been a pleasure to serve you, and we shall be happy to be of any further assistance that we can.

Sincerely yours,

Eberhardt Stempel, on behalf of
International Consultants, Inc.

Attachment

REACTIONS TO STEMPEL'S RECOMMENDATIONS

The central management group had heard Mr. Stempel's oral report, and as soon as they had had an opportunity to review the written summary, Mr. Milano called a meeting for a frank discussion of the recommendations.

Both Mr. Lopez and Mr. Peche expressed grave concern about the heavy overhead expense that the proposed organization would entail. It was far more elaborate than anything they had contemplated, and they felt the central office would be so big that personal contacts with one another would become even more difficult. Mr. Gaffney said that from the viewpoint of the automotive unit, he would much prefer to add staff under his immediate direction than be charged for a share of a central-office staff that probably would have only superficial understanding of his problems. Mrs. Rodriques expressed disappointment that the report was not specifically adapted to the needs of Milano Enterprises.

Except for the special emphasis on government representation, the organization looks as if it were designed for General Electric or Unilever.

Juan Milano endorsed this view, saying that he did not see how the particular organization would fit the hotel business or the filling-station business.

To close the meeting, Mr. Milano made a general statement of his feeling:

All of us, I'm sure, have been startled by the recommendations. I confess considerable sympathy with most of the points that have been made. And yet I ask myself whether I am rejecting recommendations because they are new and because they cast some reflection on the way I personally have been running the business. We asked Mr. Stempel to come here because we face a grave problem, the most serious problem of my entire life. I want to be sure, before I reject these recommendations, that it is not because they will require a great change in my own behavior, but because I have a better plan for the future of Milano Enterprises. One of the reasons for the success of many of our companies has been a willingness to recognize a need for a change and then to move in that direction aggressively. I would like to think that I am strong enough to apply that same doctrine to my behavior as the head of the enterprises. Unless we can come up with a better plan, I intend to start to put Mr. Stempel's ideas into effect because time does not permit us to stand still on this issue.

FOR DISCUSSION AND REPORT-WRITING

Organizing: Structural Design

1) What would be the role of staff in Stemple's scheme? If the banker's decentralization scheme were followed, where would staff assistance be needed and what role would staff play?

2) If the smaller companies were to be placed in several groups headed by general managers, what criteria should be used in making the groupings? How would such groups affect the overall adaptability of Milano Enterprises to changing conditions?

3) Discuss the implications of the span of supervision at present and under Stempel's plan.

4) What problems of dual subordination may exist under the existing organization?

5) (Summary Report Question: Part One) List and discuss the alternative forms of departmentation and degrees of decentralization possible in a reorganization of Milano Enterprises.

Human Factors in Organizing

6) Under Stempel's plan, what authority, power, or influence will staff wield? How may the diverse nature of the companies in Milano Enterprises affect your answer?

7) How would you go about developing a strong management team in each operating company under Stempel's plan? What factors would you consider in selection, motivation, and so on?

Planning: Elements of Rational Decision-Making

8) Define (as a gap) each of the potential problems Milano seeks to meet through reorganization.

9) By identifying the higher-order goals—the ends toward which solutions to question 8 were proposed—what alternatives besides reorganization do you see for meeting or avoiding these problems?

10) List the major criteria Milano should use in weighing alternative plans.

Planning: Decision-Making in an Enterprise

11) Do you feel the basic objectives expressed by Milano will have to be reflected in more formal written policies under the Stempel plan? Will more standing plans be needed? Discuss.

12) How will alternative forms of reorganization influence the need for more formal long-range planning in each of the companies and Milano Enterprises as a whole? How should such plans be developed under each alternative?

Controlling

13)   Discuss the nature of controls presently used to evaluate operating companies.

14)   What kind of controls would be required to meet Milano's three objectives for the future under each of the alternative plans of reorganization noted in your answer to question 5?

Activating

15)   What activating mode should Milano seek in gaining acceptance on reorganization from his six subordinates? If he forecasts that one or more of his subordinates may respond less positively than he feels they should, what energizing force(s) should he use to shift this response? Develop a specific plan for bringing about the desired response.

16)   What effects is the Stempel plan likely to have on effective two-way communication a) at the corporate level and b) between corporate staff and individual company management?

Summary Questions for Solution of the Case as a Whole

17)   Do you agree with Stempel's recommendations? If so, how would you respond to criticism by members of central management? If not, what do you recommend and why?

18)   What kind of changes in behavior of people now in central management does your answer to the previous question require? Do you contemplate any difficulties in bringing about these changes? What steps would you recommend be taken to induce these changes?

PART II

Organizing the *work*—both operating and managerial—that is necessary to achieve company objectives was the center of our attention in Part One. Although we often talked about the people who do the work, we focused on how organization could be used to further the *goals* of an enterprise.

In such a "work-focused" study of organization, we made implicit assumptions about how people would behave in their jobs. We assumed that organization members would do what they were told, that higher levels of management could assign goals, that for efficiency management could shift work from one job to another, and that in many other ways managers and operators would adapt their behavior to the needs of an enterprise. The use of simplifying assumptions is a fruitful device, in science and applied arts. It enables us to concentrate on particular aspects of a complex problem. But before we apply a conclusion based on such assumptions to real-life situations, we must check those assumptions. Often we find that they are only partly valid. If so, we must take additional factors into account and adjust our conclusion to fit a fuller array of facts.

In Part Two, we shall follow this procedure by examining assumptions about human behavior in light of current concepts in psychology, sociology, and anthropology. Because these sciences, as applied to business management, are "worker-focused," they can provide important insights and qualifications to the ideas set forth in Part One. Our discussion is divided among the following chapters.

Human Factors

in Organizing

Chapter 7—Personal Needs and Organization Design. Here we consider both the motivations of individuals and the adjustment of company organization to help fulfill these human needs.

Chapter 8—Group Behavior and Organization Design. This chapter deals with the pressures of culture and informal groups that may strongly influence what workers do in their jobs. Then we explore ways to guide group pressure toward company objectives—such as task teams—and to develop customs and roles in new organizations.

Chapter 9—Intergroup Conflict: Sources and Resolution. Some conflict in organizations, like friction in machines, is unavoidable. Here we explore sources of such clashes of interest, the distinctions between destructive and constructive conflict, and how we can organize to deal with conflict.

Chapter 10—Matching Jobs and Individuals. After pointing out variation in individual abilities, we shall consider how far an organization structure should be changed to suit personal strengths and weaknesses.

Many of the ideas about human behavior that we present in Part Two will be used again later, especially when we examine activating. We present them here because human considerations are fully as important in designing the structure of work as in person-to-person relationships between manager and subordinate. In Part Two, then, we focus on the impact of human factors on the process of organizing; we shall be concerned with merging the work-focused and the worker-focused viewpoints.

Personal Needs

and Organization Design

7

NEEDS SATISFIED THROUGH WORK

People are the chief resources used by a manager; he depends on their actions to achieve results. Consequently, it is important for him to understand why people behave as they do.

Formal organization is one means of guiding the behavior of people. But if we are to understand fully how an organization works, we have to appreciate the full range of influences, formal and otherwise, on the behavior of organizational members. Both personal drives and group pressures spur action. In this chapter we focus on motivations of individuals, and then we will look at internal social systems in Chapter 8.

The purpose of this chapter is threefold:

1) To present a way of thinking about human needs—an approach that will be useful later in the book as well as here
2) To consider ways an organization design can help meet human needs
3) To discuss how salaries can be related both to needs and to formal organization

The term "needs" is sometimes used to refer only to essential requirements for survival. Here, however, we shall follow the practice of psychologists and adopt a much broader meaning. Need includes both what a person must have and what he merely wants. Psychologists say that as long as a man wants something, he has a psychological need for it, regardless of what someone else may think of the justification for this desire. With this usage, we avoid making subjective judgments—for example, whether it is a matter of necessity or desire for a college student to have a car on campus.

Needs vary widely among individuals, but this variation is largely a matter of degree and of different ways of satisfying needs. There is enough similarity in the basic aspirations of most people so that we can talk of general human needs.

Many classifications of needs have been made. We shall confine our attention to those that can be satisfied to a significant degree by working in a business enterprise, for these are the needs a manager may be able to do something about. Drawing on A. H. Maslow's classic analysis, these job-related wants include: physical needs, security needs, social needs, and self-expression needs.

Physical Needs

All human beings have needs that pertain to survival and physiological maintenance of the body. The objects of these needs include such things as food, drink, shelter, rest, and exercise. Until such needs are reasonably well satisfied, they are strong, driving forces. Our society is sufficiently prosperous, however, that the minimum physiological requirements are usually met. Nevertheless, management has devoted a good deal of attention to providing adequate ventilation, heat, and light; in general, management attempts to ensure working conditions that make a workplace physically satisfactory—even attractive.

Security Needs

In an age when our entire Western society seems to have an obsession with security, we all quickly recognize needs in this area. Most of us secretly hope that some omnipotent agent will assure us that all the satisfactions we now enjoy will continue and that no misfortune will cross our path. Because such guarantees are impossible, particularly in a dynamic society, we should couch our hopes for security in more realistic terms. Both economic and psychological security are involved.

With respect to work, most attention of social reformers has been focused on *economic security*. People worry about steady employment, provisions for old age, and insurance against catastrophes that might call for large financial outlays. Private enterprise and government have both sought ways of providing at least minimum financial protection against these risks. Possibly the resulting discussions of pensions, unemployment insurance, health insurance, and similar plans have made all of us even more sensitive to economic security.

But a more subtle matter is the need for *psychological security*. This need relates to a person's confidence in dealing with the problems that confront

Figure 7–1 Jobs differ sharply in the degree to which they provide physical, social, and self-expression satisfactions.

him. His ability to meet future job requirements, the fairness of present and future supervisors, the balance of benefits and losses that result from economic and technological changes—all conjure up hopes and fears. Everyone needs assurance that he will be able to adjust satisfactorily to such new conditions.

One source of psychological security is knowing the rules of the game. For example, the student who at the beginning of a course wants to know what the final grade will be based on or how long research papers should be is trying to remove an irritating uncertainty. Uneasiness about the effect of a rumored reorganization on one's job can lead to high anxiety because the rules of the game may change. Somehow we have to develop confidence that we shall be able to cope with new situations successfully.

Social Needs

Social needs are satisfied through relations with other people, and in most of us the desire for *sociability* is strong. We need contacts with informal groups

137

as well as with close friends. Such contacts include friendly greetings, casual conversations, and amusing luncheons that a person—whether he is a mimeograph operator, foreman, or vice-president—engages in with his associates at the office or plant. Companies have found that when employees have friendly relationships on the job, absenteeism tends to be low. In fact, people often go to their jobs or to a social function despite a headache or a lack of interest in the activity itself, just to associate with other people.

Closely related to sociability is a sense of *belonging.* Everyone wants to feel that he is a recognized member of a group; that he will be included in group plans and will share informal information, both gossip and fact; that others will help him in trouble and will expect him to help them.

A third social need is desire for *status.* In a business, status depends on the value of a position in the eyes of others. Status always implies a ranking along some kind of scale, and the hierarchy of a formal organization is one of the commonly accepted gauges. In addition, occupations differ in status value in various companies and communities. For example, being an actuary at the Metropolitan Life Insurance Company may command much more respect in "nice" suburbs than being a pier boss at an ocean dock, even though the pier boss is paid more. Within companies, distinctions may be drawn between machinists and pipefitters, between locomotive engineers and firemen, or between sales clerks and cashiers. Status distinctions are drawn within classes of occupation. Everyone in a company usually knows who is the top person, the fastest typist, or the manager of the most profitable branch. Status inevitably implies competition, and competition is especially vigorous in the United States, where most people seek to improve their status. But perhaps even more pronounced than the desire to rise is the desire not to lose status. A lathe operator may refuse to sweep around his machine or an executive may refuse to answer his own telephone—even though to do so might be the simplest way to get work done—merely to maintain his status in the eyes of those about him.

Self-expression Needs

Aside from what others may think, each person is concerned with his private aspirations, and in this matter he measures himself. He asks, "Does this job permit me to do what *I* would like to do, to be what *I* want to be?" In brief, everyone needs to express himself. At the nucleus of the cluster of needs for self-expression we find self-assertion, power, personal accomplishment, and personal growth. Let us look more closely at each of these four needs.

Every mature adult wants to assert himself, to be independent at least to some extent. As we grow from childhood to adulthood, we rely less and less on other people to help us survive, to make decisions for us, and to show us how to behave and act. We want increasing control over our own destiny. In short, as we mature we progress from dependence toward independence.

By the time a person reaches maturity, he attains a level of *self-assertion* —we might say independence or initiative—that he must maintain if he is to stay happy. Being independent makes life more pleasant for him than taking advice from others. Although this drive for self-assertion varies in intensity from person to person, nearly everyone has at least some need to be independent and to exercise initiative.

In some persons, desire for self-assertion slips over into a strong urge for *power*. Like the thrill a youngster gets from driving a car, the ability to make things or persons respond to one's own will can be a strong motive.

Most of us also desire a feeling of personal *accomplishment*. Craftsmen take pride in their work, whether it be a neatly typed letter, a difficult surgical operation, or a welded joint that may never be seen by the public eye. Some people feel deeply about educating children, making highways safer, or otherwise contributing to the general welfare. For them, satisfaction comes from knowing that they have done a worthwhile job well; regardless of public acclaim or the size of tasks, they enjoy an inner sense of accomplishment. Few people, in fact, can do their best work unless they feel satisfaction of this sort.

In addition, people normally want an opportunity for *growth*. Satisfaction comes from the *process of achieving* as much as from the accomplishment itself. A college graduate in accounting may be happy while he first learns a small part of a company's cost accounting, but after he has solved problems there, he wants to move on to something else. He at least wants variety, but he probably also wants a task calling for greater skill. Individuals vary greatly in the kind and amount of growth to which they aspire. Psychologist David McClelland gives us impressive evidence that even the growth of nations is closely tied to their peoples' need for achievement. We can anticipate that with increasing education, travel, and technological change, the desire for growth opportunities will become even more pressing than it has been in the past.

POTENCY OF NEEDS

The total array of human needs seems overwhelming. Even those needs related to work—physical, security (economic, psychological), social (sociability, belonging, status), and self-expression (self-assertion, accomplishment, growth)—make us wonder, "Can man ever be satisfied?" Part of the answer lies in the relative potency of these various desires. In this connection, we shall consider marginal values, aspiration levels, and nonrational values.

Marginal Values

How intensely an individual wants more of a thing—say, food, social recognition, or job security—depends partly on how much he already has. What is an additional, or *marginal*, unit worth to him? He might sell his birth-

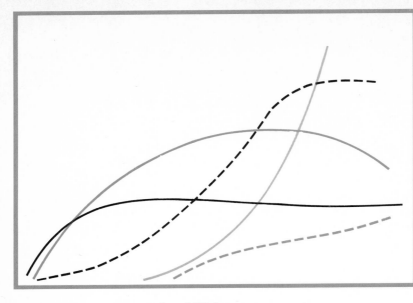

Potency of needs →

Extent needs are fulfilled ⟶

Figure 7–2 Marginal potency of needs varies with fulfillment. Some needs, such as physical protection from weather, are fully satisfied and drop off; others, like esteem of friends, keep expanding. The shapes of these curves differ among individuals, and even for the same individual over time.

right for air to breathe if he were suffocating, but when fresh air is in plentiful supply, it loses its marginal value. In times of earthquake or war, starving people have traded diamonds for food; once adequately fed, however, these same people become more interested in security and self-expression.

At a given moment, each person has a hierarchy of needs, ranging from those that seem urgent to those that are faint. As the most basic needs become satisfied—that is, when a person has sufficient water, shelter, and so on—the next most important needs become the real governors of his behavior. After they are met, some needs, such as security of employment, become dormant; but other needs, such as a drive toward personal achievement or desire for social recognition, tend to keep expanding. Frederick Herzberg applies the term "hygiene factor" to those needs that do not expand—they may cause great distress when not met but provide little drive once they are. The other needs, which keep growing, are the prime motivators.

Whether a need continues to be potent as a person derives increased satisfaction depends largely on his levels of aspiration and on his ability to draw qualitative distinctions rationally.

Aspiration Levels

The potency of a need depends on whether a person expects the need to be met. A desire to become company president, for instance, is not a strong motive for one who says to himself, "I know I'll never make it." On the other hand, a design engineer who expects ample opportunity for self-expression will be very dissatisfied if he is assigned routine drafting. To understand human needs, then, we should not only identify each need and note how well it is already being met, but also consider how much more satisfaction of each type of need a person really aspires to attain.

Incidentally, many workers—especially those on routine jobs—do not expect great things from their work. Over seventy-five percent are satisfied with their present jobs—mainly because their aspirations are not very high. We are kidding ourselves if we assume most of these people want tough, varied, and ever-expanding jobs. Nevertheless, a large minority would welcome more meaningful work, and this number will probably rise as education levels go up and as women and minorities shift their expectations.

An individual's self-image strongly influences his aspiration levels; that is, what he believes his abilities are, and what he thinks his role should be. If he regards himself as the best salesperson in a company, he will work harder to achieve top ranking than someone who considers himself a plodder, "about as good as the average." Similarly, the executive who views himself as a natural leader will be highly concerned about social approval of his ideas. Of course self-images change over time. Repeated failures to achieve an expected satisfaction normally lead to a downward adjustment in aspiration, whereas successes encourage new dreams of glory, especially if one's friends are experiencing similar failures or successes. A person typically makes these adjustments in his self-image quite slowly, however.

Social scientists have observed three things about aspiration levels that are especially pertinent for a business manager:

1) *Change* in the extent of need fulfillment—either up or down—is especially potent. For instance, a drop below a level that has become accepted is felt as a severe deprivation.

2) For many needs, people expect improvement from year to year. Indeed, the improvement is often more important than the absolute standard. (Perhaps this is why our forefathers spoke about "life, liberty, and the *pursuit* of happiness.")

3) Operators and managers recognize that in every firm there is a certain amount of dirty, routine, and otherwise unattractive work to be done. Performing such tasks satisfies few human desires directly; it is simply *necessary work.* Nevertheless, most people realistically expect to do some unattractive but necessary work as part of their jobs. Even though it does not contribute directly to meeting needs, it may be consistent with levels of expectation. Throughout life, everyone learns to mix the bitter with the sweet; we are simply seeking to devise a more pleasant mixture.

Uncalculated Values

Rarely do we calculate marginal values and aspiration levels systematically and logically; the potency of a need is more often based on our feelings. Even the person who wants to act logically is confronted with a formidable task. Our list of work-related needs is already complex, but there are still others, connected with family, religion, and other aspects of life, that also demand satisfaction. There are many ways to satisfy each of these needs, especially when we recognize *degrees* of satisfaction. For instance, we may use numerous foods of varying quality to satisfy the hunger need; we may satisfy social needs by a wide range of activities, from going to parties to working in an office together. For any given need, we may select from numerous alternative goals to fulfill it. Furthermore, we may adopt any of several alternative actions to attain each goal.

Because of the variety of our needs, the number of alternative goals that might satisfy them, and the number of alternative actions by which we might attain any one goal, we are confronted with almost unbelievably complex decisions about what to do at any one time—or *would be* if we logically determined each action. Because of this great complexity, we cannot carefully calculate all the pros and cons. Instead we rely chiefly on habits, attitudes, and emotional response.

No one can prove that as much as ninety-five percent of people's actions are uncalculated, but this is a useful approximation for a manager. It warns him that attempts to change people's behavior by logical argument will meet with limited success. Instead he must try to learn which needs have high potency for his subordinates and then try to create a work situation in which each subordinate finds his satisfactions by helping to achieve company goals.

SATISFYING NEEDS ON THE JOB

On-the-Job versus Off-the-Job Satisfactions

In our discussion of human needs, we have concentrated on those desires that can be met, at least to some degree, by working at a job. Such satisfactions, however, may arise either directly or indirectly from the work itself. This distinction has an important bearing on how a manager seeks to motivate his subordinates.

Work itself can be satisfying. A sense of achievement, for instance, arises from doing a job well. When a person performs an assigned task and at the same time satisfies his basic needs, we say he enjoys "direct," or "on-the-job," satisfactions. In such a case, it is the work itself and the normal relations with other people at work that provide satisfying experiences.

In contrast, there may be rewards for work that are not generated as an aspect of work activity. Familiar forms of this kind of reward are pay, vacations, and pensions. Let us note that the satisfactions that arise from such rewards take place *outside* the management system or work situation, and mostly outside the company. Work is simply a means of obtaining satisfaction at a later time and place. We shall refer to these as "indirect," or "off-the-job," satisfactions.

When these distinctions are applied to the human needs discussed early in this chapter, we may be surprised to note how important on-the-job satisfactions are in the total picture (see Table 7–1). Most of the literature in

TABLE 7–1—HUMAN NEEDS RELATED TO WORK

Needs	Direct, On-the-Job Satisfactions	Indirect, Off-the-Job Satisfactions
Physical needs	"Working conditions"	Money to buy necessities of life
Security needs	Psychological security	Economic security
Social needs	Sociability, belonging	Money to attain social status
	Status within company	Recognized title in reputable company
Self-expression needs	Self-assertion, power, sense of accomplishment, growth possibilities	Improved ability to engage in hobbies
		Money to seek power

economics and scientific management stresses financial, or off-the-job, compensation. But behavioral scientists have insisted—and this is one of their major contributions—that on-the-job satisfactions are also highly important.

Limitations of Off-the-Job Satisfactions

In our society off-the-job satisfactions from work depend largely on money. We use pay to buy things that satisfy physical needs and contribute toward social status. Economic security during old age or in time of catastrophe is also assured by money. But the lack of direct association between work and such satisfactions has a serious drawback—it too often leads to this familiar attitude: "I don't care about the job as long as the pay keeps rolling in."

Not all off-the-job satisfactions come through money, however. Employment with a well-known company and a good title contribute to social status away from work. Some people would rather be vice-president of a local bank than sales representative for Chilean Nitrates at a higher salary, simply because the bank job carries more prestige among their friends.

Companies may provide housing, recreation, and other off-the-job benefits. During recent years, however, most companies have withdrawn such forms of compensation because of worker resistance to "paternalism." Because of a desire for independence, which we have already discussed in connection with self-assertion, most employees prefer that their employer keep out of their private affairs. They are likely to resent even a generous program if management clearly expects them to be appreciative of the good things bestowed on them. A company can and should help build a wholesome community, provided it maintains the independence and self-respect of the citizens.

Off-the-job satisfactions, then, are essential in meeting certain types of human needs—notably the needs that can be satisfied through the use of money. But as we shall see later in the chapter, relating pay to an active interest in performing a job well is by no means easy; and many social, self-expression, and security needs must be fulfilled on the job if they are to be satisfied through work.

On-the-Job Satisfaction: A Challenge to Management

Providing on-the-job satisfactions is not a simple matter for two reasons. First, the principal difficulty lies in meeting needs for social contact, self-expression, and psychological security. Fulfilling each of these needs calls for the active participation and often the initiative of a worker himself. A manager cannot *force* a worker to enjoy his associates, be independent, take pride in his work, and be confident of the future; a manager can only create an environment in which such feelings can flourish. For a manager who is accustomed to moving equipment, shaping raw materials, and otherwise achieving goals by positive action, an approach limited to facilitating action by others may seem slow. Yet all he can do is encourage growth and foster independence.

Second, on-the-job satisfactions should arise only while *people are doing the work that is necessary to meet company goals.* The sequence of events is not that a manager first assures worker satisfaction and then hopes that the happy workers will decide to do the tasks assigned to them; as we observed in our discussion of potency, a satisfied need does not motivate behavior. Nor does a benevolent boss parcel out satisfactions as rewards. Rather, actually doing a task that leads to company success must, at the same time, be what workers derive their satisfactions from. Both parties to the transaction benefit, just as a bee in the process of making honey from a blossom fertilizes the potential fruit.

Because work must be done if an enterprise is to remain in existence, a manager may prefer to organize work purely on the basis of technology; then, as a separate issue, use "indirect" incentives to stimulate good worker performance. However, if he expects his subordinates to be self-reliant, eager, and dependable instead of apathetic, indifferent, and lazy, he must try to set up the work in ways that offer people substantial, direct, on-the-job satisfactions.

MEETING HUMAN NEEDS THROUGH ORGANIZATION

The structure of a company defines an environment of formal rules, job descriptions, and communication networks in which people live during working hours. This environment can satisfy needs or block them; it can develop good attitudes or bad attitudes; and it can determine, in part, what people think and learn. Therefore, structure—as well as planning, face-to-face leadership, and control—is highly important in getting results.

In the following paragraphs, we shall present a variety of ways in which organization structure may contribute to, or detract from, the satisfaction of human needs. There may, of course, be other, perhaps compelling, considerations in making the final choice of an organization pattern, but our purpose here is merely to point out some ways that organization alone can effect the satisfactions of the people in it.

Small Units

When many workers are required for an operation, the social satisfactions will be greater if we can assign the workers to small groups of, say, three to ten. For instance, an insurance-company typing pool of perhaps sixty typists is too large to serve as a social group. The typists would form small, informal friendship groups, of course, but their socializing would probably be a thing apart from their work. On the other hand, if we could organize the work into small units, the typists could, to some extent, serve their sociability needs *while doing assigned work*. Moreover, a sense of *belonging* would probably be stronger in the smaller unit, and if we could measure the group output, we might find that the small groups engendered a sense of personal achievement.

Isolated Jobs

Taking social needs into account in organizing should make us wary of carrying to the extreme the process of cutting down the size of work groups. We should not isolate an individual.

The personal secretary to the president of one of the country's largest corporations once remarked that in many ways she was not as happy as when her boss was a lower executive. "This office is beautifully furnished and has the latest equipment, and I do have prestige as the president's secretary. But it is quiet in here, and the door is always closed. We're so busy I never have a minute to get out and talk with Jean and Betty and Ken like I used to." This woman was isolated by space and walls, but we can produce the same result by breaking down work into such *extremely specialized* and *independent parts* that a person lacks opportunity to interact with fellow workers while performing his work. We might call this *organizational isolation*.

Consider a roomful of design engineers. We might assign one engineer to a small, specialized project with which no other engineers are concerned. Day in and day out, he designs perhaps only pipelines, whereas all other engineers collaborate in designing chemical-processing units. Because he has little reason to discuss his work with others, he must either sacrifice social satisfaction during his working hours or steal time from the company to have conversations on other matters that are either partly or wholly irrelevant to the job of designing pipelines.

As an alternative, we could include this person in a unit of engineers who design processing units and pipelines at the same time. Both his enjoyment of work and the amount he does might increase. He would derive social satisfaction in discussing problems with his colleagues and from talking to construction supervisors who come into the drafting room to seek advice on construction operations. Such "socializing" is inherent in the position and does not involve serious interruption of assigned work.

Narrow Staff Assignments

In order for a person to satisfy his social needs, his relationships with others must be *reciprocal*. We do not enjoy always giving and never receiving, any more than we enjoy a one-way conversation. For a high degree of satisfaction, the initiation of contacts and the exchange of information should be roughly equal and reciprocal.

An easy give-and-take is hard to establish when a staff expert simply tells other people what to do. Relationships in such a case tend to run in one direction. Similarly, companies often set up controls so that information flows only upward from the operating level to a staff person who measures and analyzes results. Either arrangement may accomplish its primary purpose, but it would not provide for satisfying social relationships.

The General Hardware Manufacturing Company had an organization that illustrates this point. A staff engineer who reported to the president was assigned the duty of operating a research department to plan new products and new uses for existing products. After top management approved product innovations, this product-planning director was expected to help the president convey and clarify instructions to the plant and sales managers. This one-way flow of decisions did not provide opportunity, especially for the plant manager, to enter into give-and-take discussion with the product-planning director about the work itself. Physical separation and the status of "an expert from the head office" contributed to the difficulty of establishing reciprocal relationships. The same company also located in the home office a cost expert who watched over all expenditures—labor, overhead, and manufacture of specific products. His principal duty was to request data and explanations from plant managers and pass an analysis of this information on to the president. Again, the flow was one-way, as indicated in Fig. 7–3. As we might expect, the plant managers did not look forward to their meetings with either the product-planning director or the cost analyst; similarly, dealing with plant managers was just one of the crosses the central staff had to bear.

If the company would modify the work structure so that the people concerned with product development, plant operation, and cost analysis could

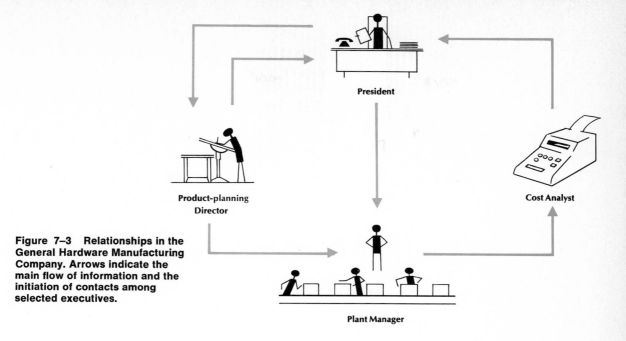

Figure 7–3 Relationships in the General Hardware Manufacturing Company. Arrows indicate the main flow of information and the initiation of contacts among selected executives.

President

Product-planning Director

Cost Analyst

Plant Manager

come together in frequent discussions of how to operate each plant in order to contribute most to company profits, the feelings and social satisfactions would be quite different. One organizational change that might bring this about would be to combine all three functions under a single executive—a plant manager with expanded duties. Another possibility would be to locate cost analysts physically in each plant, where they could serve the plant manager as well as prepare reports for the president. Even shifting greater responsibility for product development to each plant manager, with the result that he would make suggestions and ask for help from the central research group, would encourage reciprocal relations. The company would have to make any such modification in view of its total situation, but the alternatives mentioned indicate how the organization could be restructured to meet social needs more effectively.

When management sets up a committee, either temporary or continuing, it creates a vehicle for satisfying several social needs. In committees, people usually meet as equals; if meetings are properly conducted, they provide a maximum of give-and-take communication; and often, committee membership contributes to prestige within a company.

Clearly, we should not establish committees merely to make members happy. In fact, using committees that contribute little or nothing to company goals may actually have an adverse effect on morale, for members feel that the meetings are a waste of time and an interruption of their more important tasks. But if work is potentially suited to handling by a committee, an important consideration in favor of forming one is that social satisfaction will be a probable by-product.

Place in Hierarchy

Most people take pride in reporting to a high-level executive. It enhances their status, even though the executive may be too busy to see them frequently. Indirectly, it may also give independence—if the executive has many people who report to him, he *must* grant considerable freedom of action. Perhaps pride of place in an organization's hierarchy explains why over one hundred important officials report directly to the President of the United States.

Adding a supervisory level in an organization structure cuts into satisfactions from status, especially of those who report to the newly established supervisor. In one advertising agency, for instance, two department managers resigned when they discovered that they would no longer report directly to a vice president. The people in their departments felt demoted, even though no one would have suffered a reduction in pay or a change in duties.

Related to the matter of place in the hierarchy is the question of titles. Titles provide significant status satisfactions both within and outside a company. Theoretically, titles (or "rank" in military establishments) could be assigned on individual merit, irrespective of job duties or position in an organization hierarchy. But because titles are important in helping people understand a formal organization, they should usually describe where a job fits into a total organization structure. Even within this limit, however, managerial ingenuity in devising attractive titles can make substantial differences in employee satisfaction. "Let's give the guy a title instead of a raise" is not just a wisecrack; the right title may increase a person's satisfaction with his job.

Job Enlargement

Dividing up work into highly specialized jobs takes a toll on worker satisfaction. The assembly-line worker who spends day after day tightening a single bolt has become a classic example of a person who has a routine, monotonous job. Although many workers do not object to such work because of off-the-job satisfactions, they enjoy little pride of accomplishment.

Narrow specialization may also affect a person's opportunity for growth. To take a simple example from office work, a large oil company meticulously divided up work in its billing department among four employees: one typist listed in separate columns on an invoice all types and quantities of products from customer orders; a second clerk entered prices next to the products typed in the list; a calculator operator multiplied quantity by price and entered the total for each product; finally, a fourth clerk added up product totals, adjusted for special transportation charges, and entered the total amounts customers owed. With each person doing such small tasks, each one found little room for growth in his job; only by being promoted could he hope for growth. The company in question, however, changed the organization of this operation. Instead of restricting each person to a specialized task, management divided up the work so that each operator now completes a whole invoice from typing to totaling. Output has gone up and the number of errors down.

Other companies have found that similar job enlargements have improved results. Part of the benefit comes from technical improvements. Coordination is simplified, less time is wasted in moving work from one step to another, and only one person has to give attention to each piece of work—as with the invoice in the preceding example. Another benefit is increased worker satisfaction. A job becomes more challenging than under the former setup; a worker becomes aware of a natural completeness, or wholeness, to his task, and this affords him a greater sense of accomplishment. A worker on an enlarged job also becomes better prepared for other assignments.

Splitting Up Established Roles

Some jobs become firmly structured and embrace a fixed range of duties, particularly when a long period of formal training is required and when professional associations are active in the field. In hospitals, for instance, the roles of doctor, graduate nurse, and dietitian are sharply defined by tradition. Similarly, in a manufacturing concern, a first-class machinist or mechanical engineer may have a clear self-image of what he should and should not do. He has a "professional" pride in his job and the way he performs it.

Occasionally efficiency suggests reshaping such a role. Perhaps a draftsman can take over some duties that for years have been done only by engineers; or perhaps—this would be even more devastating to the engineers' pride—some aspects of design work might be shifted to salespeople. Part of the price of any such change will be a loss of self-esteem by the people whose "professional" job is being split up. The probable resistance may be strong enough to cause management to doubt whether a new organization is worth the rumpus. One large electronics firm, for instance, delayed a major reorganization because it would hurt the status and pride of its electrical engineers; at the time, good engineers were hard to recruit and hold, and the firm felt it had to provide a full range of satisfactions to retain key people.

Decentralization—Job Enrichment

By its very definition, decentralization means increasing a subordinate's freedom of action. This freedom naturally affects the fulfillment of self-expression needs. At one extreme a job description for a sales representative might simply specify, "Call on all customers in the Norfolk territory at least once a month and present company products that appear to offer most appeal at that time." At the other extreme, the guides and rules defining the same job might spell out exactly how the representative should approach customers—for instance, by presenting samples first and mentioning price only incidentally, or even by spouting a canned sales talk that he has memorized from the company manual. In the first case, a person could give his initiative free rein, but in the latter circumstance, he would have much less opportunity for independent self-assertion.

The issue of opportunity for independence is also of concern to managers throughout a company. The supervisor of a cost-accounting department in a factory, for example, may have either a high or low degree of delegation from the plant controller. He may or may not be free to work out his own methods for gathering data from heads of operating units; he may or may not be allowed to plan the vacation schedule for employees in his department; he may or may not be permitted to determine the schedule for sending summary reports to the controller.

The higher the degree of decentralization—that is, the greater freedom allowed—the more satisfaction a subordinate can expect from asserting his own ideas. Moreover, the more a person feels he is "running his own show," the more he will enjoy satisfactions of achievement. With a greater decentralization, a person has more chance to grow in his position and, in so doing, to prepare himself for more complex assignments. Clearly, decentralization ministers to self-expression needs by providing opportunities to satisfy them; but as we noted earlier, fostering opportunity is as far as management can go in satisfying this class of human need.

Organization of self-contained, semiautonomous divisions has already been described in Chapter 3 as a special form of decentralization. The separate divisions of the General Electric Company and the Du Pont Company are well-known examples of such profit decentralization. This arrangement offers the managers of such divisions unusual chances for self-assertion and growth. In fact, a recognized benefit of profit decentralization lies in the strong appeal of challenging experience it offers the managers of each division. Here, indeed, organization structure ministers to human needs.

"Task teams" also require decentralization, as we will note in the next chapter. Moreover, they are small units, and easy two-way communication becomes normal. In these respects they contribute significantly to personal needs of the members. We may encounter resistance when first establishing them, however, if a technical specialist on the team feels that his established role is being fractured (he may have to leave his office and live where "the shooting is going on") and that his status is downgraded.

In the preceding pages, we have discussed only a few of the ways a manager can creatively apply an understanding of human needs to organization design. Human needs are, of course, only one of the factors that influence the final selection of an organization structure. Nevertheless, as he considers the full range of factors, a manager should try to create positions that provide high on-the-job satisfactions.

FREEDOM VERSUS ORDER

A recurring issue in matching personal needs with an organization's is how to balance individual freedom against established order. Today nonconformity is somewhat fashionable, and many young people regard fitting into any regulated system as a sacrifice. On closer examination, however, we discover that the issue calls for sensitive balance.

One cluster of basic human needs, already discussed, hinges on security. A known, orderly way of working together is an important source of such security. Established roles, normal procedures, and planned change all help members of an organization to feel psychologically secure. They know what to expect, and they have a recognized place in the total activities. People also want opportunities for self-expression, but for most, self-expression has an underpinning of security. No person can enjoy freedom in a completely unstructured, unpredictable environment. But, as we have already noted, after a need for such security is fairly well satisfied, it drops in importance. The practical questions, then, deal with *marginal increments* of security and self-expression.

Our reaction to orderliness depends substantially on our feeling about the necessity for it. Musicians, artists, and researchers, for instance, voluntarily submit to all kinds of disciplined behavior—with no sense of lost freedom— if they regard the drill as necessary to their personal expression. Similarly, when we are committed to an objective, we accept all sorts of necessary guidance in reaching our end.

Also, for centuries most people have satisfied their self-expression needs off the job. And now, the dramatic reduction in the work week provides increasing freedom for individuals to pursue their personal interests independently. People neither want nor expect to depend solely on their jobs for opportunities for self-expression.

So we don't face a simple trade-off between the orderliness required by technology or economics on the one hand and individual freedom on the other. Nevertheless, rising living standards, increased mass education, and higher aspirations raise the marginal value attached to individual self-expression. Perhaps as a general guide, we should start with the assumption that organization designers tend to overdo systems and formal assignments. This means that we should look for opportunities to leave discretion with individual operators and managers and should be ready to modify existing organization to keep it relevant to current social moods.

INTEGRATING PAY, NEEDS, AND ORGANIZATION

Although to say that "people work for a paycheck" is a gross oversimplification (as our preceding discussion has shown), financial compensation is a vital source of satisfaction. The size of a paycheck *does* matter to virtually every worker, from president to office boy.

The real question is how pay fits into the relationship between jobs and need satisfaction. To be sure, pay enables workers to meet their physical needs and those of their families. If a paycheck is large enough, they may have steak instead of hamburgers, two cars instead of one, or even a color television set in the bedroom. But a paycheck means more than just what it buys. It is a symbol of status, a source of self-respect, an avenue to security. These primarily non-economic aspects of the paycheck often have more impact on how a person behaves in his job than its purchasing power.

Several of these "indirect" influences of pay on behavior are closely related to organization design. They also intertwine with on-the-job satisfactions. Because an alert manager will want to give attention to such interrelations, we now turn to several key issues in this area: Can we substitute money for other kinds of satisfaction? How should a pay system be related to formal organization? Can we use pay to reinforce the influence of staff and of executives? How should individual raises be related to assigned duties and company objectives? What burdens does the use of incentive pay place on organization structure?

Pay Instead of Other Satisfactions

Can a company pay high salaries and wages and disregard security, social, and self-expression satisfactions? For instance, provided pay is high, will a capable individual work as a subordinate for a supervisor who is highly critical, makes even minor decisions, and gives no opportunity for growth in the job? Experience answers, "Money isn't everything." Competent people shift to other jobs where the work is more attractive even if the pay is lower. Those who do stay on an unpleasant job are likely to develop negative attitudes toward their work and the company, to show little initiative, and perhaps even to restrict their output. Even though high pay may attract a worker, it does not win his emotional support if his job is low in direct satisfactions.

However, a job so brimful of direct satisfactions that it is "actually fun" still requires "reasonable" pay. The pay cannot be much below the prevailing rate for comparable work because of the psychological aspect of pay. The amount of compensation reflects the importance a company attaches to the work; it is a symbol recognized by other people inside and outside the company. Even though a person likes a job, he also wants others to think well of him and of the job. We can conclude, then, that a wise manager must consider *both* direct and indirect satisfactions. Most people are willing to substitute one for the other only to a limited extent. We can apply the principle of marginal value to both situations: Extra-high pay cannot compensate for the reduction of on-the-job satisfactions below a commonly accepted level, *and* a high degree of job satisfaction will not keep a person working if his pay significantly degrades his self-respect or social standing.

Exceptions to this general proposition can be found, of course. Some jobs, such as preaching or teaching, carry enough social prestige and ego satisfaction to attract people, even though business pays for comparable ability at a significantly higher rate. We can also fill dirty or risky jobs by paying premium rates. In general, however, both fair pay and satisfying work are necessary to attract and motivate good people.

This conclusion still leaves us with the question of what compensation is "reasonable" for specific jobs in a specific company. One important guide for both a manager and those who receive the pay is this: A pay rate should reflect the difficulty of a job. Jobs that require more skill, longer training, or more obligation should command higher pay. We should note that this guide is based on formal organization, for job descriptions specify duties and, at least by implication, the abilities needed to fill each position. Any pay system that is inconsistent with formally assigned duties may lead to discontent.

Status is the chief issue. A difficult or important job should have a high status. Because pay level (along with title and place in the official hierarchy) is the most conspicuous evidence of status, we should take great care in matching duties and pay. Employees at all levels are sensitive to this point. Strikes have been called over the amount of difference in wages between, say, electricians and machinists, not because of a few cents per hour, but because of

Figure 7–4   A possible salary structure for a small bank. The structure reflects the difficulties, duties, and status of jobs, the rates paid by other firms, and the possibilities for salary increases in any given position.

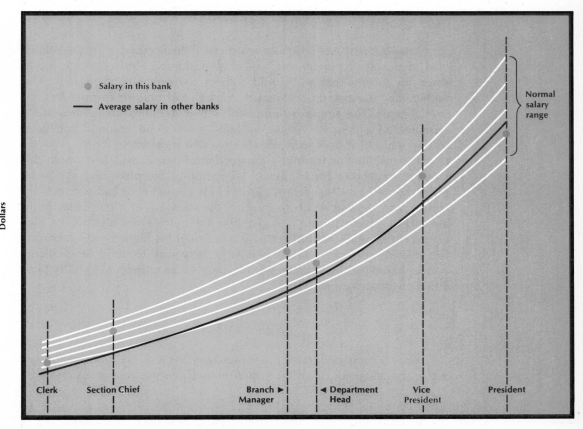

what the difference meant in relative status. On the executive level, a vice-president of a certain department store was quite satisfied with a $45,000 salary until he learned that another vice-president, whose job he considered no more important than his own, was earning $50,000; immediately, he felt insulted, downgraded, and discriminated against.

Management usually dovetails salaries and duties by a procedure called "job evaluation." Steps in an evaluation include: 1) comparing all jobs on many counts—such as scope of duties, skills, and working conditions—and placing the jobs in a series of grades; 2) establishing a general salary level for each grade based on going rates for comparable work among other firms; and 3) creating a salary range for each grade that will permit increases from minimum to maximum as an individual progresses from beginner to expert in any one job.

No matter how elaborate the job-evaluation technique we use for our pay system, it will not be successful unless it is *accepted* by the employees to whom it applies. They must believe that it fairly reflects differences in jobs; the grades assigned must coincide with the relative standing of various roles as the workers conceive of them. Without such acceptance, the status and self-esteem of some workers will suffer, and the pay system will have a negative effect on their eagerness to do their work.

Reinforcing Staff and Executives

Management has a further reason to be concerned with the relative pay level of people in supervisory and staff positions. The feeling is common in American society that we should respect the opinions of persons who earn more money than we do, whereas the opinions of persons earning less are open to challenge. The simple assumption is that earnings are a measure of the soundness of a person's views. We believe this is an unsound and dangerous assumption, but it does exist whether we like it or not.

Because of this feeling, a low-paid staff person will have more difficulty winning acceptance for his ideas. An operating executive may say to himself, "Why should I take that fellow's advice? He doesn't earn half as much as I do." Thus if management wants to increase the influence of a particular individual, one way to achieve its aim is to give him the prestige of a high salary. Similarly, a supervisor usually should get paid more than his highest-paid subordinate.

Raising a person's salary is not the only way to build his influence, but we should not overlook the impact of salary on an individual's ability to operate within an organization.

Tying Raises to Company Objectives

How a company grants merit increases has a direct influence on behavior in the organization. To an individual himself, an increase is a sign of his personal progress; he will try to continue behaving the way he thinks led to his raise. His colleagues are likewise alert. They know who gets raises more often, and who gets none at all, and they take their cues accordingly. At the same time, workers typically have strong opinions of what they feel is "fair"—that is, who deserves a raise.

Consequently, management should be careful to grant increases to those who are, in fact, improving their effectiveness and should try to get everyone to agree that the policy on giving raises is reasonable and fair. In this matter, as with most others, management's actions speak far louder than its words. Playing favorites or being soft and giving everybody a small increase just to avoid arguments will undermine appeals to do a better job. On the other hand, if management consistently matches merit increases with known contributions toward company objectives, it reinforces the whole structure of formal plans and organization.

Incentive Pay and Organization

If merit increases should go to people who perform their assignments well, how about extending the idea to "incentive pay," which varies directly and immediately with performance? Commissions for salespeople and piece rates for factory workers are common examples of incentive pay; at the managerial level, we find executive bonuses based on profits, on actual results compared with budgets, or on other quantified measures of results. Occasionally, when a whole group of people must cooperate to achieve results, a firm will offer a group bonus.

Desire for security has become so intense that today few employees on any level—president, sales supervisor, or machine operator—subsist entirely on incentive pay. Instead companies assure a degree of security either by guaranteeing minimum earnings regardless of results or by paying a base salary and adding incentive pay as a bonus. Even though incentive pay may be a small percentage of total compensation, it focuses attention on the particular achievements that management uses in determining the amount of a bonus.

Incentive pay introduces several requirements in organization design. We must sharply define the mission—the end result—of a job eligible for a bonus, and the results must be measurable. Many jobs, such as that of chief accountant or personnel director, cannot be defined in this manner. Even the work of a sales representative is not simple to describe. His primary task may be to obtain orders, but in addition he is expected to cultivate new customers, obtain information on new products, deal with complaints, and keep his own expenses low. If his bonus is based solely on new orders, he is likely to slight his other duties.

For an organization, this means one of two things. Either 1) authority should be highly decentralized—for instance, we might authorize the manager of a division to change prices, hire people, and take other action that is necessary to achieve profits, on which his bonus is based—or 2) management should standardize and control the work conditions that affect output—for a production worker who is paid a piece rate, this means that material should be readily available, machinery in good operating condition, helpers adequately trained, power and light dependable, and so forth. In both instances, the location and adequacy of staff and service work are important to the person who receives incentive pay. Again, we see that an organization pattern and a salary system are closely interrelated. If we use incentive pay, we get into questions of delegating authority, providing service and staff, and defining duties so that they conform to the bases for bonuses.

CONCLUSION

In this chapter, we have focused our attention on the personal needs of managers and operators—especially on their physical, security, social, and self-expression needs, because these can be met to a significant extent through working in an enterprise. A manager should not only identify the specific needs of the people he directs, but also be sensitive to the relative potency of these various desires. Such an understanding of his people provides a manager with a foundation for deciding how best to incorporate a high degree of motivation into his actions.

Working at a job satisfies a person's needs in two ways: indirectly through off-the-job satisfactions and directly through on-the-job satisfactions. Because many off-the-job satisfactions come from the pay a person receives for his work, a manager should try to relate pay to organization design and company aims. By tying the amount of pay to the importance and influence we wish to give various jobs, we increase the chances that the organization will actually work as we want.

A manager should also be alert to the connection between on-the-job satisfactions and organization. Often he can adjust his organization to increase the direct satisfactions of his subordinates. We discussed a variety of such possibilities, and others will occur to a manager who thinks of both work and workers as he organizes. His objective should be to design a structure in which on-the-job satisfactions are enhanced at the same time company aims are furthered.

Satisfying needs through *organization* is, of course, only one approach a manager may follow. As we shall see later, planning and activating can also contribute to, or detract from, the fulfillment of needs. We have emphasized organization in this chapter simply because we are most concerned, here in Part Two, with the impact of human factors on the process of organizing.

1) If we continue to experience relative abundance, more people will satisfy their lower-order needs earlier, and self-expression needs will take on greater potency. Because the greatest opportunity to realize self-expression needs within a large corporation has typically existed at the top management level, what problems do you see ahead? How would you deal with these problems?

2) It has been suggested that a "good" manager not only seeks to *forecast* accurately the potency of his subordinates' needs and then appeal to them, but also actively seeks to *shape* and *intensify* the potency of those needs that he can most readily satisfy. Do you feel this is practical? Is it moral?

3) "Our company works very hard to provide people with the opportuntiy to achieve status in the eyes of their fellow employees. One of the keys to making this possible is our concerted effort to eliminate status symbols." How do you interpret this statement made by the president of a successful firm?

4) What do you consider the most significant changes in America over the last two or three decades that are likely to influence the attitudes of people toward work as a means of satisfying their potent needs? Consider your answer to the first part of this question in terms of the age of the people you have in mind. Would the changes you consider significant have as much, more, or different kinds of influence on people under 25 than they would on those over 30?

5) "We cannot hope to know what the specific needs of any group of employees are, and even if we could, the knowledge wouldn't lead to any policy changes on our part. Rather than seek to adapt our operations to individual needs, we make clear what each job offers so as to attract people whose needs will be satisfied by our work." Discuss this comment by a personnel director.

6) "I have no use for all this job-enrichment stuff that is supposed to fulfill me. I get all the fulfillment I need as a mother, wife, member of a school board, and as a Sunday School teacher. I work because I'm bored between 7:30 A.M. and 3:30 P.M. and we can use the extra money. I wish these unfulfilled psychologists who keep running around the plant would leave me and my job alone." Consider this statement from a 40-year-old woman.

7) In what ways may incentive pay or rewards for employee suggestions have a negative effect on day-to-day productivity because of the implications such systems may have on human needs? Do you feel the benefits are likely to outweigh these negative effects?

8) How may some of the new approaches to structural design discussed in Chapter 6 affect the potential for meeting personal needs?

Cases

For cases involving issues covered in this chapter, see especially the following. Particularly relevant questions are listed after each case.

The Delaware Corporation (p. 113), 5, 7
Merchantville School System (p. 217), 5
Marten Fabricators (p. 316), 3

Graham, Smith, & Bendel, Inc. (p. 445), 4, 5
Central Telephone and Electronics (p. 527), 3
Household Products Company (p. 627), 3

FOR FURTHER READING

Cooper, R., *Job Motivation and Job Design.* London: Institute of Personnel Management, 1974.

Well-balanced, condensed analysis of current knowledge about designing jobs to improve worker motivation.

Davis, K., ed., *Organization Behavior: A Book of Readings,* 4th ed. New York: McGraw-Hill Book Company, 1974, Chapter 5.

Includes excellent article on job enrichment experience of A.T.&T.

Hackman, J. R., G. Oldham, R. Janson, and K. Purdy, "A New Strategy for Job Enrichment." *California Management Review,* Summer 1975.

A series of practical suggestions dealing with when and how to introduce meaningful job enrichment.

Porter, L. W., E. E. Lawler, and J. R. Hackman, *Behavior in Organizations.* New York: McGraw-Hill Book Company, 1975, Chapters 8–10.

Draws together a wide array of behavioral studies relating individual behavior to the characteristics of the work being done and especially to the job design.

Strauss, G., "Job Satisfaction, Motivation and Job Redesign," in *Organizational Behavior: Research and Issues.* Madison, Wis.: Industrial Relations Research Association, 1974.

Clear review of concepts and research findings on worker satisfaction, motivation, and the effect of redesign of jobs.

Suojanen, W. W., et al., eds., *Perspectives on Job Enrichment and Productivity.* Atlanta: School of Business, Georgia State University, 1975.

Convenient source for an array of articles on the use of job enrichment in diverse organizations.

Group Behavior

and Organization Design

8

The formal organization that describes duties and specifies relationships provides only one set of external pressures to which people respond. An organization structure that carries "official" approval is a strong influence, but there are many other pressures, and a wise manager will try to design his organization so that these other influences support, rather than detract from, desired results.

One important set of influences arises from a simple and obvious characteristic of human behavior. People live and work together. Their relationships soon result in patterns of behavior and belief, which social scientists call "cultures." Within the broader national culture, every enterprise develops its own "subculture"—that is, the beliefs and patterns of conduct that are asscciated with living and working together in that company. Two aspects of a business subculture of particular concern to a manager are the following:

1) The *customs,* habits, and ways of working together that develop informally in an expanding enterprise. These customs, which grow up around normal company activities, elaborate and extend, or perhaps modify, formal organization.
2) The informal *social groups* among employees that strongly influence their attitudes, beliefs, and behavior. These informal groups often (though not necessarily) center on personal interests and noncompany objectives.

Research on human relations in established organizations clearly demonstrates that informal social relationships have a direct bearing on effectiveness and efficiency. Formal organization is essential, but we would be foolish to *prescribe* many of the spontaneous relationships that are sure to arise. Prescribed or not, these social patterns influence how people respond to managerial action.

Striking examples of the effect of cultural attitudes and customs arise in international business. American executives have often tried to transplant to a foreign country a formal organization that worked well in the United States. They have attempted, for example, to export the concept of a budget director whose duties are the same as those of the American model, but the results have often been confusion or sabotage—and an added bit of resentment of Yankee enterprise. Unfamiliarity with the concept of staff guidance, reluctance to mix people from different social strata in informal work groups, reverence for red tape, skepticism of numerical evaluation schemes, and similar reactions have prevented superbly designed organizations from operating as they were intended.

Although social traditions and informal relationships can be annoying to an executive, they are essential for getting a day's work accomplished smoothly. Like fire, the force is destructive when improperly handled; but once a man understands how to work with a force, he can employ it for constructive purposes. A manager cannot manipulate social behavior in any way he pleases, but he can attempt to design work structures in such a way that social pressures and formal organization tend to support each other.

In the present chapter, then, we shall seek answers to the following questions: How do customs and traditional roles develop in a business enterprise? Can formal organization and informal customs be made more compatible? How do informal social groups affect the behavior of workers? What can we do to encourage such group pressure to support company objectives?

CUSTOMS AND ROLES

How Customs Develop

Only a small fraction of our behavior is deliberately chosen. During any day, we take part in many activities, and it would be impossible to analyze each separate movement or remark before we act. Acting nonrationally is not irrational; it is essential. Because purely intuitive or emotional responses are likely to get us into trouble and deliberate choices are not feasible, we rely heavily on custom and habit to direct our behavior.

Reliance on customary behavior applies to our business activities, as well as to our private lives. When a person buys a car, the dealer has a customary way of recording the sale, arranging for financing, and preparing the car for delivery. Similarly, when a company hires a new employee, it follows customary practices in arranging a medical examination, entering the person's name on the payroll, and introducing him to his new assignment and to his fellow workers. Often a situation will have unique features that call for thought—for instance, the new employee may have a physical handicap—but it is possible to give attention to these unique features because in handling the situation so much can be based on customary ways of doing business.

Once established, a customary way of doing business looks "natural." But many urban-renewal projects, for example, have floundered and sometimes failed because social mechanisms for doing unusual tasks were lacking. Often a deep-seated suspicion of procedures used in the white man's establishment has contributed to the problem. It takes time to learn how to work together.

Customs become established, or "learned," principally through personal experience. Some guidance may be provided by company planning—an organization structure assigns duties to various positions, and a company manual formally states policies and procedures. Nevertheless, only when people actually work can a custom become established. Moreover, formal plans almost never cover all aspects of a job. Any employee—be he president or janitor—acts on a problem in a way he hopes will be satisfactory. If the results are poor, he will probably try some other solution the next time he meets a similar problem. Once he finds an acceptable solution, he will probably repeat it each time a similar problem arises. As the same solution is applied over and over again, customary behavior begins to emerge.

Our emphasis on behavior based on experience should be a warning to anyone who thinks of managing purely through formal organization and written plans. Before formal instructions become customary behavior, they have to be accepted in actual use. What an employee considers "acceptable" is determined by a variety of factors, such as favorable reaction of other employees, approval by his immediate supervisor, contribution to company goals, and personal satisfaction from doing the work.

If an immediate supervisor does not insist that workers follow official plans, then other considerations are likely to determine the particular work pattern that becomes customary. For example, if employees can disregard a "no smoking" rule without serious consequences, they are likely to adopt smoking on the job as customary conduct. Similarly, if a branch manager finds that he can hire new employees without following his instructions to consult with the personnel director at headquarters, the formal plan for hiring loses its significance. On the other hand, if a branch manager consistently consults with his vice-president in charge of sales before changing sales territories even though formal organization does not require it, the practice becomes embedded in the company structure as customary behavior. Formal plans can have their full impact only when they become an integral part of custom.

Work customs are especially important when several different people work together. Each person learns to rely on the others to perform their parts of the total task in a customary manner. A hospital dietician, for instance, may assume that her order clerk will place rush orders on the top of each batch of meal requests she sends to the kitchen; if the clerk overlooks this little custom, a rush order may not get the attention it deserves. To cite an illustration from a Midwestern hardware firm, the production manager normally consulted with the sales manager before authorizing unusually long runs of a product. Once, when the sales manager was away on a trip, the production manager had to decide whether to schedule a long run of chain hoists, so he overlooked the usual cross-check. Actually, it turned out that the sales manager planned to curtail his selling efforts on this model, and only by accident was the prospect of an unusually slow-moving inventory discovered two weeks later and the order cancelled before actual production commenced. These examples show how one person may depend on the customary behavior of another—much as players on a good doubles team in tennis depend on each other to cover different parts of the court.

When each person learns what to expect of others with whom his work interlocks, coordinated effort is greatly simplified. And conversely, deviations from usual behavior call for special warnings to other people if we are to avoid confusion that might damage efficiency.

Expected Roles

As we have seen, some customs spring from the habitual actions of particular people. But, in addition, jobs often acquire traditional roles. People have preconceived ideas of how a person appointed as, say, credit manager, supervisor, or baseball umpire, should behave. In other words, each established role strongly influences the behavior that is expected of anyone in a given position. Established roles are common throughout society. We expect ministers to epitomize virtue, ship captains to be stern disciplinarians, and football coaches to be hard-driving authoritarians whose consuming interest in life is winning

Figure 8–1   When a person assumes a given role, his duties and authority and sometimes even his gestures and clothing are well defined.

games. In each case, the person who fills the established role is expected to act in a preconceived way.

In business, and especially within a single enterprise, the role for any given position may be firmly established. For instance, what a cost accountant should—and should not—undertake and what his attitude toward traditional accounting should be may be clearly defined in the minds of all people who work with him. The existence of such definite roles gives a stability to relationships in business; at least we predict from them how a person will fill a given position.

We run into difficulty, however, when complete agreement is lacking on all features of a role. Top executives may be inclined to think of a job in terms of a formal organization plan that is embellished with details contributing to company objectives. An incumbent himself may have a somewhat different point of view based on his own preferences and experiences. His subordinates may attach importance to still other features of the job, and his associates may be concerned with how his position interrelates with their work. Such lack of "role congruence" causes incompatible expectations about how a key person will behave and complaints about weak performance.

One of the best-known examples of such variation in conception of a role is the job of foreman. Top management thinks of a foreman as dedicated to getting quality production on schedule at low cost. His subordinates, on the other hand, expect him to be friendly, fair, and helpful, to represent them in dealings with higher management, and to be sympathetic to actual work difficulties. If a foreman himself tries to live up to both sets of expectations, he gets "caught in the middle." If he accepts either the labor view or the managerial view, he will be subjected to pressure from the other group.

Ideally, the job description that stems from formal organization *and* the other sets of expectations should merge into a single, consistent concept of a job. But, as we shall see further in Chapter 10, we can accomplish this only if 1) the job description is realistic in terms of both the technological and human resources available; 2) there is full communication and agreement by everyone concerned on what a person in the job is expected to do; and 3) the person actually on the job performs as anticipated. It is when these three conditions are fulfilled that a formal organization becomes a vital reality.

An additional reason why managers need to pay attention to socially accepted roles is summed up in the sociologists' concept of "legitimacy." Every complex organization is laced with a maze of contacts between different positions—requests for information, suggestions and countersuggestions, and inspection of results. Employees regard some of these contacts as entirely legitimate and deeply resent others. Their response to a suggestion or to a request is determined largely by whether it is an accepted, legitimate part of a role. If everyone expects a person occupying a particular position to become involved in the work of other people, then everyone thinks his action is legitimate. On the other hand, if he steps outside the bounds of customary behavior, he is thought to be "poking his nose into other people's affairs," and the result is sure to be friction.

Impact of Reorganization
on Customs and Roles

In Part One we described situations in which a change in organization is desirable. What does the preceding analysis of customs and roles suggest about the process of such reorganizations?

Probably most important, a manager must recognize that he cannot bring about change in customs and roles by decree alone. Social customs become the normal way of acting—even, perhaps, deep-seated habits. A person's role is a set of ideas based on experience and personal desires, often reinforced by similar sentiments of his associates.

Reorganization upsets these established customs. It redefines roles. The predictable behavior patterns, the reliable flow of information, the familiar responses of other people, the known sources of power, the confidence that arises from past successes are now all surrounded with uncertainty. Actually, many of the old ways will be carried forward. But during the transition the stability of an established social system is shaken.

To minimize worry, but at the same time to expedite intended changes within the reorganization, a wise manager should:

1) Fully understand the prevailing customs and the existing role concepts before introducing a change. Here the distinction between the formal organization and the more complex actual behavior and relationships is important. Only with such an understanding can the manager anticipate the full impact of the organization changes he is contemplating.

2) Indicate early to those affected the purposes of the reorganization, and also what is not intended. This provides a basis upon which a revised set of social relationships can be built.

3) Arrange for discussions of the change, probing its implications and examining alternative routes to the same ends. The purpose of this exchange is both to develop a common understanding of necessary shifts in roles and customs and to remove the strangeness (and hence resistance) to the new setup.

4) Relieve participants' normal anxieties about their future status and usefulness. Typically the implications of a change are not fully worked out; but insofar as the carryover from the past and the new roles are known, these can be stated, and the process and time for resolving unsettled structure can be indicated.

5) Provide opportunities to practice and demonstrate new behavior with real, current problems. As already indicated, organization design takes on meaning when the participants actually experience the new way problems will be handled.

6) Reward those who adopt desired new behavior in place of the old. Emphasize the positive benefits of change, and try to diminish the attention to "the good old days."

7) Recognize that this shift in customs and roles will take time. It is a learning experience, and like first driving a car, each person has to develop a familiarity with his new situation and skill in using his new resources.

These steps will help join together our formal organization design with the actual social behavior that produces results. A similar conversion of plans into behavior is necessary to bring policies and procedures to life, as we shall see in Part Four; and the melding of our total management design into group action is further examined in the final Part on Activating.

Where customs and roles are strongly supported by group pressures, a manager may have to supplement, or even precede, the *individual* learning process (outlined briefly in the preceding paragraph) by modifying *group* attitudes.

INFORMAL GROUPS

Social Groups within Organizations

Small social groups significantly affect the way a formal organization actually works. Informal groups of from three to perhaps a dozen members spring up naturally whenever people work together. They are common among college students and in large government offices as well as in business firms. Members of such groups see each other frequently on the job, at lunch, or riding home from work. They discover common interests and exchange ideas. A group thus forms spontaneously. If one or two members tend to be leaders, their position arises naturally out of the situation rather than from formal selection.

Most people get many of their day-to-day satisfactions from such groups. Among the "rewards" for belonging to such a group are sociability, a sense of belonging (which contributes to feelings of inner security and personal worth), a sympathetic ear for troubles, aid on the job (both information and occasional direct assistance), and some protection through a united stand against pressure from a boss or outside force. In time, these satisfactions can develop considerable group cohesiveness.

Small-group rewards are especially prized by people who work in large organizations, where, too often, the work itself provides few satisfactions. If we have fragmented the work and failed to make remote objectives significant, then the social satisfactions derived from subgroups become a major force in behavior on the job.

A small informal group—whether composed of lathe operators, members of a vice-president's staff, or senior executives in an electrical-engineering department—falls into routines for its activities. Members sit together in the lunchroom; Mary stops to chat with Steve before going home in the evening. When the members work near to one another, interchange may take place from time to time throughout the day. Sometimes a pattern of contact is extended to include off-the-job activities, such as bowling, golf, bridge, or union meetings. In addition, a group tends to evolve a pattern of attitudes, at least toward subjects of common interest. Members frequently discuss their feelings toward their boss, company, rates of output, "young squirts from college," or the accounting office; often, they all hold similar views on such subjects.

Each person normally belongs to several small informal groups. One may be founded on physical proximity at work, another on a common interest in baseball, and a third on an interest in a professional society—for example, the Society for Advancement of Management. A political-protest group draws together quite a diverse collection of people. Some of these groups may be fairly inactive, and people may drift in and out of them. But those based on daily work relationships are likely to be the strongest and most enduring.

Effect of Social Groups on Worker Behavior

It is typical of social groups to put pressure on members *to conform to group standards and routines.* This push to conformity is, of course, common throughout life. A school child gets teased by his classmates if his clothing is too fancy. Young couples who move to suburbia match their neighbors by selling the motorcycle and buying a sportscar. Even the nonconformist in college expresses his defiance in ways endorsed by his fellow nonconformists— for instance, new polished shoes must *not* be worn even if the owner has to go to a lot of trouble to get them dirty and scuffed-up. Of course, the particular matters on which to conform vary from group to group and from time to time.

Restricting output to an accepted group standard is a common practice among production operators. If a group has established a normal output per day, perhaps based on the maximum "the company will let you earn," management will find incentive bonuses of little avail in stimulating higher production. The person who steps beyond the accepted norm will be subjected to severe social censure. On the other hand, if a group endorses high output—which is likely to be true among salesmen—the low performer may find himself an outcast.

The pressure of a group on its members can be substantial, for (as we noted earlier) an individual gets many of his satisfactions in his job through group responses. If he deviates too far from group standards, other members may no longer want to associate with him and may treat him as though he were

Figure 8–2   A group may pressure deviants to conform to its standards in ways that are mild or severe. A school child may merely be teased because of his nonconformist clothing, whereas a high performer who upsets group production rates may find that his tires have been slashed in the company parking lot.

at least an oddball, if not a traitor. Such treatment is unpleasant even for those people who can move into other social groups. Moreover, a person feels immediately the rewards or punishments of his group, whereas benefits provided by a company for following its plan are usually more remote.

Managers should realize that, in addition to such standards of conduct, groups also *provide many beliefs and values* to the individual. Joe or Kathy may believe that the personnel director is a "good guy" and that the advertising director is a "screwball"—not from any personal observation or conviction, but merely because these are the sentiments passed on to them by their group. They may believe that all senior executives draw fabulous salaries, that only a Stanford graduate can get ahead in the firm, that their company has the best engineering department in the industry, and many other articles of faith, because they are strongly held by their social group. A group can also influence feelings about such matters as pilfering, accuracy in keeping reports, importance of efficient control of quality, or service to customers.

Even when an individual has direct evidence contrary to group sentiment, he may accept group judgment. In a series of experiments with groups of college students, all persons except one in each group were instructed to give incorrect answers to a simple question about which of several lines was longest. As different sets of lines were flashed on a screen, the exception in each group found his judgment consistently at odds with that of half a dozen other people in the same room; eventually, he began to distrust his own perception and started giving the group answer. At work, when facts are less clearcut, and group pressure is even greater, the temptation to accept group opinion is strong. Fortunately there continues to be a good sprinkling of rugged individualists who maintain their independence of judgment. Even these people, however, are likely simply to remain silent rather than challenge some cherished bit of lore.

Behavioral research has found one further characteristic of group behavior that is of direct interest to management. A group will probably *resist* any *change* that upsets its normal activities, especially if the change is initiated by an outsider. A new method, a change in office layout, or a reassignment of duties modifies established patterns of social relationships. Social groups may be broken up, and this disruption means loss of known satisfactions in exchange for an unknown future. Consciously or unconsciously, people resist such changes, even when offsetting advantages may benefit individual members of a group, and new groups may replace old ones. Managers should thus anticipate resistance when they upset social patterns.

HARMONIZING SOCIAL GROUPS AND FORMAL ORGANIZATION

The behavior of small groups has an impact on many facets of management, as we shall note especially in later discussions on activating, acceptance, and commitment. In the present chapter, we are particularly interested in the impact on formal organization structure. What can we do to harmonize social groups and formal organization?

Consider Adopting Group Practice

Many times people in a company think up new ways of doing things that are not only more satisfying to their group, but also better for company efficiency. For example, job descriptions in a plumbing-equipment company indicated that the sales department was simply to refer all complaints about product design to the engineering manager, so that he or his representative could talk with customers about their specific difficulties. The sales manager, however, had trouble getting minor changes made that he felt were necessary for overcoming the complaints of big customers. So the sales manager developed a habit of obtaining from these customers full information on what they wanted. Then after an engineer had been assigned to investigate the complaint, the sales manager talked at length with the engineer about what changes could be made. Actually, the engineers found that their job was simplified, and in time they began to rely heavily on the sales manager for customer data. Sometimes salespeople would provide information directly to the engineers, and on troublesome cases a meeting of salespeople, sales manager, engineer, and engineering manager would be held.

As new complaints arose, members of the sales department frequently contacted the engineers and pushed hard for changes they wanted made. At this stage, the vice-president in charge of research and engineering protested to the president. He said the salespeople were taking up too much of the engineers' time, interrupting the engineering work schedule, and "high-pressuring" his people to make too many changes. "They are violating the organization structure," he said, "and ought to be stopped."

After thorough investigation, the president decided that the company's product development was being significantly improved by the role the sales people had assumed in modifying products. So the president had the job descriptions rewritten to provide a new duty for the sales manager—that of visiting customers who complained of product design and then holding conferences with the engineering manager. The president worked closely with both executives to be sure the new statement of duties was feasible and acceptable. *Now*, even the vice-president in charge of research and engineering says that the new organization is best for the company.

Such cases indicate that our first step in dealing with informal group actions that do not "fit" the formal structure should be at least to entertain the hypothesis that the group standards and behavior are beneficial. We need not accept the group behavior, of course. After investigation, we may decide that the informal action must be changed to meet company requirements. But we should always be alert to the possibility that behavior that develops informally serves the company well and should be incorporated into the formal structure.

Figure 8–3 In an integrated task team, each member has an assigned role, but it is the immediate task itself that calls for action and voluntary coordination of effort.

Form Integrated Task Teams

A second possibility of harmonizing small-group practice with formal organization lies in the design itself. Formal organization—that is, how workers are grouped together and what the specified relationships are—provides the setting for many informal groups. Can we design a formal organization structure so as to encourage social groups that are inclined to support, rather than conflict with, the aims of an enterprise?

Organization studies in several countries—in textile mills, loading docks, sales offices, and coal mines—strongly support the formation of integrated task teams.

Three guides for organization design help foster such informal groups sympathetic to company goals:

1) Combine related tasks into clusters—or blocks—so that each cluster produces a "meaningful" end-product. First, we should identify blocks of work that have a natural unity, whose end result we can clearly visualize. Such a block may be all activities that pertain to securing a customer's order, or to making a particular product or part. Second, we should place authority for doing such a specific, complete block of work squarely on a small group of people. These people will constitute a team, and it is up to them to complete the effort. One person may be captain, but the assignment belongs to the entire *task team.*

   This proposal is in sharp contrast with the practice, encouraged by scientific management, of dividing work into highly specialized pieces and, when volume permits, of creating a specialized department to perform each narrow task. Under this latter system, detailed, centralized planning is encouraged, and supervisors are primarily concerned with seeing that operators do not deviate from the program. Such a work structure promotes informal groups that are uninterested in company goals.

   In contrast, by assigning meaningful jobs to a task team, we hope that a social group will form that is interested in achieving end-results. In fact, there is considerable evidence to indicate that indifference to company goals and restrictions on output will be less under the task-team organization than under a highly functionalized organization.

   These behavioral-science conclusions relate directly to the forming of work groups (see Chapter 2).

2) Place people with all skills necessary to complete the assigned task as close as possible to the point of action. The best arrangement is to have people with the necessary skills within the task team itself. Thus a self-contained sales team might include a sales representative, a service engineer, a delivery person and

a clerk–secretary in the office. Each person would understand how the total unit functions and could easily make direct personal contact with any other member of the unit.

Unfortunately, such an integrated unit is uneconomical for many tasks. The need in a single task team for a particular skill may be insufficient in volume or may occur at such irregular intervals that the inclusion of a qualified full-time worker on the team is unwarranted. An alternative arrangement, then, is to assign a staff or service person to work with *several* operating units and to locate him in close proximity to all units. By locating him where he can have frequent face-to-face contacts with people on the various task teams, we encourage his becoming a member—albeit a part-time one—of their respective social groups.[1]

Still another arrangement is to form a task-team for a specific project. We note here that the behavioral concept of a task-team reinforces the idea of project management explained in connection with matrix organization in Chapter 6.

In each of these arrangements, individuals with specialized skills are placed close to the scene of action, where they can form informal groups associated with the end-result rather than with their specialties.

3) Supply each task team with full facts on its work. An operating unit, such as we have been describing, should be self-regulating. Of course, being close to its work, a team will readily and immediately have available much control information. For example, if one part of the work falls behind—or gets ahead of—related activities, all members of the team will know it promptly and can adjust their efforts accordingly; or if a customer changes the specifications on his order, the whole team can quickly readjust to the new requirements. In other words, each member of the team, because he has personal contact with what is happening, knows whether all phases of the operation are proceeding as planned. Armed with such information, the team itself regulates its efforts to achieve desired results.

If control information, not obvious to the team members, becomes available elsewhere, this too should be fed back quickly to the operating unit. Data on laboratory tests or costs of materials, for instance, may first be recorded at a point remote from actual operations; this information needs to be communicated immediately to the persons who can take corrective action. Because the task group promptly receives data on its efficiency and progress and has full delegation to make changes, it may become so engrossed with results that it will avoid sparring matches with supervisors. Furthermore, the abundance of available statistical data will allow the group to base its work-related beliefs on fact rather than fiction.

The preceding guides for organizing around task teams come to us from research on small groups that usually do operating work. Practical application of these guides has been worked out for such tasks as running an open-hearth steel furnace, assembling typewriters, and handling customer orders in an office. Use of the basic ideas, however, need not be confined to operating work. We can also create task teams to do managerial work. The best-known examples in

---

[1] The effect of proximity on the ease of joining social groups has long been recognized in the auditing field. But in this instance, to ensure independence of an audit, management wishes to *prevent* close friendships, so it deliberately moves auditors from place to place before loyalties to a social group can become strong.

this field are from companies using profit decentralization. Here, as with task teams doing operating work, tasks are assigned in blocks that have a natural unity; people with the needed skills are placed within the group; and the team is self-regulating to a high degree. Very little research has been done on social-group behavior among executives, yet here lies great opportunity to discover new ways of applying insights on group action to managerial work. The applicability of the task-team concept to both managerial and operating work illustrates the feasibility of adjusting organization design so as to capture benefits from typical group behavior.

CONCLUSION

When we look at an organization as a social unit rather than as a work-producing machine, three important conclusions emerge:

1) First, the social relationships in an organization are not based on crisp decisions that remain static once they are made, but on a series of continuing personal actions and reactions over a long period. Defining relationships in an organization manual may be useful, but even sharp definitions take on their full meaning only as people learn to work together.

   In a business firm, as in a city government or a local P.T.A., we learn a great deal from organization charts, definition of duties, and other formal statements of how the enterprise is expected to work. Nevertheless, to get a full feel of an organization, we also need to know which members have the most influence on accepted beliefs, what the prevailing attitude is toward the role of the various officers and executives, what small groups exist and what their influence is, and whether strong cliques are at work.

   Moreover, social relationships evolve. For instance, circumstances and individual maturity will modify the influence an accountant has over clerks in his section. Likewise, the composition of social groups shifts with time and with changes in personnel. With these shifting social relationships, formal job descriptions tend to become obsolete.

2) Second, we should view the behavior of people in organizations objectively. When a motor will not run or a fuse blows out, we try to find the cause, correct it, and then proceed with our business. But when we deal with human behavior, our response is much more emotional. If Bob fails to do what the organization manual specifies, we get angry. Having designed a superb organization plan, we think *everyone* should behave accordingly.

   In this chapter we have suggested several reasons why people in social groups behave as they do, and research in the behavioral sciences will undoubtedly give us many more useful insights. Instead of simply getting angry when an operation falls behind schedule, a mature manager will try to find out what really happened and why.

3) Finally, if he understands the social forces at work, a manager can be more skillful in designing his formal organization and in his planning, controlling, and activating. Nothing we have said in this chapter diminishes the need for an organization structure to get work done effectively. Our emphasis on social

behavior simply indicates that organizing is a more delicate task than it appears when our attention is focused only on the work to be done.

When he includes social dimensions in the total picture, a manager may modify his organization design. Perhaps task teams or some other arrangement that recognizes social behavior in his group will be introduced; or while thinking about changes in assigned duties, he may give attention to the tugs and pulls in learning new social relationships.

FOR CLASS DISCUSSION

1) One of the real dangers of clarifying expected roles is that it can easily lead to stereotyping. What is the difference between clearly defined roles and stereotyping, and why is the latter regarded as a "danger"?

2) How does management identify the presence of social groups or cliques, and how does it determine their customs, goals, and values? How would your answer change with the organization level of the social group or clique?

3) Identify one of your habits. Think of a habitual response that is a relatively *unimportant* aspect of your behavior. Perhaps it is a speech habit or a tendency to walk from one place to another along a prescribed route. Do *not* select a habit that affects you in a *major* way, such as smoking. Having identified such a habit, try to break it. If possible, ask a friend to help by calling it to your attention. How do you feel when this unimportant habit is challenged? How do you explain this feeling?

4) Discuss the relationships between matrix management concepts, discussed in Chapter 6, and the need for clarifying expected roles.

5) "Virtually any social group or clique that forms and functions during working hours is a potential threat to satisfying a company's goals. They quite often reinforce individual tendencies, at best, to loaf and, at worst, to sabotage work efforts." How would you respond to this comment?

6) How does the concept of the "task-team" fit or conflict with the "three inescapable features of delegation" considered in Chapter 3? Relate the concept of "task-team" assignment of work to the concepts of decentralization discussed in Chapter 4.

7) What benefits and drawbacks do you see in using small-group rewards as substitutes for the rewards provided by the work itself?

8) "Whenever I contemplate an important organization change, I think it through very carefully but I do *not* discuss it with those involved. I wait until I have thought through all of the conditions needed to make the change, and I prepare for them. Then I make the change as quickly and as directly as possible. I expect, initially, some shock, resistance, and maybe even losing someone, but this is much better than the anxiety and confusion created by slow, participative attempts at organizational change." Discuss this comment by a chief executive officer of a large bank. Consider it in terms of suggestions under "Impact of Reorganization on Customs and Roles."

For cases involving issues covered in this chapter, see especially the following. Particularly relevant questions are listed after each case.

Milano Enterprises (p. 124), 6
Petersen Electronics (p. 211), 5, 6
Merchantville School System (p. 217), 6, 9
Monroe Wire and Cable (p. 436), 3
Central Telephone and Electronics (p. 527), 4
Southeast Textiles (p. 620), 3, 4
Household Products Company (p. 627), 4, 5, 6

FOR FURTHER READING

Davis, K., *Human Behavior at Work,* 4th ed. New York: McGraw-Hill Book Company, 1972, Chapter 14.

Explains informal organization, including grapevine.

Dubin, R., *Human Relations in Administration,* 4th ed. Englewood Cliffs, N.J.: Prentice-Hall, Inc., 1974, Chapter 6.

Concise examination of the interplay between informal groups and formal organization.

French, W. L. and C. H. Bell, *Organization Development.* Englewood Cliffs, N.J.: Prentice-Hall, Inc., 1973.

Excellent summary of the history, concepts, and techniques of "O.D."

Leighton, A. H., *The Governing of Men.* Princeton, N.J.: Princeton University Press, 1945.

Classic study of an American relocation camp for Japanese; shows crucial need for customs and roles.

Porter, L. W., E. E. Lawler, and J. R. Hackman, *Behavior in Organizations.* New York: McGraw-Hill Book Company, 1975, Chapter 13.

Discussion of the ways that social influences within a group of workers affect their behavior on the job.

Smith, P. B., *Groups Within Organizations: Applications of Social Psychology to Organizational Behavior.* New York: Harper & Row Publishers, Inc., 1973.

Tight, clear discussion of some aspects of small-group behavior and T-Group training, by a British social psychologist.

9 Intergroup Conflict: Sources and Resolution

INEVITABILITY OF CONFLICT

Conflict, in the sense of a clash of interests or incompatible desires, is all around us. We do not want our rustic countryside to be spoiled by civilization, and yet growing population forces us to build suburban homes connected by webs of power and telephone lines. We want full employment and at the same time no inflation. We want neighborhood schools and also integrated schools. We want freedom to drive as we please and no petroleum imports. The list goes on and on.

Similarly, within an organization some people will want assurance of jobs and stability, others the excitement of growth and modernization, and still others more pay for a selected few (including themselves). Life is not a grand harmony. Conflict exists. We have to learn how to live with it, how to use it constructively, and how to minimize its destructive aspects.

In this chapter we shall focus on *intraorganizational* conflict. For instance, when Jones's successful pursuit of his purposes would prevent Smith from carrying out his plans, management faces a conflict situation. Because both people cannot fully succeed, a lot of jockeying and infighting may arise. In fact, more effort may be devoted to internal competition than to end results. Such intraorganizational conflict often grows out of divergent goals; however, it is through clash over action—or over proposed action—rather than through a difference in motives that conflict becomes apparent.

Psychologists for some time have studied conflict *within* a person—his incompatible desires, the resulting frustration, and responses to such frustration.

However, here we are concerned with conflict *between* persons. Of course we should be aware of the possibility that an individual may have divergent motives—for instance, a worker's personal goals may not match up with those he is presumed to have for the role (job) he accepts. This particular type of conflict relates to matching jobs and people, the topic of Chapter 10.

Intraorganizational conflict poses four broad questions that are particularly significant to a manager:

1) What are the *sources* of such conflict in organizations?
2) How can we distinguish between *constructive* and *destructive* conflict?
3) How can we *organize* to increase the chances that conflict will be constructive?
4) How can we conduct our *interpersonal relations* to reconcile conflict that cannot be relieved by organization means? (This issue is considered further in Part Six.)

SOURCES OF CONFLICT

To deal constructively with conflict in his organization, a manager must be sensitive to where the conflict is likely to arise. Let us look at five typical sources.

Competition for Scarce Resources

Committed people want the resources with which to achieve their goals. The researcher looking for new products, the regional manager providing service to New England customers, and the guard charged with protecting the plant—all want equipment, personnel, supplies, and other resources. The total of such requests from all parts of the enterprise usually far exceeds the quantity of resources obtainable, and the resulting scramble is the cause of a lot of action and reaction throughout the organization.

Capital budgeting—the allocation of funds for long-run investment—often becomes a focal point for this kind of conflict. We have sophisticated techniques for making quantitative comparisons of budget requests, but these do not remove the underlying conflict. Too often the kind of rituals that characterize collective bargaining with labor unions are also present: exaggerated requests, one-sided evidence, bluffing, catering to the personal status of the bargainers, preoccupation with precedent, drawn-out negotiations. If we are not careful, this process can degenerate until both motives and honesty are distorted.

Capital is not the only scarce resource. It is often difficult to expand a company's marketing capability. If product-A is given more attention, then product-B gets less. This generates tension among those concerned with different products, a tension that is similar to that found among college department chairmen who are agitating for more courses in their respective fields. Although each chairman recognizes that only so many courses can be added, each feels that the expansion of his department should not be fettered.

Personnel is often scarce, so competition may arise over the allocation of people. In government offices and others, the number of qualified workers sharply affects the ability of a division to expand. So when employment ceilings exist, a scramble to get workers normally ensues.

Competition for scarce resources is such a pervasive feature of organization that managers devote substantial planning and control effort to wise allocations, as we shall see in Parts Four and Five. More than technology and economics are involved. If a company allocates resources to a group of employees or to a division, it in effect endorses the group's activities and assures them of their continuing value in the future company program.

Built-in Conflicts

A second normal source of conflict is deliberately created. In the process of organizing, we design jobs that breed conflict. Many staff jobs have this characteristic. An industrial engineer, for instance, may be assigned the task of finding more economical methods of making portable cassettes. His new, efficient methods often complicate life for the manager supervising cassette production: workers may resist change because their previous social relations have been upset; quality will be hard to maintain while the new method is being introduced; and schedules must be revised. For the production manager, lower costs are only one of his goals. He is concerned also with the smooth integration of: employee attitudes, quality, equipment maintenance, and so on. Consequently he tends to be cautious about new methods, and we are thus likely to find the staff person zealously pushing his special assignment while the line manager drags his feet.

This kind of conflict is aggravated when the staff person is a cocky young college graduate and the line manager is an individual who has come up from the ranks and who responds intuitively rather than analytically. Furthermore, the two people will be responding to different criteria of success. Then if the change is made successfully, the question of who gets credit is another potential sore point.

Note that we frequently establish staff jobs with the express purpose of ensuring adequate attention to an aspect of a total operation that line managers for some reason slight. Moreover, several different staff people often make demands on the same manager—personnel, quality, cost, public relations, safety, to name but a few. By design each of these has his own ax to grind.

We also know in advance that the separation of control from operations will occasionally produce conflict. The people concerned with operations are certainly not opposed to dependable quality, fast service, low cost, or other features for which we often establish separate control jobs. But the total operating assignment and the conditions under which the work is done are such that independent checks are necessary. And when an independent-control person raises an objection, the operating manager is annoyed.

The very reason we create such staff units and special-purpose operating units is to get more attention for the particular purposes of these units. Managers with other important assignments will be too preoccupied with their own focused objectives. So we build in units that will challenge normal tendencies; we *want* the conflict to occur. From the conflict will come a better-balanced, overall result.

Conflict Arising from Differences in Work Characteristics

The best way to run department-A does not necessarily fit together smoothly with the best way to run department-B. Each type of work has its own optimum technology, and vigorous pursuit of one specialty may make work more difficult for people in related activities.

Friction between production and marketing is a common illustration of this conflict over optimum technology. Most production will benefit from long runs, standardized products, limited variety, and predictable levels of activity. On the other hand, marketing benefits from a variety of products or special adaptations that fit customer desires, fast changes, and prompt delivery. Under these circumstances, the marketing manager may make requests of production that the production manager feels will hinder him from doing his job well, and vice versa.

A research director, to note another common conflict, seeks unique products or processes and insists on high quality. Long lead times are needed for experimentation, and output is limited to the test tube or pilot plant; hence a research director's priorities differ from those of a production chief or marketing manager.

Differences in technology prevail in all kinds of enterprises. In a hospital, for example, a unit treating drug addicts will often want to take action incompatible with the smooth operation of inventory control at the dispensary and with businesslike accounting, billing, and collecting.

Of course, steps are taken to mediate such conflicts. To achieve overall organization goals, some departments must deviate from practices that are optimum when each department is considered separately. Our point here is that people who know that their job could be done better if they did not have to cater to an alien activity find it hard to accept these compromises.

Divergent Personal Values and Aims

Paul R. Lawrence and Jay W. Lorsch point to a further reason for conflict between functional departments.[1] The personal values of the type of person

---

[1] *Organization and Environment: Managing Differentiation and Integration* (Boston: Harvard Graduate School of Business Administration, 1967).

Figure 9–1 Divergent values lead to intergroup conflict, especially when each group holds strong views about the use of a limited resource, such as land. Within an enterprise, too, managers and supervisors vie with one another for a share of available personnel, equipment, supplies, and funds.

who is attracted, say, to research differ sharply from those of a person in production. The researcher is usually intrigued with the unknown, places a high value on scientific "truth," is prepared to wait weeks or months to get an answer, and thinks other people should act as rationally as *he* does. In contrast, the usual production worker prefers to deal with known phenomena, has a practical and intuitive sense of what is right, wants prompt and positive action, and is more comfortable with authoritarian relationships. The typical sales executive has still another set of aims, ways of dealing with people, and time span within which he wants to see results. When people with such different orientations try to solve a mutual problem, they quickly find that they don't talk the same language.

Divergence of personal values often comes to the surface in government agencies. One person may advocate a cause (better jobs for blacks or equal rights for women); another may want to follow a strict interpretation of established law; and a third may stress current responsiveness to the electorate or party leaders. These individuals will agree on some matters but sooner or later will find themselves in conflict.

Two persons seeking the same job have a clear conflict in aims. Our system of promotion-from-within on the basis of merit deliberately places people in competition for more attractive jobs. We have traditions governing appropriate methods of competition—like the medieval codes of chivalry in combat—but ambitious individuals sometimes resort to sharp internal politics, aggressive bids for recognition, and adroit maneuvering. Even when promotion is not at stake, some compete aggressively for recognition and status.

Ambiguous Organization

Another common source of conflict in organization is lack of agreement on who should do what. For instance, in one company the president thought the controller's job was to establish accurate accounting records, to compare actual expenses with the budget, and to point out deviations to all executives directly concerned. The controller himself thought that he should press executives to avoid budget overruns and should report only unresolved deviations to the president. A newly appointed operations-research director thought the controller's task was only to maintain accounting records and to make accounting information available on request from other executives. The ill will that grew out of this role ambiguity lasted far beyond the three months required to reach a formal agreement.

Jurisdictional squabbles can arise anywhere, from the senior level down to the operating level, where, for instance, it may not be clear who can commit the company to deliver a special order on Sunday. Job scope is not a trifling matter, as nationwide strikes over jurisdictional lines demonstrate. Many firms prepare written job descriptions only irregularly, and even when more systematic attention is given, such descriptions can never be complete and are soon outdated. The more dynamic the company, the more likely are conflicts to arise from ambiguous organization.

CONSTRUCTIVE AND DESTRUCTIVE CONFLICT

Conflict within organizations can be constructive or destructive, as the preceding review of likely sources indicates. Although destructive conflict captures more attention, the positive effects can be substantial if we keep the pressures within bounds.

Constructive Conflict

Built-in conflict, as we have observed, deliberately seeks the benefits of an *additional viewpoint* or an *extra check*. Staff positions frequently are created to ensure that a particular aspect of operations—quality control, product development, personnel training, public relations, and the like—gets adequate attention. The external staff described in Chapter 6 improves the quality of major decisions, and the very existence of controls, though sometimes irritating, leads to careful performance of operations that will be evaluated.

Figure 9–2   Conflict over scarce resources, or any other conflict, can be directed toward constructive ends that are designed to benefit not only the disputing parties but also the enterprise as a whole.

Self-satisfied, complacent personnel are less likely to be found where some conflict serves as a prod. When challenge to improve is lacking, companies, like nations, tend to become soft and cater to the convenience of the persons in charge. Alternative products or other uses for capital, for instance, tend to keep managers of traditional products on their toes.

Rivalry and competition call forth extra effort. As in athletic competition, recognition, status, and the sheer fun of winning often stimulate people to try harder. Within organizations, conflict stirs people to think up new alternatives, to make sure results exceed standard, to anticipate trouble, and alter their usual patterns. The aim, of course, is to see that this extra effort is focused on company objectives.

Destructive Conflict

In contrast to the potential benefits just discussed, conflict inevitably produces emotional stress. We can all stand some degree of stress; research even suggests that a little stress serves as a tonic. But when stress goes beyond the invigorating stage, it becomes debilitating.

Furthermore, conflict pressed too energetically carries some activities beyond a useful service. The hospital clerk is overly concerned with his subgoal if he places his need for tidy files above a patient's desire to return home and keeps the patient sitting until all records are neat. Likewise, an airline-ramp service director charged with cleaning planes sometimes insists on completing his task meticulously even when his thorough cleaning of rugs conflicts with getting planes off on schedule. In terms of balanced customer service, the clerk and the service director are "suboptimizing." That is, by pursuing their subgoals to an optimum point, they are detracting so much from other desirable results that the overall service is hurt. A similar danger exists for almost all staff services.

The most detrimental effect of conflict is goal distortion. In the budgeting process, for example, if the marketing department must request double the appropriation it needs in order to end up with the correct amount, the integrity of communication becomes suspect. Likewise, legal or personnel needs may be overstated in anticipation of watering down, at the approval stage or in practice, in response to conflicting pressures. One way of describing this behavior is to say that people start "playing games"—perhaps bitter personal games— instead of pursuing their assigned mission.

Escalation of Conflict

Any internal conflict, either constructive or destructive in its original form, becomes very destructive if it is carried too far.

When a conflict gets out of control, a variety of behaviors are likely. Adversaries suspect each other's motives and read sinister intent into almost

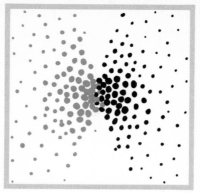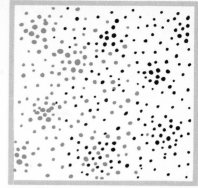

Figure 9–3   Polarization and depolarization of conflict. At left, lines of conflict are clearly defined, the clash is sharp, and all elements rally on either side of the issue. At right, vague clusters hint at potential issues, but there is some mingling of feelings; and the cluster that is forming in the center at the bottom suggests a genuine coalition.

any action. With suspicions aroused, each makes stronger demands on the other. Any failure to achieve outstanding results is blamed on the other party, and one's own behavior is defended—often in an emotional and nonrational manner. At this stage, information is withheld and distorted; so what actually happens, and why, is unknown. Soon there is deliberate sabotage of the adversary's moves. To "win" is now much more important than to accomplish any original operational goal.

In international affairs we can read accounts of such behavior in the daily papers. Within companies, an escalated conflict rarely surfaces. But unfortunately many of the same responses occur under a superficial politeness. Clearly we need mechanisms that forestall this sort of escalation.

ORGANIZING TO DEAL WITH CONFLICT

Behavioral-science writers have for many years assumed that conflict was undesirable and concentrated on ways of minimizing it. Primary attention was on individual attitudes and interpersonal responses. Recent writing, however, has shifted to channeling and harnessing constructive conflict. Actually, conflict is such a pervasive aspect of organized action that a manager has to consider it in all phases of management—planning, organizing, controlling, and activating.

At this point in our analysis, we are pulling out for special emphasis some of the ways a manager can use *organization* to create, restrain, or eliminate conflict. Later, in Parts Four, Five, and Six, we will consider other ways of dealing with conflict.

Create Desired Conflict

First, we reemphasize that some forms of conflict are useful and may be deliberately created. For instance, to secure adequate, expert, independent attention to a special aspect of an operation, a manager can establish a separate staff unit. Recently, to cite a specific activity, some company presidents have set up units to promote the employment of blacks. In addition to providing counsel and special-training facilities, such a unit prods supervisors to put forth extra effort to accommodate the new worker.

Separate control units are also commonly used. In order to permit independent action, such things as inspection, audit, and cost control are set apart from the operations they control. Such independence and divergence of objectives promote conflict, but the net effect on overall results justifies the separation.

Competition can be introduced by setting up a series of similar operating units and making regular comparisons of their results—the deadly parallel. Retail outlets, bank branches, national forests, social-security offices, and TV stations are only a few of the many activities in which this concept can be applied. When units operate at separate locations, conflict between them centers largely on status and allocation of scarce resources, so cooperation is not vital.

These examples indicate that conflict, like fire, can be a useful force when properly directed.

Establish an Umpiring System

Whenever we deliberately set up conflict units—and in many other situations when units compete for scarce resources—a mechanism for guiding the conflict is necessary. Formally established plans and objectives—considered in Part Four—set the framework within which conflict is to occur; and points in the organization are designated to make the inevitable choices.

To prevent such conflicts from escalating, we need an agency to settle the matter quickly, an *umpire* who will "call the play" promptly according to a set of known criteria so that we can proceed with the game. Not everyone may like the decision, but the issue ceases to be an open invitation for strife, and all people concerned can proceed to more constructive activities. Because the criteria for judging are known, conflicting parties can often anticipate the decisions of the umpire and adjust their behavior accordingly, thus solving the conflict even before it is necessary to arbitrate.

The usual "umpire" is the boss—the executive who directly or through intermediaries supervises the conflicting parties. In small enterprises and within single departments, the senior executive normally knows both the local facts and general objectives well enough to allocate funds and resources wisely. In addition he can maintain the desired balance between line and staff.

For more complex operations, however, the careful evaluation of the alternative uses of resources is a major task in itself. Here we need to designate an individual or committee to make the allocation. In addition a procedure specifying the information and opinions supporting a request for resources should be clearly stated. Such a setup is fairly common for capital allocation and for financial budgets, but the mechanisms for resolving other kinds of bargaining conflicts often require special designs.

The use of a committee for allocation purposes creates another organization problem. Who should be on the committee? A committee composed of competing parties merely provides a forum for continued conflict, and its decisions are likely to reflect logrolling rather than company objectives. So if group judgment is desired, a committee of objective members is clearly preferable.

A provision for appeals is common. Typically an appeal moves up the rungs of the management hierarchy. If a manager feels that a resource allocation will cause great harm, or if either line or staff people feel that their scope has been unwisely confined, a request for modification is made. Here, again, decisions by senior umpires usually become precedents—as in common law—and influence the way future choices will be made by lower-level umpires. By explicitly relating the bases for such choices to company objectives, the umpires guide conflict behavior toward desired action.

Design Integrated Units

When conflict resolution calls for frequent and varied adjustment in the activities of several people or several units, an umpire system becomes slow and unwieldy. In these circumstances, grouping together the interrelated activities may be the best way to localize the conflict. Three examples of this arrangement have already been discussed:

1) In Chapter 2 we noted that compound groups rather than functional groups enable operators to adjust their own efforts so that a completed piece of work is produced. An airplane crew and a surgical team are classic examples. The conflicting pressures are still present, for we have retained specialists with their inevitable differences in perspective and values. However, the compound group is small enough so that the need for coordination is evident and personal face-to-face communication is natural. Social pressure promotes self-coordination.

2) The concept of self-sufficient operating units, which we discussed under "profit decentralization" in Chapter 3, also encourages localized resolution of conflicts. Here again the persons whose work pulls them toward conflicting positions are placed in the same organization unit. Hopefully, the central mission becomes the overriding objective, and frequent personal contacts provide the occasions to iron out conflicts. Furthermore, a senior executive is on the spot to umpire when needed.

3) Project teams in matrix organizations, described in Chapter 6, utilize the same principle. The association of specialists needed for the project is temporary, but the hope is that these persons will be able to adapt their respective professional orientations to the task at hand. Usually this happens. If conflict arises, it typically is not within the project team but between the project team and the service departments and usually concerns the allocation of resources.

Integrated units, such as those just cited, can be very helpful in avoiding destructive conflict. Unfortunately this arrangement is not always practical. The cost of pulling a small piece of a functional unit away from the major department may be high and may result in intense disturbance. Technology may prevent the separation, or the departments may lack people with sufficient competence to exercise the decentralized authority needed in an integrated team. A piece of a complete computer cannot be split off, nor can a fraction of an advertising executive. Integrated units are a useful approach but not a panacea.

Separate the Contestants

A design that is the opposite of an integrated unit may be necessary in some circumstances. If we conclude that the conflicting parties simply cannot work together, then organizational separation *plus* a liaison mechanism can be a useful alternative.

A classic example of this approach is reported in W. F. Whyte's study of restaurant operations. The cooks—the skilled élite in a restaurant—strongly dislike taking orders from waitresses or runners who have less status. The waitresses, under pressure from customers, are persistent in their requests, and all too often the conflict over priorities and quality escalates into personal feuds with disastrous results to customer service. In this situation a mechanical system for communicating customer wants to the cooks removes the personal interaction initiated by the waitresses. The status of cooks, the evidence shows, is not hurt by receiving a sequence of inert written requests, and the waitresses learn to wait outside the kitchen until the number of their order is flashed on a screen. The opportunity for cooks and waitresses to get into a hassle is eliminated.

A comparable separation is used by successful plastics companies. In this field, frequent changes in technology and in customer requirements put pressure on relationships between research, production, and marketing. But differences in the attitudes and values of the people in these departments over time, costs, quality, and personal behavior, are so great that the individuals have difficulty communicating. Therefore they are kept apart, and an integrating unit serves as a liaison. The liaison person can talk the language of each department and so becomes an influential mediator of inherent conflict.

Incidentally a go-between is often used in Eastern cultures. To avoid the embarrassment of an open disagreement or conflict, a third person serves as an intermediary until a mutually acceptable course of action is identified. Not until then do the principals directly discuss the proposition.

Most Westerners prefer direct confrontation. But if status differences or other sources of incompatibility are major irritants, we may find that separation and the use of an intermediary are useful.

Remove Unnecessary Conflict

All the preceding suggestions for dealing with conflict assume that it will continue to be present. However, we do know that some destructive conflict is avoidable. Confusion about the approved organization, for instance, can be cleared up by managerial action. Perhaps formal job definitions have to be interpreted, and the words have to be backed up by action consistent with them. This can be done.

More complicated but also desirable is making sure that procedures, information flows, and especially control standards and evaluations match the organization design. Such clear, consistent roles do require some trade-offs, as we noted in Chapter 5, but once understood and accepted, they can remove one unnecessary source of conflict.

Even after these steps are taken, we know some conflict will remain—the tension we build in to get its benefits, and the friction that is a by-product of meeting other organizational needs. The managing of this remaining conflict will be considered in Part Six.

CONCLUSION: CONFLICT AND GROWTH

In this chapter we have considered conflict that arises in relatively stable situations. Growth or a shift in master strategy further complicates the picture. By upsetting established relationships, by introducing new priorities for allocating resources, and by increasing uncertainty, a whole array of latent conflicts flare anew.

The basic sources of conflict, its nature, and its potential usefulness and costs are still the same. But company growth means that a manager must work out a revised set of mechanisms and ground rules. The organizational arrangements that were just discussed will probably have to be adapted to the new situation. Even more demanding of managerial time will be the controlling and activating during the transition. A manager's skill in two-way communication and in gaining acceptance of new objectives will strongly affect the type of conflict that emerges during this unsettled period. We will return to these aspects of the manager's job in Part Six.

FOR CLASS DISCUSSION

1) Of the five "Sources of Conflict" discussed in this chapter, which is (are) more likely to be "managed" in a constructive and which in a destructive manner?

2) "I not only believe conflict, when it arises, to be potentially valuable, but in many situations I will seek to create conflict between evenly matched individuals or departments. There's nothing like a little competition to help find the fittest." What is your opinion of this statement by an advocate of "Managerial Darwinism"?

3) "Conflict within an organization is insidious. It may appear constructive in the short run but undermine the cooperative spirit necessary for long-run productivity." What is your opinion of this statement? Contrast the personal values and beliefs of this person with the one quoted in question 2.

4) In what ways may decisions on decentralization affect the potential for creating and identifying conflict? Relate your answers to material in Chapters 3 and 6.

5) Assume that a situation exists in which conflict arises from differences in objectives and in which outcomes are relatively certain. How may discussion of higher-level objectives (broader ends for which the conflicting objectives may be seen as means) aid in resolving such conflict?

6) In what ways may efforts to eliminate conflict between the sales, sales service, and shipping departments of an organization adversely affect the customer who tries to find out what has happened to his order?

7) How do we explain why most managers are willing to accept a financial audit of their operations as a necessity of business life even though such an audit implies a lack of complete trust in their *honesty*? At the same time, these same managers may be greatly upset by a staff audit of, say, a technical recommendation, when the latter audit implies only lack of complete trust in their *judgment*.

8) How should one deal with conflict that arises when some organization objectives are recognized as necessary to realize the purpose of the organization but also seem incompatible with the objectives of the larger society? Assume that no direct violation of the law is involved. Give a specific example of such a potential conflict before discussing possible ways of dealng with it.

Cases

For cases involving issues covered in this chapter, see especially the following. Particularly relevant questions are listed after each case.

The Delaware Corporation (p. 113), 6
Merchantville School System (p. 217), 7
Graham, Smith, & Bendel, Inc. (p. 445), 6
Family Service of Gotham (p. 532), 4
Central Telephone and Electronics (p. 527), 5

FOR FURTHER READING

Du Brin, A. J., *Fundamentals of Organizational Behavior.* New York. Pergamon Press, 1974, Chapter 10.

Uncluttered discussion of sources, consequences, and ways of reducing intergroup conflict.

Filley, A. C., R. J. House, and S. Kerr, *Managerial Process and Organizational Behavior,* 2nd ed. Glenview, Ill.: Scott Foresman and Company, 1976, Chapter 9.

Summarizes evidence on the nature of conflict and personal ways of resolving conflict in organizations.

Nightingale, D., "Conflict and Conflict Resolution," in Strauss, G., et al., eds., *Organizational Behavior, Research and Issues.* Madison, Wis.: Industrial Relations Research Association, 1974.

Clear statement of the nature of conflict as seen by a) *human relationists and* b) *pluralists, and the proposals of each group for conflict resolution. Very useful framework for sorting out diverse views about conflict in many areas of management.*

Ritzen, G., *Man and His Work: Conflict and Change.* New York: Appleton-Century-Crofts, 1972.

An examination of conflict arising between professional standards and organizational demands.

Robbins, S. P., *Managing Organizational Conflict.* Englewood Cliffs, N.J.: Prentice-Hall, Inc., 1974.

Explains why and how intraorganization conflict should be managed, including the possibility of making constructive use of conflict.

Schmidt, W. H., "Conflict: A Powerful Process for (Good or Bad) Change." *Management Review,* December 1974.

Counsel to managers about responding to conflict.

Webber, R. A., *Management.* Homewood, Ill.: Richard D. Irwin, Inc., 1975, Part Seven.

Discusses sources of stress and conflict in organizations, and ways managers resolve conflict.

10   Matching Jobs
and Individuals

ADJUSTING FOR PERSONAL
DIFFERENCES

In the preceding chapters we have considered organization and people *in general*. This approach has been a convenient simplification, but we know that *particular* individuals differ significantly in ability, learning, attitudes, and behavior. Moreover, the same person changes over time as he gains experience and as his personal needs shift.

Each specific job within an organization must be filled by a specific person, and that person may not fit neatly into a job as it has been conceived. If we find ourselves trying to fit a square peg into a round hole, we must fix either the peg or the hole or both.

PREPARING INDIVIDUAL
SPECIFICATIONS

The overall process of matching jobs and individuals resolves itself into the following subproblems: What kind of a person do we need for each job? What are the abilities of the people now in the organization? How can we best match individuals and jobs in the short run? Should we train or replace the individual, or should we adjust the job? How can we obtain people to match our long-run needs?

Clarifying Job Specifications

The first step in matching jobs and individuals takes up where organizational analysis left off. If an organization is designed properly, we have a series of *job descriptions*. A job description sets forth the objectives, duties, relationships, and results expected of a person in the job. A controller's job description, for instance, might include this duty: "Prepare monthly profit-and-loss statement." A hospital administrator's description might include such diverse statements as, "Coordinate all community relations" and "Promote outpatient services so as to relieve pressure on bed facilities."

In order to match jobs and individuals, job descriptions must frequently be made more explicit and concrete. The declaration that a controller should prepare a monthly profit-and-loss statement, for example, does not tell us whether he personally must compute the state, local, and national taxes, or whether he can delegate this task to an expert. The hospital administrator may be in charge of all community relations, but we do not know whether this duty involves delivering speeches, appearing before medical boards, or conducting health programs for school children.

In addition to specifying duties of the job, we must make explicit the *relationships required* by a position. Does the job require a lot of talking with many different people, or is it independent, calling for only short, terse communication? With what kinds of people must an incumbent deal? Are they sharp traders or indifferent, uneducated operators? Will they interpret "democratic" advice-seeking as a weakness, or have they learned to be independent and to resent orders? Do they want friendship mixed up with their work relationships, or would they prefer to keep their contacts at work matter-of-fact and impersonal?

Perhaps a job description will have to be amplified in other ways, so that it spells out, for instance, how much decentralization is intended, what frequency of innovation is expected, or what managerial techniques are to be used. In clarifying job descriptions, we need not necessarily put our thoughts in writing, but they should be clearly in the minds of everyone involved in the delicate task of matching specific individuals with specific jobs. The central point is to think through the nature of a job completely and carefully.

Translation to Individual Specifications

The second major step in matching jobs and individuals is translating the duties in our amplified job description into "individual specifications." A statement of duties often does not tell us specifically what to look for in appraising an incumbent or a candidate for a position. Suppose we are seeking a controller for a large company, and one of his duties is to "report any critical developments, as shown by accounting records, to the board of directors." How can we tell whether a man is skilled at this work? If a plant manager must "coordinate sixteen foremen," how do we recognize a person who can do so?

Of course if we are appraising an individual already in a position, his past performance, compared with the behavior and results we desire, will be the main evidence used. But when we wish to consider a new candidate or to change a position, then we want a list of crucial characteristics needed by a person in that job.

Specifications should not be so closely tied to those exhibited by previous successful executives that people with different experience and personality are automatically excluded. In particular, we want to be sure that highly qualified women and members of minority groups are kept in the talent pool used to fill vacancies.

Actually, three quite different ways of stating individual specifications are in common use:

1) Certain standardized tasks can be *tested directly.* Candidates for a lifesaving job can be run through a series of tests in a pool; prospective typists can be asked to type a sample passage; often an aspirant can be observed on an actual job for a brief period. Unfortunately, we cannot apply such standards to complicated and unusual tasks (which are typical of many executive jobs), and they tell us little about how a person will fit into a working group. So we need additional specifications, especially for executive positions.

2) Past *work experience and accomplishment* may be useful as an indication of ability to do similar work in the future. For example, a large chemical company specified that its vice-president of finance "should have served as chief financial officer for a medium or large chemical-processing company for a period of eight years; should have been responsible for tax accounting in a medium-sized company for at least two years; should have had at least fifty people reporting to him." A water company specified that its plant manager should have demonstrated ability to "reduce costs, develop subordinate personnel, and avoid stoppages and breakdowns."

3) Specifications may include a list of *personality characteristics* that are stated either in the technical jargon of behavioral scientists or in more general terms, such as "friendly temperament" and "apparent energy and ambition." The reason for resorting to personality characteristics is that experience may be an inadequate indication of the qualities needed for a position. A job may be so unusual that few candidates have pertinent experience, and experience may fail to demonstrate clearly all the qualities that might be needed for success in a new situation.

In practice, most statements of individual specifications for executive and staff jobs include a combination of desirable experience and personality characteristics stated in lay terms. The use of scientific phrasings of characteristics is limited, expensive, and complex, because such statements require people with formal training to prepare and judge them. Besides, the behavioral sciences have not yet reached a high degree of accuracy; hence, a solid record of experience, supplemented by intuitive judgments of personality, may be just as reliable for predicting managerial ability as the more intricate methods of the social scientists.

PETE ROSE							THIRD BASE CINCINNATI		

HEIGHT: 5'11" WEIGHT: 200 BATS: BOTH THROWS: RIGHT
SIGNED: REDS-1960, PRIOR TO DRAFT ACQUIRED: SIGNED AS FREE AGENT, 7-8-60
BORN: 4-14-41, CINCINNATI, OHIO HOME: CINCINNATI, OHIO

COMPLETE MAJOR LEAGUE BATTING RECORD

YEAR	CLUB	G	AB	R	H	2B	3B	HR	RBI	AVG.
1963	REDS	157	623	101	170	25	9	6	41	.273
1964	REDS	136	516	64	139	13	2	4	34	.269
1965	REDS	162	670	117	209	35	11	11	81	.312
1966	REDS	156	654	97	205	38	5	16	70	.313
1967	REDS	148	585	86	176	32	8	12	76	.301
1968	REDS	149	626	94	210	42	6	10	49	.335
1969	REDS	156	627	120	218	33	11	16	82	.348
1970	REDS	159	649	120	205	37	9	15	52	.316
1971	REDS	160	632	86	192	27	4	13	44	.304
1972	REDS	154	645	107	198	31	11	6	57	.307
1973	REDS	160	680	115	230	36	8	5	64	.338
1974	REDS	163	652	110	185	45	7	3	51	.284
1975	REDS	162	662	112	210	47	4	7	74	.317
MAJ. LEA. TOTALS:		2022	8221	1329	2547	441	95	124	775	.310

Figure 10–1 For some jobs, candidates can be examined during a trial period. But where long training is required, we put people to the test in "real-game" situations, in hopes that their full potential will be realized. Or we analyze their past performance with the assumption that it will predict future achievement.

Preparing the experience section of an individual specification is relatively simple and grows directly from analyzing the duties of a particular job. We fully recognize the value of experience specifications and urge that they be used whenever appropriate. That much of the discussion on the following pages deals with personality characteristics means not that such characteristics are more important than experience, but merely that personality specifications are more difficult to prepare and that the opportunity is greater for managers to improve this aspect of individual specifications.

IMPORTANT PERSONALITY CHARACTERISTICS OF MANAGERS

Psychologists, psychiatrists, sociologists, and cultural anthropologists have identified and classified hundreds of human characteristics. None of the classifications is "right" or "wrong." Some are useful in studying individuals in the family, others in dealing with the mentally ill, still others in analyzing small work groups. In this discussion, we have selected from both science and business practice certain characteristics that, in our opinion, are most *useful to managers* in writing individual specifications, in appraising people, and in planning personnel development. For convenience, we shall discuss these under five headings: knowledge, decision-making talent, self-reliance and self-assertion, social sensitivity, and emotional stability.

Knowledge

In matching an individual with a job, an inevitable question is, "What does he need to know?" The knowledge an aspirant to an executive position should have can often be specified in terms of specialty, depth, coordination, and management. Every managerial position calls for specialized knowledge of, say, selling methods, water pollution, petroleum economics, or bond discounts. Some jobs require knowledge in depth, whereas others demand only general acquaintance with a field. The president of a company, for instance, may need some general knowledge of public relations, but the public relations manager should have thorough knowledge of sociology, politics, communications media, and kindred subjects.

In addition to identifying the special fields and the degree of depth in each, we should consider what knowledge a manager will need to tie in his activities with related jobs. Such coordinating knowledge includes an understanding of operations—facts, technology, and problems—and of the people whose work is related to their area of the company. Managerial knowledge, on the other hand, is a grasp of management principles and techniques that are applicable to a variety of situations. Of course other kinds of knowledge may be necessary for specific decisions, but consideration of speciality, depth coordination, and management provide a good start in identifying knowledge requirements for a particular job.

Decision-Making Talent

Jobs also differ in the complexity and novelty of problems that must be solved. The president of a large aerospace firm needs a different order of decision-making ability from that needed by the head of a motel chain. Let us note several of the personality factors that contribute to decision-making talent.

Analytical ability. This ability enables a person to break a problem into parts, identify relevant facts, interpret the meaning of facts, and project the consequences of a decision. Because so many facts bear on a typical management problem, an executive needs what might be called an intuitive analytical sense in order to select key facts and eliminate the rest.

Conceptual–logical ability. To get meaning from a vast array of facts, we must assemble them under large concepts. For instance, an executive may take a chart that shows declining sales, information from competing companies, and reports on the activities of the company's own sales representatives, and pull them all together into one concept—"Poor customer service." Synthesizing facts involves both inventing concepts and using logic to connect the concepts in causal relationships.

Creativity. Tough problems usually cannot be resolved by known methods. A fresh approach, a new twist, a novel arrangement of recognized parts, or the addition of a different material or system is often necessary to find an acceptable solution. Preferably, an executive should be able to create original ideas himself; at a minimum he needs acumen in spotting the good ideas of other people.

Intuitive judgment. This aspect of decision-making ability resembles the "hunch." Up to a point a decision-maker looks at a problem analytically and logically and then suddenly seems to "know what to do" intuitively. Even though the process is only partially systematic and conscious, a decision does emerge. Intuitive judgment is particularly important when all facts cannot be gathered, when conceptual and logical arguments are fuzzy, or when immediate action is required without waiting for long, rational analysis.

Judgmental courage. Unlike a scientist, an executive must often act without careful research and foolproof logic to back up his decision. Psychologists associate ability to do so with a person's *tolerance of ambiguity* (his capacity to deal with uncertainties without breaking down) and with *frustration tolerance* (his ability to deal continually with difficulties without becoming discouraged). Courage is needed to make decisions when confronted by uncertainties and frustrations.

Open-mindedness. A sixth component of decision-making talent that is particularly important in individual specifications is the degree of receptivity to new ideas. Does a person conscientiously listen to others and try to determine the relevance of their ideas in solving current problems?

In summary, we can say that although decision-making talent is difficult to pin down, some of its elements can be identified. An executive who is analytical, logical, creative, open-minded, intuitive, and courageous is more likely to make useful decisions than a person who is weak in these qualities.

Self-reliance and Self-assertion

In satisfying needs and solving problems, people differ in how much they rely on themselves and how much on others. Jobs, too, differ in what they require of a person in the way of taking initiative, asserting his ideas with persistence over those of others, and presenting ideas forcefully and energetically.

Psychologists have studied this trait and describe degrees of self-reliance —or lack of it—in terms of a range between extremes. Some talk of dominant ←——→ submissive characteristics; others speak of independent ←——→ dependent or of active ←——→ passive behavior. Practical business executives often use the expressions "initiative," "drive," or "self-starting ability" to identify the same quality, at least for the end of the continuum they are most interested in.

This trait is one that is revealed in everyday activities. To check yourself on this quality, observe what you do when you wake up in the small hours of the night because you are cold. Do you try pulling the covers closer around your neck and hope the chilly air will go away? Or do you face the problem, climb out of bed, and get another blanket? Many executive jobs need the type of person who gets another blanket.

Closely allied with a person's self-reliance is his ambition, or his "achievement motivation." Having mastered one problem, most persons set higher goals for themselves and start working toward them. Individuals differ, however, in how much they advance their aspirations. Some aspire to make "big jumps," whereas others are content with modest progress.

Social Sensitivity

Some individuals react to a managerial problem largely in terms of the feelings of the people involved. Such "other-directed" persons are often contrasted with "inner-directed" individuals, who are predominantly concerned with their own thoughts and matters that seem important to them.

The other-directed person often has a high capacity for *empathy*—the ability to project oneself imaginatively into the thoughts, feelings, and probable reactions of another person. We might empathize with an auditor or a salesperson in Alaska without necessarily approving of his feelings and behavior; but because we really sense his reactions, we are likely to be sympathetic with, or at least understanding of, his point of view.

Social sensitivity may be helpful, of course, in almost any job, but it is of critical importance for most selling, staff, and executive positions.

Emotional Stability

Emotional stability indicates a good adjustment to life. People who are emotionally stable tend to act in the following ways: 1) they accept different people, including those they do not like, calmly and objectively; 2) they react to obstacles by calmly increasing their efforts or finding new ways to achieve their desires, rather than by denying that the obstacles exist, becoming overly depressed, lashing out aggressively, or rationalizing their inabilities; 3) they know when they cannot achieve a given goal, and shrug their shoulders and turn their attention to other matters that interest them; 4) they react to moments of success calmly and objectively, without experiencing childlike exhilaration and becoming overly optimistic; 5) they behave simply and naturally without artificiality or straining for effect.

The test of a person's emotional stability comes, of course, when he is subjected to conflict and tension; and some jobs test a person more than others. For instance, the tension experienced by the sales manager of a newly formed pharmaceutical company is likely to be greater than that felt by the chief accountant in a savings bank. So a higher degree of emotional stability would be needed in the sales job than in the accounting job.

Perceptive Use of Personality Factors

The personality factors we have been talking about will be of greatest usefulness if a custom-made list of specifications is prepared for each job. The following examples suggest how a manager should tailor specifications to a job.

Frequently we try to provide complementary abilities in an executive and his key subordinates. Thus an executive who has intuition, courage, and a penchant for fast action might want an assistant who has analytical skill and a predisposition for research and fact-finding. If a new supervisor is to be appointed over a group of subordinates who are highly dependent, he will need considerable self-reliance and self-assertion.

The position of production scheduler presents a different problem. His work must interlock frequently and closely with that of a wide variety of people—perhaps a dozen shop supervisors, inventory clerks, purchasing agents, maintenance people, sales representatives, and even others. Anyone appointed to such a job should have considerable emotional stability if he is to remain problem-centered and get along with everyone.

In contrast, the jobs of researcher and development engineer typically require persons with specialized knowledge and keen decision-making talent. Social sensitivity and emotional stability, although desirable, would not be so essential for such jobs as for a production scheduler. The position of sales representative calls for still different abilities—social sensitivity and self-reliance ranking at the top of the list.

Executives need considerable courage and self-assertiveness when a company is making frequent changes to adapt to new competition or rapid changes in technology. A high degree of emotional stability is also desirable, for major changes mean stress on everyone whose job is affected by new practices.

A final remark about individual specifications. All the preceding discussion has been couched in terms of fixed and set working environments, including a stable array of subordinates, associates, and social structure. This approach implies that an individual must adjust to fit a position. But sometimes, of course, adjustment may run in the other direction. A job may be shaped, at least to some extent, to fit the person. Nevertheless, a manager must always think closely about both the job—however it may be revised—and the characteristics of a person who could fill such a job well.

APPRAISING PERSONNEL

Job analysis and individual specifications are not ends in themselves. But they are vital preparations for a third step—appraising specific individuals to see how well they match the jobs created by an organization design. Specifications provide standards, and we must now evaluate people in terms of those standards.

Appraising Experience

Measuring what a person has done is relatively simple and direct. For example, if the specifications for a vice president in charge of production state that, "He should have ten years of experience as head of manufacturing in a medium-sized company," matching his work record to the specification is all that is necessary. The same is true if experience specifications are stated in terms of *results* rather than years; for instance, "He should have increased the sales in his territory significantly during his tenure as branch manager." But when the specified results are intangible—such as having developed good subordinates or maintained goodwill with suppliers—we run into measurement problems. Often, in a complex situation, it is difficult to know how much the person being appraised influenced the outcome, and how much of the outcome was caused by other forces. On such matters it may be desirable to pool the subjective judgments of several individuals.

Appraisal of experience is somewhat analogous to what a statistician does when he predicts the gross national product by fitting a trend line to the experience of the past ten or twenty years. He is not sure of the precise values and weights of all underlying forces; hence, without knowing the forces, he simply projects a line that is the result of all of them. Similarly, we often predict from past achievement a person's likely future success, without being sure which personal abilities determined his success. Although such prediction is admittedly risky, it is often the best way to size up an individual. In addition, the method has two attractive advantages—it is inexpensive and can be used by executives who lack technical training in psychology.

The reliability of an appraisal based on experience depends partly on the *relevance* of past experience to the new job. If a person is being evaluated in his present position, naturally the pertinent issue is whether current results are satisfactory. But when a person is being considered for transfer or promotion, we must relate his past experience to a job with different specifications. And if the candidate's background does not quite fit the new specifications, we need to decide whether the fit is close enough. In this event, past experience is probably used as evidence about personality factors, and our judgment may be improved if we frankly recognize that we have shifted from one kind of criterion to another.

A common safeguard in making promotions in many companies is a policy of testing a person in several different jobs. These assignments are useful *both* for training and for appraisal. If we have any doubt about Claire's or Pete's ability to get work out on schedule, we can assign them a task in which they can gain experience and their development can be watched closely.

Personality Appraisal by Executives

A job may be unique or so new that no previous work closely resembles it. If we insist on full experience in this case, we may pass over people, both inside and outside the company who have great ability but are short on experience. For these and related reasons, it is often a desirable practice to base a portion of our appraisals on a person's ability and personality.

Executives are rarely skilled psychologists, yet they must and do appraise personality. For years, managers have depended on their intuitive judgment in selecting personnel. Because such selection is so crucial, we should obviously adopt any measures that can improve the quality of judgment. Here are three practical rules that are applicable to large and small companies:

1) Make individual judgments on sophisticated grounds. Instead of resorting to vague terms like "personality" or "a good worker," define specifically the qualities needed in a job, as we suggested in our earlier discussion of personality. By doing so, an appraiser can detect his own biases and cultivate objectivity, which will enable him to judge people realistically.

2) Use group judgment. In order to prevent mistakes in perception and judgment, many companies insist that three or four executives appraise a person on each specification.

3) Maintain a file of key incidents in each person's performance. All of us tend to remember and overemphasize recent events. We can make more balanced appraisals if we have before us a systematic record that includes revealing incidents about the person over a period of years. Such a record should denote both strengths and weaknesses, and it may indicate the directions in which an individual is developing (perhaps he has overcome earlier knowledge deficiencies, and he may be showing more—or less—self-reliance).

Tests and Clinical Interviews

Personality and aptitude tests provide quite useful information for certain types of well-defined positions, such as salesperson, computer programmer, and routine production worker. Clinical interviews by skilled psychologists are also useful when simpler methods do not clearly indicate certain characteristics, for example, emotional stability. As our knowledge about human behavior in work situations increases, the value of such tests should also improve.

Unfortunately, in our present state of knowledge, psychological tests have only limited value as predictors of success in specific jobs. The diversity of job specifications, along with the complexity of individual motivation and behavior, makes the design of a reliable test extremely difficult. Tests may be invalid for minority candidates. Furthermore, only the largest companies can afford the great expense of designing and giving tests that are adapted to specific jobs. Except for preliminary screening of a large number of raw recruits, psychological tests and clinical interviews will probably continue to be used largely as supplements to managerial judgment. For executive posts especially, the chief value of tests lies in corroborating or questioning personal estimates. Assessing people on the basis of experience and observable personality characteristics will endure as an important management duty for a long, long time.

SHORT-RUN PERSONNEL PLANNING

Present personnel will seldom match completely the person specifications prepared for existing positions. An appraisal of personnel typically reveals that some people have less ability than desired whereas others have unused talents. What can a manager do to improve this match of human resources and organization needs? Both short-run and long-run adjustments are necessary. In the short run we have to concentrate on present employees and present jobs. The long run gives us much more flexibility, which we shall discuss later.

The Weak Incumbent

Probably the most difficult and unpleasant short-run problem arises when an individual already in a job fails to measure up. In such cases, we have three alternatives for improving the congruence of person and job:

1) Change the job. This procedure is a matter of "tinkering" with the organization structure. Three examples of such tinkering are withdrawing a duty from one position and assigning it to another, adjusting the degree of decentralization, and providing additional assistance where a person is weak.

2) Change the incumbent. Perhaps through counseling and training, the employee may overcome the gap between his present performance and what the company desires.

3) Remove the incumbent. If a person cannot be expected to become competent in a reasonable time or if the job cannot be changed to fit him, it may be necessary to transfer or dismiss him and fill the position with someone who more nearly fits the individual specifications.

Action in such situations is often painful because it upsets both expectations and established behavior. But procrastination may undercut the effectiveness of a whole department or company.

Deciding on a Matching Method

In deciding on which of the three methods to follow in matching person and job, we should answer several questions carefully.

How closely does the job interlock with other positions? The degree of interdependence between a given job and other jobs directly affects the ease or difficulty of changing the organization to fit a person. For example, the Montana sales representative of a Midwestern paint company may be ineffective without upsetting the work of others; the company simply has a somewhat reduced volume of business, and we might cut the incumbent's territory or have him concentrate on a limited number of customers, so that his duties match his abilities. But poor performance by a billing clerk may have far-reaching repercussions. Customers may get too many items of one color and not enough of another; the accounts-receivable clerk may spend extra time trying to straighten out invoice difficulties; salespeople may have trouble with customers; inventory records may be snarled up; and so on. To adjust the billing job to fit the

Figure 10–2 Short-run personnel planning. Neither subordinates nor available candidates outside the company are able to fill effectively a gap that has occurred in the company organization. There is a mismatch between the job as now conceived and the qualifications of candidates who are available to fill it.

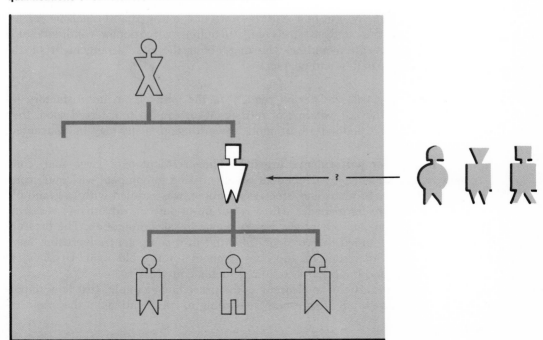

capacities of the present clerk would set off a chain reaction that would alter several other positions.

Will training make the person acceptable? Some personal deficiencies can be corrected fairly promptly, whereas others can be altered little, if at all. For instance, product knowledge or specific company knowledge can often be quickly acquired, but conceptual–logical abilities require native capacity plus many years to develop. This distinction is important, because we are always tempted to keep a person in a position because he is familiar with current facts and routines, even though he lacks the imagination and drive to do a really satisfactory job over a period of time.

Is a good replacement available? One small firm had a chief engineer who was cantankerous, uncompromising, and slow. But the company retained him because his technical knowledge of the product line was far superior to that of any subordinate or of engineers in other firms who might be attracted by the salary the company could afford to pay. Eventually, it was hoped, one of the younger engineers could take on responsibility for contacts with the sales department, production department, and customers, thereby permitting the current chief to concentrate on developing new products. Pending the event, however, the president took over some of the duties that ideally should have been the chief engineer's; the assistant production superintendent was assigned the task of expediting plans for new products; and a coordinating committee that met weekly was formed. In this instance, the organization was changed to fit an individual because a good replacement was unavailable.

In thinking about promotions and transfers, we must be wary of chain reactions. Perhaps our Canadian branch manager is well qualified to replace an ailing vice-president, but how will the work of the Canadian branch be carried on? Although our analysis starts with matching a particular candidate to a specific job, we often end up thinking about the best arrangement of the whole structure of jobs and people.

How long will the person remain on the job? If an unsatisfactory incumbent is within a few years of retirement, or can be transferred soon, then temporary and expedient adjustments in work assignments may be warranted.

Is superior performance urgent? The president of a large soap company, which was heavily dependent on advertising to compete with such companies as Lever Brothers and Procter & Gamble, was saddled with "a grand old man" as advertising manager. He was not up-to-date on advertising research, use of television, and other new developments in sales promotion. The pressure of competition forced the company to bring in a competent advertising manager in short order, despite the consequences for the old man. Urgency, in terms of time and importance, required such a course.

Most cases are not so clearcut as the preceding example. Just how important is it to have a job filled exactly according to specifications in the organization plan? What obligations does a company owe a person who has given long and perhaps distinguished service? Should any weight be given to long personal friendships? Must the need for change be clearly evident, or can changes be made on the basis of uncertain estimates of the future? Because answers to such questions of value tend to be personal and subjective, an executive should usually check his judgments with two or three associates.

How will removal affect morale? Removing a widely known, well-liked individual may cause other employees to say, "Don't go to work for this company—they fire people at the drop of a hat." Even if everyone else remains in his job, a pervasive feeling of insecurity may be created in a department by removing one popular individual. Negative effects on morale can be lessened by letting it be generally known that the person dismissed was given a fair chance to demonstrate his ability, that he was offered a transfer with dignity to another position, and that he was given a dismissal benefit for early retirement.

Sometimes, on the other hand, morale is improved by removing a person from a position for which he is not qualified. If employees see that someone is kept on a job even though his performance is mediocre, they may develop the general attitude expressed by the question, "Why push yourself?" And many a competent young person has been discouraged to find his advancement blocked by a series of inadequate people in key posts. In such situations, removal of a weak incumbent will be a signal that management is prepared to distinguish between good and poor performance, and this will boost morale among the more able employees.

The foregoing list of questions certainly indicates that no universal answer can tell a manager whether he should fit his organization to people or find people to fit the organization. Because a manager has an obligation to achieve company objectives, we urge that he give independent and detailed study to the design of an organization that will be well suited to reach these objectives. But in the short run, he must clearly meld this ideal design—as reflected in person specifications—with the abilities of available personnel.

An Unexpected Vacancy

Resignation, death, or unanticipated transfer may create a vacancy with little warning, and the empty position needs to be filled as soon as possible. In such cases, we normally have some choice of replacements, but rarely will any of the candidates completely match the specifications for the vacant position. Again we face the question of how much a job should be modified to fit a man.

Consider the sudden death of your professor or the manager of a local supermarket. The issues to be faced in seeking a successor are similar to those already discussed. Must the job be done so that it readily interlocks with other positions? What requirements for the job can be learned after the person is appointed, and what qualities must he already possess? How will the position vacated by the new appointee be filled? Is top performance immediately important, or is gradual learning and adjustment feasible? If duties are to be reassigned, what will be the impact on morale? Does this unanticipated event present an opportunity to correct previous faults in the organization or to move toward a long-range organization plan?

Expedient, compromise steps—such as having one executive cover two jobs—may be unavoidable when an unanticipated vacancy first occurs. But these moves should be clearly announced as temporary. Then prompt action should be taken to work out a more satisfactory arrangement. The danger, of course, is that the expedient action may be allowed to continue for so long that later adjustments will not be made; or if they are, people will be upset by what they regard as another reorganization.

The Strong Incumbent

Some people in every organization will have greater, rather than less, ability than their jobs call for. A familiar question arises: Should we adjust the job to fit the person? In fact, such adjustment tends to happen. There are four common situations that call for it. 1) If the work that interlocks with a person's regular duties is poorly performed, a capable individual often gives advice and checks on performance that lies beyond his assigned sphere; by doing so, he sets the stage for having duties transferred to him. 2) When a special problem arises, a capable person is often asked to help with its solution. Repeated assignments to such special projects may lead to his having additional duties as a regular part of his job. 3) Further, to paraphrase an old rule of science, "Organization abhors a vacuum"; if important activities are not being taken care of at all, the most capable person around often steps into the breach. 4) Finally, quite aside from assigned duties, the "influence" of a strong individual is apt to extend beyond his prescribed area.

Such natural, if unplanned, expansion of a job creates no difficulties until the person becomes so involved in unofficial activities that he neglects his regular duties, or until he gets promoted. The first danger can be avoided if the supervisor insists that the individual keep his main assignments in clear perspective. Promotion, however, is likely to cause a more severe jolt. The shock is like that on a football team built around a backfield star who leaves the game with an injury. Weaknesses formerly covered up suddenly become serious. A wise manager, therefore, should keep abreast of how work is actually getting done and should use his outstanding subordinates for special assignments or in other ways that do not make his organization vulnerable to serious upsets when the exceptional performer moves on to another job.

A final observation applies to all shifts of personnel, whether initiated by a manager or by a worker leaving his job. No two persons are identical; each has his own strengths and limitations. Consequently, when a person takes a new position, he will—and should—perform the work in ways that are somewhat different from those of his predecessor. At first, he may not be prepared to carry the full load, but later he will probably take on some duties that were not assigned to his predecessor; on the other hand, other duties may be more fully delegated or initiative for them transferred to staff advisors. Inevitably, then, at least minor adjustments will occur in the assignments of duties and in social structure. During this transition, while people are learning new relationships, a manager has an opportunity to make alterations in organization without treating them as special problems. Such a period is also a natural occasion to introduce features of a long-range organization plan. For all these reasons, *placing an individual should be considered in terms of organization* as well as from a strictly personnel viewpoint.

LONG-RUN PERSONNEL PLANNING

Personnel planning for the long run differs in several particulars from the short-run problems just discussed. It is concerned with all jobs and all employees at once, with matching a complete roster of personnel to total job requirements; it is concerned with filling future vacancies rather than existing jobs; and it allows time for long-term learning, especially through rotation of personnel. Three major steps are involved in the process of long-run personnel planning: 1) projecting the organization structure and the personnel that are required to operate that structure, 2) matching the projected personnel requirements with present employees, and 3) planning for individual development so that people will be qualified when job openings occur.

Projecting Personnel Requirements

The first essential step in long-run personnel planning is to forecast the organization structure that will best meet the future needs of the company. The environment of any company is constantly changing—new products are introduced, existing products are modified, production processes alter, automation is introduced, advertising policies shift, and so on. Public-service enterprises are changing even more rapidly. The whole job structure should keep pace with such changes. Adding positions because of growth and new activities may be necessary, and existing positions may be assigned quite different duties ten years hence.

With this future organization structure as a basis, we can prepare specifications for each position. Naturally, some aspects, such as personality characteristics to complement people in related jobs, cannot be included in these early individual specifications. Nevertheless the main elements of each job should be thought through. The aim is to develop a clear understanding of what our future personnel requirements will be.

The second step in long-range personnel planning starts with appraising all key personnel and cataloging their characteristics without reference to specifications for a particular position. This *inventory of talent* should include, in addition to present executives, younger men and women (including members of minority groups). For even if these younger members are not yet in key spots, a good deal of positional shifting will undoubtedly occur during the following three to ten years.

With a list of individual specifications for jobs and an inventory of talent, we are ready to start matching jobs and individuals. First consideration for any position similar to a present job goes, of course, to the incumbent. Does he have the abilities we anticipate will be needed in the future? He may be highly qualified; perhaps he needs further development; possibly he should be replaced. We must also consider his age. If he will retire within the period covered by our long-range plan, obviously a replacement should be found. As an analytical device, some companies draw up an organization chart with colored bands around the boxes: red, say, to denote a vacancy within three years, amber for five years, and purple for ten.

From the preceding steps we have spotted the initial set of vacancies—new jobs, jobs where the incumbent should be replaced, and jobs that will be vacated by retirement. Using the individual specifications for each of these vacancies, we turn to our inventory of talent to identify the *most probable* candidates to fill the vacancies. Some companies pick a single candidate for each post; others pick two or even three (at least for the major positions) because they are not certain which candidate will be best qualified by the time the vacancy opens up.

A second set of probable vacancies is created as soon as people have been identified as candidates for promotion. Do we have employees qualified to move into the present positions held by these candidates? Again, a list of most-probable candidates can be prepared by comparing individual specifications with the inventory of talent. Theoretically, a third set of vacancies could be studied to find replacements for the replacements, and so on. In practice, complete plans for replacements are rarely carried beyond the second set; because

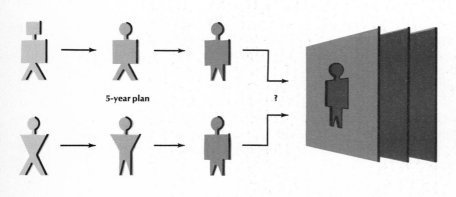

5-year plan

?

Now

2 years
from now

5 years
from now

Expected vacancy

Figure 10–3 Long-run personnel planning. To prepare for an anticipated future need, the organization guides the development of candidates, so that when the vacancy occurs, one or more individuals will have qualifications that match the requirements of the vacated position.

so many uncertainties exist, such a projection is unwarranted. Instead, division managers simply recognize that some turnover will undoubtedly occur; consequently they develop—often with the help of central staff—junior people for promotion without knowing just who will move where.

The important result of this analysis is that management foresees, several years in advance, both its need for people to fill certain key vacancies and the most promising individuals for those jobs.

Planning Individual-Development

Few if any candidates will have all the essential characteristics for the positions to which they might move. To overcome these deficiencies, management must determine what experience is needed and what personality characteristics should be developed. Some companies call the forms on which this information is listed "gap sheets."

At this stage of planning, any major difficulties in staffing the projected organization will become apparent. It may turn out to be so hard to fill certain positions with satisfactory executives that a firm will have to reconsider its organization design, at least at those points. In small firms, whose owners will undoubtedly continue to occupy key posts, adjustments may be necessary because of the owners' strengths and limitations. A three-year program, of course, is more likely to require adjustment of organization to personnel than a ten-year program, for there is obviously more opportunity to acquire and develop suitable personnel during the longer period.

Once we have decided on the gaps—the improvement and abilities a person needs to qualify for promotion—individual-development can begin. Management can help in individual-development, especially in providing needed experience. For example, a sales representative who is a candidate for branch manager might first be placed in a home-office staff position for two years. This service would broaden his perspective and acquaint him thoroughly with home-office activities and people. Executives who need broader perspective can be offered an opportunity to take part in a university's executive-development program.

Most of the individual-development, however, will depend on the person himself. He will have to choose, at several points in his development, a future "career path"—looking toward more intensive specialization, overseas assignments, managerial tasks, or other alternatives. Probably he will not be told exactly what management plans for him, but an ambitious person will guess and will act on any suggestions about where he should try to improve.

Long-run personnel plans, like any other long-range plans, should be revised periodically. With the passage of time, forecasts of operating conditions and concepts of an ideal organization for the company will change. Assessments of people will change, too, because some will develop faster and others more slowly than anticipated. In addition, resignations may require a revision of proposals for replacements. Nevertheless, if the whole process of long-range personnel planning successfully serves its purpose, qualified people will be available to fill vacancies as they arise, and short-run organization adjustments made necessary by inadequate personnel will occur less often.

CONCLUSION: ORGANIZING— A CONTINUOUS PROCESS

Matching individuals and jobs, as we have set it forth in this chapter, consists of rather sharply defined steps: clarifying jobs, preparing individual specifications, appraising personnel, making short-run adjustments, and planning long-run development of people to fit predicted organization needs. This step-by-step presentation is a useful approach to a dynamic problem. But the approach is not intended to provide a blueprint that should remain fixed once it is drawn.

Organizations are never completely established. Even the best plan soon becomes outdated by changes in work and personnel. The need for adjustment —often minor, occasionally major—is continual. Instead of being a static machine, an organization is an evolving social system.

In Part One, we were principally concerned with designing a system for getting work done. Clearly, such a plan is essential for the efficient operation of any enterprise. But emphasizing work tends to be too mechanistic. An organization will be more effective if we also give attention to the stuff of which it is made—people. So we have tried to point out in Part Two how we can pay attention to people. We need to conceive of an organization as a social system, not simply as a machine; we need to design jobs that will contribute to the satisfaction of human needs; we need to provide for conflict and conflict resolution; and, by no means least, we need to match individuals and jobs realistically.

The task of a manager, then, is to build a set of roles and relationships of living human beings that is congruent with the structure of work provided by a formal organization.

FOR CLASS DISCUSSION

1) What should be the role(s) of the following people in preparing a job specification: 1) The immediate supervisor of the man who will fill the job? 2) The immediate supervisor's superior? 3) The director of personnel or one of his subordinates? How would your answers be affected by the level of the job and by whether it was a line or staff position?

2) "Person specifications should be developed only in very general terms. As long as I have a rough idea of what I'm looking for, I select the best person for the company. If he doesn't fit the job I hired him for, but is good enough, we'll find him another job in the company. There are just too many ways to

'skin a cat' for me to write detailed person specifications." Comment on this statement by the head of a state-government agency.

3) In what ways would the technical and temperamental attributes sought in a good "external staff" man differ from those sought for men who fill the more conventional staff roles discussed in Chapter 4?

4) What should a company do about public pressure for more blacks and women in key positions?

5) George Reed was promoted from a job as senior technician in a pharmaceutical lab to supervisor of a group of technical people. After one year he was asked to go back to his former job because of low morale and poor planning in his new department. Reed said, "I never really wanted the job and I know I botched it. I took it only to get the salary increase and because I felt I should be happy to get the increased responsibility and status. Now I just can't go back to work on the bench and work with the fellows who all know I failed." How might this situation have been avoided? What might be done at least to permit men like Reed to save face and not be lost to their companies?

6) As a hedge against being caught without competent personnel, one company adheres to a policy of having at least two men capable of filling each key position. Aside from the cost of such a policy, how else might this be impractical? How else might fear of key personnel shortages be allayed?

7) As part of long-run manpower planning, what can be done to enable people to maintain their ability to learn and master new tasks? Recognize that in the short run it is more efficient to the organization and less disruptive to the person to have him do what he does best.

8) In some organizations certain positions expose managers to a great deal of conflict and stress. Although our text lists "emotional stability" as an important personality characteristic of managers, there is no mention made that some positions may require more than emotional stability. In such positions, where conflict and potential stress are high, how should person specifications reflect these factors?

Cases

For cases involving issues covered in this chapter, see especially the following. Particularly relevant questions are listed after each case.

The Delaware Corporation (p. 113), 14
Milano Enterprises (p. 124), 7
Petersen Electronics (p. 211), 7, 8
Merchantville School System (p. 217), 8
Graham, Smith, & Bendel, Inc. (p. 445), 7
Monroe Wire and Cable (p. 436), 4, 5
Household Products Company (p. 627), 6, 7

FOR FURTHER READING

Dinsmore, F. W., *Developing Tomorrow's Managers Today.* New York: AMACOM, 1975.

A businessman focuses his long experience on the process of developing managers.

Mahler, W. R. and W. F. Wrightnour, *Executive Continuity: How to Build and Retain an Effective Management Team.* Homewood, Ill.: Dow Jones–Irwin, 1973.

Practical guide to executive development, based on extensive experience.

Richards, M. D. and W. A. Nielander, *Readings in Management,* 4th ed. Cincinnati: South-Western Publishing Co., 1974, Chapter 19.

Useful articles on identifying and selecting managers.

Shaeffer, R. G., *Staffing Systems: Managerial and Professional Jobs.* New York: The Conference Board, Report 558, 1972.

Describes the process of filling managerial jobs in a systematic and planned manner. Four company systems are discussed in detail.

Warren, E. K., T. P. Ference, and J. A. F. Stoner, "Case of the Plateaued Performer." *Harvard Business Review,* January 1975.

Explores the increasingly difficult problem of what to do about executives who no longer seek promotion and have lost motivation to do more than merely acceptable performance.

Not-for-Profit Note

for Part II

HUMAN FACTORS IN ORGANIZING NOT-FOR-PROFIT ENTERPRISES

The personal and social pressures that we have been examining in Part Two bear similarly on not-for-profit enterprises. Personal needs, group behavior, and intergroup conflict call for similar modifications in the organization structure of every kind of joint venture. And the task of matching designed jobs and individuals arises in all organizations.

Certain characteristics that are strong in some—although not all—not-for-profit enterprises do, however, complicate the process of refining the organization structure.

A large number of "professionals," for example, make job enlargement and job enrichment difficult. In medicine, education, social work, and elsewhere we see increasingly narrow specialization—neurologists, psychiatrists, pediatricians, vocational counselors, music teachers, speech therapists, choreographers, anesthetists, and numerous other specialists. Each field requires special training, and most have rigid qualification examinations. Such professions develop their own code of conduct, values, and beliefs; and they have rather sharp ideas about what activities are—and are not—within their province.

One or a collection of these professions often play a crucial role in a hospital, school, welfare agency, or other not-for-profit enterprise. In fact, members of an established profession view the enterprise in which they work largely as a place for them to practice their profession. But for the enterprise manager, such high professional orientation adds rigidity. The manager runs into resistance if he tries to modify traditional boundaries of professions. In hospitals, for instance, the use of paramedics is typically regarded as unethical. On the other hand, expanding job content—commonly called job enrichment—

often encounters, "That's not my specialty; it is not what I was hired to do." To a large extent, where professionals predominate, a manager must design his organization to appeal to prevailing professional norms.

A second impact of professionalization, especially when it is reinforced by traditions transferred from government civil service, is hindrance to promotion from within. In Chapter 10 we have assumed that individuals adapt and grow as they gain experience. We also stressed that organizations change and that this change provides opportunities for people to expand the scope of their activities. In private enterprise, many of our personnel-development practices are built around such promotion from within.

This kind of personal career building based on the internal dynamics of an enterprise is difficult when employees are tied to a profession. Of course, some internal movement occurs. But we have to look harder for people who are willing to step outside their professional roles and adjust their activities to the particular needs of the enterprise. To develop managers requires extra attention, for job rotation is difficult and executives who do not come from one or two élite professions have trouble gaining respect. Only recently have doctors learned to respect a hospital administrator who does not have an M.D., and college professors are even more skeptical of a dean without a Ph.D.

Unhealthy conflict is perhaps a greater danger within not-for-profit enterprises than in profit-seeking companies. A combination of two factors may produce sharp conflict. The main creators of services—such as opera singers, research scientists, or kindergarten teachers—are likely to have aspirations and values that differ sharply from those of the financial manager of the enterprise for which they work. The football coach has aims that don't match those of the history professor, and so on. Often compounding such divergence in personal aims is the absence of a clear, overriding enterprise objective that can be used to arbitrate disagreements among the functional specialists. Many not-for-profit enterprises have multiple goals—for example, most universities promote research, teaching, community service and the glory of alma mater. The combination of differing personal values and ambiguous enterprise goals opens the way for destructive in-fighting.

As mentioned at the end of the first Note, securing voluntary cooperation from specialized personnel becomes harder as a not-for-profit enterprise grows. In a Stage-II organization, the gap between the dominant occupations—usually professionalized—and lay workers becomes wider. In large hospitals, for instance, many lay workers no longer feel the same commitment as the élite professionals to a service mission. So they unionize and press for their own ends.

There is no easy way to resolve such conflicts. A charismatic leader and a well-recognized mystique do help to resolve clearly drawn issues.

Each not-for-profit enterprise has its own characteristics. It may or may not have unusual difficulty with job enlargement, executive development, or internal conflict as briefly outlined in this Note. As cues to potential problems along these lines, we should look carefully at professionalization among employees, external restraints on rotation and promotion, and multiple or ambiguous goals that open the way for internal bickering.

PETERSEN ELECTRONICS

Petersen Electronics was founded by its current president, Benjamin Petersen, 30 years ago. The company grew rapidly during the 1950s and 1960s, and reached sales of $200 million six years ago. Growth since then has been uneven and at an average of less than five percent per year. The last 12 months, however, have been good ones, with sales and profits leaping 12 and 18 percent, respectively.

Despite the good year, Benjamin Petersen is concerned about the company as he nears retirement. One of the problems on which he would like advice involves George Briggs, vice president of marketing, and Thomas Evans, national sales manager, who is one of Briggs's four subordinates.

The comments of each of the key characters are presented for your consideration.

Benjamin Petersen, 61, president and board chairman.

When we started, a handful of people worked very hard and very closely to build something bigger than any of us. One of these people was George Briggs. George has been with me from the start, as have almost all of my vice presidents and many of my key department heads. For the next five years, I did almost all of the inventing and engineering work. Tom Carroll ran the plant and George Briggs knocked on doors and sold dreams as well as products. As the company grew, we added people, and Briggs slowly worked his way up the sales organization.

Eight years ago, when our vice president of marketing retired, I put George in the job. He has market research, product management, sales service, and the field-sales force (reporting through a national sales manager) under him, and he has really done a first-rate job.

One of the problems of having built this business with so many people who began with me is that we are all approaching retirement at about the same time. We realized this about ten years ago and began bringing in more bright young engineers and MBA's. We have moved them along as fast as we can. Turnover has been high and we have had some friction between our "young Turks" and the "Old Guard." When business slowed in the early '70s, we also had a lot of competition among the newcomers. Those who stayed have continued to move up, and a few are now in or ready for top jobs. One of the best of this group is Tom Evans. He started with us nine years ago in the sales-service area. Later, he spent three years in product management. George Briggs got him to move from head of the sales-service department to being an assistant product manager. After one year, George Briggs named him manager of the product-management group; and two years later, when the national sales manager retired, George named Evans to this post.

That move both surprised and pleased me. I felt that Evans would make a good sales manager despite his having little or no direct sales experience. I was afraid, however, that George Briggs would not want someone in that job who hadn't had years of field experience. I was even more surprised, though, when six months later (a month ago) George told me he was afraid Evans wasn't working out and asked if I might be able to find a spot for him in the corporate personnel department. Although I'm sure our recent upturn in sales is not solely Evans's doing, he certainly seems to be one of the keys. Despite his inexperience, he seems to have the field-sales organization behind him. He spends much of his time traveling with them and from what I hear has built a great team spirit.

Despite this, George Briggs claims, he is in "over his head" and it is just a matter of time before his inexperience gets him in trouble. I can't understand why George is so adamant. It's clearly not a personality clash since they have always gotten along well. In many ways, George Briggs has been Evans's greatest booster until recently.

Since George is going to need a replacement someday, I was hoping it would be Evans. If George Briggs doesn't retire before we have to give Evans another move or lose him, I'd consider moving Evans to another area. When we were growing faster, I didn't worry about a new challenge opening up for an aggressive young manager— there was always a new division or a new line or something to keep him stimulated and pleased with his progress. Now I have less flexibility, my top people are several years from retirement, and yet I have some people, like Evans, whom I would hate to lose always pushing and expecting promotion. Evans is a good example of this; I could move him but there are not that many *real* opportunities. He could go to personnel or engineering or even finance. Evans has the makings of a real fine general manager. I'd hate to move him now, however. He really isn't ready for another shift—although he will be in a few years—and despite what George Briggs claims, I think he is building team work and commitment in the sales organization as a result of his style. Finally, though I don't want to appear unduly critical of Briggs, I'm not sure he could get the job done in these competitive times without a bright young person like Evans to help him.

George Briggs, 53, vice president of marketing.

Before I say anything else, let me assure you there is nothing personal in my criticism of Evans. I like him. I have always liked him. I've done more for him than anyone else in the company. I'd tried to coach him and bring him along like a son. The simple truth is that he is in way over his head and showing a side of his personality I've never seen before. I brought him along through sales service and product management and he was always eager to learn. Although I couldn't give him a lot of help in those areas (frankly, there are aspects of them I don't yet fully understand), I still tried and he paid attention and learned from others as well. The job of national sales manager, however, is a different story. In the other jobs Evans had—staff jobs—there was always time to consult, to consider, to get more data. In sales, however, all this participative stuff he uses takes too long. The national sales manager has to be able to make quick, intuitive decisions. What's more, like the captain of a ship, he has to inspire confidence in those below him. If the going gets rough, the only thing that keeps the sailors and junior officers from panicking is confidence in the skipper. I've been there and I know. Right now with orders coming in strong, he can get away with all of his meetings and indecisiveness. The people in the field really like him and are trying to keep him out of trouble. In addition, I have been putting in 60 to 70 hours a week trying to do my job and also make sure he doesn't make any serious mistakes.

I know he is feeling the pressure, too. Despite the fact that he has been his usual cheery self with others, when I call him in to question a decision he has made or is about to make, he gets very defensive. He was never that way with me before. Now, on whatever I suggest he disagrees with me. I may have lost a little feel for what's going on in the field over the years, but I suspect I still know more about the customers and our sales people than Tom Evans will ever know. I've tried for the past seven months to get him to relax and let the "old man" help him, but it's no use. I'm convinced he just is not cut out for the job, and before we ruin him I want to transfer him somewhere else. He would probably make a fine personnel director someday. He's a very popular guy who seems genuinely interested in people and in helping them.

I have talked with Ben Petersen about the move and he has been stalling me. I understand his position. We have a lot of young comers like Tom Evans in the company, and Ben has to worry about all of them. He told me that if anyone can bring Evans along I can, and asked me to give it another try. I have, and things are getting worse. I hate to admit I made a mistake with Tom Evans, but I plan on seeing Ben about this again tomorrow. We just can't keep putting this off. I'm sure he'll see it my way and as soon as he approves, I'll have a heart-to-heart talk with Tom Evans.

Thomas Evans, 34, national sales manager.

This has been a very hectic but rewarding period for me. I've never worked as hard in my life as during the last six months, but it's paying off. I'm learning more about sales each day and more importantly, I'm building a first-rate sales team. My people are really enjoying the chance to share ideas and support each other. At first, particularly with our markets improving, it was hard to convince them to take time to meet with me and their subordinates. Gradually they have come to accept these sessions as an investment in team-building. According to them, we come up with more good new ideas and figure out ways to help each other to a greater degree than ever before.

Fortunately, I also have experience in product management and sales service. Someday, I hope to bring representatives from these departments and market research to the meetings with regional and branch people, but that will take time. This kind of direct coordination and interaction doesn't fit with the thinking of some of the oldtimers. I ran into objections when I tried this while I was working in the other departments. I'm certain, however, that in a year or so I'll be able to show, by results, that we should have more direct contact across department levels.

My boss, George Briggs, will be one of the ones I will have to convince. He comes from the old school and is slow to give up what he knows used to work well. George likes me, though, and has given me a tremendous amount of help in the past. I almost fainted when he told me he was giving me this job. Frankly, I didn't think I was ready yet, but he assured me I could handle it. I've gotten a big promotion every few years and I really like that—being challenged to learn new skills and getting more responsibility. I guess I have a real future here, although George won't be retiring for a good many years and I've gone as high as I can go until then.

George is a very demanding person but extremely fair, and he is always trying to help. I only hope I can justify the confidence he has shown in me. He stuck his neck out by giving me this chance, and I'm going to do all I can to succeed.

Recently we have had a few run-ins. George Briggs works harder than anyone else around here and perhaps the pressure of the last few years is getting to him. I wish he'd take a vacation this year and get away for a month and just relax. He hasn't taken more than a week off in the nine years I've been here, and for the last two years he hasn't taken any vacation. I can see the strain is taking its toll. Recently he has been on my back for all kinds of little things. He always was a worrier, but lately he has been testing me on numerous small issues. He keeps throwing out suggestions or second-guessing me on things I've spent weeks working on with the field people.

I try to assure him I'll be all right, and I've asked him help me with the finance and production people, who have had a tough time keeping up with our sales organization. It has been rough lately but I'm sure it will work out. Sooner or later George will accept the fact that though I will never be able to run things the way he did, I can still get the job done for him.

Victor Perkins, 39, vice president of personnel.

I feel that George Briggs is threatened by Evans's seeming success with the field sales people. I don't think he realizes it, but he is probably jealous of the speed with which Tom has taken charge. In all likelihood, he didn't expect Tom to be able to handle the field people as well as he has, as fast as he has. When George put Tom in the job, I had a feeling that he was looking forward to having him need much more help and advice from "the old skipper." Tom does need help and advice, but he is getting most of what George will offer from his own subordinates and his peers. As a result, he has created a real team spirit below and around him, but he has upset George in the process.

George not only has trouble seeing Tom depend so much on his subordinates, but I feel that he resents Tom's unwillingness to let him show him how he used to run the sales force.

I may be wrong about this, of course. I am sure that George honestly believes that Tom's style will get him in trouble sooner or later. George is no doddering old fool who has to relive his past success in lower-level jobs. In the past, I'm told, he has shown real insight and interest in the big-picture aspects of the company. The trouble is he knows he was an outstanding sales manager, but I am not sure he has the same confidence in his ability as vice president. I have seen this time and again, particularly in recent years. When a person begins to doubt his future, he sometimes drops back and begins to protect his past. With more competition from younger subordinates and the new methods that they often bring in, many of our experienced people find that doing their job the way they used to just isn't good enough anymore. Some reach out and seek new responsibilities to prove their worth. Others, however, return to the things they used to excel in and try to show that theirs is still the best way to do things. They don't even seem to realize that this puts them in direct competition with their subordinates.

What do we do about this? I wish I knew! At lower levels, where you have more room to shift people around, you have more options. When the company is growing rapidly, the problem often takes care of itself. In this case, I am not sure what I would recommend if Ben Petersen asks my advice. Moving Tom to personnel at this time not only won't help me (I really don't have a spot for him), but also won't help Briggs or Evans either. Moving Evans now would be wasteful of the time and effort we've put in his development. It may also reverse some important team-building trends Tom has begun within the sales force.

If Briggs were seven or eight years older we could wait it out. If the company were growing faster, we might be able to shift people. As things stand, however, I see only one approach as a possibility, and I'm not sure it will work. I would recommend that we get busy reinforcing Briggs's attention on the vice president's job and get him to see that there is where he must put his time and effort. Perhaps the best thing would be to send him to one of the longer senior-executive programs. Don't forget he is a very bright and experienced person who still has a great deal to offer the company if we can figure out how to help him.

Benjamin Petersen has agreed to talk with George Briggs about Tom Evans tomorrow afternoon.

FOR DISCUSSION AND REPORT-WRITING

Organizing: Structural Design

1) How might the Briggs–Evans conflict be dealt with by making structural changes in the organization? What would be the effect of any changes in organization on a) Briggs, b) Evans, c) Evans's peers, and d) Evans's subordinates?

2) Why didn't Briggs' concerns about Evans surface when Evans occupied either of his two previous staff positions?

3) If Evans continues to "succeed" in developing more participative, team-building techniques with his peers and subordinates, how will Briggs's duties, authority, and accountability be affected?

Human Factors in Organizing

4) How does Evans's style of management affect the potential for his subordinates and peers to satisfy a fuller range of needs through work?

5) How does Evans's style of management affect Briggs's capacity to satisfy his higher-order needs through work?

6) How will the power and influence of the vice president of marketing change if Evans is permitted to continue doing things his own way and sales continue to improve?

7) What would be the advantages and disadvantages to a) Evans and b) the company of shifting Evans to a job in personnel at this time?

8) If Evans is shifted to another division or leaves the company, what characteristics should Petersen press for in his replacement?

9) (Summary Report Question: Part Two) Assume the president refuses to move Evans at this time and decides to shift Briggs's focus to the broader, longer-range, strategic aspects of his job as vice president of marketing. Develop a detailed action plan for implementing this solution. Specify what steps Petersen should take, in what sequence, and give a rough timetable indicating when each step should be taken.

Planning: Elements of Rational Decision-Making

10) In what ways does Evans's lack of field-sales experience affect the chances of his contributing to creative solutions to field sales problems? Consider both pluses and minuses in your answer.

11) How does Evans's lack of field-sales experience affect his ability to make difficult judgmental decisions? Consider each of the key elements involved in "Comparing Courses of Action." If you feel that he may lack strength to carry out one or more of these elements, how should he compensate for such weaknesses?

Planning: Decision-Making in an Enterprise

12) How might standing plans relieve Briggs of some of his concerns about Evans? How might such standing plans affect Evans's ability to manage the field-sales organization?

13) In what aspects of planning does Evans most need help from Briggs? How should he go about getting this help?

Controlling

14) In what ways might Briggs measure and evaluate Evans so as to reduce his concern that Evans may get into serious difficulties?

15) Using your answer to question 14, what effect might this control system have on Evans a) personally and b) in terms of his effectiveness?

Activating

16) Assume that Petersen has decided not to approve Briggs's request to transfer or remove Evans at this time (see question 9). Prepare to play the role of Petersen and illustrate, in a role play, how this decision should be communicated to Briggs. Should Petersen seek compliance or commitment from Briggs on this decision?

17) Consider the differences in Briggs's and Evans's styles of management. From what you know of their primary styles, which is more likely to be able to shift back and forth between seeking compliance and seeking commitment from subordinates when situations require different activating modes?

Summary Question for Solution of the Case as a Whole

18) If you were Petersen, what action would you take in the Briggs–Evans situation? Consider answers to questions 9 and 16 in particular, but do not feel constrained to follow these approaches. Be specific about what steps you would take and how you would evaluate the success of your plan. If your primary plan appeared unsuccessful, what would be your contingency plan?

PART A—Top-Down

It was past midnight as Anne Forsythe closed the garage door, collected her notes from the car, and entered the house. The lights were off downstairs, but she was pleased to see the light from her husband's reading lamp as she tiptoed upstairs.

"Thank goodness Hank's awake," she thought. "I felt guilty dashing out tonight leaving instructions with Jason about their dinner. Why did I ever get involved with this school board? Now, if I can just get Hank to not insist on my rehashing tonight's meeting, perhaps I can unwind."

Anne, a tall, attractive woman, had worked for ten years as a legal secretary before "retiring" to raise a family. Her husband, a lawyer, had taken a real interest in having Anne maintain her interest in the law and now, after almost nine years of night school, she looked forward to completing a law degree this spring. With their oldest child in college and Jason leaving in the fall, Anne was determined to get out and find a full-time job.

"I agreed a year ago to serve on our local school board," she said, "as a first step to using my education to do more than ferry around four-foot-high people in stationwagons. I had no idea, however, how much time it would take and, worse, how much time was wasted on politics and on the wrong issues."

The Merchantville School System

Merchantville, Ohio, is a suburb of Cleveland, with a population of 32,000. Its board of education consists of nine members, who serve for three-year terms with a turnover of three members per year. For many years, Merchantville has been one of the most popular suburban communities because of the reputation of the school system. Real estate commands a ten to 20 percent higher price than in neghboring communities, and while these other communities rose up in arms over spiraling school costs, Merchantville residents supported systems budgets. One of the reasons for Merchantville's excellent reputation has been its superintendent of schools, John Newland. With more than 40 years experience as an educator and administrator, Newland has acquired national recognition among educational administrators. During his 18 years in Merchantville, he has maintained excellent relations with both the professional staff and the community.

Although his critics consider him more of a salesman and politician than an educator, they had little basis for faulting his results until four years ago. At that time, a bond issue for a new elementary school was presented to the voters. The proposal stirred up much controversy because of debate on where to situate the new building, and the board of education worked long hours to deal with the many problems that arose.

Citizen groups organized, took sides, and for the first time many who moved to Merchantville because of its schools got involved.

Before this time, the board met twice a month except for the last two months of the year, when teacher evaluation and budget reviews increased the number of meetings to four, or even five, a month. During the 18 months of controversy surrounding the new building, the board was required to meet at numerous hearings and citizen-sponsored "cottage parties." During this same period, legislative changes led to recognition of the Merchantville Teachers Association as a legal bargaining unit—a union. Given Merchantville's reputation, teacher union officials from all over the state sought to "help" its teachers. At that time, the Merchantville Board of Education considered hiring a professional to negotiate with their teachers. Their decision not to do so was based on a promise from the Teachers Association that they would not use state union help if the board didn't use outsiders either. As a result, the board negotiating team (three members) frequently had to meet two or three nights a week for several months to bring about a contract agreement.

John Newland

During that 18-month period four years ago [Newland said], the whole character of the board and their perception of their role changed. In the past, being a board member was an honor and required little work. Running the system was left to the professionals. During that period everything changed. Meetings ran past midnight and were frequently called for Saturday, as well as two or three meetings, "cottage parties," and hearings on weeknights. There was a great deal to be done, but it took more time than it should because the board wasn't used to doing it.

We had two elections during that period, and with the growing awareness in the community of how much work was involved, the traditional board types wouldn't run. Instead, we got a lot of candidates who were liberal thinkers and who not only supported education but also thought they knew more about it than the professionals. As a result, our board is now about evenly divided into two groups. The first are those who realize they have a full-time staff to run the system and should get involved only on broad policy matters. The second group feels the professionals are too traditional and slow to change, and thus they want to get into the details of running the system. I could keep this group out of my hair when they were busy with the new building and negotiations, but now these things have settled down and they don't have enough to do. They want all kinds of citizen, teacher, and board committees to get into every aspect of the system. Believe me, it will be a disaster if they get control of the board. I've seen these well-intentioned, frustrated "educators" ruin a school district before.

In my 40 years I have beaten back some such efforts and left communities where I couldn't. With less than five years until retirement, however, I don't feel like fighting and have no intention of moving.

A year and a half ago two high school teachers approached the new principal with a proposal for an experimental course. One, an older man, was a long-service history teacher; the other, a young woman, was a nontenured member of the English department. They asked the principal to permit them to team-teach a new elective course on current social issues. Their idea was to combine readings from history and English literature with current-events topics.

Dan Kneep, the high school principal, said, "I liked the idea, particularly when they told me they would teach the course twice in the first year and ask for only one course credit each. In this way they were bearing the extra cost of team-teaching.

"If the course was successful, I told them we would consider making this a permanent elective and providing for its staffing. As an experimental course, with no extra cost, I figured I could approve it on my own. Since I'm new and lack tenure, however, I thought I would play it safe, so I checked with the two department chairmen involved. The chairman of the history department was skeptical but, given the stature of his senior colleague in history who proposed it, he raised no objections. The chairman of the English department indicated that she thought it a good idea and so I approved it."

The course was offered in the spring of last year and again in the fall and this spring. Although the number of students was small at first, the class had to be closed at 30 both terms this year. When the two teachers requested that Kneep approve the course as a permanent elective, he did so. Formal approval of a permanent course requires approval by the superintendent after review by the director of curriculum, Jesse Lake.

The Director of Curriculum's Report

Jesse Lake is the second in command in the Merchantville school system. He had earned his doctorate in education and had taught for 15 years before becoming superintendent of a small school district. Though successful as superintendent, Lake did not like the administrative work and the politics, and accepted his present post at Merchantville nine years ago.

I thoroughly enjoy working for Dr. Newland [Lake said], "and I respect him as an educator and as a person. He knows how to pick good staff people and get the best out of them. Mine is a difficult job in many districts. Technically, I am a staff person and have no line authority over teachers and principals. Although I am legally responsible for the district in the superintendent's absence, he is the boss. In many school systems the assistant superintendent is regarded as a flunky or staff nuisance. Thanks to John, I have considerable influence here.

I think it's a crime to see him badgered by some segments of the community and some of the new-breed board members. They come in with half-baked ideas by the bushel and no real sense of their implications. Then they try to shove them down our throats, and by the time it is clear that they won't work, the instigators have left the board and start pestering the planning board or police commissioner.

Lake has reviewed Kneep's request for the new course to be made a permanent elective and recommends it be rejected. In his report he states:

. . . my opinions are based on my own experience plus interviews with all parties. I have carefully reviewed the course syllabus and find insufficient evidence of intellectual or methodological substance to justify its place in our curriculum.

Although there is no doubt that this is a popular course with the students, this popularity cannot be linked to intellectual stimulation. Rather, it is a function of their interest in what they call "relevant" issues. It is my belief that today's young people use the term "relevant" to apply to any issue that is sufficiently topical and debatable to lead them to believe that their hastily considered opinions are worth accepting as truths.

The proposed course would cater to only a relatively small number of select students, whereas the school would be better served by innovations that affect most, if not all, students. The quality of our instruction (and our general reputation) is judged by the scores our students make in national tests, and this course would contribute little toward that end. If it were an effort to bring up the lowest percentile of those scores, it would derive stronger support.

Finally, I am certain that this course's popularity is directly traceable to the pedagogical skills of the two teachers involved. I strongly recommend that these skills be applied to existing courses whose proven value to the curriculum deserves their talents. I have discussed this matter with the two department chairmen and they both support my recommendation.

Anne Forsythe

"Well, what great matters of state kept you so late tonight?" Hank asked as Anne dropped wearily in a chair.

"I was hoping you wouldn't ask," she replied. "We got a petition tonight signed by several hundred students and parents protesting our decision to drop some course. Frankly, I didn't even know we had this course, let alone that we were dropping it."

"What is the course about?" Hank asked.

"I haven't the foggiest idea. We spent three hours debating the procedure for approving courses and whether the board should get involved in this kind of issue at all. The board was split right down the middle. Four members made it clear that they feel Lake is too traditional and that Newland is not interested in getting involved in curriculum issues. They want the board involved in curriculum changes. Another four were split between those who sort of agree with the others and those who disagree and think Lake is right. These four, however, agree that it is wrong for the board to deal with this kind of issue because it opens the way for more and more board involvement in the day-to-day running of the system. I am certain that had we voted, we would have had a four-four tie."

"Aren't there nine members?" Hank asked.

"Yes," said Anne, "and I'm the ninth. Here I haven't even passed the bar exam, and I feel like a judge. I feel pulled two ways. I agree that Lake is too traditional and slow to change and that Newland won't rock the boat unless we push him. But, I don't want the board having to battle with that seasoned old campaigner. Even if we won, we would not know what to do to run the system and we certainly can't fire John."

"Well, how will you vote?"

"I hope I won't have to. John postponed a formal vote and indicated that he would review the recommendation. If he comes in tomorrow night and reverses himself to support the course, we will probably be off the hook. If he doesn't, then I will have to make up my mind. Apparently, the high school principal is wavering in his support. He is new enough to not know what is 'right' but savvy enough to know he is likely to get caught in the middle. Lake is highly regarded by Newland and by most of the teachers. Some of the newer ones get a bit impatient with him, but almost everyone respects him. Well, let's get some sleep."

PART B—BOTTOM-UP

"You can't imagine how surprised and let down, and then mad, I was when Mr. Lake and Mr. Newland vetoed our Current Social Issues course," Sandra Savas sighed. "That course is a great way of capturing student interest and making their school work relevant to the exciting events going on every day. Why the top brass is slapping us down instead of urging us on I just don't understand."

The course had been given on an experimental basis by Sandra Savas and Martin Reis. The enthusiastic response by both students and teachers led to a request that the course be made a regular elective.

Savas came to Merchantville High School as an English teacher two years ago. Because of her strong record in both academic studies and student affairs at Smith College, school officials were pleased when she accepted their offer. Savas has become a popular teacher. She also became immediately active in the county teachers' association, and especially in a workshop concerned with making the study of English more appealing to high school students. In fact, the Current Social Issues experiment was one of the projects fully discussed in the workshop this year.

Martin Reis, who team-taught the Social Issues course with Savas, is an untypical history teacher. During his 15 years at Merchantville, he has frequently given special sections of courses for bright students, and worked on outside projects with students he felt were motivated to move into college-level studies. He expects and usually gets a lot of work from his students. The joint venture with Savas was quite in character, and the precedent of previous successful ventures contributed to the prompt endorsement of the experimental course by the chairmen of the history and English departments.

Department chairmen in the Merchantville High School have a rather ambiguous position. They are regular teachers, usually with long service at Merchantville, who are asked to "coordinate materials in various courses, assist newly hired teachers, and advise the school principal on personnel matters." Department chairmen are usually given a little relief from teaching because of their duties as chairmen. In a formal sense, however, all teachers report to the principal.

The principal, Dan Kneep, is the administrative head of the school. He has an assistant principal for student counseling and a director of physical education; so he is expected to give much of his time to academic matters. Under the superintendent of schools are buildings and grounds, personnel, and financial divisions, which serve all the schools in the local system.

From typical day-to-day contacts, the history and English department chairmen have learned about the Current Social Issues experiment and the formal proposal. Over the years, the history chairman has become quite relaxed about Reis's ventures; he commented to Dan Kneep, "Reis soaks up some juvenile restlessness in a very constructive manner, and since most of his special sections come in the senior year—like this latest one on Social Issues—they don't upset our regular work."

The English department chairman likes Savas's enthusiasm but has explained to her, "We're under pressure to show up well on the state and national achievement tests. There is a lot of public outcry about students not knowing how to spell or write an English sentence, and a school like ours can't afford to be low on the lists."

Savas's response was, "We give more, not less, written work in the Social Issues course, and I watch the quality of work very closely. I'll guarantee that students in the course have scores well above the average for our senior class. And what's more important, those students will remember the value of clear, clean, convincing statements because they see its importance in what they read and in the action reports we ask them to write. Let me show you some—or all—of the reports turned in last Friday."

After further discussion, the English department chairman suggested that Savas and Reis submit a request for switching the course from experimental to regular status. Dan Kneep talked about the proposal with both of the sponsors, complimented them on their initiative, and said he would recommend that the school board approve it.

Six weeks later word came that "the need to focus resources on higher-priority objectives prevents approval of the suggested course at this time."

"What a shocker that was," said Savas. "I had assumed that with Kneep's endorsement we were all set. Before taking this Merchantville job, I asked whether teachers had freedom in designing at least some of their own courses. I was assured that 'the school is run on a decentralized basis, because we realize learning depends on the interaction between each teacher and individual students.' And until this turndown, that seemed to be the way it worked."

Savas and Reis talked about what to do next. Reis said, "We just haven't made a clear case. My impression is that plenty of support exists in Merchantville for a course like this, at least as an elective. Since we preach democracy, why don't we let the students and maybe their parents decide whether this is the kind of education they want? We might be wrong ourselves." "O.K.," responded Savas, "I know several students well enough to get their candid opinion. I'll ask them what they think."

FOR DISCUSSION AND REPORT-WRITING

Organizing: Structural Design

1) What do you think of Savas's statement that she had been "assured that 'the school is run on a decentralized basis . . .' " and that "until this turndown, that seemed to be the way it worked"?

2) How should the Board of Education reconcile its stated role as "policy makers" with the nature of the school system's organization?

3) How will Newland's decision affect Lake's a) formal authority and b) power and/or influence?

4) Could any new approaches to organization design help to balance the needs of the total organization with those of individual teachers? Discuss.

Human Factors in Organizing

5) In what ways might efforts to spell out "customs and roles" reduce potential conflict between a) board and top "management" and b) teachers and top "management"? Do you recommend such efforts? Explain.

6) How will Newland's decision affect the potential for "needs satisfied through work" of a) the board, b) Lake, c) Kneep, d) the two teachers, and e) the student body as a whole? Whose needs should be given top priority in the long-run interest of quality education?

7) How would you characterize the real or potential conflict within the board and between the board and the superintendent? How would you recommend these conflicts be reconciled? Be specific.

8) Within the school system's current organization, how should individual teachers be evaluated? How should department chairmen be evaluated? How should Lake be evaluated?

9) Since Newland and Lake both have tenure, what power does the board have in getting its "policies" implemented?

10) (Summary Report Question: Part Two) What action should Newland take on the controversy growing out of this course? What other steps should Newland take to deal with potential problems arising from your recommendations about his decision?

Planning: Elements of Rational Decision-Making

11) How would a decision by Newland to overrule Lake affect creativity in the curriculum? Consider the longer-term effect on the total curriculum, *not* on this or any other single course.

12) How should Newland weigh the costs and benefits associated with his decision to support or overrule Lake's recommendation? Consider a format or mechanism for such weighing.

Planning: Decision-Making
in an Enterprise

13) How may Lake's goals differ from those of individual teachers? How might such differences be reconciled?

14) Is it possible for the board and Newland to develop a "master strategy" for the school system? How might such a strategy be developed? How might such a strategy a) avoid such disputes as the one arising from this course or b) provide a basis for reconciling such disputes?

15) What standing plans might be developed to reduce the likelihood of such disputes a) reaching the board or b) being more easily resolved if they do come to the board?

Controlling

16) How might the board evaluate how well their policies are being implemented? Be specific about standards and measurements the board might employ.

17) Forecast the response at each level in the system to the controls suggested in your answer to question 16.

Activating

18) "Petitions from students and parents to the board are excellent means of assuring active two-way communication." Comment on this statement made by a parent at an open board meeting.

19) If Savas and Reis had anticipated Lake's negative response, what might they have done, *before* making a formal proposal, to activate a more positive response? Be specific about *a)* what, *b)* when, *c)* how they might have acted, and indicate how this might have shifted Lake's feelings about the course.

Summary Question for Solution of
the Case as a Whole

20) Assume Newland supports Lake's position and argues that this is an administrative decision and not a proper matter for board consideration. *a)* What action(s) should Anne Forsythe take? *b)* What action(s) should Savas and Reis take?

PART III

Planning is a basic management task, one that has a major place in our overall division of management functions along with organizing, controlling, and activating. In every company, managers must decide on a host of issues: production schedules, what services to provide, what price to charge, how to deal with pressure groups, whom to employ, when to collaborate with the government, and many other matters. Planning is not a manager's only task, but is certainly an essential one. Without managerial decisions about actions to be taken, employees would be as confused as ants in an upturned anthill.

Professor Graham Allison, in his trail-blazing analysis of governmental decision-making, uses three models. He 1) considers what a *rational person* would decide, 2) examines how formal organization and established procedures affect decision-making (this he calls the "bureaucratic" model), and 3) views decisions as *political* choices. In Parts Three and Four we shall apply this insightful framework to business enterprises.

From a managerial viewpoint, rational decision-making provides the best approach—or model—to start our analysis. So in Part Three we examine the main steps rational executives should follow in selecting a plan of action. Then in Part Four we complicate—and add realism to—this planning process, first by noting how organization planning is done, then by adding intraorganization political behavior. By combining Allison's three models in this sequence, a manager can blend the most recent and sophisticated planning concepts into a practical, applicable process.

In Part Three, then, our aim is to analyze rational decision-making as though one person undertook the whole process alone; at least we set aside for the moment the complications that arise when the process is divided among many people. Such a concentration on the elements of decision-making has several advantages. Many plans *are,* in fact, made largely by one person, and if we can

Planning: Elements of
Rational Decision-Making

discover ways to improve our own decision-making skills, we will be able to make such decisions better. Furthermore, by recognizing all the phases that contribute to wise decisions, we can see more clearly—in Part Four—how a particular organization setup helps or hinders the making of good decisions. And with the elements of decision-making in mind, we can also see better how political behavior modifies rational choice.

There are four essential phases in rational decision-making, each of which is examined in a separate chapter.

Chapter 11—Diagnosis: A Prerequisite for Sound Decisions. The first, perhaps the most difficult, and often an overlooked phase in decision-making is a thorough diagnosis of the problem or opportunity to be dealt with.

Chapter 12—The Creative Element in Decision-Making. Here we are concerned with finding good alternative solutions to the problems identified by diagnosis. Because no company can be a leader by copying what someone else is already doing, we give considerable attention to how new ideas are born and to what an individual can do to make maximum use of whatever creative ability he possesses.

Chapter 13—Comparing Courses of Action. To choose among alternative courses of action, we must predict for each alternative what would happen if we followed that course. We must then compare the different results. Because a projection and comparison of alternatives can become complex, this chapter includes suggestions for simplification.

Chapter 14—Making the Choice. Finally we shall discuss how to deal with differences in values and in degrees of uncertainty when making a firm decision to follow one of the alternatives.

Diagnosis: A Prerequisite
for Sound Decisions

11

RATIONAL DECISION-MAKING

A manager is more than a decision-maker. He also organizes, controls, and activates. But none of his other activities are more important than making wise decisions. We will be concerned here with managerial planning-decisions—that is, decisions about *actions to be taken* in his department or company. These are crucial.

Use of Rational Process

In Western society, with its heavy emphasis on science and utilitarianism, we take for granted that the best decisions are made by *rational* choice. There are alternative ways of selecting a plan—intuition, precedent, voting, divine guidance—but in a purposeful organization such as a business firm, it is the rational decision that is widely believed to be the best.

In spite of this very high regard for rationality, in our actual behavior there is a striking failure to follow the basic steps of rational decision-making. Our personal plans typically are not fully rational, and managers often rely on other methods in making their plans. Unfortunately, rational decision-making is hard work; and both skill and wisdom are required in its use. So as a practical matter we can use the rational process for only the more important decisions we make. Even this limited and selective use takes considerable disciplined effort.

Fundamentally, rational decision-making is quite simple The four essen-

228

PART III
Planning:
Elements of
Rational
Decision-Making

tial phases are: 1) diagnosing the problem, 2) searching for the most promising alternative solutions, 3) analyzing and comparing these alternatives, and 4) selecting the best alternative as a plan of action. Before we describe these phases in detail, let us note their general applicability.

Problem-solving in medicine. A doctor follows all four parts of this procedure in examining a patient to find out what is wrong and in prescribing a course of action. In practice the diagnosis may not be easy, because the same symptoms can result from a number of quite different causes. Special tests may be necessary to identify the underlying cause. Clearly, if the wrong cause is assumed—say, appendicitis instead of gallstones—treatment will be ineffective, even disastrous. Many of the recent advances in medicine deal with better diagnosis.

Having made a sound diagnosis, the doctor then considers possible remedies—such as changes in diet, medication, or surgery. Some remedies will be standard practice, but if the patient has limitations—a weak heart or allergies, for instance—other possible treatments must be considered. Next the doctor must weigh the advantages and disadvantages of each possible cure in a specific case. How long will the patient be incapacitated? Are the necessary resources—professional aid, equipment, money—available? Finally, the doctor uses his judgment in selecting what he believes is the best plan, or "prescription," for each case. He considers the probability of success and the risk of complications. He may decide to try a simple remedy before taking more drastic measures. Perhaps he considers it wise to do nothing at present, or he may call for an ambulance to rush his patient to a hospital. Every responsible doctor goes through these steps: diagnosis, review of possible remedies, analysis of probable results, and prescription.

Solving social problems. The decision-making process becomes less clear when we tackle social problems. Objectives, alternatives, and results are all likely to be subject to debate. Take the ownership of guns by private citizens. From one view, homicides would be reduced if fewer people had guns. But possible homicide is not the only consideration. Guns are allowed for personal protection and for sport; so the intervening objective shifts to regulation of ownership and use. The alternatives here are numerous, and nobody can be sure just how any one plan will work in practice. Nevertheless, as we start to wrestle with a problem, our thinking becomes clearer and data can be marshaled more effectively when we resort to rational analysis. What are the objectives? Have we thought of all the good alternatives? What will be the costs, side effects, and the contribution to the objectives of each alternative? Which alternative looks best in terms of the values we attach to costs, side effects, and the original objective?

In practice, getting agreement on the diagnosis, defining alternatives, obtaining reliable information from specialists on the existing situation, forecasting what will happen, especially in an uncertain environment, and winning enough support to justify positive action are by no means simple. Conflicting interest groups will deliberately muddy the waters. But these difficulties make

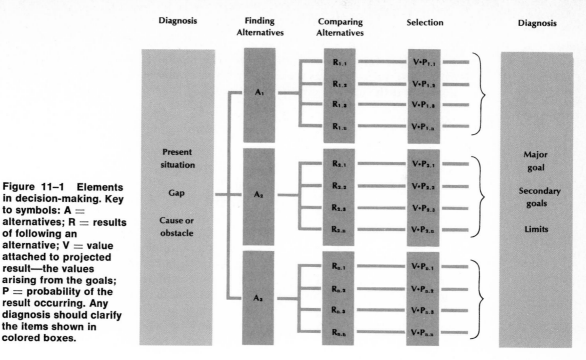

Figure 11-1 Elements in decision-making. Key to symbols: A = alternatives; R = results of following an alternative; V = value attached to projected result—the values arising from the goals; P = probability of the result occurring. Any diagnosis should clarify the items shown in colored boxes.

a firm grasp of the rational process even more valuable. Experience indicates that only a small percentage of people have the insight and self-discipline necessary to apply rational decision-making to muddied "people" problems.

Understanding All Phases

Each of the four phases of rational decision-making will be examined in a separate chapter in this Part. We will be concerned in each chapter with 1) helping incumbent and potential managers improve their personal skills, and 2) providing a basis for assessing the way subordinates are making plans. However, the four phases build one upon another, as indicated in Figure 11-1; so to solve actual managerial problems, we should bring all four phases to bear. Unusual proficiency in one phase cannot be substituted for neglect of another.[1]

The sequence of chapters aids in presenting ideas, but it is not intended to be a rigid procedure. Few problems yield to a neat step-by-step procedure: new alternatives may pop up at any time; a problem often needs to be redefined as the analysis proceeds and values are formulated; fact-gathering and judgment permeate the entire process. Therefore, we are considering a mental *framework* rather than a procedure. In a general way, we do work through the phases in the sequence listed, but our minds are apt to jump from one phase to

---

[1] A major obstacle to greater use of management science and microeconomics concepts is their heavy emphasis on comparing alternatives and making a choice, but scant or no attention to diagnosis and finding good alternatives for the particular situation facing a manager.

230

PART III
Planning:
Elements of
Rational
Decision-Making

another in a continuing effort to refine our previous thinking. We bring clear reasoning and focused attention out of such mental rambling only when we have a framework—such as the four phases just outlined—that aids us in relating facts and thoughts in a rational pattern.

THE CRUCIAL ROLE OF DIAGNOSIS

Accurate diagnosis is the essential first phase of sound decision-making. Unless the diagnosis is correct, subsequent planning will be misdirected and wasteful.

The love of quick action—and perhaps an illusion of omniscience—makes some administrators impatient with careful diagnosis and detailed planning. Even if they admit a need for planning, they are confident that they know what their problems are. They are so anxious to get moving that they neglect to take time to check the direction in which they are heading. One impetuous president, for example, pushed through extensive plans for sales promotion, brushing aside any question about who were the right customers. Later, careful diagnosis showed that he was working with a declining segment of the market; even if the sales promotion had been an outstanding success, the recovery of company sales would have been only temporary. The president might just as well have made this correct diagnosis earlier and avoided the wasted sales effort.

Sound diagnosis should cover three basic elements, which are highlighted in the following questions:

1) Just what *gaps* exist between the results we desire and the existing or predicted state of affairs?
2) What are the direct, root *cause* and the intermediate causes of the gaps?
3) Does the broader *context* of the problem place limits within which we must find a satisfactory solution?

We shall first examine the way these three elements can be used in diagnosing a *recognized need;* then at the end of the chapter, we shall consider diagnosing total situations in which attention is not yet focused on a single recognized need.

STATING THE PROBLEM OR OPPORTUNITY IN TERMS OF A GAP

When a doctor makes a diagnosis, he has as a goal a healthy person; he also has a fairly clear concept of what a healthy person is. With this model as the "desired" result, he looks for disparities in the patient's actual state of health or factors which indicate that his future health will fall short of normal.

A manager unfortunately cannot rely on a similar commonly accepted norm. The activities he deals with are so diverse that no single set of symptoms can guide him in locating what is wrong. Instead, a manager's diagnosis starts with a "felt difficulty." He may *feel* that something is wrong, or he may vaguely sense that "things could be better." Perhaps he compares other companies' accomplishments with those of his own firm, or simply desires continuing growth and ever-lower costs. Whatever the source, diagnosis starts with sensing an opportunity for improvement. To go further, however, he must sharpen this intuitive feeling as best as he can into more explicit statements of desired and actual (or predicted) results, so that the felt difficulty or opportunity can be viewed more *precisely* in terms of a gap that must be closed.

When there is a clearcut distinction between, say, quality standards and actual or anticipated quality, he can promptly move on to the next element of diagnosis. But many gaps are not so clearly defined. A manager may have only a vague feeling, which he might express as, "Our New England branch should do a lot better," or "I believe Simpson has good potential but is not living up to it." He needs to sharpen these statements before he can proceed with his diagnosis. He might restate his general dissatisfaction with the New England branch thus: "Based on performance of our other branches, and adjusting for differences between branches, New England should get twenty percent more sales without any increase in expenses." This declaration makes the problem a lot clearer. With respect to Simpson it would be more meaningful to say, "Based on aptitude and motivation, Simpson appears to have the capacity to be a regional sales manager in three to five years" (*desired*). "His failure to keep turnover of salesmen to desired levels and his inability to develop new business has produced less than expected results" (*actual*).

Likewise, a particular event that provokes our attention may not be the problem. Our company's financial statement, for instance, may show a loss for last month. In common speech we might express the problem this way: "What are we going to do about the loss?" By itself, however, this is an incomplete statement of the problem. For management to proceed, this general statement

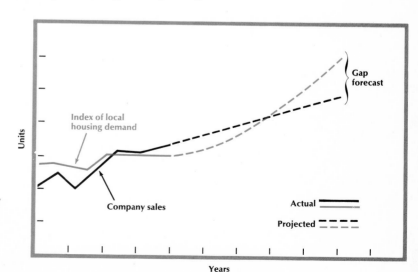

Figure 11–2   A gap may exist between forecasts of future conditions and present company plans, as shown in this five-year projection of a mobile-housing contractor.

232

PART III
Planning:
Elements of
Rational
Decision-Making

must be refined by indicating what returns are expected and the premises on which the "desired" financial picture is based.

Once a problem or opportunity is identified in terms of a gap between desired and actual or predicted results, many decision-makers move immediately to seek alternative means of closing this gap. We should avoid this temptation, though, because seeking alternatives at this stage is premature for two reasons:

1) Although the gap between desired and actual or predicted results has been brought into focus, for many situations the root cause of the gap is at this point likely to be at best vague and at worst incorrectly identified. Until that cause has been defined, alternatives designed to close it are likely to fail or to provide only costly relief of symptoms.

2) Unless the gap is defined in terms of very high-level goals, the objective that we have specified is likely to be merely a *means* of accomplishing one or more higher-level *ends* or goals. Before alternatives to closing the gap are sought, then, these higher-level goals should be identified. This exploration of the broader situation often uncovers organizational limits on such matters as time, investment, or personnel—limits that must be observed if the solution is to be consistent with the higher-level goals of the organization. Also if the stated gap proves tough to overcome, we may want to consider alternative ways of reaching the higher goal.

FINDING THE ROOT CAUSE

Search for Key Obstacle

As the decision-maker seeks alternatives for closing the gap, he usually does so with some notion of its cause. All too often, however, this intuitive and at times subconscious assumption about causality may be only symptomatic of the underlying cause or perhaps not even related to the real cause.

For example, in the early days of frozen foods, manufacturers had a difficult time reaching what they believed to be desirable sales levels. Initially, attempts to close this gap between desired and actual sales were made through consumer advertising. Lack of consumer interest in the product seemed a logical cause of low sales. Further, the manufacturers assumed that the source of the indifference was a lack of understanding about the properties and advantages of frozen food. Only after experiencing limited success with advertising designed to educate the consumer did they undertake a more careful quest for the cause.

Studies revealed that, although consumer interest in frozen foods was indeed limited, the major cause of low sales was the reluctance of retailers to stock an adequate supply. The retailers, understandably enough, wished to avoid investing several hundred dollars in refrigerated showcases. Had the manufacturers continued to bombard the consumer, they might have used customer demand to force the retailers to make the investment. This course, however, would have been an expensive way of overcoming the now-obvious obstacle of retailers' reluctance to invest in showcases. But having located the basic impediment, the manufacturers could now devise methods for lending or leasing showcases to hesitant dealers.

At times, then, in searching for a cause or an obstacle, we may have to seek the cause or the apparent cause, to push deeper and deeper until the *root* cause has been identified. Kepner-Tregoe Associates, management consultants who have focused on diagnosis, suggest two key guides for the identification of causes.[2]

First, in trying to determine why some goal is frustrated, a decision-maker should concentrate on the differences between situations where the desired goal *is* realized and those where *it is not*. Consider, as a simple illustration, the problem faced by a sales manager who is trying to unearth the cause of late field reports from his sales representatives. If some of the representatives get them in on time while others do not, the explanation may be related to the differences in the individuals or their work environment. By exploring these differences, by spelling them out in terms of *what, where,* and *when,* the manager could formulate a number of hypothetical causes. If he found that most of the late reports occurred repeatedly in certain district offices, an elaboration on the differences between district offices might lead to the cause. However, if he discovered that all districts had this problem, then he would have to look for differences in some other factor.

The second Kepner-Tregoe principle stresses the power of *negative* thinking in cause identification. Once a decision-maker has developed hypothetical causes, he should avoid seeking further evidence to support them, endeavoring instead to disprove them or "shoot them down." He should test them against all of the situations in which the problem exists and in which it does not. The logic behind this negative approach is this: Although a hundred reasons supporting a hypothetical cause as the real culprit may be found, this positive support can never *prove* guilt; however, if only *one* fact demonstrates that a suspected cause *could not* be the real one, the suspect can be eliminated.

Thus if hypothetical causes are tested against all the distinctions of what, when, and where, most proposals can be eliminated. By this process of elimination, the few candidates that remain, and thus *could* account for the differences, can be subjected to more detailed examination and testing.

Moving from Surface to Root Causes

Often in seeking the root cause of a problem, we have to move through several levels of causality. Even if the root cause can be found directly, it is well to identify intermediate levels of causality also. Later when looking for a solution, if the root cause cannot be eliminated, we may turn to symptomatic

[2] C.H. Kepner and B.B. Tregoe, *The Rational Manager* (New York: McGraw-Hill, 1965), Chaps. 5–9. Although dealing with business problems, the authors make explicit use of canons of logic expounded by John Stuart Mill over a century ago.

234

PART III
Planning:
Elements of
Rational
Decision-Making

relief by dealing with the more intermediate cause. For example, consider a situation described by a colleague of ours. A friend of his, who was in his late 60s, complained that late in the day he suffered blurred vision and then headaches and dizzy spells. An optometrist told him that his headaches and dizzy spells stemmed from moderate deterioration of the eyes, which in turn was the result of old age. Stopping the diagnosis here, the optometrist prescribed bifocal eyeglasses to compensate for the change in vision.

As a result of his difficulty in getting used to wearing his new bifocals, the man tripped on a step and bruised his hip. To be certain that it was just a bruise, he visited a doctor and in the course of his examination mentioned his blurred vision and headaches. The doctor then checked his blood pressure, which proved to be too high, and cited this as the primary cause of the vision and headache problems. To put the doctor's diagnosis in our terms, he had compared the patient's actual condition with a desired state of health and saw the announced symptoms as the cause of the difference. He, like the optometrist, did not stop there but asked, "What's causing the blurred vision and headaches?" The optometrist had assumed the basic cause was old age, but the doctor had gone one step further and had pinpointed high blood pressure as the immediate cause. He then asked, "If high blood pressure is causing the eye trouble, what's causing the high blood pressure?"

Here he made the same mistake as the optometrist and assumed that old age was the direct cause of the high blood pressure. As a result, he prescribed medication and change of diet to provide symptomatic relief for high blood pressure. He, too, treated the symptom because he could not deal with what he felt to be the root cause—old age.

Several months later, a routine visit to the dentist revealed that the doctor, like the optometrist, had failed because he had not pushed hard enough in his attempt to correctly identify all the intermediate causes of the problem. The dentist found that the doctor had missed an important link, a molar in which the nerve had died and decay had begun. The impurities introduced into the bloodstream by the decaying tooth were, in fact, the direct cause of the high blood pressure, which in turn was the cause of the eye trouble and headaches and dizziness.

This account illustrates the inadvisability of stopping a diagnosis at a first-level cause. Ask instead, "What's causing the cause?" and then, "What's causing the cause of the cause?" and so on until you have moved to the underlying fundamental cause. In our patient's situation—and the pun is built in—the root cause seems to have been the bad tooth.

The purist may argue that if we follow our own logic, we should not settle for the bad tooth as the root cause, but should ask instead, "What caused the bad tooth?" Then, with the optometrist and the medical doctor, we may point to old age. Even so, what we have accomplished by moving in a step-by-step progression to the most basic cause is to identify all the intermediary causes. This sequence is vital, for if the real root cause, old age, cannot be removed, we should focus on the next cause in the chain—the bad tooth—for it is at this level that symptomatic relief will hit closest to the root cause and hopefully be most effective.

Strictly speaking, unless we deal with the aging process directly, any treatment will be symptomatic. The closer we can come to the root cause, however, the more satisfactory the symptomatic treatment is likely to be.

Root Causes of a Motivation Problem

Because moving from superficial to ever-more-basic causes is of such great importance to effective diagnosis and thus to effective decision-making, let us consider one further example.

The BLW Company is experiencing a succession of resignations among black draftsmen in its Chicago plant. A superficial diagnosis indicates that the cause of the resignations is "low motivation." If at this point alternatives (solutions) are sought, we can imagine what they might look like: 1) higher pay (buy them happiness), 2) more office activities (another bowling team), 3) make a few awards for outstanding work (another wrist watch).

Any or all of these alternatives might work, but at this stage of investigation we are not sure whether low motivation is in fact the root cause. As a result, any alternatives based on correcting low motivation are likely to fail or at best provide symptomatic relief. Second, and more important, if low motivation is the direct cause, what is causing the low motivation? If, for example, motivation is low because the draftsmen lack proper training or must follow poor directions, none of the solutions just mentioned is likely to work. Even if one does work, it may be much more expensive than alternatives designed to get at the cause of the low motivation itself. The three proposals cited merely surround the basic problem with "human-relations gestures" in the hope that they may somehow get to the cause of the friction.

If, in this case, the low motivation is traced to poor training, which is in turn chargeable to inadequate staff, we may now tackle the root cause. But if budget constraints prevent staff additions, then the root cause, like old age in the previous example, may be taken as an unremovable obstacle, or *limiting factor,* which must be accepted as unchangeable. In that event, symptomatic relief will have to be sought by finding ways of compensating for the staff deficiencies.

Alternatively, it might be useful to reconsider higher-level goals that may be met without a prerequisite of high motivation based on sound supervision. This suggestion brings us to the step we should take after defining the problem but before searching thoroughly for alternatives.

EXAMINING THE PROBLEM IN LIGHT OF HIGHER-LEVEL GOALS

Unless a problem is defined in very sweeping terms, the recognized need is a *means* of accomplishing a more basic, higher-level *end* or goal. For instance, the problem of the late sales reports can be stated as follows:

236

PART III
Planning:
Elements of
Rational
Decision-Making

Desired: Field-sales reports for each month should be filed with district sales offices by the fifth working day of the next month.

Actual: Salespeople repeatedly submit these reports from one to six days late.

Although it is necessary to find the cause of the late reports, in many cases it would be wise to ask also, "Why do I want these reports by the fifth working day of the next month?" (see Fig. 11–3).

By asking "Why do I want . . . ," we can put this problem in perspective. Subsequently, when we seek and weigh alternatives, we can do so in light of the higher-order goals. Because getting these reports is only a *means* to an end, we are not interested in ways of reaching the means that conflict with the higher-level end. Any limits or constraints imposed by higher-level goals, then, should be stated specifically.

Suppose the answer to the question is "to provide the manufacturing department with accurate figures on which to base next month's production." Then we can be careful to seek alternative means of getting the reports in on time that are consistent with the need for accuracy. Moreover, for this purpose we are more concerned with product model numbers and delivery dates than with prices and how sales may tie into future business.

A milk company, to cite a similar example, gave the following instruction to a study team: "Do not submit any proposals unless estimated savings are over half a cent a quart." By knowing that the study aimed at finding a major gain, the team could fully understand this limit on acceptable alternatives. Product engineers often have to design not just a better product but one that is, say, faster than competitors' products or capable of being produced within a cost limit. The existence of such limits is often brought to light by extending the diagnosis of higher-level goals far enough to identify the full dimensions of a satisfactory solution.

Figure 11–3 Elementary means–end analysis. Diagnosis of a specific problem.

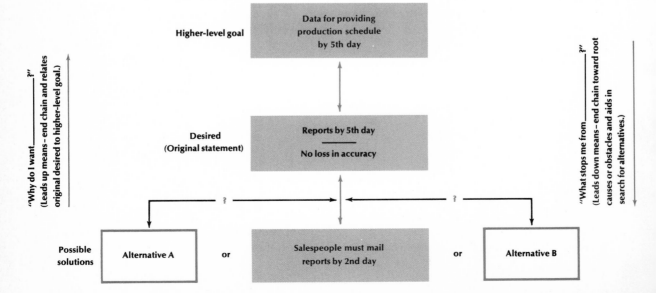

DIAGNOSIS OF THE WHOLE SITUATION

In the preceding discussion, we focused on diagnosis of a recognized need —either a specific difficulty or a known opportunity for improvement. We urged moving directly toward clarifying the gap between the actual and the desired, finding causes, and identifying limits. For most problems, such a diagnosis is all that is necessary.

At other times, though, a broader view may be essential. There are three main reasons why we may need to undertake a "diagnosis of the situation": 1) We may wish to redefine a recognized need because we cannot find an acceptable solution to the problem as originally stated. 2) Several problems may be so interdependent that we have to identify all of them and their interrelations before we can put them into a sequence for study and action. 3) We may feel that potential improvements have not been fully grasped by focusing on things piecemeal.

Broadening the Definition of the Problem

Moving up the means–end chain. The late-report problem discussed in the previous section provides a simple illustration of how diagnosis of the whole situation in terms of a means–end chain can be of great help in paving the way for a subsequent search for alternatives. If we are stymied in an attempt to speed up reports, we can seek *alternative* ways of meeting the ends toward which field reports are only one means. Stated another way, if we want these reports primarily to provide accurate information to the manufacturer by the fifth day of the month, and if we have trouble getting them on time, perhaps we should examine alternative ways of scheduling production.

Diagrammatically, this step "up" a means–end chain, wherein we move from lower- to higher-level goals, is shown in Fig. 11–4. It illustrates how we have broadened our inquiry from a diagnosis of a *specific problem*—late reports —to a diagnosis of the *situation* in which the problem exists.

Whether it proves desirable to solve our original problem or to seek ways of getting around it, can be determined after examination of the likely costs and benefits associated with various alternatives. By examining the higher-order goals before seeking alternatives to the problem, however, we open up a set of options that might otherwise have been overlooked. We can either continue to solve the "recognized need" within the context of this higher-level goal, or, if this proves difficult, we can bypass the original problem and seek alternatives that satisfy the higher-level goals by means other than field reports.

The possibility of redefining a problem by moving up a means–end chain can also be applied to the problem of low motivation in the drafting department, which we used in illustrating the search for root causes. Figure 11–5 illustrates how we might add several higher-level goals to the picture. While

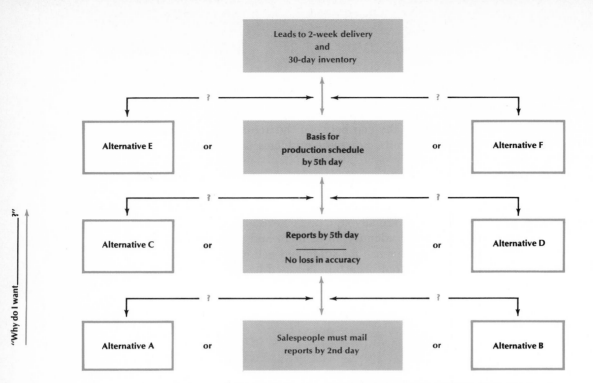

Figure 11–4   Broadened means–end analysis. Analysis moves from diagnosis of a specific problem to diagnosis of the situation in which the problem exists.

the personnel department is working on the motivation problem, the engineering department can concentrate on the goal of realizing engineering needs without low-cost drafting. Each can work independently on vastly different types of goals. The key is that some person or persons in responsible positions should attempt to determine how the several pieces relate, how they complement or substitute for one another.

By looking at this diagram, we can see how a more complicated situation might be broken down. This approach permits us to concentrate our analytical talents on each of a number of subparts of a complex problem. We can focus on each part but at the same time be able to see how it fits into the whole scheme. In many problems like the one illustrated here, what originally appears simply as a matter of personnel turnover may in fact lead to a recognition of problems and relationships in many other areas of the business. By moving from a diagnosis of the specific problem to a diagnosis of the broader situation in which the problem exists, we pave the way for recognizing and dealing with these interrelationships.[3]

[3] Note that a means–end analysis is not sufficient for making a wise choice. All we know is that each means is adequate to meet the higher-level goal; other alternatives may be even more attractive. Morover, a means–end chain shows only one consequence of a given means; other consequences may sharply affect the desirability of using the means depicted. Therefore, a final decision should be based on all four steps covered in Part Three. The chief value of means–end analysis lies in diagnosis.

Determining how far to go in diagnosing the situation. An inevitable question is how far we should go in considering ever-higher goals. Two broad guidelines help to answer this question: 1) the extent of the decision-maker's authority, and 2) the time available for analysis.

Take the first point. A district sales manager, asked to tackle the problem of late reports, may lack the perspective or the organizational authority to look farther than the reason for submitting the field reports—accurate information for scheduling. However, if the vice-president of manufacturing were brought into the decision, he might ask, "Why do I want an accurate basis for making production schedules by the fifth day of the month?"

The answer to this question would reveal the next-higher goal in the chain, which might be "to provide for delivery within two weeks of order

Figure 11–5   Extended means–end analysis. By this approach, diagnosis focuses on a specific subpart of a complex problem.

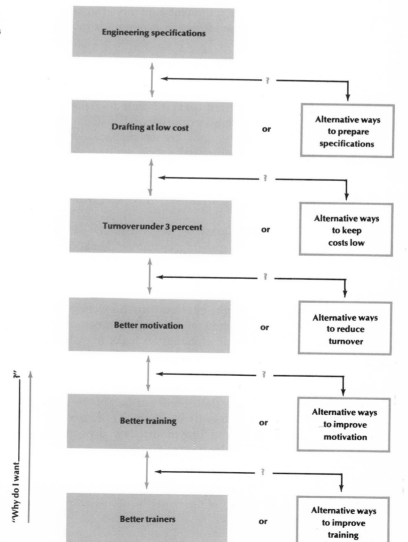

240

PART III
Planning:
Elements of
Rational
Decision-Making

placement, while maintaining a thirty-day inventory." Perhaps the vice-president of manufacturing will have the authority to search for means of achieving this goal without having an accurate basis for making production schedules by the fifth day of the month.

As a rule, the decision-maker should seek to move as far up the hierarchy of goals as his position and influence in the company permit. If the nature of the problem warrants going farther, he should seek to involve higher-level decision-makers who have the necessary perspective and influence.

When time is pressing, we should go "up" the means–end chain only as far as is necessary to get a soluble problem. In other words, we don't challenge the entire goal structure of our company each time we encounter a tough problem. Instead we push the analysis to a point at which we feel confident that one or more acceptable alternatives exist. Then we focus on this redefinition of the problem so that a decision can be made promptly and action can be started. Obviously judgment is involved in selecting the point at which prompt action (and low investigation expense) is more valuable than more exploration.

Dealing with Interrelated Problems

Problems do not remain isolated—especially in enterprises where internal and external integration (discussed in Chapter 1) is a major element of survival. In these situations, as we diagnose one facet of the business, we soon realize that any proposed action will have impact on several operations not embraced in our initial analysis. Our diagnosis should grasp all these related facets, even though in the end we may decide to deal with them one at a time. Because they are intertwined, the *sequence* of analysis and action is crucial.[4]

Difficulties faced by the Allegheny Electric Company are clearly of this sort. To serve its growing customer demand, the company must substantially expand its generating capacity. In fact, the company already is vulnerable to customer complaints of brownouts and occasional shutdowns. Any solution to this problem must concern plant size (millions of dollars will be required), timing (five-to-eight-year construction cycle), and type of fuel (nuclear, oil, or coal). But along come antipollution campaigns and interest in ecology: The public's strong fear of radiation leaks has all but eliminated the possibility of erecting a nuclear power plant, and ecological protests have forced the company to give up attempts to secure a favorable location for a coal-operated plant. In the face of all this, the company seeks a rate increase to improve its earnings, claiming that it will not be able to borrow money for the construction of new plants unless its earnings are increased. However, the public concern about pollution and brownouts may pressure the state utility commission to refuse permission for a rate increase.

---

[4] Here we endorse the concept of a total system and suggest that the diagnosis helps us decide which part of the system we should tinker with first.

Obviously, the company has half a dozen major problems, each of which should be carefully diagnosed in terms of gaps, causes and obstacles, and constraints. *In addition,* the total configuration must be analyzed in an attempt to set some kind of sequence for dealing with the related issues.

A well-established pharmaceutical firm recently faced a comparable situation. The research budget was being revised, and one significant project in question dealt with a cheaper method for producing cortisone. This project was challenged because a competitor was reported to have perfected an alternative method. Assuming the report was correct, the company might be successful in obtaining a license to use the method, or Congress might pass legislation requiring industrywide licensing. Meanwhile the company was negotiating a merger with a small drug company, which if successful and if approved by the Antitrust Division would shift the direction of new-product development for the company. Also, two leading company researchers have received attractive offers from a competitor and would be influenced by the research allotment included in the budget for their projects, even though they were not directly involved in the cortisone study.

Here again the diagnosis is "messy" because several significant problems are interdependent. There is no single answer on how to proceed with such complex diagnoses. If one problem is clearly the most important, it can be studied first; and its tentative solution would set the limits within which related problems are studied. If preliminary analysis shows that acceptable solutions exist for one or more problems, and that the range of solutions will not markedly affect other problems, then these other problems can be temporarily deferred. Another approach is to work on all major needs simultaneously. If this is done, tentative solutions for each need should be quickly provided to the people who are working on related matters so that the anticipated solutions can be used as planning premises in work on other needs and problems. This process is repeated through a series of successive refinements (assuming all the projects progress at about the same rate).

Clearly some sequencing arrangement must be developed. If each problem is diagnosed and studied separately, the opportunities for incompatability, wasted effort, and delay are overwhelming.

Exploring for Unrecognized Opportunities

Another characteristic of diagnosing the total situation is an emphasis on *future* conditions. Most diagnosis starts with a recognized need growing out of the existing scene. Obviously the here and now must not be ignored. Nevertheless, a good manager should also deliberately search out opportunities. Even though operations are proceeding well according to present standards, he knows that changes will occur in technology, politics, population, economics, competition, and other aspects of the environment. New opportunities or difficulties are sure to arise.

242

PART III
Planning:
Elements of
Rational
Decision-Making

A shoe company, for instance, predicted a change in employment practice when it opened a plant in the South. Its prediction, which was followed up by a policy of being "an equal-opportunity employer," has paid off—after a slow start. A more conspicuous example was IBM's prediction about computer needs and competitor offerings, which led the company to introduce its 360 series even though at the time its market position was already very strong. The key is to anticipate the difficulties or opportunities far enough in advance to prepare for them. By thinking in terms of future conditions, the manager can perform his diagnosis before the difficulty or opportunity fully materializes. He can make a decision based on a sound diagnosis; then, if necessary, he can wait until his guesses can be verified with more certainty before he acts on the decision. By thinking in terms of future conditions, he has time to make a thorough plan well before the decision must be implemented.

In terms of the framework of this chapter, we keep a watchful eye on the constantly changing milieu about us, and out of the hurly-burly we select those changes that can be restated in terms of opportunities or difficulties for us. By raising our expectations, or by predicting difficulty in continuing present operations, we identify new problems. Once they are recognized, we can proceed with a diagnosis of each in the manner already outlined under "Stating the Problems in Terms of a Gap." Such a diagnosis of the total situation does not create problems; rather, it shifts them from an unrecognized to a recognized state.

Such forward-looking diagnosis is difficult. Conscious, rational decision-making takes time and, what is worse, often increases the decision-maker's anxiety about the decision he must make. It forces him to bring questions and causes to a conscious level—doubts and uncertainties that might be less troublesome to his psyche (though not to his company) if left submerged. Dealing with predicted future conditions only adds to the uncertainty and anxiety. We shall return to this stumbling block in Chapter 15 when we discuss planning in organizations. What is needed is reasonable selectivity in the issues that are opened for debate and a planning climate that favors anticipating trouble rather than management by crises.

Planning in terms of the future is a recurring theme in Parts Three and Four. Especially in Chapter 13, on comparing the consequences of alternative courses of action, we shall find that forecasting is a prime consideration. In this chapter on diagnosis, however, we have been concerned with predicting independent variables—that is, those key aspects of an operating situation that are beyond our influence—whereas in Chapter 13 our attention focuses on anticipating the consequences of actions we initiate.

CONCLUSION

The essence of a good diagnosis is discernment and clarity. Usually an executive can achieve these qualities by keeping a diagnosis simple and to the point. But he should be fully aware that a high degree of personal judgment is involved. For example, he may set an unnecessary limit on acceptable solutions and thereby eliminate attractive proposals. Or, in his desire to get to a simple, concrete problem, he may move down a means–end chain too hastily and overlook broader problems that need study. The suggestions we have made should assist him in his diagnosis, but they cannot remove the need for keen discretion.

Discretion is particularly important when diagnosis shifts from a single identified need to diagnosis of the whole situation. Here the executive has to judge whether broadening the definition of a problem is warranted, what sequence should be followed in wrestling with interrelated issues, and the extent to which diagnosis should be based on predictions.

In addition, the definition of a problem should never be regarded as unalterable. Even though a diagnosis has been thorough and the conclusions about situations, gaps, causes, and limits have been put in a clear written statement, new insights may still arise. In searching for alternatives, and in analyzing and projecting such alternatives, we may uncover new evidence and new issues. If we do, we should be willing to redefine the problem. It is wise to keep an open mind about this question: "Where do we want to go and what are we up against?"

FOR CLASS DISCUSSION

1) "Decision-making, like playing golf or a musical instrument, is basically a skill. As such it may be learned through practice under the eye of a skillful tutor, but it can't be taught from textbooks." How might you respond to this statement? What is the role of books and lectures in learning such skills as those above? How might your answer differ if the skill being learned was bullfighting or mountain climbing? How does decision-making differ from playing golf or a musical instrument in terms of how it might be taught or learned?

2) How may the careful use of a rational methodology for decision-making contribute to effective decentralization?

3) In what ways may conflict (as discussed in Chapter 9), contribute to and detract from effective diagnosis?

4) "It is fine to talk about a rational process of decision-making and getting all of the pertinent facts and assumptions, but how often does a businessman have the time for such luxuries? Something happens—a competitor cuts his price or comes out with a new product—and your market is threatened and you have to act fast. This is how an executive earns his salary—by making fast, intuitive decisions under pressure." How would you reply to this statement?

5) Under what conditions might it be wise to seek solutions to symptomatic causes?

6) In an effort to stimulate sales, the sales manager of a soap company set up a contest for salespeople whereby the one selling the most soap in a one-month period would receive a $200 bonus. During the month sales soared. But during the following months, they fell off sharply, and many customers complained that they had been pressured into overstocking. 1) Draw a means–end chain to illustrate what diagnosis by the sales manager led to a sales contest

244

PART III
Planning:
Elements of
Rational
Decision-Making

as a solution. 2) Show how this diagnosis might have been broadened to avoid the undesirable outcome. 3) Explain the advantages and dangers of using a means–end chain in this case.

7) How will observing the three inescapable features of delegation (Chapter 3) aid in determining how far to move up the means–end chain?

8) "Computers may be helpful in many aspects of decision-making, but they are of little or no use until *after* a thorough diagnosis has been developed." Comment.

9) In medical cases, key elements of diagnosis may be performed by specialists rather than by the doctor who prescribes for or treats the problem. Is there a parallel in business and other nonmedical situations?

Cases

For cases involving issues covered in this chapter, see especially the following. Particularly relevant questions are listed after each case.

Milano Enterprises (p. 124), 1
Atlas Chemical Company (p. 321), 6
Marten Fabricators (p. 316), 4, 5
Graham, Smith, & Bendel, Inc. (p. 445), 8
Monroe Wire and Cable (p. 436), 6
Southeast Textiles (p. 620), 5

FOR FURTHER READING

Allison, G. T., *Essence of Decision: Explaining the Cuban Missile Crisis.* Boston: Little, Brown and Company, 1971, pp. 1–66.

Explains the purpose of this pace-setting book; develops the first of three models —the rational actor; and applies this model to the Cuban missile crisis.

Bonge, J. W., "Problem Recognition and Diagnosis: Basic Inputs to Business Policy." *Journal of Business Policy,* Spring 1972.

Explores ways of monitoring a firm's environment and of using cues to focus on potential opportunities and threats.

Harrison, E. F., *The Managerial Decision-Making Process.* Boston: Houghton Mifflin Company, 1975, Chapter 2.

Examines the nature of rational decision-making, and notes the contributions of various scholarly disciplines to our understanding of the process.

Kepner, C. H. and B. B. Tregoe, *The Rational Manager.* New York: McGraw-Hill Book Company, 1965, Chapters 3–9.

Clear, concrete instructions for diagnosing operating problems.

Leavitt, H. J., "Beyond the Analytic Manager" (in two parts). *California Management Review,* Spring and Summer, 1975.

A deliberate attempt to move beyond rationalistic ways of dealing with problems, including "far out" means of finding problems.

McKinney, J. L. and P. G. W. Keen, "How Managers' Minds Work." *Harvard Business Review,* May 1974.

A discussion of cognitive styles that gives significant emphasis to problem recognition.

Pounds, W. F., "The Process of Problem Finding." *Industrial Management Review,* Fall 1969.

Discusses four general models that managers use to identify problems: historical, planning, other people's expectations, and extra organizational.

12   The Creative Element in Decision-Making

THE QUEST FOR ALTERNATIVES

A thorough diagnosis defines both a specific problem and the situation in which the problem exists. With this definition in mind a decision-maker seeks possible solutions. Rarely does he hit upon only one perfect way to solve his problem. Usually several different approaches might work, but none is completely satisfactory; so he looks for more alternatives, hoping to find a better answer.

Like diagnosis, search for alternatives tends to be shortchanged by both busy executives and "management scientists." Finding good alternatives, especially novel ones, calls for a lot of unstructured thinking. Many managers feel uncomfortable with such ambiguous situations, preferring clearcut action along a well-defined path. So they tend to grasp the first alternative that promises a "satisfactory" (though not necessarily the best) result. Management scientists provide little help in this area of decision-making; usually their literature simply assumes that alternatives are known.[1]

---

[1] Theoretical work has been done on how much time and other resources to devote to searching (researching). The rational answer is a function of the probability of finding a better alternative than we already have, the incremental value of such an alternative, and the cost of continuing search in terms of resource inputs and of opportunities foregone during the process. As we note later, since the incremental value depends partly on levels of aspiration, there are sound psychological reasons for continuing the search until an acceptable—or satisfactory— alternative is found (but not much beyond this point).

In practice, the two most common sources of alternatives are the past experience of an executive himself and the practices followed by other executives or other companies.

Building on Relevant Experience

Faced with a problem, we naturally review our *past experience* for a similar situation that turned out well. With allowances for obvious differences between the former challenge and the present one, the successful action of the past becomes at least an alternative plan for the future.

Much business planning, as well as individual behavior, is built solely on such past experience. This is the simplest approach to a problem, and it is quite adequate in a majority of instances. As long as all goes well, we are likely to repeat past practice. Before long, it becomes habit or tradition. But the catch is that yesterday's solutions may not be adequate for today's problems, as electric-utility executives have discovered when trying to locate new plants. Workers may no longer respond to yesterday's incentive plan because their "needs" have shifted.

Originality and Selective Imitation

"How does General Motors handle this problem of dealers' inventory?"

"Pete told me he was having the same kind of trouble in collecting from foreign customers. I wonder what he is doing."

Statements such as these are made every day by executives who scrutinize the practice of other firms or other departments for solutions to their own problems. In fact, a distinctive characteristic of American business, often noted by foreign observers, is the frequency and frankness with which businessmen exchange experiences. Professional papers and trade journals are full of accounts of how the XYZ Company cut its air pollution, boosted sales, or improved quality. Ideas are exchanged at trade association meetings and through intercompany visits. Both the American Management Associations and The Conference Board regularly report business practices of successful firms. In fact, much of what we call "business research" consists of finding out what the man across the street is doing.[2]

Such examinations produce several alternatives that might not occur to executives within the company, and this practice accelerates improvement in business operations throughout the economy. But as with past experience, we should ensure that operations in one company are enough like those in a second to make transferring a practice worthwhile. We should also avoid the

---

[2] Students do the same thing. When given a case, most of them try to find what a successful company did in a similar situation so that they can follow suit.

248

PART III
Planning:
Elements of
Rational
Decision-Making

danger of too quickly falling in step with another company simply because it is a leader in its industry. Relying on past experience and imitating others produce alternatives that at best merely keep us up with the parade. Nevertheless, we should always consider *selective imitation* as a possible source of alternatives.

Although pressures of time and expense may force a company to plod along conservatively as a follower in part of its activities, it should strive to excel in some respects. In our dynamic and competitive society, at least an occasional spark of creativity is needed if a company hopes to endure. Shifts in customer demand, new technology, increased government regulation, progressive competition, new employee attitudes and mores, and similar changes limit the usefulness of past experience. The uniqueness of each company and the rapid rate of change make imitation hazardous. We need fresh, original, distinctive, and independent thinking to develop alternatives that are copied neither from the past nor from our neighbor, but rather are peculiarly adapted to the circumstances in which we find ourselves.

Creativeness

Decisions that add some *new* and useful element are creative. Not all decisions are creative in this sense, of course. Even those that are include much repetition or imitation, but in some important respect a creative decision is different and *original*.

This sort of creativeness is familiar to all of us. Every invention of a product, process, or machine contains some creative element. Sales executives who think up suburban shopping centers or package their merchandise in ready-to-use form are being creative. The person who introduced the "last-in-first-out" method of evaluating inventory was creative. Creativeness is perhaps even more familiar outside the business field and is evident in the great advances of medical science, the development of atomic energy, and in discovery of new forms in the arts.

It is natural to exemplify creativeness by dramatic discoveries such as the Salk vaccine or satellite broadcasting. But close examination will reveal that even everyday activities are shot through with strains of creativeness. A personnel manager may have a creative idea for dealing with a troublesome problem of closing a plant, or a sales clerk may think of an ingenious way to display Idaho potatoes. Every time an executive faces a problem, large or small, he has an opportunity to be creative.[3]

---

[3] In this discussion, creativeness is stressed as a means of finding alternatives to solve problems. Actually, we can bring creativeness into play throughout the decision-making process—in diagnosis, while looking for underlying causes; in analysis, while thinking of critical factors; and so on. In a strict sense, we could argue that each of these steps in planning is a little problem in itself, and that creativeness enters into finding alternatives for solving these subproblems. This reasoning becomes cumbersome, however, and it is more useful for most people simply to be aware that there may be opportunities for originality *throughout* the planning process.

Surprisingly little systematic study has been given to creativeness, either by social scientists or by business practitioners. Enough is known, though, to give us some useful leads. Scientific discoveries have probably received the greatest attention, so we do have a number of reports on how new and useful ideas were developed in the medical and physical sciences. Essays on creativeness in the arts are also plentiful. In the business world, advertising men have been particularly interested in the subject. From these and similar sources, we can draw up some suggestions on 1) the usual stages in the creative process, 2) aids to individual creativeness, and 3) aids to group creativeness. Our suggestions lack the comforting assurance of a mathematical formula, but we cannot expect to find fixed rules for developing such an elusive quality. Because creativeness is so important in dynamic planning, we must make the best use of the insights that are available to us.

USUAL STAGES IN THE CREATIVE PROCESS

Although no two persons' minds work exactly alike, the testimony of inventors and great scientists indicates that the creative process has several stages:

1) *Saturation*—becoming thoroughly familiar with a problem, with its setting, and, more broadly, with activities and ideas akin to the problem.
2) *Deliberation*—mulling over these ideas, analyzing them, challenging them, rearranging them, thinking of them from several viewpoints.
3) *Incubation*—relaxing, turning off the conscious and purposeful search, forgetting the frustrations of unproductive labor, letting the subconscious mind work.
4) *Illumination*—hitting upon a bright idea, a bit crazy perhaps, but new and fresh and full of promise, sensing that it might be the answer.
5) *Accommodation*—clarifying the idea, seeing whether it fits the requirements of the problem as it did on first thought, reframing and adapting it, putting it on paper, getting other people's reaction to it.

By recognizing these stages of creative thought, we can look for, and more effectively use, techniques that help us at the different stages.

Saturation

There is a common notion that creative ideas fall like manna from the heavens before the chosen few; one of the chosen simply sits around and waits for inspiration to strike. This impression probably arises from stories of inventions, such as Charles Goodyear's discovery of a method of vulcanizing rubber when he accidentally spilled crude rubber on his kitchen stove. We also often read of moments of inspiration in the cultural field, such as Mascagni's waking

250

PART III
Planning:
Elements of
Rational
Decision-Making

one morning with the concept of *Cavalleria Rusticana* full-blown and writing it within a few days' time. But these accounts fail to emphasize the many years of study and hard work that precede a flash of insight. Goodyear had been studying and experimenting with rubber for years before his lucky accident, and his work provided both the occasion for the discovery and his ability to recognize what he had found; Mascagni kept his family in poverty while he composed piece after piece of completely dull music. Once in a while, a novice stumbles on a great truth (probably because he is ignorant of what supposedly cannot be done, as we shall note below), but such an event is so uncommon that it offers a poor prescription for developing creative ideas. The truth is that the most likely way to get bright ideas is to work on a baffling problem, and work hard.

After careful review of a wide range of reports on creative activity, Brewster Ghiselin concludes: "Even the most energetic and original mind, in order to reorganize or extend human insight in any valuable way, must have attained more than ordinary mastery of the field in which it is to act, a strong sense of what needs to be done, and skill in the appropriate means of expression." [4]

A manager uses creative thinking in solving specific problems; and each situation dictates where he should focus attention. For him, the saturation stage normally begins in a thorough familiarity with a problem itself—its history, its importance, its relationship to other parts of the business, and its setting. Of course, if an executive has lived with a problem a long while and participates in its diagnosis, he is already intimately acquainted with it. But if he has had only casual contact with a situation, as is often true of a staff person, he is more likely to make a useful contribution if he begins by soaking up background material.

Deliberation

Knowledge alone, no matter how complete, does not produce creative ideas. Information must be mulled over until what we might call mental digestion takes place. Because we do not know just where a breakthrough to an original concept will occur, no one can say exactly how material at hand should be analyzed. In fact, an analysis of how 144 patented ideas were discovered in the Standard Oil of New Jersey (Exxon) laboratories revealed five different approaches: 1) finding a *new use* for a product or process, perhaps in another field, 2) *substituting* a better agent or way to accomplish an existing job, 3) pure *theorizing*, or sitting down and thinking, 4) going into the laboratory and *experimenting*, and 5) recognizing the significance of a *lucky accident*. The inventors who came up with the largest number of new ideas were quite adaptable in selecting the particular approach they used at any given time.

---

[4] Brewster Ghiselin, *The Creative Process* (Berkeley: University of California Press, 1961), p. 29.

Figure 12–1 As a study at Exxon Corporation revealed, new ideas have many sources, and the most creative people shift freely from one approach to another. Drawing: Richard Erdoes in *The Lamp*. Courtesy Exxon Corp.

Although there is no single and sure path to follow from information to a new and useful idea, deliberation usually includes three steps: 1) analyzing, 2) building relationships and patterns, and 3) seeking useful rearrangements or combinations.

Incubation

If we are lucky, the work we have done in the steps of saturation and deliberation has furnished us with as many useful alternatives as we want. Flashes of illumination may have occurred while we were deliberating. If so, we can omit incubation entirely and move immediately to the accommodation stage.

But not all problems yield so easily. In spite of thorough preparation and much hard thinking, we may not have discovered a really good solution to our problem. In forcing ourselves to think of yet another angle, we may only have added to our confusion. This sort of stalemate is so common that some writers list frustration as one stage in the creative process.

Advice at this point is simple and unanimous. Set the whole problem aside: go fishing, go to the theatre, pull weeds in the garden, take a long walk, listen to music, or do whatever else is relaxing. By this time, we are too steeped in a problem to wash our hands of it, but for the present we can turn it over to our subconscious mind. At least we will return to our work refreshed, and *perhaps* a creative idea will come to us.

Illumination

There are numerous accounts of sudden illumination. James Watt is said to have thought of his condenser for a steam engine while walking on a Sunday afternoon. The great mathematician Henri Poincaré reports that he grasped the significance of Fuchsian Functions as he stepped onto a bus one afternoon. The president of a large manufacturing company insists that a plan for financing a merger came to his mind while he was shaving. We could recount many other instances of flashes of insight that occurred to a person while he was not consciously thinking about a problem.

Many of us have had similar, though usually less dramatic, experiences. Often an idea is so simple and obvious that we wonder why we hadn't thought of it before. We may learn later (if we failed to saturate ourselves thoroughly in background study) that other people have had the idea before us. Nevertheless, for us it was a creative experience; a new and useful idea was born. But we cannot will such moments of illumination. The most we can do is to prepare ourselves along the lines already suggested and hope for inspiration.

So far as we know at present, illumination apparently works in the following way. We all know how speedily a complicated dream can transpire in a short interval of semiconsciousness; this experience gives us some idea of the tremendous rapidity of ideas flashing across our subconscious. It is reasonable to believe that the mind works at least as fast as an electronic computer, and we know that the number of possible relationships between ideas stored in our memory far exceeds the capacity of anything yet designed by the electronics industry. If in the subconscious the restraints of rational thought are relaxed, a myriad of new combinations and new ideas is possible. Using this hypothesis, let us consider what is truly remarkable about illumination: that, somehow, utterly wild and useless ideas are screened out. It is as though there were a filter in the subconscious that permits only the more plausible ideas to rise up to the conscious level. In those unusual cases in which illumination has unveiled a complete process or financial structure, instead of just the germ of an idea, the subconscious has been able to recognize and select a whole cluster of ideas that fit together into a workable plan.[5]

In the years ahead, science may prove that such speculation about the subconscious mind is naïve fantasy, but our analysis points up two necessary characteristics of creative thinking: Somehow, we must swiftly discard a lot of worthless ideas and learn to recognize a valuable idea when it does occur. Experience shows that there is real danger that a good idea will pass by unnoticed. Some of the aids to creative thinking suggested later in this chapter are designed to minimize this danger.

---

[5] Henri Poincaré makes the interesting and distinctly French suggestion that there is true beauty in such configurations and that the subconscious makes something like an emotional response to a thing of beauty; people are likely to be creative, then, only in those fields in which they are aesthetically sensitive to the appropriateness of a set of ideas.

Rarely is a bright idea in finished form when it is first grasped. Exciting as a newborn idea often is, we usually find, upon exposing it to the cold light of testing, that it is far from perfect.

If the new idea is for a material invention, we need to take it to a laboratory and test whether it will really work. We must write out a new mathematical formula and check it for correctness. A composer needs to commit to paper and actually play a melody that runs through his mind. So too with business ideas. We need to fit a new conception to the actual facts of a problem. Usually a check with cold reality reveals the need for adapting and refining the first conception of an idea. In this creative process, we are seeking practical alternatives for solving a problem, and our search may involve quite a little work to transform an original insight into a specific proposal for others to examine.

But rounding out an original idea does not necessarily require a complete plan of action. Perhaps at some future date, as a part of evaluation, tests may be run, pilot plants built, or budgets prepared. The point here is that the one who has had a fascinating daydream is not truly creative unless he can translate and spell out his idea in usable form.

Highly important and elusive, creativeness ordinarily emerges, then, after five stages: 1) saturation, 2) deliberation, 3) incubation, 4) illumination, and 5) accommodation. In administrative situations where we are concerned with achieving given objectives, we assume that a diagnosis of a problem has preceded all of these steps. Thus creative search in business typically starts not with unbridled effort but with a defined aim and with available background data. In pursuing his search, the creative worker must be as purposeful and diligent as any other employee.

Unfortunately, knowing about the stages in creative thinking by no means assures us that we can bubble over with new and useful ideas. Our knowledge *may* help us to develop creativeness in ourselves and in our associates, but many of us will still find it hard to create ideas. Consequently, we now turn to a number of suggestions that, experience indicates, may help individuals or groups to be creative.

PSYCHOLOGICAL AIDS TO INDIVIDUAL CREATIVITY

Two general conclusions emerge from the preceding review of the usual stages in the creative process: 1) Creativity is not an exceptional ability within the grasp only of geniuses—anyone with reasonable intelligence may have an original idea; and 2) a lot of hard mental work is usually required to produce

254

PART III
Planning:
Elements of
Rational
Decision-Making

a new idea. Prime requisites for developing creative ability, then, are the Horatio Alger qualities of self-confidence and a will to work. The imagination of a creative person is closely related to the intensity and clarity with which he senses the problem to be solved.

Can we suggest anything more about stimulating creativity? Three additional rules that people often turn to in developing new and useful ideas deserve serious attention: Recognize psychological barriers; try to change attributes of known alternatives; and be alert for serendipity.

Recognizing Psychological Barriers

Although psychologists have found no reliable machinery to generate flashes of insight, they have identified a number of common barriers to creative thought. By being alert to these barriers, we can overcome their interference to some extent. The most common obstacles are cultural and perceptual blocks.

Cultural blocks. The push toward social conformity strongly influences our thinking. All of us, consciously or unconsciously, tend to fit in with the modes of living and the attitudes of our associates. Minor exceptions may be acceptable or even desirable, but it is a daring young employee who wears pantaloons or goes barefoot to his office.

This same tendency to follow the crowd—this unwillingness to be different—affects our imagination as well as our actions. The current popularity of electronic controls and automation, for example, is so seductive that almost all young process engineers try to include these features in their new designs. Proposals that omit such features are unlikely to be submitted or, perhaps, even conceived.

For many years, credit for personal-consumption items was limited to houses and other goods whose resale value was greater than the debt. In the Puritan tradition of prudence, Americans looked askance at buying any luxury, such as jewelry, on a time-payment plan, and many people felt that the liberal extension of credit by company stores contributed to moral degeneration. In such a social climate, the idea of extending credit to thousands of mail-order customers was unthinkable.

Until we are ready to break with current fashions of thought—in a department, in a company, or in society—truly creative ideas will be scarce. On this point, C. H. Greenewalt, president of E. I. du Pont de Nemours & Company, said in a speech:

Behind every advance of the human race is a germ of creation growing in the mind of some lone individual, an individual whose dreams waken him in the night while others lie contentedly asleep.

We need those dreams, for today's dreams represent tomorrow's realities. Yet, in the very nature of our mass effort, there lies this grave danger—not that the individual may circumvent the public will, but that he will himself be conformed and shaped to the general pattern, with the loss of his unique, original contributions. The group nature of business enterprise itself will provide adequate safeguards against public affront. The great problem, the great question, is to develop within the framework of the group the creative genius of the individual. . . .

I know of no problem so pressing, of no issue so vital. For unless we can guarantee the encouragement and fruitfulness of the uncommon man, the future will lose for all men its virtue, its brightness, and its promise.

Perceptual blocks.   In addition to the barriers that arise from our social background, we often have difficulty with new ideas simply because of the way we perceive things. Psychologists have devised many experiments that demonstrate the importance of perception. In one of the simplest, they place six matchsticks before a person and ask him to make four triangles with the sticks touching each other at the ends. Most people have trouble, and may even give up, because they think only of arranging the matches on a flat surface. Once they conceive of the task as a three-dimensional problem, they quickly form a pyramid.

A dramatic instance of overcoming a perceptual barrier to creative thinking was the discovery of penicillin. For years bacteriologists had thought of mold simply as a substance that spoiled pure cultures. Mold killed all the germs in the cultures so that researchers had to throw them out and start over again. Then one day, Alexander Fleming had the bright idea that perhaps the same thing that was spoiling the cultures could be used as a germ-killer—which was, in fact, one of the objects of research. A good deal of work remained to be done before the product was refined and tested, but the original inspiration was the result of dropping a preconception about mold.

Transferring habits is one cause of perceptual blocks. The mechanics who built the first automobiles, for instance, were in the habit of thinking of carriages. It was only natural that their early designs for "horseless carriages" merely substituted a motor for a horse. Similarly, in a company where engineering has always been physically and organizationally a part of the plant, executives have a hard time devising a new organization that ties engineering closely to selling. The transfer of past habits to new situations may block out the fresh perception of possible alternative courses of action.

An additional source of difficulty is that we too readily approach a problem as an "either-or" dilemma and examine only two courses of action.

Figure 12–2   Our perception of things can be an obstacle to creativity, preventing us from seeing the wholeness or diversity of a situation, or even permitting us to see "impossible" objects. Does the silhouette show two profiles or a vase? How many stacked cubes do you count? Why is the third object called "irrational"? New perspectives are often required to enable us to break through our perceptual blocks.

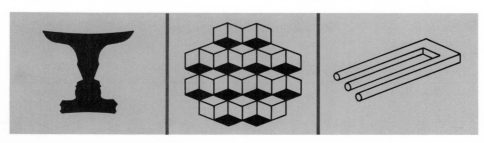

256

PART III
Planning:
Elements of
Rational
Decision-Making

When one medium-sized manufacturing concern, for example, found its plant running to capacity, its executives wrestled for several weeks with the choice between trying to attract extra capital for building an addition to its plant or giving up plans for further expansion in volume. But these were not the only two courses of action. A third possibility involved subcontracting some of the work, and a fourth one, which the company actually adopted, was the arranging of a "sale and lease-back" deal whereby the company sold its old plant and the new addition to an investor and then leased them back for a long period.

Change Attributes of Known Alternatives

The preceding review of psychological barriers to creativity is useful in suggesting attitudes and habits to guard against. But are there additional positive suggestions a person might follow? Not many, unfortunately—at least not many that appear to have widespread usefulness. But one popular approach— the changing of attributes—may be applied to a variety of problems.

In this approach, we first list the important attributes of known (though unattractive) alternatives of the problem we are studying. Next, we single out the key attribute for concentrated attention and contemplate all sorts of modifications. Then, if we can identify other attributes, we undertake a similar exploration for each. Small changes in one direction may suggest additional adjustments, and so by mentally moving from one idea to another, something truly new and useful may emerge. Because it emphasizes concentration on one attribute at a time—preferably the key attribute—this approach is really a special form of analysis, which we already discussed under saturation.

Using this approach, we might study a common window screen as shown in Table 12–1.

An industrial concern followed substantially this technique in developing an executive-compensation plan. Among the attributes of the present practice

TABLE 12–1 DEVELOPING A NEW PRODUCT—WINDOW SCREEN

Attribute	Possible Modifications
Stops insects	Repelling odor, electric beam, sonic beam, seductive trap
Passes most, not all, light	Finer strands of tough plastic, fewer heavy strands with light ones in between, fiber glass, tiny mirrors, invisible barrier suggested above
Passes air	Side ducts, small solar-cell fan, baffles
Rigid frame	Adhesive tape, elastic band over corner hooks, roll up like a window shade
Need year after year	Disposable yearly, daily

considered were these: normal amount of compensation, provision for individual incentive, form and time of payment, and method of making changes. For the first attribute—amount of compensation—the company considered many possible guides, including basing pay schedules on a fixed ratio to sales or profits, or following the pattern of neighboring concerns. Finally management decided to set the president's salary arbitrarily but to relate pay for the lowest-ranking executive with comparable salaries in the industry. All other executive positions were then arranged between these high and low points on the basis of what the president believed to be a given position's relative contribution to company profits. Although nothing especially novel developed in this instance, the new plan represented a sharply different approach from the previous practice of the company and dealt with a troublesome problem creatively.

Serendipity

Management's concern is to achieve objectives. Consequently it will direct most of its creative effort toward finding ever-more effective and efficient ways to reach its ends. Nevertheless, there is always the chance that some useful idea will turn up that is not directly related to an immediate problem.

Serendipity is the art of finding things we are *not* looking for, the knack of making unexpected discoveries. Perhaps a search for a bright idea to solve one problem turns up some interesting sidelights on quite a different issue. The real art is to recognize how we may put these by-product ideas to good use.

Alexander Fleming, as we have noted, turned what at first appeared to be a hindrance to his experiment into the discovery of penicillin. In another instance, Wilhelm Roentgen was experimenting with a cathode tube when he happened to leave a key and an undeveloped photographic plate covered with black paper over a tube. When by mistake a laboratory assistant had the plate developed, it revealed an outline of the key. Roentgen was immediately curious about how the rays from the cathode tube had miraculously passed through the black paper. Out of his investigation came the discovery of X-rays.

Probably the most striking example of serendipity in the management field occurred in Elton Mayo's famous experiments at the Western Electric Company. Mayo and his assistants set out to measure the effect of changes in working conditions on the productivity of workers. They tried changing light and noise and other factors, but with rather indifferent results. Instead, what turned out to be significant—and they were smart enough to recognize the significance—were the social relationships among the workers and the willingness of workers to cooperate with management. In one group the cooperativeness of workers led to increased output, at least temporarily, each time working conditions were changed, even though some of the changes actually made working conditions worse. In another group, differences in output were closely related to the different relationships between operators and supervisors. The researchers then directed experiments more specifically

258

PART III
Planning:
Elements of
Rational
Decision-Making

toward testing this new line of thought and thereby laid a basis for important advances in industrial psychology.

Opportunity for insight presents itself in many management fields. For example, James O. McKinsey started his career in accounting and budgetary control. He soon found that he could not work out good budgets for a company that lacked clear organization. Moreover, he needed clear statements of company objectives and policies before he could put meaningful estimates in budgets. Poking around in the areas of organization and policy proved to be more useful than working out details of a budget and accounting system. It was in these new areas that McKinsey established one of the outstanding top-management consulting firms in the world.

The chance insights on which serendipity rests are so unpredictable that no business dares to rely on them for its continuing development. Still, these opportunities do occur. They are most likely to be recognized in an enterprise that is creative in dealing with its inherent problems. A wise manager should be alert to such unexpected insights and should be hospitable to these little interlopers in his more sharply directed planning activities.

AIDS TO GROUP CREATIVITY

Under favorable conditions, a group of people may produce more creative ideas when working together than when working individually. Several different schemes have been devised by business firms to benefit from group stimulation. We shall examine two of the most popular of these schemes, brainstorming and synectics, partly for the techniques themselves but more for the light they throw on the way group activity can contribute to creativity.

Brainstorming

You may have been in a group making up a skit to mimic your professors; but even in a more formal group—perhaps a hospital board thinking about ways to gain public support for a new building—the flow of ideas might be similar. One person tosses in an offbeat idea that someone else quickly tops by another. While chuckling over these suggestions, a third person chimes in with a proposal that is really ridiculous, but can in part be salvaged to improve the earlier ideas. The animated spirit of the group is contagious. No one cares whether each idea is practical; just thinking them up is good fun. Out of such a session, an ingenious plan that no group member would have thought of alone is likely to emerge.

Alex F. Osborn has used many of the characteristics of group interaction in what he calls "brainstorming." When we are confronted with a problem that calls for an original solution, Osborn recommends that we present the problem to a group of people and ask them to think up as many possible solutions as they can. Important rules for his group procedure are:

1) *Rule out judicial judgment.* Criticism of ideas must be withheld till later.

2) *Welcome freewheeling.* The wilder the idea, the better; it is easier to tame down than to think up.

3) *Solicit quantity.* The greater the number of ideas, the more likelihood of winners.

4) *Seek combinations and improvements.* In addition to contributing ideas of their own, participants should suggest how ideas of others can be sharpened or how two or more ideas can be joined together.

Executives have used this technique on a wide variety of problems, including: how to find new uses for glass in autos, how to improve a company newspaper, how to design a new tire-making machine, how to improve highway signs, and how to cut down absenteeism. An hour session is likely to produce anywhere from 60 to 150 ideas. Most suggestions will be impractical; others will be trite. But a few of the ideas will be worth serious consideration. Note that brainstorming sessions fall under illumintion, the fourth stage in the creative process we described earlier in this chapter.

Brainstorming seems to work best when a problem is simple and specific. If an issue has too many facets, discussion lacks focus. If a problem is complicated and excessively time-consuming, and if it requires writing out a possible solution, discussion will lose its spontaneity. To overcome these difficulties, careful diagnosis to identify the "real problem" should precede any brainstorming session. Complex issues should be broken up into parts, and perhaps a separate session should be devoted to each important part.

Brainstorming has other limitations. Both the session itself and later evaluation of ideas, many of them worthless, are time-consuming. It also tends to produce superficial answers. To some extent, we can overcome these restrictions by adjusting the way sessions are handled and by selecting as members of the group people who deeply understand at least one aspect of the problem. Many business executives feel that even though brainstorming sessions do not stir up highly useful ideas every time, the stimulating effect of a session carries over into their other work. This stimulation tends to jar people out of routinized habits of thought and to force them to take a fresh look at all their activities.[6]

Synectics

A more formalized approach to creativity through group activity is synectics. The word is drawn from a Greek word meaning "the fitting together of

---

[6] Controlled experiments by psychologists indicate that during scheduled periods, motivated individuals working independently produce more ideas than when they work in groups. These findings imply that the success of brainstorming may arise largely from ensuring uninterrupted attention, engendering a relaxed and receptive attitude, and stimulating effort. In other words, the conditions surrounding a brainstorming session probably are more significant than the group action per se.

260

PART III
Planning:
Elements of
Rational
Decision-Making

diverse elements." The approach is largely the product of William J. J. Gordon, chairman and founder of a corporation called Synectics, Inc.[7]

Synectics shares with brainstorming three basic assumptions on creativity: 1) All people possess a greater degree of creativity than they are usually able to tap; 2) in seeking creative ideas, emotional and seemingly irrational elements of thought are as important as the intellectual and rational elements; and 3) the key is to harness the emotional and irrational through methodology and discipline.

Synectics differs from brainstorming in several important respects:

1) As a first step, the problem is thoroughly explored. This step provides a highly analytical treatment both of technical features and of the broad setting. Here the preceding diagnosis is reviewed and questioned. Only after all members of the synectics group are thoroughly oriented to the nature of the problem do they seek novel ideas.

2) Next, the group leader picks a key aspect of the problem and poses this as a general issue or evocative idea.

3) Then explicit devices to "invoke the preconscious mind" are used. These may induce all sorts of fantasies and wild ideas. Typically, all participants are trained in the use of direct and symbolic analogies, impersonations, and other techniques that have proven helpful in developing novel viewpoints and ideas. Thus each participant is well aware of the "method in the madness" of a synectics session.

4) Being skilled in the process, the group can move back and forth from an apparently irrelevant discussion to the real problem. A technical expert within the group assists in appraising the novelty and feasibility of various ideas. So instead of producing a large number of superficial and random ideas as in brainstorming, this group screens ideas frequently.

Because of these characteristics, synectics can deal with much more complex and technical problems than brainstorming, and do so in a sophisticated manner.

Permissive Atmosphere

What general guides to creativity do techniques like brainstorming and synectics suggest? One crucial characteristic is a permissive atmosphere. Probably the cardinal rule of both approaches is this: Postpone the evaluation of ideas. Anyone who says "That won't work" should be quickly squelched, and no one should be afraid to present an idea that is admittedly impractical. Tough, critical, searching analysis is by no means avoided, but it is deferred until a later time. Withholding judgment is psychologically sound. Social barriers, as we have already noted, tend to make all of us conform to conventional ideas,

---

[7] See G. M. Prince, *The Practice of Creativity* (New York: Macmillan, 1972); and "Synectics: Inventing by the Madness Method," *Fortune* (August 1965), pp. 165–94.

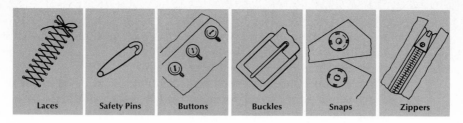

Figure 12–3 In synectics, an "evocative idea" provides the springboard for creative thought. A food company, for example, is seeking a new airtight plastic bag that can be easily opened and closed. The tough issue is how to hold the bag closed. So, various ways of holding clothing securely together is put forth as the "evocative idea." Starting with the fasteners shown here—but shifting freely to related thoughts—can you "invent" a simple and inexpensive tight seal that someone using crackers, snacks, or breakfast cereal can easily open and close several times?

and in many companies a person who makes a novel suggestion is laughed at or considered peculiar. As a result, new ideas are repressed. In such an atmosphere a person thinks about his ideas carefully and assures himself of their practicality before he dares to express them.

In contrast, brainstorming and synectics seek to remove these social barriers for at least a brief period. Because everyone recognizes the distinction between mentioning an idea and recommending it, a person's reputation for sound judgment is not at stake. The influence of social pressure is reversed. Originality is encouraged, and the desirable member of the group is the person who has lots of ideas.

Even when no formal technique like brainstorming is used, a permissive atmosphere can go far in encouraging creativity. New ideas are more likely to emerge when they receive a warm welcome. Specifically, in a permissive atmosphere 1) people are free to express ideas even though they are at variance with past practices, group norms, or the views of the leaders; 2) supervisors and colleagues give positive encouragement to a person who wants to try something new and different; and 3) mutual respect for individuality runs deep enough so that a person expresses his creative ideas without worrying about an unfavorable response. The individual who cherishes stability and respects tradition will probably be unhappy in such a permissive atmosphere, but these are the conditions in which creative thinking is most likely to flourish

Adapting and Borrowing

The encouragement of adaptation and borrowing is a second generally useful feature of both brainstorming and synectics. Each individual may have a perceptual or other mental block that limits the ideas that occur to him. But the reciprocal exchange in brainstorming and the use of analogies in synectics provide ways of hurdling these mental blocks. One member of the group picks

262

PART III
Planning:
Elements of
Rational
Decision-Making

up an idea where another leaves off, adds to it, or changes it freely. Still a third individual, not inhibited by the assumptions of the first two, may give the idea a new twist. Thus one idea builds on another.

Such a procedure may open up ideas that would never occur to "the lone wolf" who guards his secret formula until it is in a finished shape and ready to startle the world. Because credit for a creative idea may be hard to assign to a single individual, because of extensive adapting and borrowing, such free interchange is likely to work well only when participants are more interested in an end result than in personal glory. To capture the full benefits of adapting and borrowing, then, we need team spirit and dedication to overall objectives.

This analysis suggests, then, that certain kinds of group attitudes can help promote creativity. A permissive atmosphere, coupled with a free give-and-take of ideas, is necessary to harness the potential group strengths. These attitudes can be encouraged as a general policy even if particular techniques such as brainstorming and synectics do not happen to fit.

RELATING CREATIVITY TO DIAGNOSIS

Having looked at the stages involved in creative thought and at individual and group aids to creativity, we must now consider a criticism of rational diagnosis relating to its impact on creativity. A few critics contend that the methodical, highly analytical approach suggested for diagnosing a problem inhibits by its nature the decision-maker's creativity. They use the successes produced by brainstorming as evidence to support their position. We strongly believe the opposite to be true.

By clearly and sharply identifying a problem or unrealized opportunity, by clearly homing in on the root cause or obstacle to this problem or opportunity, the decision-maker should be able to utilize his creative talent to the maximum. By looking at the subparts of a complex problem and alternative means of realizing higher-level goals, the decision-maker can focus every ounce of his creative talent on seeking alternative ways of solving more precise subproblems for which no satisfactory solution is known. Further, given the nature of a thorough diagnosis, he can do so without losing sight of the relationships among the parts.

Actually, synectics combines both diagnosis and creativity. In a synectics session, the preliminary analysis of a problem is sharply analytical: The entire group's thinking is pushed to root causes and stubborn obstacles. Only then, as in brainstorming, is nonlogical thought encouraged. Moreover, in synectics the group returns to its diagnosis from time to time when someone thinks he sees a possible application of a strange thought to the identified difficulty.

Therefore, when we are faced with tough problems, we need keen diagnosis to help channel our creative efforts. The chances that a person who is unaware of a need will think of a novel solution are exceedingly small.

CONCLUSION: IMPACT OF ORGANIZATION ON CREATIVITY

In concluding our examination of creativity, we might note two points where earlier suggestions for achieving organized effort appear to conflict with proposals for stimulating creative thought:

1) Most conspicuous is the matter of conformity. To achieve the harmonious, united effort of workers in an enterprise, we need genuine acceptance of official objectives, policies, and procedures. Yet for creativity we want people to challenge existing beliefs and modes of thought freely. A manager can reconcile these two points of view at least partially by making clear when and where independent thinking is desired and when and where it is not. In our personal life we often draw such distinctions, conforming to many social mores, but defying others. Russian scientists pay homage to communist economic doctrine and still create notable engineering advances. The tough question is whether an individual, by his own volition, and in response to the needs of his enterprise, can conform to, say, a cash-and-carry policy for years and then back off for creative thinking about changes in that policy. We believe many executives— and operators—can make such a switch if they are adjusted to the idea of continual change in at least a few activities at a time in a dynamic system.

2) Organization develops status distinctions. To reinforce the influence of higher-ranking executives and of senior staff, we give them titles and other status symbols and place power in their hands. Does not such status inhibit the free expression of challenging ideas? Will a low-ranking person present an idea that contradicts one proposed by an individual of high status? Again we can in part reconcile the apparent conflict by distinguishing where and when novel ideas will be welcomed. Just as an elevator operator may feel free to tell a president about good fishing spots, so can a supervisor tell a vice-president in charge of production about possible improvement in manufacturing methods. For such suggestions to fall freely, however, the vice-president must make clear that he welcomes new ideas and recognizes that many of them may not prove to be feasible.

A theme running through our discussion in Parts One, Two, and Four is the degree of freedom of action delegated to managers and operators. One facet of such flexibility is a permissiveness that nourishes creative action. However, more than a favorable management structure is necessary for creativity to flourish. A conducive leadership style is also vital, so we shall return to the freedom–permissiveness–creativity issue in Part Six.

Knowing about creativity will not necessarily make an executive creative, but it should enable him to help build a total work situation in which creativeness can thrive.

FOR CLASS DISCUSSION

1) "A thorough, methodical, and highly rational approach to problem analysis, while it has its advantages, tends to be stultifying to the truly creative mind. Where creativity is vital, avoid overly analytical approaches." Do you agree? Discuss your answer.

2) a) "The chances of getting a truly creative idea from someone over 35 years old is slim. By that age, those who have been successful enough to be asked for creative alternatives merely try to modify their past ideas enough to make them fit the problem."

b) "Although kids under 25 might trigger creative ideas in others, it is unlikely that they can generate creative ideas. They just haven't learned or experienced enough by that age to have the raw material. Their apparent successes are a matter of pure luck."

Comment on these two ends of the "creativity generation gap."

3) In the text, the process of creative thinking is divided into five basic elements —saturation, deliberation, etc. In what ways may brainstorming and synectics contribute to each of these five steps?

4) In what ways may an organization contribute to the "incubation" stage of the creative process?

5) "Creativity in large organizations may be vital to success, but unless it is carefully coordinated or limited to only high-level managerial decisions, it can lead to chaos." Do you agree? Discuss the pros and cons of this statement. How will your answer be influenced by the degree of decentralization in a firm?

6) A four-story department store, after modernizing its elevators, was still plagued by complaints from shoppers who had long waits for an elevator. The store owners would like to avoid using any more floor space for escalators or additional elevators. Try to develop at least five creative and feasible alternatives for them. First allow yourself just to "free wheel"; then set the problem up in terms of a means–end chain and see whether this helps.

7) When it is clear that a job will require creative thinking to solve problems or realize opportunities, how should this be reflected in the preparation of person specifications as discussed in Chapter 10?

8) "Creativity is such an elusive thing I'd rather have my people work harder on mundane but tested programs than waste endless hours hoping for a creative windfall." Comment on this opinion offered by the sales manager of a small baking company.

Cases

For cases involving issues covered in this chapter, see especially the following. Particularly relevant questions are listed after each case.

The Delaware Corporation (p. 113), 8
Milano Enterprises (p. 124), 9
Petersen Electronics (p. 211), 10
Merchantville School System (p. 217), 11
Atlas Chemical Company (p. 321), 7
Marten Fabricators (p. 316), 6
Central Telephone and Electronics (p. 527), 6, 7
Southeast Textiles (p. 620), 6

Brown, J. D., *The Human Nature of Organizations.* New York: American Management Associations, 1973, Chapter 9.

Explores the conformity-versus-creativity issue, especially as it arises in large organizations.

Mair, N., ed., *Problem Solving in Individuals and Groups.* Belmont, Calif.: Brooks Cole Publishing Co., 1970.

Includes articles on creativity studies and suggestions for application in work-group settings.

Richards, M. D. and W. A. Nielander, eds., *Readings in Management,* 4th ed. Cincinnati: South-Western Publishing Co., 1974, pp. 141–75.

Three articles dealing with the creative development of alternatives.

Steele, L. W., *Innovation in Big Business.* New York: American Elsevier Publishing Company, 1975.

Explores problems of tying R&D into company planning, and of where to place R&D in the organization.

Taylor, C. W., ed., *Climate for Creativity.* New York: Pergamon Press, 1972.

Proceedings of the Seventh National Creativity Conference; includes papers on setting for creativity, identifying creative ability, and use of creative people in scientific organizations.

Zaltman, G., R. Duncan, and J. Holbek, *Innovation and Organization.* New York: John Wiley & Sons, 1973.

Moves from creative ideas to innovation in organizations.

13
Comparing
Courses of Action

PROJECTION OF ALTERNATIVES

Spotting and diagnosing a problem and then finding attractive alternative solutions is a crucial start. But it leaves us with an unanswered question: Which of the alternatives is best? The rational model for making plans, which we are examining in this Part, now stipulates two more steps: For each alternative, we must carefully project the likely results of adopting that course of action, and finally make a wise choice that accounts for the diverse values and uncertainties involved.

Projecting the probable consequences of each alternative—the subject of this chapter—should be done in a way that helps us compare these possible courses of action. To make this comparison sharp and logical, we must accept the statement of the problem that emerged from our diagnosis, and we must concentrate on our clearly identified alternative ways of dealing with that problem. If we don't maintain this focus, the entire analysis becomes very confused.

Sometimes restating a problem and adding alternatives are desirable refinements, as we have suggested in the two preceding chapters; but we should take care not to muddle a comparison of alternatives with such revision. Orderly, rational decision-making requires that we be aware of which phase in the process we are dealing with at any particular moment. If a revision of a problem appears desirable, we can and should revert to diagnosis; then, with the new issue in mind, we can analyze the ways of resolving it. Unless there is agreement on the problem being addressed, we find ourselves thinking and talking at cross purposes.

In our earlier discussion of the creative process, we emphasized such matters as stimulating the imagination, providing a permissive atmosphere, and even nurturing screwball ideas. Our purpose there was to propose ways to cultivate fresh and original thought.

The comparison of alternatives requires a different frame of mind. Here we want to be as sure as possible that we are right. Therefore we challenge evidence, stick to issues and rule out irrelevant points, prove points logically, and listen to a skeptic who says "No" in order to discover any valid reasons he might set forth. This is a time for tough, critical thinking.

People are usually adept at either creative thinking or tough-minded analysis, but rarely at both. In fact, an individual who excels in one type of thinking is likely to be impatient and scornful of the other. Yet both qualities of mind are needed for decision-making. Every manager should at least be aware of the distinction between creative thought and searching analysis in the planning process, and should understand the contributions different people may make so that he can intelligently seek help where he is weak. In the following sections we shall turn attention to making careful, rigorous comparisons of already identified alternatives.

Focus on the Future

Rational choice relies on predictions. Most of the benefits and costs of any adopted plan arise, not at the moment of decision, but over a period of time afterward. So to make a wise choice, we must *predict* what those benefits and costs will be.

An electric utility's choice of a coal versus atomic generating plant, for instance, will depend on *predictions* of construction costs, coal prices, atomic-core costs, plant efficiencies, repairs, hazards, pollution regulations, and a variety of other future events. Similarly, the selection of a TV program to use as an advertising medium will rest on forecasts of the relative popularity of that program, the quality characteristics of the audience, and their responsiveness to the message we want to deliver.

Rarely are all the future consequences of any alternative certain. Predicting some factors may be very difficult, but we can't escape the task. To consider only history and hard "facts" is a sure path to incomplete analysis.

FORECASTING BOTH ENVIRONMENT AND CONSEQUENCES

The outcome of any plan of action we select will depend upon both the environment at the time action occurs and the soundness of the plan itself. By environment we mean the whole array of conditions affecting success that

268

PART III
Planning:
Elements of
Rational
Decision-Making

cannot be controlled (adjusted) by management. In contrast, the plan (decision) refers to changes—or lack of change—that occur as a direct result of managerial choice. Our predictions must include both sets of variables.

Critical Factors
In the Changing Environment

Change is everywhere. Student attitudes, food prices, life styles, wars, medical technology, even church liturgy will change sharply within the next few years. Consequently, we cannot be sure that an action that produced delightful results last month will have similar consequences next year.

Fortunately we do not have to forecast all the shifts in environment that are likely to occur before we can make a rational decision. Many of these changes will have no noticeable effect on the set of alternatives we are considering, and they can safely be disregarded in making this choice. However, other changes may be critical to success or failure. And these variables we must forecast to the best of our ability.

The first move is to select factors in the environment that are critical to

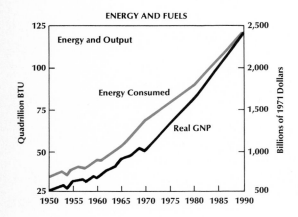

Figure 13–1 **External changes often affect the results of a particular course of action. So we must predict likely changes in key factors. Do you think the Department of Commerce forecasts shown here are high or low? What probability would you attach to the projections shown. Who cares?**

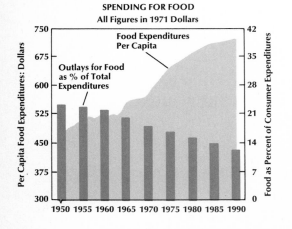

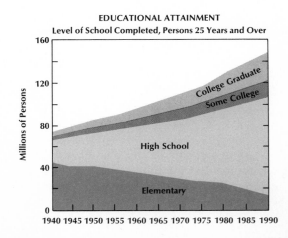

the problem at hand—critical because of their potential volatility and because their status will significantly affect the relative attractiveness of our alternatives. In the utility company example mentioned above, construction costs over the five-year span required to build a generating plant might double, with one type of plant rising much faster than the other; relative prices of coal versus atomic cores are even more uncertain; the efficiency of coal-burning plants is quite predictable, whereas atomic-energy technology is still being developed; future pollution regulations may hamper one source of energy and favor another. All such factors as these are critical to the choice and therefore should be forecast. However, for the selection of a TV program none of the above factors is relevant. In this second example, forecasts about audiences for competing programs are critical.

Of course, a start on these environmental forecasts will have been made as a part of diagnosis. Usually such early forecasts have to be sharpened and expanded to fit the critical factors for the particular set of alternatives we are analyzing with care.

Our analysis of alternatives would be simplified if we could confidently predict a single level for each critical factor. For instance, it would be helpful to have a simple conclusion that "coal prices will drop twenty-five percent by the time a coal-burning plant can be completed, and will remain stable for the next fifteen years (or rise only as fast as prices we can charge customers)"; or "there will be no additional regulations over radiation hazards of atomic plants." Unfortunately, our forecast will probably show a range of possibilities. For the radiation regulation, we might conclude:

No change	50% probability
Significant easing of regulation	35% probability
Sharp increase due to one bad accident	15% probability

Such a forecasted array of possible environments is significant. It helps us assess the degree of risk associated with each alternative. It can also be used in "expected values" and in laying out "decision-trees"—discussed in the next chapter.

Projecting Consequences of Each Alternative

A second kind of forecast is also crucial to the analysis of alternatives. We must predict what is likely to happen if we take action-A, or alternative-B, or likewise for each alternative on our list. For some decisions the tie between a proposed alternative and a result is almost mechanistic, and we can predict outcomes with precision. For example, if we install ten new machines, monthly output can be increased fifteen percent. Most predictions are not so simple. The

270

PART III
Planning:
Elements of
Rational
Decision-Making

sales increase resulting from a TV program is by no means certain, even when we know a size and quality of audience. Nor are we sure of the response to a proposed maternity-leave policy for women. So, even with the valuable aid of internal company data, we again face forecasting hurdles and may resort to projecting an array of consequences with probabilities attached to each—as was suggested for environmental forecasts.

Theoretically, for a complete analysis of each alternative, we should project an array of possible consequences for all the different environments we forecast. With several critical factors in the environment, several kinds of consequences, and several alternatives, the number of estimates quickly becomes incomprehensible. A *rational* manager will find some ways to introduce more judgment into this forecasting and analyzing. So in the rest of this chapter we shall examine ways to improve the quality of the analysis without becoming swamped in a proliferation of estimates.

IDENTIFYING ALL SIGNIFICANT CONSEQUENCES

To appraise an alternative wisely, we must try to foresee its impact on all of the various company goals. Its consequences are likely to be both desirable and undesirable, both immediate and long-range, both tangible and intangible, both certain and only possible, and we shall take all possibilities into account.

Such a comprehensive assessment is not easy. To cite a classic example, in the early days of scientific management one-sided emphasis was common. Industrial engineers often devised excellent schemes for simplifying jobs, providing mechanical aids to make work easy, and setting output standards and piece rates that enabled average workers to earn substantial bonuses. But in the application of the schemes, difficulties would crop up. Workers often felt that output standards were so much higher than what they had been accustomed to that they simply refused to try to achieve them. Sometimes women would be assigned to what traditionally was "men's work"; this practice upset status relationships and created passive resistance to a whole plan. In other instances, simplification in one department merely transferred headaches to another. These difficulties arose because management failed to foresee all significant consequences before selecting a course of action.

Predicting Impact of Proposed Action

A manager needs thorough acquaintance with an operation and a realistic imagination to anticipate fully the consequences of each alternative. Often a wide range of factors is involved. For instance, the sales manager of a manufacturer of power lawn mowers and related equipment recommended that the company establish an assembly shop on the West Coast. He said that this move would lower costs and improve customer service, thereby enabling the company to meet competition of local West Coast manufacturers. At the time, the company had only a sales office and warehouse for finished products in California. Among the questions to which the company sought answers before making a final decision were the following:

1) What will be the difference in cost between shipping parts and shipping assembled products?

2) How much will we have to pay for direct labor in the California plant? How much for indirect labor such as maintenance, janitors, and so on? What reduction, if any, in labor costs will there be at the main plant?

3) How much additional overhead will the California shop require? This includes rent (or, if we own the plant, taxes, depreciation, maintenance, and interest), power, heat, and light. How many clerks and supervisors, at what salaries, will we need for assembly work? Will there be any offsetting reduction in overhead at the main plant?

4) How much additional capital will we have to tie up in West Coast operations if the new shop is opened? This includes capital for equipment, office furniture, and other fixed assets; additional inventory; moving and setup costs; and operating losses during the period when the shop is getting under way.

5) Will the new shop be flexible enough to adjust to seasonal changes in volume of business? What minimum staff will have to be retained during low periods? Would there be greater flexibility at the main plant than at the new shop?

6) Will manufacturing in California subject the company to special state taxes or added liability insurance? Will it be advantageous to establish a separate corporation?

7) Just what will be the improvement in service to customers? How will local assembly ensure speedier deliveries than warehousing finished products? Will local repair and troubleshooting be feasible, and how much weight will this carry with customers? Will delivery of repair parts be improved?

8) In addition to actual improvement in customer service, will the "local industry" appeal have a significant effect on sales volume?

9) Will the quality of the product be as well controlled in California as in the main plant?

10) Will the union at the main plant object to transferring work to another location? Might jurisdictional problems arise if a different union organizes the West Coast operations?

11) Should the West Coast shop be under the direction of a West Coast sales manager? What responsibility, if any, will the production manager have for West Coast operations? How will accounting and personnel be coordinated with the main plant?

12) How much additional sales volume can be anticipated as a result of establishing a West Coast assembly shop? How much will company profit be increased as a result of this additional volume?

Only after checking into all of these questions was the president of the power company prepared to make a decision on the proposed West Coast assembly shop. He had a staff assistant assemble financial information and summarize it as shown in Table 13–1.

TABLE 13–1   RELATIVE INCOME AND EXPENDITURES IF NEW ASSEMBLY SHOP RESULTS IN DOUBLING WEST COAST SALES [1]

	Main Plant (assembles $200,000 worth of mowers for West Coast sales)	West Coast Shop (assembles $400,000 worth of mowers)	Difference (West Coast minus main plant)
Additions to present investment:			
Equipment	0	$ 30,000	
Starting-up costs	0	10,000	
Parts inventory	0	15,000	
Total	0	$ 55,000	$ 55,000
Annual income and expenses affected:			
Income (West Coast sales)	$200,000	$400,000	$200,000
Expenses:			
Cost of parts (increments)	90,000	170,000	
Shipping to West Coast:			
Assembled mowers	15,000		
Parts		22,000	
Assembly labor:			
Direct	12,000	24,000	
Indirect	4,000	12,000	
Overhead:			
Supervision	0	8,000	
Clerical	0	5,000	
Power, heat, light	200	800	
Shop rent	0	7,600	
Depreciation	0	2,000	
Taxes and insurance	0	500	
West Coast sales commissions	10,000	20,000	
Total	$131,200	$271,900	$140,700
Net annual gain (sales difference minus expense difference)			$ 59,300

Rate of return (before income tax):
First year $59,300 ÷ $55,000 = 108%
Average year [2] $59,300 ÷ $40,000 = 148%

[1] Only those accounts affected by the choice of one of the two alternatives are listed. The amounts shown in each column are additional expenditures or income that would occur if that alternative were selected.

[2] Equipment costs will presumably be recovered by depreciation; so the investment in equipment will drop from $30,000 to zero, or average $15,000. Using the $15,000 figure, the total investment would be $40,000 in an average year.

No managerial action has a single result. Although an action may make an important contribution to a mission, it will also result in some expense or sacrifice. Often we become so intent on one or two challenging objectives that we brush aside (undervalue) other consequences of a plan to meet the objective. For example, Americans who advocate that the United States give surplus wheat to starving people in other parts of the world tend to underestimate the political repercussions in nations whose wheat exports might be curtailed because of our gifts. On a smaller scale, a proposal to increase the proportion of women in executive positions may upset opportunities for blacks, the morale in departments where anticipated promotions will be deferred, and union contract provisions.

The production-planning section of a small company proposed a plan for eliminating overtime. By careful scheduling, and by purchasing a few additional machines and hiring operators for them, the company could cut out overtime, which had been averaging four hours per week for all workers in the shop. But one consequence the proposal did not consider was the 15 percent cut (four hours at time-and-a-half) in take-home pay that the workers would suffer. Labor supply at the time was tight, and the industrial-relations director felt sure that such a move would indirectly lead to demands for a higher base rate and perhaps to some turnover of experienced personnel. The possibility of these additional consequences was sufficiently serious that only the scheduling part of the proposal was put into effect; this cut overtime by only one and a half hours, and no conspicuous event like installing machinery called attention to the change.

We are apt to overlook "other consequences" for several reasons:

1) Other consequences do not prompt management action. The spur to a decision —the gap we want filled—gets the limelight. The unavoidable extras, whether desirable or undesirable, were not included in our diagnosis and get brushed aside as we concentrate on the major mission.

2) Long-run consequences tend to be undervalued. Pain or pleasure six months, two years, or ten years hence is remote and unreal compared with, say, pressure to make this month's expense ratios look good or quieting an irate customer.

3) The other consequences may not affect us. Even though we conscientiously want to serve the overall good, we are inevitably much more sensitive to results that hit us directly. (Social costs pose an issue of this sort.)

4) Unlikely consequences are often disregarded. Attention is naturally absorbed by the most probable outcome, and if a consequence—such as environmental damage—is viewed as a secondary effect and also has only a thirty percent chance of occurring, it may never come up for serious study.

5) Psychologically, most of us tend to perceive acceptable stimuli and to screen out unpleasant ones. So, if a secondary consequence is unattractive, we may be unaware that we are ignoring it.

One way we can overcome these tendencies and flush out "other consequences" is to ask key executives and other interest-group representatives

274

PART III
Planning:
Elements of
Rational
Decision-Making

whether they have a strong preference for one of the alternatives being considered. If the answer is "yes," then we should ask why that plan is preferred. The explanation may bring to our attention factors that should be considered.

From the preceding discussion, we can see that spelling out the consequences of alternative courses of action is no routine matter. Each managerial situation has its own distinctive characteristics. Because fact-gathering and analysis may become quite elaborate, we need to give special attention to ways of *simplifying the process*. Five useful approaches to simplifying the comparisons are: 1) focusing on differences, 2) stating differences in dollar terms, 3) simplifying the projection of intangibles, 4) narrowing the number of alternatives, and 5) concentrating on crucial factors. Let us examine each of these.

FOCUSING ON DIFFERENCES

Disregard Common Elements

One important means of simplifying the comparison of alternatives is to disregard the common aspects of all proposed plans and to focus on differences in results. This principle is clearly illustrated in the case of the West Coast assembly shop. In choosing between doing *all* assembly in the main plant and doing *part* of it in the West Coast shop, management could ignore the cost of raw materials, which would always be purchased by headquarters at uniform costs. The company could likewise disregard the West Coast sales organization and sales personnel, for no change would be anticipated as a consequence of adopting either alternative. Because the president's salary would not be affected, it too could be passed over.

When we suggest disregarding common elements, we do not mean that they are unimportant or that they may not be improved. The point is simply that for the moment we need not clutter up our thinking with them, because they will be unaffected by whatever choice we make. Later, *separate* attention can be given to improving an element that is not involved in our immediate problem—for instance, material costs in the preceding case.

This principle must be carefully applied, however, for we may be in danger of assuming too many constants. If, for example, further study of the West Coast assembly shop indicates that it would substantially increase sales volume, then management would have to revise its assumption that sales organization and sales personnel would remain unchanged. The cost of shipping finished goods from warehouse to present customers presents a similar problem. If establishing the new assembly shop would not alter the pattern of final shipment, then shipping costs could be left out of account. But if, on the other hand, the assembly shop is to be moved to a different city, or if management anticipates that sales will jump so much as a result of opening the shop that a more economical method of delivery will be possible, then costs of delivering finished goods should be included as a factor in the decision. In short,

Figure 13–2 One way to reduce the complexity of having to compare alternatives is to sort out and ignore any common factors. For example, a comparison of the left- and right-hand groups reveals only three distinctive elements in each.

there is nothing wrong with disregarding a common element so long as we are positive that the element will, in fact, be unaffected by our choice.

STATING DIFFERENCES IN DOLLAR TERMS

It is hard for any executive to keep in mind all the factors pertinent to a decision and to give each its proper relative weight. One way to reduce the complexity of the job is to translate economic factors into dollars of income, expense, or investment. Usually these dollar figures can then be combined into one or two key *net* amounts, which are concise and relatively easy to handle. But they can be dangerous as well. They may invite too much consideration because they are easier to grasp than subjective factors and because they seem more reliable than is warranted by the assumptions on which they are based. Still, for many decisions the advantages of net dollar figures outweigh the danger that they will be misused.

A choice among alternatives, as we have already discussed, depends on the *differences* in their consequences. Insofar as we can compute net income or net expenses for each alternative, it is simple to subtract one from another. Similarly, if any alternatives involve a change in investment, we can readily compute the difference. Thus, one or two net-dollar figures can summarize a whole series of factors.

276

PART III
Planning:
Elements of
Rational
Decision-Making

We can show more clearly in the following elementary examples both how consolidated dollar figures simplify decision and what the common problems in computation are.

Use of Accounting Data

A first requirement is the ability to use accounting data developed for tax or financial purposes to identify those elements of income, expense, or investment that really change with the alternatives considered. The accounting department in preparing statements for the Internal Revenue Service must follow certain conventions. On the other hand, the finance department in submitting reports to stockholders, creditors, and various governmental agencies may be required to follow different conventions. When projected in financial terms, it is entirely possible for the same group of alternatives to look quite different depending on which set of conventions is used. As decision-makers, we should be aware of how a decision will look to a tax collector, a stockholder, or a regulatory agency in Washington. But it is probably more important to know how it will look in terms of the real impact on the elements of profit that the firm can control.

For example, suppose we are trying to decide which of several materials to use in the manufacture of a special product. One type of material is in very short supply, but our company has enough to meet our needs. This material cost the company $5,000 and is carried on the books at this figure. Because the market value of the material has gone up, however, another firm is interested in purchasing it for $8,000. If we use it in making the product, what expense is incurred?

For tax purposes, we would have to enter the cost as $5,000. When reporting the change in inventory for balance-sheet calculations, we might consider it as $8,000 (market value) but would probably enter it as $5,000 (original cost). Clearly, though, in projecting the cost of the product, we should consider alternatives; and if we use this material, we should for decision-making purposes record the cost as $8,000, for this is what the material is worth today.

The decision-maker must be prepared to take income, expense, or investment figures computed for other purposes and adjust them to reflect the differences among alternatives he is considering. Because this process is so vital, we shall outline below the general concept that guides the decision-maker in carrying out these adjustments.

Incremental Concept

Here is a disarmingly simple principle that seems so logical that you may think it is certainly the way costs and revenues are commonly computed in projections. It is merely a particular form of the "disregard common elements" concept. Unfortunately, we shall find both conceptual and practical difficulties in following the proposed golden rule.

Simply stated, the principle is: In projecting any relevant revenues, expenses, or investments, seek to identify any *difference* in these flows that will arise from 1) following alternative-A compared with flows that will exist by 2) not following alternative-A. We disregard those revenues, expenses, or investments that are "sunk"—those that would be incurred or realized in any event. Thus we isolate the "incremental" revenues, savings, expenses, or investments that would result from the proposal.

As a first illustration of the incremental concept, consider the case of an international news service that sponsored the design of satellite-communications equipment. After studying the situation closely, management had decided that the undertaking would be profitable if relatively trouble-free equipment could be developed for less than two million dollars in research and development. Research people and engineers assured central management that there was a good chance of success, and the project was authorized. Today, after a few years' work, two million dollars has been spent, but satisfactory equipment has not yet been perfected.

The research people have stated that they have made great progress, even though they have been unsuccessful. They are certain that they can now produce the desired equipment with an additional expenditure of about half a million dollars.

What should management do? Even if the new machine were successfully developed with the additional outlay, the project is still doomed to lose money. As much as three million dollars will have been spent to get savings of a little more than two million dollars. It might appear unwise to spend the additional million. The company officials might be accused of throwing good money after bad. If the most recent cost estimates are correct, however, and unless the news service has much more attractive uses for its money, the expenditure should be made. We can quickly see why if we apply the marginal concept. At this point in time, if the company does nothing, it will recover none of the money already spent on research. This money represents a sunk cost, one already incurred and not affected by the present decision. Therefore, though it may be painful, we disregard it. The question to be asked is, "What additional, or incremental, costs and savings are involved?"

If the present projections are correct, the incremental (additional) costs will be less than one million dollars and the incremental (additional) saving received will be something more than two million dollars. Overall, the company will probably still lose money on this venture, but by continuing the project its loss will be reduced by at least a million dollars—the excess of incremental cost subtracted from incremental saving.

Pitfalls in Traditional Accounting Concepts

As a further illustration of the incremental concept as applied to cost and revenue, let us look at an abridged case in which we encounter problems arising out of traditional accounting concepts.

278

PART III
Planning:
Elements of
Rational
Decision-Making

The Elton Metal Products Company received an invitation to produce a specially designed pipe fitting to be used in warehouse refrigeration. Elton developed and produced 1,000 fittings at a total cost of $5,500. A large portion of this expense was the cost of developing the fitting and of converting a metal-working machine to make it suitable for manufacturing the piece. Now, on completion of this contract, Elton's sales manager has been offered an additional order from a building contractor for 500 fittings. In setting a price for the second order, the cost statement shown in Table 13–2 has been prepared.

TABLE 13–2

	Cost for 500 Units
Labor	$ 700
Material	750
Power and materials handling	50
Research and development	300
Conversion costs	400
General overhead	400
	$2,600

The first question we ask is whether some of these costs would be incurred even if Elton turned down the second order.

What of research-and-development costs, conversion costs, and general overhead? Because the research and development has been done, it is a sunk, or nonavoidable, expense. Turning down the order will not reduce this item. Therefore, these certainly are not pertinent costs. Let us assume that the same is true for conversion costs. What of "general overhead"? This entry includes the share of general operating expenses charged to this project—such costs as executive salaries, maintaining the factory, and the like. Again ask the incremental question. Will these costs be reduced if Elton does not produce the additional 500 units, and, if so, by how much? These additional overhead dollars are the crucial costs that should be considered in deciding on this order.

After carefully considering each item shown in the cost statement in Table 13–2, the Elton management has isolated certain items that would *really change* if an additional 500 units were produced (Table 13–3).

Many a cry will be raised at such an estimate because the project is not "carrying its fair share of allocated costs." Strictly speaking, this is true. But what will be accomplished if Elton holds out for a price in excess of $2,600 and does not make the sale? Suppose the top offer is $2,200. If Elton holds out for $2,600 it would be passing up $770 ($2,200 − $1,530). Stated in another way, Elton would give up a chance to get incremental revenue of $2,200 while incurring only $1,530 in incremental costs.

TABLE 13–3

279

CHAPTER 13
Comparing
Courses of Action

	Added Cost for 500 Units
Labor	$ 700
Material	750
Power and materials handling	50
General overhead	30
	$1,530

Incremental analysis dictates that unless some alternative use of the facilities represented by $1,070 in sunk costs added more than $770 in additional revenue, Elton would be foolish to turn down this proposal. It should also be noted that Elton would be wise to turn down the proposal if accepting the $2,200 offer would result in losses of more than $770 in *later* price negotiations. However, any future loss that will result from taking this order at a low price is really an incremental cost of the decision. The decision-maker can estimate the amount of "opportunity cost" (that is, income lost in other alternatives or future pricing of this fitting) and compare it with the income gained by taking the order.

Variable Versus Incremental Costs

We have just faced the first problem encountered in applying the incremental principle of costs—namely, the conventional accounting practice of allocating fixed costs. A second major problem is faced when we attempt to use standard accounting records to forecast costs. A distinction is commonly made between "fixed" and "variable" costs. From our previous observations it would seem that we could arrive at incremental costs by taking only the latter. Unfortunately, the commonly used variable costs are not the same as incremental costs, because they are normally computed as average variable costs. In addition, certain costs that are categorized as fixed in accounting terms may be incremental under other conditions. The following two situations illustrate these problems.

Suppose the Elton company received an order for 5,000 more pipe fittings. Elton would have to buy a second specialized machine to be able to accept this order. The cost of buying the machine, a fixed cost in the usual accounting sense, is an incremental cost in this instance. It is a cost that will be incurred if the proposal is accepted but would not be incurred if the proposal is turned down.

You may ask why we cannot merely add such special fixed costs to the average variable costs computed by the accountant. To see why not, let us leave

280

PART III
Planning:
Elements of
Rational
Decision-Making

TABLE 13–4

Volume	Total Variable Cost	Average Variable Cost	Incremental Cost
0	0	0	0
10	$150,000	$15,000	$150,000 (for 10 units)
11	160,000	14,545	10,000
12	168,000	14,000	8,000
13	176,000	13,769	8,000
14	185,000	13,214	9,000
15	200,000	13,333	15,000

the Elton example and examine the lists of costs for Millard Stamping Machines in Table 13–4. This table illustrates why variable costs, computed as averages, differ from incremental costs.

As you can see, the difference between average variable costs and incremental costs can be considerable, because average costs are averages of total variable costs, while incremental costs are based only on the variable costs of the additional unit or units being considered.

To illustrate how a wrong decision might be reached if it were based on average variable costs, suppose the best price the twelfth unit could fetch was $11,000. If we were to use average variable costs, we would probably turn the offer down since the incremental revenue of $11,000 does not seem to cover the costs of the twelfth unit. The pertinent cost for the twelfth unit, however, is the incremental cost figure, $8,000; using this measure, we see that incremental revenue for the twelfth unit does exceed the increase in costs incurred in producing it.

By the same token, suppose the best price offered for the fifteenth unit was $14,000. Average variable cost ($13,313) reduces the impact of the high cost of producing this fifteenth unit by averaging it in with the lower costs of the first 14 units. As a result, $14,000 of incremental revenue seems to make this price acceptable. Again, however, the significant measure of the cost of the fifteenth unit is the *additional* cost of producing it—the incremental cost of $15,000. In this case, incremental revenue ($14,000) does not exceed incremental costs ($15,000). Unless there are other reasons for taking a $1,000 loss on this sale, the offer should be turned down.

Adjusting for Differences in Time

Alternatives are difficult to compare when one produces large cash income (or requires a substantial outlay) at a much earlier date than others. If we receive cash early, we can use this capital for other purposes; we can lend it at interest if a more attractive use is not available within the company. If, on the other hand, we have to make large outlays early, the capital tied up has a direct or imputed interest cost. To remove this difference caused by *when* cash flows in and out, we can adjust all receipts and disbursements to "present cash value," just as a banker discounts a bond or some other asset that will not turn to cash for several years.

SIMPLIFYING PROJECTION
OF INTANGIBLES

The preceding section has focused on concepts for determining the relevant elements of cost and revenue associated with each alternative. In many complex situations, though, alternatives will also produce drawbacks and benefits that are difficult to translate into dollar costs and dollar revenues. Many of these intangible implications, however, can be stated in dollar terms if we avoid the temptation to evaluate them directly. Consider what happened at Millard Stamping Machines when management faced a decision on whether to accept an offer of $11,000 for one of its machines. Assuming that 11 machines had already been produced and sold for $16,000 and that this sale involves a new customer, what should they do?

Based on the tangible and relevant cost and revenue, an incremental outlay of $8,000 will bring in incremental revenue of $11,000. But what about the intangibles? For example, consider just the following two:

1) Possible difficulty in getting the normal $16,000 price from future customers.
2) Possible advantages of getting a foot in the door of the new customer, which may lead to future sales of equipment and parts.

Rather than merely try to weigh apples ($3,000 incremental gain) and oranges (plus and minus the intangibles), we should attempt to put a dollar sign on the intangibles. This is, in effect, what we would do intuitively anyway. So let us identify the elements involved in intangible factors and attempt to express the anticipated effect on these elements in dollar terms. For the first intangible, we should forecast the following:

1) How many future machines are we likely to sell at the $16,000 price if we reject this sale?
2) How many future customers are likely to know what price we charged for the 12 machines?
3) Of those who might know, how many are in a position to demand a price below $16,000?
4) How far below this price will they demand?

Answering any of these questions will indeed involve a great deal of educated guessing. However, we can make these guesses somewhat more easily

282

PART III
Planning:
Elements of
Rational
Decision-Making

and accurately than a comprehensive guess about the more general question of "upsetting normal prices."

With the second intangible, the benefits of getting "a foot in the door," the same kind of projections can be attempted:

1) How large a business does this customer do?
2) Is he likely to require additional equipment we make? If so, how much?
3) Will he be willing and able to pay normal prices for future purchases?
4) How much future parts-replacement is required, and what is the profit on such replacement?

Again, by taking the elements that determine the nature and magnitude of the intangible and projecting each in dollar terms, we can come closer to developing a dollar projection for the whole intangible factor.

In some cases, to be sure, no matter how hard we try there will be intangible consequences that defy quantification. In the field of operations research, investigators are currently attempting, through forced-choice comparisons, to develop some valid system for translating the implications of intangibles into dollar terms. However, much remains to be done before such "utility models" (as they are often called) can be widely used.

In summary, we should seek to forecast and translate into dollar terms as many of the implications of each alternative as possible. Then the remaining, nondollar considerations can be kept to a minimum and presented for final consideration, juxtaposed to the dollar projections. This process does not remove the need for some kind of forecasting theory, nor reduce the desirability of obtaining relevant data, nor make the conclusions less subjective. Its purpose is to put projections into a form that will ease comparisons of alternatives.

NARROWING THE NUMBER
OF ALTERNATIVES

The energy of managers is limited, and psychologically most of us prefer to work on plans that have a good prospect of being carried out. So the quicker we can hit paydirt, the better. To expedite getting at the main alternatives, we can do two things: accept constraint on alternatives and group similar alternatives during a first screening.

A diagnosis, as described in Chapter 11, often helps develop a list of limits that must be met by a satisfactory solution. We may treat these limits as constraints; that is, we may check proposed alternatives against limits, and if an alternative does not meet them, we can discard it. For instance, one small company seeking an additional product line might decide that a new product must be producible on existing equipment because the company has unused capacity and lacks capital to buy new facilities. Another company might say that a new product must be something its present sales organization could handle; any new product that failed to meet such a basic requirement would be eliminated from further consideration. With alternatives narrowed down by testing them against constraints, we can give closer attention to the eligible ones that remain.

In still other situations we may have such a large number of alternatives that comparing all of them even on one or two crucial factors would be tedious. To deal with this difficulty, we can group the alternatives into classes, pick a representative from each class, and compare these representative proposals. Then, having found the class that shows up best, we can concentrate on alternatives within that class. Such a procedure is often used in plant-location studies. First, a region is selected by comparing a city from each region; then cities in the most attractive region are compared; finally, specific sites in one or two of the most desirable cities are given detailed study.

In any narrowing process, such as those we have suggested in this section, we risk discarding a course of action that, if completely analyzed, would appear very desirable. Nevertheless, as a practical matter, a complete analysis of all consequences of each alternative is impossible. Using constraints and groupings to narrow down alternatives probably has the least likelihood of error.

CONCENTRATING ON CRUCIAL FACTORS

The burdensome task of projecting the consequences of following each selected alternative can be further simplified by giving primary attention to those factors that help us most in discriminating between good and not-so-good alternatives.

Satisfactory Levels for Some Factors

For some factors, it is possible to simplify by setting a satisfactory level of achievement—a level where an objective is met adequately. Any alternative that achieves this level is acceptable. If all proposed courses of action are satisfactory by this standard, there is little or no difference in incremental values. The factor then becomes a minor consideration in making the choice, or may be set aside entirely.

The concept of acceptable achievement ("satisficing") is widely used. Consider production costs. Theoretically, every manager wants to lower his costs continually—at least, so economists assume. But in practice, we find that a manager keeps his eye on critical levels of cost. When competition is sharp, the production costs of other companies set the critical level; or when a product

284

PART III
Planning:
Elements of
Rational
Decision-Making

has a popular price—say, one dollar—the important level is the one that permits a company to get the product on the market at the popular price while maintaining adequate margins to distributors in order to sustain sales volume. Production costs higher than such critical levels are unsatisfactory, and executives will press to reduce costs to the acceptable level. Even lower costs are desirable, to be sure, but the pressure to achieve them is not so great. In other words, the importance of increments in cost savings drops markedly after the critical level is achieved.

Establishing satisfactory levels for quality is also often useful. Bringing quality up to a given standard is highly important, but improvements beyond that point, though desirable, are not nearly so valuable. On the other hand, for such matters as accident prevention or sales volume, there is usually no clear-cut level at which incremental values change sharply.

Where "satisfactory" achievement levels apply, an executive finds that decision-making is simplified. He can reject a proposal if it is unsatisfactory on any count, and thereby narrow the number of alternatives for consideration. If the acceptable standard eliminates all alternatives, he seeks new proposals. As the last resort, he lowers his acceptable levels. If two or more proposals meet all the tests of acceptability, then he is back with the problem of choosing between them. Nevertheless, the problem is now simpler because fewer proposals are still in the running, and some factors can be disregarded because differences between them are insignificant.

Major Factors Affecting Choice

When we choose among alternatives, one, two, or perhaps three factors are almost always most important in making the decision. If we can single out and study these factors first, we may be able to eliminate the least-attractive alternatives promptly.[1]

A paint company was comparing candidates to head up promotional work on a product discovered in its research laboratory. The product was a new plastic that had unusually high resistance to heat and abrasion and could presumably be used for parts in machines and rockets. Because the company's regular sales organization concentrated on paint, a new job was created for this distinctive product. Little supervision would be available, and most of the work

---

[1] The advice appears to have run a full circle. In the beginning of the chapter we stressed looking at all consequences, and now we say to focus on the important consequences first. The distinction rests on two factors: 1) Taking a full perspective will ensure that the pressures of the moment, or conventional thinking, do not lead to inadequate coverage; once this perspective is achieved, wise simplification is possible and necessary. 2) A particular sequence for studying factors does not preclude full consideration of all factors for at least a few alternatives. Admittedly, unless the simplifying steps are taken with care, there is some risk of screening out prematurely a good alternative. But the surviving alternatives—the ones being considered at the time of the final choice—should have had the full screening proposed at the opening of the chapter.

would involve developing agreements with other companies for use of the product. Numerous qualifications could be listed for such a job, so all candidates who met minimum standards or limits could be compared on each qualification. The personnel director simplified the comparison, however, by selecting two qualities he considered most important for this job—initiative and decision-making talent. On the basis of these criteria, he was able to narrow the list of candidates to three men who ranked highest on these qualities. Then, he carefully compared the three men on many other factors, such as knowledge of consumer industries, emotional stability, social sensitivity, salary requirements, and so on. To have attempted to appraise all candidates on all factors would have taken more time than the executives were able to spend on this selection problem.

The use of major factors can also be illustrated by the power mower company we considered. The firm's analysis of income and costs clearly showed that a move to the West Coast was desirable only if sales would thereby increase substantially. Sales volume was thus a crucial factor. So before spending more time in analyzing factors such as quality control, corporation taxes, and labor conditions, management should thoroughly explore the likelihood of achieving a large sales increase.

CONCLUSION

In this chapter, we picked up the rational decision-making process after a management problem has been discovered and clarified through diagnosis and possible solutions have already been identified. We then must compare the proposed solutions to develop a basis for finally choosing an action.

This comparison of alternatives is based on forecasted consequences of each proposal. We have to forecast both the setting—environment—in which the plan will be executed and the effects of actions we take in that setting. However, since both environment and consequences are uncertain, forecasting alone will probably swamp us with many possible outcomes. Consequently, we take a series of steps to simplify the process; we want the comparison to be comprehensive and fair and at the same time viable.

First we try to identify all significant consequences of each proposed line of action. At this point, we are concerned with anticipating the full ramifications of our decision. Unfortunately this approach may make the comparison tedious and extended, so we must find ways of simplifying the comparison without doing serious damage to the breadth and perspective we have just urged. Five types of simplification are often helpful: 1) focusing attention on the different consequences and disregarding those aspects of a situation that will be unaffected by any alternative; 2) combining all dollar figures into one or two net totals; 3) simplifying the projection of intangibles by assigning "trade-off" dollar amounts to subjective feelings about importance; 4) narrowing the

286

PART III
Planning:
Elements of
Rational
Decision-Making

number of alternatives that are projected in detail; and 5) giving primary attention to factors that will most affect the final choice.

But a comparison is not a decision. We still must decide which set of projected results we want. Value judgment and allowances for uncertainty enter into our final choice. These matters are discussed in the next chapter.

FOR CLASS DISCUSSION

1) "I'm fed up with being 'encouraged' to be creative. We hold a meeting to solve a problem, and my boss says to suggest even wacky alternatives if they occur to us. No criticism is permitted and we toss in one idea after another. Then, after all the encouragement and permissiveness, if I ask about my suggestions a few days later, I find that behind our backs my boss and his associates have spent hours ripping our ideas to shreds. All this creativity business is just play acting." How would you reply to this complaint by a junior executive in a large advertising agency?

2) "The trouble with sophisticated forecasting techniques is that the techniques are so complicated and the predictions so precise that people tend to believe they are accurate." Comment on the several aspects of this somewhat cynical view of forecasting.

3) How is it possible to project *all* of the potentially important consequences of *all* of the possible alternatives to complex problems?

4) Fred Homer has invented a new kind of stain that is excellent for giving furniture an antique look. A large paint company has offered him royalties which would average $7,500 a year for the next 15 years, in exchange for the formula and exclusive rights for that period. For many years, however, Mr. Homer has wanted to go into business on his own, and he estimates that by working on a small scale he could make profits of $12,000. This would be his sole income, for he would have to give up his present job, in which he earns $8,000 a year. 1) What would you advise Mr. Homer to do? Show how a comparison of alternatives would support your decision. 2) How would you estimate the value to Mr. Homer of being in business on his own? 3) How would you reflect the fact that at the end of 15 years the royalties might cease while the business would presumably continue?

5) Assume a company has raw material in its inventory that it purchased months ago for $1,000. This material can be used in producing a special product that would be made and sold at a marginal price to please a good customer. If the material is not so used, it will be sold to another company for $950 in order to make room in the warehouse for other material. The material in question will ultimately be replaced, but not for at least one year. It is estimated that the cost of replacing it a year or more from now will be $1,100. What is the relevant cost of material to be added to other costs in deciding whether to produce the special product for the good customer? Explain.

6) Often a thorough comparison of alternative courses of action would require a careful analysis of the assumptions and premises on which projected payoffs are based. When such analysis is impractical, what steps might be taken to judge the soundness of a projected payoff?

7) "I will always pay more for the right questions than for the right answers!" In which situations may this be a sound idea, and in which could it lead to trouble? Give specific examples.

8) "I envy business managers because they can always weigh the benefits and costs of their alternatives in dollar terms. For most of my toughest problems, this is impossible." Comment on this observation by the head of a large municipal hospital.

Cases

For cases involving issues covered in this chapter, see especially the following. Particularly relevant questions are listed after each case.

The Delaware Corporation (p. 113), 9
Merchantville School System (p. 217), 12
Atlas Chemical Company (p. 321), 8, 9
Marten Fabricators (p. 316), 6, 7, 8, 9, 10
Monroe Wire and Cable (p. 436), 7, 8
Graham, Smith, & Bendel, Inc. (p. 445), 9
Family Service of Gotham (p. 532), 5, 6
Household Products Company (p. 627), 8

FOR FURTHER READING

Cleland, D. I. and W. R. King, eds., *Systems Analysis and Project Management,* 2nd ed. New York: McGraw-Hill Book Company, 1975, Chapter 4.

Reviews basic concepts for comparing alternatives and making a rational choice.

Dean, J., *Capital Budgeting.* New York: Columbia University Press, 1951.

Comparison of capital-expenditure projects by means of discounted cash-flow estimates—a classic on this topic.

Emory, C. W. and P. Niland, *Making Management Decisions.* Boston: Houghton Mifflin Company, 1968, Chapter 5.

Methods for evaluating alternatives, presented in operational terms. Chapters 6–13 give a good, nontechnical explanation of quantitative techniques for evaluating alternatives.

Radford, K. J., *Managerial Decision Making.* Reston, Va.: Reston Publishing Company, 1975.

A useful explanation of management-science approaches to decision-making.

Shillinglaw, G., *Cost Accounting,* rev. ed. Homewood, Ill.: Richard D. Irwin, Inc., 1967.

The management viewpoint and management problems are stressed throughout this valuable text. Chapter 3 gives introduction to "decisions and costs."

14 Making the Choice

COMPLETING THE ANALYSIS

Decision-making has many facets. Diagnosis defines a difficulty or opportunity in terms of a gap between desired and expected states. It helps pinpoint the obstacles to realizing the desired state, and it focuses attention on any limits that must be observed in seeking alternatives. Past experience and creative thought suggest possible ways of achieving the desired goals. Tough, critical analysis enables us to project and compare the consequences of the most promising ways of meeting the problem. And yet there remains the decisive act—picking one of the alternatives and saying, "This is it."

The present chapter is concerned with this final act—settling on the action to be taken. For managers who must make the decisive choice, we shall examine three groups of suggestions: placing values on projected results, adjusting for uncertainty, and testing a choice.

PLACING VALUES ON PROJECTED RESULTS

What emerges from a comparison of alternatives does not constitute a decision. Someone has to decide which set of projected results is best. And to do so, he must apply values.

A college student, in picking an elective course, makes a value judgment.

Suppose he has narrowed his choice to either History of the Soviet Union or Corporation Finance. Investigation indicates that the first course would be fun to take—good prof, air-conditioned room, current events; besides, it would be good background for the years ahead. But the Finance course is practical stuff that might really pay off, on the job or in personal investments. The Finance prof is a good egg, but he piles on the work. Tuition and credit toward a degree can be disregarded because they are the same for each course. His projections of the alternatives help him see the implications of each, but he still has to make a choice based on the weights his values place on subjective factors. What weight does he assign to enjoyable experience, cultural background, courses that may "pay off"?

Business decisions, although they include more dollar projections, also involve values. For instance, an American manufacturing firm that wished to enter the Toronto market was considering either using an agent or opening its own branch. Table 14–1 summarizes the chief differences in anticipated results.

TABLE 14–1

Considerations	Agent	Company Branch
Investment	0	$30,000
Expenses	5 percent of sales	$12,000 for year
Annual sales range [1]	$50,000 to $300,000	$100,000 to $500,000
Control	Difficult to specify behavior; agent free to quit	Responsive to specific requests; continuity more assured

[1] Profits at various sales volumes were not computed. High variable costs plus freight and import taxes indicated that gross profit per unit in Toronto would be virtually constant—and low. Hence the emphasis on sales volume and selling expense.

The firm's choice clearly depended on the relative values placed on investment, expenses, sales volume, and control. If sales volume and control were paramount, then a branch operation would be the better selection. But if the firm wished to avoid risking capital and wanted to be sure that expenses were proportionate to capital, then an agent would be the preferred choice. The fact that not all of the factors to be weighed can be summarized into a single dollar measure of "net benefit" requires a balancing of tangible and intangible payoffs. Some kind of value system, in short, is necessary for most key decisions.

Deriving Values from Objectives

The first place to look for values is within the objectives. In the example of the student who was selecting a course, knowing why he was going to college

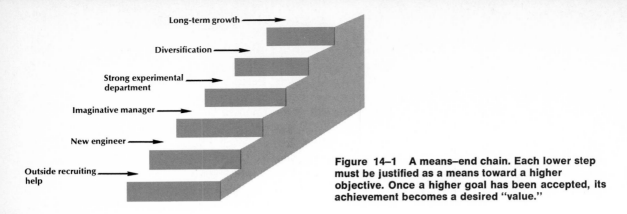

Long-term growth

Diversification

Strong experimental department

Imaginative manager

New engineer

Outside recruiting help

Figure 14–1 A means–end chain. Each lower step must be justified as a means toward a higher objective. Once a higher goal has been accepted, its achievement becomes a desired "value."

would guide him in weighing the advantages and disadvantages of the history and the finance courses. His college objective, in turn, might well be derived from a still broader objective—the kind of person he aspires to be.

In our other example, the firm that wanted to enter the Toronto market found that its objectives indicated where to put the heavier weight. This was a conservative, management-owned company with limited capital, and its executives chiefly sought a stable operation with assured profits. Consequently, they placed high value on the low risk of a sales agency. But if the dominant objective of the company had been growth, it is clear that a different set of values would have prevailed, and a sales branch might have been the final choice.

Subsidiary objectives and values are derived from major objectives through a means–end chain. Consider, for example, how the use of an executive-recruiting firm is related to the objective of long-run growth of a plastics company (as shown in Figure 14–1). Each of the steps had high value to the company. However, the lower steps (subsidiary objectives) had value only by virtue of their relationship to the principal objective through a means–end chain. This particular analysis was helpful to the company's chief engineer when he was confronted with a proposal to install a long-service, versatile mechanic as head of the experimental department. He gave the proposal no value because it was not the best-known means of reaching the ultimate end.

Obviously, if any link in such a means–end chain is faulty, the values from that point downward are unsound. Many a railroad passenger-agent has stressed the value of promoting passenger business because of its contribution to net revenues, whereas some railroad executives contend that passenger business is not a good means of increasing net revenue. If these executives are correct, then the chain between a promotion campaign for passengers and the objective of increased net revenues is faulty; even an ingenious promotional scheme will lack positive value.

Dynamic Social Values

In practice a manager often finds himself working with several means–end chains. He is trying to choose a course of action that will contribute to several objectives, and there will be a means–end chain for each. We have already run up against multiple objectives. Stable employment growth, short-run profit, low risk, ease of control are examples of internal objectives we have frequently mentioned. Theoretically all such objectives could be considered means to some single super objective, but that single goal becomes so abstract and the linkages to it so vague that it serves no practical purpose. Instead, as with our personal goals, we recognize half a dozen or more significant end results to which we would like to contribute, and we appraise a proposed action in terms of all of these objectives.[1]

Multiple goals abound in the external social arena. A quick review of the bills introduced into Congress gives a hint of the diversity of results various groups in society would like to achieve. Enterprises are inevitably caught up in this great swirl of human aspirations, for each firm can survive only if it contributes positively to fulfilling some aspirations and if it avoids serious injury to others. Situations similar to that faced by Consolidated Edison Company of New York are common: Responding to growing demand for electricity and customer complaints of brownouts, the company set an expansion goal for its generating capacity. This goal had to be reconciled with environmental objectives: A proposed nuclear plant on Long Island was dropped because of fear of radiation, and expansion of a Hudson River plant ran into thermal-pollution obstacles. Moreover, the company could not overlook profit objectives, which were necessary to support the huge loans that would be necessary when an acceptable plant site could be found. In addition to catering to these service, environment, and profit objectives, the company has goals regarding black employment, urban renewal, and other development of the area from which its future business will spring.

Furthermore, these multiple objectives must change because the environment is dynamic. Continuing the preceding example, customer service must respond to the summer peak caused by a dramatic rise in air conditioning, and generating technology must respond to reducing metropolitan air pollution.

The managers of an enterprise, we said in Chapter 1, have to devise a scheme that will effectively integrate the enterprise to its dynamic environment. Whether it be a hospital, an aerospace company, or a public utility, each needs a cluster of objectives that define the particular way it hopes to fit into the current world. As the world changes, so too will those objectives. This development of a "master strategy" is examined in Chapter 16.

It is from this set of objectives that the critical value structure of an enterprise is derived.

The stubborn fact is that the integration process results in a *set* of objectives—not just one—that must be modified as the opportunities and require-

[1] The conversion of results directed toward a social or other nonmonetary goal into dollars, in the manner proposed for intangibles in the preceding chapter, does not change the multiple-objectives situation. The purpose of the conversion is to simplify comparison of alternatives by expressing as many factors as we can in a single value scale. The objectives remain, as the term "trade-off" implies; and only when an action affects the achievement of an objective do we attach points (dollars) to it. It is important to note that the use of dollars as a convenient common denominator does not mean that we are concerned only with dollar profits.

292

PART III
Planning:
Elements of
Rational
Decision-Making

ments of the environment change. Central management selects and modifies the objectives so as to create a unique and unified enterprise. Consequently the task of formulating and reformulating a value system for the enterprise is endless. At any point in time, however, the values on which to base decisions should be tied to the prevailing objectives.

Comparing Incremental Values

When alternative plans contribute to, or detract from, several *different* goals, how does a manager set values on the various results? A simple ranking of goals is likely to be misleading. We cannot say that sales are always more important than expenses, or that investment in equipment always takes priority over labor turnover. Such a ranking may be useful for a particular set of conditions, but we get in trouble if we carry it too far. For a second helping, we might prefer lamb chops over mashed potatoes, but our digestive system (and budget) would get out of whack if we ate all lamb chops and no mashed potatoes.

Actually the importance of any element usually depends on how much of it we have; the more there is, the less value attaches to an additional supply. But this is by no means always true. Under some circumstances, increments continue to be attractive, whereas under other situations, increments are of little significance. Thus a certain amount of good, clear water is a necessity for most factories, but once this supply is ensured, additional water has little value (or, *utility* as it is called by economists).

The idea of concentrating on incremental value applies to all sorts of conditions. Suppose we are setting a purchasing policy and one factor is the number of suppliers of heating oil. The difference between no supplier and one supplier means life or death for the company. Two suppliers are more desirable than one because the competition would free the company from being at the mercy of a single source; even so, a second supplier is by no means so vital as the first. A third supplier is desirable, even though less important than the second. By the time there are five or six firms actively competing for business, each additional contender is of little significance.

It is interesting to speculate how far we can extend this general principle. In considering candidates for an executive position, a manager would normally include honesty as a minimum requirement. But is honesty a black-or-white matter, or are there degrees of honesty? How much more attractive is a fastidious candidate than one who is willing to be "reasonable" as long as everyone gets a "fair deal." High quality of work or of a product is always desirable, but what constitutes "quality" varies with the needs of a particular situation. Improvements in quality beyond an accepted standard may be welcome, but the value of successive increments of quality may not keep pace with additional costs.

In our earlier discussion of comparing alternatives, we stressed differences in results—differences in sales income, in customer goodwill, in expenses, in executive enthusiasm, and in any other factor that would be significantly affected by following plan-A instead of plan-B. Here we are considering how much value to attach to such differences—or increments—and pointing out that their value depends on the urgency of a company's need for a particular increment at a given time. When TWA was on the verge of bankruptcy in the 1970s, the incremental value it would assign to a million dollars more capital, for example, was much greater than the incremental values it would attach to a 20 percent improvement in passenger goodwill or two million dollars increase in gross revenues. If TWA had been in strong financial shape, the relationship between incremental values of capital, goodwill, and gross revenues would have been quite different.

Company Versus Individual Values

Making a choice among alternatives clearly involves many subjective judgments—first in projecting the consequences of each alternative, next in placing a value on the differences for each factor, and finally in balancing incremental values to arrive at a decision. Objective data can help, but, especially in the later phases of choosing, an executive must rely heavily on his judgment.

Reliance on subjective judgment unfortunately opens up the opportunity for substituting personal desires for company welfare. For example, customer-A may get prompt delivery of a scarce product because he is the personal friend of a manager, whereas the company good would have been better served by sending the product to customer-B. Although such deliberate mixing of company and personal values does occur, there is surprisingly little of it in American business. Most managers recognize that, in their roles as company employees, their personal preferences are irrelevant. They must view problems in terms of "what is good for the company," and the distinction between business and self is considered a matter of integrity. Ability to make the distinction is an important element in self-respect and is a criterion of central management in selecting people for responsible positions.

Unconscious biases are more critical than deliberate self-serving. A person naturally deals with a problem in terms of his experience and the pressures that weigh on him. A sales representative is more sensitive to sales needs and a production supervisor to plant needs; a person who is fearful of a layoff attaches higher value to stability than one who feels secure; an executive who recalls with nostalgia the days when his company was small—when he didn't have to fuss with so many reports and when "clearance with staff" was not part of his vocabulary—is likely to place more weight on the difficulties of further expansion than a young, aggressive president. Each of these people is sincere in his evaluation, but we can suspect that personal values have influenced his judgment.

One fact of life is that most of us are good at thinking up logical reasons for doing what we want. We kid ourselves. In making value judgments, it is entirely possible to seek earnestly for the best course for our company and at

294
PART III
Planning:
Elements of
Rational
Decision-Making

the same time unconsciously attach values that tend to favor our own interests. We must recognize that the danger of confusing personal desires with sound company values is inherent in choosing among alternatives. To avoid this danger is one reason for testing choices along the lines we outline at the end of this chapter. We shall also offer several safeguards when we discuss devices for company planning in Part Four.

ADJUSTING FOR UNCERTAINTY

One other major consideration in choosing among alternatives is *uncertainty*, which is as much a part of business life as breathing is of human life. Business cycles, weather, wars and threats of wars, competition, inventions, new laws, and a host of other dynamic situations and events make the future uncertain. Within a business firm, machine breakdowns, irregularities in human performance, and failures to maintain standard operating conditions increase our quandary.

A manager must be willing to make a decision even when he is uncertain. The same man who takes a tough, challenging attitude toward proposals that are presented to him must be willing to risk making a decision although he is fully aware that the future may play tricks with his present expectations. Let us take a look, then, at how we may best incorporate the element of uncertainty into a choice of action.

Statistical Probability

For a few types of risks, we have enough statistical evidence to compute the chances that a given event will occur. Life insurance provides the classic example. Life-insurance companies know that probably fewer than 1 percent of men age 20 will die during the ensuing five years, whereas about 5 percent of the men age 50 will die in the same period. The companies insure enough lives so that these probabilities fit their business. Thus, if an insurance executive were drawing up five-year contracts for 20-year-olds and 50-year-olds, he knows that

Figure 14–2 Businesses face a variety of uncertainties. Although careful managing can lessen the danger of some of these, managers have little or no control over others.

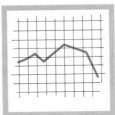

Fire   War   Strike   Prices   Timing

he should get over five times as much income from the latter to make the two policies comparable.

Similarly, if a manager had an investment opportunity with a 50 percent chance of returning $100,000 profit, a 40 percent chance of only $20,000 profit, and a 10 percent chance of losing $50,000, he could weigh these payoffs by their respective probabilities and develop an "expected value for the alternative"—in this case, $53,000; that is, ($100,000 $\times$ .5) + ($20,000 $\times$ .4) − ($50,000 $\times$ .1).

Statisticians warn us to be cautious about this simple approach to uncertainty. Rarely does a company have enough of the same kinds of risk so that losses and gains work out to the most probable result. Because it is likely that actual results will deviate from the average, we should know something about that deviation. Are the actual results of customer acceptance of bids on special jobs likely to be close to our previous 25 percent average—between 20 and 30 percent, for example—or is there a good chance that they will range anywhere from 5 to 45 percent? The central figure is 25 percent in both instances, but in the second case we would face much greater uncertainty about future sales.

In only a relatively few decisions can we use statistical probability in a strict sense to adjust for uncertainty. To make precise use of probability techniques, we need data on a large number of similar cases, and we must have a clearly defined sample. Nevertheless, probability theory does give us some useful clues to thinking about uncertain situations, two of which we have mentioned: 1) When the alternatives we are considering have different probabilities, we can multiply the appropriate values in each alternative by their respective probabilities and arrive at "expected values"; these values can then be compared, since differences in probabilities have been taken into account. 2) The width of the range within which results are likely to fall (the 20 to 30 percent and the 5 to 45 percent in the example above) may be as significant as the average or the single result that is most probable.

Inferred Probability

We often infer from limited data the probability of a particular outcome. Such predictions are common in everyday speech. "The Los Angeles Dodgers have one chance in three to win the pennant." "There's only one chance in ten that the UAW will strike at Chrysler this year." "There's a fifty-fifty likelihood we'll land that government order." "The odds are two to one that Smith will turn down the promotion."

Such inferred probabilities help us to deal with uncertainty. They at least offer a rough judgment on how serious a risk is. To say, "There's one chance in twenty our Navy contract will be canceled" is much more helpful than "There's a possibility the contract may be canceled."

Occasionally, management can put these probability guesses to more specific use. For instance, a company with annual earnings before taxes of $750,000 was rapidly approaching a stalemate in its union negotiations. The workers wanted a large wage increase that management was not ready to grant.

296

PART III
Planning:
Elements of
Rational
Decision-Making

After a long conference with his key executives, the president concluded, "I think there is a 25 percent chance of a serious strike. If it comes, our earnings will probably drop $300,000." The controller responded, "Then in comparing costs of various alternatives, we should figure the risk of a strike as a $75,000 cost [$300,000 × .25]." The comments of the president and the controller can be summarized as in Table 14–2.

TABLE 14–2

Situation	Estimated Loss of Earnings	Inferred Probability	Loss × Probability
No strike	0	75%	0
Serious strike	$300,000	25	$75,000
		100%	
	Loss adjusted for probability		$75,000

After more discussion, the president and controller worked out a probability chart that is more informative because it shows the likelihood of losses ranging from zero to $800,000 (Table 14–3). It also indicates that when a full

TABLE 14–3

Possible Length of Strike	Estimated Loss of Earnings	Inferred Probability	Loss × Probability
0 days	0	35%	0
3-5 days	$ 50,000	40	$ 20,000
3 weeks	200,000	15	30,000
6 weeks	400,000	7	28,000
10 weeks	800,000	3	24,000
		100%	
	Loss adjusted for probability		$102,000

range of possible consequences is included, the seriousness of a strike threat is somewhat worse than the company first thought.

A similar analysis would be helpful to the president of the power mower company considering a new West Coast assembly shop. Estimates indicate that $19,000 will be lost if the proposed shop handles only the current volume of business in that territory, whereas a net gain of $59,000 will be realized if a local

TABLE 14–4

297

CHAPTER 14
Making
the Choice

Possible Sales Volume (Annual)	Estimated Net Gain	Probability Inferred by President	Net Gain × Probability
$200,000	$−19,000	0	0
250,000	600	50%	$ 300
300,000	20,100	30	6,030
350,000	39,700	15	5,955
400,000	59,300	5	2,965
		100%	
	Net gain adjusted for probability		$15,250

Rate of return on initial investment of
$55,000 = 28% (i.e., $15,250 ÷ $55,000)

assembly plant doubles sales, as the sales manager predicts. The chief uncertainty in the picture is sales volume. The president feels the sales manager is overoptimistic. He grants that some increase in volume is likely, but he believes that there is only a small chance to achieve the $400,000 volume within a few years. Table 14–4 sharpens these feelings and relates them to estimates of gain for different sales levels.

The president's informed guess is that sales volume will be between $250,000 and $400,000 per year, with the lower volume much more likely. When he adjusts the net-gain estimates by the inferred probabilities, the final value he assigns to the new shop is about $15,000 per year. Although this figure is not so enticing as what the optimistic sales manager would forecast, it still represents an attractive 28 percent return on added investment in West Coast operations.

Unfortunately, these final figures "adjusted for probability"—the $15,250 in the power mower illustration and the $102,000 in the strike example—are quite synthetic. If we want a single value, they are the best we can do. If the companies in these cases had hundreds of similar (though independent) problems, then the average results might be close to the adjusted figures. In a single instance, however, the actual outcome is almost certain to differ from the adjusted total. In deciding whether to open a West Coast branch, the president of the power mower company may be equally interested in the fact that there is a fifty-fifty chance that the operation will just break even as he is in the synthetic adjusted total. If he had plenty of capital, he might say, "I don't think we'll lose any money, and we might make a handsome profit, so go ahead." On the other hand, if he is short of capital and pressed for earnings, he might decide, "We should allocate our capital and our time to projects where we feel sure of making some profit, even though the potential may not be so high as that in the West Coast operation." In other words, a distribution of probabilities may be as important in making a value judgment as a weighted average.

298

PART III
Planning:
Elements of
Rational
Decision-Making

Similarly, the president of the company confronted with a strike threat may be concerned about the range of chances he is taking. For example, if the company has large payments to make on a bank loan, even a small risk that earnings will be wiped out is serious. But under other circumstances, the company might be quite prepared to take this risk in exchange for other gains. Whenever we face uncertainties, using probabilities—whether by putting them on paper or just estimating them mentally—helps in forming judgments.

Unreliable Data

The vast majority of decisions must be based in part on evidence that is not fully reliable. Trade-association figures might not be representative of an entire industry; equipment salesmen present their products in the best possible light; social tradition requires that the published statements by company presidents bristle with confidence; market surveys by advertising agencies usually point to the need for more advertising; Army generals foresee grave dangers if their appropriation requests are not met in full; and so on. Such data are apt to be only part of the whole truth, and the manner of presentation may be slanted to produce a desired impression.

Of course, a manager who must make a decision tries to get data that is as reliable as possible. But usually he cannot get the full story from his sources. He has to pick up grains of truth and new insights whenever or wherever he can find them. He can ill afford to disregard the opinions of well-informed persons, even though they may be tarnished with bias.

We are all familiar with unreliable data in our daily lives. We learn a lot from food advertising without being upset by copywriters' superlatives. When a high school girl pleads, "Everybody is wearing them," parents interpret the remark to mean that three or four of her friends are sporting the style in question. Such information is not as precise as we might like, but we learn to live with it and even to take effective action on it.

Two simple rules are helpful in using unreliable data: 1) Keep aware of the limitations of the information we are working with; label it "suspect," and perhaps adjust it to what we believe is reasonable. 2) Appraise the person supplying the data. What are his interests, ability, judgment, integrity? The more we know of an individual, the better able we are to evaluate what he says. We can usually reduce uncertainty by considering unreliable as well as reliable data, provided we use it with discretion.

Incomplete Data

The manager who must choose a course of action is on the horns of a dilemma: more information versus more time and expense.

The expense of planning may be substantial. Boeing Aircraft spent over $4,000,000 in designing its K-135 and 707 jet planes before a single order was on the books; a consulting firm was recently paid $60,000 for advice on locating a suburban shopping center; a new layout for a large industrial plant may require several engineer-years of effort. Simpler decisions naturally require less effort, but even they entail expense. Selecting a desk calculator for an office, for instance, calls for studying different kinds of equipment, the needs of the particular office, necessary operating skills, maintenance problems, and so on. Although detailed information on all these points might improve the quality of his decision, we cannot expect an office manager to become an expert in calculating equipment just for the purchase of a single machine.

Timely action may also compete for priority with more complete information. When a competitor cuts prices, or an important customer inquires when delivery can be promised, or the still at an oil refinery breaks down, the executive in charge must decide what to do without delay. The costs and risk incurred by delay may be more serious than the probable error inherent in judging on incomplete information.

Overcoming incompleteness of data is a small decision-making problem in itself. Diagnosis, alternatives, projection, and value judgments are needed. Among the ways of increasing the store of information while keeping expenses of obtaining it within bounds are these: bravely singling out one or two crucial factors and concentrating on gathering facts about them; taking just a sample of the total data we might like to have; and, if feasible, postponing decision until good information becomes available.

Reasonably complete information and prompt decision-making are often hard to combine. The chief hope for conquering this problem is to anticipate the need for such a decision—for instance, guessing that a competitor might cut his prices—and to have pertinent current data already assembled; possibly the military practice of preparing in advance tentative courses of action might even be warranted. Another approach is to split an activity into parts and try to postpone that part where information is the weakest. A multiproduct company, for instance, may plan a weekly television program for months ahead, but may defer writing commercials until market conditions reveal which product will benefit most from advertising at a particular time.

When balancing increased accuracy against expense and time, an executive should think in terms of increments, as with other problems. Will the improved accuracy of a decision that arises from additional data be worth the added expense and time to obtain it?

To summarize: Uncertainty is inherent in choosing a course of action, and, at best, an executive can only reduce it. Thinking in terms of probabilities; being sensitive to, and adjusting for, the bias in the opinion of others; balancing the cost of more data against likely improvement in judgment—these are all ways of dealing with this troublesome issue. Like levees against floods on the Mississippi River, they are helpful primarily as devices for coping with uncertainty rather than for removing it.

CONTRIBUTIONS OF
OPERATIONS RESEARCH

A manager, as we have seen, must often make a choice that involves both a variety of consequences and uncertainty regarding, perhaps, all of these outcomes. So many considerations are involved that devices for summarizing and condensing are very helpful. We shall briefly describe two: operations-research condensations and matrices.

Operations-Research Models

One major contribution of operations research is the concept of a model that summarizes in a few numbers many of the factors involved in a complex choice.[2] Basically, three features are involved in this method of summarizing:

1) Problems are stated in mathematical symbols. Symbols and equations, which make up a convenient shorthand widely used in science, provide a form of expression that is concise and easy for an expert to manipulate. (It also provides the appeal of a professional jargon. To the operations researcher, stating a problem in words is clumsy and vague.)

2) A cardinal rule of the operations researcher is: Build a model. The use of physical models is, of course, a common practice in industry. Aircraft engineers use small models to test new designs in wind tunnels; models of new automobile styles are common in the automobile industry; scale models are often used in studying plant layout. Each model is a symbolic picture that represents certain aspects of a real thing. A model of a management problem in mathematical symbols is similar, except that both the thing being pictured and the way of describing it are more abstract. A model of this sort familiar to business students is the balance-sheet equation:

$$A = L + P$$

where A represents total assets, L total liabilities, and P total proprietorship. This can be elaborated:

$$P_n = P_{(n-1)} + \{I_{(n-1) \to n} - E_{(n-1) \to n}\}$$

in which the proprietorship at the end of year n equals the proprietorship at the end of the previous year plus income (I) during the past year minus expenses (E) during the year, and so on.

But instead of using a conventional model like those for financial accounting, the operations-research man is prepared to build a new model for each problem

[2] We should note that for some kinds of problems, operations-research models also permit us to expand the *number* of alternatives from which a choice is made. When a linear relation exists between *degrees* of input and resulting output, the equations enable us to consider a full spectrum of alternatives involving that relationship. Consequently, by using the equations, we can choose the theoretical optimum degree of, say, investment and inventory.

he studies. He seeks a set of equations that will project consequences, attach values to these consequences, and make allowances for uncertainty. The model hopefully presents an orderly picture of the total problem that otherwise would be dealt with unsystematically in the mind of an executive.

3) The third essential feature of operations research is quantitative measurement of the several independent variables and the dependent variables (predicted results) in the equations. Just as a chemist must measure the temperatures, pressures, and other factors he works with, so must the operations researcher express in quantitative terms the elements in a managerial situation if his model is to be useful in making a choice. This requirement means a tremendous amount of "digging" for facts. It also requires that values be expressed in a uniform scale—usually dollars.

Operations-research models have been applied to a number of complicated management problems. For example, oil companies use them in scheduling refinery runs. Here the problem is determining what proportion of various products to manufacture from a barrel of crude oil. The variables include: different sales prices for gasoline, heating oil, lubricants, asphalt, and other end-products; availability and price of several types of crude oil, each with its own composition and refining characteristics; variations in yields and operating costs of the refinery when a specific crude oil is used to make different proportions of end-products; and costs of storing excess output of specific products during slack seasons. The equations dealing with such refinery-run problems are complex, and electronic computers are necessary to handle the masses of data promptly.

Generally, the situations in which operations research has paid off have these characteristics: 1) A problem is so complicated or involves such a sheer mass of data that it cannot be fully grasped by one person's mind; yet its parts are so interrelated that dividing it into comprehensible units would not necessarily yield the best answer. 2) The relationships are known, clearcut, and of a type that can be expressed by available mathematical formulas. 3) Statistical data is available for all important variables.

The first of these requirements makes the study worth the trouble, the second is necessary to build a satisfactory model, and the third is a requisite for practical application.

Decision Trees

Some decisions involve a series of steps, the second step depending on the outcome of the first, the third depending on the outcome of the second, and so on. Often uncertainty surrounds each step, so we face uncertainty piled on uncertainty. "Decision trees" are a model to deal with such a problem. Here is an illustration.

Exports from Organic Fibers, Inc., to Australia have been expanding. The local Australian sales agent is now insisting on a ten-year contract, but Organic Fibers' overseas manager recommends opening a company sales office as a first step toward building a plant three or four years later. Decision-A is this

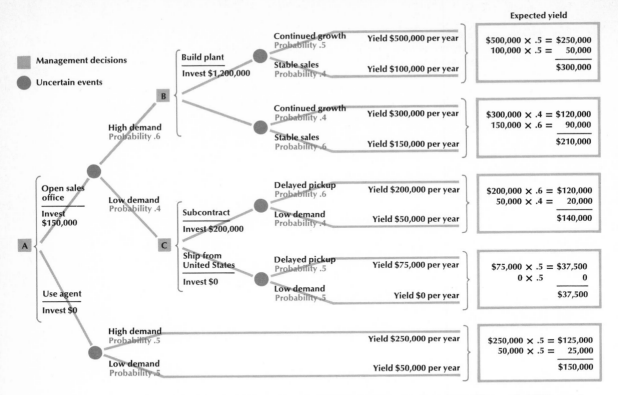

Figure 14–3 **A decision tree for projected Australian expansion. The probabilities and amounts of investments and yields as shown represent management's best estimates on the basis of present knowledge.**

choice between the sales agent or a sales office. Decision-B, to build a plant, will be made only after sales growth has been demonstrated. An alternative to Organic Fibers' building its own plant is to subcontract. In fact if a sales office is opened and growth is slow, subcontracting would still be an alternative to exporting from the United States; this would be decision-C.

To clarify 1) the decisions to be made, 2) the key uncertainties and probabilities, and 3) the estimated yields, the decision tree shown in Fig. 14–3 was prepared. Laying out on a chart the alternative series of events along with estimates of probabilities and estimated net profit is a very helpful device by itself. However, to sharpen the choice even more, we should calculate the "position value" of an established sales office. This can be done by rolling back the expected values as follows:

1) On the basis of our best estimates, *decision-B will be to subcontract.* The difference in expected return from the plant and subcontracting ($300,000 — $210,000 = $90,000) is not large enough to justify the difference in additional investment ($1,200,000 — $200,000 = $1,000,000). So we assume the outcome of decision-B will be an expected yield of $210,000 and an investment of $200,000.

2) *Decision-C will also be to subcontract.* The difference in expected return be-

tween subcontracting and exporting ($140,000 — $37,500 = $102,500) is large enough to justify the additional investment of $200,000. So we assume the outcome of decision-C will be an expected yield of $140,000 and an investment of $200,000.

3) Using the probabilities of high and low demand, which dictate whether we will be faced with decision-B or-C, we can compare the two alternatives at decision point-A. If the company opens the sales office, the expected yield from decision-B is $126,000 ($210,000 × .6), while the yield from decision-C is $56,000 ($140,000 × .4). The total expected yield from opening the sales office is therefore $182,000 ($126,000 + $56,000) on a total investment of $350,000 ($150,000 to open the sales office and $200,000 to subcontract). On the other hand if the company uses a sales agent, the total yield that can be expected is $150,000, without any initial investment.

4) *Decision-A will be to use the agent.* The difference in expected yield of opening a sales office or using the agent ($182,000 — $150,000 = $32,000) is not large enough to justify the initial investment in the sales office plus the investment necessary to subcontract in Australia ($150,000 + $200,000 = $350,000).

Decision trees can be drawn to fit all sorts of situations, and refinements of the preceding illustration—such as more alternatives, more than two levels of risk, discounting for when income and outflows will occur, and risk of losing the investment—suggest themselves as soon as the problem and premises are explicitly stated. But even this relatively simple illustration points up the inherent complexity and difficulty in making precise quantitative projections.

Computer Simulation

In decision trees and most other operations-research models, uncertainty is stated in terms of "expected value"—the weighting of various possible outcomes by their probability. Such practice enables us to take account of differences in the chances of success, but the resulting figures are only synthetic scores, not a picture of any result we may actually face. One way to get a better sense of what our world might be like *if* this happened or *if* that happened is through simulation.

With this technique, a model—admittedly incomplete but the best we can design—is used to project possible results of different alternatives under varying assumptions. Usually the model is programmed into a computer; then we can easily try out all sorts of contingencies—tight money, high demand, and so on—and various actions to deal with such situations. It is like running through football plays on a practice field, knowing that in actual play the situation will be much more complicated. The simulation is helpful in making a choice because it has summarized and condensed at least part of the many considerations.

Unfortunately, in many management situations the factors involved and the relationships between them are not sharp enough for mathematical expression; and if the simulation is oversimplified it loses much of its usefulness.

In conclusion, then, operations-research models are helpful in making a choice in certain types of complex situations. But even where data is available

304

PART III
Planning:
Elements of
Rational
Decision-Making

and a useful model can be constructed, we always face the question, "Is it worth the trouble?" For the myriad of relatively simple problems, use of symbolism and models probably will not improve the quality of decisions.

MATRIX SUMMARIES

Many decision-makers want some means, simpler and more flexible than an operations-research model, for summarizing the projections they must weigh in choosing among alternatives. Especially, they need a way to get the intangibles into the same focus. Matrix summaries are helpful for this purpose.

Here is an example—one of many variations—of how matrices can be used. The president of a large paper company had to choose a new mill location. He had narrowed his choice to four locations and had consolidated as well as he could the dollar benefits of each into an estimated rate of return on incremental investment. He then identified five other factors that, while they were partially reflected in the dollar figures, had additional intangible implications. For each of these intangibles the president faced two questions:

1) What *degree of satisfaction* may I expect for each intangible at each mill site?
2) How *important* is each intangible to me—in the range being considered?

The first question seeks to determine the extent to which a desired intangible need is met by each alternative. The second question recognizes that a favorable position with respect to one intangible may be more important than a favorable position with respect to another.

Because the president could not avoid answering these two questions, at least subjectively, he went one step further and translated his feelings into numbers. He ranked each alternative on a scale from zero to ten for each question, low ranking reflecting low satisfaction or low importance. These evaluations of the intangibles are summarized on the matrix shown in Fig. 14–4.

To arrive at a rough indication of the relative significance of intangibles for each site, the degree of satisfaction (in color) in each cell of the matrix has been multiplied by the relative importance (in black). The resulting numbers are a rough index of the relative degree and importance of each intangible for all four sites.

Then, to summarize, the index numbers have been added to show a combined score for each site. This total score had significance only for comparing the alternative sites. Nevertheless, it did help the president make a choice. By concentrating on the last two columns of the matrix, he quickly decided that site 2 was preferable to site 1: The score for the intangibles was about the same, and site 2 had a decided edge in rate of return. After a little thought the president decided that site 3 was preferable to site 4: The significant intangible advantage of site 4 simply could not offset a 50 percent higher rate of return at site 3. That selection left a final choice between sites 2 and 3.

Alternative Sites	Predicted Availability of Desired Labor/ Skill Mix	Predicted Favorable Union Relations	Predicted Favorable Local Legislation and Taxes	Predicted Ability to Hold Capable Mill Managers in This Location	Predicted Unlikelihood of Competitors Moving Nearby	Weighted Total Score for Intangibles	Estimated Incremental Return on Investment Compared with Doing Nothing
Site 1	6 × 9 = 54	5 × 8 = 40	6 × 9 = 54	9 × 9 = 81	4 × 3 = 12	241	12.1%
Site 2	5 × 6 = 30	8 × 8 = 64	6 × 9 = 54	9 × 9 = 81	3 × 3 = 9	238	14.7
Site 3	5 × 6 = 30	1 × 8 = 8	8 × 9 = 72	5 × 9 = 45	4 × 3 = 12	167	16.1
Site 4	10 × 6 = 60	6 × 8 = 48	8 × 9 = 72	8 × 9 = 72	5 × 3 = 15	267	10.8

Figure 14–4   A matrix for choosing mill locations, showing the president's subjective evaluation of intangibles. Sites below minimum acceptable level on any factor have already been eliminated. The company can easily finance the dollar investment required at any of these locations with an 8 percent bond issue. Quantity and quality of output will not be affected by the choice of site. Key: colored numbers—degree factor is achieved at each site; black numbers—relative importance of a factor; colored underscore—weighted score.

Were the intangible advantages of site 2 worth sacrificing an estimated 1.4 percent difference in rate of return? Looking at the cells in the matrix, the president could see that the chief difference in intangibles was in the favorability of predicted union relations; after further reflection he decided to sacrifice rate of return rather than build a plant where union relations would probably be quite troublesome.

Although this matrix did not give the president an automatic answer, it did two things. First, it forced him to clarify his judgments about the intangibles. Second, it provided a mechanism to help him balance them in his mind. Crude though the weightings were, use of the matrix helped integrate the implications of each alternative into a final choice.

All sorts of matrices are possible. Verbal statements instead of numbers may be placed in the cells. Probability estimates may be added. Predictions based on very flimsy evidence may be flagged, weights adjusted for degree of satisfaction, and so on. Basically the matrix is useful because it enables us to summarize a variety of projections in a systematic fashion.[3]

[3] Some experienced executives make a tentative decision first and then prepare a matrix with data necessary to justify that decision. Such a practice is not so silly as it first appears, because the executive is testing his intuitive feeling against its logical implications. If the implications appear unsound when they are clearly exposed, he can revise his intuitive judgment.

TESTING A CHOICE

Is there any way a manager can tell when he has arrived at a correct choice among alternatives? Unfortunately, there is no sure test. The most he can do is to reduce the chance of serious error. Over the years, several different ways of checking the soundness of a decision have proved useful. Every manager should be familiar with these techniques so that he can pick those that are appropriate for each specific decision. Urgency of action, what is at stake, and degree of doubt will determine how many checks to use and how far to press them.

Reexamining the Analysis and the Evidence

Most people prefer to stick to a line of thinking once it is well drawn in their minds, especially if the ideas are familiar, accepted, and attractive. Consequently, a comfortable decision—right or wrong—tends to go unchallenged. To catch errors in such thinking, the following devices are helpful.

Listen to the "devil's advocate."   For centuries, the Catholic Church has used the institution of the "devil's advocate" as a way of testing decisions, especially those relating to the canonization of new saints. A person is assigned the task of pointing out weaknesses and errors in proposed action. He assembles the best negative arguments he can. If a proposal cannot withstand such an attack, action is postponed.

In business, a decision-maker himself often makes a deliberate effort to stand aside and think of all the reasons why a proposed action won't work. Before a manager says, "Go ahead," he should take time to calculate everything that may go wrong. But this negative approach may be difficult and unpleasant for an aggressive executive, and if a problem is complicated or involves strong emotions, he should perhaps assign the task to someone else. The role is apt to be unpopular, so a manager should make sure everyone recognizes that the devil's advocate is not passing judgment on a matter, but simply seeing to it that all negative points have been carefully considered.

A decision may be challenged on the basis of evidence, logic, values, or other grounds. At the time of the cross-examination by the devil's advocate, all sorts of embarrassing questions are raised. For example, "If officers need the proposed three-week vacation, why not all employees?" Or, "True, our annual reports do show a high correlation of sales volume and advertising expense, but does this mean that more advertising will increase sales? Maybe the causation runs the other way or does not exist. Remember, the United States leads India in heart disease and baths per capita, but it does not follow therefore that baths cause heart trouble." A decision is sound only if it can be defended by good answers to such challenges as these.

Project a decision into detailed plans.   Often we can check on the wisdom and practicability of a decision by spelling out its consequences in more detail. A very large manufacturing company, for example, tested its tentative decision to decentralize into product divisions by using this approach of projecting consequences. It allocated customers, outlined a proposed divisional organization, devised a tentative placement of executives, and estimated the administrative cost of the new setup. This analysis uncovered so many weaknesses and difficulties that the original decentralization plan was abandoned. Not until a year later was a substantially modified reorganization put into effect.

Reconsider planning premises. Every management decision is based on assumptions, or planning premises. They may be assumptions supported by sketchy data about future demands for company products; about the availability of raw materials; about the attitudes and future behavior of employees, perhaps based on reports of staff people or hearsay evidence; or about company values that are as much a reflection of personal desires as of company goals. In checking a decision, a manager often finds it useful to ask himself just which assumptions are crucial to the success of a proposed action and to try to obtain further clarification on these pivotal premises.

All premises cannot be verified, of course. We will always have to contend with incomplete data, errors in perception of facts, and distortion in communication. But an executive should reconsider assumptions so that he at least knows what risks he is taking rather than proceed naïvely. In addition, as the future becomes history, premises can be checked against events, and the need for reconsidering the decision may be clearly seen.

Review abruptly discarded alternatives. Too often an otherwise excellent alternative has been discarded because of a single drawback. In such cases, we should ask whether the assumed drawback is insurmountable.

Consider the following situation: When additional tests were required by the F.D.A., one pharmaceutical firm decided to discontinue its research on a skin-allergy product. The potential market was not great, and the increased—the firm felt unnecessary—investment in testing and launching the product made the investment high. "The potential return is now so low we aren't justified in taking the fifty percent chance of success," said the president. Then the international vice-president proposed that the product be launched in countries where F.D.A. approval is not required—a reversal of the firm's usual practice of first proving products in the U.S. before taking them abroad. Although this revised plan is not very attractive, it does make feasible finishing the R&D effort and removing these uncertainties before trying to satisfy the F.D.A.

Thus, if a critical drawback can be removed, a worthwhile alternative may come back into consideration. The manager may still reject the alternative, but not until he has reexamined the assumed disadvantage.

Securing Consensus

A director of Exxon Corporation has observed, "When a proposal comes before our Board for decision, there is rarely sharp difference of opinion. We

308

PART III
Planning:
Elements of
Rational
Decision-Making

try to anticipate problems, and then we discuss possible solutions with every-one directly affected and those who might have useful views. These discussions often seem slow, but by the time we are ready to act, a clear consensus backing the proposal has usually developed."

Most of us use this technique, at least occasionally. We make a tentative decision—whether or not to accept a job—but before taking action, we get the frank opinion of one or two friends. In so doing, we are testing the decision.

Formal arrangements are sometimes made to get consensus on important decisions. The United States Supreme Court is a notable example. Boards of directors and some company committees presumably provide group review and endorsement of key plans. The "independent staff" described in Chapter 6 is specifically designed to provide a second judgment. But the use of consensus to test decisions need not be limited to such bodies. Informal advice from individuals may contribute just as much to the wisdom of a decision.

If the assent or dissent of others is to be meaningful, the advisor should be both well informed about a situation and seriously concerned with the soundness of the decision. Neither polite agreement nor logrolling politics nor cavalier advice is desirable.

Pilot Runs

The surest way to test a decision is to try it out. A test will not tell us whether some other decision might work better, but it will tell us whether a proposed plan is at least promising. Sometimes a new product or process can be tried out on a limited scale with custom-made models or equipment. Automobile companies give their new chassis and new engines severe road tests before the products are put into mass production and sold to the public. A chemical company with a new detergent may have its laboratory make up

Figure 14–5 Before a new automobile is put into production, specially made trial cars are subjected to severe tests to check the validity of previous engineering estimates.

limited quantities for market tests in a restricted area. As these cases show, even if a tentative decision looks good on paper or in the laboratory, a further test under more nearly normal operating conditions is desirable.

Pilot operations have their limitations, of course. They are often costly; they may consume valuable time; and they may not be feasible for some actions (such as floating a bond issue while interest rates are low). Consequently, this test is appropriate for only a few major decisions a manager must make.

Sequential Decisions

Occasionally, we can make a decision one part at a time; when the results of the first part are known, we can use them in deciding the second part; and so on with each succeeding part. Thus we make a series of decisions to solve one main problem.[4]

This form of decision is often used for executive promotions. Suppose a company president has his eye on a salesman named John Baker as a likely replacement for the sales manager who will retire in three years. The president's first step might be to bring Baker into the home office as sales-promotion director. If Baker does that job well, he may be put in charge of sales planning. If his work continues to be effective, he may be named assistant sales manager six months before he is to be moved into the key spot. These successive assignments serve a double purpose. Baker gets experience and learns about home-office operations, and the company can make a *series* of appraisals of his capability to be sales manager. The results of each move provide data used in deciding what the next move should be.

Sequential decisions are in sharp contrast to the bear-by-the-tail decisions familiar in sales promotion campaigns, where it is difficult to discontinue a project after it is launched. Sequential decisions should also be distinguished from the proverbial British habit of "muddling through," whereby one step is taken with the simple faith that some way will open up for the next move. In sequential decisions a tentative plan or a new alternative for dealing with a major problem is in mind from the beginning. The plan is then tested against newly acquired evidence and perhaps revised at each stage.

All these proposed devices for testing decisions have their usefulness. Some fit one situation better than another, but in general, they may be applied in the following order: 1) checking our own thinking by the devil's-advocate approach, projecting detailed plans for implementation, reconsidering assumptions, or reviewing discarded alternatives; 2) securing consensus from other

[4] Decision trees, already discussed, also deal with this kind of situation. However, they focus only on the first decision and assume that subsequent decisions will follow in the projected fashion. In the sequential-decision process, we plan to reconsider each step on the basis of newly acquired information. A decision-tree analysis can be used to clarify any one of the steps in a sequential decision, but the two techniques are distinct and may be used separately. As the example to follow above suggests, the sequential-decision technique has much wider applicability.

competent people; and then, whenever suitable, 3) making test runs either by pilot operation or by sequential decision.

CONCLUSION

A manager can rarely follow the phases of rational decision-making in the neat order of our discussion: defining the problem, finding alternatives, projecting and comparing alternatives, choosing a single course of action. Even if our minds tried to follow a disciplined path, the trails through the phases would crisscross. In testing a choice, for instance, we may want to get more data, and the added information might suggest new alternatives. Or using a means–end chain to establish values might cause us to revise our diagnosis. Similarly, in discarding alternatives—by setting limits or focusing first on one or two crucial factors—we are in effect making negative choices.

Although we have not discovered a simple procedure for making wise plans, a formal analysis of decision-making, such as we have covered in Part Three, is highly useful as a framework for putting our thoughts and planning efforts into an orderly, understandable arrangement. With this framework, random thoughts can be put in place, and any necessary backtracking need not confuse us.

The more specific suggestions made in the last four chapters about each of the four phases of decision-making apply to all types of management problems, from the daily questions that face a first-line supervisor to the fundamental policy issues that confront central management. Incidentally, these suggestions can be used both for intangible problems, such as how to organize a branch office, and for concrete problems, such as what products to make or what machine to buy. The tough task for each of us is, of course, not merely to be acquainted with an approach to decision-making, but rather to master the concept so well that we use it skillfully and perhaps almost unconsciously.

We call this process laid out in Part Three "rational decision-making." It is the first of three models or approaches to decision-making examined in this book. The emphasis here has been on rational analysis and choice by a single manager. Basic concepts from logic, decision theory, managerial economics, and management science have been incorporated into the model—though with a concerted effort to avoid specialized jargon. We have also drawn freely from psychology. The selection of concepts and language, however, is based on what will have practical usefulness for an active manager.

This rational, individualistic model provides the starting point for studying, in Part Four, the more complex bureaucratic and political decision models. No one person, unaided, can follow through all phases of rational decision-making for the many problems confronting a business enterprise. We need the joint effort of many people. So we turn to decision-making in an organization.

1) Often a manager will develop alternative ways of solving a problem and find one clearly superior to the others except for one major disadvantage. Before eliminating this alternative, what should the manager do?

2) "I try to shield my good intuitive decision-makers from too much in the way of subjective probability estimates, decision trees and matrices. They are like expert marksmen who can hit a moving target at 100 yards in a windstorm. If you gave such marksmen too much wind, speed, and distance data, you would just confuse them." Discuss this comment by the managing partner of a small investment bank.

3) What are the advantages and limitations of having the same person(s) who gathered data for comparing courses of action also make the final choice? Give your answer before and after reading Chapter 15.

4) List and discuss the major pitfalls a decision-maker should consider in seeking to develop and use subjective, numerical estimates of probability. How will your answer differ if the probabilities are to be used in decision trees rather than in a matrix summary of a choice that does *not* involve sequential decisions?

5) Consider the data shown in Table 14–3. Assume the president was certain that he could create conditions in which *if* there was any strike at all, it would last for no more than three to five days. To do so he would have to add a sum of money to his latest salary offer. Given the data in Table 14–3, what is the maximum amount he should add to his salary offer? Consider only one year's effect.

6) A friend of yours has narrowed his alternative uses of a $10,000 inheritance to three: 1) Invest in common stock of a small company not currently on the open market, and, if the company is successful, stand to make anywhere from 50 to 200 percent return. 2) Invest in a guaranteed 8 percent note that will be repaid in five years but that is not transferable without the issuer's authorization. 3) Deposit the $10,000 in a savings bank paying 3¾ percent, compounded quarterly. What additional information would you need to advise your friend in making his choice? Which alternative would *you* choose? Why?

7) The use of simulation techniques for making a choice requires the combination of knowledge of computer and mathematical techniques with practical experience with the elements of the decision to be made. Because few managers are likely to be strong in both areas, how should the different types of expertise and experience be brought together? What problems do you foresee in this effort?

8) What are the major similarities and differences between "means–end" networks and "decision trees"?

Cases

For cases involving issues covered in this chapter, see especially the following. Particularly relevant questions are listed after each case.

FOR FURTHER READING

Allison, G. T., *Essence of Decision: Explaining the Cuban Missile Crisis.* Boston: Little, Brown and Company, 1971, Chapters 1 and 2.

Model I: The Rational Actor is the first of three approaches Allison uses to explain American and Soviet decisions in the Cuban missile crisis. See pages 28–32 and 286–88 for a summary of basic concepts on rational choice derived from business and economic theory.

Brown, R. V., "Do Managers Find Decision Theory Useful?" *Harvard Business Review,* May 1970.

Surveys the extent of use of, and problems in applying, modern decision theory.

Harrison, E. F., *The Managerial Decision-Making Process.* Boston: Houghton Mifflin Company, 1975, Chapters 3, 5, and 8.

Systematic examination of several aspects of choice—maximizing versus satisficing, values used, probability, utility, and game theory.

Miller, D. W. and M. K. Starr, *Executive Decisions and Operations Research,* 2nd ed. Englewood Cliffs, N.J.: Prentice-Hall, Inc., 1969, Chapters 4–6.

Cogent summary of decision theory and role of operations research; clearly stated without the overlay of mathematical symbolism.

Not-for-Profit Note

for Part III

The underlying steps in making a decision rationally are the same for all sorts of problems and situations. Diagnosis, search for alternatives, comparing courses of action, and choice based on values and uncertainty relate to not-for-profit activities just as much as to profit-seeking ventures. The critical difference, of course, arises in the values used in making choices.[1]

In concept, a person making a rational choice in a not-for-profit venture simply derives his values from the service mission of the venture—through a means–end chain, as already explained. In practice, the selection of appropriate values is often complicated. Several factors are likely to add complications:

1) *Divergent goals* often exist within a not-for-profit enterprise. A nursery school, for instance, may aim at day care for children of working mothers, child socialization, a head start on the three R's, creative expression, psychological counsel, or just plain fun. A labor union—to cite a different example—has economic, political, and social goals. And the aims of particular professions within the enterprise may add to this array of goals. Consequently, a decision-maker in such an organization has no single criterion to use in choosing.

2) The concept of whole *sets of values* relating to various dimensions is characteristic of not-for-profit enterprises. Typically, as in nursery schools and unions

---

[1] Multiple and ambiguous goals in not-for-profit enterprises also complicate diagnosis and comparison of courses of action. In diagnosis the limits on acceptable solutions are more difficult to establish, and in comparing alternatives, just which consequences should be carefully projected is unclear. Nevertheless, the crux of the difference between rational decision-making in profit-seeking and not-for-profit enterprises lies in the values used in the final stage of choice. If these key values are established, they can easily be introduced into the earlier phases of the rational model.

314

PART III
Planning:
Elements of
Rational
Decision-Making

mentioned above, several kinds of results are desired simultaneously. There is no recognized priority among these goals, nor is there a common denominator (such as dollars in a profit-making firm) that enables a decision-maker to compare the incremental outputs of diverse results. So he must assess each proposed course of action in terms of several different values simultaneously.

3) Contributors of funds and other resources often have strong feelings about the goals an enterprise should pursue and about the degree of risk that is warranted. Thus, the conservative donor to a college may inject his values into the decision process, or a congressman may have pet projects. A decision-maker who is aware of these *external pressures* must at least weigh the likelihood and seriousness of antagonizing important resource contributors.

4) A further complication is that the consumer of the service provided—the student, hospital patient, concert-goer, and the like—is in a weaker position than the customer of a typical business firm. Customers of not-for-profit enterprises usually pay only a fraction of the service cost, and often there is a presumption that the producer knows best what the customer should receive. Such *reduced influence of customers* of a not-for-profit enterprise permits the diversity of values noted above to continue without a clear market check.

When we recognize these various influences, it is not surprising that the value pattern in not-for-profit enterprises is often vague and multidimensional. Values in profit-seeking firms are not nearly as simple as economic and mathematic models suggest (see Chapter 14); but long-run profit does serve as a theoretical basis for resolving conflicts. This convenient criterion is not available for the decision-maker in a not-for-profit venture.

Two main mechanisms are often used in not-for-profit enterprises to provide direction and priority among the various goals that each enterprise typically has. One is a *charismatic leader*. Especially in Stage-I ventures, a dynamic and forceful individual often "calls the plays." He has personal convictions about the values to be used in decision-making; and he either has enough power to make important choices himself, or is so influential that his values are accepted by others who make decisions. Field studies indicate that the charismatic leader is even more vital to success of a not-for-profit enterprise than is an outstanding entrepreneur for a profit-seeking firm.

Another way value conflicts are resolved is a *mystique* that dominates the enterprise. As explained in the first Note, we use the term "mystique" to describe a strong conviction about the importance of a particular service mission and the unusual capacity of the enterprise to provide that service. The Mayo Clinic, Ford Foundation, Rotary Club, and Red Cross each has an international mystique, and many local not-for-profit ventures have a comparable tradition. Once established, the mystique defines a respected role in society. For decision-makers the mystique sets the character and values one is expected to follow.

A charismatic leader and/or a widely accepted mystique—by endorsing a particular set of values—help make rational decisions possible. With priority of goals known, the entire process of diagnosis–search–projection–choice can be accomplished on the rational basis in profit-seeking and not-for-profit firms alike.

But if a charismatic leader or accepted mystique is lacking, rational decision-making in most not-for-profit enterprises is virtually impossible. Instead, decision-making by some kind of consensus, often based on politics, becomes dominant.

Moreover, as we shall see in Part Four, the extension of the rational, individual model into the social structure of an enterprise creates an additional set of problems. When we disperse the phases of decision-making among different people and over the months—as we must in medium- and large-size firms—a variety of further planning tools are needed. As these planning tools are examined in the following chapters, their applicability to not-for-profit ventures is a continuing pertinent question.

Case Studies

for Part III

For the first time in four days, Ken Marten, president of Marten Fabricators, felt comfortable with the subject under discussion. He had enrolled in a week-long seminar on decision-making offered by a leading Southern business school.

"The faculty are good," he said, "and they try to illustrate their material with real situations; but I find it hard to see how I can apply much of it to a small business like mine."

The subjects covered thus far in the seminar were:

1) Problem analysis and cause identification
2) Accounting for top-management decisions
3) Probability, uncertainty, and risk
4) Decision trees and model building

The final subject was to be a brief look at various ways of using computers to aid in top-level decision-making.

When Marten mentioned his concern to a member of the faculty, Edgar Winter, Professor Winter suggested that he bring one of his own situations to the group and see if collectively they could use the course techniques to help him deal with it. The next day and several telephone calls later, Marten presented a problem he was facing and asked the group for their advice.

Marten Fabricators is a small, family-owned business located on the outskirts of Houston. Total sales for the past five years have fluctuated between two and three million dollars and profits between $25,000 and $185,000.

We are metal fabricators who seek subcontract work from larger companies and contractors [Marten explained]. Although we have a few stock items we specialize in and can occasionally inventory on speculation, the bulk of our work is on the basis of our successfully bidding on a piece or pieces of a large job.

We have about 30 to 35 first-rate machinists, operators, welders, and engineers who work the year round with us; then we add people as needed if we get more business than our full-time staff can handle. I have four people reporting to me.

Emily Jones, *chief accountant*
Conrad Ericson, *engineering and estimating*
Will Craig, *plant superintendent*
Edward Aker, *sales manager*

Last week, Aker came in to see me with a proposal that we submit a bid to Westex Engineering that would be well below our costs. Things have been a bit slow lately and I would like to bring this project in, but I worry about bidding below cost. It can hurt in several ways. First, your competitors get nervous and may do the same to you on the next proposals. We are already seeing some of this as business continues to be slow. Second, the contractor may regard the bid as a sign of trouble and question your reliability and quality. Finally, I don't want to spoil our people. If they get used to us making below-cost bids just to keep things going, they may not work as hard to keep costs down and look for profitable projects.

THE WESTEX PROPOSAL

Ed Aker really wants this project [Marten continued]. He says that Westex is on its way to becoming one of the biggest contractors to the chemical and oil companies in our area. Though Ed may be a bit optimistic, I agree that they are going to be one of the best around these parts. Ed wants us to bid quite low on a piece of a big project Westex has successfully bid on. He feels that we must get this job because of its demand for the kind of quality work we can do. It is a perfect job for us to show our work, but I'm less certain that we can count on Westex to remember us in the future for our quality rather than as a hungry subcontractor.

The cost estimates that Aker submitted to Marten are summarized in Exhibit I, which follows. Emily Jones, chief accountant, has reviewed this estimate in summary form and has reviewed the detailed drafting and plant estimates that underlie it.

318

PART III
Planning:
Elements of
Rational
Decision-Making

EXHIBIT I

Cost Estimates for Westex Bid

Alloy-clad materials and fittings	$ 1,500
Other materials	15,000
Labor	17,000
Overhead (direct)	7,000
Shipping, etc.	1,800
	$43,300

It's not for me to decide what we bid [she told Marten] but I do think Ed is being unrealistic. If you and he want the business that's fine with me, but you ought to look at more realistic costs. If this project were to carry its fair share of overhead, you should add about $10,000 to Ed's estimate. Further, those alloy-clad materials and fittings should be estimated at a figure of at least $4,000. As I see it, a more realistic estimate for this project is $55,800. Since Ed feels we must bid under $45,000 to be assured that we get the work, I figure we will take a $10,000 loss. If you think it's worth it, fine, but you ought to know what it will cost us.

I checked with Ericson and Craig [said Marten] and they agree with Emily on the figures. Craig woud like to get the order to keep his plant busy, but he doesn't feel as strongly as Aker about the project.

One of the trickiest questions about our cost estimate is the question of how much to put in for a number of alloy-clad fittings, which are one of the key elements in the project.

THE ALLOY-CLAD MATERIALS AND FITTINGS

Over a year ago, Marten successfully bid on a project similar to the one now being considered. Materials were ordered and work had begun when the project was canceled. As part of a settlement plan, Marten was paid for its completed work and for any materials that had been ordered especially for the project.

Included in this project were a number of high-quality, alloy-clad materials and fittings that Marten had purchased. These materials were special-ordered, and at settlement they were conservatively valued at the price they would bring for scrap—$1,500. Marten, as part of the settlement, received the difference between its purchase price and the scrap value, or $3,300.

We didn't scrap them, however [Craig said], because we hoped to get another project where we could use them; or if we failed to get a new project, we would sell them to whoever did. Well, this proposal of Aker's is the first one we have seen in 15 months that calls for these materials and fittings. I looked at them the other day and they are not in great shape. They were stored in a yard shed and are a bit weathered. Before they can be used, they will have to be sanded, buffed, and quite a few will need to be rebonded and others reclad. If we get the Westex order, we will have to have this work on the materials and fittings done outside, because our equipment and people will be tied up. If we don't get the Westex order, then we can use a little of our excess capacity to get the materials and fittings in shape and try to sell them to whoever gets the order. Since alloy and labor prices have shot up since we bought these materials, they would cost at least $9,000 now and have to be special-ordered. Therefore, I am sure that we could get them in shape before a special order could be ready and sell them for $9,000.

Marten presented his classmates with the following estimates pertaining to these fittings. See Exhibit II.

EXHIBIT II

Alloy-Clad Fittings

Original cost	$4,800
Book value	1,500
Current scrap value	2,000
Sale to successful bidder (as is)	6,200
Sale to successful bidder (refurbished)	9,000
Refurbish cost if done by Marten with excess capacity	800
Refurbish cost if done outside	2,800

CONCLUSION

In response to questions raised by his "classmates," Marten placed several phone calls to his subordinates and asked them to estimate the probability of various outcomes.

They didn't like trying to give me numbers to reflect their feelings but here are our best efforts to quantify what you asked for. [See Exhibit III.]

EXHIBIT III

Probabilities of Various Outcomes

1)	Getting Westex order with a bid of $45,000:	90%
2)	Getting Westex order with a bid of $55,000:	45%
3)	Getting Westex order with a bid of between $45,000–$50,000:	50%
4)	Getting Westex order with a bid of between $50,000–$55,000:	?
5)	Getting major Westex orders as a result of this order—Aker:	100%
6)	Getting major Westex orders as a result of this order—Marten:	50%
7)	Getting major Westex orders without this order—Aker:	20%
8)	Getting major Westex orders without this order—Marten:	30%
9)	Selling fittings as is to a successful bidder for $6,200:	75%
10)	Selling fittings refurbished to a successful-bidder for $9,000:	90%

By major orders [Marten explained], I mean ones that might bring us at least $15,000–$20,000 a year in profits.

FOR DISCUSSION AND REPORT-WRITING

Organizing: Structural Design

1) If the president accepts Aker's recommendation on the Westex proposal and Marten gets the job, who is accountable for the impact of this decision on *future* profits stemming from work with Westex? Consider several forms or levels of accountability relative to tasks and authority.

2) Assume Marten grew to three or four times its current size through subcontracting for electronics firms (they now concentrate on the chemical and petroleum industries). What changes in structure might they contemplate? Then suppose instead that this growth came entirely through more business to the chemical and petroleum industries, but that Marten expanded geographically to Oklahoma and Southern California.

Human Factors in Organizing

3) How may Marten's decision affect "customs and roles" in the organization?

Planning: Elements of Rational Decision-Making

4) Draw a means–end diagram that places Marten's decision on the Westex bid in the context of parallel or higher-level goals.

5) How might the diagram drawn for question 4 assist Marten in deciding what to do about Aker's request?

6) How may Marten's decision affect creativity in Craig's and Aker's areas of accountability?

7) What are the criteria for determining the cost of the alloy-clad materials and fittings?

8) List all the significant consequences of approving Aker's request to bid $45,000 or less. Separate those consequences that can be measured in tangible terms from those that cannot.

9) How should Marten assign values to the intangibles noted in your answer to question 8?

10) How should Marten make use of the estimates of probability shown in Exhibit III?

11) What additional data should Marten seek? How should he get it? How should he use what he is likely to get?

12) (Summary Report Question: Part Three) Develop what you consider the relevant costs and benefits associated with the project, and present a mechanism by which Marten can see the significant implications of his major alternatives.

*Planning: Decision-Making
in an Enterprise*

321

Case 3-2
Atlas Chemical
Company

13)   What steps might Aker have taken to gain broader political support for his recommendation?

14)   Could Marten, through standing plans, keep problems like this one from reaching his desk? Should he develop such plans?

15)   Could Aker have made a stronger case for this project by developing a formal (written) integrated sales strategy? Illustrate your answer.

Controlling

16)   How will Marten's decision on this project affect the general use of budgetary controls in the company?

17)   How should Marten evaluate the results of his decision if *a*) he requires Aker to submit a bid of $55,000 or *b*) he permits Aker to submit whatever bid he feels appropriate as long as it is $45,000 or more?

Activating

18)   If Marten decides to submit a bid of $55,000, what activating response should he seek from Aker? Discuss.

Summary Question for Solution of the Case as a Whole

19)   What action do you recommend to Marten? Show numerical and other bases for your choice.

CASE 3-2

ATLAS CHEMICAL COMPANY

Atlas Chemical Company is a wholly owned subsidiary of Atlas Oil International. With the growth of the petrochemical industry in the late 1940s and early 1950s, Atlas Chemical has grown from a small division of Atlas Oil to the point where it now accounts for more than 20 percent of the sales and 25 percent of the profits of Atlas Oil. Atlas Oil International's consolidated sales last year amounted to more than one billion dollars.

Atlas Chemical produces a wide variety of chemical and petrochemical products, most of which are sold to manufacturing and processing companies. Although the chemical company has more than 2,000 products in its line,

322

PART III
Planning:
Elements of
Rational
Decision-Making

70 to 80 percent of its annual sales come from roughly 200 basic chemicals. One of these high-volume chemicals is synthetic phylozine.[1] Phylozine is employed primarily as an additive to the bonding agents used in the lamination of wood and plastic products. Although it is not an adhesive, it is a necessary ingredient in the lamination process.

THE PHYLOZINE MARKET

Until ten years ago, phylozine was available only as a by-product of the refining of crude rubber. Before 1937, when its value as an additive in lamination was discovered, crude phylozine had been considered a waste product by the rubber companies. With its discovery, it suddenly became a highly profitable product to the rubber industry, even though it has never constituted more than three percent of its total sales. Although large investments were needed to convert crude phylozine to a finished product, the cost of this conversion by the large rubber companies, who produce and/or complete the refining of 95 percent of domestic crude, is estimated as less than 14¢/lb.

As a by-product, the supply of natural phylozine is limited by the amount of crude rubber processed. Since 1937, the demand for phylozine typically outstripped available supply; and with the growth of plastics and lamination, the gap between the supply of natural phylozine and total demand increased. As a result, the price of phylozine had increased irregularly from 19¢/lb. in 1937 to almost 60 cents a pound ten years ago. To fill the gap and hedge against rising prices, many users of phylozine sought a substitute. Other additives were used, but none proved particularly successful.

Ten years ago the domestic supply of by-product phylozine amounted to roughly 200 million pounds. Imports of crude phylozine, refined domestically by a handful of independent refiners, added another 22 million pounds to the supply. It was estimated that even at the existing price of 60¢, more than 250 million pounds could have been sold. Had the price been reduced below 50¢/lb., virtually all of the subsititutes used to fill the gap could have been driven from the market, which would have approached 300 million pounds.

SYNTHETIC PHYLOZINE

Faced with these conditions plus periodic drops in the production of crude rubber and the resulting decreases in supply of natural phylozine, many

---

[1] To maintain the anonymity of the company called Atlas Chemical, we have not only given the company a fictitious name, but also changed the name and use of the actual synthetic product involved.

of the large chemical and petrochemical companies poured great amounts of money into finding either a more satisfactory and cheaper substitute or methods of lamination that did not require such an additive. Ten years ago, Atlas Chemical marketed a synthetic phylozine that possessed all of the key characteristics of the natural product. In addition, it possessed a slightly clearer color, which had some advantages to companies using it in the lamination of certain plastic products. Large-scale production of synthetic phylozine required a sizeable capital investment by Atlas, and it approached the market cautiously. Since many others had been seeking substitutes or new lamination techniques, Atlas could not be sure how long the market for synthetic phylozine would last. To ensure a market large enough to cover the investment, Atlas negotiated five-year cost-plus contracts with a limited number of major phylozine users at prices ranging from 44¢/lb. to 47¢/lb. Atlas received favorable customer recognition for providing a quality product at attractive prices, and during the contract period, Atlas sold its full capacity of about 50 million pounds. Five years ago, just before the expiration of these contracts, the Oakline Chemical Company introduced a synthetic phylozine that was virtually identical with the Atlas product. Although there was a brief effort to stop Oakline from entering the market by claiming patent infringements, Atlas's legal department decided the likelihood of a successful suit was too small to press the issue against the smaller Oakline company. Furthermore, the size of the market and obstacles facing other potential synthetic producers left Atlas fairly sure of selling to full capacity. Oakline appeared to be the only company willing, at that time, to face the obstacles of 1) making the large initial capital investment required, 2) gaining processing know-how, and 3) living with uncertainty about the response of the rubber companies. Oakline's original capacity was estimated at 15 million pounds per year, which it sold without contracts at prices ranging from 46¢/lb. to 50¢/lb.

THE SYNTHETIC MARKET TODAY

By June of last year, Atlas and Oakline had increased both capacity and sales and were operating at near-capacity levels. Atlas had doubled its capacity five years ago to a level of 100 million pounds, while Oakline, through more efficient use of its facilities, had increased its capacity to 20 million pounds. Atlas had sales last year of 84 million pounds, while Oakline sold 18 million pounds. Oakline is presently completing a major addition to its phylozine capacity and expects to have capacity up to 40 million pounds some time this year. Atlas, at present, has no plans for a sizeable increase.

Customer response to synthetic phylozine has been excellent. In tests of applications and performance, the synthetic product has done as well as "natural" phylozine; and for certain applications (roughly 10 percent), its slightly clearer color, while not a necessity, has proved to be an advantage.

MARKET OUTLOOK

With the introduction of synthetic phylozine, most of the substitute products were dropped from the market. Last year, sales of synthetic and natural phylozine reached 330 million pounds, with the rubber industry accounting for 216 million pounds. The synthetic producers sold 102 million pounds, and net imports made up the difference. Despite a current surplus of crude phylozine outside the U.S., imports have declined steadily since the introduction of the lower-cost synthetic product. Demand for phylozine has been increasing steadily since the initial jump that followed the introduction of the synthetic product. For the past five years, with the additional synthetic capacity, the total market grew at an annual rate of seven to eight million pounds.

During the same period the available supply of natural phylozine grew in proportion to the slower growth of the rubber-refining industry, at an annual rate of roughly two million pounds.

REACTION OF RUBBER COMPANIES TO SYNTHETIC PHYLOZINE

The introduction of a limited amount of synthetic phylozine ten years ago had no noticeable effect initially on the price of the natural product. Over the past four years, however, the rubber companies have dropped their prices to meet those of the synthetic producers. For several years, prices of both synthetic and natural phylozine were virtually identical, averaging 45¢/lb. In the summer of last year, the rubber companies cut their price by ½¢/lb., while the synthetic producers held the line. Before this time, such cuts would have been met immediately by Atlas and Oakline since the only reason for a cut had been to reduce the domestic price of phylozine to prevent a sizeable increase of foreign crude. Periodically, when the supply of foreign crude became too large, the fear of a large increase of imports would lead to a drop in domestic prices of up to two or three cents a pound. When the fear passed, prices would then return to their earlier level.

The management of Atlas Chemical did not feel that last summer's ½¢ drop by the rubber companies stemmed from fear of imports. With an increase in competition between Atlas and Oakline for the gap between the supply of natural phylozine and total demand, some of the rubber companies were beginning to fear an incursion on their sales from the synthetic producers. The rubber companies had no sales forces set up to sell phylozine. They had sold their by-product in the past through manufacturers' representatives on a price basis. The chemical companies, like Atlas and Oakline, on the other hand, could justify using their own field-sales personnel, since they sold many other chemical products to the same customers who buy phylozine.

Although Atlas held its price in the face of the ½¢ cut, its salespeople reported that considerable pressure was being exerted by customers to meet the price of natural phylozine. According to George Hagen, general sales manager of Atlas, "Our people had a rough time with the purchasing agents, but by stressing our quality, clarity, and dependability, they were able to keep most of them, if not happy, at least willing to stay with us. We lost some accounts but picked up others, and our sales for the last six months of last year, in fact, were up over the same period the year before. Oakline followed the same strategy and apparently had the same results."

THE LATEST PRICE CUT

In February of this year, one of the medium-sized rubber companies reduced the price of natural phylozine by an additional ¼¢/lb., to 44¼¢/lb. Within two days, all other rubber companies had matched the cut.

I just can't figure this one out [said Hagen]. With the general increase of industrial activity overseas, I don't see any new pressure from imports. As far as I know, no major user of phylozine has switched over to synthetic in the last few years. Maybe the rubber people want to generate a better cash flow by working their inventories down faster than usual. Or, perhaps the one who started it has misread the market. I frankly can't figure it out. Regardless of the reason, I have to give my sales people an answer right away about whether we meet the cut or hold our price. We had a heck of a time convincing most of our customers that we weren't being unfair when we let the ½¢ differential stand. Now that it has reached a ¾¢ differential, we may have to do something. So far, Oakline hasn't reacted, and unless I want to risk a visit from the Justice Department, we won't know what they have in mind until they show their hand.

FOR DISCUSSION AND REPORT-WRITING

Organizing: Structural Design

1) As the parent company, what influence should Atlas Oil International have on the operations of Atlas Chemical Company? How may the parent company be affected by decisions made by Atlas Chemical? What authority should they have over the operations of Atlas Chemical? Why?

2) What should be the nature of departmentation within the Atlas Chemical Company? How should the activities related to development, production, and sales of synthetic phylozine be related to those of other Atlas Chemical products?

3) Based on your answer to question 2, who should have the ultimate authority to make the pricing decision? Explain.

Human Factors in Organizing

4) If Atlas decided to allow the ¾¢ margin to remain, what conflicts might arise between the goals of the company and some of its personnel?

326

PART III
Planning:
Elements of
Rational
Decision-Making

5)   In what ways will sound communication networks within Atlas Chemical influence making and implementing a decision on the price of phylozine?

Planning: Elements of Rational Decision-Making

6)   What "desired" objectives are threatened in this case? What gap between desired and actual might you anticipate? What would cause this gap?

7)   Seek a creative way of solving the problem and test it against the desired goals and obstacles.

8)   Develop rough cost estimates in dollar terms for your alternatives.

9)   In what ways might subjective-probability concepts prove helpful in this case?

10)   In making the choice, what factors (other than those shown in answer to question 8) would have to be weighed?

11)   (Summary Report Question: Part Three) Using your answers to questions 6 and 7, develop a full, graphic means–end chain to depict the elements of your diagnosis. Where necessary, give a written explanation.

Planning: Decision-Making in an Enterprise

12)   How might standing plans aid in a more rapid solution to this problem? In what ways might they reduce the likelihood of the right action being taken?

13)   Who should participate in making this decision, and in what ways?

14)   How does the pricing decision relate to the longer-range goals and strategies of Atlas Chemical? Of Atlas Oil?

Controlling

15)   For each of the alternatives that you see open to Atlas Chemical on the pricing question, indicate what factors you would measure if that alternative were implemented.

16)   How would you measure the factors indicated in your answer to question 15?

Activating

17)   How should the Atlas Chemical salespeople be directed to explain a decision not to reduce prices? A decision to cut ¼¢? Under what conditions can the sales staff settle for "compliance" as a response from customers? Under what conditions must they seek commitment from customers?

Summary Question for Solution of the Case as a Whole

18)   Based on your answers to questions 7 through 11, what course of action would you recommend? Support your answer by explaining your choice.

PART IV

Who should make plans for a company was a major consideration in examining formal organization in Part One. We examined decentralization of planning, the use of staff to assist in planning, and structural arrangements to coordinate planning. In Part Three, we have just explored suggestions on *how* sound decisions could be made. Now we shall integrate the *who* and the *how* by studying the way concepts from Parts One and Three can be joined.

In this synthesis, we must keep in mind group influences on behavior, personal needs and beliefs, and the existence of conflict and power. These forces, as we noted in Part Two, affect decision-making in an organization as much as does a formal assignment of duties.

When a manager shifts his viewpoint on decision-making from individual to enterprise, his task is both simplified and complicated. The availability of more minds to work on problems is a great advantage. But when several persons take part, we must introduce ways of securing consistency among decisions, coordination of various planning units, and economy in planning effort. Various types of plans—or planning instruments—are used to obtain such consistency, coordination, and economy; and we shall look carefully at how these instruments aid in the planning process.

Moreover, an objective examination of group decision-making—in contrast to individual decision-making—will reveal *political* behavior. In fact, politics is Allison's third decision model. And such intraorganization politics must be harnessed, as we shall see in Chapter 20, if the planning system is to function as intended. These issues will be considered in the following chapters.

Chapter 15—Decision-Making as Group Behavior. Here we shall explore the benefits and difficulties arising from a division of labor when the elements of decision-making are dispersed throughout an enterprise.

Planning: Decision-Making

in an Enterprise

Chapter 16—Master Strategy and Long-range Programming. Central to systematic planning is continuing appraisal of the major services that a firm seeks to provide and of the best way to produce those services. Moreover, the timing of moves to carry out this strategy must be fitted into long-range programs.

Chapter 17—Operating Objectives. If planning is dispersed to many people, the broad strategy must then be recast in terms of specific goals and subgoals. In this chapter, we shall consider how to set up a hierarchy of objectives so that effective action follows.

Chapter 18—Planning for Stabilized Action. Policies, procedures, and standard methods contribute substantially to consistent and economical decisions. But, as we shall now see, there is serious question about how far to carry this type of planning.

Chapter 19—Adaptive Programming. A substantial part of every company's planning deals with nonrepetitive situations. Managers must set up programs and decide on tactics to follow. We shall note how such plans must frequently be adapted to new problems and opportunities.

Chapter 20—Intraorganization Politics. Who will be helped and who hurt are prime issues to a company politician. These decision guides are especially potent when used by persons with power. And coalitions of powerful persons in support of a cause may further increase political pressure. So, to keep a company on course we must develop congruence between political motives and company objectives.

Future success will depend significantly on how management distributes this increasingly difficult task of planning and *simultaneously* maintains a dynamic, integrated operation.

Decision-Making as
Group Behavior

15

THREE MODELS OF DECISION-MAKING

In the preceding chapters on decision-making, we explored the basic elements of developing creative and wise solutions to management problems. That analysis was simplified by assuming that the process was being carried on in a single person's mind. Planning in an enterprise is more complicated. Many people take part over an extended period; yet numerous specific decisions must fit together to produce coordinated action. So in Part Four we shall examine ways to deal with this added complexity.

Allison's Models for National Decisions

Political scientists are especially concerned about how decisions are made in governmental organizations, for one of their jobs is to predict what actions governments are likely to take. Professor Graham T. Allison suggests a three-stage approach to such prediction, which he has used in a revealing study of the Cuban Missile Crisis.[1] Allison contends that we need to consider 1) rational

[1] See G. T. Allison, *Essence of Decision: Explaining the Cuban Missile Crisis*, Little, Brown & Company, 1971. Allison and his colleagues are extending this approach to many different situations.

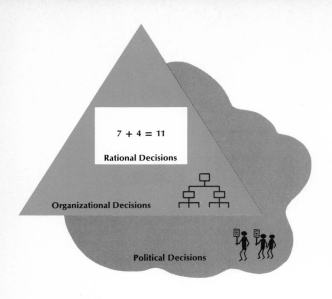

Figure 15–1 Allison's three models of decision-making overlap. Rational decisions on focussed problems are often made by an individual. In a more complex organizational setting the division of labor, problems of communication, uncertainty absorption, and conflict create the need for formal planning mechanisms. But these mechanisms may be conditioned by political pressures. An effective manager must understand all three models.

behavior, 2) bureaucratic behavior, and 3) political behavior. Only by considering all three viewpoints was he able to explain how the Russian and U.S. governments came very close to, and then avoided, triggering another world war during the Cuban crisis.

The same three sets of forces exist in a business enterprise. Business, too, has its formal procedures and political maneuvering, as well as cool rationality. Of course, the structure and the weights differ, but each viewpoint will help us understand how planning actually occurs. By pursuing all three models we will: 1) get a better grasp of the overall system, 2) utilize and combine insights from several disciplines (political science as well as management, behavioral science, economics, operations research, logic, etc.), and 3) be able to devise better guides for practical managerial action.

A Three-Stage Approach to Business Decisions

Our concern is to improve managerial practice. For this purpose, the three models for analyzing decision-making can be briefly described as follows:

 I *Rational decision-making* As already developed in Part Three, rational decision-making involves diagnosis, search, projection, and choice. In its simple form, we assume a single person performs all four elements. The focus, of course, is on decisions about future action—that is, planning.

 II *Organization decision-making* [2] Here planning is done by a "formal" organization. The organization sets up approved guides and mechanisms that its mem-

[2] In technical political-science terms, this model would be called "bureaucratic" decision-making. However, to many people "bureaucracy" suggests rigidity and indifference to changing social goals. So to avoid confusion we use a more neutral word.

bers follow in responding to cues and pressures. The emerging decisions are shaped by this segmented, group-planning process.

III   *Political decision-making*   This deals with the way *internal* politics—based on swapping favors and on power and coalitions—modifies plans that are made. It does not refer to external, party politics.

As developed in this book, each of these models is treated as a modification and elaboration of the preceding one. In other words, the models are not alternatives; in our scheme each model extends the previous one, and helps us sense more fully the complexities of group planning.

Since Number I—Rational decision-making—has been explored in Part Three, we turn now in Chapters 15–19 to Number II—Organization decision-making. Here we are concerned with how a manager can design a total planning system for his organization, thereby greatly enlarging his personal capacity to make plans. Number III—Political decision-making—is then discussed in Chapter 20.

DECISION-MAKING IN ORGANIZATIONS

A variety of managerial tools and practices are available to aid decision-making within organizations. These practices, which are based on years of experience and on recent innovations in management design, must be thoroughly understood by every modern manager. (We will examine these in Chapters 16–19.) As a basis for this analysis, we must note the strengths and the limitations that organizations inevitably add to the decision-making process.

While reviewing these strengths and limitations, we can also appraise the capacity of organizations to perform each of the elements in rational decision-making. Clearly, if the steps outlined in Part Three lead to wise decisions by an individual, it is desirable to incorporate those same steps in organization planning. Actually, under the right conditions an organization has a much greater capacity to plan than a single person. To see how and why this jump in capability occurs, we need to link the elements of rational decision-making with organization design. That is, we need to build bridges connecting concepts of individual decision-making (Part Three) with insights about organization (identified in Parts One and Two).

Dispersion of Inputs

Organizations have the potential for making better decisions than an individual because more experts contribute their specialized judgments. This requires, however, that the decision-making is *dispersed* a) among more people, and b) over a longer period of time. A decision to retreat from a decaying urban location to the suburbs requires inputs from personnel, sales, accounting, finance, legal, office services, and other affected departments. And months, perhaps years, will pass before a clear consensus develops to make the move.

Succession of Premises

Decision-making in an organization differs from individual decision-making in still another way. The help we get from other people and the guides ("restraints") provided by the enterprise itself rarely come together in a single grand array. Theoretically, if we follow the rationalistic-model approach, we might consolidate all the forecasts and guesses, relate them to selected alternatives, make allowances for time and uncertainty, apply a formally approved value scale, and emerge with *the* decision. Actually, only in small organizations and for relatively simple decisions can we get all the issues and "facts" on the table at the same moment.

Instead, conclusions are reached in *sequence*—often by different individuals—and one conclusion becomes a premise for the next. Thus in diagnosis a district sales manager may conclude that the company's new plastic-base paint is unsuited for the blistering sunshine in his district; the plant engineer, accepting this fact, reports on the technical difficulties of making a special mix for that district; and, on the basis of the engineer's report, the cost accountant prepares some figures on producing two different mixes. These are all preliminary data, but note how one builds on another.

Such interlocking of one conclusion into another is particularly significant in projecting consequences after a problem has been defined and the alternatives identified. Suppose that the difficulty with paint blistering has been diagnosed and we have a proposed second line of "sunproof" paint. The company is now trying to project the results of adding this new line. As general background, the company economist predicts general business conditions and the level of business activity for the next five years. Accepting this forecast, the sales manager predicts sales volume with and without the new line. Then, given these volumes, the chief engineer estimates the new equipment that would be needed and other effects on production; he reports that if the new line is added an automatic grinding mill will be feasible. Now, the purchasing agent, learning from the engineer the kind and quantity of raw materials needed, prepares a cost estimate for raw materials; and the personnel director, using the sales and production forecasts, estimates training and wage costs. With these data, the controller makes a summary estimate of total outlays and receipts.

Note in this illustration that the estimates of each person are built on conclusions of one or more other people. Stated another way, the conclusions of the sales manager become premises for the engineer, the conclusions of the engineer become premises for the purchasing agent, and so forth. Consequently, if we want to be confident that the final decision emerging from this sequence is sound, we must give careful attention to how each premise is set. Personal bias and faulty communication may introduce substantial error in the process. Even officially approved premises need to be reviewed.

Problems differ in the number of people who become involved and in the amount of special effort required.[3] The more rare and complex the problem, the more pooling of diverse management talents is necessary. Here are two situations that we shall use as examples throughout the chapter.

The president of Frosty Foods, a successful frozen-food processing company, is aware of the growth in "fast-food" restaurant chains such as McDonald's Hamburgers. These chains use large quantities of frozen food, and variations of basic products especially designed to fit the fashion trends of this market might increase that volume. Possibly Frosty Foods should buy up a chain of outlets. The move of the Howard Johnson chain to sell food products carrying its name through supermarkets suggests the possibility of synergistic benefits; that is, the combined effect of restaurant and supermarket promotion may be greater than the sum of separate promotion of restaurant and supermarket sales. In other words, the president of Frosty Foods feels that opportunity for some kind of action in the "fast-food" industry exists, but he is not clear on what action should be taken. We are concerned here with how a plan of action responding to such an opportunity can best be devised in an organization.

Resolution of the situation just described will obviously involve many people. And the manner in which they will work is quite different from that of a food buyer of a motel chain who telephones to request information about frozen meat dishes suitable for cooking in an infrared oven when the regular kitchen crew is off duty.

For these and similar problem situations a manager concerned with the decision-making process should know *who* will do the following: 1) sense and diagnose opportunities, 2) come up with creative alternatives, 3) make projections of probable results, and 4) meld separate projections into a component picture and select one alternative for positive action.

SENSING AND DIAGNOSING NEEDS

In the diagnosis stage of rational decision-making, an individual starts with his own "felt need" and proceeds to look for causes and limits. But when many people are involved, we face serious risks that important opportunities will pass by unnoticed, or ills be detected too late. "Let purchasing worry about it" is all too easy.

Of course, many management problems or opportunities will surface in normal operations. The control system (Part Five) flags significant deviations from the plan. A customer, supplier, or other outsider makes a request, as did the motel food buyer mentioned above. Or a conscientious operator or manager

---

[3] Throughout this discussion we use the term "problem" to include opportunities as well as present and anticipated difficulties.

has an idea for improving the work he is doing. Some of these wheels will squeak louder than others, but at least the noise is there to be heard.

Discerning New Opportunities

Anticipating obstacles *before* they arise and sensing opportunities in the dynamic environment is more difficult. Managers, such as the president of Frosty Foods, certainly watch major developments, but they also need the help of a mechanism that is alert to all sorts of developments.

Sensing-units. Because employees ordinarily give their chief attention to facts and ideas that directly relate to current problems, they often fail to report other facts and ideas to key executives. Perhaps the unreported information deals with a minor but nonetheless significant aspect of the work; perhaps it is an early warning of impending difficulties; or a lead to a great opportunity. Somehow, someone in the communication network should recognize the significance of this bit of information and tell the appropriate executive about it.

To search out just such information, we may assign a person—or perhaps a research unit. He may watch consumer behavior, new patents, employee complaints, proposed legislation, or some other special area. Although he will probably be overimpressed with the significance of his specialty, his purpose is to call attention to valuable information that might go unnoticed.

Interest-group representatives. Government agencies, especially, often provide a clear avenue for representatives of various interest groups (labor, small business, environmental protection, and so on) to present information and suggestions. These communication devices bypass the points of routine contact; they enable stimuli from the fringe of the complex to reach decision centers with maximum speed and minimum distortion. We indicated earlier that a comparable arrangement seems to serve business enterprises better than does

Figure 15–2 Companies, like nations, must scan their environment to detect threats and opportunities.

the placement of interest-group representatives on the board of directors (see Chapter 6).

It is hard to keep formal interest-group representation and sensing-units alert. After a time they, like managers, tend to accept established institutions and to think in terms of modest changes. Yet we very much need some mechanism to help keep the enterprise relevant to its shifting social, technological, and economic setting. The formal organization is not enough; it must be staffed with perceptive, constructive people.

Communication Barriers

Even with such sensing-units, information has to reach someone who perceives its significance, and many bits and pieces of data bear no label as to their relevance. In fact, much information does not flow freely for two reasons:

1) Experience and experiments have shown that people are poor transmitters of ideas. We know, for example, that people who witness the same automobile accident describe it differently. If these descriptions are later passed on orally from Pete to Karen to Joe, the chances are slim that Joe will have an accurate picture of the accident. As information passes through additional intermediaries, the errors of transmission are compounded. Such decay in accuracy is found within businesses as well as outside.

2) Additional distortion occurs when a message passes up or down a channel of command. *Protective screening* tends to intervene between subordinate and superior. A subordinate is apt to tell his boss what the boss likes to hear and will omit or soften what is unpleasant. Perhaps, too, a subordinate will cover up his own weaknesses. We all adopt this procedure, at least mildly, in ordinary conversation with our friends; we do so even more when we talk to a person in a position of power. After two or three successive screenings of this sort, a report is likely to be considerably distorted. Messages coming down the channel are similarly screened. Each supervisor puts his own interpretation on a message, and probably withholds information that he feels his subordinates do not need to know.

The combined result of normal losses in transmission and protective screening is called *organizational distance*. Workers removed from one another by several steps in an organization hierarchy are in serious danger of being estranged. It is difficult for one to know how another really feels and thinks. If they differ in experience, education, and outlook, the inadequacies of communication are further increased.

Initiators

In face of the diffusion of potentially useful information and the normal communication barriers, we dare not assume that unusual and subtle problems will be recognized. Here we have no predetermined controls nor insistent petitioners. Instead, if the opportunity or potential obstacle is to be identified early, we need an "initiator"—a person who 1) is exposed to the information cues, often through his own initiative, 2) perceives the significance of the cues to company plans and objectives, and 3) insists that careful consideration be given to the perceived problem. An initiator may be a manager or a staff person who has been assigned the duty of discovering problems; or he may be any alert member of the organization with ability to "sense" problems. Rarely is it wise for a manager to rely entirely on himself for this elusive work; so in his staffing (see Chapter 10) he should seek at least a sprinkling of people with this initiating flair.

Completing the Diagnosis

Spotting a potential problem is only the start of a diagnosis. Defining the problem in terms of a gap, identifying causes and obstacles, and establishing limits within which a solution must fall—all need attention (as we saw in Chapter 11). Who in the organization performs this part of the diagnosis?

Complex problems. For complex and unique problems several people should participate in the diagnosis. The initiator, the manager or managers whose sphere of activities will be affected, and perhaps several other experts or investigators can all contribute. For example, the president of Frosty Foods needs more information about the "fast-food" business: critical factors for success, capital requirements, food-buying practices, and so on. A staff person can dig up this information. The maximum size of an appropriate merger partner should be discussed with the treasurer; the effect of the merger on company sales to other chains should be gone over with the sales manager; antitrust issues, with the company's attorney; and impact on management motivation, with the chairman. These early discussions are very tentative; the whole idea is still very fluid. Actually the discussion will undoubtedly slide over to specific alternatives and rough projections of results, but the main purpose is to sharpen the concept of what is desired and to identify major obstacles early. The whole idea may be dropped at any stage if the prospects for success look dim.

Participation by a number of people serves several purposes. The initiator is needed for his insights and also to keep the idea alive. The experts consulted help clarify the objective and are the major source of information on obstacles. Starting with the premise that the new objective is compatible with other company objectives, operating executives define acceptable limits. As we noted in Chapter 11, the senior executive involved shapes the breadth of the study by stipulating how far it should go up the means–end chain and by deciding which company policies are to be regarded as constraints.

At this stage a manager has an exceptional opportunity to guide his organization. He can easily encourage or discourage creative planning in areas he selects. Having endorsed a direction in which a search for improvement should move, he can resort to management by objectives. He can create enthusiasm by having key people participate actively in the formative phases of planning. Because of all these factors, a manager should play an active part in this phase of decision-making and should become as involved here as he does in making the final choice.

Simple problems. Diagnosing the more customary and simple case of the motel buyer who requests information on food for off-hours service involves a very different process. The initiator—the buyer—is an outsider. His request is specific and most if not all of the response comes from established decision guides. If Frosty Foods normally carries products that fit the inquiry, the company has only to convince the buyer that he should deal with Frosty Foods; after this, agreement on price and delivery can be sought. Even if the buyer wants a variation from stock items, the problem can be immediately narrowed by company policy toward special orders.

Such simple diagnosis is possible because a whole set of policies and procedures have been designed to resolve promptly just this kind of problem. Obviously if Frosty Foods had just opened its doors and had no standard array of products, production specifications, or sales policies, the inquiry would precipitate a great deal of diagnosis and problem-solving. However, the planning structure, which we shall examine in the next four chapters, is formulated for the express purpose of avoiding the need for much diagnosis of single transactions. In advance of the specific request, decisions have been made that cover a whole series of similar situations.

To summarize: The main questions a manager must answer when thinking about how diagnosis occurs in his organization are these: 1) What provision should he make for scanning both the external environment and internal operation to detect future opportunities and problems? 2) How can he minimize the effect of "organizational distance," so that cues once discovered do not get lost? 3) Who should participate in completing the diagnosis and in revising it as the decision-making process evolves? 4) What role should previously established plans play in simplifying and expediting diagnoses?

The two Frosty Foods illustrations make clear that no single set of answers can be given to these questions. Companies vary in the number of unique and complex problems they face, and so do departments within companies. The provisions for diagnosis should reflect this variation. Even in this first stage of decision-making, we see the benefits and complexities that arise from having several different people participate.

SOURCES OF FRESH IDEAS

Finding good alternatives is the second basic stage in rational decision-making. Here we certainly expect an organization of many people to have many more good ideas than a single individual. Nevertheless, special arrangements are necessary to stimulate and detect these bright ideas.

338

PART IV
Planning:
Decision-Making
in an Enterprise

Relying on Operating Personnel

Sometimes acceptable alternatives emerge during the diagnosis stage. The people consulted about the problem also know what other firms are doing, and they add ideas of their own. In fact, the cue that triggered the recognition of a problem may have been an action taken by someone else—a proposal by a supplier, or a request by a client.

Yet sooner or later, someone has to decide that searching for additional alternatives is not worth the trouble. This decision is often made promptly. When at least one satisfactory alternative is at hand, the person who suggests further search is given the burden of explaining why he thinks a better way might be uncovered.

This tendency to end a search for alternatives too early leads a few wise managers to insist always on serious consideration of at least four alternatives. Such a rule of thumb does not ensure a careful search, but it does avoid the tempting simplicity of an *either* A *or* B formulation. Another tack is to invite suggestions from all key people who would be affected by the contemplated change. Too often this is really an early move to prepare them for an imminent change, and proposals submitted are brushed aside as biased or as ploys to avoid the inevitable. Nevertheless, several fairly good alternatives can often be assembled promptly from such key people.

Separate Creative Units

What happens when no acceptable alternative bubbles to the surface? The constraints built into the diagnosis (capital, ownership, time, impact on community, and so on) or a tough obstacle may eliminate all the obvious courses of action. We then turn to creativity.

When the need for creative ideas is predictable and recurs in a known field, we organize to get fresh ideas. Product or process research in a pharmaceutical firm is an example. Specialists are hired and a laboratory is built to create a flow of new, useful drugs, typically within certain predetermined classes. The results are uncertain, but the approach is straightforward. Advertising agencies similarly hire experts to produce fresh themes. A variation occurs in new designs for women's dresses. Small firms often buy designs from an independent designer, but the approach still involves a specialist who creates alternatives for a predicted need. The researchers and creative people may share in short-run diagnosis, but they are primarily a separate group of specialists.

One drawback of relying on specialized people is the possibility of friction. In Chapter 9 we noted that sharp differences in attitudes and values of personnel in sales and production are a source of organizational conflict. The same type of conflict is very often found between "creative guys" and "tough operators." The imaginative person who is ready to entertain all sorts of fanciful notions has an outlook that is very different from that of the operator who carefully distinguishes between fact and fiction, right and wrong, established practicality and daydreaming. Because of this contrast in orientation, we must anticipate friction when two such people are asked to collaborate. To minimize this difficulty, physical separation and relatively few interactions are probably desirable. On the other hand, if we choose to make different types learn to live together, we should use carefully supervised project teams whenever feasible.

Temporary Assignment to Produce Ideas

The use of specialists is unsuitable when the need for creative alternatives is irregular or unpredictable. Frosty Foods cannot afford to maintain a specialist on mergers with restaurant chains, even if such an expert could be located. Instead, people who have other jobs in the company must temporarily become creators of alternatives.

Conditions that foster creativity were discussed in Chapter 11. A permissive atmosphere, for instance, is conducive to a flow of fresh ideas. Note, however, that the need for alternatives to a unique problem is temporary. We may ask three or four individuals to be creative for a week or only a morning, after which they return to jobs where stress is on analysis and where supervisors tolerate no mistakes. Both the people and their supervisors are asked to shift attitudes and standards for only a brief period. Some of us have this flexibility, but a lot of sophistication about different styles of work is required.

Management consultants can be brought in if the problem is large enough to warrant the cost of the special arrangements. Consultants will have ready-made alternatives for only a few fairly standard problems. These advisors usually work with their client on the entire project—diagnosis, alternatives, projection, and choice—and their chief contribution is typically objective, undivided attention to the project and skill in digging out and arranging facts and ideas. Consultants provide ability much more than specific ideas, for the client personnel who work with them supply many of these. Therefore, company personnel work on a strange and temporary assignment as before; but in this case they are under the skillful guidance of the consultants.

Internal generation of creative alternatives for unique problems should therefore be assigned to people who have considerable flexibility, in addition to the required knowledge of the situation being studied.[4]

Most significant for successful use of any of these arrangements—relying on operating personnel, using separate creative units, or making temporary assignments—is recognition that the mental attitude and surrounding support needed for creativity differs sharply from that needed for projection and choice.

---

[4] *Synectics*—discussed in Chapter 11—is an exception. With this technique only one or two participants have to be qualified to build bridges from fresh ideas to the actual situation.

What would happen if we follow alternative-A? If we follow alternative-B? We should predict such results for each alternative.

When such projections are made in an organization, people from many departments normally help make them. Also, as we noted at the beginning of this chapter, one forecast often becomes the planning premise of a related forecast; thus a whole succession of estimates may be interdependent. This ability to tap the understanding and judgment of a variety of specialists is a great strength, because it allows organizations to deal intelligently with complex issues that are far beyond the comprehension of a single individual.

The use of different specialists to make projections, however, is not an unmixed blessing. The very fact that each of several individuals contributes a piece of the total picture poses some unique difficulties in consolidating the pieces. We need to appreciate these difficulties and understand what we can do about them, in order to grasp fully the potential benefits to be gained from group projections of results.

"Absorbing" Uncertainty

All the estimates used in decision-making deal with the future, and all involve some uncertainty. Future sales, for instance, depend on a host of unknowns—competitors' actions, consumer reaction to our tie-in advertising, health of our sales manager, a civil-rights boycott, and the like. When our sales manager makes an estimate of sales for the next five years, he might hedge his answer with a lot of "ifs"—*if* competitors cut prices by five percent, *if* the advertising plan really clicks, *if* everyone is healthy, *then* sales will probably be around four million or maybe five million.

Such an answer is quite unsatisfactory for the engineer. He says, "I don't have time to guess whether your advertising campaign is any good. Just tell me how much you want, because I have plenty of problems of my own." He prefers a single figure, or at most a narrow range. So the sales manager makes the best guess he can, realizing that his figure may not be accurate. If he is a conservative individual (or experience has taught him that he gets into less trouble when his estimates are low), he picks a low volume. Or, if he is optimistic, does not mind taking a risk, and wants to impress the boss, he picks a higher volume. In any event, he "absorbs" a lot of uncertainty when he finally tells the engineer to assume that sales will be, say, four and a half million.

The engineer is in a similar predicament. Will the refrigeration pumps break down in the near future? Can quality be maintained if a new product line is added? How long will it take to make a changeover to new raw material? And so forth. Again, we do not want an answer full of "ifs." Instead, we ask the engineer to use his judgment, which means that he absorbs uncertainty about a group of factors. Virtually everyone else who provides estimates used in our projection for expanded production will likewise absorb uncertainty.

Such uncertainty absorption is inevitable and desirable. Without it the analysis of problems becomes hopelessly complex. If we attempted to give attention to all the possibilities as one estimate is built on another, the number of possible outcomes would increase at a geometric rate and would soon become incomprehensible. So we accept uncertainty absorption, but try to minimize its dangers.

Recognizing the Bias of Estimates

Whenever we depend upon an estimate prepared by someone else, we naturally want to know whether it is reliable. We want to know whether it is optimistic or pessimistic. We want to know of any bias, especially when we are aware that a particular individual has absorbed a lot of uncertainty in a prediction that is used in other estimates.

Bias of some sort is almost inevitable in a set of projections made by different people. Here are four common reasons why one person's projections of results may not be just what the decision-maker needs:

1) *Differences in the perception of objectives.* A manager who is making a decision may have objectives different from those of the people who are giving him advice. This situation is especially true when the advisors have strong, professional indoctrination, as in accounting, law, social work, and, to a lesser extent, engineering. The advice and other help such people provide may be strongly influenced by what they believe to be important. If a decision-maker is trying to achieve different objectives, the sympathetic help he is expecting may turn out to be suggestions leading off on a tangent. The help may still be of some value, but he has to make allowance for its source.

     Difference in objectives was found to be an important factor in a study of seventy-four companies' decisions on the use of outside contractors for maintenance work. The study showed that senior executives place high values on stable union relations, whereas maintenance superintendents give greater weight to keeping their costs low and to the number of their employees who might be laid off. We cannot tell from the available information which objectives deserve priority, but clearly the difference in objectives affects the way the two leadership groups respond to this problem.

2) *The "persuasive" advisor.* People vary in their persuasive ability, and it is entirely possible that a person who is making a projection will be unduly swayed by the counsel he receives from an impressive individual. A review of the role of business economists in twenty firms revealed that the use made of economic forecasts was significantly influenced by the personal feeling toward the company economist and by how well he "sold" his conclusions.

     Status and company politics are factors here, as well as manner of speech. The treasurer of a food chain served as chairman of its capital-expenditures committee, and his views carried heavy weight in decisions on which division received the largest share of capital for expansion. Partly because of this "power," his recommendations on other matters were seldom challenged. Such influence, again, makes it difficult to reach completely objective decisions.

3) *Special pressure.* Informal groups, as we noted in Chapter 8, have a strong influence on the values, beliefs, and socially acceptable actions of their members. All of us are members of several such groups, and we take part of our counsel from these unofficial sources as well as from the advisors and information centers provided in the formal organization. Informal groups, particularly among executives, may strongly support official company objectives and plans—but not necessarily. When we base our planning on numerous personal interchanges, we must be prepared for this reality: Social relations cannot be prescribed by an organization manual.

4) *Personal needs.* The aspirations and beliefs, as well as the sweet or bitter experience, of a person making a projction affect his response to the array of help provided by an organization. To be sure, supervisory review keeps reminding the advisor of company objectives and other basic "premises." Nevertheless, there is still room for personal bias to affect the predictions the advisor makes. The fallibility of human nature is simply another source of conflict to bear in mind as we contemplate the organization as a machine for making plans.

When several different projections have to be consolidated, as is necessary to appraise expansion alternatives open to Frosty Foods, the cumulative effect of bias can be substantial.

Credibility Structure

Faced with uncertainty absorption and likely bias in the estimates he receives from his expert advisors, what can the manager who makes the final choice among alternatives do? He wants to achieve key objectives, and he will be accountable for results; yet he is aware that the projections on which he bases his choice are synthetic and questionable.

Identify reliable projectors. Among the various individuals who analyze alternatives and predict outcomes, a few stand out as persons whose conclusions can be relied upon. "If Jeanne says it will work, that's good enough for me." "No one knows for sure, but I'll bet on Philip's estimate." These are highly subjective judgments about specific persons. This is the way the manager who has to make the final decision feels about participants in the decision-making process. The "reliable" person might be disliked or perhaps is ineffective in other kinds of work, but his opinion is respected.

Usually we regard a person as reliable on a particular subject, not on everything. One individual has a good feel for labor relations, another for European economic developments, someone else for production feasibility, and so on. One person may possess keen technical insight, whereas another keeps divergent trends in good balance.

Among the qualities that inspire confidence are: knowledge of relevant facts; integrity (not saying things to manipulate other people); sensitivity to a broad range of influences; capacity to visualize change, but not be carried away with one possibility; willingness to accept a given premise and use it as a basis for further thought. Also, a capacity to explain why his projections differ from others is helpful but not essential.

No list of personal qualities, however, substitutes for the judgment of the final decision-maker concerning those on whom he can rely for different kinds of inputs. S. L. Andersen of the Du Pont Company calls this array of dependable advisors the "credibility structure." It is built on an assessment of persons, not on written job descriptions.

Distinguish credibility structure from formal organization. A widely held role concept is that the administrative head of a unit 1) provides the official opinions of activities within the scope of the unit, or at least 2) reviews, amends, and communicates the business opinions of anyone within his unit. More specifically, the concept holds that the head of the marketing division makes the official market projections, the chief engineer provides the official engineering projections, and so on. Each one normally consults with his subordinates and may authorize them to speak for his unit, but any projection coming from the unit is subject to the approval of its titular head.

The credibility structure may not agree with the concept just stated. In

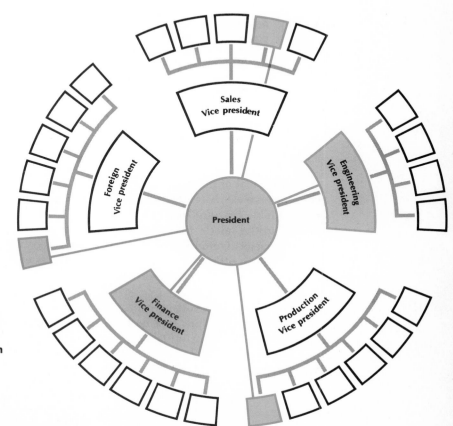

Figure 15–3 A circular organization chart. Colored boxes show the president's "credibility chart" for a decision on whether to open a new mine in Latin America.

forecasting the results of a set of alternatives, a respected staff person may have views that differ from those of the operating executives. Perhaps the opinions of a subordinate carry more weight than those of his boss; or an outsider, such as a former division executive, may have the highest credibility. The reason for such a discrepancy between the credibility structure and the administrative organization is that assisting in making projections is only one, perhaps minor, part of the total job of a line manager. The sales manager, for instance, has to plan an annual campaign, maintain good relations with distributors, build and inspire his own sales force, cultivate key customers, exercise control over sales expense, and so on. The optimism, enthusiasm, and drive needed for these duties may actually interfere with the objectivity and discernment that contribute to reliable projections. Similarly, a first-rate engineering manager may be a wizard at adapting present plants to variation in the product line, but this does not mean that he is necessarily qualified to predict the cost of building a small plant in New Zealand.

Dealing with divergence. Strong operating executives have confidence in their own opinions. They do not relish the thought that another's projections are more highly regarded than their own. So when the credibility structure diverges from the administrative structure, we face a delicate relationship. Among the ways to sidestep this kind of embarrassment are these:

1) Point out not only the importance but also the difficulty of making a reliable projection in the manager's area; it will follow then that this is one area where expert outside judgment is warranted.

2) If necessary to maintain morale, carry forward two sets of projections, one based on the executive premise and one on the more reliable premise of another person. Rarely will the final choice depend solely on this discrepancy, and the difference will be submerged in the total balance.

The important point is never to lose sight of the confidence that can be attached to the projections being consolidated into the final balancing of alternatives.

Approval of premises. Especially when one projection becomes the basis of successive estimates, the manager making the final choice may try to control the premises that are fed into the process at early stages. Unless he has confidence in the sales estimates upon which production forecasts are based or in the engineer's assurance that ecology issues will cause no delay, the entire exercise may have little value. To avoid such fruitless effort, the decision-maker can insist upon his review and approval of conclusions that become premises for the next set of projections.

Control of this sort may also be necessary if a person in the midst of the estimating process finds that he lacks confidence in the premises given to him; in this case he privately makes his own corrections. For instance, if a production manager says, "I know those sales estimates are always twenty-five percent too high" or "The engineers never turn loose a new product when they say they will," and then bases his estimates on a less ambitious assumption, the consolidated projections are not internally consistent. A review and approval of premises at key stages should reduce this need for hidden adjustments. Here again, the control of premises seeks to keep the successive projections in line with the credibility structure.

The whole issue of credibility structure relates especially to complex, unique decisions. For simpler, repetitive decisions the future results of various actions are better known, and there is less use of dubious premises for successive estimates. At Frosty Foods, the credibility structure is highly significant when projecting different merger alternatives; but for the motel inquiry the projections are more reliable and bias is more easily assessed.

Analysis of Risk

In a projection, greater uncertainty can surround some points more than others. For example, in a massive sewage-disposal experiment in western Michigan, the rate of biological decomposition affects the feasibility of the entire scheme, whereas the cost of building a dam can change the total capital outlay by less than one percent. Both points are uncertain, but the risk related to the speed of decomposition is critical because 1) the *range* of possible results is wide—from very slow to fast—and 2) the *effect of variations* will determine the capacity of the entire system. In contrast, building costs of the dam are unlikely to deviate by more than twenty-five percent, and even if they do, this variation has repercussions on only a few aspects of the total venture.

Risk analysis identifies the critical points of uncertainty in a projection—the decomposition rate in the previous example. These points can be identified by careful thought, as was possible for the multimillion-dollar project just cited. If a mathematical model has been prepared to assist in the projection, the critical risk points can be derived from the model.

Having spotted the critical uncertainties, a manager can: 1) give close personal attention to the forecasts made for these factors and can probably personally approve premises about these factors; 2) provide for later rechecking as better evidence becomes available; and/or 3) make multiple projections using two or more points on the range. By concentrating only on critical uncertainties, multiple projections may become technically feasible.

Stabilizing Projections

Most of the difficulties of making projections in organizations apply especially to complex, unique problems. To the extent that we can simplify such problems by dividing them into parts and by making the parts less unique, we reduce these difficulties. A company planning structure does just that.

Explicit objectives and subobjectives tend to remove bias arising from bureaucratic maneuvering. Policies, standing operating procedures, and standard methods help establish a customary way of dealing with problems. This customary practice provides a historical basis upon which to base projections and creates a stabilized environment in which predictions are more accurate. In addition, consolidation of estimates is easier when each person preparing an estimate visualizes the same consistent manner of operation. Because of these and other benefits of structured planning, we shall carefully examine important planning practices in the next four chapters.

To summarize: The underlying process of projecting the probable results of different alternatives was explored in Chapter 13. In this chapter we placed that process in an organizational setting. Within an organization a wide variety of expert talent can be drawn upon to round out the projections. We inevitably must face uncertainty absorption and biased estimates, but we can reduce the undesirable effects of these factors by recognizing and utilizing the credibility structure, employing risk analysis, and creating a stabilized setting for the projected activities.

OFFICIAL CHOICES OF THE ORGANIZATION

The final act in decision-making, which follows diagnosis, identification of alternatives, and projection of results of each alternative, is choice of the one alternative to be followed. In organization decision-making, the formal organization design designates who makes this choice.

Fruitless arguments can be held on who *really* makes the decision. As we have stressed, many people often get into the act. They may affect the way a problem is formulated or decide which alternatives should receive consideration or which consequences should be forecast. They may influence the values used by the decision-maker in his choice and may block effective execution so that a new decision must be made. But influence is not the official act. In every organized effort, we need a mechanism for decisiveness. If action is to proceed effectively, an official stamp of approval must be provided.

The authority to make decisions, in the sense of selecting one alternative and giving it official sanction, may be delegated, as we saw in Chapter 3. The delegation may be surrounded with limitations on scope or with policy constraints. Perhaps decisions will require the endorsement of other executives. Nevertheless, we continue to look to the "formal organization" for information on who makes the final choice.[5]

Because the final choice is made in an organizational context rather than by an isolated individual, the decision-maker makes his choices by using a set of values quite different from those that would govern simply a *personal* preference. He is strongly guided 1) by company objectives, departmental

---

[5] Formal organization structure is not always clearcut; perhaps it needs clarification, using the guidelines already discussed in Part One. Nevertheless, it is the formal organization —not the informal one—that tells us who can give the official stamp of approval for a particular kind of decision.

objectives, company traditions and norms, and other institutional values; 2) by the company incentive and control system as related to him; and 3) by company politics growing out of conflict within the organization.

347

CHAPTER 15
Decision-Making
as Group Behavior

CONCLUSION

When we superimpose the rational decision-making model over the formal organization design, we have seen that each element—diagnosis, search, projection, and choice—can indeed be carried out in a typical organization. However, bringing to bear the full potential strength of the organization on each element calls for special managerial attention. Clearcut provisions are needed, especially to flag new opportunities, to encourage creative suggestions, to watch for biased estimates, and to clarify who has the authority to make the final choice.

Several new concepts aid in securing rational decisions—sensing units, initiators, uncertainty absorption, credibility structure, and risk analysis.

Even more significant is the cost to the company of making an important, unique decision within its organization. Each of the many people who contribute to the decision use valuable time becoming oriented and contributing. In addition, managers must coordinate the many efforts, keep attention focused on dominant objectives, communicate back and forth as the decision evolves, know how uncertainty is resolved, maintain consistency with related decisions, get action before it is too late—all of which absorbs even more effort. Clearly all the numerous decisions that must be made in an active enterprise do not warrant such costs (just as an individual cannot take time to make all his decisions rationally).

Instead, we need simplifying mechanisms that enable the organization to approach the ideal of rational decision-making but do not entail such high costs. We must provide the organization with a planning system that encourages consistent and persistent effort, timely action, efficient use of resources, morale among the members—and does all this with a bearable input of managerial time. The next four chapters discuss the design of such a planning system.

In terms of the three decision models identified under "A Three-Stage Approach to Business Decisions," the present chapter has provided an introduction to Number II—Organization decision-making. However, the main features of that model are still to be developed as we examine company planning systems.

FOR CLASS DISCUSSION

1) "A truly rational decision will also involve *rational* consideration of 1) how the organization may be used to reach and activate a decision, and of 2) the political implications." How do you respond to this statement in light of Allison's three-pronged approach?

2) Leo Cherne says, "Only the man who sits in that tiny space where the information, the problems, and the authority intersect can really see the picture in all its aspects and confusions." Reconcile this view, to the extent you can, with the concept of planning in an organization.

3) A product manager of a food company explained that all major decisions on the group of breakfast foods he was "responsible" for were made not by him but by a product-management committee. He was chairman of the committee, which includes vice presidents in charge of the production, sales, and research departments. What advantages do you see to such an arrangement? What potential drawbacks?

4) Apart from formal suggestion systems, what could be done to increase the value of inputs from hourly workers to higher-level decisions? Consider both opportunities and difficulties with respect to each part of the decision-making process.

5) "Group judgment is fiction. If delegation has been carried out properly, one man and not a group has the obligation for making the decision. If this one man wants the advice of others, he can get it by conversing with them or through staff and control reports. Forming a committee is a sure way to get men to abrogate their responsibilities and is a costly and time-consuming use of executive time." How would you reply to this statement?

6) Realizing the transmission losses and protective screening that take place as information passes through successive layers of management, why not encourage more direct communication between those who have data and those who need it, rather than insist on following the chain of command?

7) "One way to increase the soundness of key figures on which I must base decisions is to insist that those who furnish them state in writing the assumptions, premises, and techniques used to arrive at them. Although I don't have the time and, in some cases, the background to verify these assumptions, I keep them on file to help sort out reasons for mistakes." What do you think of this approach as described by a vice president of marketing?

8) The controller of a large company regularly receives sales forecasts from the marketing vice president. The forecasts are developed after corporate assumptions are sent to field representatives. These people then put together their estimated sales. By the time the controller receives these forecasts, they have been reviewed by three or four levels of sales management. Although the controller's primary job is to consolidate these forecasts with production, engineering, finance, and other budgets, he plays another, unofficial role: "I sit down with the president and help him decide how much to raise or lower these forecasts, based on our estimates of sales optimism or pessimism." Discuss this unofficial task.

Cases

For cases involving issues covered in this chapter, see especially the following. Particularly relevant questions are listed after each case.

Allison, G. T., *Essence of Decision: Explaining the Cuban Missile Crisis.* Boston: Little, Brown and Company, 1971. Chapters 3 and 4.

Develops the second of three models used by Allison in his pace-setting study— the organization decision process; and applies this model to the Cuban missile crisis.

Bower, J. L., *Managing the Resource Allocation Process: A Study of Corporate Planning and Investment.* Boston: Harvard Graduate School of Business Administration, 1970.

Careful study of the way several major investment projects were conceived, examined, and eventually approved in a large corporation.

Cleland, D. I. and W. R. King, eds., *Systems Analysis and Project Management,* 2nd ed. New York: McGraw-Hill Book Company, 1975, Chapter 8.

Discusses planning in an organization from a systems viewpoint.

Roberts, M. J., "An Evolutionary and Institutional View of the Behavior of Public and Private Companies," *American Economic Review,* May 1975.

An up-to-date, sophisticated discussion of decision-making in public-utility companies.

Simon, H. A., *Administrative Behavior,* 3rd ed. New York: The Free Press, 1976.

Provides conceptual and theoretical insights into decision-making in organizations. This edition enlarges, but leaves intact, the now-classic formulation of the first edition in 1947.

Wortman, M. S. and F. Luthans, *Emerging Concepts in Management,* 2nd ed. New York: The Macmillan Company, 1975, pp. 84–95.

Two concise articles on the planning process in large organizations written for managers.

16 Master Strategy and Long-range Programming

RELEVANCE AND SURVIVAL

Every enterprise needs a central purpose expressed in terms of the services it will render to society. In addition, it needs a basic concept of how it will create these services. Because it will be competing with other enterprises for resources, it must have some distinctive relevance—in its services or in its method of creating them. Moreover, because it will inevitably cooperate with an array of other firms, it must have the means for maintaining viable coalitions with them. Added to these issues are the elements of change, growth, and adaptation. Master strategy is a company's basic plan for dealing with these factors.

One familiar way of delving into company strategy is to ask, "What business are we in?" or, "What business do we want to be in?" "Why should society tolerate our existence?" Answers to these questions are often difficult. A certain tuberculosis sanitarium almost went bankrupt when antibiotics reduced the need for long rest cure, but it revived by becoming a beautifully located retirement home. Less fortunate was a cooperage firm that defined its business in terms of wooden boxes and barrels and had to shut down when paperboard containers took over the field.

Product line is only part of the picture, however. An ability to supply services economically is also crucial. For example, most local bakeries have closed, not for lack of demand for bread, but because they became technologically inefficient. Many a paper mill has exhausted its sources of pulpwood. The independent motel operator is having difficulty meeting competition from franchised chains. Yet in all these industries some firms have prospered—the ones that have had the foresight and adaptability (and probably some luck, too) to take advantage of their changing environment. These firms pursued a master strategy that enabled them to increase the services rendered and to attract greater resources.

Master strategy is of such cardinal importance, and it so permeates other planning within a firm, that we devote most of this chapter to it. Although our illustrations will be largely from business, the central concept is just as crucial for hospitals, universities, and other nonprofit ventures.

A practical way to develop a master strategy is to 1) pick particular roles or niches for the company that are propitious in view of society's needs and the company's resources, 2) combine various niches and other facets of the company's efforts to obtain synergistic effects, 3) express the plans in terms of targets, and 4) set up sequences and timing of changes that reflect company capabilities and external conditions. Let us look at each of these steps in turn and then see how long-range programming ties into the concept of the company mission.

PICKING PROPITIOUS NICHES

Most enterprises fill more than one niche. Often they provide several lines of products or services. Even when a single line is produced, an enterprise may sell it to several distinct types of customers. Especially as a firm grows, it seeks expansion by tapping new markets or by selling different services to its existing customers. In designing a company strategy we can avoid pitfalls by first examining each of these markets separately.

Because of the long time required to develop new products or services, a wise executive looks beyond modifications of his present line. He focuses on changed conditions in the world that will alter the needs of customers he might serve. Basically we are searching for changing, growing customer needs where

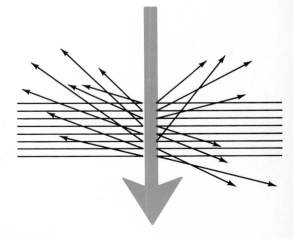

Figure 16–1 Company strategy gives overall direction to operations and takes priority over the often-diverging interests of various departments.

adroit use of our unique resources will make our services distinctive and in that sense give us a competitive advantage. In these particular spots, we hope to give the customer an irresistible value at relatively low expense. A bank, for example, may devise a way of financing the purchase of an automobile that is particularly well suited to farmers; but it must then consider whether it is in a good position to serve such a market.

Identifying such propitious niches is not easy. Here is one approach that works well in a wide variety of situations. Focus first on the industry as a whole —growth prospects, competition, key factors required for success—and then on the strengths and weaknesses of the specific company as matched against these key success factors. As we describe this approach more fully, keep in mind that we are interested in segments of markets as well as entire markets.

Industry Outlook

The sales volume and profits of an industry or one of its segments depend on the demand for its services, the supply of these services, and the competitive conditions. (We use "service" here to include both physical products and intangible values provided by an enterprise.) Predicting future demand, supply, and competition is an exciting endeavor. In the following paragraphs we suggest a few of the important considerations that may vitally affect a company's strategy.

Demand for industry services. The strength of the *desire* for a service affects its demand. For instance, we keenly want a small amount of dental care, but place little value on additional quantities. Our desire for more and better automobiles does not have this same sort of cut-off level; and our desire for pay-television (no commercials, select programs) or supersonic air travel is highly uncertain, falling in quite a different category from that of dental care.

Possible *substitutes* to satisfy a given desire must be weighed—beef for lamb, motorboats for baseball, gas for coal, Aureomycin for sulfa, weldments for castings, and so forth. The frequency of such substitution is affected, of course, by the relative prices.

Desire has to be backed up by *ability to pay,* and here business cycles enter in. Furthermore, in some industries large amounts of capital are necessarily tied up in equipment. The relative efficiency, quality of work, and nature of existing machinery influence the money that will be available for new equipment. Another consideration: If we hope to sell in foreign markets, then foreign-exchange issues arise.

The *structure of markets* also requires analysis. Where, on what terms, and in response to what appeals do people buy jet planes, sulphuric acid, or dental floss? Does a manufacturer deal directly with consumers, or are intermediaries, such as retailers or brokers, a more effective means of distribution?

Although an entire industry is often affected by these factors—desire, substitutes, ability to pay, structure of markets—a local variation in demand sometimes provides a unique opportunity for a particular firm. Thus most drugstores carry cosmetics, candy, and a wide variety of items besides drugs; but a store located in a medical center might develop a highly profitable business by dealing exclusively with prescriptions and other medical supplies.

All these elements of demand are subject to change—some of it quite rapid. Because the kind of strategic plans we are considering here typically extend over a period of years, we need both an identification of the key factors that will affect industry demand and an estimate of how that picture will change over time.

Supply related to demand. The attractiveness of any industry depends on more than potential growth arising from strong demand. In designing a company strategy we must also consider the probable supply of services and the conditions under which they will be offered.

The *capacity* of an industry to fill demand for its services clearly affects profit margins. The importance of overcapacity or undercapacity, however, depends on the ease of entry and withdrawal from the industry. When capital costs are high, as in the hotel or cement business, adjustments to demand tend to lag. Thus overcapacity may depress profits for a long period; even bankruptcies do not remove the capacity if plants are bought up at bargain prices and are operated by new owners. On the other hand, low capital requirements —as in electronic-assembly work—permit new firms to enter quickly, and shortages of supply tend to be short-lived. Of course more than the physical plant is involved; an effective organization of competent people is also necessary. Here again the ease of expansion or contraction should be appraised.

Costs also need to be predicted—labor costs, material costs, and, for some industries, transportation costs or excise taxes. If increases in operating costs affect all members of an industry alike and can be passed on to the consumer in the form of higher prices, this factor becomes less significant in company strategy. However, rarely do both conditions prevail. Sharp rises in labor costs in Hawaii, for example, place its sugar industry at a disadvantage in the world market.

A highly dynamic aspect of supply is *technology*. New methods for producing established products—for example, basic oxygen conversion of steel displacing open-hearth furnaces, and mechanical cottonpickers displacing centuries-old handpicking techniques—are part of the picture. Technology may change the availability and price of raw materials; witness the growth of synthetic rubber and industrial diamonds. Similarly, air-cargo planes and other new forms of transportation are expanding the sources of supply that may serve a given market.

For an individual producer, anticipating these shifts in industrial supply may be a matter of prosperity or bankruptcy.

Competitive conditions in the industry. The way the interplay between demand and supply works out depends partly on the nature of competition in the industry. *Size, strength, and attitude of companies* in an industry—say, the dress industry, where entrance is easy and style critical—may lead to very sharp competition. On the other hand, oligopolistic competition among the giants of the aluminum industry produces a more stable situation, at least in the short run. The resources and managerial talent needed to enter one industry differ greatly from what it takes to get ahead in another.

A strong *trade association* often helps to create a favorable climate in its industry. The Association of Consulting Management Engineers, to cite one case, has actively promoted professional conduct in the management-consulting field. Other associations compile valuable industry statistics, help reduce unnecessary variations in size of products, run training conferences, hold trade shows, and aid members in a variety of other ways.

Government regulation also modifies competition. A few industries like banking and insurance are supervised by national or state bodies that place limits on prices, sales promotion, and the variety of services rendered. Airlines are regulated as a utility and subsidized as an infant industry. Farm subsidies affect large segments of agriculture, and tariffs have long protected selected manufacturers. Our patent laws also bear directly on the nature of competition, as is evident in the heated discussion of how pharmaceutical patents may be used. Clearly, future government action is a significant factor in the outlook of many industries.

Key factors for success in the industry. This brief review suggests the dynamic nature of business and the uncertainties in outlook for virtually all industries. A crucial task of every top management is to assess the forces at play in its industry and identify those factors that will be crucial for future success. These we call "key success factors." Leadership in research and development may be very important in one industry, low costs in another, and adaptability to local needs in a third; large financial resources may be a *sine qua non* for mining, whereas creative imagination is the touchstone in advertising.

We stressed earlier the desirability of making such analyses for narrow segments as well as for broad industry categories. The success factors for each segment are likely to differ from those for others in at least one or two respects. For example, General Foods Corporation discovered to its sorrow that the key success factors in gourmet foods differ significantly from those for coffee and Jell-O.

Moreover, the analysis of industry outlook should provide a forecast of the *growth potentials* and the *profit prospects* for the various industry segments.

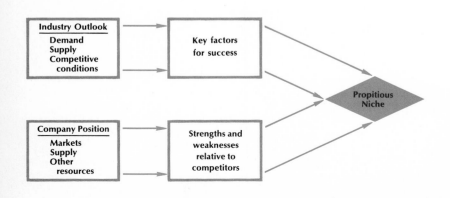

Figure 16–2 Locating a propitious niche involves matching a firm's specific qualities against the industry outlook.

These conclusions, along with key success factors, are vital guideposts in setting up a company's master strategy.

Company Strengths and Limitations

The range of opportunities for distinctive service is wide. In picking its particular niche out of this array, a company naturally favors those opportunities that will utilize its strengths and bypass its limitations. This calls for a candid appraisal of the company itself.

Market strengths of a company. A direct measure of *market position* is the percentage that company sales represent of 1) industry sales and 2) major competitors' sales. Such figures quickly indicate whether a company is so big that its activities are likely to bring prompt responses from other leading companies. On the other hand, a company may be small enough to enjoy independent maneuverability. Of course, to be most meaningful, these percentages should be computed separately for geographical areas, product lines, and types of customers—if suitable industry data is available.

More intangible, but no less significant, are the relative standing of *company products* and their *reputation* in major markets. Kodak products for instance, are widely and favorably known; they enjoy a reputation for high quality and dependability. Clearly this reputation will be a factor in Eastman Kodak Company strategy, and any new, unknown firm must overcome this prestige if it seeks even a small share in a segment of the film market. Market reputation is tenacious. Especially when we try to "trade up," our previous low quality, poor service, and sharp dealing will be an obstacle. Any strategy we adopt must have enough persistency and consistency so that our firm is assigned a "role" in the minds of the customers we wish to reach.

The relationship between a company and the *distribution system* is another vital aspect of market position. The large United States automobile companies, for example, are strong partly because each has a network of dealers throughout the country. In contrast, foreign car manufacturers have difficulty selling here until they can arrange with dealers to provide dependable service.

All these aspects of market position—a relative share of the market, comparative quality of the product, reputation with consumers, and ties with a distributive system—help define the strengths and limitations of a company.

Supply strengths of a company. To pick propitious niches we also should appraise our company's relative strength in creating goods and services. Such ability to supply services fitted to consumer needs will be built largely on the firm's resources of labor and material, effective productive facilities, and perhaps pioneering research and development.

Labor in the United States is fairly mobile. People tend to gravitate to good jobs. But the process takes time—a shoe plant in the South needed ten years to build up an adequate number of skilled workers—and it may be expensive. Consequently, immediate availability of competent personnel at normal industry wages is a source of strength. In addition, the relationships between the company and its work force are important. All too often, both custom and formal agreements freeze inefficient practices. The classic example is New England textiles; here, union-supported work habits give even modern mills high labor costs. Only recently have a few companies been able to match their more flourishing competitors located in the South.

Access to *low-cost materials* is often a significant factor in a company's supply position. The development of the paper industry in the South, for example, is keyed to the use of fast-growing forests that can be cut on a rotational basis to provide a continuing supply of pulpwood. Of course, if raw materials can be easily transported—such as iron ore and crude oil by enormous ships—plants need not be located at the original source.

Availability of materials involves more than physical handling. Ownership, or long-term contracts with those who do own, may ensure a continuing source at low cost. Much of the strategy of companies producing basic metals —iron, copper, aluminum, or nickel—includes huge investments in ore properties. But all sorts of companies are concerned with the availability of materials. So whenever supplies are scarce, a potential opportunity exists. Even in retailing, Sears, Roebuck and Company discovered in its Latin American expansion that a continuing flow of merchandise of standard quality was difficult to ensure; but once established, such sources became a great advantage.

Physical facilities—office buildings, plants, oil wells—often tie up a large portion of a company's assets. In the short run, at least, these facilities may be an advantage or a disadvantage. The character of many colleges, for instance, has been shaped by their location, whether in a plush suburb or a degenerating urban area; and the cost of moving facilities is so great that adaptation to the existing neighborhood is often an absolute necessity.

Established organizations with people highly trained to perform particular tasks also give a company a distinctive capability. Thus a good research-and-development department may enable a company to expand in pharmaceuticals, whereas a processing firm without such a technical staff is virtually barred from this profitable field.

Perhaps the company we are analyzing will enjoy other distinctive abilities to produce services. Our central concern at this point is to identify strengths and to see how these compare with strengths of other firms.

Other company resources. The propitious niche for an enterprise also depends on its financial strength and the character of its management.

Some strategies will require large quantities of capital. Any oil company that seeks foreign sources of crude oil, for instance, must be prepared to invest millions of dollars. Few firms maintain cash reserves of this size, so *financial capacity* to enter this kind of business depends either on an ability to attract new capital—through borrowing or sale of stock—or on a flow of profits (and depreciation allowances) from existing operations. On the other hand, perhaps a strategy can be devised that calls for relatively small cash advances; in these fields a company that has low financial strength will still be able to compete with the affluent firms.

A more subtle factor in company capacity is its *management*. The age and vitality of key executives, their willingness to risk profit and capital, their urge to gain personal prestige through company growth, their desire to ensure stable employment for present workers—all affect the suitability of any proposed strategy. For example, the expansion of Hilton Hotels into a worldwide chain certainly reflects the personality of Conrad Hilton; with a different management at the helm, a modification in strategy is most appropriate because Conrad Hilton's successors do not have his particular drives and values.

Related to the capabilities of key executives is the company's organization structure. A Stage III divisional structure, for instance, facilitates movement into new fields of business whereas a Stage II functional structure with fine specialization is better suited to expansion in closely related lines (see Chapter 5).

Matching Company Strengths with Key Success Factors

Armed with a careful analysis of the strengths and limitations of our company, we are prepared to pick desirable niches for company concentration. Naturally we will look for fields where company strengths correspond with the key success factors that we have developed in our industry analyses. In the process, we will set aside possibilities in which company limitations create serious handicaps.

Potential growth and profits in each niche must, of course, be added to the analysis. Clearly a low potential will make a niche unattractive even though the company strengths and success factors fit neatly; but we may become keenly interested in a niche where the fit is only fair if the potential is great.

Typically several intriguing possibilities emerge. These are the various niches—in terms of market lines, market segments, or combinations of production functions—that the company might pursue. Also typically, a series of positive actions is necessary in order for the company to move into each area. So we need to list not only each niche and its potential, but also the limitations to overcome and other steps necessary for the company to succeed in each area. These are the propitious niches—nestled in anticipated social and economic conditions and tailored to the strengths and limitations of a particular enterprise.

COMBINING EFFORTS FOR SYNERGISTIC EFFECTS

An enterprise always pursues a variety of efforts to serve even a single niche, and usually it tries to fill several related niches. Considerable choice is possible, at least in the degree to which these many efforts are pushed. In other

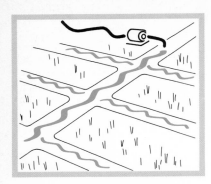  

Figure 16–3   The benefits of synergy. Irrigation or fertilizer used alone will increase crop production somewhat. If the two are used together, though, the increase may be more than the total of the two separate increases.

words, management decides how many markets to cover, to what degree to automate production, what stress to place on consumer engineering, and a host of other actions. One vital aspect of master strategy is fitting these numerous efforts together. In fact, our choice of niches will depend, in part, on how well we can combine the total effort they require.

Synergy is a powerful ally for this purpose. Basically, synergy means that the combined effect of two or more cooperative acts is greater than the sum that would result if the actions were taken independently. A simple example in marketing is that widespread dealer stocks *combined with* advertising in one locality will produce much greater sales volume than widespread dealer stocks in Virginia and advertising in Minnesota. Often the possibility of obtaining synergistic effects will shape the master strategy of the company, as the following examples will suggest.

Fuller Use of Existing Resources

Synergistic effects may be uncovered in any phase of company operations. One possibility is that present activities include a "capability" that can be applied to additional uses. Thus watch companies in the United States undertook the manufacture of tiny gyroscopes and electronic components for spacecraft because they already possessed technical skill in the production of miniature, precision products. They adopted this strategy on the premise that they could make both watches and components for spacecraft with less effort than could separate firms devoted to only one line of products.

The original concept of General Foods Corporation sought a similar synergistic effect in marketing. Here the basic capability was marketing prepared foods. By having the same sales organization handle several product lines, a larger and more effective sales effort could be provided, and/or the selling cost per product line could be reduced. Clearly the combined sales activity was more powerful than separate sales efforts for each product line would have been.

Expansion to Obtain a Resource

359

CHAPTER 16
Master Strategy
and Long-range
Programming

Vertical integration may have synergistic effects. This occurred when the Apollo Printing Machine Company bought a foundry. Apollo was unsatisfied with the quality of its castings, and with tardy delivery and was looking for a new supplier. In its search, it learned that a nearby foundry could be purchased. The foundry was just breaking even, primarily because the volume of its work fluctuated widely. Following the purchase, Apollo gave the foundry a more steady flow of work, and through close technical cooperation the quality of casting received by the new parent firm was improved. The consolidated setup was better for both enterprises.

The results of vertical integration are not always so good, however; problems of balance, flexibility, and managerial capacity must be carefully weighed. Nevertheless, control of a critical resource is often a significant part of company strategy.

Expansion to Enhance Market Position

Efforts to improve market position provide many examples of the whole being better than the sum of its parts. The leading can companies, for example, moved from exclusive concentration on metal containers into glass, plastic, and paper containers. They expected their new divisions to be profitable by themselves, but an additional reason for the expansion lay in anticipated synergistic effects of being able to supply a customer's total container requirements. With the entire packaging field changing so rapidly, a company that can quickly supply more than one type of container to another offers a distinctive service to its customers.

A few years ago, International Harvester added a very large tractor to its line. The prospects for profit on this line alone were far from certain. However, the new tractor was important to give dealers "a full line"; its availability removed the temptation for dealers to carry some products of competing manufacturers. So when viewed in combination with other International Harvester products, the new tractor looked much more significant than as an isolated project.

Compatibility of Efforts

In considering additional niches for a company, we may be confronted with negative synergy; that is, the combined effort is worse than the sum of independent efforts. This occurred when a producer of high-quality television and hi-fi sets introduced a small color television receiver. When first offered, the small unit was as good as most competing sets and probably had an attractive potential market. However, it was definitely inferior in performance to other products of the company and consequently undermined public confidence in the quality of the entire line. Moreover, customers had high expectations for the small set because of the general reputation of the company, and they became very critical when the new product did not live up to their expectations. Both the former products and the new product suffered.

To summarize: We have seen that some combinations of efforts are strongly reinforcing. The combination accelerates the total effect, or reduces the cost for the same effect, or solidifies our supply or market position. On the other hand, we must watch for incompatible efforts that may have a disruptive effect in the same cumulative manner. So when we select niches as a part of our master strategy, one vital aspect is the possibility of such synergistic effects.

CRITERIA OF SUCCESS

Thus far we have discussed strategy in *operational* terms—services to perform, resources to acquire, synergistic benefits to seek. These are the terms that lead directly into managerial action. To say, for example, that a hospital is going to try to cut costs by opening a new wing for ambulatory patients provides positive direction.

Another way to view strategic plans is to look at their potential *results* expressed in terms of selected *criteria*. Here we ask: If we follow a proposed strategy, will the results, as measured by our selected criteria, be satisfactory? The key is to pick the criteria, or values, we are concerned about and then translate the proposed action into its effects on these criteria.

Two reasons for making this translation from operational plans to expected results are: 1) The results of the strategy can be compared with general objectives—if the results are not acceptable, a search for a better proposal will be called for. Also 2) assuming approval, the strategy results become targets for the more detailed planning (see Chapters 17, 18, and 19).[1]

Values Sought

The array of values (criteria) sought by various enterprises is endless. Here are a few: stable employment, filling a specific need of consumers, improving urban slums, assistance to the government of our country, promoting the economic growth of Oshkosh, increasing trade with Central Africa, elimination of the boll weevil, protecting savings of widows and orphans, maximizing short-run profits, improving company position in the industry, having a high percent of graduates in *Who's Who*, optimizing long-run return per share of common stock, perpetuating the enterprise.

---

[1] This approach to targets implies that targets without operational strategy have little value. A statement that the company seeks fifteen percent return on capital is not by itself a strategy. Until it is tied into an operational design, it is little more than hopeful thinking.

Every enterprise, like every individual, pursues several objectives. Theoretically these objectives could all be converted into one common denominator such as profit, but in practice the conversion becomes so abstract it serves no useful purpose. Instead a few objectives are singled out, and the predicted results of a strategy are compared with these values. Thus, the Metropole Power Company is primarily giving attention to the following: long-run survival, profits high enough to attract needed capital, minimum government interference, contribution to the economic growth of its geographic area. Hopefully Metropole's strategy will contribute to all four criteria. An important function of central management is developing a widely understood consensus on the primary criteria for values for that firm. These values should be known while strategy is being formulated. Emphasis will undoubtedly shift when the firm's success or environment changes. But at any point in time the chief value criteria should be recognized.

Strategic targets.   We should aim not merely in the direction of a target but rather at the bull's-eye within the target. It is ambiguous to say, "More major medical insurance." "Twenty percent of our policy holders covered for major-medical expense by 1979" adds both a quantitative and a time dimension. Similarly, "Sixteen percent return on book value of equity capital" sharpens a loose statement about "increasing profits." So when we convert our operational strategy into targets, we should, whenever feasible, express the expected results in *specific degrees of achievement* for each criterion.

With such targets as an added dimension, our master strategy sets forth 1) the services to be provided and to whom, 2) the major ways these services will be created or obtained, *and* 3) the primary results expressed as degrees of achievement for selected criteria. The mission is now defined.

SEQUENCE AND TIMING OF EFFORTS

Many actions will be necessary to achieve the mission, and senior executives must decide what to do first, how many activities can be done concurrently, how fast to move, what risks to take, what to postpone. Here we are dealing with major allocations of company efforts; detailed programs for putting plans into action are discussed later in Chapter 19.

Choice of Sequence

A perennial issue when entering a new niche is what to do first—for instance, whether to develop markets before working on production economies or vice versa.

A striking example of strategy involving sequence confronted Boeing

Aircraft when it first conceived of a large four-engine jet plane suitable for handling cargo or large passenger loads. At the time, Air Force officers saw little need for such a plane, believing that propeller-driven planes provided the most desirable means for carrying cargo. Because this eliminated the military market, most companies would have stopped at this point. However, Boeing executives decided to invest a significant portion of the company's liquid assets to develop the new plane. Over two years later, Boeing was able to present evidence that caused Air Force officials to change their minds—and the K-135 was born. Only Boeing was prepared to produce the new type of craft, which proved to be both faster and more economical than propeller-driven planes. Moreover, the company was able to convert the design into the Boeing 707 passenger plane, which, within a few years, dominated the airline passenger business. Competing firms were left far behind, and Convair almost went bankrupt in its attempt to catch up. In this instance, a decision to let engineering and production run far ahead of marketing paid off handsomely.

Straining Scarce Resources

Every enterprise has limits—perhaps severe limits—on its resources. The amount of capital, the number and quality of key personnel, the physical production capacity, the adaptability of its social structure—none of these are ever boundless. The tricky issue is how to use these limited resources to best advantage.

The scarce resource affecting master strategy may be managerial personnel. A management-consulting firm, for instance, reluctantly postponed entry into the international arena because only two of its partners had the combination of interest, capacity, and vitality to spend a large amount of time abroad, and these people were also needed to ensure continuity of the practice in the United States. The firm felt that a later start would be better than weak action immediately, even though this decision meant losing several desirable clients.

The weight we should attach to scarce resources in the timing of master strategy often requires delicate judgment. Some strain may be endured. But how much, and for how long? For example, in its switch from purchased to company-produced tires, a European rubber company fell behind on deliveries for six months; but through heroic efforts and pleading with customers, the company weathered the squeeze. Now, company executives believe the timing was wise. If the delay had lasted a full year—and this was a real possibility—the consequence would have been a catastrophe.

Forming Coalitions

A cooperative agreement with firms in related fields occasionally provides a way to overcome scarce resources. The early development of frozen foods provides a good example of fruitful coalition. Birdseye had to get freezer cabinets into retail stores, but it lacked the capability to produce them. So it entered into a coalition with a refrigerator manufacturer to make and sell (or lease) the cabinets to retail stores. This mutual agreement enabled Birdseye to move ahead with its marketing program much more quickly. With the tremendous growth of frozen foods, support of the cabinet manufacturer is no longer necessary, but without assistance in the early days, widespread use of frozen foods would have been delayed three to five years. From the coalition the cabinet manufacturer obtained early entry into a growing market.

Coalitions may be formed for reasons other than "buying time." Nevertheless, when we are trying to round out a workable master strategy, coalitions—or even mergers—may provide the quickest way to overcome a serious deficiency in vital resources.

Receptive Environment

Judging the right time to act is difficult. Thus, one of the contributing factors to the multimillion-dollar Edsel fiasco was poor timing. The same automobile launched a year or two earlier might have been favorably received. But buyer tastes changed between the time elaborate market research studies were made and the time the new car finally appeared in dealer showrooms. By then, preference was swinging away from a big car that "had everything" toward compacts. This mistake in timing, and associated errors in strategy, cost the Ford Motor Company over a hundred million dollars.

The preceding discussion of sequence and timing suggests no simple rules for this critical aspect of basic strategy. But the factors we have mentioned 1) for deciding which front(s) to push first (where is a head start valuable, early attention to major uncertainties, lead times, significance of secrecy), and 2) for deciding how fast to move (strain on scarce resources, possible coalition to provide resources, and receptivity of the environment) do bear directly on many strategy decisions.

LONG-RANGE PROGRAMS

Moving from a master strategy to short-run programs is a grand leap. Many companies prefer to go first from strategy to long-range programs and then to short-range programs.[2] Because the tie between long-range programs and strategy is so close, we will take a quick look now at this form of programming.

[2] The expression "long-range planning" is loosely used. It may refer merely to carefully considering long-run results of today's decisions. In other contexts it embraces both strategy and long-range programming. Because strategy and programming are quite distinct forms of planning, we prefer to use separate designations.

Strategy, as we have just seen, provides targets and major moves, along with general guides for sequence and timing. The long-range program is a comprehensive, companywide plan that spells out more fully the steps to be taken to execute that strategy. It serves as a bridge between current operations and those necessary to pursue the new mission.

For most companies, the results expected in five years provide a reasonable span, but some other period, such as three or ten years, may be used if it fits better into a cycle of planning. With the strategy established, the actions necessary to achieve it should be laid out for each department or aspect of the business. These actions include not only programs for sales, production, finance, and similar functions, but also plans to provide the necessary resources, such as offices, machinery, plants, executive personnel, trained operators, organization structure, and capital. Typically the progress to be made in each part of the total program is specified for annual intervals. The essential characteristics of such a master plan are that it is *comprehensive*—that is, it covers all major elements of the business—and that it is *integrated* into a balanced and synchronized program for the entire operation.

Many companies use their existing budget machinery to prepare their "five-year plans." Income, expense, assets, and other accounts are simply projected for the period covered by a plan. This practice provides an easy way to express a future plan because existing records and systems for consolidating figures can be followed. But long-range planning, in terms of budgets, involves some risk. The figures for years ahead may be merely financial guesses rather than actual plans of responsible executives; the entire long-range planning effort may be dominated by financial people instead of being a genuine group effort of all key executives; and planning may be restricted to what shows up directly in accounting records and may omit intangible items like product development, executive personnel, and organization.

To avoid these risks, other companies build their five-year programs around product lines. First, they work out programs that include sales volume in physical units, plant and equipment, key personnel, and specific activities necessary to reach the goal. *Then* they translate these programs into budgetary terms. Cash requirements, of course, must be computed, and the entire program checked for financial soundness. But whatever the sequence of planning, the final result is a set of blueprints that lay out in broad terms the course of action the company hopes to follow over a given period of years.

Such a five-year program can lead to dangers as well as benefits. Inability to forecast feasible action is at the root of the major drawbacks: 1) Commitments may be made too soon for plant, equipment, people, and so on. The existence of a plan naturally encourages an executive to get ready for it, but if a plan has to be modified, an executive may find that he is committed to an expansion that no longer fits into the scheme. 2) Most of us are reluctant to change our plans after we have invested time and energy in their preparation. The more elaborate the plans, the more likely that rigidity will be serious. 3) Planning entails a good deal of effort and expense, which may be wasted if the plan proves inappropriate.

If a five-year plan is to be used, top management must seek ways to reap the benefits and at the same time minimize the dangers. The purpose is to anticipate difficulties and opportunities, to prepare to meet these problems when they arise, and to stimulate the motivation that comes with a feeling of "knowing where you are going and how you are going to get there." Here are three guides for reducing the dangers:

1) Distinguish sharply between plans and commitments. Use the plan as a preview of things to come; but take action only when there is a distinct advantage in doing so today rather than waiting until better information about the future is available.

2) Spell out the long-range program only in such detail as is necessary to test its validity and to provide the basis for sound action today. This practice means that projects with long lead times, such as constructing a dam, will be planned in much greater detail than projects that can be adjusted in a relatively short period, such as an advertising campaign.

3) Provide for at least annual revisions of the long-range program, so that objectives, steps, and schedules are reconsidered in light of new information and forecasts that were unavailable at the time of the last revision. Unless executives are prepared for this continuing reassessment, they will find long-range programming of little value.

These three concepts are illustrated in the planning procedures of electric-utility firms. Long-term projections of the demand for electricity are made for fifteen to twenty years in advance. These projections are later revised and broken down by geographic areas for a ten-year advance period; at that time sites are purchased for generating plants and for transmission lines. Seven years in advance of the anticipated need for service, estimates of capital requirements are prepared and tentative financial plans are laid. Later, a formal construction budget based on engineering studies is prepared. Actual orders for equipment and construction are issued as late as possible but still in time to have service available when needed. At any of these stages, adjustment is likely in anticipated dates, volume, technology, or other aspects of the program.

To jump immediately into a five-year budget without first thinking through the master strategy will almost surely result in a superficial plan. There is no easy formula for long-range programming. Unless executives can forecast the future of their industry with considerable reliability, and unless they have time and objectivity to divorce themselves from day-to-day problems, the benefits they derive will probably not warrant the effort long-range programming requires.

Figure 16-4 Provision of natural resources often calls for long-range programming. One of the longest cycles is reforestation by paper companies.

CONCLUSION:
REAPPRAISAL AND ADAPTATION

Master strategy involves deliberately relating a company's effort to its particular future environment. We recognize, of course, that both the company's capabilities and its environment continually evolve; consequently, strategy should always be based not on existing conditions but on forecasts. Such forecasts, however, are never one-hundred percent correct; instead, strategy often seeks to take advantage of uncertainty about future conditions.

This dynamic aspect of strategy should be underscored. The industry outlook will shift for any of numerous reasons. These forces may accelerate growth in some sectors and spell decline in others, may shift social pressures, may squeeze supply of resources, or may open new possibilities and snuff out others. Meanwhile, the company itself is also changing because of the success or failure of its own efforts and the actions of competitors and cooperating firms. In addition, with all of these internal and external changes, the combination of thrusts that will provide optimum synergistic effects will undoubtedly be altered. Timing of actions is the most volatile element of all. It should be adjusted to both the new external situation and the degrees of internal progress on various fronts.

Consequently, frequent reappraisal of master strategy is essential. We must build into our planning mechanisms sources of fresh data that will tell us how well we are doing and what new opportunities and obstacles are appearing on the horizon. The feedback features of control—examined in Part Five—will provide some of this data. In addition, senior managers and others who have contact with various parts of the environment must be ever sensitive to new developments that established screening devices might not detect.

We hope such reappraisal will not call for sharp reversals in strategy. Typically a master strategy requires several years to execute, and some features may endure much longer. The kind of plan we are discussing here sets the direction. In the following chapters we delve into the planning of these more immediate and specific activities.

FOR CLASS DISCUSSION

1) It is usually assumed that a company's structure follows from its strategy. List and discuss the kinds of strategies that might lead to a "matrix form" of structure (Chapter 6).

2) Use the general outline of this chapter to analyze and explain the strategy of the United States in its dealings with South Africa (or some other foreign nation with whom our foreign relations are strained). In what respects does the concept of national strategy differ from a company's master strategy?

3) Much has been made of the statement that the present problems faced by many railroads stem from the tendency of their leaders, years ago, to see

themselves as being in the *railroad* business rather than in the *transportation* business. How does this accusation fit with this chapter's advice on selecting a propitious niche?

4) The president of a large and successful cosmetics firm attributes his success to waiting for his competitors to do his innovating, forecasting, and testing for him. "We let them dream up the new products and promotions and we watch the results. If they go over, we copy all of the best features and add a few of our own. Sometimes we get a little less for being second; but considering the number of flops they have that we don't copy and the cost they incur by 'pioneering,' we come off far better than they." What do you think of this approach to developing, forecasting, and testing innovations? Under what conditions will it be most, and least, successful?

5) "The greatest danger in developing a master strategy is to fail to appraise your key competitors' strengths and weaknesses accurately. Companies constantly over- or underestimate their competitors." Comment on this observation made by a successful management consultant.

6) What role(s) might an outside consultant play in developing a strategic plan? Consider specific tasks they might best carry out or assist in and tasks for which they would be of least help.

7) "Our line managers are too involved in running our current business to do any really imaginative strategic planning. As a result, I have been considering the creation of a strategic planning department and having two or three really bright people put it together for us on an ongoing basis." What do you think of this idea? What duties should be given such a department? What criteria would you use to select the head of this department? To whom should he report?

8) In forming a master strategy, it may be just as vital to consider "forming internal coalitions" as the kind of external coalitions discussed in the chapter. Relate this concept to the Graham Allison material in the previous chapter.

Cases

For cases involving issues covered in this chapter, see especially the following. Particularly relevant questions are listed after each case.

FOR FURTHER READING

Ansoff, H. I., "The Concept of Strategic Management." *Journal of Business Policy,* Summer 1972.

Argues for a distinction between operations management and strategic management, and the need for both.

Ewing, D. W., ed., *Long-Range Planning for Management, 3rd ed.* New York: Harper & Row, 1972.

Collection of practical articles on the process of long-range planning.

Hofer, C. W., "Toward a Contingency Theory of Business Strategy." *Academy of Management Journal,* December 1975.

Brings together a variety of studies and propositions dealing with variables that affect company strategy.

Katz, R. L., *Cases and Concepts in Corporate Strategy.* Englewood Cliffs, N.J.: Prentice-Hall, Inc., 1970, Chapters 4–7.

Chapter introductions lay out the cycle of strategic analysis, planning, and action in clear, operational terms.

Miller, E. C., *Advanced Techniques for Strategic Planning.* New York: American Management Associations, 1971.

Examines successful applications of "management-science" techniques in strategic planning. Essential reading for the operations-researcher who wants to tackle strategy problems.

Newman, W. H. and J. P. Logan, *Strategy, Policy, and Central Management,* 7th ed. Cincinnati: South-Western Publishing Co., 1976.

Strategy selection (Part 1); policies needed to support strategy (Part 2); organizing and executive strategy (Parts 3 and 4).

Schoeffler, S., R. D. Buzzell, and D. F. Heany, "The Impact of Strategic Planning on Profit Performance." *Harvard Business Review,* March 1974.

Report on key factors affecting company profitability, based on the most comprehensive analysis of company experience yet made.

Warren, E. K., *Long-Range Planning: The Executive Viewpoint.* Englewood Cliffs, N.J.: Prentice-Hall, Inc., 1966.

Response of managers to different forms of long-range planning.

Operating
Objectives
17

FROM STRATEGY TO ACTION

Bridges must be built between broad company strategy (discussed in the previous chapter) and specific objectives that must be carried out next week. Once strategy has been set and long-range programs developed, operating objectives come into play. Strategy gets translated into effective action only when each member of the organization understands what he is supposed to do about a given situation.

Three kinds of issues arise in setting operating objectives so that a master strategy will become a driving force. First is the translation—the spelling out—of broad goals into smaller and more specific assignments for each part of the organization. Next we make these specific objectives a vital focus in the local managing process; and for this "Management-by-Objectives" (MBO) is a proven instrument. Finally, problems of melding and adjusting operating objectives must be resolved. These are the issues examined in this chapter.

Scope of Operating Objectives

For managerial purposes, it is useful to think of objectives as the results we want to achieve. The words "goal," "aim," and "purpose" also have much the same meaning, because they, too, imply effort directed toward a preselected result.

In this book, we use the word "objectives" broadly. It covers long-range company aims, more specific department goals, and even individual assignments. Thus objectives may pertain to a wide or narrow part of an enterprise, and they may be either long- or short-range. A salesperson may have an immediate objective of clearing up a misunderstanding with a customer, and he may have a five-year objective of cultivating his territory to provide $25,000 in sales each month. Similarly, a company may have a short-term objective of providing stable employment during the next summer and a long-range objective of being a product leader in its industry. These are all results to be achieved.

Often objectives of a particular nature are given a special name. For instance, we may speak of equal-opportunity quotas, expense ratios, budgets, absentee rates, or market positions. The use of such descriptive terms does not remove them from the broad category of objectives.

Military and church officials frequently prefer to use the word "mission" instead of objective. A military commander, for instance, may be assigned a mission of protecting a city or a coastline; the mission of a church-worker may be to reduce juvenile delinquency in the neighborhood. A mission is an objective that has been psychologically accepted by the doer; he is dedicated to its fulfillment. When we speak of a mission, then, we imply moral compulsion to achieve the result. Ideally, in business, all well-thought-out objectives should be accepted as missions, and many are. How to secure such dedication is a recurring issue in this book, and we discuss it explicitly under Management-by-Objectives and in Part Six.

Hierarchy of Objectives

The process of assigning part of a major mission to a particular department and then further subdividing the assignment among sections and individuals creates a hierarchy of objectives. The goals of each subunit contribute to the aims of the larger unit of which it is a part. We have already used this hierarchy concept, in Chapter 11, to place a problem in a ladder of objectives, but there we did not tie the goal hierarchy to organization units.

The concept of hierarchy was useful to a diversified equipment company. One of the objectives of this firm was to become a leader in the motor-scooter business. Toward this end the engineering department was charged with an intermediate goal of designing rugged, easy-to-use, economical, and efficient scooters. Because the test of a scooter's design was whether it continued to work in the hands of users, the engineering department established a small dealer-service section. The objective of this unit, derived from the broader goal of the engineering department, was to keep scooters operating up to the level of their design potential. (The unit also fed back information that was useful in improving designs.) One engineer in the dealer-service section was given the still narrower task of writing clear, useful instructions, both for repairmen in dealers' shops and for owners of scooters. Specifying the audience in this objective was important because it told the engineer to avoid technical jargon, to remember that the reader of his instructions did not have elaborate testing equipment, and to anticipate difficulties caused by customer abuse and foolishness. As in the means–end chains we examined in Part Three, each of the subgoals in this example derived its worthiness and its character from its contribution to a broader goal.

Meaningful Objectives for Each Job

In the preceding illustration, the aim of being a leader in the industry was too vague to provide a guide to action for most members of the company. What bearing specific decisions have on the objective is often indirect, and particular activities tend to lose their significance when they are merged into a large, total result. Seeing the broad picture, desirable as it is, does not replace the need for more specific goals for each job. In fact, it is entirely possible for an effective worker to be dedicated to doing his job well and at the same time be indifferent to the broad company objectives.

One task of every manager, then, is to help clarify intermediate objectives for each of his subordinates. A subgoal may be a dominant market position in a particular city, leadership in salary administration, keeping abreast of new techniques in the industry, or well-kept grounds around the plant. This is the kind of goal a subordinate executive or operator can "go to work on."

Setting such subgoals combines two processes we have already explored —decision-making and organizing. The subgoal should not only contribute to a broader objective; it should be the best of the known ways to do so. This is a rational decision-making problem we analyzed in Part Three. In addition, carrying out the selected route must be tied to a job (person), and this involves organizing, which we analyzed in Parts One and Two. Unfortunately, the two processes don't always match. Do we select methods that fit a division of labor already set by the organization, or do we reassign duties to fit an attractive way of achieving a result?

Care and ingenuity are needed in refining these subobjectives. A total system is involved. All of the contributions to a broad objective—not just one or two—must be assigned to somebody. Often these contributions interact, so that if we change Irene's subgoal it may upset Bob's. Moreover, such jobs always have several subgoals—various aspects of one end result (quantity, quality, cost, etc.) and often several end results (financial reports, management information, protection from fraud for a controller). Tinkering with one of these subgoals may complicate another. Actually, this multidimensional interrelatedness creates so much inertia that we have difficulty adjusting operating objectives to support shifts in strategy.

Clarifying objectives and subobjectives is a continuing task. We often like to think that objectives are fixed, but this is only partially true. We shift company strategy to seize a new opportunity; and because the specific objective assigned to individuals are derived from the broad company goals, a change in strategy is likely to require adjustments in the "missions" of several supervisors and operators. In fact, little effective change will occur until assignments down the line are revised. Clearly, defining objectives is neither static nor automatic.

MANAGEMENT-BY-OBJECTIVES

Once operating objectives are specified, how do we induce executives and workers to accomplish them? This is largely a matter of activating—the subject of Part Six. However, one approach—Management-by-Objectives—is so widespread and so intimately related to the setting of objectives that it should be briefly explained here.

Elements of MBO

MBO represents a whole cluster of management techniques. It combines selected, but by no means all, aspects of organizing, planning, controlling, and activating. Having become a fashionable term, MBO is given personal meanings by different writers.[1] Nevertheless, virtually all definitions stress the following elements:

1) *Agreement.* At regular intervals a manager and his subordinate agree on the *results* (objectives) that the subordinate will try to achieve during the next period (quarter, half-year, or year). The subordinate *participates* actively in spelling out the meaning and feasibility of the assignment he accepts. The broad purpose and the organizational constraints, however, are dictated by the strategy of the enterprise and the mission of the supervisor (as we have explained in the preceding pages). We hope that both the subordinate and his supervisor will understand and feel committed to this statement of what will constitute good performance.

2) *Delegation.* The supervisor then makes a high degree of delegation to the subordinate. During this period the main role of the supervisor is to *assist* his subordinate(s) in fulfilling the agreement(s). As part of the agreement, he may be committed to provide certain help, and the subordinate may call for more. But the subordinate is expected to take whatever initiative is necessary to achieve the agreed-upon results.

3) *Evaluation of results.* At the end of the period actual results are measured, and the supervisor and subordinate discuss reasons for success and failure. This evaluation becomes the basis for making another agreement (perhaps at a later meeting) for the next period. And so the cycle continues.

4) *Associated activities.* The evaluation of results often serves as the basis of setting salaries and bonuses and for planning personal development. Also,

---

[1] E. H. Schleh prefers the term "Management-by-Results" because the word "results" emphasizes what actually takes place instead of stopping with intentions. All writers, however, urge that the approach be carried through to measurement and evaluation of results.

the negotiation of agreements may lead to modifications in organization, procedures, policies, and controls. But these associated activities are not essential parts of MBO.

Main Benefits of MBO

The potential benefits from MBO are impressive. Foremost is the greater *personal motivation* of the people who commit themselves to achieve a set of results. Through participation in setting meaningful and realistic targets, and the accompanying delegation of initiative, many individuals "internalize" their role in meeting company objectives.

A sense of accomplishment—of meeting objectives—is desired by people at all levels. The captain of a ship takes pride in keeping his vessel on schedule; a telephone lineman wants to "keep the circuits open"; a chief engineer works overtime to make sure that a newly designed product will not break down under operating conditions. Without a recognized objective, none of these people would put forth such effort.

Each person has a variety of needs that he strives to fulfill, as we explained in Chapter 7. To the extent that an individual accepts business objectives as desirable, fulfilling them becomes one of his needs. Especially today, as a worker's physical and security needs are more fully satisfied and as the desire for self-expression becomes relatively more pressing, the achievement of explicit work goals becomes relevant.

Figure 17–1   Steps in Management-by-Objectives (MBO).

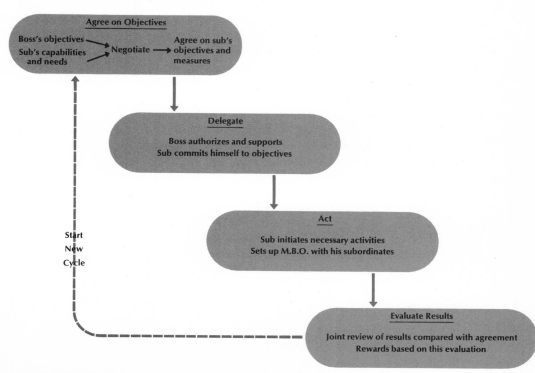

A second benefit of MBO is a *clarification* of the results that will best serve the enterprise. Especially in large organizations, the mission of a particular section often becomes distorted. And as strategy changes over time, the desired results may be blurred even more.

A situation that illustrates unclear objectives arose in the training section of an urban-renewal center. The training director was pushing hard to increase the number of people trained and placed in regular jobs. Consequently he encouraged registration and gave first attention to highly competent people who could be placed quickly. Welfare workers in the area, however, reported that as far as they could detect, the training center was not relieving economic distress. The people who needed jobs most were not being trained; welfare workers encouraged their clients to sign up for training, but few stayed more than a couple of days, and most said there was "no use going there." Only after the objective of the training center was redefined and understood did the coordination between the center and the welfare workers improve.

Focus of thought and effort *on results* is a third benefit. All too often we treat mere activity as a goal. Under MBO the activity "call on new customers" is unsatisfactory; instead, a result is stated, such as "firm orders from eight new customers each month." Similarly, "monitor smoke-stack emissions" is unsatisfactory; instead we say "hourly stack emissions always within federal standards, and temporary excess never more than five minutes in any hour." The supporting activity may well be necessary, but management's attention is on results.

Personnel evaluation reflects this same emphasis on results. Instead of relying on personality traits, under MBO we assess people in terms of the results they produce. And fresh data is available at the close of each period. Perhaps some personality analysis will help us explain good or bad performance, but we start from the more objective and clearly pertinent comparison of actual results with planned results.

Better response to controls is a fourth benefit of MBO. Both the control standards—the objectives for the period—and the way performance will be measured are part of the agreement between the manager and his subordinate. So the subordinate usually regards the controls as being fair—they are not unexpected or arbitrary. Moreover, with the subordinate himself desiring the objectives, control feedback is helping him achieve his personal goals as well as company goals. As we shall see in Chapter 23—"Behavior Responses to Controls"—such understanding and acceptance alter one's feeling about controls; they become like the gas gauge on your car—aids in reaching a destination instead of instruments of repression.

Finally, MBO has a synergistic effect. The delegation is feasible because of the agreement on objectives; the participation in setting the objectives adds to motivation, as does delegation; and the evaluation based on these same objectives reinforces their significance. Furthermore, in the broader scope, the forward planning for the specific job is consistent with the job duties laid out by organization design; and this job mission has significance and value because its contribution to broader company objectives can be easily traced.

The objectivity and impersonality arising from the stress on agreed-upon results reduces feelings of personal dominance and increases the sense of joint endeavor. Each of these features builds upon and reinforces the others; and because they are combined together under the banner of MBO, the psychological effect is synergistic.[2]

Establishing MBO

Because MBO embraces a cluster of management techniques, it requires hard work to establish. Organizing is involved. Job duties and delegation must be carefully developed, keeping in mind the factors we discussed in Parts One and Two. Communication and leadership style are also essential aspects; the options and issues in this area are examined in Part Six. Controlling, the third phase of the MBO cycle, has its own set of problems, as we shall see in Part Five. And objectives, the take-off pad for MBO, should reflect a rational selection process outlined in Part Two. Of course, in a successful *going* enterprise, most of the necessary managerial system will already be operating. So installing MBO calls only for adjustments and refinements. Nevertheless, any needed changes should be made only after a review of the total situation as proposed in these other Parts. MBO provides no easy shortcut around these problems.

Defining the operating objectives for each job included in the MBO system is by no means simple. In addition to specific substantive questions, several general issues—discussed below—reappear.

HOPES VERSUS EXPECTATIONS

An objective may be optimistic, in that the results we hope for will occur if everything works just right—like par on the golf course. Or it may be realistic, a statement of what we actually expect can be accomplished—like par plus our handicap. Both types of goals have their uses, but it is important to distinguish between them.

---

[2] Management-by-Objectives has no monopoly on such synergy. All good management design is inherently made up of highly interdependent parts; it is a system. Theoretically, we can start with *any* one part and then relate the other parts to it in a consistent manner. When the interacting parts of the system are well integrated, synergy results. Historically in the U.S. we have had waves of enthusiasm for scientific management, budgetary control, organization planning, executive leadership, management-information systems, organization development—each of which can be broadly conceived to embrace virtually the entire management process. For a particular company at a given point in its development, one approach often has a tactical advantage. In skillful hands it can open the way for many related improvements, just as Management-by-Objectives starts with defining objectives for a job and expands into an activating system.

Advocates of optimistic objectives believe that a person will accomplish more if he sets his sights high. If we have the courage to dream great dreams, then we can bend our efforts to make them come true.

Everyone knows of examples of such determination succeeding. The largest transatlantic air-cargo line would never have been more than a small charter carrier without the high objectives of its president. The company spent years obtaining government permission to operate scheduled flights. In the midst of these negotiations, a decision to place a multimillion-dollar order for new jets was made. In this instance acting on hope, rather than on "sound" expectation, led to significantly better results.

In all such cases, the aimed-at results are at least possible, with supreme effort, good luck, and favorable operating conditions. Occasionally, even objectives known to be unattainable are used—this, for example: "Give every employee the maximum opportunity to use his highest potential ability." This is an ideal to strive for. It provides direction, as stars do for sailors, but it is never reached.

In contrast, we may choose to state objectives in realistic terms—seeking levels that can be achieved without superhuman effort and uncanny luck. Thus reasonable sales quotas can be filled by most sales representatives; with normal diligence, expense ratios can be met by good managers; personnel programs come up with able workers, if not geniuses; profit targets bear some resemblance to last year's results. These are goals that management expects to be met. In some areas, performance may surpass the objectives, and this good fortune may help offset lagging performance at other spots.

In business planning, emphasis is generally on tough, but achievable, objectives. There are two reasons for this preference: 1) Frustration or indifference is apt to develop if stated goals are rarely, if ever, achieved. 2) Objectives are used for planning and coordination as well as for motivation; so related activities may go awry if management tries to synchronize them with an objective that proves to be more hope than reasonable prediction.

SHORT-RUN OBJECTIVES AS STEPS TOWARD LONG-RUN GOALS

A major task becomes more manageable when it is divided into small pieces. This analytical concept is, of course, employed in setting up hierarchies of objectives and in organizing work by departments. Another manner of breakdown is by steps, or results, to be achieved within a given period of time. This method is commonly used in personal career decisions. For instance, suppose Joan Casey wants to become an executive in a local publishing firm (long-run objective). She may decide that a business education (intermediate objective) will help her achieve this goal. So she takes a course in management as one of several steps toward a formal business education.

A step-by-step breakdown is particularly valuable in complicated business projects. The use of satellites in telephonic and TV communication, for example, is a vast and complex undertaking. Receiving and broadcasting stations have to be located on the basis of technical, economic, and political considerations; equipment has to be designed and built, personnel trained, satellites launched, users of the service educated, rates set, and a staggering amount of capital acquired. A job of this sort becomes manageable only when it is broken down into a series of steps. In fact, each major step will be divided and subdivided.

Even relatively simple assignments, such as giving polio shots to all children in a city, may well be divided up into small work units.

The creation of such short-run objectives has several advantages:

1) *It helps make the objective tangible and meaningful.* We all find it easy to project ourselves into the immediate future, whereas the more distant future is filled with uncertainties; besides, we have no compelling reasons to face remote problems now.

2) *Short-run objectives provide a means of bridging the gap between hopes and expectations.* It is entirely possible to have optimistic long-run goals and at the same time be quite realistic about the immediate steps to be taken toward these ends. Working on a tangible, immediate project tends to relieve the frustration that can arise from the magnitude and difficulty of a major objective. This tendency is an asset, provided a manager himself does not become so engrossed with a short-run objective that he loses sight of the existence and nature of the long-run objective.

3) *An outstanding advantage of setting up short-run objectives is that they provide benchmarks for measuring progress.* This advantage is a great aid in motivation and control. When a person sees that he is making progress, he gets a sense of accomplishment even though a job is not yet finished, and he also builds his confidence to tackle the work still ahead.

MULTIPLE OBJECTIVES

Never does a job, department, or company have a single objective. It may have a dominant mission, but other goals will also demand recognition.

The manager of an airport, for instance, may be charged with making it

Figure 17–2 In dealing with so vast an undertaking as an urban-renewal project, it is necessary to break down the project into a series of subobjectives—financing, excavation, construction, and selection of tenants. This practice can be useful on a smaller scale as well.

easy to move planes, people, and freight in and out of his facility. But, among other things, he will also be expected to keep operating costs low, use only as much capital for equipment and inventory as is necessary, maintain an efficient work force, and develop employees for promotion to key jobs. Just as each of us aspires to a variety of goals—for example, good health, challenging work, enjoyable leisure, happy family life, service to our fellow beings—so too is a manager confronted with diverse, and perhaps competing, goals.

Multiple Objectives of a Company

The common belief that "the purpose of a business firm is to make a profit" is part of American folklore. It probably started as an *assumption* made to simplify economic theory. Being a half-truth, it proved to be an easy way for even business executives to talk about a complex problem. Then when public accounting made the profit-and-loss statement one of the few universal measures of business performance, the notion became ingrained.

But the suggestion that profits are the sole objective of a company is *misleading*. Obviously a company must earn a profit if it is to continue in existence; earnings are necessary to attract additional capital and to provide a cushion for meeting the risks inherent in business activity. But for survival it is also essential that a company produce goods or services customers want, that its conditions of employment continue to attract competent employees, that it be a desirable customer to the people who supply raw materials, and that it be an acceptable corporate citizen in the community in which its operates. Remove any one of these essentials, and the enterprise might collapse. To argue that profit is the supreme objective is like saying that blood circulation is more important to survival than breathing, digestion, or proper functioning of the nervous system.[3]

In discussing strategy in the preceding chapter, we pointed to the need for multiple criteria, in practice if not in abstract theory, for overall company targets. Now, when we are seeking ways to state objectives that have operational relevance, the principle of multiple objectives takes on added significance. For the manager, no enterprise—public or private—has a single objective.

To assist the managers of the enterprise in setting objectives, the General Electric Company has singled out eight "key-result areas":

1) Profitability—in both percentage of sales and return on investment.
2) Market position.

---

[3] Suitable measurement of profit poses an additional drawback. Profit figures reported by existing accounting systems are based on past costs. A new system that attempts to be a common denominator for setting and measuring all company objectives would have to deal with the present worth of future values. This would call for estimates of future conditions and of the influence of intangibles such as morale and customer goodwill; comparability from year to year and between companies would be desirable. The theoretical and practical difficulties in designing such a system are overwhelming.

3) Productivity—improving costs as well as sales.
4) Leadership in technological research.
5) Development of future employees, both technical or functional and managerial.
6) Employee attitudes and relations.
7) Public attitudes.
8) Balance of long-range and short-range objectives.

Several other companies use variations of this format. Note that the list identifies only areas; each firm must fill in specific subjects and levels of achievement that fit its circumstances at a particular time.

Service enterprises likewise should determine their key-result areas. Here is such a list for a public library: circulation (loans and in-library), reference questions answered, cooperation with schools and other libraries, percentage of population using the library, contribution to community cohesiveness, collection of books and reference materials, personnel development, operation within financial budget. As soon as we start dealing with objectives that can readily be translated into action, we are faced with multiple goals.

Each of the objectives of the enterprise will, of course, call forth an array of more specific operating goals, and this fanning out continues through to the detailed objectives for each person in the organization.

Number of Objectives for Each Person

Having too many objectives can be troublesome, especially for one person. When a company's multiple objectives are subdivided and elaborated into an array of specific, short-term objectives, we also split up the work among various people. Nevertheless, one manager may be confronted with thirty or forty identified results he is expected to achieve—quality output, meeting deadlines, overtime pay, self-development, training of others, aid to other departments, plans for next year, budgeted expense, customer service, and many others.

Such a large array of objectives tends to disperse attention and fails to provide clear direction of effort. Consequently, the number of objectives any one individual is expected to focus on should be limited. Some executives feel the number should be narrowed to the range of two to five, thereby ensuring concentrated attention; others contend that a person can keep a dozen objectives in mind. In either case, agreement exists that motivation is improved by reducing the number.

Two methods are used to narrow the number of objectives for an individual. First, a distinction is drawn between what Herbert Simon calls satisficing and optimizing. For a variety of results we simply try to achieve a satisfactory standard. Only when results—say, quality, honesty, or maintenance—fail to meet the standard do we give the matter attention. In a sense, these are passive objectives, at least for the time being. Other objectives call for improvement. These are the stimulants to action, and they are fewer in number.

Consolidating several objectives that are means to some higher goal is a

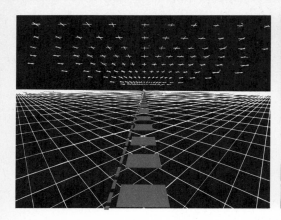

Figure 17–3 Too many objectives for one person can be hazardous. In a conventional aircraft, the pilot must contend with a bewildering variety of informational devices. New instruments, such as the contact analog (color, left), condense information about the plane's movement and position and present it to the pilot in forms that can easily be grasped. Deviations from the intended course are thus instantly revealed. Matters related to course—speed, position, and so on—can be ignored until deviation is indicated. The analog demonstrates two ways of reducing the problem of multiple objectives: 1) integrating a variety of elements under a few headings and 2) adopting the "exception principle" of ignoring any given factor as long as it is in a satisfactory range.

second way of limiting the number of key objectives for a job. For example, we might say that the head of the Atlanta office of an accounting firm should obtain ten new accounts next year; embraced in this objective are subgoals regarding speeches, public-service activities, contacts with bankers and other influential people, and visits with potential clients. To be sure, most of the subgoals have to be met if the accountant is to get his ten new clients. Yet focusing on one net result is easier to deal with, and it encourages delegation of the problem of how to achieve results.

ADJUSTING SHORT-RUN EMPHASIS

Problems of Balance

Even half a dozen objectives create difficulties, for emphasis on any one goal tends to reduce attention given to others. The welfare worker urged to process more cases gives less consideration to individualized problems.

All of us, in planning our own work or in correcting that of others, like to assume that we can give more effort to some goal that is pressing at the moment *without* slackening off on other work. Sometimes we can. Sooner or later, however, a point is reached where attention and effort are simply diverted from one activity to another. More time on football or campus politics means less with the books, and vice versa.

Keeping the emphasis on diverse objectives in balance is hard. A common difficulty is that the tangible, measurable ends receive undue attention. It would be easy for a professor to stress the appearance of a report rather than the learning that went into its preparation, simply because the paper itself is so much easier to see. Similarly, in business those results that show up directly in accounting reports often command priority; thus, avoiding overtime expense may be preferred to maintaining quality in advertising copy.

Furthermore, immediate problems tend to take precedence over long-run issues. The dilemma of choosing recurs time and again in engineering departments. Customers' orders for immediate delivery have a "here-and-now" quality about them. If he is not careful, an engineer will find himself simply going from one order to the next, always leaving for tomorrow the design of a new product.

The case of one's own work versus teamwork may also pose a balancing problem. We all know friendly individuals who are so ready to help with another person's problems that they have difficulty getting their own work done on time. But a self-centered view may also cause trouble. Some results for the company can be created only by teamwork; the task cannot be divided into parts and accountability assigned to separate jobs. Task teams, described in Chapter 7, and the combined work of line and staff are of this nature. So we say that several people are jointly accountable; we measure the result of their combined effort and give each of them credit for the success or failure. But then the problem is this: Smith is a member of a team, and he also has several individual objectives. Does he give priority to those results for which he alone is accountable, and let teamwork slide; or does he stress the team project even though other results that are more clearly his may suffer?

According to rational decision theory, we should pursue each of our diverse objectives to the point where added increments of achievement have equal value. Actually—behavioral research suggests—most of us give attention first to one objective and then turn to another, the sequence and direction of effort being determined largely by momentary social pressures.

The desirable balance among objectives shifts over time. With success or failure and with external changes, the incremental values also change. So the wise manager must reappraise his preferences. This job is like that of a captain of a large ship who is continually changing his speed and direction in relation to his present position, tides, winds, and other conditions.

A regional sales manager of a well-known computer company uses MBO for such a reappraisal on a systematic basis. Every month, he sits down with each of his branch managers to review past performance; together they agree on three, four, or at most five goals that will be emphasized during the following month. This list may include any of several desirable aims: calling on new customers, pushing the sale of a particular product, recruiting additional salesmen, clearing up customer complaints, or reducing expenses. Sometimes the same item appears on the list for several months. It is generally understood that the branch managers will not completely neglect items missing from the list, but special emphasis will be given to only a few goals. This manager contends that he gets better results by *highlighting* a few items than by talking about many. He is able to maintain an overall balance by the frequent reviews and by shifting from one objective to another as necessary.

The details of this technique are not important here. But we should note several of its desirable features: 1) Any misunderstanding about the quality, timing, or costs of a specific objective can be cleared up at the monthly discussions. 2) Plans are adjusted in light of progress already being made. This practice permits comparison of incremental values. 3) New information and new pressure from headquarters can be promptly incorporated into the action taken at each branch—thus giving recognition to the problems and needs of the many branches, instead of blithely following blanket orders from headquarters. 4) Broad objectives are translated into meaningful and immediately applicable terms for each branch manager.

CONCLUSION

Master strategy deals with the company as a whole. It stakes out the role in society that the enterprise wishes to play. But this strategy can be achieved only if it has an impact on the behavior of people working in the company. Consequently we have to give close attention to fashioning objectives and sub-objectives that are understandable and significant to the executives and other workers affected by them.

These operating objectives are tied to jobs and thus to individual managers and operators who hold these jobs. In terms of "decision-making within organizations," this goal structure is the starting point for diagnosis. Each responsible person predicts potential gaps between his objectives and actual results, and these gaps become the focus of his search, decision, and action.

Since in the hurly-burly of organization life each of us is bombarded by all sorts of information and influences, operating objectives serve the important role of leading us to purposeful, consistent action. MBO especially builds this focus. It also encourages commitment and enthusiasm for accomplishing the objectives.

In practice, the definition of clearcut objectives for each job is far from simple. To make operating objectives a vital, energizing managerial tool, we deal with the following: distinguishing between hopes and expectations, setting short-run objectives as steps toward long-run goals, recognizing the presence of multiple objectives, and adjusting the short-run emphasis on various objectives. When we have clarified objectives in this manner, they provide the guiding, unifying core of company planning.

FOR CLASS DISCUSSION

1) The more precise the standards and the more detailed the directions for achieving them, the better the coordination of tasks and the greater the ability to take corrective action. Do you agree? What effect would such standards have on employee morale and creativity?

2) "I am frequently asked what my strategic objectives are. I have two: profit and growth. I want to get as much of both as I can. Though I have to send numbers in to headquarters, they don't mean much. I just go after all I can get." What do you think of this statement by the successful general manager of a division of a large chemical company?

3) A standard such as a sales or production quota is of little value unless the assumptions and methods of reaching the quota are spelled out and understood both by the man who is to achieve it and by the man who is to evaluate his performance. Comment. Do you agree? Explain.

4) In what ways may the demand for clarity and, wherever possible, quantification of objectives lead to difficulties when seeking to balance long- and short-run objectives?

5) "My key subordinates and I spend one day each month reviewing and updating our objectives. We try to quantify the results of our discussions in order more easily to communicate them to others in the organization. But I doubt that these quantified objectives are as meaningful to the others as the discussions that produce them are to us." How do you interpret this statement by the director of a volunteer family-service agency? Would a vice president of a bank be as likely to say the same thing?

6) The importance of periodically adjusting objectives is stressed in this chapter. List ways in which a superior may judge whether a subordinate's requests for frequent changes in longer-term obejctives are the result of good or poor planning by the subordinate.

7) Where superior and subordinate seek to set goals jointly for the subordinate, would it make any difference which is the first to present his expectations?

8) The text suggests that objectives are the tangible outgrowth of strategic planning. What about the notion that setting objectives should come first and *then* strategies should be developed to determine how to get them?

Cases

For cases involving issues covered in this chapter, see especially the following. Particularly relevant questions are listed after each case.

Milano Enterprises (p. 124), 11
Merchantville School System (p. 217), 13
Graham, Smith, & Bendel, Inc. (p. 445), 11
Monroe Wire and Cable (p. 436), 10, 13
Central Telephone and Electronics (p. 527), 8

FOR FURTHER READING

Bennett, P. W., "Participation in Planning." *Journal of General Management,* Autumn 1974.

Describes a participative-planning system used in a large British retail–wholesale company, W. H. Smith & Son.

Brown, J. K. and R. O'Connor, *Planning and the Corporate Planning Director.* New York: The Conference Board, 1974.

Examines the way companies use corporate planners in formulating strategy and extending formal planning into operating units.

Carroll, S. J. and H. L. Tosi, *Management by Objectives.* New York: The Macmillan Company, 1973.

Practical guide to the use of M.B.O., with an analysis of problems arising in the integration of M.B.O. with budgeting and management development.

Simon, H. A., *Administrative Behavior,* 3rd ed. New York: The Free Press, 1976, Chapter 12.

Theoretical discussion of multiple organizational goals and the way these are resolved into useful operational goals for personnel action. See also Chapter 10.

Stonich, P. J., "Formal Planning Pitfalls and How to Avoid Them." *Management Review,* June and July, 1975.

A management consultant stresses the need to move from data-gathering and broad generalizations to specific plans for operating units.

Planning for
Stabilized Action

18

CONSISTENT AND ENDURING
BEHAVIOR PATTERNS

Objectives, however soundly conceived and clearly communicated, provide only part of the guidance essential to united effort. Even the most highly motivated people need some plan of action, as has become painfully clear in several urban-renewal projects where the absence of customary patterns for joint effort has thwarted lofty aims.

Basically, management uses two kinds of plans to direct activities toward established goals: *single-use* plans and *standing* plans. Single-use plans include programs, schedules, and special methods designed for a unique set of circumstances. We shall examine these plans in the next chapter. In this chapter, we shall consider standing plans, a group that includes policies, standard methods, and standing operating procedures, all of which are designed to deal with recurring problems. Each time a particular, but familiar, problem arises, a standing plan provides a ready guide to action.

Need for Standing Plans

A wildlife magazine ran into serious difficulties with three firms that bought considerable advertising space in the publication. These firms objected to articles on conservation appearing in the magazine. The editor contended that he was serving readers by reporting to them on critical conservation issues. The advertising manager argued that there were two sides to every question and that the magazine did not have to join in the popular clamor for more regulations. The problem arose because the magazine lacked a clear, well-known editorial policy.

In this instance the editor won. The policy became "Challenging, informative articles that would excite the interest of readers." With this new policy firmly established, the advertising manager had to shift his approach to advertisers; he now says, "You may not like it but our editorial policy builds an audience you would like to reach." The new policy has removed internal conflict; it enables all magazine personnel to work in a consistent direction.

Moreover, procedures have to be adjusted to support policies. This became dramatically evident when the City University of New York adopted an "open-admission" policy. The number of entering freshmen jumped fifty percent, and their academic preparation varied drastically. This change had been anticipated—it was the aim of the new admission policy. But the procedures for registering this heterogeneous group and assigning members to appropriate classes were grossly inadequate. For weeks, students shifted from class to class, and no one was sure who should report where.

For any group of people to live or work together, they must be able to anticipate one another's actions. There must be some consistency or pattern of behavior. The more interdependent the activities, the more important the ability to anticipate. Without this ability, an individual cannot know what he should do; he is doubtful about what he can depend on from others; and he is unsure whether his own efforts will be helpful or harmful. This is true for a symphony orchestra, football team, diplomatic corps, ship's crew, bank, coffee plantation, and for any other similar situations.

Standing plans are one of the important means for building predictable patterns of behavior in a business firm. If these patterns clearly contribute to the achievement of objectives, they tend to breed confidence and good morale. There is a limit, to be sure. Although every organization requires the stability and aid to coordination afforded by good standing plans, the plans could become too numerous or too rigid, and flexibility and initiative could be snuffed out.

TYPES OF STANDING PLANS

Within the broad category of standing plans, a manager has a choice of several types, notably policies, standard methods, and standing operating procedures. Like formations for a football team, one type of plan may be more useful than another in a certain situation. So a manager needs to know the characteristics of the tools he has to work with if he is to be effective in achieving balanced results. Let us look at the characteristics of the principal types of standing plans.

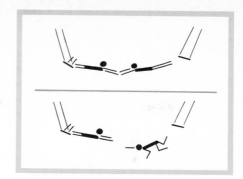

Figure 18–1 In organizations there is a continual need for consistent, dependable behavior. If behavior becomes unpredictable and erratic, disaster could follow.

Policies

A policy is a general guide to action. Typically it does not tell a person exactly what to do, but it does point out the direction. Familiar policies are summed up in these statements: "We sell only for cash." "We lease, rather than buy, office space." "We insure all property worth more than $10,000 against fire loss." In each instance, some important aspect of a recurring problem has been singled out, and a guide established for dealing with it.

Although policies are often desirable, the wise way for a manager to use them is by no means obvious. He has to give considerable attention to these questions: What kinds of problems are covered? How precise should a policy be? Should it give explicit guidance or merely set limits?

Some policies provide only broad guidance. For example, "Our policy is to make college education available to all students graduating from an in-state high school" leaves much leeway as to what is done about classroom space and about keeping up with standards. Similarly a statement that "Preference will be given to goods made by union labor" indicates intent but leaves the purchasing agent free to decide whether the preference comes first or only when all other considerations are equal.

But policies can be much more specific. An investment-banking firm makes the following statement on length of vacations:

> *Employees shall normally be entitled to vacations according to the following schedule:*
>
> 1) On payroll six to eighteen months prior to March 1—*one week.*
> 2) On payroll nineteen months to ten years prior to March 1—*two weeks.*
> 3) On payroll eleven to twenty years prior to March 1—*three weeks.*
> 4) On payroll over twenty years prior to March 1—*four weeks.*

What subjects policies should cover and what policies should say about these subjects depend entirely on what will be helpful in solving specific problems. Take customer policies. Many companies believe it is wise to establish lower limits and perhaps upper limits on the size of customer they want; location limits are also common. These guides are useful not only to the selling organization, but also to people who must plan production scheduling, warehousing, and shipping. Establishing a useful policy covering the quality characteristics of customers is more difficult. Credit rating, stability of demand, desire for special service, history on cancellation of orders—all contribute to a definition of "a good firm to do business with." Few companies, however, attempt to incorporate these considerations in a policy, because most customers are good in some respects and weak in others; thus a general guide applicable to many situations is hard to formulate. For guidance on this aspect of selecting customers, certain companies have a policy that simply lists all factors that must be considered in arriving at a decision.

Even when most aspects of a problem do not lend themselves to policy guidance, perhaps one or two aspects do. The selection of suppliers of raw materials and parts is a good example. To a large extent, a purchasing agent must make a separate analysis of possible suppliers for each item he buys. Nevertheless, most companies have a few policies about selecting suppliers. A company may have a policy of buying no more than seventy-five percent of its needs for any one product from a single supplier. The purpose is to avoid being dependent on a single source and so run the risk of a shortage if that firm is shut down. Another policy may be to secure bids from at least three sources to encourage competition for the company's business. Note that such policies deal only with the number of suppliers, leaving open the selection of specific firms.

A policy, then, may 1) be specific or general in its instruction, 2) deal with one, or many, aspects of a problem, 3) place limits within which action is to be taken, or 4) specify the steps in making a decision. The skill of a manager in using policies lies in how he decides just *what kind of guidance* will be helpful.

For convenience of reference, policies are often classified by subject, such as sales, production, purchasing, personnel, or finance. But at other times, we refer to *general* policies and *departmental* policies, depending on the scope of activities to which they apply. Such groupings do not, of course, change the character of policies as a management tool.

Standard Methods

The distinction between a policy and a standard method is chiefly one of degree, because both provide guidance about how a problem should be handled. The chief differences relate to viewpoint, completeness, and the attempt to control operating conditions.

Viewpoint. A policy is a general guide, whereas a standard method deals with detailed activities. But what is general and what is detailed? The answer depends on our point of view. For example, a vice-president in charge of personnel would probably say that a general rule to pay wages comparable to those prevailing in the local community was a policy, whereas job evaluation was simply a method for carrying out this policy. But the chief of the wage and salary division would look on a decision to use job evaluation in establishing pay rates as a major policy covering his work; he would consider a particular way of relating one job to another—say, factor comparison—a method. What about still a third person, a job analyst who works for the wage and salary chief? He, too, has his own point of view. He thinks the choice of factor comparison is a policy decision; for him, methods are such things as determining whom to contact and how to conduct interviews in analyzing each job. Clearly, then, whether a particular guide to action is called a policy or a standard method depends on the perspective of the person who is talking.

Still, even such a slippery distinction as this is useful. In planning the work of each job, at whatever level, an executive should think of both the broad framework in which he operates and the more detailed methods he will use. Good planning requires both viewpoints, and we need terms that distinguish between them.

Completeness.   Standard methods, like policies, never cover every aspect of an activity, although typically they do provide fuller guidance than a policy. Their greater completeness is scarcely surprising, however, because standard methods apply to a narrower scope of activities. Therefore, it is easier to find general guides that fit most cases. Besides, thanks to Frederick W. Taylor's attempt to plan everything in detail, tradition favors developing detailed methods on the assumption that the more completely a method is planned, the more efficient it will be.

Control of environment.   The pioneers of Scientific Management—Frank Gilbreth, Taylor, and others—quickly discovered that the conditions surrounding a job often had more influence on output than the performance of the person holding the job. The successful use of standard methods called for standard conditions.

The scientific managers therefore set about to control raw materials, machine maintenance, work flow, tools, training, and other factors that affect output. After such work conditions were controlled, it became reasonable to expect an individual to follow a standard method of work and to achieve a standard output.

Today we can see many applications of this basic idea of controlling conditions so that standard methods will be applicable. An automobile assembly plant is perhaps the most widely known example. In this case, standardized parts reach the assembly line precisely on schedule. Necessary tools are placed within easy reach of the worker. Special instructions for auxiliary equipment are readily available. In fact management has gone to great lengths to make sure that standard methods are applicable to car after car. Although most industries do not go to this extreme, attempts to maintain uniform and effective working conditions are common.

Standard methods are essential in the use of electronic computers to make automated decisions. Several conditions are necessary for a computer to "decide"—that is, issue instructions to another machine or to a person about action to be taken: 1) The significant variables in the situation must be measured and this information fed into the machine. (The rest of the environment is assumed to be constant.) 2) Any deviation from acceptable performance flashes a specific cue. 3) Each cue trips a "programmed" response—a standard method for dealing with the situation. All three conditions call for intense standardization. It is clear that unless an operating situation lends itself to a very high use of standard methods, automation is not applicable.

One drawback of developing standard methods and standard working conditions is the cost. Industrial engineers may spend months developing "the one best way" to perform a single operation. In a large plant, thousands of similar studies may be needed. Even after all of these studies, the engineers may be unable to discover a feasible way to control one or two factors. All this detailed planning obviously is expensive, and the resulting standard method must apply to a large enough volume of work so that the cost can be recovered by more efficiency in doing the work.

A shortcut is to standardize a method already in use, probably the method of the best workers.[1] This approach enables a company to predict processing costs and delivery times. Careful analysis, however, usually reveals places where methods that have simply evolved over the years can be improved. If a company is going to adopt a standard method at all, it normally pays to adopt a good one. It is particularly dangerous to introduce incentive pay in order to increase output until a thorough analysis of methods has been completed. Once a production norm has been established, most of us resent an attempt to increase it.

Standard methods are more difficult to apply to sales and other client contact than they are within a plant. The former activities tend to be varied, and the diversity of individual behavior is often an important consideration. Consequently, two approaches already mentioned in connection with policies are often used. First, we can standardize certain parts or aspects of the total activity —for instance, in sales work, the presenting of merchandise and the writing of sales orders; and in a hospital, the handling of admissions, routine tests, and accounting. Second, for some activities, we can specify a series of steps, as in conducting an interview or reconciling a bank statement. An executive or operator can use these standard parts in whatever combination seems appropriate for a day's work. This practice permits flexibility while still achieving some of the benefits of standard methods.

Standing Operating Procedures

A procedure details the *sequence of steps* several individuals must take to achieve a specific purpose. When a procedure for dealing with recurring problems becomes formalized, we call it a standing operating procedure.

---

[1] Standing plans are not always consciously and deliberately established. Some are like common law; they are practices that just grow, become accepted behavior, and are then enforced by those in official positions.

There is no sharp line that divides a company's traditions and customs from its standing plans. From a manager's point of view, we might say that a custom becomes a standing plan when 1) it is clearly enough recognized so that those it affects can describe it, and 2) individuals would be subject to criticism if they disregarded it merely on their own initiative. Other customs and traditions undoubtedly influence behavior, but they can scarcely be considered a part of a planning structure, because they are not sharply enough defined to be enforced.

Company action on even relatively small matters usually requires the work of several individuals. A procedure helps to integrate their bits of work into a meaningful whole. Consider the standing operating procedure set by an insurance company for the employment of exempt personnel (that is, employees not subject to wage-and-hour regulations):

1) A supervisor decides he needs an additional person to help with technical problems.

2) The budget officer must approve the addition unless the supervisor's existing budget has funds available for this purpose (which is unlikely).

3) The supervisor advises the personnel director by phone or in writing of his new need.

4) The personnel director sends a job analyst to the supervisor; the analyst writes a description of job duties and qualifications of the person needed to fill the job, and gets the supervisor's OK.

5) This job description is reviewed by the wage and salary administrator, who classifies the job and thereby sets the salary range for the new job.

6) The employment manager looks for candidates who have the qualifications stated in the job description. He first checks present employees who might be qualified and interested. If necessary, he turns to outside sources. He then picks the two or three most promising candidates.

7) The supervisor interviews the candidates sent to him by the employment manager; he selects the one he prefers or asks for more candidates.

8) The employment manager checks the references and tries to uncover other pertinent information about the leading candidate.

9) This individual is called back for a second interview with the supervisor. They try to reach a tentative understanding about the job duties, salary range, and other matters.

10) The supervisor's boss interviews the candidate.

11) If everything is in order, the supervisor makes a firm offer.

12) The candidate reports to the office of the employment manager, fills in company forms, retirement instructions, and so on. The employment manager gives him background information on the company and its personnel policies.

13) The person takes a medical examination from the company doctor.

14) He reports for duty.

15) The employment manager sends instructions to the payroll clerk about starting date, rate of pay, deductions, and so forth.

Most companies have literally hundreds of such procedures—for grievances, capital expenditures, arranging to use the company car—and most are essential for smooth operation. Picture the confusion if there were no standard procedure for customers' orders. Somehow each order must get immediately from the sales representative to the shipping clerk, the credit manager, and the accounts-receivable clerk; later the persons responsible for billing, inventory records, sales analysis, and sales compensation must be advised. Without a regular routine for handling such matters, customer service would be poor, salespeople would be angry, bills would have errors and become troublesome to collect, and inventory controls would collapse.

Most standing operating procedures apply to the flow of business papers —orders, bills, requests, reports, applications, and so forth. The papers are simply vehicles for information and ideas. But there can be standing procedures with no papers at all; for example, when an exception to a normal price is at issue, the three or four people involved may have a well-established understanding about the steps necessary in making a decision.

Although standard forms are not an essential part of a standing operating procedure, they can be very helpful for a large volume of routine transactions. A well-designed form with space for all essential information aids accuracy of communication, permits rapid handling, and serves as a convenient record.

Relation to organization. Formal organization divides the total work of a company into parts, thus permitting concentrated and specialized attention where necessary. Procedures help tie all the parts together. Like an automatic shuttle on a loom passing back and forth through the warp threads, the procedures weave woof threads that bind a firm fabric. Some of the weaving must be done by hand, as we shall see in the next chapter, but a large part of it must become routine and standardized. This is the role of the standing operating procedure.

Clearly, the way a company is organized affects the number and sequence of steps in any procedure. For instance, if each supervisor in the life-insurance company referred to earlier recruited his own technical personnel (as is the case in some companies), at least steps 6, 8, and 10 of the procedure would be changed. Fifty years ago, when there would have been no central personnel department, a supervisor might well have done all the work himself, except for steps 2, 10, and 15. But if the company had more personnel specialists, the procedure might well be more elaborate—as anyone who has been recruited into the Armed Services can testify.

Keeping procedures simple. Standing operating procedures tend to become complex and rigid for several reasons. Each unit takes jurisdictional pride in performing its part accurately. Control points are added to avoid difficulties that are often temporary, and these controls then survive like the proverbial cat with nine lives. Executives habitually look for information at certain spots, not realizing that it might be more simply compiled elsewhere. Standard forms acquire a sanctity that few dare challenge.

To avoid the choking effect of overelaborate procedures is a continuing task for a manager. A variety of techniques are open to him. He may hire a special procedures-analyst for assistance in this area alone. Among the many possibilities for simplification are mechanical devices for communication and duplication. Perhaps a procedure can be revised so that some steps are taken concurrently. One company found that checking all invoices from vendors was unnecessary; by concentrating on those for over $100, 74 percent of the invoices could be handled more promptly, with a likely annual loss of only $200; furthermore, the work of two clerks was eliminated.

Job enlargement is receiving increasing emphasis in business organizations. Instead of dividing work into narrower specialities, companies are combining a wide variety of duties into a single job, as we noted in Part Two. Job enlargement affects procedures because it reduces the number of stops in a total flow. Often much more time is used in *moving* customers' orders from desk-A to desk-B than in performing the two steps. So merely a reduction in the number of stops is itself an advantage.

In appraising a standing procedure, a manager wants to ensure that 1) the action each person must take is clear, 2) the information each person requires is provided, 3) the work proceeds promptly, 4) economies are obtained where feasible, 5) control checks are made at strategic points, and 6) necessary records are kept. Meeting these tests and also keeping procedures simple often calls for keen resourcefulness.

HOW STRICT SHOULD PLANS BE?

There is much double talk about the flexibility of standing plans. An executive may spend ten minutes emphasizing the need for a policy, standard method, or standing operating procedure, and then finish by saying, "Of course, we want to keep it flexible." In a single breath, he has cast out his whole point. How flexible? Flexible in what way? The catch is that the executive has several available courses of action.

One approach is to change standing plans frequently: A policy, method, or procedure remains in effect until a new guide is established, but such revisions are made promptly whenever operating conditions change. Unfortunately, this approach has serious limitations. Many of the advantages of dependability, habitual behavior, customary social relations, and predictable results are lost. Communication about changes in standing plans is difficult, especially if a large number of people are involved; the reasons for the new plan and its full meaning become confused, and loyalty to informal groups encourages resistance to new alignments. Therefore, using frequent change to secure flexibility in standing plans needs to be confined to a few issues—such as a special procedure to handle the Christmas rush—and preferably applied to a small group that understands why the change is necessary.

Another approach to flexibility is to state a standing plan generally, or loosely, in order to permit a wide range of variation within the plan. Or we may list many exceptions to which the plan does not apply. In effect, this simply restricts the scope of the plan; flexibility is achieved by not giving full guidance.

Still a third way is to think of standing plans partly as guides and partly as rules. If we can draw this distinction clearly, the usefulness of standing plans can be greatly extended. Let us examine this approach more fully.

Guides Versus Rules

Some policies are intended to be definite rules having no exceptions. For example, the Cluett, Peabody Company, manufacturer of Arrow shirts and related products, has this policy: "No advertising allowance will be made to our customers." This does not mean that the company *prefers* not to pay advertising allowances or that *only* the sales manager may authorize such allowances; it means just what it says. This company wants its products carried by many small stores as well as by large ones. By making no allowances to favored customers, it believes that a greater number of outlets will stock its products. Hence the policy is rigidly enforced. This company also has a policy that no second-quality merchandise will be sold with its Arrow label, and it makes sure that this policy, like the other, is strictly observed.

Contrast these Cluett, Peabody policies with this employment policy of a large consulting firm: "Individuals added to the professional staff should be between the ages of thirty and thirty-eight when first hired." The reason the minimum age was instituted was that clients might object to paying high fees unless all staff personnel have some maturity and experience. The maximum age was designed to avoid embarrassment if either an individual or the firm decided that his employment should be terminated. In the company's experience, it often took three or four years to reach such a conclusion, and if a person was still in his early forties when he left or was let go, he could find another good job with ease. An analysis of this firm after the policy had been in effect for ten years showed that 36 percent of the staff had been employed at ages outside the established limits. What good, then, was the policy? Senior members of the firm insisted that the policy was very helpful. "It is a distillation of our experience. It reminds us that any time we step outside these bounds, we are asking for trouble. However, finding good staff is so difficult, we do not believe that we should be bound by this single consideration. Because of the policy, we are doubly careful when we stand outside the age limits." In short, this policy served as a guide but not a rule.

Variations in strictness of application will also be found among standard methods. Even the sales pitch of a Fuller Brush representative is only suggested, and good representatives adapt their sales presentation to individual customers. On the other hand, the methods for running a test in a medical laboratory are usually followed precisely so that results will be reliable.

Because standing operating procedures always involve several people, less freedom is possible than with standard methods. Each person relies on the other links in the chain. When exceptions to a usual routine are necessary, everyone affected should be notified, for the very existence of the standing

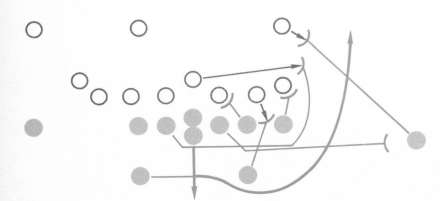

Figure 18–2 Plans should be clearly plotted in advance. But they should also be flexible enough to allow for necessary adjustments in the field of action.

procedure creates a presumption that everyone will follow his customary path. Sometimes there is even a standing procedure for making an exception to a standing procedure! Handling rush orders at a plant or registering a special student at a university, for instance, may call for this refinement.

Restrained Use of Rules

Variation in strictness can cause confusion, however. In some cases, the reliability of a standing plan is its virtue. In other instances, rigidity is anything but a virtue. We should recognize the dilemma and deal with it in the following ways.

Making intentions clear. An executive who had built his company from scratch supposedly had a large rubber stamp that read, "And this time I mean it." When he wanted his orders followed precisely, he used the stamp on any documents involved. Modern executives who are otherwise fond of "flexible policies" might well adopt a similar device. Subordinates are often uncertain whether a standing plan is a guide or a rule. Simply making clear how much flexibility is intended will remove much of the confusion.

Establishing rules only for compelling reasons. When we set up a policy, method, or procedure, we often have a strong conviction about the soundness of that plan, and we believe others should follow it to the letter. Our natural tendency is to state it as though it should be strictly observed. But we should remember that a standing plan may remain in effect for a long time. Circumstances may change. Those who apply the plan later will probably be in a better position to judge its fitness. If they are permitted to treat the policy or method as "recommended practice," they profit by the guidance but are not pushed into an action that fails to accomplish major objectives. Consequently we should have compelling reasons for insisting on strict observance.

Strong reasons for strict observance may indeed exist. *Consistency* of action by several people may be necessary, as in pricing to avoid illegal discrimination. Or consistency over time may be desirable; for instance, accounting reports should be comparable from one year to the next. *Dependability* may be crucial if several people must rely on knowing what others will do, as when a plane lands on an aircraft carrier. *Doers may clearly lack judgment* on the subject covered by a standing plan; most operators of electronic computers do not know enough about the inner mechanism to deviate from standard instructions, nor does the student who is selling magazines to get through college have enough background to adjust subscription rates. In circumstances such as these, standing plans should be strictly observed.

Using the exception principle. The so-called "exception principle" simply refers to an understanding an executive may have with his subordinates that so long as operations are proceeding as planned, the subordinates should not bother him. But when exceptions arise, they should consult him. The principle applies to standing plans in this way: Subordinates are expected to abide by policies, standard methods, and standing procedures in most instances; but if an unusual condition arises in which a standing plan does not seem suitable, they turn the matter over to a higher authority, who decides whether an exception should be made. Perhaps the "higher authority" will be the executive who established the standing plan in the first place; at other times, permission to make exceptions may be assigned to lower-level executives. Note that in this setup, the standing plans are strict *rules* for operating people, but they are only *guides* for the executives who handle the exceptional cases. Of course, successful operation of the scheme requires that operating people be able to recognize when a situation may merit an exception and demand the attention of the "higher authority."

WHAT TO COVER
AND IN HOW MUCH DETAIL

For what activities should standing plans be established? More specifically: What aspects of such activities? With what type of standing plan—policy, standard method, or standing procedure? In how much detail?

Reasons for Standing Plans

Because the ways of using standing plans and the extent to which they are applied always depend upon specific situations, a manager cannot avoid the continuing task of deciding when to add or drop policies, procedures, or standard methods. Here are several reasons why a standing plan may be introduced:

1) The need for *consistency* and close *coordination* of work, as we have noted, affects the desirability of detailed planning. Where consistency is crucial, as in accounting, pricing, wages, vacations, and the like, the pressure for detailed plans is strong. Where adjustment to local conditions is paramount, detailed plans are apt to get in the way. Similarly if the activities of several persons must interlock (in timing or quality), detailed planning may be necessary. To the extent that work is independent, or coordination is easy to achieve through personal contact, a compelling reason for detailed planning may be lacking.

2) Higher executives may lighten their work load by using standing plans. Once a policy, method, or procedure is developed, an *executive can delegate* to subordinates the job of applying the plan to specific cases. This delegation relieves him of the need to become personally familiar with each case, while still giving him confidence that work will proceed according to his wishes. One decision—like a pattern in a foundry or a dress shop—can shape the output of many workers.

3) The *quality* of operating decisions may be improved. Because a standing plan is followed repeatedly, a manager can afford to give careful thought to the formation of the plan. A policy is one means of transmitting the company's heritage of knowledge to many people. The painstaking analysis upon which a standard method is based will benefit many operators when they follow "the one best way."

4) If it uses standing plans extensively, a company may find that it can employ people with less experience or ability to do certain jobs. If so, *payroll economies* should result.

5) Standing plans also lay the *groundwork for control*. By setting up limits within which activities take place, and perhaps by specifying how those activities are to be performed, it is easier to predict results. These predictions can then be translated into control standards (as explained in Chapter 21). In fact, establishing detailed plans encourages tight supervision and control, which may or may not be desirable.

6) A manager should also take heed of the people who do the work as well as of the work itself, in deciding how detailed his plans must be.[2] The greater the dependency of subordinates, the greater the need for detailed plans. Such people want guidance, and they feel ill at ease without it. But if subordinates are highly self-assertive, general rather than detailed plans will be more applicable. Ability also plays a part in deciding on degree of detail. The greater the decision-making talent of most subordinates, and the greater their knowledge about the business, the less detail in planning is necessary.

Drawbacks to Standing Plans

A manager must remember, however, that these possible benefits are offset by several inherent drawbacks; the more detailed the planning, the greater the drawbacks. Standing plans introduce *rigidity*. Indeed, the *purpose* of plans is to limit and direct action in a prescribed manner, and such plans become ingrained attitudes and habitual behavior. Especially if the plans are written down, they tend to be followed until new plans are written and approved. Naturally enough, the executives who spend time developing such plans are inclined to defend them. All this means that it will be hard to change standing plans once they are well accepted. In dynamic situations, where frequent change is desirable, such rigidity is a drawback.

Planning also involves *expense*. Fully as important as direct outlays for industrial engineering and management research is the time that operating executives devote to analysis, discussion, and decision. Teaching people to understand and follow a new plan also takes effort. Unless particular kinds of problems keep recurring, there is no point in even considering standing plans. The more the repetition, either inherent or contrived, the more useful standing plans will be. But as planning is extended to more areas of a business and is

---

[2] Typically a manager is not free to change those already on the job, and their replacements are likely to have about the same attitudes and abilities. Consequently, plans have to be suited to the people, unless a drastic reorganization of the activity, including recruiting new workers, is contemplated.

Figure 18–3 For each position, these questions arise: What aspects of the job should be covered by standing plans? In how much detail? Should these plans be guides or rules?

increasingly detailed, a point will be reached where the improvements in results do not justify the cost of further planning.

Time taken in preparing and installing standing plans—time for analysis, to secure approvals, to develop understanding and skill in their use—may also have strategic value. A customer may want prompt delivery, or the board of directors may want a report next week. In such situations, immediate action may be more important than taking time to discover the best possible method.

Clearly, then, the choice of what a standing plan should cover and how detailed it should be is strongly influenced by the particular work and people involved. Essentially, it is the operating situation, not the personal preference of the manager, that dictates a specific structure of planning. The task of a manager is to identify the salient features of each situation.

CONCLUSIONS: FREEDOM VERSUS REGULATION

Standing plans are a significant part of a company environment in which workers (managers and operators) make decisions. Policies, standard plans, and standing operating procedures provide decision-makers with limits, alternatives, and other premises. These premises have a double effect: They simplify the task of deciding how a specific problem is to be resolved; and they ensure a degree of consistency, dependability, and quality of decision throughout the company.

Nevertheless, the farther standing plans are extended, the more pressing becomes the dilemma of freedom versus regulation. This is an age-old issue that men have faced as long as they have participated in joint communal activities. But urban living and working together in specialized, purposeful organizations accentuate the problem. How much regulation of individual action is desirable? This question takes many forms and is common in many areas of human activity.

In political philosophy, the problem takes the form of a conflict of authority versus freedom. Every time a law is enacted, it limits someone's freedom. Yet we must have laws when people live together, in order that the actions of one person will not unduly infringe on the actions of others. In psychology and sociology, this is the problem of individual self-expression, initiative, and creativity versus group norms, rules, and customs. Every time a social group derives a customary way of thinking or acting, somebody's decision-making "on his own" is thereby circumscribed. Yet without such customs the group would disintegrate. In ethics, this is the problem of individual dignity versus the common good; and in law, it is a major issue in rendering justice. Finally, in business management, this is the problem of making plans that coordinate the action of people and regulate their job activities and their communications— plans that at the same time do not stifle the creativeness and energies of people who are contributing to the group effort.

Unfortunately, no plan is perfect for resolving the conflict between freedom and coordination. In our discussion, we have suggested several key factors a manager should consider in resolving these issues, but his final array of standing plans can be established only on the basis of the specific needs within his organization.

Two important aspects of the use of standing plans have not been discussed in this chapter because they are treated in other sections of the book. One is the intimate relation between decentralizing (considered in Chapter 3) and the degree of detailed planning. For instance, if we wish to decentralize, we should do the following: Whenever possible, make the detailed plans *guides* to be followed at a subordinate's discretion; if this is not feasible, provide for quick exceptions to the rule through appeal to some higher executive; and only as a last resort, make the plans a "law" from which no deviations are permitted. Contrariwise, centralization and the wide use of unalterable standing plans go hand in hand.

A second aspect, participation in the preparation of plans, will be explored in Part Six. As we shall see there, the basic conflict between regulation and freedom can at least be relieved by following these guides: In the preparation of a plan, seek the participation of those affected by it; let them help determine the most satisfactory extent of detail incorporated into the plan; and let them present their views on how various alternatives will work. In addition, allow subordinates continuing freedom to suggest changes in the plan, not only to improve operations, but also to take advantage of their initiative in adjusting details. By such means as these, we must meld the formal planning structure with the interests of the people doing the work.

FOR CLASS DISCUSSION

1) What factors should be considered when determining the degree of detail required in a standing plan—namely, whether to write a broad policy, general procedure, or detailed method?

2) "Why talk about flexibility in standing plans? If a situation arises that is not covered by a plan, then change the plan to cover it. Eventually the plan will be broad enough to apply to all likely situations." Discuss this from the viewpoint of someone who must operate under these plans—and then from the viewpoint of someone who designs them.

3) "Standing plans are really substitutes for thinking. They are organizational habits formalized to make sure that no one uses his head as long as he can remember what page in the manual the answer is on." Comment on this position.

4) The president of a large chain of retail stores said: "I estimate that we lose more than $100,000 a year in sales and goodwill by having our sales staff follow very specific operating procedures. Though I would like to reduce it, I must regard this loss as a necessary cost of doing business." Explain what you think he meant by this. Do you agree or disagree?

5) Consider a fairly significant change in policy that you would like to see implemented in your organization (business, school, class). a) List other policies affected by this change. b) List and discuss changes in procedures and methods that would be needed if the policy were made and then smoothly integrated.

6) In what ways will the emergence of more complex organization forms (e.g., matrix management, etc., in Chapter 6) affect the number and type of standing plans?

7) a) "One should never write a standing plan unless he intends to ensure it has been followed to the 'T.' "

b) "Standing plans are merely guides to action. One should not waste a lot of time checking to see if they have been followed. Instead, check results; if they are acceptable forget about the standing plans."

Discuss these two statements fully. With which do you more nearly agree? Why?

8) The Ace Auto Finance Company has operated for years as a distinctly local enterprise in which the granting of credit and the insistence on repayments has reflected knowledge about and often acquaintance with borrowers. Now, with population growth and increasing competition from national finance companies and banks, the directors of Ace Finance have decided that the company is getting a disproportionate share of poor-risk and slow-paying customers— "business our competitors are glad to push our way." Consequently, the directors have adopted a revised master strategy of "more sales promotion coupled with tightening up on collections and repossessions."

a) The collection manager of Ace Finance has been informed of the new master strategy and is wondering how he can interpret it to his five collectors. Most of these men have worked for Ace Finance for several years; their "reasonable" treatment of slow-paying borrowers has helped build a favorable reputation. The new strategy will certainly not make their job easier.

What kind of objectives do you suggest be set for the five collectors? How rigid should the objectives be? Should they be hopes or expectations? Should the form of objectives be different during this transition period from, say, a year hence? Who should formulate the objectives for each collector?

b) Typically, loans are made in the front of the office. Only when records show that an applicant has been delinquent on a previous loan is the collection manager consulted, and he may or may not consult the collector who handled the account. The new master strategy will of course affect those granting credit as well as collectors. How should objectives be set for granting credit so that they contribute to the new strategy and at the same time are compatible with revised objectives for the collectors?

Cases

For cases involving issues covered in this chapter, see especially the following. Particularly relevant questions are listed after each case.

Petersen Electronics (p. 211), 12
Merchantville School System (p. 217), 15
Atlas Chemical Company (p. 321), 12
Marten Fabricators (p. 316), 14
Graham, Smith, & Bendel, Inc. (p. 445), 13
Monroe Wire and Cable (p. 436), 12
Family Service of Gotham (p. 532), 10
Central Telephone and Electronics (p. 527), 10

FOR FURTHER READING

Bower, M., *The Will to Manage.* New York: McGraw-Hill Book Company, 1966, Chapter 4.

Management consultant explains the need for policies and procedures to carry out strategy effectively.

Filley, A. C., R. J. House and S. Kerr, *Managerial Process and Organizational Behavior,* 2nd ed. Glenview, Ill.: Scott, Foresman & Company, 1976, Chapter 14.

Discusses the role of objectives and policies in achieving organizational goals, and examines research evidence on significance of clearly defined goals and policies.

Mockler, R. J., *Business Planning and Policy Formulation.* New York: Appleton-Century-Crofts, 1972, Chapters 5 and 8.

Explores the process of establishing policies and procedures, and illustrates their use in specific companies.

O'Shaughnessy, J., *Analysing and Controlling Business Procedures.* London: Cassell & Company, 1969.

Remarkably concise and specific guide for improving business procedures.

Twedt, D., "Management Handbooks for Continuing Education." *Harvard Business Review,* July 1975.

Briefly describes 33 handbooks on general management, marketing, finance, production, and human relations. Each book includes detailed discussion of policies and procedures.

19

Adaptive Programming

SINGLE-USE PLANS

In the preceding chapters we have examined two broad types of plans: master strategy and objectives, which focus on desired results, and standing plans, which establish a structure of customary behavior for achieving these results. Both types are highly useful devices for managerial decision-making. But they do not exhaust the arsenal of weapons a manager can use in attacking problems.

A third type of managerial plan, equally essential for effective management of any group effort, deals with single, rather than repetitive, situations. In such cases, a manager decides in advance what action to take within a given period or what to do to meet a particular problem. Once the time has passed or the problem has been met, a new plan is devised for the next problem. We call these single-use plans.

PROGRAMMING

The basic characteristics of single-use plans can be explained best in terms of programs; other forms, such as schedules and projects, can then be viewed as particular kinds of programs. After examining several types of programs, we shall turn to the more uncertain problems of adjusting programs to a dynamic and uncertain environment.

The synchronization of customary, repetitive work is achieved primarily through standing operating procedures and other work habits, as we noted in Chapter 18.

But opening a new office in Harlem, changing organization structure, and countless other executive actions are not routine. They are distinctive, or special, in at least some respects, and their timing calls for specific attention. For such activities, a *program* is needed. A program lays out the principal steps for accomplishing a mission and sets an approximate time for carrying out each step. For an entirely new activity, a program also indicates who should take each step. To cite a very simple example, a program for a branch managers' conference should indicate what topics will be covered, who should lead the discussion on each topic, and when and where each subject will be considered.

Good programming is often crucial to smooth and efficient operations. Consider, for instance, the problem faced by an airline in introducing a new type of plane, such as the Boeing 747. Flight crews and ground personnel— literally thousands of people—have to learn new skills. To postpone a reeducation program until the planes are delivered would result in chaos. Instead, a company must anticipate by two years the need for competent maintenance people, experienced flight crews, different weather information, and solutions to other new problems. Some personnel need classes of only a few hours; others must spend several months learning complex theories and skills. All this training has to be carried on while regular operations with older plans are maintained.

Only through careful programming can an airline 1) anticipate possible crises and make provisions for them, 2) review the subprograms to be sure that they fit together into a consistent whole, 3) avoid hurried decisions that would just get by in favor of taking sound and economical steps, and 4) use its limited (and expensive) training facilities most effectively.

Skill in programming is a major asset for any operating executive. A personnel director, for instance, needs a program for recruiting more blacks. A treasurer is concerned with a program for selling new bonds; an executive vice-president works out a program for introducing a new product. Programs, in fact, are useful at all levels in a firm: The president may develop a program for merging two companies, and a first-line supervisor may have a program for training Sally to take over Lorraine's job.

Basic Steps in Programming

Many programming problems can be solved by following six basic steps.[1] In some situations, of course, this approach will not fit exactly, but the basic stages are these:

[1] Adapted from a fuller discussion in W. H. Newman and J. P. Logan, *Strategy, Policy, and Central Management*, 7th ed. (Cincinnati: South-Western, 1976), Chap. 20.

1) *Divide into steps the activities necessary to achieve the objective.* Dividing work into steps is useful for planning, organizing, and controlling. Planning is improved because concentrated attention can be given to one step at a time. Organizing is facilitated because the steps or projects can be assigned to different persons to effect speedier or more efficient action. Controlling is also enhanced because an executive can watch each step and determine whether progress is satisfactory while work is actually being done, instead of waiting for final results. If the division into parts is to be most effective, we should clearly define the purpose of each step, indicating the kind of work, the quality, and the quantity we expect.

2) *Note the relationships among steps, especially any necessary sequences.* Usually the parts of a program are closely dependent on one another. The amount of work, the specifications, and the time for one step often affect the ease or difficulty of taking the next. Unless these relationships are closely watched, the very process of subdividing the work may cause more inefficiency than it eliminates.

    Necessary sequences are particularly significant relationships. In a drug-addiction program, for example, local counseling centers must be set up and staffed before general publicity is released; otherwise early interest turns into frustration, and the entire effort is regarded as a sham. Necessary sequences have an important bearing on scheduling because they tend to lengthen the overall time required for an operation; since a shorter cycle gives a company more flexibility, we should carefully check the need for delaying one action until another is completed.

3) *Decide who is to be responsible for doing each step.* If we are programming a company's normal operation, the existing organization structure will already have determined who is to perform each activity. But if the program covers an unusual event—merging with another company, for instance—we should give careful attention to deciding who is accountable for each step. These special assignments may create a temporary set of authorizations and obligations. A special team may be formed to carry out the program.

4) *Determine the resources needed for each step.* For realistic programming, we must recognize the need for facilities, materials and supplies, and personnel. Next we should appraise the availability of these necessary resources. If any one of them is not available, we should set up another project designed to obtain this resource. For example, if a company is short on qualified personnel, it should make plans for hiring and training new employees. Many a program breaks down because the executive who prepares it does not realistically understand what resources will be required.

5) *Estimate the time required for each step.* This act really breaks down into two aspects: 1) the date when a step can begin and 2) the time required to complete an operation once it is started. Starting time, of course, depends on the availability of the necessary resources: How soon key personnel can be transferred to a new assignment, what work is already scheduled for a machine, the likelihood of getting delivery of materials from suppliers, the possibility of subcontracting part of the work—all have an effect on the time any given steps may begin.

    Processing time, once the activity has begun, is usually estimated on the basis of past experience. In addition, for detailed production operations, time-study data may permit tight scheduling. But for a great many operations, more time is consumed in securing approvals, conveying instructions, and getting people to work than is required for doing the work itself. Unless this "nonproductive time" can be eliminated, however, we should include it as part of the estimated time.

6) *Assign definite dates for each part.* An overall schedule is of course based on the sequences noted under step 2 and the timing information assembled under step 5. The resulting schedule should show both the starting date and the completion date for each part of the program.

A good deal of adjustment may be necessary to make a final schedule realistic, however. A useful procedure is to try working backward and forward from some fixed controlling date. Availability of materials or facilities may set the time around which the rest of the schedule pivots. In sales, a particular selling season, such as Christmas or Easter, may be the fixed point. We must, of course, dovetail any one program with other company commitments. We must also make some allowance for delay. Allowances all along the line are not desirable, because they would encourage inefficient performance, but a few safety allowances are wise so that an unavoidable delay at one point will not throw off an entire schedule.

In summary, a well-conceived program covers all actions that are necessary to achieve a mission, and indicates who should do what and at what time. Note how all the programming elements arise even in this simple example. The

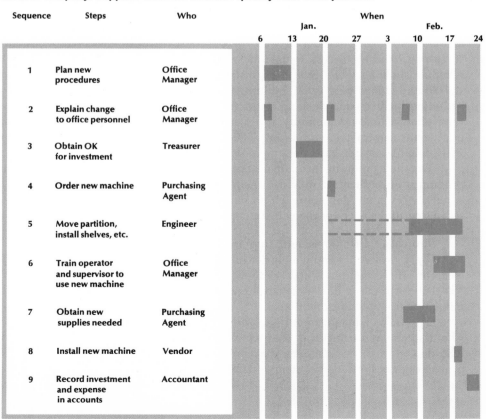

Figure 19–1   A program for installing a new duplicating machine in the controller's office. Starting and completion dates for each step are indicated here by the colored bars. The moving of partitions was delayed so that the office would not be torn up at the end of the month. Training included a visit to see a similar machine in operation in another company. Supplies could be obtained quickly from local jobbers.

controller of a pharmaceutical company decided to install a large Xerox duplicating machine to make multiple copies of the many reports his office issued. The Xerox salesman said, "All you have to do is plug in the machine." But the controller realized that a shift in the office routine was more complicated than this. After some thought he developed the program summarized in Fig. 19–1. With this plan, he was able not only to specify when he wanted the machine delivered but also to prepare both the physical setup and his personnel for the change. He avoided having the office torn up when people were busy with month-end closing, and he had a plan that could easily serve as a control as the work progressed. Most programs are more complicated than this, of course, but their essential nature is the same.

Wide Use of Programming

Hierarchy of programs.   For some firms, a major program encompasses a large part of company activity. This situation is true in the automobile industry, where annual model changes pace the work of all major manufacturing departments. Lead times are long, because there is a necessary sequence between market and environmental research, functional design, engineering, tooling, and actual production and sales. In fact, in any one year a company must do preparatory work for models that will be sold two, three, and four years later.

Such programming of major steps must necessarily lump together large amounts of work. But each step, in turn, has a program of its own. Thus the stage of providing necessary facilities may be divided into a more detailed schedule showing when building construction and machine purchase must be started and completed. Again, building construction will have its own program, including such steps as defining requirements, selecting a site, getting architectural plans, gaining community approval, completing engineering plans, selecting a chief contractor, and so on. The executive charged with finding a site will probably establish an even more detailed program for his own chore.

Detailed programs are not necessarily connected to successively broader programs; any executive may use them by himself if he wishes. Nevertheless, when the programming approach permeates managerial thinking at all levels, it sets a tone and a pace for the entire company.

Projects.   Often a single step in a program is set up as a "project." Actually, a project is simply a cluster of activities that is relatively separate and clearcut. Building a hospital, designing a new package, soliciting gifts of $500,000 for a men's dormitory are examples. A project typically has a distinct mission and a clear termination point—the achievement of the mission.

The task of management is eased when work can be set up in projects. The assignment of duties is sharpened, control is simplified, and the people who do the work can sense their accomplishment. Calling a cluster of work a project does not, of course, change its nature. It may still be part of a broader program, and programming the project itself may be desirable. The chief virtue of a project lies in identifying a nice, neat work package within a bewildering array of objectives, alternatives, and activities.

Schedules.   A schedule specifies the time when each of a series of actions should take place. It is one aspect of programs, as we are using that term. When, as a result of standing plans, the tasks to be done and the persons who must do them are clear, then scheduling may be the only element that needs management's attention. This would be the case, for example, in a frozen-food plant where the line is all set to go, as soon as the manager decides when to start and how many of each size package to produce. Under some conditions, then, planning is simplified by focusing separately on scheduling. In thinking about management broadly, however, the more inclusive concept of programming has wider usefulness.

Complex schedules are also closely linked to control, as we shall see in Chapter 22, in which a special control technique—PERT—is discussed.

STATIC VERSUS ADAPTIVE PROGRAMMING

Our discussion of programming so far has been based on several assumptions that are realistic only part of the time. We have assumed 1) that most of the actions necessary to achieve an objective are subject to direction and manipulation by management, and 2) that management can forecast the time factors—both availability and elapsed time—with considerable accuracy. For a good many problems, notably those that occur chiefly *within* company offices and plants, these assumptions are usually correct.

But when the timing of several important steps is outside management's control and is uncertain, the character of programming changes. Sound attitudes, competition, and business cycles are indeed independent variables. When we cannot make such events conform to our master plan, we need more adaptability, more resourcefulness, and more hedges and retreats. We must still think in terms of major steps, sequences, and timing and duration of each step, but now we must do so creatively rather than perfunctorily as though we were dealing with a routine engineering problem.

Contingency Programs

Typically we draw up a single program; it is the best way we can devise to get from our present position to a stipulated objective. But such a single program requires much uncertainty absorption. We are aware that external events may not occur as predicted and that the results of our actions may not turn out as anticipated. These uncertainties may be serious—perhaps catastrophic. If we stick with our single program, we may get into deep trouble.

The most elaborate way to plan for such uncertain events is to prepare contingency programs. Here we prepare in advance a set of programs. Each is ready to use if a particular circumstance arises. In planning flights to the moon, for instance, a whole array of contingency programs are developed in detail. On the Apollo 13 moon shot, such a contingency plan permitted partial completion of the mission and probably saved the lives of the crew. Contingency planning is also common in military operations.

In contrast little contingency planning is done by most enterprises. Aside from limited plans for action in the event of fire, we prefer to focus on making our single program come true. Is this disregard of admitted uncertainty wise?

The reasons for shunning contingency programs are plain. 1) The effort and expense of preparing such programs is large. Contingencies are many, so the number of programs could quickly multiply—as the decision tree (in Fig. 14–3) suggests.[2] To keep the programs viable, necessary preparations have to be put into effect. 2) Contingency programs are disconcerting. A manager tries hard to develop enthusiastic, committed effort behind the preferred program. Discussing and preparing for a lot of "ifs" adds confusion and distraction. 3) Postponement of planning until the contingency arrives (or can be more reliably forecast) *usually* permits us to get by without very serious losses.

The prudent manager, however, should identify those contingencies whose risks are so large that special programs are justified; and he should ensure that sequential adjustments—discussed in the next section—are promptly made.

Sequential Adjustments

An alternative to setting up contingency programs is making successive modifications in a program as unpredicted (or unassumed) conditions move to center stage.

Anticipating that feedback data will lead to revisions.   One way to deal with unpredictable and uncontrollable conditions is to ensure a flow of current information as work progresses and to adjust the program when necessary. A surgeon has a general plan of action before an operation starts; a football coach may have a game plan in mind before the kickoff. But each of these specialists expects to be guided more by current developments than by his prediction. An executive-development program is similar; a company may have a tentative ten-year plan for the progression of its outstanding young employees; but every-

---

[2] In theory, decision trees differ sharply from contingency programs. A decision tree is designed to help make a single decision now; the spelling out of various courses, results, and probabilities is intended to throw light on a present choice among alternatives. A contingency program, on the other hand, is concerned with future action; it does not weigh probabilities, but says what to do if a given situation occurs. In reality, however, the decision-tree predictions lack reliability unless they are based on some kind of programs; and the by-product of thinking through how various contingencies will be met is likely to be the chief benefit of decision-tree analysis. So the two concepts do tend to merge.

one expects that the actual performance of these people and the needs of the company will lead to drastic modifications long before the ten years are up.

On the matter of revising plans, the key distinction between static and adaptive programming lies in executive attitude toward change. When a program is regarded as a blueprint, an executive is heavily motivated to make the plan work; changes, he feels, are a confession of partial defeat. But under the adaptive approach, the manager considers some change normal and responds readily when reasons appear for modifying plans.

Long-range programming, which we have already discussed in Chapter 16 as a device for rounding out a company's master strategy, is always periodically revised. It is a prime example of anticipating that feedback data will lead to revision of the program. In other programs the feedback and revision cycle occurs more frequently, perhaps monthly or when key steps are completed—for example, after test marketing, or when the quantity of available funds is firmly established.

Restricting scheduling to the near future. When a pharmaceutical company put a new tranquilizer on the market, all executives were confident of a rapid growth in sales; there was talk of enlarging the plant, opening new branch offices, and using profits for additional research. Until the hoped-for sales volume actually developed, however, specific programming was confined to promoting the new product. Timing and determining the magnitude of other moves were held in abeyance until sales prospects became more certain.

A manufacturer of women's shoes got into trouble for not following a similar course. The firm opened a new plant in the South; it borrowed money and changed executive personnel on the assumption that most of its production could be transferred to the new plant within two years. Actually, the company had great difficulty in securing quality production from its new plant, and training expenses and spoilage made costs even higher than at the old plant. Consequently, the company was forced to postpone the move and found itself in serious financial difficulty. Had this firm merely scheduled the opening of the new plant, while leaving the time of closing the old factory unsettled, it might have avoided the crisis.

These devices for flexibility—anticipating changes and deferring program commitments except for the near future—sacrifice some benefits of a clear, positive program. Preparing for the future is more difficult and some economies may be lost. But these drawbacks are simply the price paid for a somewhat cautious approach to an unpredictable future.

Adjusting to leads and lags in the flow of goods. A program for a continuing flow of goods and services differs in important respects from a program for a single event. Producers and distributors of goods, such as gasoline or even aspirin, must think in terms of a *rate* of output for a week or month. Such companies may be affected by seasonal fluctuations in consumption and by the buildup or cutback of inventory in the hands of distributors and perhaps consumers. Thus production must precede seasonal peaks in demand, and if a stable level of operations is desired, a firm must build inventories.

Programs that deal with the flow of goods rarely provide exactly the rate of activity that proves to be needed. The rates of flow must be adjusted, a little here and a little there, somewhat as we adjust the hot and cold water taps in a shower. When a variety of products is involved, this adjusting process becomes complex.[3] Most companies have operating programs for some months ahead, but revise them at least monthly on the basis of feedback information. For perishable products, like bread, adjustments may be more frequent—even daily.

A program, then, must be suited to the operations it covers, but its essentials remain the same. By anticipating the what, who, how, and when, it enables a manager to prepare systematically and carefully for difficulties before they arise.

TIMING AND CONFRONTATION MODE

Importance of Timing

Timing deserves special emphasis. Many a program, sound in all other respects, has failed in application because action was taken at the wrong time. A shipping company built a large dock on Lake Erie, anticipating the movement of ocean freight through the St. Lawrence Waterway. The volume of business has been so slow in developing that the dock is now closed down. Perhaps ten years hence the necessary traffic *will* develop, but clearly the construction was premature. On the other hand, many a product has reached its market after the demand has waned—witness the multimillion-dollar loss on the oversized Edsel automobile. Similarly, there are better and poorer times to ask the boss for a raise, to buy raw materials, and to float a bond issue.

Two major sources of timing errors are economic shifts and the moods of key people. Our programs inevitably rest on forecasts (or unstated assumptions) about *when* economic and social conditions will be attractive. If we are early or late, the program suffers.

Adjusting to Economic Conditions

One strength a company may have, in contrast to an individual decision-maker, is its own economic-forecasting staff. These experts gather data from many sources and make predictions about factors that directly affect company

---

[3] Programming in terms of flows rather than for specific projects is a source of confusion in government planning. The national-income accounts, which reflect flows, are frequently used to express fiscal policy, but Congress makes appropriations primarily for a particular project or on an annual-appropriation basis. Aside from Federal Reserve actions, we have few good mechanisms (like hot and cold water taps) to adjust the flows of goods and services.

planning (as we noted in Chapter 15). Although no systematic appraisal of the "batting average" of company economists has been published, they undoubtedly provide useful insights on questions of timing.

Unfortunately for the forecasters, their occasional errors are often quite conspicuous. The public knows, for instance, that when Dacron fiber was first introduced to the market, du Pont built production facilities that far exceeded the demand. As a result, a new eighteen-million-dollar plant was idle for more than two years. The demand eventually developed, but the mistake lay in how fast it would do so.

Objective appraisal. A review of a variety of examples of poor timing suggests that executive attitude is more likely to be faulty than the forecasting and programming techniques. As already noted, executives become strongly committed to programs; they believe in them, and desperately want them to succeed. Because of this feeling, it is only natural for them to underrate information that might hint at a need for modification.

Unwillingness to face fairly clear trends in the wallpaper industry, for instance, led one company to postpone closing an old and inefficient plant; this decision prevented the company from taking the necessary steps to pull itself out of serious debt.

Prudence requires an objective appraisal. Somehow, either through checking with outsiders or through self-discipline, we should make a detached forecast of when key wants will occur. Moreover, as we will see in Part Five on controlling, the key planning assumptions should be monitored as the program gets underway. This sort of objective appraisal will not ensure perfect timing in our fast-moving world, but it will avoid a significant number of pitfalls.

Keeping flexible. When forecasts are not fully reliable—and few are —a wise executive seeks to *avoid making commitments until necessary.* He tries to distinguish between a bear-by-the-tail situation and one that consists of independent steps. For example, in a marketing program one move, such as

Figure 19–2 Timing the construction of a major facility calls for adroit adjustment to economic need, to political support or opposition, and to availability of vital supplies and capital. The speed of building the Alaskan pipeline, for example, has required careful balancing of U.S. need for crude oil, political relations with O.P.E.C. countries, strength of popular ecological concern, and conditions in the capital markets.

national advertising, may necessitate a string of accompanying moves. As in passing a car on a crowded two-lane highway, once we start we have to follow through. But in many research projects, a process may be halted at the end of any of several steps and then begun again without major loss. In the latter situation, because we are not yet committed to subsequent steps, new timing is possible.

A related way to retain flexibility in timing is to *keep two or more alternatives open.* At one stage in its development, Boeing Aircraft had a large military contract that would eventually necessitate a new plant. The time arrived when the firm had to acquire a plant site and begin engineering work if the terms of the military contract were to be met; yet there was sharp disagreement among several parties about the location of the plant. To avoid being caught later in a time squeeze, the company took options on land in both Seattle and San Francisco and hired engineers to make detailed plans for plants in both localities. More than a year later, but before any building contracts were let, the Seattle location was selected. The company kept two alternatives open until it became clear which one should be followed. Of course, substantial costs were involved in obtaining this flexibility. Boeing had to pay for two land options and two sets of engineering plans, though it knew that only one would eventually be used. Often, it seems, flexibility can be achieved only at a price.

Anticipating Reactions of Key People

Among the many forecasts needed for good timing of executive action is a prediction of how key people will react to parts of a program. Temptation is always strong to concentrate on tangible, quantitative elements and slide over the more evasive human factors. Yet the responses of people may make or break a program. Often a proposed action calls for a major effort or readjustment on the part of several individuals or groups, for their behavior patterns, beliefs, and values may be involved. Perhaps political behavior (to be explored in the next chapter) will also be involved. In timing, we have to judge when the situation is ripe for a new move.

For years a leading Midwestern department store had never used blacks in sales positions. The personnel director believed this tradition should be changed, but he anticipated resistance from supervisors and salesclerks. So he waited until there was a shortage of well-qualified salespeople and then hired two blacks, placing them under supervisors who were sympathetic to the change. Actually, these two were noticeably better qualified than most of the whites who could have been employed at the time. Word got around that they were unusually competent, and soon several other supervisors were asking for similar help. Had this change been introduced when well-qualified white applicants were in ample supply and were being turned down, the response might have been quite different.

A large bank had just installed a long-needed job-evaluation system. Officers and supervisors were pleased with the way the system was working, and the vice-president was anxious to move on to a training program that was also badly needed. The president turned down the proposal, explaining that job evaluation had not yet become normal behavior. To introduce a second change on the heels of the first "might give us indigestion." This was the president's judgment on how fast his group could comfortably adapt to a new personnel practice. Not until a year and a half later did he launch the training program.

An executive with a good feel for timing must be socially perceptive. He must know enough about people's needs, hopes, and fears to be able to anticipate their reaction to a proposed plan.

Confrontation Mode

A company's master strategy, as described in Chapter 16, includes the timing of major moves. The timing features of strategy broadened to cover the speed, effort, and aggressiveness with which changes are sought is called the "confrontation mode."

The choice of a confrontation mode is based on many factors: urgency of achieving an objective, available resources, temperament of the executive who is making the decision, as well as predictions of external conditions and of responses of key people (which we have just discussed). Several illustrations of implementing-strategies will demonstrate their nature and importance.[4]

Mass, concentrated offensive. Occasionally, an executive will decide to push through a plan despite opposition and obstacles. Ralph Cordiner did so when he decided to decentralize the management of the General Electric Company. Orders were given, positions were abolished, the gospel was preached, new organization plans were carefully prepared, the most elaborate management education program ever tried in industry was launched, and a few recalcitrants were fired. Within a mere three years, thousands of executives had changed their way of thinking, and the company was prepared to handle the largest volume of business in its history. Rarely has such a large company been changed so drastically so fast.

Fabianism—avoiding decisive engagement. This mode seeks gradual changes rather than revolutionary ones. The head of an industrial-equipment company chose this approach in his engineering department. The engineers, he felt, were too professional in their outlook and not sufficiently oriented to customer needs. Drastic action would have upset morale and probably caused valuable men to resign. So the president made arrangements to have the engineers visit customers' plants: They were invited to sit in with the salespeople when bids on important jobs were being prepared; those engineers who helped meet tough problems posed by a customer were given public commendation; the chief engineer counseled with his people about how they could make their

---

[4] For additional examples of implementing-strategies, see W. H. Newman, *Administrative Action,* 2nd ed. (Englewood Cliffs, N.J.: Prentice-Hall, 1963), pp. 86–98.

work more valuable to the company. Thus, although management ventured no single dramatic action, the point of view of the engineers changed substantially over a period of time.

Letting someone else pull your chestnuts out of the fire. For years, the thought of variable annuities was shocking to the life-insurance industry. But gradually, more companies could see that here was a new form of insurance that would be tied roughly to the general price level. Still, many of the firms that favored variable annuities were happy to let the Prudential Insurance Company carry the brunt of the bitter fight to obtain government permission to sell this new type of coverage. While secretly hoping Prudential would win, they maintained a neutral and respectable position in the industry.

Boring from within. Here, people already within the organization initiate the change. The potency of this mode in the hands of Communists is well known, but a similar approach may be used in many different situations. One company used it to get its executives to take an active part in community affairs. No general program was announced. Instead, management identified managers sympathetic to this cause throughout the branches of the company, and used them to spread the point of view. Occasionally these individuals would have dinner with one of the vice-presidents, at which time they talked over progress and problems; more often, however, just two or three would meet together for a discussion. All shared a missionary zeal for "having businessmen live up to civic responsibilities." Although top management let its endorsement of this type of activity be known, the effective ferment really started with these dedicated people—and it took hold in several branches in which the local manager was far from enthusiastic.

Things must get worse before they get better. The treasurer of a family-owned company with a five-million-dollar sales volume was convinced that companywide budgets should be installed. Other members of top management were ambivalent toward this "big company device." In view of their position, the treasurer might have prepared some estimates simply for his own use. Instead, he waited until the company had a poor six months during which expenses went up while sales went down. There was a good deal of grumbling about who should have done what. At this point, the treasurer again suggested budgetary control. The potential benefits were now clear, and all the executives took an active part in operating the new system.

Striking while the iron is hot. This mode calls for prompt action while a situation is propitious. When the sales manager of a chemical company decided to retire because of ill health three years before the normal retirement age, simply replacing him would have been relatively easy. But because several readjustments in the whole sales-management organization were due, the president seized this opportunity to push through other modifications that would have been resisted if they had been initiated as separate, conspicuous moves.

Keeping one jump ahead. In some circumstances, being the leader is a decided advantage. The management of IBM followed this strategy when that company received orders from the Army for two electronic computers of advanced design. Although the engineering was incomplete and several tough production problems remained to be solved, the company decided to go ahead with the production of twenty such machines in order to lead its competitors in marketing this type of computer. The gamble was great for two reasons: 1) several million dollars were poured into the project, and 2) by seeking commercial orders, the company risked damaging its reputation if the machines could not be successfully produced. Fortunately for IBM, this tactic paid off handsomely, although at the time it was by no means clear that the move was a wise one.

Red herring across the trail. With this mode, a deliberate attempt is made to divert attention. The manager of a European office for an American manufacturer was a master in the use of this method. Whenever he had a sour deal or a tough situation to clear up, he would meet his colleagues in the home office, bubbling with enthusiasm about some new proposition with great possibilities. Once the home-office executives became intrigued with the new proposal, they had difficulty finding time to examine the trouble spots throughly. The resulting delay gave the foreign representative more time to work out of his difficulties.

These examples of confrontation modes carry us a long way from the rather mechanistic concept of programming discussed in the beginning of this chapter. They strongly suggest the need for some qualitative inputs in the framing of a program. The confrontation mode selected clearly affects the timing of the initial program, and it is often one of the considerations in making adaptive adjustments.

CONCLUSION

Having just reviewed in the preceding chapters a whole array of planning methods and problems, we notice that the complexity of the process stands out. The power and benefits tend to be forgotten. Actually, as experience amply

Figure 19–3 Various ways of moving toward the goal of racial equality. On each front, issues arise concerning the confrontation mode to be used and the pace with which to proceed.

demonstrates, using the resources of an organization to do the planning has potential strengths vastly greater than individual decision-making. Our task as managers is to use this potential skillfully.

Design of Planning Systems

To take advantage of the specialized knowledge, ideas, and energies of the various members of an organization, we divide the planning work (as we do other kinds of work) into bits and pieces. Planning in any except Stage-I organizations requires many people and much time. This gives us numerous inputs; but we must also develop ways to fit all these pieces together, and to ensure that our farflung planning team is pulling in the same direction.

The best-known mechanisms for achieving such integrated planning have been discussed in the last five chapters. Master strategy sets the mission; operating objectives spell out the goals for each executive, and serve as company values in making short-run choices. The strategy and objectives together provide the coordinated direction so essential to purposeful endeavor.

Then to simplify planning while taking advantage of accumulated wisdom, we create standard patterns—policies, methods, procedures—for dealing with recurring problems. Added benefits of this established social behavior are a dependable flow of information and an ability to predict and depend upon the actions of others. And by no means the least of our planning instruments are various programming techniques that tell scattered people how to fit their actions into a united effort.

Interdependence of Organization Structure and Planning Systems

Our organization structure significantly affects the particular form of planning that will be most effective. For example, the more we decentralize a branch office the greater reliance we place on objectives and the less on rule-governed standard operating procedures. Especially as we move to Stage-III and Stage-IV structures, centrally established operating objectives become the dominant planning device at the corporate level. Thus, when such organizations define the role of a staff unit—say, public relations or industrial engineering—they often imply the way planning in that function will be done. Also, we have just seen that programming may stipulate who is to perform each step; yet the design of organization strongly influences the way programs are put together. Organizing and planning are not a one–two punch. Instead they are a kind of reciprocal motion, like the push and pull on a double-handled saw.

A recurring theme in both organizing and planning is that of freedom versus the regulation of individual behavior. As managers, we want unified effort *and* individual initiative, commitment to enterprise objectives *and* fulfillment of personal needs, use of expert judgment *and* creative imagination, coordinated action *and* individual resourcefulness. Fortunately, wise management can provide some of both. In many chapters we have indicated explicitly the factors a manager should weigh in deciding when the benefits of giving individuals discretion counterbalance the advantages of regulation. But the choice is not easy, especially in view of changing values and expectations of the contemporary work force.

Fitting the System to the Situation

Throughout our analysis of both organizing and planning, we have stressed managerial options. The company's size, resources, technology, competition, and traditions, and the managers' personal values all affect the specific organization and planning arrangement that should be adopted at a given time. Much of our discussion has dealt with alternatives available and factors to consider in selecting among them. The manager of the future, we believe, will have to be highly flexible in adapting his management design to changing requirements.

One of the unsettling factors in most situations is intraorganization politics —the topic of the next chapter.

FOR CLASS DISCUSSION

1) a) "The people who develop programs should be the same people who will be responsible for carrying them out. This is the only way to get real accountability and realism!"

   b) "Programs should always be written by staff or by those one level higher than whose who will be responsible for carrying them out. This is the only way to get real objectivity and completeness."

   With which of these two statements do you more nearly agree? Under what conditions might each be right?

2) In what ways will the degree of decentralization influence the way in which the basic steps in programming are taken and coordinated?

3) How should a manager determine when to develop a contingency program rather than write a more flexible plan that allows those who must implement it to make on-the-spot adjustments if circumstances require?

4) "Since all good programs must sooner or later be stated in budget terms, the controller's office should have primary responsibility for determining the form of the program and overseeing its development." What do you think of this suggestion from the controller of a large multinational company?

5) Contingency plans can be expensive to develop and may require a costly monitoring system to determine whether and when to activate them. To minimize the expense, what are the two most important factors to consider when determining whether to build a contingency program? Relate your answer to material in Chapters 13 and 14.

6) You have been asked by the mayor of Suburbia, Illinois, population 7,000, to organize and direct a one-day outing for the town's children. The mayor would like to hold the outing in a state park some 25 miles from town and agrees

to put up $1,500 to cover the cost of food, transportation, and other expenses. *a*) Set up a program for carrying out this assignment, indicating where and how you have employed each of the six basic steps in programming. *b*) Illustrate how you might reduce the amount of detailed planning you would face by delegating projects to townspeople willing to help. *c*) What schedules would you have to devise to make the outing run smoothly? *d*) How would you provide for the possibility of rain or a larger turnout then estimated?

7) Planning is meaningless without accurate predictions about the future. Yet with accurate predictions, anyone can develop good plans. Do you agree with all or any part of this statement? Discuss.

8) In what ways must techniques designed to test the soundness of single-use plans differ from those used to test the soundness of standing plans?

Cases

For cases involving issues covered in this chapter, see especially the following. Particularly relevant questions are listed after each case.

FOR FURTHER READING

Argenti, J., *Systematic Corporate Planning.* New York: Halsted Press/John Wiley & Sons, 1974.

A step-by-step process of planning to reach a company profit goal.

Bower, J. L., "Planning and Control: Bottom Up or Top Down." *Journal of General Management,* Spring 1974.

Excellent summary of the tie between the strategy and the capital-allocation process in diversified companies contrasted with conglomerate companies.

Mann, R., ed., *The Arts of Top Management.* New York: McGraw-Hill Book Company, 1971, Chapter 20.

Good, nontechnical discussion of the use of project management.

Scheck, A., "A Death in the Bureaucracy: The Demise of Federal P.P.B." *Public Administration Review,* March 1973.

Describes forces leading to the ineffectiveness and abandonment of "Planning, Programming, and Budgeting" as a government-wide planning technique—despite the enthusiasm with which it was adopted only a few years earlier.

Vancil, R. F. and P. Lorange, "Strategic Planning in Diversified Companies." *Harvard Business Review,* January 1975.

Describes planning steps in moving from broad corporate strategy to action programs for the operating divisions of a diversified company.

Intraorganization Politics

POLITICS IN COMPANY DECISION-MAKING

No exploration of managerial decision-making is complete without considering internal company politics. Having examined the rational individual approach and the formal organization approach, we now turn to the impact of intraorganization politics on choices managers make.

A constructive way to think about internal political maneuvering is as a modification, or additional dimension, of the more official decision-making structure described in the last five chapters. In other words, the political process takes place within an established planning system; it modifies the way the planning system actually works, but it is not a substitute for such a system. So, as we look more closely at the main features of internal politics, keep in mind that the setting is an established organization that encompasses a planning mechanism with its objectives, policies, programs, and standing procedures.

For some writers "politics" is a dirty word. E. E. Jennings, for instance, implies that company politics are "devious, indirect, and underhanded." [1] Political action is often treated as the antithesis of organization development.[2] In contrast, for a political scientist, political behavior is a normal, essential element in "winning the consent of the governed."

---

[1] *The Mobile Manager: A Study of the New Generation of Top Executives* (Ann Arbor: University of Michigan Press, 1967).

[2] See A. J. DuBrin, *Fundamentals of Organizational Behavior: An Applied Perspective* (New York: Pergamon Press, 1974).

In the present discussion we treat politics as necessary and unavoidable, and consequently we must deal with it. However, from the viewpoint of effective management, political action can have both good and bad effects; so we should try to guide this behavior into those areas where it is a constructive influence.

Since our concern here is with planning within an organization, we will focus on the pursuit of individually held objectives *by doing reciprocal favors* and *by using power to reward or to punish.* This use, or definition, of "politics" sets aside the politics of external relationships—an important subject but beyond the scope of this chapter. To be able to harness intracompany political behavior, a manager must understand the:

1) Distinguishing features of internal politics
2) "Causes" and coalitions
3) Relation of politics to rational and bureaucratic decision-making
4) Channeling of political behavior

DISTINGUISHING FEATURES OF INTERNAL POLITICS

Exchange of Favors

Politics starts with the exchange of favors. As in the pioneer days when neighbors helped each other when either was in need, mutual assistance with a rush order or filling-in for a sick coworker is normal social behavior within any organization. In this process, implied obligations arise. If a person has

Figure 20–1 The exchange of favors in business is usually unspecified. Here, setting budgets and handling rush orders are presumably handled in a purely objective fashion. But if a production manager receives kindly treatment in his budget request, he is likely to ensure that the rush order of interest to the budget officer gets prompt attention; or perhaps the sequence is reversed. The favors may consist of prompt attention and sympathetic attitudes.

helped you several times, you are expected to help him when the opportunity occurs. Typically, in this elementary form, no attempt is made to precisely balance the good turns done; in fact, a statement that any direct return was expected would probably be emphatically denied. Rather, the practice is one of mutual helpfulness.

Whatever etiquette may require us to say, however, a person is expected to help his friend. Thus, if I have upset my normal shipping schedules several times to help you placate customers, I do expect your support in a negotiation with central personnel about a revised job evaluation. The subtlety here is the extent, if any, to which either you or I deviate from official instructions or professional conduct. Clearly, I can get things done faster and better if I have friends at key points where help is needed.

There is nothing inherently sinister about this kind of behavior, as critics of politics imply. Much voluntary coordination is achieved through trading of favors, and deep personal satisfactions arise from mutual helping. It is the amplification of the practice that *may* lead to negative complications.

Choice Based on Who Is Helped and Who Is Hurt

Each organization member has the opportunity, if not the necessity, to play one or more political games. In our jobs we all have some discretion to allocate our effort and to set priorities; and in many managerial jobs a person has great latitude in deciding what his organization unit will do. The way a person allocates his energies can assist some fellow workers and perhaps hurt others. His action or inaction, therefore, has political implications. Everyone from receptionist to chairman of the board has this political dimension to his behavior, for he is inevitably helping some people more than others.

People vary in the degree to which they act with political motives in mind. (Also, those affected vary in the extent to which they perceive an act as a personal favor or disfavor.) Some individuals concentrate on objective results and appear to be quite insensitive to who may be helped or hurt, while others become preoccupied with how their actions will be viewed by influential persons. Most of us are in between. A "company politician" is an organization member who chooses his actions primarily on the basis of who will be helped and who, if anyone, will be hurt.

Use of Power

The possession of power greatly adds to a person's political strength. Here we use "power" to mean the ability to supply or withhold something another person wants. For example, the receptionist has power to help (or hinder) a visiting salesperson to see the purchasing agent; the chairman of the board has power to make capital appropriations and to appoint people to attractive jobs. The ability to inflict penalties—such as restrictions on the scope of freedom or loss of a job—is the negative form of power. Clearly, if a person has power and is willing to use it in exchange for favors, he can generate a great support for moves he would like to see made. Even an advisor to someone with power has political strength.

Power is so important to political effectiveness that its acquisition becomes part of the game. The politically motivated person does things he hopes will place him in a powerful position; and once in such a position, he has added capacity—by granting or withholding favors—to increase his power even more. Consequently, the sources of power and the way it is used within an organization deserve very careful attention.

Sources of Power

Individuals can develop political power in an organization in a variety of ways. The more common ways include:

1) Formal appointment to a line position that by tradition or design gives the incumbent authority to make key decisions. For instance, the appointment enables one to add or withdraw products, select locations, grant discounts, appoint executives, promote and pay bonuses, select vendors, and the like. Clearly the more options the incumbent has—that is, the more decentralized and less constrained his job—the more power he possesses.

2) Opportunity to review and veto plans. Typical examples are a controller's authority to review budgets, a legal counsel's authority to review contracts, an environmental advisor's authority to examine ecological impact, and other staff—especially when they have concurring authority.

3) Direct supervision of the resources necessary to carry out essential steps in the plan. The person who supervises the troops in the field, the computer, the plant, or even the mimeograph room can help get a project done quickly and well, or his opposition can add to delays and mistakes. Personal indispensability is even more effective. A government official once remarked, "Let them pass all the laws they want as long as I administer them."

4) Access to, and especially control over, the flow of information that is needed to identify opportunities or problems, and/or information that tells what actually is being implemented.[3] With this knowledge a person can easily pass tips to his friends and embarrass his competitor.

5) Quick, direct access to persons with power, coupled with ability to influence them—a "power behind the throne." Usually this influential-advisor status arises through personal friendship and confidence; or it may reflect the advisor's active or latent ability to rally support from a pressure group—union, banks for a financially troubled company, or college alumni.

If a person with power from such sources as these elects to "take care of

---

[3] A similar power is control over "the agenda" of a key committee—some proposals are argued to death, others slide through in a last-minute rush, some are shunted aside.

his friends and punish his enemies," he can encourage considerable support for programs he wants to sponsor. Rarely is the power used blatantly; it is usually clothed with plausible rationalization, and may take the form of expediting or foot-dragging rather than open support or opposition. For instance, an announcement will explain, "This appointment is an exception based on unusual need," or "The proposal for a new plant is being sent back for further studies because of unexpected technological problems." Nevertheless, the political message comes through to those who live in the company society.

We should note that restraints do arise on the use of power for political purposes.

1) The formal managerial structure places limits on the use of power—as we shall see in the closing section of this chapter.

2) Favoring one person often deprives another, and an individual in power soon faces the dilemma of whom to help. The "art" of politics lies in aiding as many people as possible in ways they feel important without seriously antagonizing anyone.

3) Several persons are active in any political game, and in many situations they tend to check one another (though not necessarily in a way that benefits the enterprise).

Summarizing briefly, the distinguishing characteristics of political behavior within organizations are 1) the exchange of favors, 2) choices based on who will be helped or hurt—and the effect of this on returned favors, and 3) the acquisition and use of power to reinforce this "you scratch my back and I'll scratch yours" process. Innumerable variations in scope, method, and effectiveness arise, but these features will be found at the heart of all internal politics.

"CAUSES" AND COALITIONS

Political Objectives

Thus far we have discussed political behavior without reference to the motives of the politicians. Although a few company politicians are interested in power alone, most are strong supporters of a "cause." The cause is an ideal or goal—or set of these—to which the person is dedicated. In public life a cause may be better housing for blacks or tariff protection for local industry; within a company it may be higher-rank jobs for women, increased use of computers, keeping production concentrated in the Toledo plant, or a larger market share than the XYZ Company. Often the cause is tied to loyalty to one's department or profession.

With such a commitment the politician can proceed with zeal. The distinction between his personal benefit and the cause becomes fuzzy—if it is

TABLE 20-1 CAUSES THAT MAY LEAD
TO INTERNAL COALITIONS

Type of Organization	Examples
Military	Nuclear submarines
	Women in command posts
Church	Ecumenical movement
	Medical missionaries
Local government	Lotteries to support schools
	Family-planning clinics
Private business	Geographical dispersion of offices
	Addition of low-priced, fighting brand
	Retention of all production in U.S.A.

drawn at all.[4] He is still exchanging favors, making choices based on who is helped or hurt, and seeking power. But the criterion for whom to help and how to use the power is tied to the cause.

Moreover, devotion to a cause may be shared by other members who prefer not to take political initiative. These people become supporters of a political leader who espouses their cause (or uses symbols that they feel represent their interests). Although such support is normally passive, it does provide voluntary service and also potentially active backing, which the political leader can arouse in case of a showdown. Clearly this latent support strengthens the political potency of the leader who champions a popular cause.[5]

Forming Coalitions

A popular cause is often joined by other politicians. In fact, support from a variety of directions is essential for any complex endeavor. So *coalitions* are formed. Persons whose main interests may be quite diverse join such a tempo-

[4] Protecting one's career and advancing a cause are especially likely to be entwined. A person may demonstrate ability while advocating a cause; thus his career prospects are improved by successful promotion of a cause. Drawbacks arise, however. Powerful people may disagree with the cause, and any advocate may be damned—currently or in the future—along with the cause. Of course, we may support a cause only temporarily, vacillating according to our assessment of the feelings of executives who can affect our career. Carried to the extreme this attempt to curry favor with anyone in power will be interpreted as purely opportunistic and as lacking character and integrity. So, the person concerned about building his career has to select his causes thoughtfully and sincerely.

[5] For an early discussion of this phenomenon in public affairs, see H. D. Lasswell, *Politics: Who Gets What, When, How* (New York: McGraw-Hill Book Company, 1936).

rary alliance to support the cause. Members of a coalition do not give up their independence, and they may continue to differ sharply on some issues; but they do agree on joint action with respect to the cause.[6]

For several years the marketing manager of a furniture company had been recommending adding an upholstered line—but other executives were preoccupied with the expanding volume of dining and bedroom furniture. Then, when sales dropped, both the personnel and manufacturing managers joined the cause—the personnel manager to provide promotion opportunities for trainees, and the manufacturing manager to use the space and service facilities of a new plant. With this support, a decision to add upholstered furniture was made.

Coalitions are easier to form in opposition to a proposed change or to a person than for a positive action. Among people with diverse goals, we are more likely to agree on what we don't like. The dean of a school of architecture, for example, became intrigued with matrix organization. However, several of his department heads viewed the proposal as a threat to their domains and decided to buck it. Each kept raising problems and drawbacks to such an extent that the plan became surrounded by doubt and was finally dropped.

In a coalition, each member contributes his influence—and if necessary uses his power—to bring about the desired results. Most coalitions in companies are quite informal and spontaneous, although on major controversial issues the coalition leaders may systematically seek support and modify the proposed plan to obtain crucial backing.[7] By participating in coalitions an individual can extend the scope and impact of his political behavior.

RELATION OF POLITICS TO RATIONAL AND ORGANIZATIONAL DECISION-MAKING

Political Process Fills Some Gaps

We find political activity within organizations partly because neither the purely rational nor the organizational approaches to decision-making provide complete guidance for action. Gaps in explicit plans open the way for the trading of favors.

The rational–individual concept (discussed in Part Three) runs into diffi-

---

[6] This definition of coalition differs from that of R. M. Cyert and J. G. March in their *Behavioral Theory of the Firm* (Englewood Cliffs: Prentice-Hall, Inc., 1963) in its more limited scope and uncertain duration. Thus in our terminology, senior executives make a much stronger commitment to their company than merely joining a coalition.

[7] This (negotiation of an agreement among independent participants) is akin to "participative supervision." Although power is present in both situations, the participants do have an opportunity to influence the selection of action taken.

culty when it is applied to a dynamic, multidimension enterprise. Multiple objectives, at least at the operating level, replace the single overriding goal; even a single objective may have different dimensions, such as jobs that are both secure *and* challenging. So the criteria for making a choice are not clearcut. Also, although a means–end chain does tie a specific action to a general objective, there may be alternative routes that receive scant attention. And often uncertainty about the future environment or long-run results is so high that we must act on faith. All this leaves room for debate about the optimum decision, for plausible arguments can be advanced for several. And with strong-minded executives in a growing enterprise, timely resolution of such a debate may require a "political" action.

Nor does the organizational approach give full guidance on how members are to act. Everything cannot be planned; expense, rigidity, and external changes impose limits on the extent of planning. Moreover, delegating some authority helps build commitment and fulfills personal needs (see Chapters 3 and 8). To secure prompt action, we deliberately create several local power centers and then find that we cannot measure the use of that power against specified goals—at least in the short run. In addition, we often deliberately build conflict into our organizations (to ensure adequate attention to, say, consumer safety) and then encounter difficulty keeping our specialized units focused on some larger goal (see Chapter 9). Again, the absence of clear guidance opens the way for politics.

These practical limitations on our customary approaches to organizational decision-making create the arena for political behavior. Frequently, whether we like it or not, a single right decision is by no means obvious. Necessarily, you and I and a lot of our coworkers have some freedom in the choices we make. And in this gray, unspecified area politics will color, if not determine, the shape of company action.

When Harnessed, Politics May Have Beneficial Effects

The exchange of favors in its elementary form is a necessary ingredient of voluntary coordination. Such reciprocal give-and-take facilitates all sorts of helpful operating adjustments that are impractical to plan in advance. Although we may prefer to think that our colleagues are generous with their help whenever opportunity arises, reinforcement for that generosity comes from a recognition that failure to join in mutual help can have serious personal consequences of a political nature.

The credit analysts in a Chicago commercial bank, for instance, each follow a separate set of customers, but they frequently exchange industry and company data to help each other. If requested, an analyst will devote great effort to obtain information desired by a coworker. However, one analyst chose to "stick to his own accounts"; he felt that he had all he could do watching his customers, and could not take time doing someone else's research. As a consequence, this analyst not only failed to get cues and supporting data from other analysts, but his suggestions for improving procedures in the department were resisted—"We had fun shooting down all his bright ideas," explained another analyst—and he was socially isolated. After two years in the credit department he left the bank.

Politics also engenders other kinds of motivation. For instance, commitment to causes can create great enthusiasm and drive. Personal loyalty is likewise a practical motivator, and often a psychological need satisfier. Political behavior is by no means the only way to generate such feelings, but we should recognize this potential energizing force. Obviously, directing such energy toward constructive ends becomes essential.

Since political behavior is one of the facts of organizational life—for reasons already noted—it would be a mistake to overlook the positive contributions such behavior can provide.

Debilitating Effects of Political Behavior

Unless it is very carefully channeled, however, intraorganization politics can undermine the effectiveness of an enterprise. Four influences call for specific attention.

1) Pursuit of the personal goals of politicians (either self-selected causes or personal drive for power or promotion) usually detracts from the central objectives of the enterprise. To the extent that political action succeeds in diverting resources and/or blocking efforts toward central objectives, effectiveness suffers. Perhaps there is doubt about the wisdom of officially endorsed objectives, but that is a separate issue (discussed in Chapter 16). Internal politics tend to subvert resources, whatever the central objectives may be.

2) If internal politics escalate into a major power struggle, a substantial amount of attention and energy is devoted to the internecine warfare itself. "We spend more time outmaneuvering each other than we do serving the customer," one disillusioned executive remarked.

3) The company incentive mechanisms directed toward company objectives may be undermined by the rewards and punishments meted out by those with political power. And the more imprecise the company measurement-and-reward system, the more vulnerable it will be to counterproductive internal political pressures.

4) Politics often focuses on short-run tradeoffs. In this process long-run programs tend to be sacrificed because both the measurements and payoffs from long-range programs occur well into the future.[8]

[8] This disregard of long-run results can be mitigated to some extent by setting up "milestone" control points and offering strong incentives to achieving these intermediate goals. See Chapter 22.

CHANNELING POLITICAL BEHAVIOR

The preceding analysis indicates that, although some features of political behavior can be beneficial, there is serious danger that such behavior will dissipate the concerted effort that an organization is intended to deliver. What we need, then, are ways to harness and direct the energies of persons who have a bent for this form of "winning friends and influencing people." The following measures will move us a long way toward this end.

Sharpen Objectives of the Enterprise

Troubles start when political pressures pull away from the central mission of an enterprise. Consequently, a good place to start is to clarify objectives. The results sought by the enterprise (or department) and the balance between them should be clear and agreed upon. Then numerous supporting activities (and political maneuvering) can be evaluated in terms of their contribution toward achieving these goals.

Such defining of objectives is easier to propose than to do. Objectives are multiple and sometimes competing; they shift over time; the optimum way of attaining them is always uncertain; and in subdividing necessary work we often create conflicting subobjectives. Nevertheless, mechanisms exist in an organization (that is, in a well-organized bureaucracy!) for identifying the objectives which, for a given period, carry official endorsement. These must be articulated if undesirable political activity is to be flagged and checked.[9] With approved objectives known, we hope political efforts will be directed toward their achievement. What we want is congruence in the results sought by politicians and by the enterprise.

Tie Resource Allocations and Rewards to Objectives

The capacity to give or withhold resources and rewards is a foundation of political power. The key modification that we must introduce here is to structure the allocation and reward processes so that the best payoffs clearly go to people who are actively contributing to achievement of official goals—and not to mere political allies. Note that again the ideal arrangement is one in which political payoffs and rewards—as well as company rewards—support the enterprise's objectives because the same results are being sought.

[9] If an approved objective also becomes a political cause—or vice versa—then we have the best of both worlds. This can happen. For instance, in a publishing firm catering to commercial schools, modernizing the product line became a political cause as well as an official objective; and in a rug company, cutting costs so that the Yonkers plant could continue to operate had both political and official backing.

To tie approved objectives into resource allocations and rewards, these procedures and criteria must be carefully watched:

1) For standard, repetitive situations the steps to be taken to obtain resources and rewards and the criteria that will be used in allocating them should be known in advance. Thus, the procedures and the standards used in extending customer credit or in granting an extra week's vacation should be explicitly stated. Then individual discretion—aside from assessing the facts in each case—is reduced to a minimum. And there is little occasion for intramural politics.

2) Budget allocations, promotions, assignment to high-potential project teams, provision of R&D support, personnel quotas, and the like cannot be treated in the "programmed" manner as just suggested in 1). The possible alternatives and the criteria used to choose among them are too numerous and shifting to fit a single model. However, we can insist that decisions on such matters be made jointly and openly—that is, several executives and/or staff people should participate, opportunities for suggestions from even more people should be provided, and final approval should be given by a senior executive after he is informed of the disagreements or doubts of qualified people. Such open consultation provides opportunities to check political maneuvering and to test the compatibility of proposed action with central objectives.[10] In those situations where conflict has been deliberately built into the organization—to ensure adequate attention or to provide competition—decisions on resource allocations and rewards must be approved at least by a common superior who is aware of the inherent potential for "politicking."

3) Even more subtle is tying rewards to informal cooperation in achieving company goals. Cooperation here refers to the flow of key information, the energy applied to unexpected problems, a willingness to make changes that primarily aid some other division, the provision of minor but necessary services such as duplication and supplies, and the like. The measurement of such cooperation or the lack of it is difficult, and no specific decision warrants the kind of review suggested in 2) above. So a formal measurement-and-reward system is unwarranted. Nevertheless, persons who can grant or withhold such aid may use this power politically. Whenever possible, procedures and jobs that give people power to interrupt communication and work flows should be avoided, even at some extra expense, thereby reducing the potential for a strong political base. However, if power positions are unavoidable, then such jobs should be filled by individuals who are loyal to overall company goals.

   The underlying aim of these various arrangements is to create a situation in which "virtue is rewarded" and "crime does not pay"—virtue being decisions contributing to central objectives and crime being decisions calculated to enhance political strength even though they are dysfunctional.

Punish Deviant Power-Seekers

This is a secondary step. The primary way to avoid undesirable political activity is to create a setting in which the desired results are known and the

---

[10] We are assuming here that the senior executive is committed to company objectives and is not himself playing political games which are incongruent with company interests. Actually, the open participation of several people with different viewpoints also restrains a senior executive; if he indulges in personal politics many people will know about it, and the potential adverse consequences on motivation and morale will be so serious that the political gain may not be worth the price.

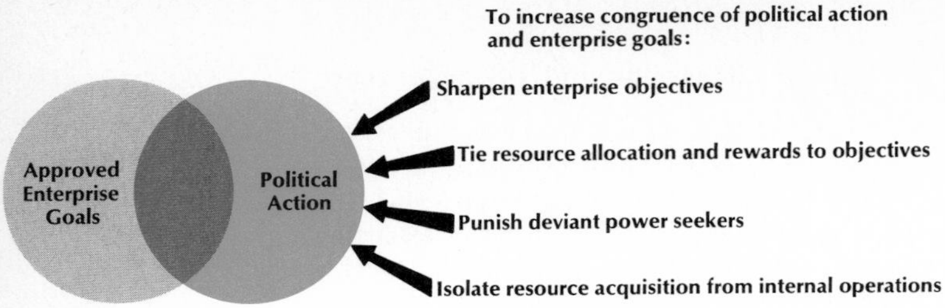

To increase congruence of political action and enterprise goals:

Sharpen enterprise objectives

Tie resource allocation and rewards to objectives

Punish deviant power seekers

Isolate resource acquisition from internal operations

Figure 20–2   Ways to harmonize political and company goals.

major sources of power are administered in support of those goals—as recommended above. However, in spite of these positive influences, some individuals will occasionally become so obsessed with promoting their private goals that they resort to politics that run contrary to company interests. Specifically, they reward and punish and start building coalitions for actions inconsistent with recognized company goals.

When such behavior is discovered, it should be promptly and openly reprimanded; if continued it should be punished by more severe measures—such as transfer to a powerless position or by dismissal. Every organization develops a climate—a set of traditions, mores, habits, attitudes, values, standards—that subtly shape behavior. Tolerance or intolerance toward independent power bases is part of this climate. And if a company wishes to avoid becoming infested with petty power-players, the practice must be explicitly frowned upon. Just as people sense (and anticipate in their decisions) the existence of political pressures, so too will they sense firm disapproval of private politics contrary to company interests.

Isolate Resource Acquisition from Internal Operations

Every company must attract a variety of resources—people of different skills, capital, materials and services, government support, customers, and the like. Although each resource group finds association with the company mutually beneficial, there is inevitably some bargaining over the terms of cooperation. And this bargaining is very similar to the political process we have been examining—an exchange of favors and mutual help, the development of relative power positions, and perhaps informal coalitions in concluding agreements.

If this external bargaining with resource suppliers gets mixed up with internal decision-making, the likelihood of deviant internal politics jumps sharply. For instance, if a banker is given a veto on expenditures or a union leader controls work assignments, each becomes a member of the decision-making apparatus; then, if either pushes for his parochial interest while internal choices are being made, we find ourselves in the same fix as with a self-centered politician.

An examination of numerous institutional arrangements for bargaining with resource contributors is not the primary focus of this chapter. Broadly speaking, to keep internal politics adequately channeled, arrangements for resource inputs should be set for a year or more; and once set, team behavior should be expected. After ground rules for contributing the resource have been established, integrated company action takes over. The concept of "no divided interest" becomes paramount. This does not mean that company decisions are indifferent to the need to reach future agreements with resource contributors; it does mean that the two categories of decisions are separate.[11]

CONCLUSION

This set of proposals for channeling intraorganization politics obviously proposes "bureaucratic" devices to prevent political behavior from upsetting the organizational model. The reason for giving priority to the organizational approach is simple. The political model lacks any modus operandi for securing concerted group effort toward common goals. Neither theoretically nor practically does it guide decision-making in a manner that would permit enterprises to survive and serve their social ends.

The political approach is nonetheless useful. It does help us predict what decision an organization is likely to make, as Allison has so dramatically shown. It points to potential deviant behavior that should be harnessed. And it suggests some political motivations that may be turned to constructive purposes if we are able to identify them with the organizational objectives being pursued.

Although we conclude that a manager should view intraorganization politics as an added dimension to the planning and organizing systems, the harnessing of political behavior calls for measuring and controlling mechanisms (to be considered in Part Five) and for understanding of and commitment to company objectives (to be considered in Part Six). So again the interdependence of various parts of managing stands out. The challenge for each manager is to put all these parts together in a way that best suits his own opportunities.

FOR CLASS DISCUSSION

1) "Politics is not only necessary but a *noble* art. It's only that politics gets done by politicians as contaminates the noble end it's all about." How do you interpret this paraphrasing of an old Yankee maxim on politics? Would it apply to corporate politics as well as to governmental politics?

[11] A major difficulty in government administration is the never-ending concern with maintaining support of the electorate. Being "responsive" to groups of voters often means that active interest groups can intervene at almost every step of a program. This assures us of a kind of protection but at the price of cumbersome and often indecisive action.

2) As business becomes more and more complex, is there more or less potential for politics to emerge from its traditional role as a medium of favor exchange?

3) "A politician's power stems less from what he legally can force others to do than it does from his skill in using his skills as a 'broker' to get others with more power than he to join him." To what extent does this comment, made by an early 19th century American statesman apply to today's governmental politicians? How about today's corporate politicians?

4) In general, do you feel that effective use of organization politics is more important at high management levels or among first-line supervisors?

5) Staff personnel are more frequently expected to use politics than their line counterparts. Why do you think this notion is commonly held? Review Chapter 4 and consider what can be done if someone sought to reduce staff dependence on politics.

6) "Politics is essentially the art of the *practical*. Managers, since they don't have to get elected, should be less concerned about what is practical and more concerned about what is *best*. I don't want politics in my bank." Comment on this from the president of a large bank.

7) Would politics be more or less useful in a matrix organization than in a centralized functional structure?

8) How may the absence of clear objectives and standing plans affect the political process within companies?

Cases

For cases involving issues covered in this chapter, see especially the following. Particularly relevant questions are listed after each case.

Petersen Electronics (p. 211), 13
Marten Fabricators (p. 316), 13, 15
Monroe Wire and Cable (p. 436), 14
Central Telephone and Electronics (p. 527), 9

FOR FURTHER READING

Allison, G. T., *Essence of Decision: Explaining the Cuban Missile Crisis.* Boston: Little, Brown and Company, 1971, Chapters 5 and 6.

Develops the third of three models used by Allison in his pace-setting study—government politics; and applies this model to the Cuban missile crisis.

Du Brin, A. J., *Fundamentals of Organizational Behavior.* New York: Pergamon Press, 1974, Chapter 5.

Describes various forms of "political maneuvering" in organizations.

Hinnings, C. R., et al., "Structural Conditions of Interorganizational Power." *Administrative Science Quarterly,* March 1974.

An interesting study for those who can cope with sociological jargon.

MacMillan, I. C., "The Political System in Business." *Journal of General Management,* Autumn 1973.

A practical model for analyzing political behavior of individuals within an organization and of firms in their economic and social environment. See also "Business Strategies for Political Action," in Journal of General Management, *Autumn 1974.*

Pettigrew, A. M., *The Politics of Organizational Decision-Making.* London: Tavistock Publications, Ltd., 1973.

Detailed study of the power and politics involved in selecting computer equipment in a large British firm.

Pfeffer, J. and G. R. Salanick, "Organizational Decision Making as a Political Process: The Case of the University Budget." *Administrative Science Quarterly,* June 1974; and "The Bases and Uses of Power in Organizational Decision-Making: The Case of a University." *Administrative Science Quarterly,* December 1974.

A sociological Study that may intrigue professors.

Zald, M. N., ed., *Power in Organizations: Proceeding of the First Annual Vanderbilt Sociology Conference.* Nashville: Vanderbilt University Press, 1970.

Leading sociologists look at the origins and role of power in organizations. Useful background for developing insights into intraorganization politics.

Not-for-Profit Note

for Part IV

PLANNING WITHIN
NOT-FOR-PROFIT ENTERPRISES

As not-for-profit enterprises grow, they face the same problems as profit-seeking companies in involving more people in the planning process and in extending the plans to cover more activities. And the same instruments we have been examining in Part Four lie at the heart of their planning process—strategies for adapting to the environment, operating objectives, policies and procedures, programs and schedules.

Multiple goals—that are perhaps also vague and often hard to measure—may complicate internal planning in a not-for-profit enterprise. Such a mixture of goals not only creates difficulty in making a rational choice (as mentioned in the third Note); it also tends to muddle the operating objectives of departments, sections, and subsections. Theoretically, the priority among various goals could be resolved by central management so that assignments to an orchestra leader or vocational counselor could be sharply pointed toward specific results. Instead, the multiple ends are too often passed along for subordinate personnel to wrestle with. Thus, *the uncertainty about just what is wanted permeates the entire planning process*.

When goal achievements are hard to measure—as is true in education, welfare, and many other not-for-profit services—we often shift operating objectives from results to the activities that we hope will create the desired results. For example, because measuring what students actually learn is difficult, we shift the operating objectives for a teacher to the number of classes conducted or of reports turned in. Actually, much planning in not-for-profit organizations moves even further back and *focuses on resources allocated for various purposes*—a dollar budget or the assigned personnel—simply assuming that the resources will be used for proper activities, which in turn will produce desired results.

When fuzzy objectives are combined with planning in terms of resources only, operating executives have considerable leeway in what they actually do. And such leeway permits *political maneuvering* for personal ends. It is a tribute to thousands of lower-level managers in not-for-profit enterprises that the potential for maneuvering is not often abused and that results in most instances are reasonably satisfactory. Nevertheless, if we can devise ways to apply the "management-by-objectives" concept to major operations in the enterprise, both planning and final results are likely to be substantially improved.

The use of standing plans—policies, standard operating procedures, and the like—in not-for-profit enterprises raises the inevitable issues of dependability and simplification versus individual freedom and flexibility. Where professionals hold dominant roles, as in hospitals and schools, many standard methods and procedures are dictated by the professions rather than enterprise management. In fact, professional traditions may be so strong that the enterprise managers have difficulty changing conventional behavior patterns to fit new service missions. The availability of *professional methods and standards* does simplify local planning, but it also imposes rigidity in adjusting to new needs, such as education of hard-core unemployed and modern birth control.

Another potential difference in planning within not-for-profit enterprises arises from the way operating income is obtained. When voluntary contributions or government grants are a prime source of income, the donors may *intrude into the planning process*. For instance, the government may insist on an "affirmative-action program" for the employment of minorities and women. A different kind of impact results if contributions are made only one year ahead; *long-range planning* then faces the added uncertainty about a continuing flow of income—both as to size and the restraints attached to it. Such uncertainty discourages long-range strategic planning.

These characteristics of multiple, hard-to-measure goals, high professionalization, and dependence on financial contributions—to the extent that they exist—do complicate planning in not-for-profit enterprises. But the ambiguity that they create also makes some form of systematic planning even more vital. The tie between such planning and control is considered in Part Five.

Case Studies

for Part IV

CASE 4-1
MONROE WIRE AND CABLE

"Two years ago we realized the biggest profit in the history of the company, but did we ever pay for it last year! This year will be a little better, but we have to find a better way to plan our sales and profits."

This statement was made by Henry "Hank" Simpson, newly appointed vice president of marketing for the Monroe Wire and Cable Company. It was December 8th and Simpson had just completed a meeting with the president and the vice presidents of finance and operations.

We have finished with a rush and we'll show market share and volume figures for this last quarter that are almost as good as those of two years ago [Simpson continued]. But our margins are much lower and we have a great deal of work to do.

THE COMPANY

Monroe Wire and Cable, as its name implies, originally manufactured wire and cable products. As competition in these markets intensified, the company shifted its emphasis to the steel-service-center industry. At present, with total sales approaching 80 million, 75 percent of its volume comes from the sale of basic steel products to customers whose needs do not justify their dealing directly with a major steel-producing company.

Essentially we are a service business [Simpson explained]. We do not produce any steel and perform only minor fabricating functions. We are really wholesalers and warehousers. We buy from the big steel companies and store bulk shipments in our five steel-service centers. Basically, these are warehouses that can do some minor finishing, shaping, and slitting work. Although we still make some wire rope, cable, and conduits, our real profit comes from sales of basic steel products. To make a profit we have to know what to buy, at what prices, when, and where to store it. Then we have to offer the right prices and service packages to the thousands of steel users whose needs are either too small or too specialized for them to deal directly with a steel producer. I work very closely with the vice president of operations to guide him on purchasing, storage, and fabrication. Officially, the president makes most of the key decisions on price, product emphasis, and so on. However, if the vice president of operations and I agree, we usually can get what we ask for. Occasionally we disagree on something and have to go to the president for his inputs; but we directly coordinate as much as possible.

Several steel producers have their own "service centers" and compete with Monroe. In addition, there are more than 30 independent companies like Monroe; some are national companies many times the size. Others, like Monroe, are primarily regional marketers with sales under $100 million.

Ours is a very competitive business [says John Eggleston, president]. We steel-service-center companies really survive because we can fill a variety of small or specialty customer needs that aren't big enough to be attractive to most of the big steel producers.

Eggleston indicated that the company had five main competitive "weapons" in their arsenal. They are:

1) Price (including discounts and deals)
2) Reliable delivery
3) Credit
4) Ability to meet specialty needs and rush requirements quickly
5) Ability to help "good customers" during occasional steel shortages

The problem [according to Eggleston] is that all of our competitors have the same weapons. None of us is big enough to establish any real competitive advantage. Further, we can't hope for some technological advantage to give us cost or other benefits. As a service business, our success depends almost entirely on whether our people do their jobs *better* than their counterparts with our competitors. This translates into get the best, train them, support them, and keep them. They don't have to make a lot of decisions, but their inputs shape our key decisions on price and what we buy. Then they make our decisions look good or bad depending on how well they interpret and sell them to the customer.

Sales personnel can modify price within a small range through discounts, and Simpson can do so within a wider range. The basic price and discount structure, however, is set by Eggleston. The president also makes decisions on any major changes in inventory, product emphasis, and credit policies. Although all of his subordinates agree that he listens to their recommendations and seeks their agreement on difficult decisions, he is a very decisive person. As one executive put it,

John encourages us to make our own decisions and to settle our differences before we come to him with recommendations. If we disagree on a big price issue or inventory decision, however, he gives each party about one minute to make his case and then he ends debate. Usually, it is the next day before we find out what he has decided.

Two years ago Monroe enjoyed its most profitable year. Though sales tonnage was up only 4 percent, profits on sales increased by 30 percent. Last year, sales tonnage dropped by 15 percent, and the company recorded a loss of three million dollars.

Simpson estimates that for the current year, sales tonnage will approach that of two years ago but that the company will show only a small profit. Before his appointment as vice president, Simpson attended a seminar on marketing offered by a leading business school. He was much impressed by sessions conducted by two professors and invited them to the company's offices to consider how they might help him develop a "strategic integrated marketing plan."

The professors agreed to spend a day at headquarters. Simpson arranged to talk with them and have them interview the following people (see Exhibit I):

John Eggleston, *president*
Grant Dooley, *national sales manager*
Richard Kopez, *service-center sales manage* (one of five)
Alex David, *sales representative* (one of 27)
Francis de Haas, *marketing planning manager*
Emile Kasian, *vice president of finance*

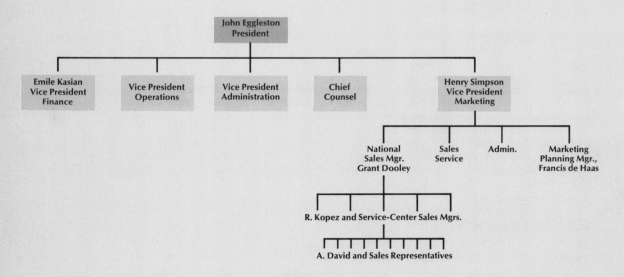

Exhibit I   Partial organization chart.

The following are summaries of these interviews.

Simpson, at 43, has almost 20 years experience at Monroe. Starting as a sales correspondent (order clerk), he worked his way up the sales-management ladder and was in charge of several service centers. After serving briefly as marketing planning manager, he spent eight years as national sales manager.

Thirteen months ago he was named vice president of marketing when his predecessor left Monroe to take a similar post with a larger competitor. The former president of Monroe had left several months earlier to become president of this same firm, and succeeded in getting Simpon's predecessor to join him. Simpson described the current situation at Monroe and his objectives as follows.

Bill Reed [past president] was a nut for planning and he tried to get everybody into the act. The trouble was that he was so dynamic and capable that he did almost all of it himself. Every division submitted forecasts, budgets, and profit plans for one and five years, but no one ever heard what happened to what he sent in. Reed used the plans to establish tough quarterly objectives, and performance was measured strictly according to these objectives. I'm sure Bill had strategies and longer-range plans, but none of us had any idea what they were.

Two years ago we found ourselves in a real seller's market. Apparently Bill decided to "skim" it, because we not only raised our prices but also shifted our emphasis almost entirely to our high-margin products. In the process we made a lot of money but really angered many of our customers. Last year they got their revenge. We had to cut our margins way back and handle a number of loss items. We lost market share and really went through a terrible period. This year we have fought to regain our market share, and while tonnage and sales-dollar figures will be up, our profits will be very low.

As I look back at it, most of our problems could have been avoided if we had had a marketing strategy and better marketing plans three years ago. I learned a lot from you [the visiting professors], and I want you to show my people the benefits of marketing planning and how to do it. We have a "marketing plan" for next year but it is really just a forecast. We show tonnage figures for each of our 24 basic product lines. We started with a 12-month breakdown per item, per customer. Then we divided by 12 and adjusted for normal seasonal fluctuation. Thus, we have tonnage figures for each item for each customer on a monthly basis. I had all of our sales "reps" estimate what they can do next year. Their estimates were reviewed by several levels of management, and my marketing-planning people, as well as by me. The president has bought our plan and supports me in my efforts to develop more comprehensive and more strategic marketing plans. I am sure we can count on him for support in whatever you and I agree on. What bothers me is that what we have is really just a forecast based on past trends and on our best estimates of what kinds of price and product-line changes we will make during the year. We really don't have any strategies *per se,* and none of the logic behind the numbers has been put down on paper.

JOHN EGGLESTON, PRESIDENT

John Eggleston, an engineer by training, rose to his current position 16 months ago after serving for four years as vice president of operations. Though courteous to the professors, he expressed concern about their ability to help.

My predecessor [he said] was a great advocate of planning. He constantly hammered home its importance. The trouble was that he talked about it but didn't really use it or do much of it himself. The rest of us sent up forecasts, budget reports, and so on, and he built a "library" of green books that were supposed to be our plans. We even used to send him a "prose plan," which contained the premises underlying our numbers. He seldom told any of us *his* strategies or objectives, however; he just asked for ours. After we went through the exercise of giving him our forecasts and plans, he would disappear for several days, then come back with what he called "the adjusted consolidated plan." It contained modifications of our numbers and supporting logic. If we didn't like it, we had a few hours to try to change his mind. But we seldom bothered because we learned that whatever he approved was, by year-end, no longer of any value in assessing performance. Within a month of approving the annual and five-year plan, he would start pressuring various people and, as a result, goals, budgets, and any sales programs we may have had would shift so much that by year-end they bore no resemblance to the plans he approved. He always told us how helpful our plans were to him, and maybe they were, but we generally regarded the effort as a ritualistic waste of time.

I want to get away from that game-playing. I want people to set their own goals—tough but reachable goals—and then feel committed to achieve them. I want everybody concentrating on gross tonnage. That's really all a salesperson can control, so that's all they worry about. Their bonuses are based on tonnage. We set prices and priorities at the top and then they sell. I can't stand the phoney numbers game people play in setting objectives and then justifying such absurdity. I like simple, realistic goals and hard work to achieve them—not elaborate green books full of plans. Unfortunately, I still get a lot of numbers I don't have much confidence in, but at least I no longer get the profuse justifications Reed asked for and then ignored.

It seems to me that most people use formal planning either to avoid decisions or to cover up mistakes. I'm not against it but I have yet to figure out how to use it. Now, you two "Svengalis" have Simpson convinced there is but one God and his name is planning. I'm worried because Simpson is a very bright guy who is desperately searching for some way to turn around a difficult situation. I'm afraid he is going too far in his enthusiasm for planning as a panacea. When I ask him what he really means by planning and what specific benefits he hopes to achieve, he really can't answer me. I think that is why he has asked for your help.

I don't want to puncture his balloon because, heaven knows, he works harder than anyone else I know. I will help all I can but I ask you to be very careful. He may well be overly dependent on you having the *answers.*

The president went on to note that he felt the sales organization did not need to learn more about strategic or long-range planning.

What they need [he continued] is more bread-and-butter knowledge of things like forecasting, communication, and professional selling. Simpson wants you to help them write a great novel, and I would rather he got someone to teach more of them how to spell.

GRANT DOOLEY, NATIONAL SALES MANAGER

Dooley, at 53, had once been Hank Simpson's superior. He indicated that he had great respect for Simpson and wished him well.

Hank is a man with a mission [said Dooley]. He is committed to improving things, and I will do everything I can to help him. For the first time, we used "bottom-up" forecasting under Hank's insistence, and our profit plan for next year will see us back to solid volume, market-share, and profit figures. I made sure that our salespeople know that they will really have to stretch next year. The numbers they sent up may be a bit optimistic in places, but with a little luck and a lot of hard work they can do it. Hank, Frank de Haas [marketing planning manager], and I went over the figures the service-center sales manager sent up; and though we raised a few and lowered others, the totals are just about the same as the grand totals approved by the service-center managers.

Dooley indicated that though he really didn't know what Simpson meant by strategic marketing planning, he was sure that

Your professors can explain it and help us do a fine job. You really have an open field because right now we really don't have any planning at all in a formal sense. I hope you can get Hank clear on what he wants us to do. Just let me know what I can do to help and I'll try. But I hope you will keep in mind that next year is going to be a very important and tough one. Our sales people took an awful beating last year and they need successes.

RICHARD KOPEZ, SERVICE-CENTER SALES MANAGER, CLEVELAND

The interview with Richard Kopez was a puzzling one. He repeatedly pledged loyalty to Simpson and recognition of the need for planning, but seemed to lack any real sense of what planning meant. At times he used the term as if it were synonymous with forecasting, at other times he described budgets and/or tonnage objectives as plans. When asked why he felt planning to be so important, he said,

It is the only way to keep us from getting into trouble by constantly changing signals. Right now, we never know for sure what prices we will be quoting next week. Our priorities are constantly being changed—we push one product, then another. Our inventory records are awful. I spend half my time on the phone with other service-center managers, trying to find out who has what, and making swaps. The marketing-planning people should be doing all this but, frankly, they spend most of their time working with our sales representatives on big accounts or trying to shift and expedite orders with our purchasing and operations people. If we had comprehensive strategic planning, we wouldn't have all this scrambling confusion. I'm really hoping that you people can help us. We need it.

ALEX DAVID, SALES REPRESENTATIVE, CLEVELAND

David was one of seven men and one woman working as sales "reps" in Cleveland.

This planning stuff is really new to most of our people [he said]. I just finished my BBA last year, so I have had a lot of it. Maria Gonzalez and I were the first college graduates to be hired for this center. A few of the guys haven't even finished high school. They are mostly all good salesmen, but they don't understand planning like I do. They learned the hard way and most of them still make sales by doing a lot of bull-throwing, drinking with purchasing agents, and getting tickets to games and things. They don't know how to build a proprietary relationship between our organization and the customers, but they do hustle. Last year, apparently, they really got burned and this year has been a wild one; but they tell me next year will be a good one.

Although they haven't really gotten used to Maria, they have helped me a lot. Six weeks ago we had to put together a forecast, customer by customer, product by product, for next year. Even with fewer accounts than the rest, I had a rough time. I couldn't figure out how to do it without any price, discount, credit, delivery, or priority policies; but they showed me how to use past practices to work up a reasonable forecast. Then they helped me adjust the numbers to come out at levels that would be acceptable at headquarters.

FRANCIS DE HAAS, MARKETING PLANNING MANAGER

Francis de Haas labeled himself "a survivor."

I'm not a hero [he said]. I guess I'm just not sure about the hereafter. My philosophy is to do the best I can and not expose any vital organs. At 57, I have outlasted a lot of the hotshots in this organization, and I expect to be here until *I* am ready to retire. Simpson's predecessor was a "scrambler." He filled out all the planning forms for Reed and I helped him. Then we found out what Reed wanted and we got it. I have four product planners working for me, but they are really our top salespeople, not planners. Sixty percent of their time is spent traveling around to our service centers and calling on key accounts with the sales "reps." Forty percent of the time they spend expediting orders at headquarters or with service-center operations people. The rest of their time they spend on planning.

Simpson says he wants us to help him do more strategic integrated marketing planning. He probably knows what *he* means by this, but I don't. I hope you guys can help him clarify to us old country boys what he wants, because I know everyone would like to help him. By the way, have you spoken to Mr. Eggleston yet? He is someone we have all known for years, but becoming president sometimes changes people. How does he feel about all this strategic planning? I'm sure he can help you if you figure out what he is looking for.

EMILE KASIAN, VICE PRESIDENT OF FINANCE

It was late in the day when the professors met with Kasian. He greeted them warmly in his office, reaching over a cluttered desk to shake their hands.

Year's end is a frantic time [he said], but we always survive it. I hear you are in to give Hank a hand by teaching his people to plan. Good. They really need it. Only yesterday I reviewed his profit plan with him and John Eggleston. It isn't a plan at all; it's just a forecast. He has a set of figures down, product by product, for each account in each center. It really must have taken a lot of time to write up, but it's laughable to read. I'm sure they will hit some of their forecasts, but most of his "plan" is nothing more than unduly optimistic extrapolations. I asked him why, in several cases, he is assuming market-share figures for customers or products that he has never reached before. I didn't get any real answers.

It's a shame, but I think he is playing games with us. John Eggleston is a real "stretch man." If he expects you to reach 300, he insists that you accept 330 as your objective. Then he says to himself, "Maybe they can even reach 310 if they think I want 330." In that respect, he is just like his predecessor, Bill Reed. I think Henry realizes this because he brought in promises that are even higher than Eggleston could hope for.

Next week I hope to sit down with the president and help him adjust the profit plan and set more realistic targets for our internal-planning purposes. It would be crazy to peg our financial, purchasing, and operations planning to these marketing figures. I use to help Reed in the same way, but it would be nice to stop all this game-playing. If Henry would only take a more realistic, hardnosed approach with his people, I wouldn't have to adjust all his figures.

If nothing else, I hope you can help him come up with more realistic forecasts. Everyone will benefit.

CONCLUSION

At six-thirty P.M. the professors waited in Simpson's office for him to return from a meeting with a large customer. They were reviewing their notes and considering what to suggest to Simpson when he arrived, he observed,

Well, I hear that you have had a busy day. I'll be glad to set up other interviews for tomorrow if it would help but, first, perhaps you can give me some dates for our first planning workshop. I was hoping that we could get all of our key people together next month for a few days and have them work with you on developing strategic-marketing approaches for our key markets.

FOR DISCUSSION AND REPORT-WRITING

Organizing: Structural Design

1) If the president wished to push "profit-center" responsibility down to individual service centers, what changes in organization structure would be necessary? Consider how he would provide relative autonomy for the service-center managers and still enjoy the benefits of high-level coordination of operations and marketing.

2) Would it be 1) possible and 2) desirable to organize individual service centers as compound work groups or on a matrix-management basis?

444

PART IV
Planning:
Decision-Making
in an Enterprise

Human Factors in Organizing

3)   Discuss the nature of Kasian's power as opposed to his formal authority. What is (are) the source(s) of this power? If Simpson succeeds in developing sound market-planning systems, how may Kasian's 1) power and 2) authority change?

4)   How may the changing demands on service-center sales representatives affect the job descriptions and person specifications for these positions?

5)   Which of the people working in Simpson's division do you feel can be most helpful to him in accomplishing the tasks he must perform? Why?

Planning: Elements of Rational Decision-Making

6)   Draw a means–end diagram to show the relationships among the several problems that Simpson is trying to solve. Which of these should he tackle first? Why?

7)   What are the strengths and weaknesses of the process by which the president makes decisions on price and purchasing when his subordinates do not agree?

8)   Reed's decisions to "skim the market" and focus only on profitable items obviously involved risks. How should someone in Reed's position assess these risks and factor them into his decisions?

Planning: Decision-Making in an Enterprise

9)   Before Simpson can expect to develop better marketing plans, what should be "given" to him by Eggleston?

10)   What do you think of Eggleston's stated approach to setting objectives? How does it compare with Kasian's description of Eggleston's approach?

11)   What effect is Kasian's "help" in adjusting sales forecasts likely to have on developing unified plans?

12)   If Eggleston wished to arbitrate fewer debates between marketing and operations, what standing plans should he develop and pass down the line?

13)   In what ways will success in upgrading the quality of those working as service-center sales representatives affect the need for and type of standing plans developed by Simpson and Dooley?

14)   What would have to be included in Simpson's "plans" to convince Kasian that they were real plans and not merely forecasts?

15)   (Summary Report Question: Part Four) Develop a formal marketing-planning system for Simpson to implement. Indicate what the key elements of this system should be and who should carry out each key step in what sequence. Be certain to indicate also how the key elements should be consolidated.

Controlling

16)   If Kasian's description of how Eggleston develops key objectives is accurate, how should Eggleston measure and evaluate results versus the plan?

17) In what ways would more detailed marketing plans 1) facilitate and 2) complicate control of marketing operations?

Activating

18) How may Simpson's efforts to involve sales representatives more fully in developing marketing plans affect the potential for his getting commitment to these plans from the sales representatives?

19) For which aspects of the sales representatives' jobs should Simpson "settle" for compliance rather than seek commitment? Why?

20) How will your answer to question 19 affect the choice of communication patterns between Simpson and Kopez? Between Kopez and lower levels?

Summary Question for Solution of the Case as a Whole

21) What advice should the "consultants" give to Simpson? Be specific about what they should help him to do and how they should help him do it. Are there specific things they should advise him *not* to do at this time? Why?

CASE 4-2
GRAHAM, SMITH, & BENDEL, INC.

INTRODUCTION

The Graham, Smith, & Bendel organization is a highly respected management-consulting firm. Though not among the industry leaders, in gross billings GSB has a highly impressive list of past and present clients. For more than 30 years, under the direction of William Graham, GSB had been a profitable but conservative consulting firm.

Our fees are a bit higher than our competitors' [Graham said], but our clients know we will not take on an assignment unless we have the expertise to do it right. We have been very cautious when adding staff, and we bring them along slowly until we and our clients are confident that they have proved themselves ready.

While their competitors were expanding rapidly during the 1960s, GSB refused to recruit inexperienced staff. They frequently turned down assignments rather than add "unproven" staff to do the work. As a result, the 1970s found GSB with a solid profit picture but with slow growth and a declining market share.

At the time of his retirement two years ago, 11 functions reported directly to Graham. Basic consulting services were grouped in five departments. Each was headed by a senior consultant, who reported to Graham. In addition, six service departments also reported to the president.

Before his retirement, Graham named Aaron Nettles as his replacement. Nettles, 59, has been with the firm for 27 years and was director of consulting projects, which deals with marketing issues.

AARON NETTLES, PRESIDENT

Mr. Graham was a consultant's consultant [said Nettles]. He headed up a number of our key account projects even while running the business. His secret was his ability to find good people, groom them slowly, and then give them almost complete freedom to do their job. Once he felt you were ready, he told you explicitly what objectives he wanted met, listened, altered them if you made a good case, and then gave you autonomy. If you did well, you heard from him only once a year to congratulate you and update your goals. If you did poorly, he would call you in and ask how he could help. If you could tell him, he would provide what you asked for and possibly adjust your objectives. Normally, if you did not show marked improvement within a year, he let you go. He followed this practice with all of his subordinates and expected them to do the same with theirs. He was extremely tough but very fair. Although some very senior people were fired in this way, I never heard anyone blame Graham.

With this highly decentralized style and his many talents, he probably could have had 50 people reporting to him.

Nettles went on to explain that, though he respected Graham, he was neither comfortable with Graham's style nor content with slow growth. Within six months, he acquired two smaller consulting firms. One, Executive Recruiting and Placement, was regarded as an ethical and effective management-search firm, which operated on a regional basis from Los Angeles. The second, Arista, Inc., was also a highly regarded firm that specialized in sophisticated research and engineering studies. With its headquarters in Cambridge, Massachusetts, and offices in Houston, Texas and San José, California, Arista had a growing reputation in high-technology industries. About three months ago, Nettles acquired Filer Associates, a New York-based market-research firm. Filer, highly regarded for the quality and integrity of their work, had become overextended and resisted laying off personnel during recent slow periods. As a result, they were close to bankruptcy when they agreed to join GSB.

Although all three acquisitions were made by exchange of stock, Nettles felt that the firm would have to accelerate its growth and generate more volume and profits. As he stated,

We have an excellent reputation and great opportunities to grow. Mr. Graham built an outstanding group of people but never really tried to capitalize on what he built; his view was that our sales promotion should be as "professional" as an M.D. I believe we must seek to make fuller use of the talents of our three new divisions, and we have to get more synergy out of our existing groups.

REORGANIZATION

After the Filer acquisition three months ago, Nettles announced a major reorganization. Three long-service GSB consultants, Shamtun, Reldan, and Leon, were named vice presidents and put in charge of groups that had hitherto reported directly to the president (see Exhibit I). In addition, several service activities were divided into smaller departments.

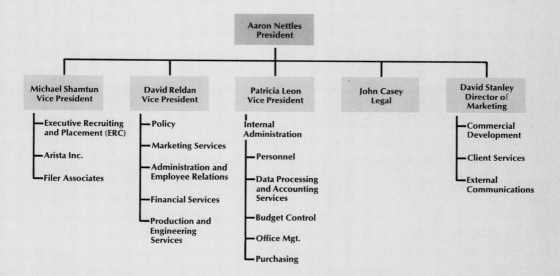

Exhibit I   Partial organization chart.

I want to maintain our decentralized structure, but I also want more coordination among key departments and more time to devote personally to key accounts [Nettles explained]. When we get a project it usually falls within the scope of one of our five consulting departments (policy, marketing, administration, finance, or production and engineering). It is assigned to a senior consultant from that area and he builds a project team. He may draw on people from other areas by checking with their department heads. This works pretty well, but with Reldan heading up all five groups, he can save me a lot of time overseeing the makeup of key project teams and balancing workloads.

I also expect Reldan to get more business from our current customers. Frequently, for example, while working on a financial project with a client, the potential for a marketing or personnel project will emerge. In the past, our people were virtually conditioned not to seek such a project for another group within our firm. Mr. Graham felt this was "solicitation" and not ethical. "If the client needs more work and feels we can handle it," he used to say, "then he will invite us to make a proposal." We have missed too many opportunities this way.

DAVID STANLEY, DIRECTOR OF MARKETING

To assist Reldan and Shamtun in marketing GSB services, Nettles named David Stanley to the new position of director of marketing. Stanley is a relative newcomer at GSB, having been brought in less than two years ago by Nettles. Stanley, at 37, had been a professor of marketing at several leading business schools before accepting Nettles' offer to join GSB.

I had hoped Stanley would become head of our client-marketing group [Nettles said], but he had problems with some of our older consultants. They are slow to accept a newcomer and a few regarded him as too much of an academic. It was really unfair stereotyping on their part. I have watched Stanley and he will make a first-rate consultant. Dave Reldan didn't want him to head up his marketing group, though; so I put Stanley in charge of our firm's personal-marketing efforts. This is a new job and it will be up to Stanley to make it work.

Stanley has one man and one woman working for him who carry out commercial-development activities.

They do some missionary selling with prospective clients [Stanley said], but their main function is to work with our consultants and our acquisitions and to help them develop and sell proposals to existing clients.

Stanley also has a small client service and an external-communications department under him. But he considers his most important responsibility to be his post as chairman of the New Business Committee, which was created by Nettles at the time of the reorganization.

NEW-BUSINESS COMMITTEE

To foster greater interchange of ideas within the firm and to promote new business, Nettles has asked David Stanley to chair this committee. The head of each of the five consulting groups under David Reldan also serves on this committee. In addition, one representative from each of Shamtun's three divisions was designated by Shamtun. Since GSB's headquarters are in New York, of Shamtun's people only the representative from Filer attends the committee's fortnightly meetings. The representatives of Executive Recruiting and Arista are kept informed of committee work and are expected to attend three major meetings held in March, September, and December.

In addition to these, Patricia Leon, vice president of internal administration, is also a member of this ten-person committee.

I wrote a memo to each member as soon as the committee was announced three months ago [Stanley explained]. In it I laid out two basic objectives and suggested some procedural guides. But I left things open until we met and sorted things out face to face.

The two basic objectives stated in the memo were:

1) To facilitate communication among organizational units with an eye to sharing successful techniques and helpful data.

2) To develop an integrated mission for business that will foster growth greater than the sum of what is possible in individual segments.

So far [Stanley observed], I am getting nowhere. Over the last three months, 11 meetings have been scheduled, but three were cancelled because key people were out of town on client business. Of the eight we held, only our last one included all ten members, and that was the biggest fiasco of all. I prepared a detailed agenda and asked each representative to be prepared to make a one-hour report on his department's plans and opportunities for synergy. They had all agreed to do their homework, and I blocked out two days to give us ample time to hear and criticize each unit's inputs.

I was optimistic that we would really develop the basis for a more integrated marketing approach because our earlier two meetings generated a lot of good discussion. These previous two meetings dealt strictly with exchange of techniques, and everyone there said they got a lot out of them. As soon as we shift from information to planning, however, they clam up.

I'll bet that half of the people from Reldan's group hadn't spent more than ten minutes preparing their presentations. It was particularly embarrassing because it was the first meeting the Arista and Executive Recruiting representatives attended; and they had both put a lot of time into their presentations, even if they were more descriptive than prescriptive.

I specifically asked Reldan to assign the heads of each of his five groups to this committee to get their commitment, and he went along. Perhaps they are just too busy and I ought to get them either to name an alternate or send their junior people to the fortnightly meetings.

Then the top people need come only to the three meetings attended by Arista and Executive Recruiting. Perhaps I could get more debate and honest exchange of ideas from their subordinates. Reldan's department heads virtually refuse to dig in and criticize one another's operation. Nettles is looking to me to generate a lot of new business from existing clients, and I know I can do it if these people would take off their department hats and try to think in terms of the whole organizaion. He promised to help when he gave me this job and I certainly need it. It's just that I'm not sure what to ask for. He is very busy and has a lot of confidence in me. I would hate to let him down.

Following the most recent committee meeting, Stanley asked his two subordinates (who constitute the commercial-development department) to develop a list of planning possibilities which, if approved by Nettles, would improve GSB's marketing efforts.

They each developed a number of ideas [Stanley said], and then we discussed them and added some more. It was a real brainstorming session. Though we eliminated the wildest ones, the following list of ideas still needs further pruning before going to Nettles for approval. (See Exhibit II.)

EXHIBIT II
MARKET-PLANNING POSSIBILITIES

1) Codification of Marketing Techniques

A manual listing the marketing techniques that had been presented and discussed at previous committee meetings. Make this a looseleaf manual to encourage additions.

2) New-Business-Opportunity Reports

Require each project manager, before completing a major consulting project, to fill out a form (prepared by commercial development) listing and describing opportunities for additional consulting work. (No decision on whether Stanley or Nettles should determine who receives copies of this report and on who pursues each lead.)

3) Client-Review Meetings

Require each project manager to meet monthly with Stanley, Reldan, and Shamtun to discuss potential for additional business.

4) Market-Analysis Reports

Seek funds to develop a detailed market analysis for each of eight major industry categories.

5) Assessment of Internal Capabilities

Develop a detailed report on GSB strengths and weaknesses relative to the five areas under Reldan's direction and the three subsidiaries under Shamtun's direction.

6) Strategy Formulation Workshops

Get Nettles to hold several strategy-formulation workshops. Here, the top 12 to 15 people in the firm would use the results of items 4 and 5 (above) to recommend overall GSB strategy and specific planning programs.

7) Research and Publications Policy

Develop a policy that directs GSB consultants to seek opportunities, wherever possible, to contribute to business research and writing. These activities would be coordinated and evaluated by Stanley, though client clearance would remain with the project managers.

8) International-Expansion Policy

Seek funds to have market analysis carried out with regard to expanding GSB activities overseas. (At present all GSB work overseas is based on U.S. contracts and coordinated in the U.S.) Stanley would be authorized to study and recommend programs for greater involvement in markets outside the U.S.

9) Assessment Standards

Develop standards to use for evaluating how well each segment of the firm is meeting its market potential. These standards would be developed jointly by Reldan, Shamtun, and Stanley; then be reviewed, modified (if necessary), and approved by Nettles and administered by Leon.

10) Policy Clarification of Marketing Responsibilities

Request that Nettles carefully review the authority and accountability needed by Stanley to play a more active role in shaping policies and carrying out programs designed to generate new business.

As I reread this list [Stanley said], it seems clear that we can't push for all of these. I don't want people thinking I am trying to build an empire. On the contrary, I would rather that most (if not all) of the things contained in these ten proposals were carried out by Reldan's and Shamtun's people. I just don't think they will do it, however. Too many of the things we should be doing are foreign to the firm's history. The only written policies we have were last reviewed 20 years ago and deal with ethics of client–firm relationship and expense-account procedures.

Next week I will meet with my people again and try to trim this list of ten and assign priorities to the ones that remain. Then I will meet with Nettles and see just how far and how fast he is willing to move.

FOR DISCUSSION AND REPORT-WRITING

Organizing: Structural Design

1) What are the pluses and minuses of the GSB departmental structure in terms of "harnessing" specialized efforts?

2) Assume GSB were to seek further growth by establishing small offices and offering the five major services now under Reldan's direction. These offices would be located in Washington, Chicago, Los Angeles, Brussels, and Tokyo. a) What changes in overall organization would you recommend? b) Might the larger New York office be organized differently from the "branch" offices? Discuss.

3) How might a more complex structure, such as a matrix organization, fit GSB's current needs? How might it contribute to Nettle's growth objectives?

Human Factors in Organizing

4) How might differences in customs and roles between the subsidiary divisions and Reldan's group be dealt with? Should differences be a) maintained, b) encouraged to increase, or c) encouraged to decrease?

5) Indicate, in relation to question 4, how you would go about maintaining, increasing, or decreasing differences.

6) What forms of conflict may arise from each of the ten marketing-planning possibilities being considered by Stanley? In *each* case indicate whether such conflict is likely to be constructive or destructive.

7) Based on Nettles's objectives, does Stanley seem to fit the specifications of the person who should occupy the director of marketing job?

Planning: Elements of Rational Decision-Making

8) State Stanley's major problem(s) as a gap(s) between desired and actual or predicted results, and then develop a causal chain(s).

9) How many of the suggestions offered for "comparing courses of action" and "making the choice" apply to the decisions Stanley must make?

Planning: Decision-Making in an Enterprise

10) Should Nettles attempt to develop a written master strategy for GSB at this time? If not, indicate your reasons and when, if ever, he should do so. If you feel he should, indicate how he would go about developing and writing it.

11) If Nettles were to seek explicit profit goals from Reldan and Shamtun for each of their departments, how should he go about getting these goals set? Should he follow the same approach with each? If yes, why should they be the same? If no, how and why would they differ?

12) Consider your answer to question 11. If Nettles took your advice, how might his action help or hinder Stanley's tasks as director of marketing?

13) Which of Stanley's ten market-planning possibilities would result in standing plans? Indicate for each whether they are most nearly policies, standard methods, or standard operating procedures.

14) Was the idea of a New Business Committee a good one?

15) How, politically, might Stanley have acted to increase the success of his New-Business Committee?

16) (Summary Report Question: Part Four) Which of the ten market-planning possibilities should Stanley recommend to Nettles? Indicate which should have highest priority and the sequence and timing with which they should be instituted.

Controlling

17) For each of the ten market-planning possibilities, indicate a) which you consider standing plans and b) how controls could be developed to ensure compliance. What standards would be set and by whom? What measures would be taken and by whom? How frequently would they be measured? How would the results be analyzed, and who would recommend corrective action?

18) Which of the controls discussed in answer to question 17 would be most likely to evoke negative response from Reldan?

Activating

19) For each of the ten market-planning possibilities, if approved by Nettles, forecast Reldan's likely response.

20) Based on your answers to question 19, for which of the ten would you seek compliance and for which commitment? Where the forecast response differs from the desired response, what energizing force should be applied, how, and by whom?

Summary Question for Solution of the Case as a Whole

21) Based on your analysis of this situation, what action would you take if you were in Stanley's position?

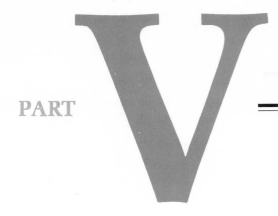

PART V

Controlling is the counterpart to planning. Less glamorous than planning and often annoying, control provides the measurement and evaluation of results that is so essential to ensuring that plans are not mere pipedreams. No plan is complete until we have designed ways of assessing its outcome.

Much more than recording history is involved. A good control system includes three kinds of controls: steering-controls, yes–no checks as work progresses, and postaction evaluations.

Also, controls are effective only to the extent that they influence people's behavior. So when designing controls we must carefully consider how those affected by each control will respond to the feedback provided.

In Part Five we shall first examine the basic elements of a control system, and then explore ways of integrating controls with a company's behavioral and formal management structures.

Chapter 21—Basic Elements of Control. Here we shall discuss selecting strategic control points, setting levels of desired performance, evaluating results on the basis of various kinds of evidence, and making reports that lead to timely corrective action.

Chapter 22—PERT and Budgetary Control. These two control mechanisms are of special interest, for they are companywide in scope. PERT provides coordinated control of the timing of diverse actions involved in major programs. Bud-

Controlling

gets give a comprehensive view of financial plans and results. Both concepts can be used in many circumstances, but we must understand their limitations as well as their advantages.

Chapter 23—Behavioral Responses to Controls. The idea of being controlled is repugnant to most people, even though they readily accept controls as a normal part of civilized living. We shall explore why people react as they do to controlling and shall consider how we can design and administer controls in order to engender a positive feeling about them.

Chapter 24—Integrating Controls with Other Management Processes. Here we explore interrelationships between controlling, on the one hand, and planning, organizing, and activating, on the other. We shall deal with a series of special problems that arise in keeping the various aspects of managerial action coordinated and integrated.

Controlling depends on, and contributes to, the other management processes —organizing, planning, and activating. Without organization, guidance would be lacking about who should make evaluations and who should take corrective action. Without plans to set objectives and specify activities, control would serve no purpose. Without effective activating, a whole carload of measurement reports would have no impact on actual performance. Consequently, we must carefully fit together executive action in all these phases of management.

Basic Elements
of Control

21

Plans without corresponding controls are apt to be hollow hopes. So, to make managers really effective, we must couple controlling with the planning that we have just discussed in the preceding Part.

The primary aim of controlling is to ensure that results of operations conform as closely as possible to established goals. A secondary aim is to provide timely information that may prompt the revision of goals. These aims are achieved by setting standards, comparing predicted and actual results against these standards, and taking corrective action.

Types of Control

In practice, controlling is often poorly done; conflict arises about when to control and who should do it. One way to avoid part of this difficulty is to distinguish three different types of controls:

1) *Steering-controls.* Results are predicted and corrective action taken before the total operation is completed. For example, flight control of the spacecraft aimed for the moon began with trajectory measurements immediately after take-off, and corrections were made days before the actual arrival.
2) *Yes–no controls.* Here, work may not proceed to the next step until it passes a screening test. Approval to continue is required. Examples are legal approval of contracts, quality checks on food, and test flights of aircraft.

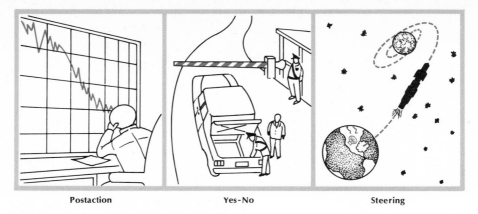

| Postaction | Yes-No | Steering |

Figure 21–1 Three basic types of control.

3) *Postaction controls.* In this type of control, action is first completed; then results are measured and compared with a standard. The typical budgetary control and school report cards illustrate this approach.

All three types may be needed to control a department or major activity. But it is steering-controls that offer the greatest opportunity for constructive effect. The chief purpose of all controls is to bring actual results as close as possible to desired results, and steering-controls provide a mechanism for remedial action while the actual results are still being shaped. Much of the discussion in the following chapters will focus on the design of good steering-controls.

Yes–no controls are essentially safety devices. The consequences of a faulty parachute or spoiled food are so serious that we take extra precautions to make sure that the quality is up to specifications. Avoidable expense or poor allocation of resources can also be checked by yes–no controls. If we could be confident that our steering-controls were effective, the yes–no controls would be unnecessary; unfortunately, steering-controls may not be fully reliable, or may be too expensive, so yes–no controls are applied.

Postaction controls, by definition, seem to be applied too late to be very effective. The work is already completed before it is measured. Actually, such controls do serve two purposes. 1) If rewards (a medal, bonus, discharge, self-esteem, etc.) based on actual results have been promised, these results must be measured and the appropriate rewards made. The aim is psychological reinforcement of the incentive scheme. The pay-off in this reinforcement lies in future behavior. 2) Postaction controls also provide planning data if similar work is undertaken in the future.

Phases in Controlling

Even though controls are placed at different stages of operations, as the preceding classification suggests, three phases are always present in each control cycle:

1) *Set standards that represent desired performance.* These standards may be tangible or intangible, vague or specific, but until everyone concerned understands what results are desired, control will create confusion.

2) *Compare predicted or actual results against the standards.* This evaluation must be reported to the people who can do something about it.

3) *Take corrective action.* Control measurements and reports serve little purpose unless corrective action is taken.

Regardless of what is being controlled, these elements are always involved.

Expense control, from the use of electric lights to the total cost of goods; quality control, from the appearance of a typed letter to the dependability of an airplane engine; investment control, from the number of spare parts in a repairman's kit to the capital investment in a fleet of tankers—all involve standards, evaluation, and corrective action. A closer look at each of these phases will help us design controls for specific purposes.

SETTING CONTROL STANDARDS

The first step in setting control standards is to be clear about the results we desire. What shall we accept as satisfactory performance? Usually we must answer this question in terms of 1) the outcome characteristics that are important in a particular situation and 2) the level of achievement, or "par," for each characteristic.

Characteristics That Determine Good Performance

An executive who wishes to control an operation under his supervision often finds that the work has several characteristics, and he must conceive of good performance in terms of these characteristics. A furniture store, for instance, found that it had to think about the following factors in appraising its credit department: the attitude of customers who had dealings with the department, the total credit extended, the operating profit earned on goods sold on credit, credit losses, department operating expenses, gross income from credit charges, net expense of running the department, and departmental cooperation with the treasurer, sales manager, and other company executives. It was decided that the credit manager had to perform well on all these counts if his work was to be rated as satisfactory.

In an earlier discussion of objectives (Chapter 17), we noted that companies with decentralized operating divisions have found that profits are an inadequate measure of success. In addition to profits, a number of companies are now considering market position, productivity, leadership, personnel development, employee attitudes, and public responsibility. It is, of course, possible to focus controls on one aspect of a job, such as current profits or market position. But to do so without first thinking through *all* the characteristics that contribute to good performance and without making provision for these characteristics in the control system is to court trouble.

Each time a manager designs a new control, he faces this question of what characteristics to consider. An approach that could benefit some jobs would be to give thought to these three matters:

1) *Output.* What services or functions must be performed? Perhaps each of these services can be defined in terms of quantity, quality, and time.

2) *Expense.* What direct dollar expenses are reasonable to secure such an output? What should be normal indirect expenses in terms of supervision, staff assistance, interference with the work of other people, and opportunities foregone to perform other kinds of work?

3) *Resources.* Does the operation require capital investment in inventories, equipment, or other assets?[1] Are scarce human resources or company reputation being committed? If so, effective use of resources should also be considered.

Par for Each Characteristic

Having identified the characteristics of good performance, we must then determine how high a level of achievement we desire for each characteristic. More precisely, what is a reasonable expectation, or par, for good performance? For example, pars for the credit department in the furniture store mentioned earlier might be as shown in Table 21–1.

TABLE 21–1

Characteristic	Standard
Attitude of customers	90 percent of furniture purchased on time, financed by the store
Total credit extended	Outstanding loans approximately equal to last 90 days' sales
Operating profit earned on goods sold on credit	$250,000
Credit losses	0.5 percent of credit extended ($3,500 in normal year)
Department operating expenses	$12,000 per year
Gross income from credit charges (above interest paid to bank)	$14,000 per year
Net expense of running department	$1,500 per year

[1] Although the cost of developing a well-trained corps of workers, a smooth-running organization, or a good reputation with outside groups does not appear on a company balance sheet, such assets do require investment in the same way that machinery does. Such investment is essential if future "output" is to be achieved within desired future "expenses."

For most performance characteristics, par is simply an ordinarily feasible achievement level. Variations beyond this level are usually desirable—such as output above par or expenses below par. But in special circumstances, such as the rate of production on an assembly line, there may be only narrow tolerance limits for deviation above or below the established par.

On highways, the speed limit is a single standard that is applicable to all drivers. Similarly in business, a single standard may be applicable to such things as quality of delivery service. But for many other situations we may adjust the standard for a particular individual or local circumstance. A branch manager of a national sales organization who tried this individualistic approach reports as follows:

Don't compare an individual to the group average, but rather to a "standard" set for him. I have tried this on quotas for growth and for new customers and during the current canvass, and the results are good. The salespeople are more quota-conscious than I have ever before known them to be. I find they will work much harder to make their own standards than they will to "beat the high man" or surpass crew average. Also—each one is much more aware of his own quota (through interest) and the total book standing than previously.

Securing flexibility through adjustment of par. In control, as in other phases of management, we have a legitimate need for flexibility. For instance, a firm may increase inventories if there is reason to anticipate a shortage of raw materials; it may cut its price to meet competition, knowing that dollar sales figures will be thrown out of line; during a depression it may decide not to cut employment in proportion to the drop in production; and so forth.

Unfortunately, "flexibility" is sometimes used as an excuse to disregard control entirely. Because the previous standards are no longer reasonable, there is a temptation to say that control is not feasible. A more sensible way of dealing with unforeseen conditions is to adjust par. The performance characteristics being watched, the measurements, and the reports continue to be useful; we need to change only the levels of expectation. As we shall note in Chapter 23, this is precisely the result of "flexible" budgets, and this concept may be adapted to many other control standards.[2]

Relating Results to Individual Accountability

Control standards are most effective when they are related to the performance of a specific individual. Thus both the person himself and his supervisors

---

[2] Both automatic and semiautomatic adjustments of par are usually based on a variation of a key external variable (that is, external to the domain of the person being controlled) such as volume, price, or wage rates. The original pars are based on a set of *planning premises;* and when these premises shift through no fault of the controllee, some offsetting revision of pars is called for. In a broader scope, this kind of adjustment suggests that when control is used for personal evaluation, the key planning premises should be identified and then *their accuracy* observed as well as the results of a person's efforts.

can know whether he should be praised or blamed. In addition, fixing accountability for a deviation helps focus the search for causes and thereby sharpens corrective action.

But accountability for a desired result is not always simply assigned. A company's investment in inventory, for example, is affected by purchases, rate of production, and sales. Each employee to whom one of these three activities is assigned looks on inventory from his own point of view, as does the treasurer, who is concerned with the financial strength of the company. In some companies, only one person, who has the task of coordinating these different viewpoints, is accountable for the level of inventories. In other companies, the task is divided: For instance, the sales manager estimates sales, the plant manager schedules production and indicates the quantities of raw materials he will need each month, and the purchasing agent decides when it will be advantageous to buy the materials specified by the plant manager. In such a situation, in which no one person is accountable for the level of inventories, standards may be set for each step. Then if there is trouble with inventories, we can ascertain where the system broke down.

An alternative to dividing complex tasks into separate steps that can be assigned to single individuals is dual accountability. When cooperative effort is crucial and contributions of each person are hard to distinguish (as in a surveying crew and in many methods-improvement studies involving both line and staff personnel), we may say that each member is accountable for the team result. The control then keeps the focus on results, with strong emphasis on cooperation.

Clearly, the establishment of standards for control purposes is heavily dependent on the previous management decisions on plans and organization. Specifically, objectives (discussed in Chapter 17) are the direct counterpart of "desired results"—the starting point in a control cycle. Similarly, the assignment of duties (discussed in Chapters 2 and 3) is the key to the assignment of accountability for achieving control standards. Theoretically, setting objectives and defining job duties need not be reconsidered when we set control standards. But in practice this is rarely so. Workable control almost always calls for refining and clarifying objectives and duties. Without fail, though, we should start with the plans that have already been developed. Then the process of developing standards for purposes of control is really a matter of refinement.

Checking on Strategic Points

"Desired results" have been urged as a good starting point for designing managerial controls. We now want to turn to several refinements of this principle.

1) To attempt to evaluate all the results of everyone's work would be very burdensome. Instead we usually measure results only at various intervals. For instance, a dairy farmer may measure his output only in terms of pounds of butterfat produced per week. Moreover, as we shall discuss in the section on

evaluation, sometimes only samples of the output are measured. The aim is to watch enough to keep track of what is happening, without going to the expense of watching everything. That is, the aim is to pick *strategic points* that will, at least indirectly, reflect the total operation. If results at these points are off standard, a more detailed check can be made of intermediate stages to find the reasons for the deviation.

 The president of an automobile-parts manufacturing company keeps his eye on four key items that reflect operations in the plant: total output, efficiency, back orders, and inventory. By watching the ratio of standard man-hours to actual man-hours worked every month, the president believes he can detect any major difficulties with equipment or with operating personnel, and so keep track of overall efficiency. The back orders indicate whether the plant is meeting sales requirements. The inventory figures show whether good deliveries and plant efficiency are being achieved by large accumulation. There are, of course, many other local controls, but the four points are what the president watches closely.

2) When we use steering-controls, we want to move before the final results have occurred. For this purpose, we seek out points to serve as warning posts. Here the aim is to *direct attention* rather than to evaluate. The Hilton Hotels, to cite an example, keep close tabs on advance bookings of conventions—one, two, or even three years ahead. With this warning of the ups and downs of business volume, they can undertake special promotions to fill in valleys. On a month-to-month basis, when it is too late to change booking volume, knowledge of advance bookings is used to expand or contract staff to fit the expected level of operations.

 In safety work, control is achieved largely through training in safety methods and through maintaining safe operating conditions. In other words, management locates strategic control points in the formative stages, and inspections are made to try to prevent trouble from ever arising.

3) By using yes–no controls, we are utilizing screening devices to catch serious errors. Actual results to date are measured, and work is permitted to proceed only if the results are satisfactory. Such controls may be placed anywhere in the flow of work at which safety can be checked—the earlier the better.

In many companies, requests for capital expenditures for such things as new buildings, equipment, and sources of raw materials have to be presented in writing with an explanation of why each investment will be advantageous to the company. The request then passes a yes–no hurdle. By controlling approval of the projects at this formative stage, the president or financial officer can exercise an influence that would be futile after orders are placed and contracts let.

Checking on Methods of Work

In the preceding discussion of control standards, we have emphasized the results of work rather than the method for accomplishing it. Even strategic control points at early stages are basically devices for anticipating results. This emphasis is consistent with our stress on objectives, in the earlier discussions of planning and decentralizing. Nevertheless, there are times when control over method is more expeditious than control over results.

Sometimes we set controls on work methods simply because it is more economical to watch the methods than the results. Diamond-cutting and quality control in the manufacture of spacecraft or parachutes are undertakings in which control will probably be exercised over methods as well as results.

Then there are baffling situations for which it is extremely difficult to know just how good results should be. Cancer research or negotiating with a group that is protesting ecological abuses are examples. In these situations we may resort to evaluating the method by which work was done.

Whenever control is undertaken, then—from the entire company down to the work of a single employee—we need to consider what kinds of results and what level of par to incorporate into our standards. And since busy executives cannot give regular attention to a complete array of standards, we should identify strategic points to watch: summaries of overall results, results of key activities, warnings of impending trouble, and—for some jobs—*methods* of work. One of the arts of good management is setting the right standards at the right control points.

THE TASK OF MEASURING

Once standards are set, the second basic step in control is the evaluation of performance. This step involves 1) measuring the work that is done, or predicting what will be done, in terms of the control standards and 2) communicating the appraisal to persons who search for reasons for deviations and take corrective action. Broadly speaking, control measurements seek to answer the question, "How are we doing?"

The specific methods of measuring results are almost as diverse as the activities of business. Because at best we could give only a few suggestive examples here, it will be more useful to examine some of the common difficulties in measuring for control and to note several promising ways of dealing with these difficulties.

Need for Ingenuity

Engineers are far ahead of managers in their ability to measure what is going on. For one thing, we have tended to rely on accounting far beyond its intended purpose and inherent capacity. To be sure, surveys of employee attitudes and morale, and Nielsen reports (which provide current data on the sale of goods in the grocery and drug fields by brand, region, and type of outlet) are steps in overcoming this deficiency. But great opportunity remains for improvement.

Actually, many companies have information they do not fully utilize. For example, an employment office may be able to provide a lead on labor costs long before these figures show up in accounting reports. A market-research department may be able to provide both control data and planning data. The information necessary for production scheduling can be used to measure productivity. These illustrations indicate that facts for use in control may be found in a variety of places.[3]

Leadership in product design was set as a major control point for the engineering department of one company. Because product leadership is very difficult to measure, the company decided to try to summarize personal opinion systematically. Each year a committee composed of the general manager, sales manager, chief engineer, and two outside experts try to agree on the following points:

1) The number of the company's significant "firsts" introduced each year versus competitors' "firsts."

2) A comparison of company products with competitors' products in terms of market requirements for performance, special features, attractiveness, and price.

3) The percentages of sales of products appraised to be superior to competition, equal to competition, or inferior to competition, together with corresponding market position and gross margin ratios of each category.

4) The percentage of company products in the total of machines used in the plants of the twenty most efficient customers in the country.

In spite of the high degree of personal judgment involved in several of these criteria, this company has substantially better control over its product development than before it undertook such measurement. As this example shows, the design of managerial controls can benefit greatly from ingenuity.

Considering Qualitative as Well as Quantitative Results

Because measurement is often difficult, it is only natural to use any available figures. This is to be commended. There is the danger, however, that those

---

[3] Auditing is concerned with control, but not the type of managerial control we are discussing in this chapter. A manager focuses on achieving certain results. Financial auditing, on the other hand, is designed chiefly to ensure that no skullduggery has taken place. An auditor deals with the accuracy of financial reports—be they bearers of good tidings or bad—and especially with making sure that there has been no pilfering of cash or valuable inventory and no fraud or embezzlement.

Occasionally the concept of auditing is broadened beyond the financial matters just discussed. If an auditor is asked to verify "proper execution of policies and programs," then he moves into the area of managerial control. Rarely is this a desirable arrangement. Measuring for managerial control is far from exact; it tends to be intimately associated with operations themselves; and its usefulness is enhanced by a cooperative relation between those who are making the measurements and those who are doing the work. Auditing, on the other hand, needs to be specific and objective, and independence from operating personnel is to be encouraged. In a well-run company, evaluating managerial control should have taken place long before an audit is completed.

characteristics of an operation that can be easily measured will receive far greater attention than their importance warrants.

An office-equipment manufacturer relied heavily on dollar-sales figures to control its ten regional sales representatives. As the sales manager was fond of saying, "The signed order tells who's on the ball." The representative in the Southern territory was an older man, and for two years before his retirement, he and the company had a clear understanding that he planned to settle down in Florida when he reached sixty-five. His sales held up reasonably well. But when he was replaced, it was discovered that he had neglected to cultivate new customers. He had called only on his old accounts, and even with them he had glossed over troublesome service problems and had failed to cultivate the younger people in the customers' organizations. Several years of hard work were required before the territory again produced the volume it should. This unsatisfactory condition developed because the firm relied only on the easy measurement of results. If other, more intangible, factors had been watched, the deficiency in the representative's performance would have been noted before too much damage was done.

The danger that ease of measurement will dictate what gets attention is even more serious in operations where quantitative results are hard to pin down. The public-relations department of a pharmaceutical company kept close track of the number of letters received as a result of the news releases it issued. "Letters received" became one of the department's few quantitative measures of performance, and soon public relations was issuing news releases written expressly for the purpose of creating a flow of mail. Unfortunately, although controversial subjects and hints that a remedy was being developed for a widespread malady did produce a lot of letters, publicity on these topics distorted the public image of reliability that the company wished to establish.

Besides public relations, another chance for quantitative and qualitative considerations to get out of balance is in expense control. Zealousness in controlling travel or telephone expenses occasionally causes people to pay as much attention to these minor aspects as to the results of the work.

Using Symptoms for Control

Just as the smell of smoke is an indication of fire, or bloodshot eyes and a haggard look at examination time are an indication of cramming, so in business we may use symptoms as indications of what is going on.

Employee attitudes, for example, are hard to measure directly and economically. Consequently, several companies have used such criteria as turnover, the number of absences and tardinesses, the number and content of grievances, and the number of suggestions submitted in a formal suggestion system. Under normal conditions, such factors probably do reflect employee attitudes. But we must exercise care in using symptoms as measuring devices, because 1) outside factors may cause a symptom to vary, and 2) when it becomes known that a

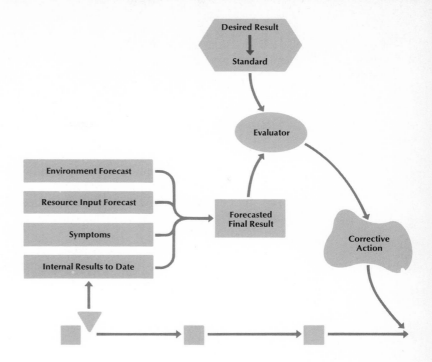

Figure 21–2 Steering-control is based on predicted results.

symptom is being used as a measure, it may be possible to manipulate the measuring stick—for instance, tardiness in one office may be low because the office manager is a tyrant and not because employee attitudes are good.

Using Predictions in Control

In steering-controls we often use predictions as a basis for corrective action. As with the use of symptoms, we do not measure actual results. But here the reason for using less-reliable criteria is our desire for prompt action. Customer inquiries may be used to predict a rise or fall in sales; a machine's vibration may be used to predict a breakdown; or grievances may be used to predict a strike. The prediction in such a case initiates corrective action; we don't wait for the predicted event to occur.

One of the large can companies has a control procedure that encourages corrective action based on predictions. A monthly profit-and-loss budget is prepared for each operating division and plant. Then, ten days before the start of the month, the various managers are asked to estimate how close they will come to the budget. Each prepares a revised estimate about ten days after the beginning of the month. A major advantage of preparing these two estimates lies in forcing the manager to predict what is likely to happen and to adjust his operations to current conditions. Because local demands for vegetable cans vary with the weather, short-run expansion or contraction of operations—and of expenses—is very important. Top executives do compare the performance of each division and branch against the original budget, but they give more emphasis to the ability of their managers to predict results accurately and take prompt corrective action.

Sampling

A familiar way of simplifying the measurement task is to consider only a sample, which is presumably typical of the whole. For example, the quality of most food products, from kippered herring to corn meal, is tested by sampling. And students are well aware that an examination is only a sample of what they know, just as office workers realize that in his periodic visits, their supervisor samples their behavior.

Sampling is better suited to some activities than others. If a machine set to perform a particular operation turns out good-quality products both when the run is started and at the end, we can usually assume that the intervening production has also been satisfactory in quality. In a check of routine sales correspondence, if a random sample indicates that letter-writers are using good judgment and diplomacy, a supervisor will probably assume that all the work is satisfactory. On the other hand, a one-hundred percent check is desirable for some operations. A manufacturer of hearing aids, for instance, may sample at the early stages of production, but will undoubtedly insist on a careful inspection of every finished product for performance before it is shipped.

Broadly speaking, to determine what portion of an operation should be measured, we try to balance the cost of incremental measurements against the increased value that might accrue from catching more errors. "Statistical quality control" is a special application of this general idea. When products are produced in large quantities, we can use statistical probabilities to decide when the number of errors is large enough to warrant stopping production and finding the cause. Substantial economies in inspection costs may result in situations where this technique applies. Unfortunately, the vast majority of managerial control situations do not involve the large number of similar actions that are needed for this refined statistical technique.

Personal Observations and Conferences

Even with all the measurements that we have suggested in the preceding paragraphs, a supervising executive still needs to hold informal discussions with the persons whose work is being controlled; and, at least occasionally, he should visit the actual operations. Anyone who has corresponded over a period of time with another person whom he knows only by letter, and then has an opportunity to meet and talk with him, knows that there are certain impressions that can be conveyed only in face-to-face contact, personal observation, and conversation.

More importantly, personal observation has a flexibility that permits an executive to keep his eye on what is "hot" at the moment. Ability to make prompt delivery to customers may be crucial at one moment and the number of executives worthy of promotion at another. When a person is new in a job, a supervising executive will want to watch his work more closely than he would that of an experienced operator. Even if we could incorporate these factors into a formalized, continuing flow of information, to do so would probably be undesirable because of the cost and the added burden.

Discussions in other Parts of this book dealing with organization, planning, and activating present compelling reasons for close personal contact between an executive and those who work with him. To those reasons we should now add this: effective measurement of results.

CONTROL REPORTS

Measurement of performance is of little value until the resulting appraisals are communicated to executives who can take corrective action.

The smaller the operating unit, the simpler the control reports need to be. In fact, in a small company or within a small unit, a supervising executive often evaluates results himself, and the only report is an oral discussion with the person doing the work that is being evaluated. A great many controls, perhaps the most effective ones, have this informal character. The basic steps of control are present—setting standards evaluating results, taking corrective action—but the formal recording of results and of comparisons with standards is simple and rudimentary. Few people are involved and the facts are known to everyone, so the control deals primarily with initiating corrective action.

As more people are involved, the task of reporting evaluation becomes more important. People work in different places, they are concerned with different parts of a total task, and there are more detailed facts than any one person can keep in his mind. A need arises, therefore, for control reports that summarize and communicate the conclusions of the measurements that have been undertaken.

Who Should Receive Control Reports?

Control information should be sent immediately to the person whose work is being controlled. He is the one most likely to be able to do something about it. Not that the information should go to a machine operator or a clerk who is merely carrying out specific instructions. Rather it should go to the purchasing agent who decides how much to buy, to the supervisor who decides when overtime work is necessary, to the sales representative who may be able to secure additional orders for slow-moving products, or to the foreign manager who might decide to withdraw from a market. In other words, information should reach the person who, by his own actions, can have a strong influence on final results.

Prompt feedback to the point of action encourages use of the "law of the situation," one of the means for obtaining voluntary cooperation discussed in Chapter 26. In most instances, the person on the firing line will start corrective action as soon as he knows that results are falling short of the established norm.

In addition, control information should flow, perhaps as a summary at a later date, to the controllee's boss. The person on the firing line may need help or he may need prodding; it is the duty of the supervisor to see that he gets either or both as the situation warrants.

These elementary observations about the flow of control reports are meant to emphasize that action which results from control measurements should be taken by the people who have primary responsibility for an activity being measured. Only in rare circumstances is it desirable to separate the action, or dynamic, phase of control from the duties of the one who initiates and supervises performance of the activity. But other people are often interested in these reports, to be sure: 1) executives who will use the control information to help formulate new plans, and 2) staff personnel who are expected to be familiar with, and give advice about, the particular activity under control. These people should be provided with such reports as they find helpful. But their claim is secondary to those of operators and immediate supervisors.

Timeliness Versus Accuracy

Promptness is a great virtue in control reports. If some job is being mishandled, the sooner it is reported and corrected, the less damage will be done. Moreover, if the cause of a difficulty is not obvious, a prompt investigation is more likely to turn up true causes.

The distinction between postaction controls for overall evaluation and steering- or yes–no controls affects the importance of promptness. Timeliness is especially urgent with the latter group, because they lose most of their potency if they are tardy.

Unfortunately, it is often difficult to be both prompt and accurate. An accurate evaluation may require a certain amount of investigation and double-checking. The person making an evaluation naturally wants to be sure he can justify his conclusions, especially if they draw attention to inadequacies in someone's work. In addition, delay is likely to be compounded if a report is prepared by someone who is trained to balance accounts to the last penny. A hospital administrator, for example, was having great difficulty keeping down expenses, partly because expense reports—laboriously compiled at the end of each month—did not become available until six to eight weeks following the events presumably being controlled.

Executives who use control reports should be fully aware of the kind of information they are getting. If they insist on prompt reports, they must learn

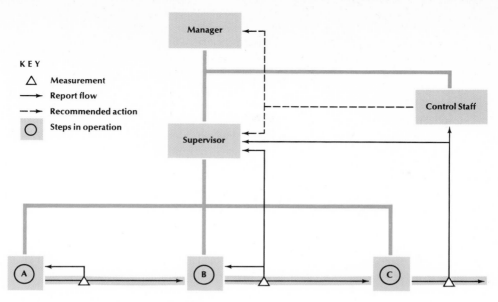

Figure 21-3   Alternative flows of control reports.

to disregard insignificant variations and to expect some false alarms. On the other hand, if we are interested in having the full facts and being deliberate in taking action, then we need a different kind of report.

Form and Content of Reports

Most control reports can be kept simple and present only key comparisons.[4] They are not intended to present a full analysis; furthermore the people using them are intimately familiar with the operations they reflect. These reports are not designed to impress the public; they are valuable if they give the operating people the facts they need quickly and understandably.

In addition to showing a comparison of performance against standard, control reports often reveal whether a situation is getting better or worse. They do so by comparing present performance with that in the recent past and with that during the same period a year ago. Such "trend" information is a helpful guide to a manager in deciding what kind of corrective action is appropriate.

CORRECTIVE ACTION

Control reports call attention to deviations of performance from plans, but they only signal trouble. The pay-off comes when corrective action is taken.

---

[4] As we learn to put our management-information systems on computers, the detail need not accompany the summary report. Instead, the detail will be stored in the memory bank and retrieved on request.

The control information should lead to investigating difficulties, promptly deciding how to overcome them, and then adjusting operations.

Sometimes a control report will start a new management cycle: new planning and organizing, more activating, and another set of measurements and reports. But often, the original objectives and program are retained, and we simply make minor adjustments at one point and push a little harder at another. These adjustments may be necessary anywhere along the line—needling a supplier; pinch-hitting for Joe Zilch, who is ill; running department-A overtime; and so on. In such situations a manager is like a captain who gets information on the location and bearing of his ship, and then adjusts his course in order to arrive at his planned destination.

The distinction between replanning and corrective adjustments is not sharp. For convenience, we speak of "corrective action" if plans and the final result remain the same. If our appraisal indicates that major changes in plans or goals are in order, then we should "replan." In both kinds of action, data from measuring is fed back to executives, who modify their operation.

Finding Reasons for Deviation

That actual operations do not always turn out just as planned is not surprising when we think back over the planning process described in Parts Three and Four. To proceed with planning, we must often adopt predictions as premises—predictions of sales, competitive prices, availability of capital, research results, productivity of new machines, and a host of other things. Such premises are our best estimate at the time, although we recognize they may not be accurate. Also, many plans involve a calculated risk; for we may know that there is, say, about one chance in five that an assumed event may not occur.

So, when our control measurements indicate that all is not well, we have to investigate many possible causes to discover the one that is creating the difficulty. Perhaps some person is at fault, but it is likelier that one of our premises is wrong or that we have unluckily run into the one chance that we hoped could be avoided. At this stage, we are more interested in identifying the cause than the culprit, so that necessary adjustments in operations can be made promptly.

Moreover, the control measurements themselves may lead us astray. We may deliberately watch symptoms or estimates for early warnings of trouble—sales inquiries or employee absences, for instance. But we know from our discussion of diagnosis that symptoms can mislead us (see especially Chapter 11, "Finding the Root Cause"). A similar situation is possible if we use the "exception principle"—that is, watch only for exceptionally high or low performance. An exception may flag serious trouble, or it may be a unique instance that probably will not recur.

In some highly routinized operations, we can act like a servomechanism on a machine, automatically making a given adjustment when certain conditions are detected. Automatic pilots on airplanes and thermostats on furnaces work this way. But most managerial situations are not so simple; we have to identify which of many possible causes is creating difficulty and then devise appropriate corrective action.

Corrective Adjustments

Once a difficulty is spotted, as a result of an investigation prompted by an unfavorable control report, we move quickly to corrective adjustments. If the operating situation has shifted from what was planned—perhaps raw materials are delayed by a dock strike or our computer breaks down—we will take steps to get the working conditions back to normal. If our subordinates are ineffective, we will clarify our directions to them, provide additional training where necessary, consider motivational lacks, and perhaps reassign work. Or, if it is not within our power to overcome the difficulties—say, customers simply will not buy our product—we must then recast goals and programs. From a managerial point of view, a control is not effective until such corrective action as may be necessary has been undertaken.

CONCLUSION

Controlling, like many other aspects of management, is simple in its basic elements but calls for ingenuity and deftness in its application. Setting control standards at strategic points, sampling and measuring qualitative results, balancing timeliness and accuracy in reports, translating reports into corrective action—all are examples of the many issues we must skillfully resolve for a control system to be potent.

Distinguishing between steering-, yes–no, and postaction controls assists greatly in control design. The selection of strategic control points, the use of predictions before work is completed, the balance of promptness versus accuracy in reporting, and the nature of corrective action are all affected by a choice among these control types.

Although we have seen in this chapter a range of issues a manager should consider in the controlling phase of his work, other vital factors remain to be considered. The design of comprehensive control systems will be illustrated in the following chapter. Next, we will review the responses of people to controls, and finally, the integration of controls to other areas of management. These further considerations are important in making control an integral and consistent part of our total management structure and behavior.

FOR CLASS DISCUSSION

1) A fan of professional football and a keen analyst of the game commented that in a professional football game one may find an almost perfect control system. In what ways does the measurement and control system used in professional football reflect the elements of control discussed in this chapter?

2) In what ways do you think the growth of high-speed computers will affect the elements of control? Where are they likely to be most helpful? Where least?

3) "Controls and plans are two sides of the same thing. Without good plans one cannot have good controls and vice versa." Discuss this statement and indicate in detail how you agree and disagree.

4) How can one develop control systems for a decentralized company that balance concern for long- vs. short-run, strategic vs. tactical, and total company vs. unit goals?

5) What type(s) of control would be most useful in a continuous-process chemical plant?

6) In most foreign countries, the Pepsi-Cola Company grants a franchise to a local bottling and distributing firm. The franchised firm must use Pepsi's secret extract shipped from the United States. All other activities are performed by local nationals. The American company provides advice on production and distribution and permits use of the well-known Pepsi-Cola trademark. The company in the United States is naturally concerned about both short- and long-run profits in the foreign countries and about the worldwide reputation of Pepsi-Cola. What controls should the company establish over the activities of a franchised dealer in a foreign country?

7) "The essential difference between *freedom* and *license* is that freedom carries the obligation to provide the grantor with sufficient control to determine how it has been used." *a*) What historical figure might have made this statement? *b*) How do you feel about it? *c*) Relate your answer particularly to the section "Relating Results to Individual Accountability."

8) "Our greatest weakness in control systems is our inability to determine the reasons for failure in sufficient detail and with sufficient certainty to be able to take sharply focused corrective action." Do you feel this is the "greatest weakness"? What can be done to deal with it?

Cases

For cases involving issues covered in this chapter, see especially the following. Particularly relevant questions are listed after each case.

Koontz, H. and R. W. Bradspies, "Managing Through Feedforward Control." *Business Horizons,* June 1972.

Develops concept of control based on inputs rather than results.

Litterer, J. A., *The Analysis of Organizations,* 2nd ed. New York: John Wiley & Sons, 1973, Chapter 21.

Basic elements in the design of a management-control system.

Mockler, R. J., *The Management Control Process. New York: Appleton-Century-Crofts, 1972.*

Comprehensive text covering concepts and techniques related to managerial control. The frequent references provide leads into control literature.

Newman, W. H., *Constructive Control: Design and Use of Control Systems.* Englewood Cliffs, N.J.: Prentice-Hall, Inc., 1975.

Comprehensive analysis of managerial control, including—in addition to topics in this Part—chapters on control of repetitive operations, projects and programs, resources, creative activities, and strategy; and a chapter on balancing the total control structure.

Richards M. D. and W. A. Nielander, eds., *Readings in Management,* 4th ed. Cincinnati: South-Western Publishing Co., 1974, Chapter 11.

Excellent articles on measuring nonfinancial factors in business operations.

Starr, M. K., *Production Management: Systems and Synthesis,* 2nd ed. Englewood Cliffs, N.J.: Prentice-Hall, Inc., 1972.

A more readable exposition of modern quantitative treatment of production problems, including a good chapter on quality control.

PERT

and Budgetary Control

Two mechanisms of control are examined in this chapter. We pick them out for special attention because each can be applied to a wide variety of situations, and each aids planning and coordination as well as control. By discussing them here in Part Five, we underscore the interdependence between planning and control.

Financial budgeting is widely accepted, whereas PERT (Program Evaluation and Review Technique) is relatively new and its potentialities are not yet fully understood. Let us look first at budgeting.

Elements in Budgetary Control

Basically, financial budgeting involves these three steps:

1) *Expressing in dollars the results of plans anticipated in a future period.* These dollar figures are typically set up in the same way as the accounts in a company's accounting system. The budget shows how the accounts should look if present plans are carried out.

2) *Coordinating these estimates into a well-balanced program.* The figures for sales, production, advertising, and other divisions must be matched to be sure that

they are mutually consistent; the financial feasibility of all plans added together must be ensured; and the combined results must be examined in terms of overall objectives. Some adjustments will probably be necessary to obtain such a balanced program.

3) *Comparing actual results with the program estimates that emerge from step 2.* Any significant differences point to the need for corrective action. In short, the budget becomes a standard for appraising operating results.

These steps will be illustrated first by an extended example of a small company. Then we shall discuss the implication of the budgeting concept for larger firms and for special situations. Finally, we shall look into ways of securing flexibility and also into some of the dangers and limitations of budgetary control. Our aim is to see how financial budgeting fits into the management processes; we are not concerned here with the details of budgetary procedure.

BUDGETING IN A NEW ENTERPRISE

Examining budgets for a new, small company enables us to see readily how operating plans can be translated into financial figures and how budgets provide an opportunity for overall coordination. For this purpose, we shall use Belafonte Fashions, Inc., as an illustration.

General Plans of Belafonte Fashions, Inc.

After working as a stock boy, presser, and, more recently, foreman in several apparel plants, Paul Bailey went into business for himself. He had an opportunity to buy the total equipment of a defunct ski-suit plant and to take over a lease on the space it occupied. The $40,000 price was attractive, especially since the equipment was already installed and experienced labor was available in the area. Bailey, a black himself, had a strong desire to establish an all-black enterprise in a depressed area on the Near-West side of Chicago. His new venture was made possible by an investment by High Horizons, a private urban-renewal corporation. High Horizons matched Bailey's capital contribution of $30,000, arranged for an equipment mortgage with a bank, and made a temporary working-capital loan of $23,000. Because Bailey had little background in finance and accounting, High Horizons stipulated that he use the "MBA Consultants" from Northwestern University for help in this area; Morris Barkin is the student assigned to this client.

Bailey decided to concentrate on a limited line of women's pants, which are relatively simple to manufacture and use existing skills of the work force. Purchased fabric of polyester and cotton or wool is cut, sewn, and pressed; permanent-press finishing is subcontracted to a nearby company. Bailey started in business in the autumn, a season when the demand for pants is brisk; and by the end of the year he had a going concern. The balance sheet at that time is shown in Table 22–1.

TABLE 22–1 BELAFONTE FASHIONS, INC.:
Balance Sheet—January 1

Cash		$ 8,700	Accounts payable		$ 17,200
Accounts receivable		33,600	Accrued taxes, etc.		2,700
			Current liabilities		19,900
Inventories:			Mortgage on		
			equipment		16,000
Raw material	$20,500		Loan from		
Finished goods	16,800	37,300	High Horizons		23,000
			Total liabilities		58,900
Current assets		79,600	Equity		
			Common stock	$60,000	
Equipment	40,000		Loss for first		
			three months	800	59,200
Less depreciation	1,500	38,500			
			Total liabilities		
Total assets		$118,100	and equity		$118,100

Morris Barkin, after a careful industry survey, urged Bailey to prepare a profit-and-loss budget for his new company. At the beginning of the new year, Bailey had the following plans in mind:

1) The company would first establish itself by making four fairly standard pants at low cost. With this operation as a base, more highly styled and novelty items could be added later to provide wider profit margins. But to attempt to operate a business on novelty items alone was too risky.

2) The four types of pants Bailey had in mind usually sold to retailers at an average price of $45.50 per dozen. Even with allowances and markdowns, Bailey hoped his average selling price would be at least $42.00 per dozen.

3) Selling would be done through manufacturers' agents, one in New York, covering the territory east of the Mississippi, except for Illinois and Wisconsin, and one in Chicago, covering the remainder of the United States. In the plant, Bailey figured, he needed an experienced cutter and a sewing foreman, each of whom would be paid $250 a week. He expected to take care of designing, buying, marketing, and general administrative work himself. However, he had hired a man to act as bookkeeper and general office assistant at $10,000 per year. All other employees were to be paid on an hourly or piece-rate basis. While the business was getting on its feet, Bailey planned to pay himself only $700 per month.

4) Experience during the fall had indicated that fabric, zippers, and other mate-

rials would cost about $21.50 per dozen finished pants. Provided the work was well planned, direct labor amounted to $10.00 per dozen.

5) Every apparel company is torn between being able to make prompt deliveries and avoiding a large obsolete inventory. Bailey sought to meet this problem 1) by keeping well stocked with fabric (each month he would purchase the fabric needed for producing the pants he expected to sell during the next 30 to 60 days) and 2) by restricting his stock of finished goods to expected shipments during the following two weeks. This plan was intended to permit him to adapt the sizes and styles of pants being produced to the orders being received (assuming the right kinds of fabric were on hand).

Profit-and-Loss Budget for the New Year

After talking with his sales agents, Bailey estimated he could sell 10,000 dozen pants during his first full year of operations. In fact, the New York agent talked of large sales to chain-store buyers, but this would have involved making price concessions and maintaining a large inventory that Bailey wanted to avoid at this time.

By translating his plans and estimates into dollar values, Bailey and Barkin came up with an estimated profit-and-loss statement, which is shown in Table 22–2. The young proprietor was pleased about two features of this budget: It

TABLE 22–2 BELAFONTE FASHIONS, INC.:
Profit-and-Loss Budget for the Year

Net Sales (10,000 dozen @ $42)	$420,000
Expenses:	
Materials ($21.50 per dozen)	215,000
Labor ($10.00 per dozen)	100,000
Plant supervisors' salaries	26,000
Repairs	7,200
Heat, light, janitor	7,200
Rent	8,200
Depreciation	6,000
Office salaries	18,400
Travel expenses	2,000
Office miscellaneous	1,200
Sales commissions (2.5 percent)	10,500
Shipping (1 percent)	4,200
Interest and financing charges	4,720
Total expenses	410,620
Operating profit	9,380
Income tax	1,380
Net profit	$ 8,000

indicated that he should be able to earn a modest profit, and it showed that a large part of total expenses could be adjusted downward if sales volume did not develop. Thus, through close control of "variable expenses" he should be able to avoid large losses, even if sales were smaller than anticipated. He now saw more clearly the financial results he might expect, and he had a standard to guide him while attempting to achieve these results.

Monthly Cash Budget

Morris Barkin was dubious. He did not challenge the annual-profit budget, but he was worried that the company might go bankrupt before the end of the year arrived. He pointed out 1) that wide seasonal fluctuations in sales would cause temporary demands for larger inventory and accounts receivable; 2) that High Horizons hoped to get back $10,000 of its loan by the middle of the year; and 3) that the company might have to make additional investments in equipment. An examination of this last point revealed that Bailey was using his personal car for company business and that a station wagon ($4,000) would be needed before the end of the year. Additionally, a different kind of fabric was needed for the autumn lines, and this would require the purchase of second-hand sewing machines for a total of $4,800.

Faced with these facts, Bailey and Barkin undertook to prepare a monthly budget of cash receipts and disbursements. For this purpose Bailey assumed that customers would pay for merchandise within thirty days after shipment and that he would pay for his purchases within a similar period. But it was more difficult to estimate how his annual sales volume would be distributed by months throughout the year. Industry figures supplied by the local sales agent indicated that the distribution would probably be as shown in Table 22–3.

TABLE 22–3   BELAFONTE FASHIONS, INC.:
Estimated Monthly Sales

Month	Sales (dozens)	Month	Sales (dozens)
January	800	July	400
February	800	August	500
March	1,100	September	1,200
April	900	October	1,300
May	600	November	1,200
June	400	December	800

With the data he already had and with his inventory policy, Bailey was now able to budget his monthly flow of cash. This analysis indicated that he might just squeeze by the March sales peak and that cash would accumulate rapidly in April and May, as he collected from customers and reduced his inventories. May and June, then, appeared to be the best time to buy the new equipment and reduce the loan to High Horizons.

Serious trouble would arise in August and September, however, as inventories and accounts receivable would rise to an autumn peak. Without financial aid Belafonte Fashions, Inc., could not possibly meet its budgeted annual sales.

The crucial assistance was found in a finance company. An agreement was made for Belafonte Fashions, Inc., to borrow whatever it needed up to 80 percent of its accounts receivable. The accounts were pledged as collateral, and special records and collection procedures were established. For its services, the finance company would be paid both a flat annual fee of $1,000 to set up the arrangement and also interest on any money borrowed, at the rate of ten percent per annum. With this assistance, the estimates indicated, Paul Bailey would be able to weather the financial crisis forecast for the autumn.

The budget that reflects all these plans is shown in Table 22–4. Note that the preparation of this budget required some adjustment in financial plans in order to arrive at a feasible balanced program.

Comparison of Actual Results with the Budget

During the first six months of the year, the operating results of Belafonte Fashions, Inc., were surprisingly close to the budget. Sales during March, April, and May were 400 dozen below the budget, but the comfortable accumulation of cash tended to obscure the influence of this drop. More serious trouble arose in November and December when business failed to meet expectations. Mild weather in the fall left retailers well stocked with the type of pants Belafonte made, so reorders did not come in as anticipated. This in turn left Bailey with a high inventory of raw materials; also Bailey could not pay off the finance company in December because of inadequate receipts. Price-cutting was necessary in order to move the finished stock, and even with this action sales were 800 dozen below the budget forecast for the last two months. The final profit-and-loss figures for the year compared with the budget are shown in Table 22–5.

A first glance at actual results compared with the budget indicates that virtually all the unsatisfactory showing can be ascribed to the drop in sales. This is somewhat misleading. Price-cutting to an average of $41.50 explains over $4,000 lost in revenue even on the 8,800-dozen volume. In addition, direct-labor cost was $.74 per dozen higher than the budget, which points to an inefficiency here; the total labor cost went down, but not as much as it should have. Fortunately, material costs dropped even more than might be expected from the shrinkage in volume. Variations in other expenses were minor: Sales

TABLE 22–4 BELAFONTE FASHIONS, INC.:
Budget of Monthly Cash Receipts and Disbursements

	Jan.	Feb.	Mar.	Apr.
Sales (dollars)	33,600	33,600	46,200	37,800
Sales (dozens)	800	800	1,100	900
Goods produced (dozens)	800	950	1,000	750
Cash received from sales	$33,600	$33,600	$33,600	$46,200
Disbursements:				
Materials	17,200	20,425	21,500	16,125
Direct labor	8,000	9,500	10,000	7,500
Plant supervision ⎫				
Repairs ⎬	4,050	4,050	4,050	4,050
Heat, light, janitor ⎭				
Rent	0	0	0	0
Depreciation				
Office salaries ⎫				
Travel expenses ⎬	1,800	1,800	1,800	1,800
Office miscellaneous ⎭				
Sales commissions ⎫	1,170	1,170	1,620	1,325
Shipping ⎭				
Interest and financing charges	0	0	780	0
Disbursements for operations	32,220	36,945	39,750	30,800
Cash gain or **loss** from operations	1,380	— 3,345	— 6,150	15,400
Loans received or **paid**				
Investment in equipment				
Cash balance at end of month	10,080	6,735	585	15,985

TABLE 22–5 BELAFONTE FASHIONS, INC.:
Comparison of Actual Profit and Loss with Budget for Year

	Budget	Actual	Difference
Net sales	$420,000	$365,200	$ — 54,800
Expenses:			
Materials	215,000	185,800	— **29,200**
Direct labor	100,000	94,500	— **5,500**
Plant supervisors' salaries	26,000	26,000	0
Repairs	7,200	5,900	— 1,300
Heat, light, janitor	7,200	7,300	100
Rent	8,200	8,200	0
Depreciation	6,000	6,400	400
Office salaries	18,400	18,400	0
Travel expenses	2,000	2,500	500

	May	June	July	Aug.	Sept.	Oct.	Nov.	Dec.
	25,200	16,800	16,800	21,000	50,400	54,600	50,400	33,600
	600	400	400	500	1,200	1,300	1,200	800
	500	400	450	850	1,250	1,250	1,000	800
	$37,800	$25,200	$16,800	$16,800	$21,000	$50,400	$54,600	$50,400
	10,750	8,600	9,675	18,275	26,875	26,875	21,500	17,200
	5,000	4,000	4,500	8,500	12,500	12,500	10,000	8,000
	4,050	4,050	4,050	4,050	4,050	4,050	4,050	4,050
	0	0	0	0	0	0	0	0
	1,800	1,800	1,800	1,800	1,800	1,800	1,800	1,800
	880	590	590	735	1,770	1,910	1,770	1,170
	0	780	0	1,000	580	0	0	1,580
	22,480	19,820	20,615	34,360	47,575	47,135	39,120	33,800
	15,320	5,380	— 3,815	— 17,560	— 26,575	3,265	15,480	16,600
		— 10,000		10,000	30,000		— 10,000	— 30,000
	— 4,000	— 4,800						
	27,305	17,885	14,070	6,510	9,935	13,200	18,680	5,280

	Budget	Actual	Difference
Office miscellaneous	1,200	1,600	400
Sales commissions	10,500	9,130	— 1,370
Shipping	4,200	3,700	— 500
Interest and financing charges	4,720	4,720	0
Total expenses	410,620	374,150	— 36,470
Operating profit	9,380	— 8,950	— 18,330
Income tax	1,380	0	— 1,380
Net profit	$ 8,000	$ — 8,950	$ — 16,950

commissions and shipping naturally went down, and tighter control of other expenses would have made only a minor difference in the final outcome. In short, this comparison points directly to sales volume, price, and direct labor costs as the areas where improvement must be made if the company is to become profitable.

The revised budgets that proved suitable for the first year of operation of Belafonte Fashions, Inc., provide a simple example of the three basic steps in budgeting. Plans were translated into accounting results, plans were adjusted where the combined picture proved to be unworkable, and the resulting budgets served as a useful standard in highlighting places that need corrective action. For Paul Bailey, planning became more comprehensive and rigorous, and post-action control became a reality. Clearly, budgets need not be elaborate to be a useful management tool.

BUDGETING IN A LARGE FIRM

Company size does not affect the essentials of budgeting, but it does influence the complexity of the budgetary system. As a company grows, several things are likely to happen to the budgeting process:

1) Separate budgets are prepared for each department or division of the company. Because each operating unit is somewhat independent, standards to measure its particular performance are needed. Moreover, detailed budget information is often helpful for control within the division. In a large company there may be literally hundreds of subsidiary budgets dealing with the sales, expenses, or other appropriate items of many different operating centers.

2) Communication of "planning premises" is important if these numerous subsidiary budgets are to be prepared consistently. Each person who prepares or interprets a budget needs to know what assumptions to make about, for instance, wage increases during the budgeting period. The plant manager is dependent on the sales department for information on volume of activity. Are prices and the availability of raw materials going to change? How soon will a new product be ready for the market? Such matters will affect the budgets of several departments. Therefore, someone must provide a forecast that can be used consistently in all subsidiary budgets.

3) Coordinating the many subsidiary budgets into a balanced program becomes complicated. A big company tends to have a large number of specialized units, and a good deal of effort is needed to synchronize their activities. Even in highly decentralized companies, the total activities of the various units, as reflected in their budgets, must not exceed the company's resources. In other words, preparing a consolidated budget for a large company entails more than merely adding the budgets of the various divisions; the budget should represent a feasible program that is in the best interest of the company as a whole.

4) A special unit that concentrates only on budgeting may be desirable. Such a unit can help design the budgetary emphases and procedures that are best adapted to the particular needs of its company. A budgeting unit may provide routine clerical services in processing figures and in compiling and circulating

reports; perhaps it will also make substantive analyses of both proposed budgets and actual experience, with recommendations for action. This staff unit, however, should neither prepare the budgets nor try to enforce them; budgeting is a tool for operating executives to use and not a device for usurping their duties.

APPROPRIATION BUDGETS

The budgets we have discussed thus far are concerned mainly with managerial actions that produce observable results within a given accounting period —a month, a quarter, or at most a year. Other managerial actions are taken that are not expected to yield results for two years, five years, and often longer. Such actions pose special control problems; appropriation budgets help meet this need. These budgets cover expenditures for items such as: [1]

1) Land, building, and equipment.
2) Research for new products and new processes.
3) Institutional advertising.
4) Personnel development.
5) New-market development.

Expenditures of the type just listed deserve management attention for several reasons. When wisely made, they are often crucial to the long-run success of the company. But on these items management has a wider latitude of discretion—it can expand, contract, or even discontinue them—than it has for most current expenses, which must be met in order for the company to continue operations.

Appropriation budgets provide some help by their planning and control. Typically, all large requests for new buildings and equipment are submitted once a year to top management, which examines the justifications for each project, compares prospective yields, considers the relation of each to long-term objectives, matches the total requests against available financial resources, and finally makes an overall appropriation. This appropriation, which usually includes an allowance for small and emergency requests, becomes the approved budget for the year. A similar procedure is often followed for research and advertising appropriations. Budgets for development expenses, however, are apt to be less formally established.

A great deal of work is devoted to preparing these appropriation budgets, and in large companies we find elaborate procedures for review and approval— especially for new equipment and buildings. In essence, these procedures pro-

---

[1] Conventional accounting spreads the costs of buildings, equipment, and inventions over their presumed useful life, whereas the other items listed are treated as an expense at the time they are incurred. From the viewpoint of management planning and control, however, all expenses of this type present similar problems.

vide yes/no control to proceed with—or hold back on—proposed expenditures *before* any money is spent or contracts signed.

Usually, purchasing or hiring commitments are not permitted unless they are covered by an appropriation. But note that this provides a one-sided check. It does not even attempt to measure the results—which is the original purpose of making the investment.

Unfortunately, a useful check on the results of long-term investment is extremely difficult to devise. The period from initial decision to fruition is long—extending far beyond the time when corrective action during the formative stages would be possible. During this long interval, many other events occur, making a clear chain of cause and effect difficult to establish. Such efforts as we can make to match an appropriation with specific results are more for "learning from our experience" than for control. (One company, however, does check results of capital expenditures two years after installation "just so operating executives won't forecast all sorts of benefits they can't deliver.")

Nevertheless, appropriation budgets have some clear benefits: 1) They keep disbursements for the purposes they cover within known limits. 2) They provide an opportunity for key executives to review and compare alternative uses of limited funds. 3) They provide important information for cash budgets and permit coordination of investment and financing plans.

BENEFITS AND DANGERS OF BUDGETARY CONTROL

Budgeting is no panacea. We need to understand its strengths and weaknesses so that we may fit it into the total control structure we design for a company or subdivision.

Unique Advantages

First, the greatest strength of budgeting is probably its use of a single common denominator—dollars—for many diverse actions and things. TV advertising, tons of coal, and liability insurance can all be reflected in a budget of dollar cost and dollar result. Dollar language has its limitations, as we shall see, but it does lend itself to summaries and comparisons. The dollar, more than any other measuring device in business, government, or even military and church administration, can be applied to a wide range of work; and financial budgets capitalize on this unique feature of a monetary unit.

Second, budgeting uses records and systems already in existence. We must keep elaborate accounting records for tax returns, financial reporting, and internal management. In budgeting we utilize this system, rather than a new set of records. Figures on past experience are likely to be already prepared.

Some new accounts or reports may have to be added, but the basic information system is available and easy to use.

Finally, budgeting deals *directly* with one of the central objectives of a business enterprise—making a profit. What shows up in budgets is what affects recorded profit or loss. Thus the relevance of items being controlled by a budget can be easily traced to the profit objective.

Stimulus to Good Management Practices

Budgeting often makes its greatest contribution as a stimulus to other good management practices. These are practices an executive might wisely use without budgets, but the adoption of budgetary control may bring them to life. For instance, here are several critical management requirements, with suggestions of how budgeting can help vitalize them.

1) Formal organization should be clear. An understanding of who is assigned to make each type of plan should be a prerequisite to the translation of such plans into budget form. Similarly, accountability for execution has to be clear if comparisons of actual performance with a budget are to have their full impact.

2) Financial accounts must be set up for each department or other unit of administration. When expenses, investments, and income are readily traceable to specific managers, they are more easily controlled. Such correspondence between accounts and departments is especially important in both the preparation and the evaluation phases of budgeting.[2]

3) Planning must be done well in advance and should be highly specific. Without such plans, a budget for the year ahead would be little more than a guess Precision in planning, in turn, calls for clarifying objectives and for coordinating the plans of interrelated departments.

4) Once annual budgets are well established, tentative budgets for three or five years become feasible. In Chapter 16 we noted that this was one form of long-range planning. Experience with budgeting is also very useful in what some companies call "profit planning"—setting targets for profits and related matters and then working back through financial accounts to determine the actions that will be necessary to achieve these targets.

[2] A major drawback of budgets when used to evaluate personal performance is their tie to a single forecast of external conditions. When external conditions (volume, prices, strikes, and so on) deviate from the forecast, a new standard is needed if a budget is to be fair. Two ways of obtaining flexibility are 1) a "flexible budget" that permits the calculation of expense standards based on the actual volume of work (an interpolation between high- and low-volume budgets) and 2) "standard costs" that permit calculation of expense standards based on the actual product-mix. The greatest flexibility, however, is obtained through periodic budget revisions. For example, each month a twelve-month budget can be drawn up, including a revision of previous estimates for the period immediately ahead. This modified budget can take account of inflation or any other external change and thus become a realistic standard. Additionally, if the person who will be evaluated participates in the budget revision, he is motivated to adjust his operations to the new external conditions. The realistic standard plus the improved motivation lead toward changed behavior— which is the aim of controls. Incidentally, although "expected values" and "decision trees" are useful devices for dealing with uncertainty in *planning*, they tend to confuse the setting of reasonable standards for *control*.

5) When line managers use budgets as a key management tool, they at least provide an opportunity for clear directing and constructive counseling. Because budget figures are objective and tangible, everyone can avoid misunderstandings and all parties can focus on improving results.

When we dream about a "turkey dinner and all the fixin's," it is hard to tell whether the turkey itself or what goes with it is the most attractive. And so with budgeting. Budgets are useful as a financial control, but when they are accompanied by other elements of good management they can be an even more cogent force.[3]

Dangers in Using Budgets for Control

The most serious risk in using budgets is an *unbalanced emphasis* on factors that happen to be the easiest to observe. For example, the operating expenses of the engineering or personnel department stand out clearly in budget reports, and the supervising executives are under pressure to keep expenses within prescribed limits. But the services such departments perform are of even greater importance. Inadequate service, unfortunately, is reflected only indirectly in the profit-and-loss figures—perhaps in costs or in low sales—and is difficult to trace back to the service division. In terms of budget controls, a service department can look good by keeping expenses in line even though it performs its major mission poorly.

At the same time, a budget emphasizes the orders received by the sales department and low cost in the production department. Executives of these departments make a good budget showing by demanding more, rather than less, help from related operating and service divisions. Consequently, a budget tends to create *internal conflict* and pressures. Intangible results may not be measured at all, or they may not be properly associated with the units that produce them.

A related danger of budgetary control is that we may *treat symptoms* as though they were basic problems. We may become involved in a numbers game rather than probe the reality that lies behind the numbers. If total office salaries look high, for example, a manager may withhold merit increases and fill vacancies with low-salaried, inexperienced help. This remedy may make a bad situation worse. Perhaps the salary figure is a symptom of poor office organization, and a realignment of jobs is what is really needed.

To cite another example, high material costs do not necessarily mean that the supervisor in the processing department is ineffective. Such costs may be a symptom of any of the following weaknesses: unnecessarily rigid specifications, competition for limited supply of raw stock, inept purchasing, inadequate inspection of materials put into the production process, poor process engineer-

[3] A similar effect arises from other management tools. The introduction of organization planning, operations research, and output standards, for instance, all stimulate many associated improvements. Consequently, as noted in connection with Management-by-Objectives, we can pick a tool that is appealing at the moment and use it to overcome resistance to an array of improvements.

ing, or old or poorly maintained equipment. A financial budget cannot and should not be expected to reveal the real cause of difficulty.

In addition, a budget system opens the way for *dictatorial* action. The terse, objective figures of a budget make it easy for an executive to say, "Cut that expense by thirty percent." If the executive is pressed for time or does not know what else to do, he may order a change in the budget without thinking through the ramifications.

Finally, there is the danger that a company will go through the *form* of budgetary control *without the substance*. All too often some staff man in the controller's office merely predicts what the accounts will look like several months in the future, with little or no actual planning by operating managers. In other instances, budgets are prepared routinely and mechanically, with no thought given to how operations might be improved. Later the managers simply make excuses if performance compares unfavorably with the budget. In such circumstances, budgeting is a nuisance rather than an aid to management; it simply adds paper work and red tape to an already complex task. Budgetary control can be helpful only if key executives incorporate it as a dynamic part of their way of managing.

PERT

Dollar incomes and dollar expenses are the grist of financial budgeting. Although the timing of action from one budget period to the next is considered, synchronization of work is a secondary aspect of budgeting. With PERT, the emphasis is reversed. Timing is primary; expense control is an accessory. Consequently, PERT serves quite a different role in a total control system.

Time is crucial in many management situations. Quick results are often important. In addition, by synchronizing activities we can utilize resources more fully and maintain a steady pace of work. The control of when events occur is especially important in complex, interdependent ventures like launching a new product or erecting a bridge. For these reasons, a manager often needs a control device that focuses on the timing of each step necessary to arrive at an established goal.

A recently developed means to analyze and control the timing aspects of a major project is PERT (Program Evaluation and Review Technique). Originally developed for the highly complex task of producing Polaris missiles, PERT has been adapted to a wide variety of undertakings, including hospital fund-raising drives and the construction of the World Trade Center.

Recording the Network

As with any control, we start with a plan of action. Suppose our goal is to launch a new product or place a communications satellite in orbit, and we determine the actions that will be necessary to achieve our goal. The first phase of a PERT analysis is to note carefully each of these steps, the sequence in which they must be performed, and the time required for each. This informa-

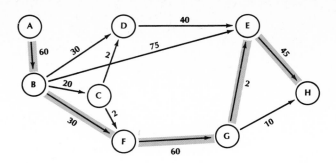

EVENTS

- (A) Decision to add product
- (B) Engineering work completed
- (C) Financing arranged
- (D) Material purchase orders placed
- (E) Production started
- (F) Sales campaign arranged
- (G) Initial orders received
- (H) Initial orders shipped

Figure 22–1   A simplified PERT chart. Events—that is, the start or completion of a step—are indicated by circles. Arrows show the sequence between events. The time (in days) required to move from one event to another appears on each arrow. The critical path—the longest sequence—is shown in color.

tion is recorded in the form of a network—usually on a chart such as those shown in Figs. 22–1 and 22–2.

The chart in Fig. 22–1 is highly simplified so that we can easily grasp its main features. It shows the main steps that an American auto-equipment manufacturer would have to follow to market a new antismog muffler. The manufacturer has purchased a tested European patent so that engineering to domestic requirements is simple; furthermore, he already has a well-organized plant and distribution setup. Arrows on the chart indicate the sequence of events he must follow to get his new product on the market; the numbers on the arrows show the required time for each step.

Note that the network is really one way of recording a "program"—a concept we examined early in Chapter 19. This list of events, the sequences, and the elapsed times are all the data necessary for program planning. The network does not show the resources needed for each step, but an understanding of men, machines, and money underlies the estimated time for each step. The chief advantage of expressing a program as a network is its emphasis on sequences and interrelationships.

The Critical Path

Because we are focusing here on time, we wish to know where delay, should it occur, would be most serious. The network is very helpful for this purpose. By tracing each necessary sequence and adding the time estimates for each step, we can identify which sequence will require the most time. This is the "critical path." Other sequences will take less time and hence are less critical.

The critical path is especially important in planning and control. Any delay along this path will postpone the completion date of the entire project. On the other hand, by knowing in advance which series of steps are critical, we might be able to replan (allocate more resources, perform part of the work simultaneously, and so on) in order to shorten the total time. In other words

1) we focus control where it is most essential; 2) we are in a good position to spot potential trouble early; and 3) we can avoid putting pressure on activities that will do nothing to hasten completion.

Moreover, as work progresses, reports on activities that are ahead of or behind schedule will enable us to reexamine the timing. Perhaps an unexpected delay has created a new critical path. (For example, if "tooling up"—B to E in Fig. 22–1—required an additional thirty days, a new critical path would be created.) Then corrective action can be shifted to this new sequence in which no slack time exists. In this way PERT becomes a strong control.

Control of Major Projects

PERT is typically applied to a much more complicated network than the illustration we have just used; in practice, each of the major steps would be programmed in more detail. The preparation of the sales campaign, for instance, would involve packaging, pricing, sales brochures, installation manuals, training of sales people, placing of advertisements, and the like; and each of these activities should be shown separately in the network. Such delineation improves our chances of catching delays early, and it also spells out the need for coordination at numerous points.

For a complex project, such as the construction of a large plant, the network becomes complicated indeed. A network with 137 events is shown in Fig. 22–2. PERT is especially suited to large "single-use" programs having clearcut steps and measurable output.

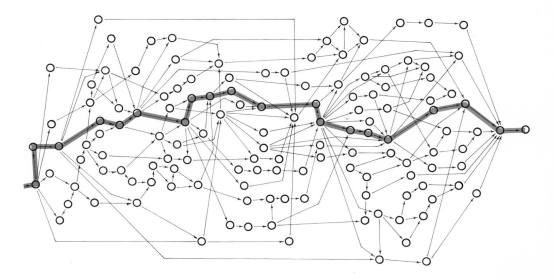

Figure 22–2 PERT in an actual situation.

PERT/COST Systems

PERT's forte is control of time. However, as we noted in the preceding chapter, control over one aspect of performance tends to diminish attention to other aspects. So, if timing is stressed, costs are likely to get out of line. To counteract this tendency the original PERT concept has been expanded to include both time and cost.

To put it in a nutshell, most PERT/COST systems merely add an estimated—or budgeted—cost for each step in the network. Then, as work progresses, the actual cost to date is compared with the estimate, just as actual time is compared with estimated time. Basically, the cost-control mechanism is the same as the normal budgetary control of costs.

The distinctive aspect of PERT/COST is its direct association with each separate step in the total operation. PERT provides a unique way to measure how much progress has been made; and if we have a standard for *costs* for each step, we can also tell whether costs are running ahead of accomplishment. Normal accounting does not keep track of costs in this way.

The unique features of PERT/COST are also its drawbacks. Costs for each step in a network are both hard to budget and hard to keep track of. Even when several minor steps are combined, companies have trouble setting standards and making measurements. PERT frequently deals with activities that are new, and this makes estimating of costs difficult; also, it often stresses joint contributions of different departments, which makes the allocating of overhead difficult. Consequently, we still have much to learn about making a PERT/COST system work smoothly.

Uses of PERT

Currently, PERT controls are fashionable. They are associated with spacecraft and other scientific achievements; they often, though not necessarily, use computers for tabulations and reports; and they are described in terms of "systems," "networks," and other management-science lingo. Naturally, this phase of popularity will pass. From a basic management viewpoint, we need to know where PERT will fit as a continuing instrument of control.

Lasting applications will probably be of two sorts. First, we will use PERT to plan and control the progress of highly complex projects. Here, the design, engineering, purchase or production, testing, and assembly of hundreds of parts must be synchronized.[4] The task of controlling such work differs sharply from

[4] The Department of Defense requires its contractors for major projects—supersonic planes, submarines, and the like—to develop a Cost/Schedule Planning-and-Control System. Such a system normally includes a network of steps such as we have described, with the added features of 1) "milestone" events to be used as control points, 2) dates related to each step, 3) cost estimates broken down by material, labor, and overhead for each step, 4) regular reviews and reports of actual time and cost versus the plan, and 5) revised "estimated-to-complete" costs and time. Such systems are the most elaborate planning and control mechanisms used in non-Communist countries.

control of repetitive operations. Second, we will use a simplified version of PERT for all sorts of single-use programs, such as a sales promotion or floating a bond issue. The concepts of a network of events and of the critical path can be applied to many kinds of situations in which we are interested in getting a job done on time.

CONCLUSION

One striking aspect of both PERT and budgetary control is the need for careful planning before the control feature can be effective. In fact, the pressure to refine and clarify plans when setting up these controls may be a major contribution in itself. Also, although neither device ensures corrective action at early stages, both permit prompt identification of trouble, and both provide us with a framework for making adjustments that recognize the ramifications of the actions taken.

In this review of budgeting and PERT, we have made only passing reference to the way people respond to the controls. Actually, the effects of both instruments depend greatly on getting executives and operators to accept and use the data provided. We shall explore this subject in the next chapter.

FOR CLASS DISCUSSION

1) What do you feel to be the single most important benefit (to Mr. Bailey) of detailed budgeting for the *first six months* of Belafonte Fashions' existence?

2) "A company might have good plans and even good controls without good budgets, but one cannot have good budgets without first having good plans and controls." Do you agree with this comment? Discuss.

3) The sales manager of a company making electric clocks complained, "I can't draw up a sales budget until I know how much the products will cost us, so I can estimate price and sales volume." The production vice president asked, "How can I draw up production budgets and give the sales manager the data he wants until he gives me an idea of what sales volume to plan for?" How would you resolve this apparent stalemate in the preparation of departmental budgets?

4) A number of companies now present forecasts on key variables not as single-point estimates but in terms of "best, worst, and most likely" estimates. How should these multiple-point estimates be handled when they must be recorded as budget targets?

5) In what ways has computer technology contributed to budgetary control? Has it created any problems with using budgets for control?

6) In what ways does good budgeting depend on clearcut organization?

7) "The trouble with systems like PERT," said the experienced director of a key federal agency, "is that the person responsible for planning and controlling

results becomes unduly dependent on the technicians who have to put all of the plans into these networks and then interpret them." How do you feel about this criticism?

8) "The thing I like best about budgets and PERT systems is that they are the real basis for control. I can keep track of what's happening and know who to go after if results are not what was promised." Discuss this statement by the head of a state agency. Would your answer differ if the speaker were the controller of a large retail store?

Cases

For cases involving issues covered in this chapter, see especially the following. Particularly relevant questions are listed after each case.

Atlas Chemical Company (p. 321), 15, 16
Marten Fabricators (p. 316), 16, 17
Family Service of Gotham (p. 532), 12
Southeast Textiles (p. 620), 11
Household Products Company (p. 627), 13

FOR FURTHER READING

Bacon, J., *Managing the Budget Function.* New York: National Industrial Conference Board, 1970.
Clear summary of the use of budgets for management purposes, based on survey of company practice.

Schoderbek, P. P., ed., *Management Systems,* 2nd ed. New York: John Wiley & Sons, 1971.
Part III includes excellent articles on PERT, PERT/Cost, and related techniques. The book is more concerned with systems than with programming.

Shillinglaw, G., *Cost Accounting: Analysis and Control,* 3rd ed. Homewood, Ill.: Richard D. Irwin, Inc., 1972, Part III.
Thorough explanation of budgeting, standard costs, responsibility accounting, and reporting systems; emphasis is on managerial use of data.

Vatter, W. J., *Operating Budgets.* Belmont, Calif.: Wadsworth Publishing Co., 1969.
Lucid, condensed description of the budgeting process as a managerial tool.

Welsch, G. A., *Budgeting: Profit Planning and Control,* 4th ed. Englewood Cliffs, N.J.: Prentice-Hall, Inc., 1976.
Comprehensive treatment of budgeting from an accounting viewpoint.

Behavioral Responses
to Controls

23

A fire siren never put out a fire. Nor has an on-line computer printout secured a new customer. Only when some person responds to the signal or takes action in anticipation of it, does a managerial control become effective. An adjustment in behavior is crucial.

In the two preceding chapters, we have considered controls primarily from an engineering, or mechanistic point of view. Control standards derived from company objectives, control points selected in light of technology and administrative organization, financial budgeting made attractive by the existence of an accounting system—these are valid considerations, but they are not enough. The pay-off comes only when somebody—manager or operator—does his work better because the controls are in operation.

In fact, responses to controls may ill serve the purpose for which they were designed. The controls may be mistrusted and disregarded, and they may have significant side effects. So this chapter explores ways to create positive responses to controls—and ways to minimize the negative reactions. Although people's feelings about controls vary widely, we do have some data on typical responses; behavioral scientists have described controlled behavior, and executives have reported on an even wider range of experience. Our aim here is to translate these findings into guides that can be used in designing and operating a control system.

Each element in a control cycle can provoke constructive or negative responses. The goals that receive attention, the pars, or standards, set, the reliability of measurements and reports, and the manner of corrective action—all affect the eagerness or sullenness of the people being controlled. So in addition to the rational, mission-focused aspects of control design discussed in the preceding chapters, we need to incorporate behavioral dimensions.

RELATING CONTROLS TO MEANINGFUL AND ACCEPTED GOALS

Meaningful Goals

A desirable end-result from the viewpoint of a central manager may be regarded as vague and inapplicable by an operating supervisor. The operating vice-president of a large textile firm, for example, is deeply concerned that each company mill keeps its production costs in line with the quarterly budget; for him the financial budget provides the natural criterion for cost control. However, the mill supervisors, who are in the best position to change costs, regard budgets as a nuisance. Most of them realize the competitive necessity of keeping costs down, but in their eyes budgets merely absorb time that they could better devote to actually doing something about costs. The supervisors think—and act—in terms of machine loading, output per man-hour, spoilage or material usage, machine maintenance to avoid stoppages, and indirect labor on the mill payroll. They know what happens to these factors long before budget reports are received, and explaining budget variances is merely a chore imposed upon them by "the pencil pushers in the office." Controls that have a constructive impact on the mill supervisors must provide prompt data on operating factors.

"Client satisfaction," to cite another example, is a poor control criterion for the printing shop superintendent of a public-relations firm. This individual has unique talent for producing beautiful brochures, announcements, and reports. But he takes no part in deciding what message is important or what media are most suitable. His finest creations may or may not satisfy clients. Instead of the broader goal of client satisfaction, relevant control criteria for the printing superintendent are unique and attractive publications, on-time production, and reasonable costs.

A control criterion is meaningful to a person 1) when it is expressed in terms that are operational to him—that is, in terms of actions and results within his sphere of activities; 2) when he can significantly affect the outcome being considered; and 3) especially when the outcome is clearly measurable.

Accepted Goals

To spark a constructive response, a control criterion must also be *accepted* as reflecting a valuable part of the job. Psychologically, the person being influenced should feel that measuring his results in this respect is normal and legitimate.

"Why heckle me about late deliveries?" asked one irate shipping clerk. "I handle the orders as they come to me." Here, the control on late deliveries was probably causing more harm than good, at least for the individual who felt the pressure.

Goals may be accepted for a variety of reasons. The person accepting them feels that they are relevant to his job, they are the way the game is scored, they are worthy, they represent "professional" conduct, or they bring punishment or reward. Whatever its origin and reinforcement, psychological acceptance is a prerequisite for the success of any control. Without acceptance of the goal, the control is sure to be resented; evasion, manipulation of reports, buck-passing then become normal responses.

Acceptance is often passive. The person being controlled recognizes the objective as part of his responsibility, but beyond that he is indifferent to the outcome. The typical taxi driver, for example, conscientiously takes his passenger to the stated destination without the slightest concern with why the trip is being made. Many of us, as will be pointed out in Part Six, have wide "zones of acceptance" with respect to parts of our work.

Although passive acceptance permits the control to function adequately, active commitment to the goal is obviously superior. Psychologists speak of a goal being "internalized"—the individual includes the aim as part of his own desires. When an individual gains personal satisfaction from achieving a result that is also a company goal, his feeling about control shifts. Control now aids him in gaining personal satisfaction. Steering-controls, especially, become aids rather than irritants.

Active acceptance is common. Typically, the carpenter does take pride in the quality of his work; the teacher does want his students to learn; the gardener does like to see a flourishing flower bed; and likewise with many, many people. Although questions arise about levels of achievement and about competing goals, as we shall soon see, a completely indifferent person is very rare.

Control, then, is much easier and more effective when it is related to goals that are meaningful and actively accepted by the people who really shape the result. So when designing a control system, it pays to seek out ways to match company objectives and personal values.

Participation to Secure Understanding and Acceptance

Participation in setting standards is widely advocated as a way of gaining positive commitment to control. Sales representatives in a large frozen-food company were asked to develop a picture of a first-class representative in terms of his duties and performance. Following a thorough and frank discussion of this ideal person, everyone was asked to prepare for himself a statement of what he thought he would accomplish during the next year. The representatives were expected to cover all the functions that had been listed, but they were free to set whatever outputs they believed were reasonable. Managment then used these statements as standards of performance for the following year.[1] The only adjustments—and these were made with the concurrence of the individuals involved—were to scale down some of the outputs if the representatives had set too high a standard for themselves.

The success of participation in a wide variety of instances attests its usefulness. But the way participation is employed is critical. Hypocrisy is an ever-present danger. Usually the end-result sought by a control is fixed by plans that are already settled. To pretend that these goals can be changed in participative discussions is misleading, and the participants will soon recognize this. Such discussions lead to a cynical mistrust of the whole system.

Participation does help, however, 1) to develop a mutual understanding of the aims and mechanisms used, 2) to translate broad goals into criteria that are meaningful and operational for the persons being controlled, and 3) to set stimulating pars—as indicated in the following pages. These are the subjects on which the controllee can make definite contributions, and having done so, is more likely to psychologically accept—and possibly feel a commitment to—the control endeavor.

SET TOUGH BUT ATTAINABLE PARS

Meaningful and acceptable control targets create a situation in which various control mechanisms can function. There is agreement about the aims of cooperative effort. However, further refinement of goals is necessary. The specific level of quality, amount of output, and expected degree of perfection must also be agreed upon. So we turn now to the psychological aspects of establishing pars.

Much criticism of controls comes from trying to enforce "unreasonable" levels of achievement. Some kind of speed limit, sales quota, or deadline, for instance, may be quite acceptable; but tempers rise if the standard is felt to be impossible or unnecessary. Unacceptable pars turn positive effort into all sorts of scheming to evade the pressure.

Dual Purpose of Pars

Pars serve two distinct purposes: 1) a motivational target we hope to achieve, and 2) an expected result used in planning and coordination. Although actual practice varies, most evidence indicates that people generally respond

---

[1] No trickery was involved. The representatives knew when they started discussing the ideal salesperson how the description would be used.

to a challenging target. We get more personal satisfaction and pride out of meeting a tough assignment than through exceeding an easy standard. Not everyone will meet the tough standard every time, but some will; and the overall result is higher than with an easy one. Notice, however, that with such high pars, some deficiencies will occur. For planning and coordination these shortcomings must be anticipated; thus, the estimated sales volume used for coordination purposes will be lower than the total sales quotas for individual sales representatives or separate product groups.

Pars that Motivate

Tough pars will motivate people only if several conditions are met. The individuals responding must feel that the target is attainable with reasonable effort and luck. Perhaps, like a handicap in golf, the person will privately set his aspirations a bit lower than the stated standard. But to stimulate determination and willingness to be inconvenienced, he needs a personal belief that he has a reasonable chance of success in achieving the adjusted target.

Also, a supportive atmosphere is necessary. Supervisors and staff can provide help; they *join in the game* of meeting a challenge—like climbing a mountain or swimming the English Channel.[2] Success is emphasized and rewarded; failure is a disappointment but is not treated as a catastrophe. If the par can be adapted to unpredictable, external variables—as with quotas tied to industry activity or cost tied to orders processed—the feeling of being supported in the venture is increased.

Motivating pars cannot flaunt social norms. Peer groups have their own ideas about acceptable behavior—output ceilings in a factory is the classic example. If a control pushes a person to take actions that are not approved by his friends, he is likely to abide by their social standards. Of course, there are plenty of instances—especially in the executive ranks—in which social pressures support controls. The attitudes that really count are those of associates whose friendship and respect the individual wants to keep. If these persons feel that a control standard and its measurement are fair and that cooperating with management is the right thing to do, they will constitute a social force supporting that standard.

Between the two extremes of direct opposition and strong support are many shades of group attitudes. Perhaps a group is indifferent to what management wants to accomplish, but it may have certain norms of its own, such as keeping the gang together or deciding who may legitimately set a standard. So exactly how peer groups affect responses to controls should be examined for each case.

---

[2] In *The Game of Budget Control* (London: Tavistock Publications Limited, 1968), G. H. Hofstede cites an array of psychological studies showing the role of the game spirit in adult motivation.

Figure 23–1   Even if a person wants to achieve a given goal, he may resent a standard of performance that seems extremely demanding.

Pars that Breed Dissension

If a par is so difficult that controllees consider it "impossible" to achieve, a strong negative, emotional response is likely. In fact, the behavioral-science literature is so full of gruesome cases of unattainable pars that naive readers assume that control always produces bad results. Sending incomplete or shoddy work to the next department, falsifying records, and transferring blame are common devices used by workers under pressure of appearing to meet a standard. If such defenses are inadequate, a person may become indifferent about his entire job, irritable to work with, and hostile to his boss. To relieve his frustration, he often joins in horseplay, slips a dead mouse into a can of soup, and takes an active part in any available protest movement.

Confronted with such behavior, a supervisor who wants to meet his commitments often increases pressure on the alienated operator. We are then faced with a vicious circle—more pressure, more resistance; and the adverse response undermines the social system that the controls were supposed to stimulate.

One way to avoid such a collapse is to lower performance standards to a level that the performer regards as realistic. Even if this lower par is insufficient to attain some broader output or quality objective, it is better than a standard that precipitates negative behavior of the kind just described. Fortunately, there are a variety of other steps we can take to reconcile gaps between what is needed and what the person responsible for the work regards as realistic; for example, redesigning the job, training, demonstrating, transferring people, and the like.

Participation in Setting Pars

Since feelings about what is reasonable and unreasonable affect the response to a control so sharply, we should make extra effort to uncover those feelings. Participation in setting the pars provides this communication. Each supervisor—from the president to the foreman—can frankly discuss with his subordinates the levels of expected results that will be used in each major control.

Such participation includes fact-finding, communication, prediction, negotiation, and mutual agreement. Although the supervisor has the stronger bargaining position, sincere agreement by the subordinate is essential if the control is to induce a positive response. And this feeling cannot be ordered by the boss. The process of participation itself has beneficial side effects, but these depend on consenting to standards that the subordinate really feels are attainable.[3]

Technical pars, such as man-hours per telephone installed or credit losses per dollar of sales, tend to be stable and must be renegotiated only when significant changes occur in the environment or technology. On the other hand, broader-output pars, such as sales quotas or budgeted profits, are reset for each period of time.

Participation in setting the broader-output pars is akin to bidding in contract bridge. A player first negotiates a tough but realistic standard based on his new situation and then strives to achieve the contract.

Thus, if our controls are to induce positive responses, we must approach the establishment of pars not just in terms of company needs. These standards also connote fairness, challenge, self-respect, social norm, winning, and related attributes for people. Consequently, we need to perceive the attitudes and values of the people whose behavior we hope to influence—a process explored in Part Six.

LIMIT CONTROLS AND MINIMIZE COMPETITION FOR ATTENTION

A third cluster of behavioral considerations, in addition to feelings about goals and pars, relates to the total load. We must avoid "the straw that breaks the camel's back."

Every one of us is subject to a whole array of controls. This multitude of controls creates some psychological problems in addition to those already discussed. The combined total may be so oppressive that we rebel. Also, the various controls compete for attention, and the stress of these conflicting pressures can lead to irrational, emotional response.

Consider the controls on a purchasing agent. Quality of materials and supplies obtained must meet exacting production standards. Delivery dates must anticipate actual use. Inventory levels will be checked against capital allocations. Prices paid will be measured in terms of cost estimates. Departmental operating expenses must stay within budgets, and a wide variety of

---

[3] The Management-by-Objectives technique, when properly applied, creates individualized objectives. These objectives become the acceptable pars for the control systems that we are discussing here.

personnel and accounting procedures should be followed. No personal gifts can be accepted. In addition, there are informal controls on intangible factors, such as obtaining data on new materials, responding to normal pressures for reciprocity, and minimizing risk arising from strikes and other shutdowns of suppliers. Tight controls over all these facets add up to a great deal of pressure; the purchasing agent can justifiably feel that he is buffeted from all sides.

Psychological Tolerance for Controls

People differ in their desire for freedom—and in the areas in which they feel that controls are repressive. One person may feel that regular working hours and scheduled tasks infringe on his rhythm of work, whereas another welcomes specific working assignments and checks on his progress, but is irritated by controls designed to monitor how he gets the work done. To some extent, by carefully selecting people for specific jobs, we can match these individual differences in security and freedom needs with the number of controls inherent in the work assigned. However, in this age of reaction against "the establishment," the number of controls necessary for management is likely to seem excessive to most people.

An emphasis on steering-controls, rather than yes–no controls, will reduce the feelings of constraint. Although steering-controls may prod and signal a need for action, they do not restrict the action. Also, participation in selecting criteria and in setting pars—already recommended—helps to incorporate the resulting controls into the normal activities associated with the job.

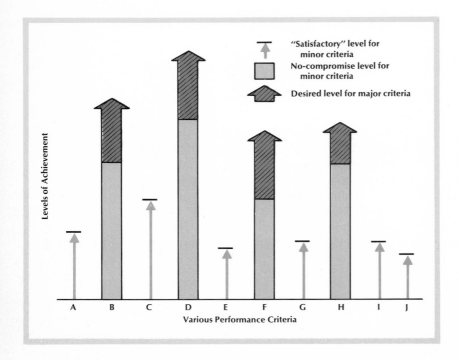

Figure 23–3 Pars for multiple goals.

*"Satisfactory" Targets
for Minor Criteria*

501

CHAPTER 23
Behavioral
Responses
to Controls

The main way to make a variety of controls tolerable is to associate "satisfactory" levels of achievement with most of them. As long as a satisfactory level for personnel turnover or equipment maintenance is achieved, no one gives it much attention; there is little or no pressure to improve performance beyond a satisfactory level. In any going concern, experienced personnel carry on many activities in this fashion. Controls exist but most of them are rarely brought into play, for people have learned to do satisfactory work; and these satisfied controls do not seem oppressive.

Obviously, if only a satisfactory achievement is accepted for a particular criterion, additional improvement in that area will probably be sacrificed. In effect, we are saying that the potential benefit of a tighter control here is not worth the psychological cost and the reduced effort in other areas. So we must carefully select areas where the effects of not pushing hard are relatively minor. Experience indicates that most people can give serious attention to only four to six different objectives. This rule-of-thumb suggests that controls above this number should require merely an adequate level of performance. Even four prime controls may be too many if they deal with complex and urgent matters.[4]

Reduce Competition for Attention

Even a limited number of controls, each with a tough par, can place an operator in a psychological vise. For instance, the purchasing agent mentioned above may find pressures for ready availability of materials, high quality, low cost, and low inventories competing for his attention. He may be forced to trade off low cost for higher inventory, low cost for less quality, and so on. He feels frustrated because he recognizes that meeting one goal will hurt him on some other front.

Such compound pressures can be relieved in several ways. Simple priorities may be established—in the preceding example, instructions might be given to meet targets in the following sequence: quality, availability, cost, inventory level. A more sophisticated guide would set "no-compromise" levels below the desired pars, and then set a priority to fill the gaps between the "no-compromise" levels and pars. In financial budgeting, three levels are sometimes specified for various accounts—optimistic, expected, and minimum. More often, an implicit tolerance range is understood by people using the controls.

The key in all these arrangements is to relieve the pressure at least to the extent of providing guidance for allocating effort among competing controls. By itself each control may be desirable and acceptable, but we must also consider how that control fits into the total.

---

[4] A simple arrangement for dealing with targets that merely need to be "satisfied" is "Management-by-Exception"—a signal is raised only on the exceptional occasions when the satisfactory level of attainment is not being met.

CONFINING CONTROL OF DETAILS
TO SELF-ADJUSTMENT

Running One's Own Show

Interference with the way a person does his work can be very annoying. A branch manager may be fully committed to training new sales representatives and have in operation his steps to meet an agreed-upon training target. But if he is then subjected to detailed control over the selection of trainees, their job assignments, and how they are supervised, he is likely to resent the control. Most experienced people—from bus drivers to atomic scientists—have a set of activities that they feel they know how to do well; and they regard interference by outsiders as lack of confidence and respect for this skill.

Expense budgets are a case in point. Such budgets frequently include great detail. (The amount of detail often arises mainly from the availability of expense records.) Once specific items for telephone or overtime are in the budget, a supervisor or staff controller is tempted to watch these items closely and to insist on an explanation each time actual expense exceeds the budget. The typical manager will resent such "needling," especially if his *total* expense is in line.

Feedback that Assists Self-Adjustment

In behavioral terms, the person who feels that his domain is being invaded by a control is likely to be the one who can best initiate corrective action. He knows the local facts and is aware of the effect of manipulating one part of a total operation. Consequently, the control on overtime, for instance, will probably be most effective if the standard and the feedback on overtime become an integral part of *local* management.

In controlling detail, then, a desirable arrangement is to 1) design control mechanisms for elements worthy of systematic attention, but 2) route the feedback to the lowest level of decision-making for that element. The aim is to encourage self-control and to avoid interference by an outsider. Obviously such a scheme will work best when some evaluation of the overall results can be made, and when the local decision-maker recognizes that the detailed feedback will aid him in achieving that desired overall result. In other words, for important details we design local, quick, operational feedbacks—and then encourage their use by the man who wants to run his own show.[5]

[5] This situation of considerable freedom in selecting local means to achieve an overall result is also well suited to participation in setting pars for local performance. Theoretically, the supervisor could withdraw entirely. In many cases, however, the supervisor wishes to strongly encourage the local operator to use particular controls, and periodic participation in setting pars is one way to indicate continuing respect for a control mechanism.

Conrad Hilton applied a variation of this arrangement in the management of his hotel chain. Each hotel, for the Waldorf-Astoria to the Shamrock, regularly computed and reported many ratios (e.g., number of meals per guest-day and coffee shop sales per guest-day). Occasionally, at an unpredictable time (one manager claimed 1 A.M. to 3 A.M. was most likely), Mr. Hilton phoned a hotel manager to ask what was being done to correct an off-target situation. If corrective action was underway, Mr. Hilton was satisfied; he relied on the hotel manager to decide what action fit the local situation. The effect of the system was that local managers retained a feeling of autonomy in operating their hotels, but they were alert to the control mechanism that central management had designed for local use.

DEVELOP A DISCERNING VIEW OF MEASUREMENTS

The human problems discussed thus far relate to the design of a control system—what criteria are acceptable, how tough standards should be, how many controls a person can tolerate, how to build on desires for self-control. We now turn to a different kind of issue, the *integrity* of the system. Can we believe what the control reports say?

Your response to the gasoline gauge on your auto or to the scales in your bathroom depends heavily on your belief in the accuracy and significance of

Figure 23–3   Prompt feedback directly to the person performing a job encourages voluntary self-adjustment and learning.

the message the device is sending to you. Neither device is fully reliable, so you allow for a margin of error. But if the error is unexpectedly large, you become annoyed about the false alarm (or lack of alarm). Here, as with all controls, one's feeling about the measurement can significantly affect the response.

Attitude Toward
Promptness Versus Accuracy

A prompt warning is often more useful than a tardy precise one, as we pointed out in Chapter 21. For instance, flood warnings by the weather bureau fortunately turn out to be "wrong" (a flood does not occur) two-thirds of the time, but we don't want to wait until the water is at our doorstep before starting suitable action.

Psychologically, early but unreliable measurements are a potential source of tension. The person making the measurement (or prediction) may be criticized because of his "mistakes," and the person receiving the report may become resentful if he is pushed to act on "wrong" information. Only when all persons concerned recognize the inherent limitations of such measurements (or predictions) can such friction be avoided.[6]

Preliminary estimates and probabilities can be used for control in a variety of ways. Perhaps they merely alert the operator, or they may set in motion a series of more elaborate measurements. If a large number of similar events are involved—as in quality control of long runs of machine-made parts or in extending credit to customers of mail-order retailers—statistical ranges of normal variability help distinguish between random and significant deviations. In all such uses, a clear awareness that the measurement itself may be misleading is coupled with precautionary action. Everyone knows that uncertainty exists. They are prepared to shrug off the false alarms.

Credibility Attached to Control Data

Uncertainty arising from a small, early sample (as just discussed) is fairly easy to understand and to accept psychologically. A different sort of problem arises from the use of symptoms and subjective measurements. Here the significance of the measurement is open to question. For instance, how valid a control instrument is the number of "laughs" at a Broadway play or the number of lunch dates scheduled by an aspiring young management consultant?

Such information is often helpful feedback; it provides some additional "feel" about what is happening. Both the measuring and the evaluating can

---

[6] Some individuals are so reluctant to take risks that they are incapable of dealing with unreliable data. These people either cry "wolf" for every distant shadow they see or do nothing until they are sure the wolf is at the door. They are misfits in a dynamic-control job.

be challenged. And this doubt about its meaning makes such data poor input for strict controls.

Such "soft" data can be used for *self*-control, and for supplementing more objective measurements. But until such a measurement has gained credibility in the minds of both the controller and the controllee, its use for yes–no controls or for postaction evaluation is likely to evoke a negative response.

RESPONSES TO
THREE TYPES OF CONTROLS

Behavioral reactions to each control element (goals, pars, measurements, feedback, and the like) are vital parts of every control design. To ensure that these human dimensions are recognized, we can also relate normal responses to each of the three basic types of control singled out in Chapter 21. The underlying response patterns are those already described, but regrouping them by types of control shows their significance in a new light.

Positive Response to Steering-Controls

The great virtue of steering-controls is that most people regard them as helpful rather than as pressure devices. If the goal is accepted, then the various feedbacks are treated as aids in achieving the desired result. Even though a control report sometimes conveys unwelcome news and prods a person to extra effort, the warning is constructive. Coming before work is completed, the signal is seen in terms of action needed rather than personal evaluation.

Since steering-controls provide inputs early enough for the principals concerned to use the data in their own decisions, their personal involvement in the control cycle is high. And this close involvement adds to the positive response.

Goal acceptance is crucial. Unless the sales representative wants to increase his sales, reports of deviation from course and of potential obstacles are merely so much static. And an unreasonable par can sour the reaction to the latest word about competitors or planned shipping dates. Steering-controls stimulate a positive response only when the people on the giving and receiving ends of the control effort are steering in the same direction.

Who steers is also an issue. As already mentioned, outside regulation of detailed operations annoys those who see themselves as experts in that area; consequently, self-regulation is more welcome. This suggests that steering-controls should be translated into action as close to the actual operation as possible. The positive response to the control activity then spreads among operating personnel.

Too many reports can swamp the system. Unimportant information diverts attention from the main goals; frequent needling is irritating. So for many dimensions, "satisfactory" conditions should not be reported. Feedback should center on key variables and on major shifts in the work environment. Steering can then focus on goals we wish to maximize and on serious obstacles.

Neutral or Negative Reaction to Yes–No Controls

Yes–no controls set hurdles to be crossed. They ensure that quality standards are met, that a proposed action is within budgetary restraints, and the like. For the "professional" who takes pride in his work, being able to clear such hurdles easily may provide reassurance. But the check is only whether work is good enough to pass. If it is better than standard, little or no praise is given; if it is below standard, the work is rejected. And rejection of work often creates delays and resentment. On the whole, when yes–no controls demand attention, they proclaim bad news.

Negative feelings about yes–no controls are often increased: 1) when a person is unable to achieve other goals because his work is blocked by this hurdle; 2) when the par is felt to be unreasonable (e.g., the budget is too tight or the requirement for a salary increase is too strict); or 3) when the standard is vague and unpredictable. The legality of a contract, the impact of a public-relations release, or the qualifications required for promotion are typical examples in which standards are likely to be vague and unpredictable. Unpredictable standards are particularly troublesome, for people lack guides on how to prepare for the control. Then if the standards applied to separate cases appear to be inconsistent, charges of favoritism and politics will follow.

Such reactions to yes–no controls can be reduced, first, by making clear that the control is necessary for attainment of company or department objectives. Both the aspect being measured and the par should be directly traceable to a basic objective. Second, keep the measurements as objective as possible, and insist on consistency in their application.[7] These steps will rarely make the control popular, but they will cut down frustration and foster a feeling of fair play.

Postaction Controls as Scorecards

In a strict sense, measurement and evaluation after work is completed cannot alter what is already done. Like Monday-morning quarterbacking, talking about what might have been won't change matters. Nevertheless, as pre-

---

[7] Occasional exceptions will, of course, be necessary. In fact, people working under the system may strongly advocate exceptions—to achieve justice or meet an emergency. But exceptions have little meaning until we have established a stable, predictable social system as a base.

viously indicated, postaction controls do serve two general purposes: 1) If we are going to play another game next week, the Monday-morning review of successes and failures helps us *plan* the *next* engagement.[8] 2) If some kind of reward is tied to how well actual results match selected goals, then the *anticipation* of that comparison and pay-off may be a strong incentive.

The influence of anticipated rewards depends upon the strength of the rewards (or punishments) and upon the perceived basis on which the rewards will be allocated. We are not here exploring the nature of rewards—they vary from bonuses and promotions to commendations and scoring well in the game. But we are directly concerned with the scorecards that determine, in fact, when a person receives a reward. Postaction control reports are such scorecards.

Control design affects what is put down on that scorecard—the factors that are watched, how they are measured, and the expected levels of performance. Their impact on behavior has several dimensions.

1) People in the system will be sensitive to factors measured and reported; if valued rewards are closely allied to control reports, the participants will watch the scoring like bettors at a racetrack watch the horses. Consequently, tying controls to the desired emphasis among objectives is important.
2) A lack of confidence in the reliability of measuring and reporting mechanisms will create a feeling that granting of rewards is probably inequitable.
3) In a rapidly changing environment, people may discover that their final score is affected more by their skill in renegotiating pars after-the-fact than by efforts to improve actual results.

When the purpose of a control is to produce a scorecard, several ways of automatically adjusting par after-the-fact are available. A "flexible budget" that is adjusted on the basis of actual volume—sales quotas adjusted for actual disposable income in each territory—illustrate an attempt to make the final standard reflect changes in the environment. Such devices usually increase the chances that the participants believe the par is fair—even though they recognize that the par may move up as well as down.

CONCLUSION

Managerial controls are concerned with achieving results—with a balance between inputs and outputs that pushes toward the company mission. These controls, however, take effect only when they influence the behavior of people. It is behavioral response, not the mechanics of a control, that really matters. So when designing a specific control or a control system, we must consider how

---

[8] Notice that analysis and evaluation for purposes of future planning need not adhere to a control format of predetermined standards and feedback. The aim of the analysis is to help devise better plans, whereas control is predominantly concerned with restraining and motivating behavior toward selected objectives.

executives and other people involved will react. This chapter highlights conclusions drawn from behavioral-science studies that relate to the process of controlling.

Controls typically have a poor reputation, at least in terms of their popularity with persons being controlled. Fortunately, such a negative feeling need not prevail. By including behavioral aspects in the design and execution of controls, these devices can become normal aids in cooperative effort. Important in this respect are meaningful and accepted goals, challenging but attainable pars, restraint on the number of controls, means for resolving conflicting pressures, encouragement of self-adjustments, and acknowledged uncertainty in some of the measurements. Participation in designing and setting standards also helps.

All these ways to secure positive responses to controls are only parts of a total management design. Remember that the need for controls arises from managerial planning and that controls function in an organization structure. So as we shape the control process, we must also be sensitive to harmony with our planning and organizing. This integration of control with other concerns of management is explored in the next chapter.

FOR CLASS DISCUSSION

1) Evaluate your feeling about such controls as a gasoline gauge, time clock, department store shopper, telephone supervising operator, customs inspector of luggage, auto safety inspector, medical exam to participate in sports. Why does your response to these controls differ?

2) "One of the major advantages of using Management by Objectives (MBO) in our planning is that now my subordinates have no basis for objecting to controls. Since the controls are based on jointly set standards, they must regard them as fair." Discuss this assertion.

3) "The fewer restrictions placed on *how* a job is to be done, the greater the obligation of the person who is assigned the job." Do you agree? Why? Why not? Even if true, what dangers should be watched for?

4) How may changes in personal needs, as discussed in Chapter 8, influence a person's acceptance of controls?

5) If "par" must serve two purposes, why not have two pars? The first par would be the basis for planning coordinated effort and the second par, a higher target, the basis of motivation. Comment on this approach to setting pars.

6) This chapter presents several reasons why people resist controls and offers ideas on how to minimize this resistance. Some people, however, seem to thrive on controls and in fact seem uncomfortable without tight controls. What should management do in this latter case?

7) How will the degrees and types of delegation followed in an organization affect the number of controls needed?

8) When may it be safely argued that postaction controls are both the most important and least-liked controls?

For cases involving issues covered in this chapter, see especially the following. Particularly relevant questions are listed after each case.

Petersen Electronics (p. 211), 14, 15
Merchantville School System (p. 217), 17
Graham, Smith, & Bendel, Inc. (p. 445), 18
Family Service of Gotham (p. 532), 11
Central Telephone and Electronics (p. 527), 11

FOR FURTHER READING

Cammann, C. and D. A. Nadler, "Fit Control Systems to Your Managerial Style." *Harvard Business Review,* January 1976.

Relates selection and design of controls to leadership style and internal motivation of subordinates.

Dubin, R., *Human Relations in Administration,* 4th ed. Englewood Cliffs, N.J.: Prentice-Hall, Inc., 1974, Chapter 19.

Cogent description of workers' responses to controls.

Hofstede, G. H., *The Game of Budget Control.* London: Tavistock Publications, Ltd., 1968 (U.S. distributor, Barnes & Noble, Inc., New York).

Actual operation and impact of budgets in six plants in the Netherlands; a thorough, unique, and very useful behavioral study.

Lawler, E. E. and J. G. Rhode, *Information and Control in Organizations.* Pacific Palisades, Calif.: Goodyear Publishing Co., 1976.

Uses behavioral-science research findings to explain responses to control mechanisms in organizations.

Morrisey, G. L., "Without Control, MBO Is a Waste of Time." *Management Review,* February 1975.

Stresses the need for systematic measurement and feedback to make M.B.O. effective.

Tosi, H. L., "The Human Effects of Budgeting Systems in Management." *MSU Business Topics,* Autumn 1974.

Good summary statement of the behavioral effects of budgets.

24

Integrating Controls with Other Management Processes

MANAGEMENT SYNTHESIS

The intimate relationship of controls to other management processes has been indicated throughout the last three chapters. Objectives and other goals, for instance, underlie the selection of control standards; programs find their financial expression in budgets; decentralization and participation have a marked influence on the acceptance of controls; and so on. Many control designs can be made more effective by modifying the company's organizing, planning, or activating. Conversely, sometimes the control design should be adjusted to aid the planning, organizing, or activating. Obviously such trade-offs should be considered, especially if synergistic effects in the total management design are possible.

In this chapter, we shall single out several ways controls can be fitted together with other management processes. These opportunities do not begin to cover all the interrelations. Rather, they are issues that arise time and again in actual practice, and resolving them wisely can be a great aid to effective management. These issues are: decentralizing without loss of control, harmonizing departmentation with controls, using staff in control, clarifying planned results to aid control, relating control to *new* planning, creating profit centers, and matching controls with activating modes.

The concepts involved are already familiar, for we have explained them elsewhere in the book. In this chapter, we are concerned largely with reconciling, refining, and combining these ideas.

Each time a manager delegates work (operating or managing) to a subordinate, he creates the problem of knowing whether the work is performed satisfactorily; hence, delegating inevitably raises the question of control. Often the degree of decentralization a manager will adopt is tied to how far he can do so "without losing control."

Modify Control
as Decentralization Increases

A manager need not lose control when he delegates a large measure of planning, but he should be prepared to change his controls. This alteration is illustrated in Table 24–1. First, the appropriate control standard changes. When

TABLE 24–1 EFFECT OF DECENTRALIZATION ON CONTROL

Degree of Decentralization	Nature of Control	
	Type of Standard	Frequency of Measurement
Centralization of all but routine decisions.	Detailed specifications on how work is to be done, and on output of each worker.	Daily for output; hourly to continuous for methods and for quality.
Action within policies, programs, standard methods; use of "exception principle."	Output at each stage of operations, expense ratios, efficiency rates, turnover, and the like.	Weekly to daily for output; monthly for ratios and for other operating data.
Profit decentralization.	Overall results, and a few key danger signals.	Monthly for main results and for signals; quarterly or annually for other results.

decisions are centralized, the manager himself will establish rather detailed standards for the method and output of each phase of the work. But as he delegates increasing amounts of authority to plan and decide, the manager should shift his attention away from operating details to the results that are achieved.

The frequency of appraisals also changes. Because the manager is no longer trying to keep an eye on detailed activities, most if not all daily reports can be dropped. As his attention shifts more and more toward overall results, the span of time covered by reports can typically be lengthened. For a division that operates on a profit-decentralization basis, monthly profit-and-loss statements and balance sheets come as frequently as most top managers want reports. Other factors, such as market position or product development, may be reported only quarterly.

Retain Safeguards

The shift from frequent, detailed control reports to periodic, general-appraisal reports does not preclude the use of a few danger-signal controls. A common practice is to expect a subordinate to *keep his manager informed* of impending difficulties rather than bother him with control data when conditions are satisfactory. A manager may ask to be notified when deviations from standard exceed a certain norm, thus applying the "exception principle" to control. Moreover, yes–no controls can be used for certain major moves, such as large capital expenditures or the appointment of key executives. Here again, the number of proposed actions that *require confirmation* will decrease as the degree of decentralization increases.

Still another kind of safeguard is to *insist that lower levels of management use specific control devices* even though an upper executive himself neither sets the standards nor receives reports on performance. A vice-president in charge of production may be vitally concerned that a reliable quality-inspection plan is in use, but he may take no personal part in its operation. He expects sufficient control data to be handy if the need for determining the cause of any problem arises.

As more authority is delegated, *self-control* by the subordinate becomes crucial. Such self-control is partly a matter of attitude and habit. In a situation in which centralized control has been the traditional practice, operating personnel naturally rely on senior executives or their staff to catch errors and initiate corrective action. If authority is then passed down to them, they need to formulate a new attitude. It may also be necessary to redirect the flow of information so that these people down the line have what they need to do their own controlling.

With heavier reliance on self-control by subordinates, the manager should act more as a *coach* than as the one who decides on corrective action. Ideally, the initiative for corrective action comes from the subordinate. To foster a relationship in which a subordinate is not reluctant to seek advice on tough problems, a manager should 1) avoid giving the impression that he feels an admission of difficulties is a sign of weakness, and 2) be careful not to make unilateral decisions that, in effect, take authority back from the subordinate.

Set the Stage

The kinds of controls and their associated relationships we are discussing grow only in a favorable climate. To create such an environment, we must think out a clear set of objectives for a task that is being delegated and develop ways of measuring their achievement. Also necessary is a clear understanding of which policies, organization, management methods, and other company rules *must* be followed and which may be regarded only as recommended practice. Moreover, those actions that require prior approval by a boss need to be labeled as such.

In addition to the substantial amount of planning and clarification of organization just outlined, high decentralization requires the right people. Subordinates able to perform the delegated duties must be selected, trained, and properly motivated. An executive himself must be able and willing to adjust his behavior, and the two people involved in each delegation must trust each other. Remove or significantly diminish any one of these aspects of an operating situation, and there will be a corresponding reduction in the degree of decentralization that is possible without loss of control.

HARMONIZING DEPARTMENTATION WITH CONTROLS

The ease of control is significantly affected by the way the company is grouped into departments and divisions. Important here are the concepts of clean breaks, deadly parallel, and direct interaction.

The simplest way departmentation can aid control is by separating departments or sections where a clean break in work occurs. Thus, a farmers' buying co-op will separate bulk fertilizer, seeds, fuel oil and gasoline, and garden supplies; each requires distinct storage and delivery equipment. Likewise, a well-run ski resort will have separate divisions for its ski run, its ski shop, and its housing and food; to separate control of its restaurant from its bar, however, becomes more difficult because the service is so interrelated. Control is easier when either the physical separation of operations or distinct stages of work make it simple for everyone to understand the organization structure.

A second suggestion is to set up two or more operating units in deadly parallel. A telephone company may create a series of nearly identical divisions; or finance companies may organize each of many offices on the same general pattern. Control is enhanced because the results from any one office may be

Figure 24–1 Establishing a series of virtually identical operating units introduces a deadly parallel and enhances control by making it easy to identify any unit that is out of line.

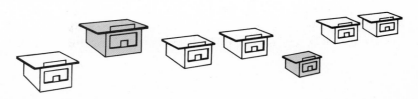

compared with the performance in the others. This deadly-parallel arrangement removes a great deal of personal opinion in setting standards. As we noted in the last chapter, it is important that employees accept standards as reasonable; if one branch meets a given standard, an aura of reasonableness is created for that standard, and a wholesome attitude toward it tends to develop throughout all branches.

A proper grouping of activities can aid control in still another way. By placing together activities that are closely interdependent, we can reduce the amount of "overhead" control. When interrelated work is done in several different departments, we have to control with precision the quality and flow of work as it moves from one department to another. Even with the best of controls a mistake is likely to result in arguments and buck-passing. So a more satisfactory arrangement is to assign the interrelated work to a single department or "project team," or to an individual.

Product divisions of a decentralized company are perhaps the best examples of this basic idea. Each division is in charge of its own production, selling, engineering, and other essential functions. Key people in the various departments know one another and exchange information freely and informally. If production falls behind schedule, the sales manager probably knows it almost as soon as the production manager; so the former adjusts sales efforts and delivery promises accordingly. Or if price competition is very keen on a particular item, the engineering and production men find out about it and adapt their activities with an eye to cutting costs. In short, the division functions as a team. Elaborate controls are not imposed from someone several organizational levels higher; instead, control information is promptly available to the people best able to do something about it.

In an organization where interdependent work is combined in a single unit, supervisory control focuses on end results. Data on in-process activities do not pass through several layers of supervision but are fed promptly to the appropriate members of the team, where they serve as a basis for self-regulation. Control is not only simplified, but there is also a much better chance for developing constructive attitudes toward control.

USING STAFF IN CONTROL

Staff assists in performing managerial work. As we explained in Chapter 4, most staff assistance is concerned with planning, but it is not necessarily limited to this one process of management. To what extent, then, should staff also be used in control?

We have noted that people naturally dislike controls, and they are especially sensitive about who may legitimately exercise control. Consequently, as we think about assigning control duties to staff, we must be sure 1) that the tasks are well suited to a person in an auxiliary position, and 2) that the control duties will not make it difficult for him to perform his other staff work.

Staff is often used in setting control standards. Since the early days of Scientific Management, industrial engineers—by employing time and motion study—have set output standards; product engineers have set quality standards; and cost accountants have set detailed standards for product and process costs. Often a market-research man takes part in establishing sales quotas for individual sales representatives.

The reasons for using staff to help set standards are clear. Special skills in engineering or research methodology may be required. Besides, setting standards is often very time-consuming, and an operating manager cannot give attention to all the necessary details. Of course, when we think of the whole range of control standards a company uses, it becomes evident that many standards are established without the aid of staff. However, when controls are formalized and detailed, staff help may lead to better standards.

But the active participation of staff is also a major source of human problems with control. All too often the people being controlled feel that standards are unreasonable and that control pressure comes from illegitimate sources. The technical jargon of a staff person—his preoccupation with certain aspects of a problem, his different values, and his desire to make a good showing all contribute to a lack of confidence by workers and lower-level supervisors in the standards he sets. If, in addition, the staff person applies pressure to meet the standards and suggests corrective action, fuel is added to the flames. "Who does that slide-rule artist think he is?" is likely to be the response.

The remedy appears to lie in two directions: 1) Operating managers should be instructed to give more attention to the review of standards before they are put into effect and to discuss these standards with people who will be expected to live up to them. 2) Staff people should be made to realize that their most constructive contribution lies in providing sound advice up and down the organizational hierarchy without usurping the functions that legitimately belong to the line managers.

Objective Appraisal

When control standards are expressed in terms of inches or dollars, the comparison of actual performance—as in auditing—is relatively simple. But measurements are often vague, and the allowances we must make—for illness, competition, and numerous other influences—are a matter of subjective judgment. There is widespread debate about the value of staff participation in this kind of appraisal.

Operating managers, it is pointed out, often lack objectivity in making appraisals. They are committed to a program, and the drive they need to make the program succeed calls for optimism and a determination to "do the impossible." Besides, a manager must appraise the work of his friends, and he is sensitive to the effect of appraisal on their morale. On the other hand, it is

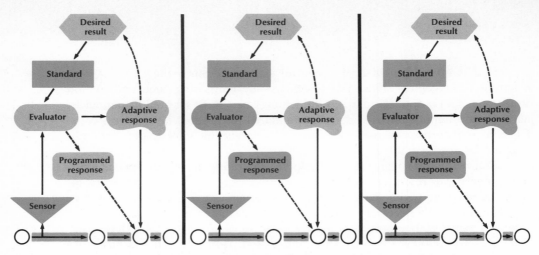

Figure 24–2   Staff may take various roles in the control process. In these three examples, staff assumes the roles indicated by the **darker color**.

argued that although a staff person has greater objectivity, he also has a less intimate knowledge of the facts. He, too, may have a bias, especially if he is looking at a situation only from the point of view of, say, personnel, engineering, or public relations.

Management needs both kinds of appraisals. The objective views of staff can be extremely valuable. But such appraisal finds its greatest use when we are formulating *new* plans rather than attempting to control activities so that they conform to *existing* plans. Corrective action is predominantly a line activity; so inevitably, an operating manager will rely primarily on his own judgment. When formulating new plans, however, an operating manager normally has more time for contemplation; and in this activity both the appraisals and proposals of staff can make their greatest contribution.

Yes–No Control

In special circumstances, a staff unit, like an operating manager, may exercise yes–no control. The personnel department, for example, may have to give its approval before the sales manager can make a final commitment to hire a new representative. Similarly, capital expenditures may require the approval of the controller; changes in organization, the approval of the management-planning section; or property leases, the approval of the legal staff. When yes–no control is exercised by a staff person, we say that he has "concurring authority."

Concurring authority works best when the criteria on which a staff person can either concur on or reject a particular proposal are specified. And, for those transactions where a mistake would be very serious and where time is not critical, concurring authority may be desirable as a safety measure. Serious difficulties with yes–no staff control arise when a decision to turn down a proposal is based principally on subjective judgment. It is one thing for a controller to say that an advertising appropriation has been used up, and another for him to turn down a proposal because he believes that advertising is unwise during a recession. An alternative arrangement is simply to have the staff person give advice; we may insist that a consultation take place, but specify that the operating manager's judgment prevails.

A final reason for carefully defining and restricting staff participation in control is that it undermines the constructive role staff usually plays in other areas. An unpopular assignment makes a staff person unwelcome; so his ability to be a friendly advisor is lessened if he goes too far into control.

AIDING CONTROL BY CLARIFYING PLANNED RESULTS

The basic concept that planned results become the goals of control is simple enough. However, achieving this neat relationship requires continuing managerial attention. Deciding to increase the ratio of women executives or to obtain more stainless steel from European sources merely states an end result. Since control becomes effective only through modifying the behavior of persons, these new goals have to be translated into more individualized standards.

Planning must be pushed from broad objectives to successively narrower and more specific tasks, until each necessary move or component is assigned to a particular person. Then controls at the subsidiary level will contribute to the final result. If the completed plans for the construction of a building are properly integrated—and then controls set up over the work of the foundation subcontractor, the structural-steel subcontractor, the electrical subcontractor, and everyone else who makes a contribution to the total structure—the final result should be a building as conceived by the architect.

Unfortunately, this sort of matching of the control structure with company objectives is hard to achieve. Often the planning is not extended to the point where we can safely rely on individual discretion to complete the task. And if a new objective is unusual, our normal measuring devices may not reflect its distinctive features. So, two questions should be asked: 1) Who must achieve what results if the new objective is to be obtained? 2) How will we know that the necessary contributions to the final result are being made? *Planning is incomplete until concrete steps have been identified and provision made to control this implementation.*

The elaboration of a plan down to results required from the many individual operators or units need not be prepared by a single central-planning body. A large block of the total work may be delegated to, say, the purchasing division, and the elaboration of plans for that block developed within the division. Such decentralization, however, does not reduce the need for full planning and subsequent control; only the location of who does the planning and control is changed by the decentralization.

This elaboration of planning and the creating of controls to check on the results—as just recommended—is hard to keep flexible. The controls, once established, tend not to be readjusted as objectives are changed. Take even the simple matter of a cutback in the sales of a product line because of a change in competition or technology. It is entirely possible that although the overall income and expense objectives will be adjusted to the new conditions, the control standards for engineering and other service departments will remain unchanged. Or suppose the company president decides to increase the number of broadly trained young men and women in the organization as a reservoir for filling top management positions. If the job specifications that control the representatives who actually hire college students are not adjusted, the specific actions at the various recruiting centers will not be attuned to the new objective.

The several steps involved in translating the new company objective into revised divisional subobjectives, securing understanding and acceptance of these objectives, adjusting the control standards and measurements accordingly, and using the control mechanism to influence behavior all take time and effort. In extreme cases, the inertia is so great that inconsistency between company objectives and ineffective controls continues indefinitely.

So the need to link planned results to control standards arises over and over. Whenever new plans are laid, we should ask, "What corresponding adjustments in controls must be made?"

RELATING CONTROL TO
NEW PLANNING

Three types of control were identified in Chapter 21: steering-controls, yes–no controls, and postaction controls. Normally, steering-controls and yes–no controls are used to adjust activities so that a predetermined objective will be achieved. A thermostat turns heat on or off; bacteria tests in a milk plant flash warnings to the processing units and to the whole collection system; and so forth. Corrective action may involve detailed planning, renewed motivation, and other managerial acts. In this sense, control may prompt action in any of the other managerial processes. Nevertheless, objectives usually remain the same, and the adjustments are like those of a ship's pilot who modifies his course with the winds and tide to reach home port. Only if there is a terrible storm or breakdown is the pilot likely to change (replan) his destination.

In contrast, postaction controls almost always lead to planning. For example, if a sales campaign is only partially successful, both the objectives and methods of the next campaign are likely to be modified; similarly, executive-development activities planned for next year will be strongly influenced by an appraisal of results achieved this year. In situations such as these, control reports serve as a basis for an entirely new cycle of managerial activity—planning, perhaps organizing, activating, and controlling the new activities.

But the concept that postaction controls rather than steering-controls are of principal use in planning needs one important qualification. Often we must lay plans for new activities before a present cycle is completed. University budgets, for example, are often prepared in preliminary form in December and January for the following school year. This means that the results of the fall-semester activities are not yet known, and the spring semester has not even begun, when the first steps of planning for new courses and size of classes have to be taken. Automobile companies have an even greater lead time in planning for their new models; commitments on design and engineering are often made with little or no measure of the popularity of the current year's model.

When new plans must be made before the results of the old ones are known, the results must be predicted. Control information of the steering type is naturally used in making these predictions. In some situations, then, we use information on how we are doing both as a guide to current operations and as part of the data on which the outcome of present and new plans are predicted.[1]

Care is necessary when the same data is used for both planning and controlling. The over-zealous vice-president of a furniture-manufacturing company used the expense ratios projected for a new method of operation as a standard in appraising current activities; this discouraged and annoyed the people in the plant, because they felt the new standards did not apply to their current operations. On the other hand, we may sacrifice accuracy for promptness in compiling control data, thereby limiting the value of our figures for planning. So, as we shift back and forth between planning and controlling, we must recognize the way basic "facts" were compiled.

CREATING PROFIT CENTERS

"Profit centers" are a valuable control device if organization and controls are well matched. A product division with its own engineering, production, and marketing can be judged in terms of the profit it earns. Since the profit figure shows the *net* result of all divisional activities, its use as a control standard encourages coordinated and balanced effort. Also, executives within the division must keep their activities in tune with the external environment in order to sustain profits. Although insensitive and slow to reflect intangibles, the profit standard is the best comprehensive measurement that we have.

---

[1] The benefits of control to planning, however, should not be exaggerated. If we want planning to be dynamic, we must consider new ways of performing work. Operating conditions change, and future opportunities may improve or diminish; consequently, more complete, or different, information is often needed for planning than control activities provide.

The temptation is to over-use the idea of the profit center. Some companies try to make each plant, each branch office, each warehouse, and even service units (such as purchasing) a so-called profit center. A profit is calculated for each unit. In effect, each unit buys its materials (often from other units), hires its own labor, and sells its products or services (perhaps to other units). Then after charges for overhead, a profit for the unit is computed. But how suitable is this resulting profit figure as a control standard?

Many profit-center managers devote more energy to negotiating the artificial prices used to transfer goods in and out of their unit and the amount of overhead charged to them than they give to improving the activities they can actually improve. Because of the profit control, they spend a lot of unproductive time playing games with transfer prices. The trouble arises because the control measurement—profit—is much more comprehensive than the activities assigned to the unit they direct. Most plant managers, for instance, do not decide the specifications of what they make, how much to produce, nor whom to sell it to at selected prices. Consequently, control standards focusing on cost, quality, and delivery are more appropriate for such a plant manager than total profit.

Profit-center control makes sense when 1) semi-autonomous, self-contained operating units are part of the organization structure, and 2) the primary objective of such a unit is profit. Managers of the semi-autonomous unit are free to adjust to new opportunities, and we want to encourage their initiative. But we must be careful that the control directs that initiative to the desired result. If the main purpose of a district office is to build sales volume, we will confuse matters by calling the office a profit center. The control we select should reinforce the intent of the organization.

Figure 24–3   Alternative approaches to product control. Product divisions, shown on the far right, serve as clear-cut "profit centers."

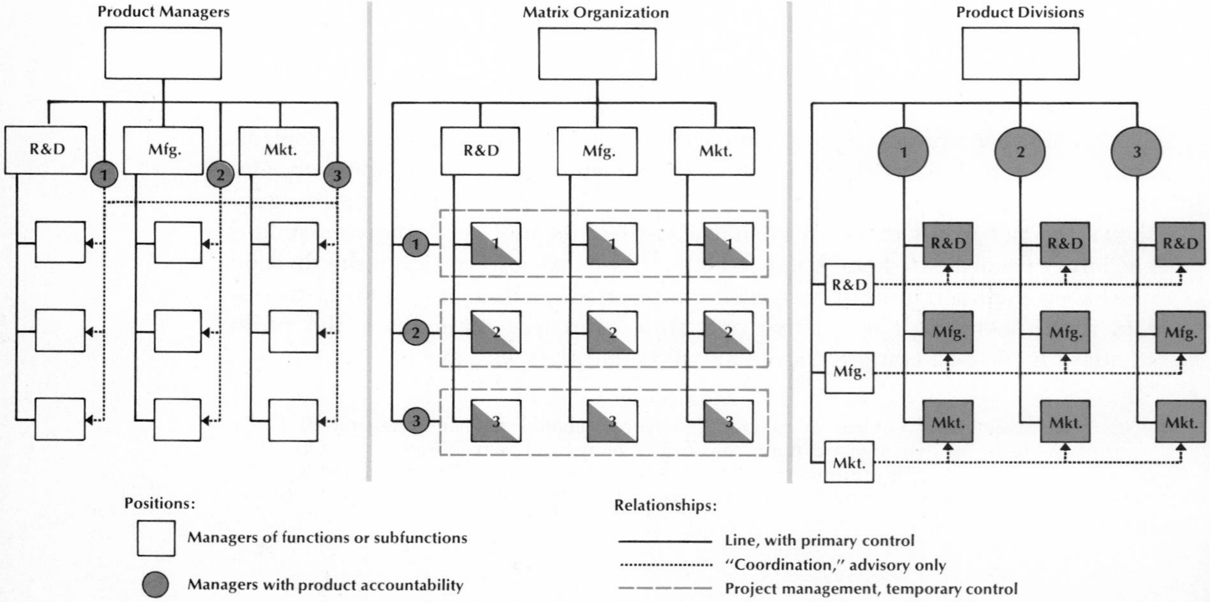

Positions:

☐ Managers of functions or subfunctions

⬤ Managers with product accountability

Relationships:

——————— Line, with primary control

····················· "Coordination," advisory only

– – – – – – Project management, temporary control

When activating a plan, as we shall see in Part Six, a manager has many options—ranging from coercion, through compromise and bargaining, to obtaining commitment. The control system in a company has a direct bearing on which of these activating modes is most likely to succeed. Three such links between controls and activating deserve special attention.

Coercion Calls for Close Controls

Often we do work which we dislike. We do it because we have to. Someone with power to withhold rewards or impose punishments may insist that we do the work. Or in bargaining with a powerful person, we may agree to do a disagreeable task in order to gain some other benefit.

One activating mode that managers use (in circumstances to be examined in Part Six) is this sort of strong pressure—or, coercion. If the work is not too onerous, subordinates become accustomed to it and treat it as a normal part of life—just like getting out of bed promptly in the morning. Nevertheless, the desire to behave differently remains.

When coercion is used, control becomes necessary to ensure that the work is done promptly, efficiently, and is up to quality standards. Without such close control, performance will drop. At some steps yes–no controls may be required; more generally, persistent and consistent postaction measurement will suffice. The crucial point is the need to couple coercion with close control. When a manager elects to seek results through coercion, he should be sure that corresponding controls are available or set them up promptly; otherwise action will not flow in the desired direction.

Control and Rewards Communicate

Clear communication by the manager of the results he wants is an essential element in activating. And actions speak louder than words. Enforced standards communicate. Regardless of what a boss or a manual may say, enforced controls are to the persons being controlled an unembellished guide to what they must do well and what they can do indifferently. Workers soon learn, for example, whether a "no-smoking" rule means what it says or is merely a suggestion of desirable behavior. It is the action of the supervisor in disregarding or insisting upon the standard that gives meaning to his instructions.

Similarly, rewards communicate. And in this connection a manager should be careful that his rewards reinforce both his activating requests and the control system he has established. Every production man knows that a bonus based on volume alone leads to neglect of quality. Similarly, if professors get promoted on the basis of publications, their teaching suffers. Perhaps the most common error in management practice is to reward people for short-run results while urging them to take a long-run viewpoint; such short-run payoffs are particularly insidious because long-run results are hard to measure and control. With a recognized reward (or penalty) associated with one kind of result, even the best-designed controls on other results will receive secondary attention.

Especially when making changes in established ways of doing business, a manager must be wary of stressing his new plan while leaving his control and reward system unrevised. Instead, updated controls and rewards should communicate the same "desired action" as the announced plan.

Link Steering-Controls with Commitment

When a manager is able to rely on commitment for executing his plans, the accompanying controls should primarily be steering ones. Commitment— as an activating mode—exists when subordinates want to carry out company plans because of the direct satisfactions they themselves get from the action. Since subordinates want the same outcomes as the company, controls can focus more on steering efforts toward those results. Less prodding is required to stimulate effort, and less checking is needed to make sure such effort is properly directed. Instead, because of the congruence of individual and company goals, we feed back information directly to persons doing the work so *they* can quickly adjust their own activities as necessary to achieve the mutually desired result.

CONCLUSION

Like the human nervous system, control is only one of the vital subsystems in effective management. Planning, organizing, and activating are also essential; and all these subsystems interact. If we change one, we may need to redesign the others also.

This interaction is a potential source of strength. By designing an organization suited to company plans, and by reinforcing both with compatible activating and controls, we can create a highly synergistic force.

Several ways to obtain such an integrated management design have been flagged in this chapter: decentralizing without loss of control, creating departments and profit centers that aid control, using staff properly, maintaining clear control targets, using control data for new planning, and enhancing control by consistent activating and rewards.

The design of good controls is an intriguing task. Fitting them neatly into a balanced management structure is even more challenging—and rewarding.

1) When "self-control" is possible, it is suggested that the superior should act as more of a "coach" to his subordinates. What are the key control devices needed to be a good coach?

2) How do recent trends toward wide diversification, if not conglomeration, affect the design and implementation of sound control systems?

3) A major reason for removing a group of activities from an operating unit and turning them over to an auxiliary division is to ensure that these activities receive adequate attention. Would it not be as effective and less expensive to provide the operating unit with the incentive needed to ensure adequate attention by stressing that these activities will be subject to close scrutiny in the evaluation of the operating unit? Discuss the pros and cons of this viewpoint.

4) "Essentially the results of staff work overlap the results of line executives' work. Therefore, you must define results you expect of staff people so that they will be harmonious with the results of line people. Both line and staff should get full credit for whatever is accomplished, just as though either had done it himself." Do you agree? What difficulties might arise in applying this concept?

5) "The fewer people involved in making a decision, the easier it is to control." Do you agree? Discuss.

6) *a)* Even if standards are set and corrective action by line management is taken, what problems may arise if the evaluation phase of the control process is carried out by staff personnel? How would you deal with these problems? *b)* Is it *possible* for subordinates to feel that a staff person has a more legitimate right to set standards and take corrective action than their line supervisor? Under what conditions might this occur?

7) Make a list, without referring to the text, of what you regard as key factors that must be considered in designing and using a sound control system. Ask yourself where else in the book, besides Part Five, each item has been discussed. You will probably find that virtually all of the items were considered in Parts One to Four. What does this tell you about the design and use of control systems?

8) "Profit centers" can be very valuable as control devices in business. Can profit centers be created in a way that offers the same benefits to a nonprofit organization that has no tangible measure of profit? Illustrate your answer.

Cases

For cases involving issues covered in this chapter, see especially the following. Particularly relevant questions are listed after each case.

FOR FURTHER READING

Bower, J. L., *Managing the Resource Allocation Process.* Boston: Harvard Graduate School of Business Administration, 1970.

Four case studies of capital allocation in large corporations. The actual process was found to be much more diffused and complex than capital-budgeting theory assumes.

Corey, E. R. and S. H. Star, *Organization Strategy: A Marketing Approach.* Boston: Harvard Graduate School of Business Administration, 1971.

A recurring theme is the inherent conflict between resource controls and product divisions.

Newman, W. H. and J. P. Logan, *Strategy, Policy, and Central Management,* 7th ed. Cincinnati: South-Western Publishing Co., 1976, Chapters 23 and 24.

Discussion of central management's use of controls to secure united action, and role of control in managing multinational enterprises.

Schleh, E. C., "Grabbing Profits by the Roots: A Case Study in 'Results Management'." *Management Review,* July 1972.

Shows the need for a close tie between planning, organizing, and controlling.

Vancil, R. F., "What Kind of Management Control Do You Need?" *Harvard Business Review,* March 1973.

Selecting financial controls that fit objectives and organization design; cautions against indiscriminate use of profit centers.

Not-for-Profit Note

for Part V

The application of control concepts within not-for-profit enterprises poses special problems. Unclear standards and difficulties in measurement, coupled with sharp restraints on the use of rewards (discussed in Note Six), undermine the effectiveness of control processes, which in profit-seeking firms have widespread and successful use. Several characteristics often present in not-for-profit ventures contribute to such lame control.

The intangible output of museums, orchestras, schools, and retirement homes is *hard to measure* in terms of objective standards. Because quality of the service is often judged subjectively by persons with varying expectations, pars lack consistent definition. Of course, some aspects of the activity can be measured—such as the number of people served and direct financial expenses —but these aspects tend to receive disproportionate attention merely because they can be measured.

In profit-seeking concerns the adequacy of their service relative to its cost is repeatedly appraised by consumers. But such a *market test is unclear* for those not-for-profit enterprises that rely on gifts or subsidies. Especially when the enterprise has a local monopoly, as is often true for schools, hospitals, and other service establishments, patronage alone does not give us a full evaluation of service rendered. For sensitive control, additional measures of quality of service and consumer response are needed.

One source of standards for a local service establishment is a comparable unit in another locality. Schools, hospitals, and even zoos, for example, can be compared with neighboring institutions or with "industry" averages. Such comparisons always need to be adjusted for differences in size, service objectives, existing facilities, and the like; nevertheless, they do provide some control benchmarks where standards of performance are hard to set. Unfortunately, these *cross-comparisons* usually focus on expenses, activity, and other easy-to-measure aspects; they are of limited help where qualitative judgment is required.

If an enterprise has not just one but several hard-to-measure objectives, control is further complicated. As we observed in Note Four, *priority* among these objectives—for instance the relative weight to be given in a school to the 3 R's, social development, character, creativity, culture, and vocational training—is often ill defined and left to the teacher. And if the operating objectives are fuzzy, then control standards and corrective action lack their necessary base. In such circumstances, systematic control systems focused on results are rarely attempted.

Because of these limitations of output controls, many not-for-profit enterprises emphasize the *control of inputs*—expenses and use of personnel—and of the volume of activities. Such controls on the use of resources and on rates of activity are typically treated as restraints, and there is little or no positive reward for meeting the control standards. Quite understandably, the personal response of people affected by these restraining controls is usually negative.

Of course, managers do give attention to the quality and quantity of output. Certainly orchestra conductors evaluate results and take corrective action. However, this kind of control is necessarily individualistic and subjective; especially in medium- and large-size enterprises, it lacks the *consistency and predictability* that is so important in developing widely accepted norms of behavior. And if busy managers are "hit and miss" in their exercise of these controls, employees are likely to feel that corrective action is arbitrary and unwarranted.

All too often, then, controlling in not-for-profit ventures is still in an elementary and uninspiring stage. The most prevalent controls are merely postaction checks on expenses. Steering-control, as described in Chapter 21, is rarely used. The concept of a balanced control structure cannot be applied where so many key areas lack acceptable measurement.

The rather rudimentary stage of control, which is typical of many not-for-profit enterprises, has a direct bearing on the activating process discussed in the next Part. Where tight control is not feasible, a manager has a limited choice of his activating mode. As we shall see, he must rely primarily on personal commitment.

Case Studies

for Part V

CENTRAL TELEPHONE AND ELECTRONICS (CTE)

Central Telephone and Electronics is a large telephone company servicing one of the central provinces of Canada. While maintaining a loose affiliation with the Bell System, CTE operates as an independent corporation. At one time, the company also developed, produced, and sold electronic devices used in the communications industry, but these activities were abandoned 30 years ago.

Philip Stephenson, president of the company, expresses great pride in his organization.

> We have over 18,000 loyal, dedicated workers and managers [he said]. They stretch across hundreds of miles of the province. They work in small three-person offices in isolated farm communities and in large offices serving several of our major cities. They are as different as the communities they work in, but they are linked by one common goal: their desire to "Do more! Do better!" That is our company's motto—"Do more! Do better!"

THE PAST FIVE YEARS

Although Stephenson's comments might strike an outsider as "corny," until five years ago there was a great deal of evidence to support his claims. Problems brought on by the combination of a decade of rapid expansion and then recession during the past five years necessitated a number of changes in company policy. Many long-service employees were unhappy about these changes.

The company has reduced its personnel from over 23,000 to about 18,000 in the last five years, while simultaneously servicing a larger market. This reduction in force has been accomplished primarily through attrition, but was accelerated by some early retirements, and several hundred dismissals. Although continued automation has been a major factor in making this reduction possible, every employee has in addition been asked to "pull a little harder."

"It came as quite a shock to many of the old-timers," said one company official, "to learn that some long-service employees were being terminated for unsatisfactory performance. For more than 50 years, anyone who lasted more than three had a job for life."

During the rapid-growth period, CTE had hired several hundred college, engineering, and business-school graduates to be groomed for management positions. Referred to as "jets" by management, these young people were given accelerated training and promotion opportunities. Although fewer than 40 percent of the jets remain with the company, those who do occupy responsible, middle-management positions.

No jets have been hired, however, for the past five years. In fact, the company has had a virtual hiring freeze in effect, with only a few replacements for technical personnel and operators brought in.

DECENTRALIZATION, DEVELOPMENT, AND CONTROL

The keys to our business now [Stephenson said], can be stated in three words—"Decentralization, Development, and Control." In the past we had a rather centralized functional organization. Since we are forced by economic and political conditions to do more with less, we have to get more out of each and every employee.

Stephenson went on to note that over the past three and a half years, the company has made a concerted effort to encourage more initiative and decision-making "down the line." It has introduced Management by Objectives and run numerous seminars on participative planning and team building.

Jim Prince, director of personnel, has organized these programs.

We are fighting a difficult battle [he explains]. With such major reductions in staff, we have the potential for serious morale problems. The "worriers" are fearful that our new, forced ranking-appraisal system will lead to their demotion or discharge. The former jets have slowed down in their climb to the top and hence are becoming concerned. We will not have a great many promotions for another ten to 12 years, at which time a large segment of our top executives retire. In addition, everybody is being pressed to do more. Although our customer service is holding up fairly well, there have been, according to our records, more complaints from customers about higher rates and poorer service.

Prince indicated that it is his responsibility to provide the appraisal, counseling, education, and resource-planning systems needed to satisfy the president's desire for "development."

I have to convince every manager [Prince said] that one of his major responsibilities is to invest in the development of his people. Then I have to offer the facilitating programs to make this possible. If there isn't enough room to grow hierarchically, we have to give people the challenge to grow in their current jobs and to move laterally.

Prince has met with a number of problems in his effort to increase human-resource development. One experienced middle manager, Norb Evans, summed up the thoughts of many attending one of Prince's seminars. As he said:

Top management talks about us investing in the development of our people; then they call for increased productivity in every part of the business and impose hundreds of controls to measure productivity. Rewards and penalties are dished out according to these control standards, and I have yet to see any that really recognize investments in development.

Another experienced manager, Mary Dyer, said,

About five years ago the "manual monsters" took over. We have always had many policies and procedures but they were general guidelines. Though we had access to Bell System procedures and standards, we never used most of them. In fact, many of us wondered how we would survive if be *had* to live by those manuals. Now we are finding out! As part of our MBO program, I have 14 "objectives" that my superior and I have to agree to. But I now have to send in control reports that measure performance in my department against *117 standards*. Each month my department's results are compared to those of 20 others like mine across the province. If we miss a standard by more than an acceptable margin, it is red-circled. If we miss by a wider margin or miss any of 25 standards in two successive months or in three out of any six months, we have to file a report explaining the deviations. What a waste of time and an insult to our ability! We will soon strangle in a sea of red tape.

Last month I wasted two days at headquarters explaining why one of the ratios they use to measure maintenance efficiency had dropped from the 9.5 standard to 8.3 and 8.7 for the last two months. This ratio, an indicator of how efficiently we have maintained our open-country lines, is only one of seven maintenance ratios reviewed each month. There are at least five ways I could have doctored the figures to show this ratio at 9.5. Or I could have authorized material expenditures that would have cost the company more than it's worth to meet the 9.5 figure. By spreading these expenditures over four accounts, I could have stayed within my material-expenditure standards, too. I mentioned this to one of the staff people whom my boss called in to help him "interpret my justification." The staff person didn't even understand what I was talking about. It is just plain silly. Here we are cutting back in areas where I need more people, and we have these staff types falling over each other trying to find new ways of measuring things they don't understand.

A third manager, Bud Scibilli, explained,

I understand what they are doing. They want to decentralize operating decisions but increase and centralize controls. To set good controls is hard. Although they try to adjust standards to reflect differences in departments, it is very difficult to be fair. For example, we have one standard that sets a maximum of three "rings" for an operator to answer. If our office can average anywhere between 0.5 and 2 rings per operator call, we are graded excellent. Between 0.5 and 1.4 and between 2 and 2.9 are acceptable. More than 3 rings or less than 0.5 is unsatisfactory. The reason for less than 0.5 being unsatisfactory is that too quick a response average is supposed to indicate that we have more personnel than necessary and should consider a reduction or reassignment of personnel.

To begin with, these averages may mean something in a big-city office, but out in the farm country we have many ups and downs based on weather, fire, flooding, and so on. Second, how long do you think it takes an experienced person to figure out how to get around the standards? For every genius at the home office dreaming up a new standard, there are several thousand working people relieving the tedium of the day by coming up with imaginative ways of getting around them. This leads to more standards to plug the loopholes and more red tape.

I wish we could go back to the old days when we were told what to do and had to live with only three or four measurable standards—such as total costs per unit of "throughput," customer service, and employee turnover. All this freedom and growth they are talking about seems to be negated by the controls.

CONCLUSION

Jim Prince, having heard these and similar comments, indicated growing concern.

The president wrote a very strong policy statement for me [Prince said], indicating that human-resource development is every manager's job and must be given high priority. I am trying to help with seminars, career-planning programs, and a host of supporting services. But the fact remains that it is very hard to measure the results of an investment in human development. The "graphite engineers" [methods and industrial engineers] keep increasing the number of measures of productivity but haven't much to offer for measuring contributions to resource development.

In addition, many of our experienced middle managers do not like MBO or participative-management systems. It's not their style, and some are running scared and are using the pressure for productivity to jump back into the details of subordinates' work. They use control to block real decentralization and give lip service to development. The president is right—we need "decentralization, development, and control"; but how do we balance the three instead of having them neutralize each other?

FOR DISCUSSION AND REPORT-WRITING

Organizing: Structural Design

1) "Decentralization, development, and control is viewed by top management as a way of securing organizational balance. I regard the statement as a contradiction in terms." Comment on this statement by a CTE department head.

2) How might we deal with Mary Dyer's reaction to the staff person who "didn't even understand what I was talking about" and her further observations on staff?

Human Factors in Organizing

3) What might have been done (and by whom) to deal with existing customs when the need for change became evident five or six years ago?

4) How may the changing economic and work environment in recent years have affected human needs and their potential for satisfaction through work?

5) In what ways might CTE management have reduced the potential for destructive conflict when they realized the need for reducing the work force?

Planning: Elements of Rational Decision-Making

6) In the current environment at CTE, is there likely to be a greater or lesser need for creativity at lower levels of management? Explain.

7) What can be done *now* by CTE management to increase or decrease creativity at lower levels? Tie this answer to your answer to question 6.

Planning: Decision-Making in an Enterprise

8) Is the need for formalizing the hierarchy of objectives more than, less than, or the same as it was during CTE's rapid growth? Explain.

9) Will the need for considering political factors be higher than, lower than, or the same as it was during CTE's rapid growth? Explain.

10) "To deal with our current problems, we need more standing plans to ensure coordination, since everyone is working under greater pressure."

"To deal with our current problems, we need fewer standing plans to provide us with the flexibility we need to adapt to current pressures."

With which the two statements do you more nearly agree? Why?

Controlling

11) Based on the number of controls now being instituted in CTE, is high participation in setting standards as sound an idea as it was when there were many fewer controls?

12) Should the same staff personnel who play a major role in determining where to set standards and what those standards should be also play a major role in measuring and interpreting results?

13) Does the company appear to be giving proper recognition to the need for qualitative as well as quantitative standards?

14) When the number of controls applied to a manager's performance increases, is it more or less desirable to have his assumptions regarding his goals written down?

15) How should top management deal with the need for control over longer-term, less-tangible "investments" in person development?

16) (Summary Report Question: Part Five) What actions should the president take to increase the effectiveness of his control system and to elicit more positive responses to controls?

Activating

17) What criteria would you use to determine when to seek compliance rather than commitment to a particular control?

18) What criteria would you use to determine when to use power (coercion) versus compromise to elicit a more positive response to a control?

Summary Question for Solution of the Case as a Whole

19) What action should the president take to increase congruence between his desire for decentralization and development and his need for assuring greater operating efficiency?

CASE 5-2
FAMILY SERVICE OF GOTHAM

Freda Maurer is regarded as a kind and considerate friend but an awesome enemy if she "really gets her dander up." And she is dangerously close to getting her dander up, according to Jim Torrent, director of casework for Family Service of Gotham.

Mrs. Maurer has been executive director of this agency for almost 25 years [Torrent said]. I have only been here for six years, and in that time I have come to admire Mrs. Maurer as an executive as well as a humanitarian. Jan Blossom [office manager] and I have tried to persuade her to bring in a consultant to help her implement the board's request for tighter controls, but she says she doesn't need any help from consultants at this time.

THE AGENCY

Family Service of Gotham is a private, nonsectarian agency that provides a range of social services to the people of Gotham. The bulk of its budget of

$2.7 million stems from the Gotham Community Chest. Approximately 25 percent comes from fees; direct gifts and endowments make up the balance.

It is very frustrating to try to expand our services Torrent said, because invariably for every extra dollar we raise through fees or gifts, the Chest reduces our annual allocation by 80 to 90 cents.

The agency is one of more than 1,000 private agencies in the United States that operate on a local, community basis. Most, like Family Service of Gotham, are members of a trade association of family-service agencies headquartered in New York City. The motto of this association, "Strength to Families Under Stress," typifies the goals and frustrations of the member agencies. Their goal is to provide help, through professional social workers and volunteers, to individual family members, but primarily to strengthen the family unit. With limited resources, however, the motto highlights the dilemma. "What help, to which families, and under what kinds of stress?' 'is the three-part question that has been debated at length in individual agencies and at local and national priority conferences.

Family Service of Gotham (FSG) is one of three private family-service agencies serving Gotham's 200,000 population. Although each of these agencies offers several services, FSG offers the fullest range. Its services include:

1) Individual and group counseling
2) Infant day care
3) Foster-home placement
4) Drug and alcohol treatment
5) Senior-citizen services

In addition to the other two private, sectarian agencies, there are public-welfare and-assistance services and a number of other agencies offering one or more special services.

FSG has approximately 50 people on its staff, including 37 with degrees in social work. Freda Maurer, the executive director, is a youthful 60 years. She has three immediate subordinates: Jim Torrent, director of casework, supervises 30 caseworkers through four section heads. Jane Blossom, who has an MBA and CPA, manages the office and directs accounting services. Clark Whitman, the executive director's third subordinate, supervises the agency's day-care and senior-citizens programs.

Mrs. Maurer is the chief executive officer, but she is responsible to a board of directors. The board is made up of local business and professional people, clergy, and several wealthy philanthropists. Although Mrs. Maurer has great influence with the board, it selects its own members and elects a board president each year. Last month, the board selected William Garcia. A Mexican-American, Garcia has risen from poverty to prominence in his 43 years. He has been active in community affairs and is president of a large insurance and real-estate brokerage firm. He has served on the FSG board for three years and has been perhaps its most outspoken member on the need for (in his words) "running the agency in a more businesslike way."

As a result of recent inflation, recession, and pressures for reduction in government spending, agencies such as FSG are faced with more clients, who have more problems and less money. The Community Chest has indicated that it will have to reduce its allocation to FSG next year, but the amount has not been disclosed. For three of the last five years, the agency has operated at a deficit, reducing its already small endowment fund.

Garcia was elected by a six to four vote of the board on the promise that he would play an active role in assisting the director to set priorities for the agency and develop tighter controls to ensure greater efficiency.

GARCIA'S VIEWS

Freda Maurer is an amazing woman [said Garcia]. I respect her for what she wants to do and love her for what she tries to do. Despite our differences on how to deal with our current crisis, I think she is a good executive. Her problem is not lack of strength or the toughness to stand up to a difficult situation, but that she is too strong and refuses to believe she can't do everything she wants. She is a builder but not a planner. She has visions of how to change social evils, and they require time, patience and, unfortunately, a lot of money. When I point out that we don't have the money, she laughs and says, "Don't worry, Willie, we'll get it if we need it." Well, we can't keep spending more than we have. We must set priorities and make sure that our personnel follow them. They must be supervised more closely to keep them within the bounds of our agency priorities; and they must increase their efficiency even if the quality of their work has to drop off a bit. Agencies like ours may soon be fighting for survival; so we have to get more efficient or we won't be around to help anyone.

Once we get our basic cost studies done, we can set standards and control performance in any of the following ways. The first is very simple. For each branch of our work, select a unit of service—such as a day of care for one child, placement of a child in a new home, families counseled, senior-citizen lunches served, and number of participants in recreational activities—and then show total cost per unit of service against our original estimates. This would at least make supervisors cost/output-conscious and would give the board an idea of relative costs for the different services and of where people are working to reduce costs per unit of service.

Second, there could well be a system that got closer to individual productivity. If the service units cannot be assigned to single social workers, then keep track of the volume of the major activities they do perform: for instance, number of counseling interviews or, for placement workers, the number of home visits, number of telephone inquiries, and number of new homes investigated. A simple daily tally could easily be kept and then summarized for each two-week period to average out the variation in specific calls. Incidentally, by evaluating several caseworkers, everyone would know who was most productive. If some unusual event absorbed a lot of time, this could be noted on the summary report. Of course, the board would not be concerned with such reports, but the supervisors and Freda would. Our task would be to make sure that the system was being used conscientiously. With this sort of attention to output, even though not exact, I'm sure FSG would generate more service for its expenditures. Also, we would know where necessary cutbacks could be made with the least pain.

Third, we might use MBO. This would get each worker—or a unit of two or three people who do a job together—to participate in setting short-run goals and then reviewing output. We have well-motivated people, and if we really challenge them—and give them a chance to challenge themselves—the results will be impressive. MBO is a way to keep people thinking about getting the important aspects of their job done. And they get a real feeling of accomplishment. This system could involve everyone from caseworker to executive director.

If there are even better ways to improve productivity, let's use them. I'm not wedded to any particular forms. But it is clear to me and to a majority of the board that we now have virtually no control and yet are accountable to our supporters for spending their money. We have to do something.

BOARD SENTIMENT

Garcia has considerable support from other members of the board, though not all feel as strongly as he does. Peter Carbonara, chief of surgery at Mother Cabrini Hospital, typifies the ambivalence of several board members:

There is no question that we have to get Freda to cut back, to set some priorities and live with them. That's as far as I go, however! I don't want to get into the details of how she does it. Bill [Garcia] wants to set up a series of cost studies on each of our major programs. Then he wants to have each program evaluated. Based on these evaluations, he envisions setting standards and controls to make certain that necessary levels of efficiency are achieved. Presumably, if the standards aren't met for a program, it will be reevaluated and perhaps even dropped.

Carbonara expressed great reluctance to try to force Mrs. Maurer to prepare such studies and develop the ensuing detailed plans and controls:

I've seen what happens at the hospital when this starts. Within 18 months the bureaucrats take over and suffocate you with forms and control reports; and costs keep going up anyway. I say we should give Freda a flat sum, a dollar limit, for each major service and monitor her quarterly. If she goes over in one place, we can force her to shift it from another. She knows this agency better than all of us put together. We don't have the time or knowledge to try to hold her in line with detailed controls. If we try, we will waste money on the studies and controls, make people angry, and probably have Freda outfox us anyway.

Other board members, however, support Garcia's approach. Edward Nelson, president of a large pharmaceutical firm headquartered in Gotham, said:

We have to help Freda. She's a great leader but she is not a planner. She may know where every nickle is being spent but it's mostly in her head. We don't have any real detailed information on how effectively the money is being spent. We need facts to guide us with tough priority decisions. We have to know just how much more we can get for each dollar we spend and where we get the best return. I recognize that we are dealing with tangible costs and intangible benefits, but this doesn't pose an impossible situation. Heaven knows, I have worked with enough research people in my company to know that one can set priorities and control expenses while being uncertain about the payoffs.

Nancy Morgan, another member of the board, represents a third point of view:

To tell the truth, I'm confused by all the debate. Garcia, Nelson, and others keep talking about "cost-benefit studies," which will lead to setting "priorities," and about creating "control standards" to "monitor results" and "shift resource comitments." Frankly, it sounds like a lot of jargon to me. I don't have a lot of business experience, but I have worked with enough charities to know that most of the so-called efficiency techniques brought in from business end up lowering morale more than costs. Freda Maurer knows more about how to run this agency than any of us. I think we should listen to her. Let *her* tell *us* the minimum she needs to do the job *she* thinks should be done. Then, we should get out of her way and spend our time raising the money and squeezing more out of the Community Chest rather than creating and studying a lot of reports on agency operation.

FREDA MAURER'S THOUGHTS

I am very concerned about recent events. No matter how they put it, the board's support for Willie Garcia's position shows less than full confidence in me. I am certain not only that Willie's studies and reports will not help, but also that they will hurt morale and reduce the respect the people in the agency have for my position.

Mrs. Maurer went on to point out that her agency differed from business in that it had no measure equivalent to revenue or profit. The services the agency provides cannot be measured in tangible terms. Therefore, she felt that if there would be measures only for cost, they—the costs—would be unduly controlled to the detriment of long- and short-run benefits.

I can do things that would seem to improve the "efficiency" of the agency [she said], but only because we can't measure the loss of benefits that will accompany cost-cutting. For example, my family counselors could handle twice the caseload they now have if I required it. In the short run, they could still deal with current crises, but they would not have time to probe for the causes or develop the trust necessary to anticipate and prevent problems. Within six months they would start losing control of the situation and be giving "first aid" instead of curing and preventing family problems. Within another six months we would have *more* and *worse* problems to deal with if people still trusted us enough to come back.

Another example Mrs. Maurer gave dealt with priorities:

I'm sure Willie could show that we should give up our day-care center. If I let him, it wouldn't be hard to find figures to show that other agencies can pick up our children and service them at a lower cost per day. But where will Willie get the figures that show how much we lose in our counseling and foster-care programs when we lose the opportunity to get to know families through the day-care program?

A final example of the difference in viewpoint deals with applying efficiency techniques to foster-care programs.

The social workers in the office [Garcia said] can be more closely supervised than those in the field. They also monitor each other. If someone isn't pulling his or her share, the others know it. But the caseworkers who are out in the field seeking and checking on foster homes are hard to supervise. I am sure we could set standards for their case loads and get more out of them. They would have to spend less time drinking coffee and gabbing, but they could help a lot more kids who need foster homes if they worked harder.

Mrs. Maurer disagrees.

If I have a loafer or foot-dragger in the field, I find out. I don't need standards and reports, which make people think I don't trust them, in order to catch one sluggard. All those reports will do is force everyone to do less careful investigations on prospective foster homes and less careful review of how our kids are doing with our current foster parents.

At first, I was hurt by the board's support of Willie [she concluded]. Then I got angry and considered resigning. Now, I have calmed down. I know they want to be helpful. Things are very tough now. Money is hard to come by and everybody is nervous. But we will weather this storm like all the others. We can work harder and smarter without all these studies and reports. My concern is not survival. We will survive! My concern is how I keep Willie and his allies from making it even harder. I could fight him, and I daresay I have enough friends in town and on the board to force him to back off if it comes to a "him or me" situation. That is wrong, though. It polarizes, and it would deeply hurt Willie; and, after all, he means well.

As an alternative, I could appear to go along with Willie. It would cost us a bit in time and energy but if I can't "bury" him in useless studies and inconclusive, contradictory reports, then I should be ashamed of myself. I fought these battles years ago with the bureaucrats who were seeking to take over welfare from private agencies. I won more than I lost even then, and I'm a lot smarter now. I could probably get Willie so confused and frustrated he would go looking for another place to make more efficient. I would hate to do that, too, because Willie has helped us a lot in the past and still can help if he would just realize that many of his ideas do not fit our kind of business. Maybe if we had a heart-to-heart talk, I could convince him to slow down and let me help him help us.

FOR DISCUSSION AND REPORT-WRITING

Organizing: Structural Design

1) If Garcia wished to initiate one of the three approaches he discusses, how might the addition of "staff" help facilitate one or more of these approaches?

2) Assume the agency was ten times larger, located in a much larger city, but

offered the same services. How might the organization design differ from the one you would recommend for the current agency?

Human Factors in Organizing

3) In what ways may imposing of controls, such as those proposed by Garcia, affect "controls" that may arise from current customers and informal-group pressures?

4) How would you characterize the "conflict" that seems to be arising between Maurer and Garcia? What is (are) its source(s)? Is there any likelihood that this conflict could be constructive?

Planning: Elements of Rational Decision-Making

5) List the crucial factors that Garcia should consider in deciding where to apply more specific controls over agency operation.

6) How may one make program decisions in situations where direct, short-run costs can be measured but where both short- and long-range benefits resist quantification? In what ways do you believe Dr. Nelson's experiences would be helpful in answering this question?

Planning: Decision-Making in an Enterprise

7) Based on the nature of the organization—namely, its 1) mission, 2) personnel, 3) situation, and 4) executive director—how effective would be an effort to generate cost-reduction suggestions from the employees?

8) Is it possible for the agency to develop a strategy based on "picking a propitious niche"? Consider each of the steps suggested as a basis for such a choice, and indicate how it might be applied to the agency.

9) Based on the agency's dependence on short-term funding, can it realistically develop long-range plans? How?

10) In what ways would each of Garcia's three suggested approaches affect the need for formalized standing plans?

Controlling

11) If a management-by-objectives system were developed and supported by Mrs. Maurer, what effect should resulting controls have on the motivation of the social workers?

12) What problems may be encountered in developing total costs per unit of service? Is it necessary to develop such cost per unit figures in order to set control standards?

13) How useful would Garcia's second approach to setting standards based on individual productivity be? What would determine the success or failure of this approach?

14) How would the board "make sure that the system [Garcia's second suggestion] was being used conscientiously?"

15) How effective would Dr. Carbonara's suggested approach to controlling the agency's expenses be?

16) (Summary Report Question: Part Five) Based on your analysis of the situation, how would you go about instituting controls designed to reduce agency costs with a minimum impact on agency service? Assume you had a majority of the board's support for your scheme but had yet to get Mrs. Maurer's reactions.

Activating

17) How might the activating mode sought to activate tighter controls on the agency office differ from the one sought with regard to social workers who spend most of their time in the field?

18) Assume the board felt they could gain ambivalent compliance from Mrs. Maurer for tighter controls, in exchange for assured support for one of her favorite projects. Should the board "settle" for this compliance or seek her commitment?

Summary Question for Solution of the Case as a Whole

19) From the perspective of Freda Maurer, what action would you take on Garcia's impending proposals to institute formal planning and control systems? Develop a step-by-step plan of action; and based on your (Mrs. Maurer's) perspective, experience, and value system, indicate why you feel this is the soundest approach?

PART **VI** ——————

Activating puts plans into action. In a sense, all the planning, organizing, and designing of controls heretofore discussed are preparation. Now we are ready to go. Activating is the "make happen" phase of managing.

Instructions must be given. But much more is needed. Wise managers first predict how their subordinates will respond to their requests, based on the prevailing set of conditions. If the expected responses are inadequate, we then seek means of changing them. Building commitment to shared goals, providing additional rewards, removing objections, or using power may all be tried. The activating mode selected must be suited to the specific situation and to the need for prompt action.

Clearly, in thinking about activating, we make use of an array of behavioral concepts—many of which we have already encountered. Personal needs, group norms, conflict, rewards, and perception are all involved in the motivation we are seeking. A main feature of Part Six, however, is the framework that enables a manager to relate these forces to executing his specific plans.

This process of activating is explored in four chapters.

Chapter 25—Choosing an Activating Mode. The normal first step in activating is to predict how persons receiving a request will respond. Then we compare this predicted response with what we as managers consider satisfactory in the

Activating

circumstances. Possible responses range from opposition, to ambivalent or indifferent compliance, to full commitment. In this chapter a series of criteria are listed for selecting the kind of response to strive for in various settings.

Chapter 26—Gaining Commitment or Compliance. When the predicted response is unacceptable, the manager must take steps to change that response. Depending on the immediate circumstances, we may try to build congruence in goals, work out a compromise, or resort to coercion. Here we will consider an array of potential motivating, energizing forces.

Chapter 27—Gaining Understanding. Good person-to-person communication is vital to a manager, both to develop a basis for predicting how subordinates will respond and to convey the full meaning and intent of an instruction. This chapter explores the art of listening and of conveying meaning to others.

Chapter 28—Activating in a Dynamic Setting. In this chapter we use two cases to highlight the need for prompt, adroit behavior in activating situations. The most suitable activating mode depends upon past practices and future plans.

In Part Six many of the ideas coming from recent research on leadership and motivation are placed in a focus on purposeful managerial action. It is in the pressure of getting things done that these ideas have their primary social value.

25

Choosing
an Activating Mode

John F. Kennedy was at the peak of his career in 1962 when he ordered the removal of U.S. missiles from their locations in Turkey. His decision had been taken after careful review of the alternative plans prepared by many layers of different organizations. The Joint Chiefs of Staff, the State Department, and the National Security Council had carefully coordinated these data and added their recommendations. When President Kennedy decided on the removal, clear written directions began their spiral path from the Oval Room in the White House toward the silos in Turkey.

Yet, months later, during the height of the Cuban Missile Crisis, Kennedy learned that his decision had not been carried out. In his famous confrontations with Soviet Premier Nikita Khrushchev, Kennedy was told that the Russians would withdraw their missiles from Cuba if we would remove ours from Turkey. President Kennedy was shocked to discover both that his decision had not been executed and that his "control" systems had failed to keep him as well informed as his "competitor" about the status of his decision.

What went wrong? Is is possible that those responsible for carrying out this decision did not "understand" what they were to do? Were they unwilling to "comply" with the decision? Or did they lack the "commitment" necessary to execute the decision when confronted by obstacles? Moreover, if this could happen to one of the two or three most powerful executives in the world, imagine how much more likely it is to happen to the average manager.

There may of course be unexpected reasons why sound decisions, developed and implemented by a good organization, fail to achieve desired results —even though the decisions are understood and acted on with commitment. Similarly, even the best control systems occasionally will fail to spot problems on time or help in pinpointing causality. After all, in an unpredictable and frequently competitive world, imperfect planners, organizers, and controllers will guess wrong or be beaten by competitors. However, just as we sought to improve the quality of other management functions, so too we must focus now on achieving optimum performance in the remaining management function—activating.

Function of Activating

"Activating" deals with the steps that a manager takes to get subordinates and others to carry out plans. It bridges the gap between managerial decisions and actual execution by other people. It is the "make-happen" phase of management.[1]

Although many forms of human effort are required to build organizations, develop plans, and design control systems, they are all for naught unless their outcomes are put into action. A construction superintendent has to convert blueprints into a power dam. A football coach has to transform plays that look foolproof on paper into touchdowns on the field. A director has to turn a Gilbert and Sullivan score and libretto into a lively stage production. Such a conversion of ideas into results is an essential element in every manager's job, and how skillfully he does it can profoundly affect the returns from all other phases of management.

Personal Interaction

All phases of management have vital behavioral aspects. Organizations should be structured to meet human needs and to harness interpersonal conflict, as we saw in Part Two. Both the content of plans and the process of preparing such plans have deep social and individual impact, as noted in Parts Three and Four. And in the preceding chapter, the human factors in controlling were examined. To think of managing in purely mechanistic and financial terms up to the stage of activating, and only then to confront human needs and responses, would be folly indeed.

---

[1] The term "leadership" is commonly used for this phase of managing—as indeed we did in earlier editions of this book. Now we strongly prefer "activating" for three reasons.

1) Leadership has too many meanings, ranging from being first to initiate a change to inspiring bravery on the battlefield.

2) Within the management field, leadership deals only with inducing positive sentiments, whereas activating covers a range of actions from coercion to creating congruence.

3) Activating is more directly tied to company goals and plans.

Nevertheless, it is in activating that success or failure in dealing wisely with human considerations becomes most apparent. If gross oversights have occurred in organizing, planning, or controlling, these will become painfully evident when the activating phase is reached. Goals will be missed, morale will sink, and workers will evade instructions or oppose them openly. But even if we skillfully include human aspects in our organizing, planning, and controlling, some loose ends always remain. The organization plan may not quite fit the employees we have; external pressures may force us to adopt unpopular plans; controls may clash with individual preferences.

In activating, a manager starts with this background of plans and structures, and with people's feelings about such plans and structures. The time for action has arrived, and a manager must deal with his situation as it exists—with its inevitable mixture of strengths and drawbacks.

Activating is highly personal. Each human being whom the manager directs has his unique set of beliefs, hopes, and needs. These feelings and ideas will be influenced by co-workers, to be sure, but the manager must think in terms of the willingness of specific individuals to do specific tasks. Moreover, the manager himself has his own attitudes, disposition, and skills. All these personalities and behavior drives interact. Nevertheless, from this milieu a series of purposeful, effective actions should emerge—for this is the task of activating.

THE ACTIVATING PROCESS

The Need for a Contingency Approach

Throughout this book we have urged that managers select the particular form of organization, the type of planning, and the system of control that best suits the specific problems confronted. There is no universal solution; instead, a wise manager looks at his needs and available resources, then charts his course to fit that "contingency." In each Part our discussion of issues, various options, and factors affecting final design provides guidelines for adjusting the way of managing to a particular set of circumstances.

Activating should also be shaped by a contingency approach. The measures adopted should be suited to the situation.

This concept that the best way to activate a person depends upon the local situation is not always accepted. Instead, we find advocates for Theory-Y, management-by-objectives, self-actualization, and a variety of other motivational techniques. The originators, or more likely some of their disciples, have missionary zeal for what they believe to be the "one best way." Such single-mindedness can perhaps be explained because a) advocating a single technique is simpler, or b) the technique fosters some human values that appeal to the advocate. Usually such techniques have considerable merit when used in the proper setting; but they may waste time and actually be harmful when the necessary support for them is lacking.

Managers need an approach to activating that they can fairly easily apply to a wide variety of people and situations. Good managers do intuitively adjust their behavior, but they can make such adjustments more quickly and with more sensitivity if they have a framework—or approach—to guide their analysis.

Elements in the Activating Process

A managerial approach to more effective activating involves these elements:

1) Forecasting the likely response of workers to the activating request.
2) Choosing a preferred activating mode that suits the task, and matching this with the forecasted response.
3) Selecting an energizing force or method of shifting responses when a mismatch between expected and desired results is forecast.
4) Developing modes of personal communication and follow-up consistent with 1), 2), and 3).

Throughout this chapter we shall deal with the first two of these elements —the forecast of how affected persons are likely to respond and the choice of a preferred way of activating in a specific setting. The next chapter explores the controversial issue of trying to shift expected responses, when necessary, through such means as coercion, compromise, and congruence. Chapter 27 focuses on the fourth element—selecting and developing communication patterns consistent with the first three elements. And in Chapter 28, by examining a case in which a difficult set of activating decisions were called for, we will illustrate the knitting together of all elements in the activating process as well as the relation between activating and other processes of management.

In practice, the elements of activating are closely interdependent. Forecasted responses are one factor in selecting a preferred activating mode; two-way communication improves the accuracy of a forecasted response to an activating request; bargaining and coercion may upset communications; and so forth. Moreover, the process is quite dynamic, shifting with both internal and external events. Such fluid interaction may make the activating process messy, but it also increases the value of a designed approach such as we are proposing here in Part Six.

POTENTIAL RESPONSES
TO ACTIVATING REQUEST

To decide how best to convert plans into action, a manager must predict how his subordinates and other people involved will respond to his request for an action. Will they simply refuse to comply (mutiny), or grasp the opportunity

TABLE 25–1   RANGE OF RESPONSES TO AN ACTIVATING REQUEST

	Negative Sentiment		Ambivalence	
Range	Strong negative feeling toward request	Mild negative feeling toward request	*I don't feel like it but . . . .* *I'll try*	*I'll do it*
of Feelings				

	Opposition		Ambivalent Compliance	
Range	Fight or flight	Deceit Avoidance	Minimum compli- ance	Full compli- ance
of Actions			Inertia	Momentum
			As long as external pressure is maintained	

for action like a charged-up football player (fanaticism), or do something in between?

A useful way to think about possible responses to activating requests is suggested in Table 25–1. This diagram shows a range of *feelings* and a corresponding range of *actions*, moving from a strong negative response, through ambivalence and indifference, to positive, internalized commitment. For convenience the diagram is divided into four stages, although in practice responses may fall anywhere along the continuum.

Since the predicted response is fundamental to choosing an activating mode, we should note several key types.

Opposition

Refusal to carry out instructions does occur. The person receiving the request may believe that the task is too dangerous, that it is outside the kind of work he was hired to perform, that it is demeaning or will subject him to ridicule. He may object to dirty assignments or to work in cold or wet locations —"I don't have to put up with that." Tasks he feels are unethical or nonprofessional may be refused. An assignment that means moving his family to an undesired location ("Siberia"), or travel that interferes with a cherished hobby can create opposition. Unfair allocation of tough and easy jobs may stir up revolt.

Strong negative feelings from causes such as these may lead to one of several actions by the individual who receives the request. If he feels very strongly, he may insist that he will quit the job unless the instruction is changed.

Indifference		Positive Sentiment	
Why should I?	*Why shouldn't I?*	Mild internalized positive feelings	*Strong internalized positive feelings*

Indifferent Compliance		Commitment	
Minimum compliance	Full compliance	Minimum commitment	Full commitment
Inertia	Momentum		
As long as no counter pressure exists			

Or if resignation is untenable, he can object, appeal, and seek support of colleagues for his case—and meanwhile refuse to comply.

Mild negative feelings are likelier to result in more subtle responses. Instead of open opposition, the assignment may just not get done. Some excuse is found for successive postponement—necessary supplies or outside help is for some mysterious reason not available when needed; papers get lost; other more important work interferes; illness occurs. If necessary a bit of deceit about what actually has been done avoids a confrontation.

Whenever a manager predicts such opposition behavior, he clearly should either modify his request or take steps to modify the response.[2] Ways to shift such a response, ranging from coercion to cultivating cooperation, will be discussed in the next chapter.

Compliance

Any time someone carries out another's request, we might say that he is "complying." As we will use the term, however, compliance signifies actions that result from either ambivalence or indifference.

Ambivalent compliance. Ambivalence was once defined as the feeling one would get watching his $20,000 sportscar being driven off a cliff by his

---

[2] A maxim in political science says, "Never pass a law that cannot be enforced." Applied to management this suggests, "Never issue an order unless you predict it will be acceptable or unless you are prepared to take steps to ensure its acceptance."

most hated enemy. Many times an individual complies with a request with some degree of ambivalence. Both negative and positive feelings are present. The prevailing mood is likely to be, "I don't want to do it but considering what happens if I do, I will."

The ambivalence arises because negative feelings—such as those listed directly under "Opposition," or perhaps merely dislike of the work—are coupled with positive inducements—such as pay, economic security, fellowship with peers, respect of outsiders, and the like. The single action of complying with the manager's request results in mixture of feelings.

In ambivalent compliance that borders on opposition, most of the positive feelings come from external sources—from other people who want the request to be acted upon. The actor himself has no direct interest in the outcome, but he does respond to the pressures (rewards or punishments) that these other concerned people place upon him. The external pressures may stem from any of the following or, usually, from some combination.

1) A hierarchical superior
2) Peers
3) Subordinates
4) Spouse, friends, family
5) General societal values or perceived expectations

In the absence of these *external* pressures, the individual would not comply. Mild pressure brings minimal compliance. Greater pressure may produce full compliance. The moment that pressure disappears or is avoided, however, effort will probably slacken or cease.

Indifferent compliance. Individuals may also *comply* with a request without experiencing either ambivalence or commitment. They are simply indifferent to the request, and compliance may be activated with only the

Figure 25–1 Ambivalence—simultaneous attraction and repulsion. People in organizations also feel ambivalent about requests they receive from their superiors.

slightest "push." This is the "zone of indifference" that Chester I. Barnard wrote about several decades ago.[3]

One of the authors recalls an incident that took place during the stormy 1968 academic year. Shortly after a campus protest, the author approached an elevator with an armload of books. Two students stood chatting near the elevator and the author asked one, "Would you please push the 'up' button for me?" The student in a calm, but obviously defiant tone answered, "Why should I?"

Taken aback and at a loss for a suitable retort to this rude rebel, the author blurted out, "Why not?" Then it was the student who blinked and, after a moment's hesitation, said, "Sure, why not?" as he pushed the button. In this encounter, as in many other situations, the "Why not?" may be as difficult to answer as the "Why?" In an era in which everything from soap to virtue is "sold" or at least legitimized as "relevant" or "meaningful," we are likely to forget that many responses are positive simply because there is no real reason for not complying with a request.

Most of us expect to accept instructions when we take a job. Such a response is part of our role. Especially when the overall work situation is pleasant, we are quite prepared to give passive compliance to requests that fit within prevailing work patterns.

Of course, if bare compliance is inadequate to achieve company goals, or falls so far short of what workers want from their jobs, the manager will have to seek commitment. And moving workers from compliance to commitment requires special managerial effort, much as shifting from opposition to compliance. But first we have to decide whether expending the effort to encourage such a shift is necessary.

Commitment

Still another response to a manager's request is commitment—the other extreme from opposition on the continuum of potential reactions to activating requests shown in Table 25–1.

Commitment connotes a positive, welcoming feeling about the requested performance. The more positive the feeling, the greater the commitment. In addition, this feeling comes from *inside* the individual. He reacts favorably because the task is something he wants to do; it helps him serve directly one or several of his own "needs."

All sorts of people engage in committed action. A mail carrier, for instance, may feel that delivering mail accurately, promptly, and without damage is a satisfying activity; he does the job well, not to avoid punishment, but because he personally believes this is the right way to do an important job. Similarly, a life-insurance "counselor" usually feels that he is really helping his

---

[3] In *Functions of the Executive* (Cambridge, Mass.: Harvard University Press, 1938).

NEITHER LETHARGY, INDIFFERENCE, NOR THE GENERAL COLLAPSE OF STANDARDS WILL PREVENT THESE COURIERS FROM EVENTUALLY DELIVERING SOME OF YOUR MAIL

Figure 25–2   A choice of activating mode should reflect shifts in workers' attitudes. The actual inscription carved in stone on the face of the New York Post Office is: "Neither snow, nor rain, nor heat, nor gloom of night stays these couriers from the swift completion of their appointed rounds." Drawing by Handelsman; © 1976 The New Yorker Magazine, Inc.

clients by selling them large policies; he is pleased each time another bread-winner protects his family from a severe catastrophe. Likewise, the superintendent of a telephone exchange may want his to be the lowest cost unit in the company—as a matter of pride and personal satisfaction.

The reasons that a person feels committed toward a particular goal vary widely. The person may believe that his work is making a significant contribution toward a social objective that he strongly endorses. Or, often the person holds a view of how a job or task should be performed—say, a firstclass truck driver or a surgeon—and takes pride in performing work that meets such a standard. A game spirit may be invoked—being better than a competitor or exceeding self-imposed standards. But whatever the underlying motivation, the important feature from a manager's viewpoint is that the individual derives personal satisfactions from an activity that is also helping to meet company goals.

In full commitment, the "pressure" to carry out the task must be *internal*. The actor seeks to carry out the task, not because his boss or peers or friends think he should, but rather because *he* himself feels that he should. In contrast to compliance, the primary pressure to act is no longer external.

In stressing the internal aspect of commitment, we are not saying that fair treatment, bonuses, and other rewards that a manager makes to a committed worker have no influence. A favorable climate and overall satisfying job certainly pave the way for commitment. However, when commitment is present, these highly acceptable rewards have merged with other motivations in such a way that the task itself takes on positive value for the individual. No longer does the individual perform the task, as in ambivalent compliance, merely as a means of obtaining some payoffs. Instead, the internalized values— of the mail carrier, the life-insurance counselor, the telephone company superintendent—are now congruent with company goals. And with commitment comes energetic, flexible, creative effort to achieve enterprise tasks.

PREDICTING RESPONSE
IN SPECIFIC SETTINGS

Activating starts when a manager has arrived at a plan of action that he wants to put into operation. He has a specific plan for a specific setting. This may be President Kennedy's decision to remove U.S. missiles from Turkey, or a sales-promotion director's plan to mail out 10,000 more circulars. Much planning effort precedes the decision, and a lot of previous experience will have conditioned the organization that is to carry out the decision. But for the manager, the activating step has a distinct *here-and-now* quality.

A sound initial move, we believe, is to consciously predict how individuals receiving the activating request— the "order"—will respond. And the format of potential responses that we have just described is a very useful form in which a manager can express his predictions. The divisions of that format— opposition, ambivalent compliance, indifferent compliance, commitment—all relate directly to the execution of the request. By this device, behavioral-science insights are focused on desired action.

To make such predictions reliably, a manager has to know each of his subordinates well. He must be aware of their feelings about different kinds of work, the motivation and values that they esteem, their loyalties, and something of their experiences that will color their present beliefs and attitudes. And if the request the manager is about to make is unusual or calls for a sharp change from previous behavior, then predicting the response calls for an even deeper understanding of the individuals involved.

The likely response to requests that are very similar to previous requests can, of course, be more easily predicted. A pattern of behavior has been established, and we assume the pattern will be repeated—*unless* the needs, aspirations, or beliefs of the subordinate have changed. To detect and evaluate such changes, a manager should have open communication with each of his subordinates. Open communication also provides the facts on which predictions about responses to unusual requests are made. So important is this communication between manager and subordinates that we devote a separate chapter to it, Chapter 27.

Having forecast the response to his request, the manager then decides whether that response will be satisfactory. "Do I like what I foresee?" If the answer is yes, the request is made and action proceeds. If the answer is no, the manager then must think through ways to change the response or perhaps his request. In the next chapter we will explore this second process of accommodation. But what are the criteria used to judge whether the predicted response is satisfactory? When is mere compliance acceptable, and when should a manager strive for commitment?

The answer to these questions affects the entire character of operations; it shapes the enthusiasm with which work is performed. This choice of activating mode is much more subtle and difficult than is generally recognized. Let us look at the options and some criteria more closely.

ACTIVATING MODES

Our review of potential responses to an activating request—opposition, ambivalent compliance, indifferent compliance, commitment—points to several alternative ways that managers can convert decisions into actions.

Opposition is obviously unacceptable. If opposition to a request is predicted, the manager must immediately devise steps to shift the expected response to the right on the scale shown in Table 25–1—at least to ambivalent compliance or, theoretically, all the way to commitment.

Both compliance and commitment, however, may get the desired work done. So here a manager has a choice. He faces a question for each plan to be executed: Which would be preferable—compliance or commitment? Furthermore, if the preferred response does not match the predicted reaction, what can be done to bring the two together?

We call the answer to these questions an "activating mode." The primary aspect of a mode is the choice between compliance and commitment. The secondary aspect is how to shift the response when the predicted (or actual) behavior does not match the chosen response. Since the primary issue arises frequently in practice, it should be squarely faced.

Seek Compliance?

Why might a manager elect the compliance mode for activating in certain situations? First, if he has just been confronted with opposition, even ambivalent compliance may be a great improvement—and to strive for more in the press of getting things done may involve too much delay and expense. Second, for many activities compliance is quite adequate. Routine activities often call for no more than dependable performance—filing expense reports, keeping the car greased, sending out sales literature. Even more significant activities like maintaining standard temperature on a refinery still may require little judgment. Every position from president to janitor contains substantial amounts of such work—for which compliant action produces acceptable results.

Mere compliance, however, has limitations. External pressure must be always present, and supervision close. More seriously, it fails to bring out much latent energy and initiative.

Seek Commitment?

Committed workers can ease a manager's burdens in several ways. A person with commitment to a task works more energetically and with more imagination. He is his own "energy source" and requires less close control.

The behavioral scientists build an even stronger argument for this activating mode. Writers with humanistic values like McGregor, Argyris, McClelland, and Myers contend that in today's society we should appeal to such higher-order needs as self-expression (see the discussion of individuals' needs in the early part of Chapter 7). Rising expectations, they say, will make more and more people dissatisfied if their work serves only their physical and security needs. Instead, the illness of alienation can and should be cured by commitment. Incidentally, research findings show a closer link between what we call commitment and worker satisfaction than between commitment and productivity.[4]

By relying on commitment as an activating mode, then, a manager serves two objectives—greater effort toward company tasks and greater satisfaction of employee higher-order needs.

But not all situations lend themselves to this ideal solution. One kind of limitation is technological. Some work, such as operating a paper-making machine or collecting tolls on a bridge, has so little opportunity for variation that the strongly committed worker may feel constrained and frustrated. Another limitation is the cost of establishing commitment relative to its benefits in particular settings.

Because of these pros and cons for both compliance and commitment, the wise manager adjusts his choice of activating modes according to the situation.

CRITERIA FOR SELECTING AN ACTIVATING MODE

When a manager turns to the activating phase of his total job, his main concern is to execute the planned actions that will produce desired results. His focus is necessarily on getting a particular set of tasks accomplished. Consequently, for him the most useful operational guides will be those stated in

---

[4] F. Herzberg's distinction between hygienic and motivating needs, explained briefly in Chapter 7, provides a more direct tie to company productivity. Commitment contributes primarily to not-fully-satisfied motivating needs, and this in Herzberg's scheme builds productivity.

terms of the work to be done. The following criteria for selecting an activating mode for use at a particular time have this practical quality.

1. *Can extra effort by the performer of the task substantially improve results?*

In any organization, there are numerous tasks for which work has been so designed as to make "extra effort" wasted. Such tasks are like light switches without rheostats. Flip the switch and the light goes on; don't flip it and the light stays off. How hard or soft, how fast or slow the switch is flipped makes no difference in the intensity of the light. Many tasks, like the light switch, are either "on" or "off." The assembly-line operator who connects seven wires either connects them or he doesn't. The insurance-company clerk stamps three pages and initials them or he doesn't. The pilot preparing for takeoff goes through each item on his checklist or he doesn't. In each case, there are pre-scribed tasks to carry out. Although they must be carried out properly, it is unlikely that the extra *effort* that comes with commitment will produce any significant additional benefits.

One might argue that such mechanistic tasks that require no more than compliant performance should be eliminated. Clearly, much of the job-enrich-ment literature strives to make that point. If a careful analysis of an individual's or group's total tasks leads to the decision to reorganize the job, then indeed a new method of activating may be practical. Until such a change in duties takes place, however, compliance is an acceptable means of activating these tasks.

On the other hand, there are many tasks for which results are directly related to the degree of effort expended. A football player who executes a play with technical perfection may succeed or fail, depending on whether he makes that "second effort." The salesperson who follows every step in the manual will probably still find that his energy level influences sales. If the automatic landing gear shorts out, how hard the co-pilot works the manual crank will directly affect results. In all of these and thousands of other tasks, the degree of success is fairly directly related to the degree of effort expended. In these cases the greater the commitment sought and achieved, the greater the likeli-hood of success.

2. *Will the environment in which the work is performed be controlled so that there is little need for flexibility and creativity.*

A primary benefit of committed performance is that it is characterized by greater flexibility and creativity. A significant question, then, is how valuable these characteristics will be. If the task performance is unlikely to be improved or if the environment can be controlled to reduce the need for flexibility and creativity, a manager should seek compliance. In each of our examples for which extra effort was unlikely to produce extra results, the environment has been "controlled" to reduce the need for flexibility and creativity. The assembly line is designed to control as much of the environment as possible and to acti-vate contingency plans when needed. It would be quite unusual for the wire connector or the clerical employee to find much need for flexible, creative behavior. Similarly, though other aspects of a pilot's job call for considerable flexibility and creativity, his preflight checklist does not.

On the other hand, the salesperson whose extra effort can produce extra sales may be asked to "comply" with specific travel routines. Here, the controlled world of planned itineraries and scheduled airlines may not allow the salesperson or pilot much flexibility and creativity. However, if the salesperson's travel and entertainment environment is not susceptible to careful control, if trips cannot be planned and opportunities must be seized when they arise, then his commitment to the task will determine how well or poorly he responds to the less-controllable environment.

The research scientist who strives in the laboratory to control the environment of his experiments, if successful, also creates a situation in which less-experienced, less-committed technicians can carry out parts of the experiments. A budget meeting, however, where the scientist's research budget for next year is being determined, is a less-controllable environment. As a result, his own "committed" attendance, accompanied by all the creativity and flexibility he can muster, is necessary instead of the "compliant" attendance of one of his lab managers.

3. *How practical is close supervision and strong control?*

The service people who maintain complex computers are subject to close supervision and control when they are being trained. As they learn their trade in the classroom, or under the eye of an experienced person, they can be activated by a host of external pressures. But when that service engineer goes out in the field, performance will depend largely on commitment. The nature of his field work makes close supervision and control too costly. How well he performs now is much more a function of his skills and of whether he is committed to his task.

The assembly-line wirer, on the other hand, is almost continuously subjected to close supervision and tight controls. Because of the decision to design work in this way, the cost of close supervision and control are presumed to be offset by close adherence to prescribed standards. Even the indirect costs of

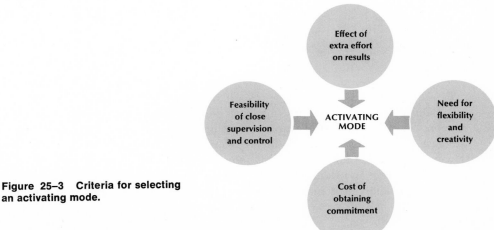

Figure 25–3   Criteria for selecting an activating mode.

boredom and undetected "deviant behavior" are calculated to be acceptable. And here *compliance* is the activating mode that is compatible with the organization and control structure.

A third type of situation is one in which close control is possible, but in which high decentralization is elected, to secure job enrichment or other benefits. By design we have given subordinates great latitude. Close control is not consistent with this arrangement. So here, as with the service engineer in the field, we must rely on commitment for dependable, effective, day-to-day performance.

4. *Where commitment is preferable but not essential, how will the cost of obtaining commitment compare with the improvement in performance?*

The preceding criteria will identify some situations in which compliance is adequate and others in which commitment is essential. More difficult to resolve is another class of situations, in which a committed response to a manager's request is desirable though not essential. A manager must then weigh the cost of obtaining commitment against the improvement in results that such commitment will create. (We presume that if commitment already exists, the manager will choose to maintain it.)

The manager of a gasoline station, for example, would certainly prefer committed attendants who are responsive to each customer's needs. But the cost and difficulty of obtaining such commitment may be so high that the manager decides to settle for indifferent compliance. A similar dilemma often confronts the manager of bargain-price chain-store outlets.

Normally, shifting a response from compliance to commitment entails significant costs—as we shall see in more detail in Chapter 26. Always the manager must invest a lot of his own effort. Changes in work structure or technology may be necessary. Perhaps some new personnel will have to be brought in and indifferent workers retired. A new group morale will be needed. And all this takes time.

The manager must estimate 1) how strong a sense of commitment he can create by these steps, and 2) how beneficial will be the resulting additional effort, self-control, flexibility, and initiative.

COMPATIBILITY AMONG
ACTIVATING MODES

Our discussion up to this point has deliberately focused on the predicted response and the preferred response to *single* activating requests. We clearly suggest that an activating mode be selected for each separate request. By always considering how each of his requests will be activated, a manager can build a sensitive and dynamic relationship with each of his subordinates.

Nevertheless, it is important to recognize that the mode used today may affect both the response and what is feasible for another request tomorrow. Separate attention to each request does not mean the activating choices are unrelated. Quite the contrary—in some circumstances a mode is selected largely in light of the impact it will have on activating important subsequent requests.

Prevalence of Mixed Modes

A manager's desire for compliance for some tasks and commitment for others, in dealing with the same individual, is in fact quite common. Both parties expect different modes to be employed.

A salesperson, for instance, is usually committed to his product but compliant on reports and pricing—and both he and his manager expect the activating modes to be adjusted accordingly. Similarly, a design engineer typically is strongly committed to the effectiveness of the product or process on which he is working, whereas he is likely to be ambivalently compliant about completion dates and perhaps indifferently compliant about his expenses. Here again, if he and his supervisor consider different modes suitable for the various issues, mixed styles of activating create no difficulty.

This mutual expectation that some aspects of work will be treated differently from others has a parallel in planning and in decentralizing. In Chapter 18 we noted that the amount of detailed planning varies greatly from subject to subject. The degree of decentralization, as explained in Chapter 3, necessarily varies by subject. Activating modes are normally adjusted to these variations in planning and decentralizing.

Of course, if the manager expects commitment but the subordinate feels compliance is good enough—or vice versa—friction will arise. But this sort of misunderstanding is simply a mismatch between desired and actual response and can be dealt with as any other mismatch.

Pervasive Response

Much more significant is the extension of a response generated by one request to many other requests. This extension can work either way. Thus, if a sales manager can get a salesperson highly committed to the product line, that commitment behavior *may* spill over to other aspects of the job, even though in isolation the response to the secondary requests would be indifference. Or, a request that provokes a strong ambivalent response—perhaps involving a bit of heated bargaining—may undermine commitment to other tasks. A professor may say, "I find it hard to be steamed up about this new course when the Dean keeps asking me to serve on unnecessary committees."

Very little scientific data exists to throw light on which responses are most likely to have a pervasive influence. Clearly, the more *intense* the feeling about a single request the more likely it is to be carried over to other requests. Also, if the manager *changes* his activating mode in a particular area, and takes steps to shift the previous response pattern, the attention created by change itself gives the new response temporary dominance.

So, when a manager is selecting an activating mode, an additional factor to consider is its possible effect on future responses in other areas. This should be part of the cost/benefit analysis. The most obvious dilemma is whether to use coercion if doing so may upset some carefully nurtured commitment—a question we return to in the next chapter.

A final aspect of using different activating modes is consistency in the eyes of subordinates. As noted, different modes are normal and expected. But unpredictable shifting from one to another can be very disturbing to subordinates. If a manager seeks commitment one month, then next month indicates that ambivalent compliance is all he expects, subordinates will not only be confused; they will also question their boss's integrity. The principle involved here is communication. If a manager chooses to modify his previous activating practice, subordinates should be made aware of the change and reasons for it.

CONCLUSION

Activating is an inescapable, vital part of the process of managing. More systematic attention to how it is done, we believe, can often significantly improve a manager's effectiveness.

A constructive approach to activating—one that is more comprehensive and more tightly related to organizing, planning, and control than the usual leadership guides—is to recognize that a manager's request of a subordinate may receive opposition, ambivalent compliance, indifferent compliance, or commitment.

Using this framework, a manager should predict the probable response to each activating request he makes, and compare that predicted response with an acceptable (optimum) response for that task in the existing setting. When there is a good match between the predicted and acceptable response, the request is made and action proceeds. But when a mismatch is predicted—when the likely response will be inadequate—the manager then must consider what he can do to shift the response or perhaps modify the request.

Commitment is an "ideal" response. Many situations arise, however, for which compliance is both normal and acceptable. So, making a realistic choice among these activating modes for specific requests is a recurring task for every manager. Criteria for making such choices have been reviewed in the last part of the present chapter. These choices are not secondary issues; they affect the entire tone and effectiveness of a company's operations.

The tough phase of activating, of course, is overcoming mismatches between an activating mode selected as necessary and the predicted behavior. Ways to bring about such agreement are explored in the next chapter.

1) What is the major difference between "activating" and "motivating," if by motivating we mean causing people to want to do what they are asked to do by management?

2) Under what conditions may a local union help management in forecasting likely responses of workers to an activating request?

3) How does a manager choose a preferred activating mode if he forecasts that key members of his department will respond in quite different ways to a single request?

4) Give a personal example in which someone with formal authority over you tried to "activate" you to do something that elicited a strong negative feeling, and in which, further, you managed to avoid doing it without punishment.

5) Based on your answer to question 4, was there any way the "activator" could have forecast your response and changed either the request or the response?

6) Which is a better response—ambivalent or indifferent compliance?

7) Assume that ambivalent compliance is an acceptable response to an activating request. The pressure to comply may stem from any one or a combination of five external sources. In general, which of these sources is likely to be the best means of assuring full compliance over time?

8) The text suggests that it is not only necessary but also desirable to seek, from the same individual, compliance to some requests and commitment to others. Consider the desirability of seeking or accepting different responses to the *same request* from several members of a group who must share in carrying it out. What should be considered before accepting this situation? What are the dangers? Might there be advantages?

Cases

For cases involving issues covered in this chapter, see especially the following. Particularly relevant questions are listed after each case.

FOR FURTHER READING

Fiedler, F. E. and M. M. Chermers, *Leadership and Effective Management.* Glenview, Ill.: Scott, Foresman and Company, 1974.

Surveys various leadership theories, then develops a "contingency model" for selecting leadership behavior.

Gibson, F. K. and C. E. Teasley, "The Humanistic Model of Organizational Motivation: A Review of Research Support." *Public Administration Review,* January 1973.

Useful brief summary of theories of Argyris, Bennis, Herzberg, Maslow, McGregor, and Likert regarding motivation in organizations. Notes the inadequacy of research support.

Malone, E. L., "The Non-Linear Systems Experiment in Participative Management." *Journal of Business,* January 1975.

Clear description of the serious difficulties one company encountered when the president instituted participative management in a bold fashion.

Tannenbaum, R. and W. H. Schmidt, "How to Choose a Leadership Pattern." *Harvard Business Review,* May 1973.

A classic article on selecting an activating mode suited to local conditions. In this presentation the authors update their first statement.

Willcoxon, S. R. and C. J. Brocato, "Improving Results Through an Integrated Management System: A Case Study." *Management Review,* February and March 1976.

Report of A.T.&T. long-lines program aimed at setting goals and gaining commitment to them, as seen by two managers.

Gaining Commitment
Or Compliance

26

"You don't have to like it, just do it!" This command certainly echoed along the Nile as pyramids were begun, and quite likely the medieval monastic scribe heard it from the head monk. And the power of the overseer was strong enough to get obedience.

Not so today. In our world of growing affluence and desire to protect individual freedom, "Why should I?" has become a much more legitimate question. In a modern enterprise the response to a manager's request can range anywhere from enthusiastic, committed behavior to opposition and refusal to carry out the instruction, as we noted in the preceding chapter.

The perceptive manager can predict the response that a specific request is likely to provoke. Often this expected response will be quite acceptable, and instructions can be issued immediately. But if the predicted response fails to match what the manager feels is desirable, he must seek an energizing force that will improve it.

Many options exist. In terms of their impact on behavior, there are four broad ways to induce subordinates to be more willing to act as desired:

1) Coercion
2) Cultivating cooperation
3) Compromise
4) Seeking congruence

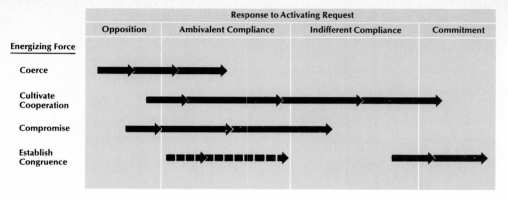

Figure 26–1   Situations in which various energizing forces are used to _shift_ response to an activating request.

Each of these energizing forces has distinct strengths and limitations, and consequently must be carefully fitted to a selected activating mode.

The typical place where these four types of motivation are used to shift responses to activating requests is indicated in Figure 26–1. In actual practice the steps taken to change a response must be finely tuned to the specific setting; but the chart does introduce us to the normal relationship between the range of responses outlined in the last chapter and the energizing forces discussed in this.

USE OF COERCION
TO SECURE COMPLIANCE

Throughout history coercion has been used to secure obedience. Here we are concerned with a manager's use of coercion to overcome opposition and shift that response to at least minimum compliance.

What Coercion Is

Coercion involves the imposition by one individual or group of _its goals_ onto another. If you have been coerced, you have _not_ been led to alter your basic goals or your feelings toward the goals of the coercer. You pursue his goals (with varying degrees of effort) without accepting them because you see such pursuit as the lesser of several evils. Thus, coercion can only move responses from negative toward ambivalent compliance.

Coercion is achieved through the _use of power_. In the pure form of coercion, the person wielding power disregards the needs and wishes of the weaker one, and pursues only his own ends. If compliance is not forthcoming, increased pressure is exerted until the subordinate gives in. Rarely, however, can power be used in such an unrestrained fashion in a modern business firm. Instead, we find varying degrees of power employed in indirect as well as direct ways. Every manager should understand these subtleties about exercising power.

Ability to Coerce

In the broadest sense, we have power over another person when we can supply something he wants and cannot get elsewhere. A small child with the only football in the neighborhood, for example, has power over other children who would like to play football. A monopoly on salt can be a source of power for a government or a company. Control over the transportation of oil several decades ago gave John D. Rockefeller great power over the petroleum industry. Of course, if there are alternative—even if less convenient—ways of satisfying a need, the degree of power is correspondingly reduced.

Ability to inflict penalties is the negative side of power. In this sense, power results when we can deprive a person of something he has or wants. The "something" can be his freedom, his possessions, or even his head. The political power of dictators rests largely on the use of such penalties, whereas political power in democracies often rests on rewards.

An essential element of a coercive relationship is fear of punishment. We behave as a wielder of power wishes us to behave, for we fear that he will deprive us of important satisfactions. Sometimes we are not sure that deprivation is inevitable, but we simply do not wish to risk the chance. Unfortunately, if a relationship is dominated by fear and uncertainty, it is difficult for the weaker person to be self-reliant and to feel friendly toward the powerful person.

These general concepts can be applied to the internal operations of a business enterprise. Management can design jobs, assign work, transfer, promote, demote, discharge, set pay, provide benefits, select titles, and recognize achievements. If subordinates obey because of fear—fear that rewards will be withheld or punishments inflicted if directions are not carried out—then we can say that a manager is clearly depending solely on the use of power in an attempt to gain compliance with his orders.[1]

At times a manager may lack the personal power to coerce a subordinate but have enough influence over those who do exercise power so that the net effect is much the same. Thus, in one shop the superintendent rather than the foremen allocated overtime. However, the workers believed that the superintendent always took the foremen's advice, and this belief enhanced the power

---

[1] Power relationships, of course, are not confined to managers and subordinates. A salesperson with close ties to key customers can wield power over his employer by threatening to go to work for another concern. A plant manager can have power over salespeople if he is free to decide which orders to fill promptly. A vice president's secretary can even develop some power by regulating the flow of visitors and information to this key executive. And, of course, a labor union with a monopoly of certain skilled technicians has power over industries that require those technicians. The matrix of relationships in a company includes all such sources of power, whether potential or realized; and a manager must often determine how best to channel, reconcile, or curb the interplay among people with different sorts of power. See the discussion of intraorganization politics in Chapter 20.

of the foremen. Also, through political maneuvering—described in Chapter 20 —an executive can increase his ability to coerce.

Use of Coercion to Shift Behavior Patterns

Coercion has its principal effect in its potential use, rather than in its actual use. We can see this most clearly in the use of penalties. An actual demotion or a withdrawal of a challenging assignment, for example, contributes little directly toward meeting an objective of either employee or firm; indeed, the immediate effect may even be a drop in output. What is important is fearful *anticipation* of such a penalty, for it motivates an employee to behave as the company wants.

The actual use of a penalty is, of course, significant—not because it gives a person "what is coming to him," but because it makes clear what will happen if there are further digressions. A two-week layoff for repeated tardiness, for instance, benefits a company only if the fear of future layoffs leads to punctuality.

Rewards work similarly. Fear of missing a raise in pay or a transfer to a more interesting job—sometime in the future—stimulates effort now. But a policy of making promotions and pay increases routinely, on the basis of length of service or seniority, provides little power to secure obedience because a person gets his reward even though he fails to obey instructions conscientiously.

The effect of a discharge, transfer, or pay increase is often as great on associates as on the individual directly concerned. Everyone in an organization anticipates the consequences of his own actions, and he takes his cues from what has happened to others. When Sally Hardin, who has been casual about her work, is passed over for a promotion in favor of an ardent supporter of a new company policy, the handwriting is on the wall for all to see: "If you want a promotion, support the new policy." Thus, the occasional exercise of power can set a pattern of expectation—and behavior—for a large number of people.

Management naturally hopes that it can induce widespread acceptance of desirable behavior patterns and that its power can remain latent. But to achieve such a widespread effect on behavior, management must use power consistently. Penalties should regularly follow undesirable behavior, and rewards should follow desired behavior. Moreover, the reasons for penalties and rewards must be made clear to the entire group. Each consistent action reinforces existing beliefs about when management will use coercion. But if an executive is capricious—using his power first one way and then another—he will merely stimulate fear without positively influencing behavior patterns.

Limits on Coercion

Accounts of early railroading, sailing, mining, and other industries report frequent use of power to get results. But today coercion plays a lesser role.

There are three broad reasons for this. First, to avoid its corrupting effect, we have placed sharp restrictions on power. Second, coercion sometimes actually increases negative feelings. Third, while achieving compliance we may undermine the possibilities of building commitment.

Checks on executive power.   People of free countries have an ingrained mistrust of putting vast powers in the hands of a single individual or small group. Past experience with sovereign kings and dictators, coupled with a high value on justice for the individual, makes us wary.

This antiauthoritarian sentiment has been carried over into our business practices, especially in recent years. Enterprises have introduced numerous safeguards to prevent any single executive from abusing the power that resides in the firms. Policies often place limits or conditions on permissible actions, and power is often divided so that two or more executives must concur on an action. Here are some company rules that are typical examples of safeguards:

1) Except for specified causes (for example, smoking in an oil refinery), a worker can be discharged only after one (or two) written warnings and an opportunity to improve.
2) Two levels of supervision and the personnel director must concur before pay increases or decreases can be made. Increases must fall within established ranges; no one may be paid less than the minimum for the job he holds.
3) Executives must submit to grievance procedures that provide an opportunity for objective review of any action an employee feels is unfair or malicious.

Negative effects.   The open use of power is often resented. It may create antagonism toward the user and toward the existence of power. When such a negative reaction occurs, even more positive inducements will be needed to offset the reaction, and this high pressure will have to be maintained.

· So when contemplating forceful use of power, a manager must predict whether his action will a) build greater resentment and resistance, *or* b) establish a pattern of behavior and expectations that will gradually become accepted as normal.

Inadequacy of coercion.   A third drawback of relying solely on coercion to secure obedience to authorized instructions is its inadequacy to the task. Attempts to use power are in certain circumstances simply ineffective. A threat of discharge is not serious to the person who can readily obtain as good a job elsewhere. Similarly, the prospect of promotion holds no lure for an individual who dislikes added burden and authority over his associates. Because power rests on ability to deprive a person of a satisfaction, its strength depends on the marginal value the person attaches to that satisfaction. A point is often reached at which the satisfactions an executive controls have little value for his subordinates.

Power is inadequate in other ways. We have already mentioned certain counterpowers that can neutralize managerial power. As noted in Chapter 8, informal groups can occasionally enforce standards that are inconsistent with those set by the formal hierarchy. Labor unions, too, may have sufficient power to counteract the strength of management in certain areas. Even a large stock-holder, an important customer, or a crucial supplier can occasionally use his power to countermand the directives of company management. Such counter-powers, like the safeguards a company voluntarily imposes on its use of power, reduce an executive's ability to enforce his will.

But the most significant drawback of coercion is its failure to generate the initiative and enthusiasm that are vital for many jobs in an enterprise. When people respond to power alone, they offer only ambivalent compliance. They give answers they guess a supervisor wants to hear rather than give their own honest judgment. They are likely to stress superficial accomplishments and neglect hard-to-measure elements, for there will be little payoff for unnoticed quality. Unless tight controls are maintained, they may postpone or forget disagreeable work. In short, in a power-centered concern, a worker (manager or operator) focuses his attention on pleasing his boss rather than on achieving results he himself believes worthwhile. Dependency, a psychologist would say, snuffs out self-expression and personal drive.

While stressing the limitations of coercion, we must recognize that short-run or extreme situations do arise in which coercion is the only feasible way to move people from opposition to ambivalent compliance. Moreover, power need not be blatantly used. Power exists and it plays a crucial role in every organized endeavor of society. In all the other means for shifting responses to activating requests (to which we now turn our attention), power lurks in the background —a latent force that a manager can call upon.

CULTIVATE COOPERATION

"Build cooperation—not coercion" is the underlying tenet of the "human-relation" advocates. Following this approach, a manager tries to create a total job setting that employees feel is acceptable and pleasant. And because the work situation is pleasant, it is presumed that employees will carry out instructions.

This approach to activating has great appeal. It places value on worker satisfaction as well as on productivity. It fits our concern for the common man— our egalitarian traditions. It stresses contentment and harmony rather than rest-less ambition and conflict.

Before examining how this approach fits into our activating model of opposition, compliance, and commitment, let us review briefly several important ways that a manager can create such a cooperative work situation.

Structural Prerequisites
to Voluntary Cooperation

The total process of managing must be reasonably well performed for voluntary cooperation to flourish. We cannot do a poor job of organizing, planning, and controlling, and then expect a kindly leader to pull us out of our troubles miraculously.

Managerial leadership operates within a structure—a structure of organization, plans, and controls. And on the basis of this formally designed structure, a social structure develops—as we have seen earlier in the book. Many of the habits and persistent feelings of workers (both managers and operators) arise from the formal and social structures we create as a part of managing, and these feelings affect workers' responses to activating requests. Major points at which our structural design may have a significant bearing on the responses of workers include the following.

Clear organization. When a person has known duties—and corresponding authority—he can develop a pride in his work, a recognized status, and a sense of inner security. By making clear the role of staff, we avoid a source of confusion and perhaps conflicting obligations.

Individuals well matched with jobs. A person's feeling about his work also depends on whether his job is suited to his abilities. Through personnel planning we try to make full use of an individual's abilities, but at the same time we try not to put him in a spot where he becomes discouraged and defensive because he cannot meet his obligations. Minor modifications in organization structure are often made, either enlarging or contracting an assignment, so that the person and his job are well matched. Such matching fosters a cooperative feeling.

Effective communication networks. With each person necessarily doing only a piece of the total work in a company, we must design systems that provide him with the information he needs, promptly and accurately. If he is kept well informed, his work can proceed smoothly and he can take pride in his accomplishment; whereas poor communication leads to confusion, frustration, and negative attitudes toward meeting company goals.

Sound objectives. To create personal satisfactions, broad goals should be translated into specific aims that are meaningful to each employee, and then reasonable levels of achievement should be agreed on. Such specific goals can become the basis for a great deal of voluntary cooperation, and achieving them can give a worker a significant sense of accomplishment.

Workable policies, methods, and procedures. A structure of plans for handling repetitive problems creates a necessary stability and a pattern of behavior that make work more satisfying to most employees. For aside from an occasional rebel, most people derive a sense of security from an established, known set of norms.

Balanced control systems. In Part Five we saw that control systems, too, can be designed to minimize the usual negative reaction to controls and to provide constructive help to individuals in meeting their accepted goals.

In the following discussion of personal actions by a manager that help develop cooperation, we are assuming that the total management structure is conducive to effective person-to-person leadership.

Thoughtful Supervision

A second category of managerial actions that increase the likelihood of a cooperative response to activating requests deals with the manner of supervision.

Friendliness and approval. The kind of friendliness we are concerned with here runs deeper than mere cordiality and politeness. A subordinate is dependent on his supervisor for a variety of things—job assignments, information, help in overcoming problems, and the like—and he wants assurance of *approval* from this strategic person. Being friendly is one way a supervisor can convey approval.

Consistency and fairness. Inconsistent treatment by a boss can upset workers to a point where they become disgusted with their entire job. The president of a medium-sized import-export company, for instance, was so unpredictable in his demands that his chief accountant resigned. The accountant explained: "I can't live with a guy like that. One day he's hounding you for figures—'guesstimates' if necessary. The next day accuracy is all important, right down to the last penny. The Dr. Jekyll–Mr. Hyde act was driving me nuts." Consistent supervision enables subordinates to develop normal patterns of behavior. Knowing what to expect and how to respond, they feel more secure and self-confident.

Even more important to a spirit of cooperation than consistency over time is consistency—or fairness—of treatment among subordinates. A feeling among workers that a boss plays favorites ("Pete gets all the soft assignments." "Sure, he's the fair-haired boy; he can take a day off and nobody kicks.") can quickly reduce voluntary cooperation to zero.

Here we get into difficulty in determining just what is fair. The principle of equal treatment clashes with another strong belief. Every person should be treated as an individual. If Joe has thirty years of service with the company, or his leg is in a cast because of an automobile accident, or he is going to be sent abroad in six months, should he be given special consideration?

To build a spirit of cooperation, we must give rewards and punishments and perform other supervisory acts in a manner that *subordinates feel* is consistent or at least reasonable. Equal treatment is only a starting point. Many exceptions to strict equality are regarded as fair. Joe can be given special treatment—because of his long service, or accident, or future job—if the reason is known and accepted as legitimate and if subordinates believe that future exceptions will be made consistently for others in a similar situation. Among many employees, in fact, fairness actually requires that those with long service or in poor health be given special treatment.

Support for subordinates. A manager can provide a wide range of supports for his subordinates. One is simply to help in getting a job done. For example, machines may need repairing, tough customers may need to be impressed by an executive from the home office, letters should be answered while a subordinate is in bed with the flu, and so on. A subordinate will feel more secure and confident if he knows he can get help from his boss *if and when* he asks for it.

A supervisor may also support his people outside the department. He may vigorously seek every salary increase his people deserve; he may try to keep work flowing to his people at a steady pace—that is, avoid critical demands one week and layoffs the next; he may negotiate frictions with related departments —perhaps getting engineers to modify unworkable specifications or answering complaints from customer-service people; he may push for better offices or equipment; and he may keep his people informed about changes that affect them. When subordinates know their boss is representing their "needs" with a fair measure of success, they are inclined to follow his lead.

Law of the situation. Whenever possible, a supervisor should let the facts of a situation tell his subordinates what should be done—rather than to say, in effect, "Do this because *I* tell you to." An American manufacturer of

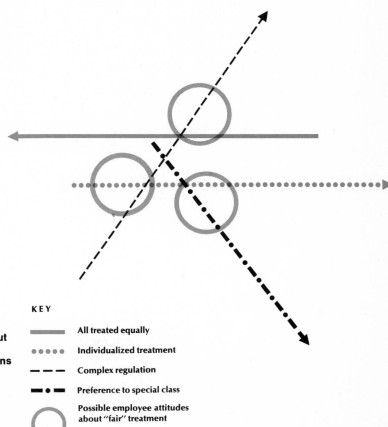

KEY

Figure 26–2 **Attitudes differ about how managers should treat subordinates. Four possible patterns of treatment are shown. Circles indicate which methods three separate groups of subordinates consider "fair."**

——— All treated equally

••••• Individualized treatment

— — — Complex regulation

—•— Preference to special class

◯ Possible employee attitudes about "fair" treatment

electrical equipment lost a big order to a foreign competitor who quoted an appreciably lower price, and the domestic firm faced the prospect of losing substantially more business for the same reason. The general manager might well have issued a lot of edicts about cutting costs. Instead, he laid the full facts before his engineers and production people, announcing, "We have a problem." The situation rather than the general manager issued the order to cut costs.

Similar reliance on the law of the situation can be used for small problems as well as large ones. For instance, a customer's complaint about an error in billing or the illness of a key person in a department obviously requires some kind of action. A manager may in the end decide precisely what is to be done, but the *need* for action is accepted by subordinates not because he says so, but because they recognize an objective to be met. When men respond to a situation rather than to an order, they have a sense of self-expression. Their identification with the desired result fosters a willingness to cooperate with a program of action.

Settlement of grievances. Over time we can expect subordinates to have occasional work-related grievances. Most of these will be *minor:* a 50-cent error on a paycheck, a chair that snags stockings, lost telephone messages, failure to announce a new title, and the like. Any minor grievance by itself is not particularly important, but until it is settled, it is a continuing source of personal annoyance. By prompt attention to such matters, a manager not only removes the irritation but also shows his concern for the feelings of his subordinates. Even if a grievance cannot be resolved in just the way the subordinate wishes, the boss clearly demonstrates that he considers even the minor needs of his people worthy of respect.

Progressive Off-the-Job Benefits

The most conspicuous way to cultivate cooperation is to be progressive (generous) with off-the-job benefits. In addition to paying relatively high salaries (see Chapter 7), a company may be a leader in cutting hours of work, granting holidays, providing paid vacations, giving liberal pensions, guaranteeing employment, arranging for health and other insurance, sponsoring recreational activities, and providing still other fringe benefits.

Such added compensation obviously increases the attractiveness of employment by a "progressive" company. Here again the way employees feel about what they are receiving is crucial. To create positive sentiments, a benefit must a) be generous relative to historical patterns and b) be at least as good as benefits provided by other well-known employers. Thus there is a built-in escalation in the costs of such provisions, and a risk that even slowing down on increases will lead to disappointment because worker expectations have not been fulfilled.

Does Cooperation Lead
to Compliance or Commitment?

571

CHAPTER 26
Gaining
Commitment
or Compliance

Well-designed structure, thoughtful supervision, and generous benefits do indeed create an appealing work setting. They go a long way toward building a cooperative work force. But in terms of activating, two aspects of this approach to motivation call for emphasis.

First, cultivating cooperation along the lines just reviewed leads to indifferent compliance but not to commitment. When skillfully used, these measures should make subordinates favorably disposed to carrying out activating requests. Contrariwise, the absence or bungling of these measures will lead to discontent and perhaps to opposition. So they are significant in creating a favorable environment. But in Frederick Herzberg's language, these measures are hygienic, not motivators. Lacking in the preceding review are steps that lead to commitment to achieve particular goals. The feelings created relate to one's job in general, but they do not tie personal goals with company goals. Consequently, compliance rather than commitment is the most we can expect.

Second, time is required. The cooperative feeling—growing out of the management structure, the supervision, and the benefits—must be nurtured. Confidence, expected relationships, and attitudes must be built up over a considerable period. The cooperative spirit we are discussing here cannot be turned on by a manager just for a particular request. In fact, the feeling is largely unrelated to specific company tasks and goals. Selective flexibility is very limited.

Finally, we should note that our discussion of cultivating cooperation has assumed that management carries the initiative for creating an acceptable work setting. Responding to workers' needs, management selects and designs—in a rather paternalistic fashion. This view fits many situations but not all. Certainly when a labor union is present, and often in individual arrangements, bargaining about the terms of employment takes place. And when bargaining occurs, a manager normally reverts to compromise. The manager and the subordinates both make concessions. To the extent that bargaining takes over, we can expect ambivalent compliance instead of indifferent compliance.

USE OF COMPROMISE

A third basic way to shift responses to an activating request is compromise. Compromise differs from coercion and cultivating cooperation in its flexibility and its treatment of subordinates' wishes. When using coercion, a manager keeps his aims (both short- and long-range results) intact, and simply employs as much power as necessary to gain compliance. When cultivating cooperation, a manager starts by creating an attractive work setting, and then expects that his contented, appreciative subordinates will gladly comply. In compromising, a manager draws on both his power and cooperation inducements, but finds an expedient mixture that wins at least ambivalent compliance in the immediate future.

To compromise, according to Webster, is "to settle by mutual concessions." In activating, compromise requires that both the manager and his subordinates modify or give up part of what they want, but they do reach agreement on the conditions under which action will proceed. Neither party is completely satisfied, so we have ambivalent compliance.

Those captains of industry—and of ships—who like to think that they have absolute power balk at the idea of compromising. They feel that compromise invades their managerial prerogatives. A modern manager, however, is well aware that he has no divine right to command. Instead, he has to consider objectively how he can best obtain adequate responses to his requests—and compromise is one of the means. Compromise in the meaning used here is a normal fact of life, and we believe it should be treated as such.

A manager in an activating situation typically arrives at a compromise either by initiating the compromise himself, voluntarily composing the terms, or by bargaining.

Self-Composed Compromise

A manager turns to compromise when 1) the predicted response to his activating request is unsatisfactory, 2) prompt action is desired, and 3) the cost and possible failure of other methods (coercing, cultivating cooperation, establishing congruence) are high. And we often find ourselves in such a predicament.

Sensing the need for a compromise, the astute manager may try to think of one that is likely to be acceptable to all parties, and then try to initiate this proposal. By anticipating the need for mutual concessions, he hopes to avoid the rancor of bargaining and also to maintain his leadership role. For example, if his subordinates are becoming increasingly annoyed with computer print-outs and the barrage of accompanying requests, he may decide (or arrange with the controller) to discontinue several existing reports. Then when he announces a newly devised "computer aid," he can simultaneously tell of relief from other pressure.

Whereas the power to coerce has its principal effect in its potential rather than actual use, compromise is most effective in shifting behavior toward compliance when it is actively used. In fact, compromise may make its most significant contribution toward eliciting positive responses when it is used by a manager who has the power to coerce. The manager who is able to coerce or exact a lopsided compromise (in his favor), but who refrains from doing so, may create a climate favorable to future cases in which he must compromise or seek commitment.

The use of compromise involves three dangers.

1) It may be perceived as a sign of weakness, and thereby invite opposition to later requests.
2) It may create embarrassing precedents.
3) It may be an "easy" treatment of a situation in which a more difficult co-operative or congruent resolution would give more lasting benefits.

All three of these dangers were faced by the supervisor of seven draftsmen in an engineering consulting firm. The prevailing practice for overtime pay was quite flexible: When work was slack, the draftsmen left the office early with no loss in pay; in exchange, when rush projects required overtime, they worked up to an extra ten hours per week with no additional pay; beyond the ten hours, they received overtime pay at their regular hourly rate. This arrangement was quite acceptable until a union organizer started preaching "time-and-a-half for all hours over the regular 35-hour week."

The supervisor predicted that the draftsmen would neither quit nor join the union in the near future even though he insisted on continuing the past practice. However, the draftsmen clearly felt that they should get time-and-a-half for all extra hours beyond ten per week. Rather than say no, which he had the power to do, he devised a compromise that still was simple and flexible. "I told them that instead of making an issue in the personnel department, I would handle it informally. I promised to get them some extra money by approving payment for one and one-half hours for every overtime hour over ten. It worked well because they trust me to do right by them and I trust them not to drag their feet. I told my boss and he liked it too."

"Now," the supervisor continued, "I have another touchy one. For this summer we just got several big projects we hadn't planned on. Normally our summers are our slow times. To get these projects our salespeople submitted very low bids. To complete the work on time, I will have to ask our people to give up a total of five weeks' vacation. Four of my people get three weeks of vacation, two get four weeks, and one gets two weeks. I'm sure we can get them to allocate this time among themselves. I don't want to have to hire someone else to do the work. My problem is that while I can pay them for the vacation time they give up, these low-margin projects will not permit me to pay them the equivalent of time and one-half. I'm sure that most of them won't like the idea of giving up vacation time with no bonus involved."

To illustrate the three possible dangers of compromise, consider first how the draftsmen perceived their superior's prior actions. If they see a pattern of compromise on his part (in the decision on added pay for overtime) stemming from his fear of a union, they may interpret that decision as a sign of weakness and thus might resist his request for giving up vacations with no bonus.

With respect to the second danger, the supervisor developed the overtime compromise at least in part to avoid "changing our compensation practices every time a problem comes up." In the process, however, he created a potentially dangerous precedent with his compromise if, this time, he must say no and his people do not accept his reasons.

To illustrate the third danger, he may again work out an acceptable compromise and move their expected response from opposition to ambivalent or indifferent compliance. By so doing, however, is he missing an opportunity to review the entire work-compensation area and develop a longer-term, flexible program that is more congruent with the company's goals and those of his people? Developing such a program may take time, and creativity has its risks. A rational appraisal might lead him to invest the time and take the risks in light of potentially greater commitment from his people. But the ease of another compromise may well lead him away from a better long-run approach.

Bargaining

Many compromises are reached through bargaining—rather than being composed almost entirely by the manager. Collective bargaining with labor unions is required by law, but informal bargaining between a manager and single subordinate or group of subordinates is even more widespread.

In the bargaining process, each party indicates (with varying degrees of candor) what he would like; he listens to the other person; and he expects some give-and-take in reaching a compromise agreement.

The style of bargaining varies. One style is showmanship and bluffing—so common in union negotiations that it has become a ritual. Quite different is open, candid confrontation—all cards on the table; this style is often used in person-to-person bargaining. But perhaps even more prevalent is submerged bargaining, in which the demands and threats and even the proposed concessions are not openly stated but are nonetheless recognized as part of a negotiation.

Both parties in manager–employee bargaining should recognize that more than a single, immediate request for action is involved. More important is developing a sound basis for *continuing* cooperative efforts. Also, the potential use of power by either party is always in the background—both the amount of power and the willingness to use it; this inevitably affects the concessions made and agreements reached.

The choice of whether or not to use bargaining to reach a compromise, and of the style of bargaining, is made by subordinates as well as managers. If subordinates insist on bargaining, their manager must join in the process.

An advantage of open bargaining is that subordinates' "needs" will be more accurately known—the compromise will not be based on what a manager guesses someone else wants. Moreover, because each person decides the concessions he will make, the compromise will lessen his regret. In this regard, during the bargaining process we should look for changes in the activating request and in the work situation that are of high value to one party and of little or no significance to the other. Bargaining is not entirely a "You win, I lose" affair; a creative solution more attractive to all parties may be found.

The great disadvantage of bargaining, of course, is its strong emphasis on conflict. Areas of disagreement are stressed, perhaps magnified out of proportion to their real significance. In formalized collective bargaining we even have specialists whose positions depend on uncovering and increasing sensitivity to sources of discontent. Such emphasis on conflicting goals makes ambivalent compliance the best response that a manager can hope to achieve.

Fortunately, bargaining need not take center stage. For some issues, such as level of pay, it is possible to agree on criteria for adjustments (cost of living, prevailing rates in the labor market, or matching a leading company). A permanent arbitrator can establish a "common law" pattern for resolving other kinds of disputes, or a company by its own actions may build such a tradition. Open communication (discussed in the next chapter) can lead to quick resolution of conflicts that do arise. And, long-term agreements, formal and informal, can make bargaining only an occasional affair.

Avoiding frequent discussion of conflicting goals is especially important to the manager who seeks commitment to his activating requests. Bargaining that involves acrimony and bluffing is especially injurious to feelings of trust and confidence that accompany commitment. Some conflict is inevitable, as we have noted throughout this book, and means for resolving it—perhaps through bargaining—must be found. But if we seek commitment, this resolution must be made promptly and adroitly to establish a climate favorable to positive, enthusiastic action.

CONGRUENCE: GATEWAY TO COMMITMENT

The ways of shifting responses to activating requests already discussed—coercion, cultivating cooperation, compromise—lead to ambivalent or indifferent compliance. They may (or may not) also help set the stage for commitment. But to switch subordinates to a committed response requires that a manager resort to another kind of energizing force.

Commitment, as defined in the preceding chapter, involves a subordinate's desire to carry out the activating request *for his own satisfaction*. This is an internal, emotional feeling. For instance, if you are the West Coast manager and your marketing vice president asks you to increase the company's share of the market from ten to twelve percent, your response is likely to be a strong commitment to that goal. The goal becomes a personal challenge; you believe your company should have even more of the market; you'll have fun showing other managers how strong your district is; customers on the West Coast really need your product; building up the territory carries with it more recognition in headquarters and a good bonus; and you have a lot of ideas about how the job can be done. A different example—your warehouse manager on the West Coast is an old-timer and less exuberant than you; nevertheless, he takes great pride in running an efficient operation, and is strongly committed to keeping his expense ratios in line.

The primary way a manager can encourage such feelings of commitment is to establish *congruence* between his aims and those of his subordinates. Congruence is the gateway to commitment. It exists when both the manager and his subordinates want the same immediate results from the subordinates' efforts.

Broadly speaking, a manager can develop congruence by 1) encouraging subordinates to embrace general company objectives, and/or 2) increasing the personal satisfactions arising from the immediate work assignment. Although these two approaches overlap, they do provide a convenient framework for tackling the delicate task of building congruence.

Embracing General Company Objectives

Frequently employees identify themselves closely with their company. They genuinely feel, for example, that "What's good for General Motors is good for me." Even more common is identification with a division or a department, just as a professor wants his department to be successful and well respected. If, in addition to such identification, the employee feels that his work contributes to the strength of his department or company, then his work takes on a special significance for him. He is contributing to a cause.

No manager can order a subordinate to embrace company or departmental objectives, but he can encourage such feelings. Rational persuasion about the importance of company activities has only limited effect because of the emotional basis for the choice of missions or causes. Equally important is the charismatic charm of key executives, coupled with feelings of loyalty to important executives. Moreover, successful companies that enjoy public goodwill develop their own mystique; there is significant prestige in being associated with such an institution. By drawing attention to such appeals as these, a manager can often develop an endorsement of company (or departmental) objectives.

A separate factor is the feeling of being "on the team"—especially on a successful team. When an individual feels that he is making perhaps a small yet significant contribution to group accomplishment, and he is recognized for that contribution, he tends to identify with the group and its goals. The group achievement represents a projection of his own achievement. And when he feels that he has had some participation in setting group goals, the group (company or departmental) objectives become even more his own. By helping people sense the importance of the roles they play, a manager nourishes this feeling of group affiliation.

Then, if the personal endorsement of a company or department is coupled with a feeling of significant participation in its activities, a basis is laid for the individual to embrace the company or departmental objectives. And we are well on the road to congruence.

Such embracing of group objectives is, of course, easier to develop among people higher in the organization, where their individual contributions are easy to recognize. In fact, a recent survey by the American Management Associations of over 2,500 managers found that ninety-nine percent feel that their work is worth doing.[2] The survey did not attempt to measure the strength of this feeling compared with other values, but the implication is clear—high congruence with company objectives. For people at lower organization levels, it is probably more reasonable to seek congruence with departmental or other intermediate objectives, rather than congruence between individual and corporate objectives.

Personal Satisfactions
Arising from Immediate Assignment

Embracing company or departmental objectives is one path to congruence; but, while always desirable, it is not the only means. Congruence can also arise from the specific work a person is asked to do. Provided company objectives do not directly clash with his personal values, an individual may become strongly committed to only his segment of the total operations.

Every activity has a variety of consequences. The work that Sue Smith does, for example, results in beautiful sales-promotion brochures that the company likes, and it also gives her an opportunity to use her flair for artistic photography. Sue observes:

Sure, what my supervisor asks me to do is a means of reaching his own and company ends. Though I don't care as much as he or the president about such ends, they aren't in conflict with my own goals or values. And, if I do what he asks, I get to

---

[2] Ninety-four percent are proud of their company, ninety-six percent enjoy their work, eighty-eight percent feel that their salary is equitable, and seventy-five percent believe their fringe benefits are rewarding. Although the sample is biased toward favorable answers, the weight of the evidence is substantial. See P. G. McLean and K. Jillson, *The Manager and Self-Respect* (American Management Associations, 1975).

achieve my ends in a way I would choose for myself if I were my own boss. I'm far from indifferent, because I want the same results as he wants—but for different reasons [ends].

Productive work may provide many kinds of satisfactions. Pride in the output, sense of creativity, self-expression, and demonstration of professional skill are among the psychological rewards of a well-done job. Although we usually think of such satisfactions in connection with crafts, professions, or other individualistic work, managers and team workers may get the same sort of elation from the results of group effort.

With care a manager can design his organization so that there is opportunity for people to get these satisfactions from their particular work—as we recommended in Part Two. Job enlargement (more activities) and job enrichment (more decentralization) are ways of expanding the scope of a position so that the incumbent finds his work more rewarding. Of course, it is necessary to assign an individual to a job that provides opportunities for work satisfactions that appeal to him.

Through this process of skillfully designing jobs and matching people to them, a manager can build congruence. Then if he actively assists and supports people in those positions in achieving their immediate goals, a high degree of commitment normally follows.

In addition, such off-the-job rewards as bonuses, external recognition, and consideration for promotion can reinforce the positive feelings about an already-attractive assignment. To help build congruence, however, these off-the-job rewards must be closely tied to results that the company wants. The subordinate (laborer or vice president) must be aware of a direct, consistent, and predictable relation between rewards received and achievement of his assigned mission. Then, the work that he already finds personally satisfying is made even more attractive by its subsequent off-the-job endorsement.

In other circumstances the off-the-job rewards may be simply part of a package of "goodies" that the company uses to cultivate cooperation, and the bonuses might be part of a negotiated compromise leading to ambivalent compliance. The distinction here is that these off-the-job rewards are coupled with an already attractive assignment. Their presence enhances the satisfactions a person gets from doing his job well and makes it easy for him to internalize his desire to achieve the immediate goals.

To summarize, congruence—both the manager and his subordinates wanting the same immediate result from the subordinates' efforts—may arise from the subordinate embracing company goals and feeling that his work is making a significant contribution toward these goals; or it may be based on satisfactions the subordinate gets from good performance of assignments that he likes—especially when doing such good work is reinforced with off-the-job rewards. Obviously, if the manager who wants to build congruence can arrange a combination of these forces—an embracing of company objectives, feeling one's work is important, satisfactions from the immediate task, and off-the-job rewards—he has the basis for very strong commitment.

How to change responses to activating requests is the central issue of this chapter. When a manager forecasts an unsatisfactory response—opposition when he wants compliance, or compliance when he wants commitment—he must immediately consider what he can do to shift that response. Coercion, cultivating cooperation, compromise, and establishing congruence are all possible means he can try to bring about a different response. We have now looked at each of these energizing forces, but in discussing them separately we have oversimplified the manager's quandary about how to proceed. In addition to the factors already laid out, these three integrating situations should be faced.

Interaction Among Modes

In the normal relationship between a manager and his subordinates, different activating modes will be used concurrently—ambivalent compliance for keeping regular office hours but commitment for their role in training new workers. And when we add to the basic modes the selected steps for shifting some predicted responses, the activating pattern may be further varied.

For the subordinate, these pieces of his boss's behavior interact and perhaps get mixed up. There are two common sources of overlap:

1) Different kinds of requests are activated by different modes, as in the office-hours and training example mentioned above.
2) The methods used to shift responses are not mutually exclusive—power is a silent partner in bargaining, for instance, and voluntary cooperation provides an important background for establishing congruence.

Insofar as possible, the manager should follow a consistent pattern for each type of activity, and help his subordinate recognize this pattern. Even so, the reactions will merge. Consequently, when considering action on a particular problem, the manager should weigh its likely influence on responses to other activating requests. He is dealing with whole persons, and their psychological moods carry over from one encounter to the next.

Influence of Peers

Most of our discussion has focused on person-to-person relationships. But activating normally takes place in a social context. The way a manager treats one subordinate will be known and have an effect on his peers. Also, the beliefs and values of peers will influence the way an individual responds to a request. Because of this permeating effect, any attempt to alter responses should take into account both its broader impact on others and the fact that the response will be conditioned by group norms.

Activating is a continuing process. Past arguments, disappointments, use of power, surprises, and gratifications are the prologue for today. We build (or destroy) confidence, set precedents, engender commitment by a whole series of specific actions. Part of each setting (contingency) that we as managers must carefully assess is this heritage. In activating, we do not start each day with a clean slate; instead, we start today where we left off yesterday. When we act on a concrete, immediate issue—as we must for work to proceed—we are also setting the stage for the next problem.

FOR CLASS DISCUSSION

1) The text deals with the normal situation in which a manager seeks to shift a predicted response from *less* to *more* positive. Can you conceive of a situation in which it would be important for a manager to shift from a *more* to a *less* positive response?

2) "Power is a managerial resource that must be used fairly but regularly. If it is used infrequently and only as a last resort after other approaches have failed, it is much more likely to fail." Discuss this comment made by a successful director of a large museum.

3) What is the distinction between a manager's effort to "cultivate cooperation" and what has come to be frowned on in the United States as "paternalism"?

4) "Sometimes I feel like laughing out loud when my boss comes to me and tells me how important my acceptance of some new scheme of his is. We both know that, accept it or not, I have to follow it. Yet he tries to make me feel that I should be willing to devote the same time and energy to making his plan work that he did in dreaming it up. To me, this is a job, a way of supporting my family. Maybe if I owned as much stock in the company as the boss, I'd see things his way; but as it is, why should I get all involved?" *a)* Diagnose this reaction of a production supervisor to his boss, the production vice president. *b)* If you were the production vice president and overheard this statement, what would you do?

5) "Frequently, when I predict a negative reaction to an order I have to give, I will ask for something my subordinates will like even less. Then after a certain amount of debate, I back off and 'settle' for what I originally wanted. Invariably I get a better reception than I would have otherwise." Comment on this "compromise" approach by a successful magazine editor.

6) In general, do you feel it is more or less important to develop voluntary cooperation at high management levels rather than between first-line managers and their hourly workers?

7) The supervisor of maintenance in an ink and dye factory has to get two of his men to repair the inside of one of the plant's large mixing vats. This is a highly unpleasant job and the supervisor sees no way of making his men want to associate their needs with this project. Of course, he can order them to climb into the vat and make repairs. What response should he seek? What energizing force should he use if he predicts mild resistance to the request?

8) In what way may "open bargaining" contribute to a manager's ability to pre-dict responses to future activating requests?

Cases

For cases involving issues covered in this chapter, see especially the following. Particularly relevant questions are listed after each case.

FOR FURTHER READING

Hersey, P. and K. H. Blanchard, "What's Missing in MBO?" *Management Review,* October 1974.

Recommends that leadership style—in addition to performance goals—be negoti-ated between boss and subordinate.

McMurry, R. N., "Power and the Ambitious Executive." *Harvard Business Review,* November 1973.

Argues that the use of power is essential in organizational life, then discusses con-structive ways a senior manager can gain and keep power.

Oates, D., "McClelland: An Advocate of Power." *International Management,* July 1975 (condensed version in *Management Review,* December 1975).

Contends that successful managers need and use power—despite the dislike of power expressed by popular behavioral scientists.

Schleh, E. C., *The Management Tactician.* New York: McGraw-Hill Book Com-pany, 1974.

A how-to book on Management by Results by a successful consultant. Schleh advocates carefully structuring the total job relationships so as to make commitment likely.

Sherwin, D. S., "Strategy for Winning Employee Commitment." *Harvard Business Review,* May 1972.

A company executive proposes a series of managerial steps that will enrich jobs and develop employee commitment.

(NOTE: See also the recommended readings on organizational change at the end of Chapter 28.)

27 Gaining Understanding

PERSONAL COMMUNICATION: FOUNDATION FOR ACTIVATING

Mutual understanding is essential to successful activating. Throughout our discussion of the activating process—predicting responses, selecting modes, deciding on energizing forces to shift responses, moving into action—we have assumed that the manager understands his subordinates and that they understand him. In practice, deficiencies in such understanding are a major stumbling block.

The critical element here is an ability to communicate person-to-person. A manager must learn from his subordinate the latter's thoughts, feelings, and motivations. He must also clearly convey his explicit and implicit instructions, along with their significance and the feeling that lies behind them. Because skill in such interpersonal communication is so vital, it is the focus of this chapter.

Many other forms of communication are important in managing an enterprise. As we have seen in Parts Four and Five, both planning and control depend on a vast flow of data. Division of labor, decentralization, staff, and other features of organization—analyzed in Parts One and Two—create the need for management information systems. But this kind of information flow does not provide the highly personal understandings that underlie activating.

To improve one's ability to communicate person-to-person, one should:

1) be aware of common obstacles to gaining understanding, 2) recognize several psychological prerequisites, 3) understand the process of empathetic listening, and 4) know how to make clear activating requests. Throughout our discussion of these topics, however, we should think of their relevance and suitability to each of the activating modes explored in Chapters 25 and 26. In person-to-person communication, as in virtually all other areas of managing, the value of a concept or technique depends upon the situation to which it is being applied.

OBSTACLES TO UNDERSTANDING

Differences in Viewpoints

One reason comunicating is not easy lies in the different point of view of receiver and sender. Let us take an example. Joan Brown is sales manager for one of the leading American manufacturers of men's and women's apparel; her salesman in the Atlanta territory is Al Williams. Brown has always gotten along with Williams, enjoys talking with him, and likes to help Williams when she can. Recently Brown has been looking at figures on population and buying power; these indicate that the Atlanta district has greatly increased in both categories. So on a visit to the Atlanta office, Brown said to Williams, "I've been wondering if the Atlanta territory is the right size for one person to cover."

In making this apparently simple observation, Brown meant to imply that the work load in Atlanta has apparently increased, and that some arrangement must be made to keep the company growing and profitable in relation to its competitors. She is also trying to convey a feeling toward Williams—that she likes him and is concerned about his satisfaction with his job.

Al Williams, however, has just returned from 300 miles of travel on a July day with temperatures over 90 degrees, a trip that included 60 miles of a dusty, unpaved road. Before his boss came in, he read his mail and found a routine communication from New York asking him to fill out a complete set of forms on forecasting purchases by each customer and to "get these back to us next week if possible." Williams knows that he will have to work a couple of nights to finish the forms in time. In addition, Brown is the first woman Williams has ever worked for. So when Brown says, "I've been wondering if the Atlanta territory is about the right size for one person to cover," this series of thoughts runs through Williams' mind: "Brown has never been over the back part of the territory; she doesn't know what the territory is really like; she thinks of it as a big smooth map; now she thinks I'm not working hard enough so she's asking why I'm not producing more sales."

Situations like this occur in industry every day. An executive makes a seemingly simple statement, and a responsible subordinate who gets along well

Figure 27–1   A person's perception of a situation—here, a power failure—depends on his particular viewpoint. A different attitude toward the same situation can lead to a breakdown in communication.

with his boss receives quite a different communication. Why was Brown's communication ineffective?

First, we should note that to Brown and Williams the word "territory" means different things, as a factual, intellectual matter. Williams has seen 30 towns in the back part of the territory, known 45 customers in those towns, traversed 30 roads connecting them, and experienced how much time it took to talk to Al Jackson in Marietta compared with the time it took to talk to Jack Freeman in Valdosta. These 107 facts, along with hundreds of others, he has lumped together in his head, into a construct called the "territory." From literally thousands of things he has felt and seen, Williams has abstracted a "territory." It has *meaning* to him. Brown, on the other hand, has looked at many maps, reviewed statistics on the number and names of customers, measured distances, looked at population and buying-power statistics, and has lumped all these facts together into something she calls a "territory." The word clearly has another meaning for her.

In addition to such differences in intellectual content, the feelings a person wants to transmit may not correspond to those that are received. Joan Brown, when she spoke, actually felt friendly toward Al Williams; but Al did not, at least in this particular communication, receive that impression. He may generally feel that Brown likes him, but this one statement did not convey or reinforce that feeling. At this point, then, just as each person is thinking of different intellectual abstractions, so each one is feeling different emotions.

If Al Williams is to understand Joan Brown, the latter must find some way to overcome this semantic barrier, a barrier created by both the difference between her own factual experience and that of Williams and the differences in her feelings and his.

Incidentally, Brown will gain very little by asking Williams, "You know what I mean by the Atlanta territory, don't you?" Williams can really only answer, "Yes." If he says anything else, his boss is likely to think he is not too bright. Furthermore, if by saying "Yes" Williams really believes that he does understand, he can only mean, "I understand what *I* heard," not "I understand what you heard yourself say."

Any subordinate naturally wants to look good in his boss's eyes. Consequently he selects the information he passes up the line so as to create a good impression, and he holds back information that makes him look bad. In organization jargon, he protectively screens the information that he transmits. A boss, likewise, may feel that, because of his position, he should not be completely candid with his subordinate. Individuals differ, of course, in the extent to which they permit a status discrepancy to interfere with a free exchange of ideas and feelings, and in extreme instances organizational distance blocks all except formal communication.

Perfunctory Attention

Often in our conversations with others, we only half-listen to what they say. We are so busy with our own thoughts that we tend to give attention only to those ideas we expect to hear. When an accountant talks to the controller, the controller may pay attention only to how work is progressing and may disregard clues on morale or friction with staff. In fact, psychological studies show that many of us ignore information that conflicts with our established patterns of thought; we simply do not believe that Steve is serious about quitting or that a key customer would buy foreign-made equipment, because such thoughts do not conform with the ideas we already hold. Especially if we are deeply committed to, or emotionally involved in, some matter, we prefer to pay no more attention to bad news than Hitler did to reports of inadequate supplies during the latter part of his regime. We tend to retain our private concept of the world by saying to ourselves, "I just don't believe———is so."

A manager is especially likely to give perfunctory attention to incoming communications when he is very busy with other matters. He simply has so many other distractions that he selects those parts of a total communication that can be readily used. Novel and irreconcilable bits of information or unexpected feelings get brushed aside. Under some circumstances, an executive may be justified in such cursory treatment of messages, but he pays a price in being superficially informed.

Repressed Feelings

Western culture stresses "objective evidence," "full knowledge of the facts," and "exchange of information." But at the same time we are taught to hide our emotions. Unlike a small child whose feelings are openly expressed, a mature adult is expected to moderate his emotions—or at least *appear* to moderate them. Likewise, our culture encourages us not to publicly recognize emotions in others. Except with one's closest friends, it isn't polite to discuss strong feelings.

A result of this repression of feelings is that we are inept in communicating them. Of course, there are such cues as the so-called body language. But particularly in a business or other organizational setting, special effort is required to detect how many people feel, and we rarely find an opportunity to verify our guesses directly.

Inferred Meanings

Still another difficulty we face in developing a clear, mutual understanding with our boss and our subordinates is the meaning—or interpretation—that we give a message. We do—and should—consider the source of a message: The sender may be biased, he may draw his ideas from an unrepresentative sample, or he may deliberately twist the evidence. But we get into trouble by lumping everyone in broad classes—for example, assuming all salespeople exaggerate. True, the typical salesperson tends to be too optimistic, but we must not assume from that trait that everything he says is unreliable. Moreover, our hopes may lead us to infer a meaning that was never intended; for example, a friendly talk with the boss does not necessarily mean we are in line for a promotion.

Then, too, the particular situation at the time a message is received may *accidentally* affect the meaning we attach to it. If Al Williams had been working over his prospect list instead of just returning from a hot, dusty trip, the meaning he drew from Joan Brown's comment about the size of the Atlanta territory might have been quite different. To take a similar example from another company, a plant superintendent was talking with one of his foremen about the high cost of certain products on the same day that the company controller distributed a bulletin on keeping time cards posted accurately. The foreman inferred that the superintendent thought he was faking his time reports. Actually, the superintendent had no such idea in mind; the arrival of the two messages on the same day was a pure accident.

Sensitivity to these common difficulties with person-to-person communication within organizations helps us spot misunderstandings. We may not be able to correct the difficulties—most are imbedded in our social customs—but we can sharpen our own communicating skills so as to work around them.

PREPARATION FOR UNDERSTANDING

As managers, we are dealing with the reactions of individual personalities to one another. If we are to understand, predict, and to some extent guide these interactions, we must be highly perceptive about the people involved. Three qualities contribute greatly to such perception: *empathy, self-awareness,* and *objectivity.*

Of course knowing about the importance of these qualities will not ensure that we develop them—just as knowing we should not get mad and actually controlling our anger are two different matters. Still, by understanding which qualities contribute to gaining understanding, we can at least discover where each of us should try to improve.

Empathy

Empathy is the ability to look at things from another person's point of view. If a manager is to understand, be understood by, and forecast the responses of a subordinate, he needs this capacity to project himself into that person's position. How does that person feel about the company and his job? What values does he attach to friendships, security, titles, and the many other things affected by his work? How will he interpret the words and actions of his boss, his associates, and his subordinates? What are his hopes and aspirations? What difficulties are bothering him at the moment? Whom does he trust, and whom does he fear?

Empathy is not a case of asking, "What would *I* do if I were in your position?" because any one of us might bring to the position quite different knowledge and feelings. We are empathetic only when we can sense and feel, almost intuitively, how another person is likely to react to a certain situation. An executive may set up a new vacation policy or make some other change he intends as an aid to his subordinates. But if he thinks of the change in terms of how *he* would like it rather than how the people affected will like it, the move is likely to be forecast badly.

To be empathetic we need *respect* for the other person as an individual. We may disagree sharply with his values and consider his reasoning false, but we should still recognize that his feelings and beliefs seem just as valid to him as ours to us. A salesperson, for instance, often finds he needs such attitudes; if he is a good salesperson, he has a high degree of empathy for his customer, but he does not necessarily endorse the customer's behavior or beliefs.

Self-Awareness

Knowing oneself ranks with empathy as a requisite for activating. We want to stress that each executive must be *aware* of the impact he makes. He should know his own predilections for taking action hastily, being brusque with people who don't understand instructions the first time, getting so involved in problems that he bypasses supervisors in resolving them, and so forth.

Moreover, a manager should know how he appears to other people. Many of us have an image of ourselves that differs from the way others see us. A manager may think of himself as fair and objective, but some of his subordinates may consider him biased in favor of young women with college degrees. Regardless of which view is correct, the manager may have difficulty in understanding and being understood by such a subordinate unless he knows how that subordinate feels.

Finally, with an awareness of his own preferences, weaknesses, and habits, and of what others think of him, a manager should learn what impression his actions make on other people. One high-ranking executive, for instance, growled over the telephone at the secretaries and assistants of his immediate subordinates when the latter were "not in." In so doing, he unwittingly created morale problems for his subordinates and virtually cut himself off from any understanding of lower-level personnel. But this executive, whose manner with his immediate subordinates was much less gruff, was unaware that by expressing his displeasure to secretaries he was creating this barrier to communications.

Objectivity

A third attribute that is crucial to good understanding is objectivity. Something causes everyone to behave as he does. If we can identify the influences on Joe Jones's actions, we have taken an important step toward forecasting his behavior. Instead of getting angry with Joe for resisting a new method, we should recognize his response and try to find out what caused it. Or if one of our sales representatives is unusually energetic, we should try to understand what motivates him, in the hope of discovering a way to induce similar behavior in our other representatives.

Such detachment may not be easy to maintain. We commonly react to the behavior of others emotionally instead of coolly and analytically. Besides, a manager is often deeply concerned with the outcome of his subordinate's activities and therefore lets his intense feelings cloud his objectivity.

Complicating the quest for objectivity is the fact that empathy fosters sympathy and personal identification with other people; yet a good activator should be both objective and empathetic. The viewpoint of a physician is similar to what a manager needs to reconcile these two attitudes. A good physi-

Figure 27–2 Objectivity in times of stress is vital to full, clear communication.

cian understands his patient's feelings—he is empathetic to a high degree; but his *own emotional involvement* must be limited if he is to make an objective diagnosis and perhaps take action that he knows involves substantial risk. He is well aware of the problems of his patients as individuals; yet he deals with such problems in a detached, scientific manner. A good manager, likewise, understands the feelings and problems of his subordinates; yet he keeps enough psychological distance to be fair, just, and constructively concerned with performance.

Many qualities contribute to a manager's ability to understand his people. We cannot make a complete and unassailable list of such qualities, partly because they vary with the people being activated and with the circumstances in which the activating takes place. Nevertheless, these three qualities—empathy, self-awareness, and objectivity—are all needed in the vast majority of cases. The importance of these abilities will become increasingly apparent as we consider two specific processes that aid in gaining mutual understanding—empathetic listening and making meaningful requests.

EMPATHETIC LISTENING

The kind of understanding we are exploring in this chapter requires the mutual exchange of ideas and feelings between manager and subordinate. The manager must *listen* and he must also *impart* facts and feelings. But for the interchange to be most effective, he should emphasize listening. If he starts by giving his views to a subordinate, as many managers are inclined to do, he is likely to stifle upward communication because of his status and latent power. Of course, a manager does give directions, as we shall soon note; but the form of communication we are examining here builds understandings and relationships that underlie and greatly simplify his task of directing.

What Empathetic Listening Involves

When listening empathetically, a person opens the way for another to talk freely about his ideas and feelings without having to justify each statement he makes. The listener reserves his own views and preconceived ideas, while giving close attention to the sentiments the other person is trying to express. The listener is simply trying to gain an insight into what is "on the other fellow's mind." Although this is a valuable skill at all levels, it is hardest, but probably most valuable, to the high-level manager. Because of his status, he frequently has difficulty getting subordinates to give him their "whole message."

Empathetic listening makes use of certain techniques employed in psychiatry; ideally, a patient first expresses his feelings, then recognizes the facts of his problem, and finally develops a workable adjustment of these facts. A manager, of course, should not undertake psychotherapy of deep-seated personal problems, but he can use some of the elementary concepts to nurture a mutual understanding of day-to-day problems at work. The manager can listen sympathetically, without injecting his own views, to a subordinate's attitudes and emotions about his job; and in so doing, the manager may help the other to gain a more objective appreciation of the total situation.

For a manager, this kind of nondirected interview may be the only way he can learn the full feelings and operating problems of his subordinates. Without such an understanding, a manager is in a poor position to predict responses to activating requests or to energize forces to shift those responses.

Example of Free Response

An illustration of empathetic listening will give concreteness to the free-response technique we have been discussing in general terms. Let us compare the way two different executives approach the same situation. The following facts were presented to executives at a management-development program; then members of the group interviewed a person who knew the full story and who responded as Tony Flynn probably would have.[1]

Tony Flynn works in the assembly department of a company that manufactures television-broadcasting equipment. The operation requires that men work in teams. Tony has been employed by the company six years. During the first two years he showed aptitude for the job, but his attendance record was so irregular he was warned twice that he would be dismissed unless he got to work steadily. For the past four years he has a good attendance record and is a competent, experienced workman. Although Tony gets along well with his fellow workers, he has always been very quiet and reserved, and company records do not contain any explanation of his early absences. Three days ago (Monday) Tony did not show up for work, nor did he phone that he was sick—which company rules require a man to do when he is ill. Tuesday the same thing happened, and the employment manager got no answer when he tried to call Tony's home. Again, on Wednesday, no Tony. This morning Tony appeared on time, but looking a bit disheveled and glum. The superintendent of the assembly department asked the lead-man under whom Tony works to send him to his office.

One interview with Tony developed as follows:

SUPT.: Hello, Tony, it's good to see you. Sit down a minute.
TONY: (*Taking chair beside desk*) Thanks.
SUPT.: Tony, we've missed you the last few days.
TONY: (*Half to himself*) Yeah, been out all week, until this morning.
SUPT.: That's right, I'm sorry to say, and you know how one man out upsets your crew. We didn't have a substitute most of the time.

---

[1] Professor Alex Bavelas assumed the role of Tony in both of the "role-playing" views digested here. The persons who took the position of superintendent were given only the facts known to management before the interview; they were free to conduct the interview as they chose and did not listen to anyone else before their turn. The two interviews selected represent contrasting approaches. The conversations have been condensed to conserve space.

TONY: (*Pause*) Yeah, afraid I caused some trouble.

SUPT.: And not calling in, Tony, that made matters worse because we didn't know what to plan on. You've been here long enough to know how important it is to keep full crews in assembly.

TONY: (*Again, half to himself*) Should have called in, that's right.

SUPT.: Tell me, when you realize how important it is, how could you just disappear for three days? We couldn't even get an answer at your home.

TONY: I just couldn't make it, and been too messed up to call in. Sorry I caused so much trouble.

SUPT.: Tony, I've looked over your record. The last four years have been fine. We need good men like you. A few years back the absences were pretty serious, and I sure hope we're not going to slide back to that trouble again. Yet, the recent record looks real good. (*Pause*) What do you think, Tony, can you keep that record as clean as it has been the last couple of years?

TONY: I'd sure like to. I've been trying. (*Pause*)

SUPT.: We need good men like you. You know the work, and you pitch in when we have to get work out in a rush. But we have to be able to depend on the men we keep in your spot. If you think this won't happen again, we're mighty glad to have you back.

TONY: Well, I need my job, and I'll do the best I can.

Another executive took a different tack with Tony:

SUPT.: Hello, Tony, we've been missing you. Sit down and let's talk about it.

TONY: (*Taking chair beside desk*) Thanks.

SUPT.: You been under the weather, Tony?

TONY: I'm all right, I guess.

SUPT.: Gee, Tony, the way you say that, you don't sound very sure.

TONY: (*Half to himself*) Well, I've got to feel all right.

SUPT.: Hmm?

TONY: (*Pause*) I just gotta keep going somehow.

SUPT.: It takes some real push, sometimes.

TONY: Lost three days' pay already. Not sure I can stay awake today.

SUPT.: Been losing sleep?

TONY: Can't sleep even when I get to bed. (*Pause*) Took Mary to the hospital Sunday— no, that would be Monday—about 2 a.m. She darned near died that morning. Went home to see about Patsy that evening. She was bawling to see her mother, but I left her with the neighbors anyway. Spent most of the night at the hospital. Tuesday, Mary at least knew who I was. Tuesday night I took Patsy home—the neighbors got kids of their own—and she cried and fussed most of the night. Last night I tried to give her supper. It was awful. Mary's getting better, they say, but she still looks like a ghost. Well, I figured I had to get back to work this morning.

SUPT.: No wonder you look bushed. Think you can keep going?

TONY: Guess I can get through to the weekend. The neighbors will keep Patsy in the day and a high school girl is coming to sit with her in the evening so I can go see Mary. But we can't keep this up forever, and I don't know how to pay the doctor's bills and blood transfusions and all that. (Pause) Guess I'd better take Patsy down to Mary's sister's. Could do that Sunday without losing any more pay.

SUPT.: Tony, you don't have to settle everything right away. You say your wife is getting better, and that's most important. If you can get Patsy taken care of for a couple of weeks, maybe the public-nursing service can help your wife get back on her feet. The personnel department could tell you about that.

TONY: Sure, we might make out that way for a while.

SUPT.: I'll phone Joe [Tony's lead-man] to find a few minutes you can talk with the personnel people today. And if you do have to take time off, be sure to phone us, Tony. You know how important it is to make up a full crew.

TONY: (*Leaving*) Yeah, thanks. I'll call in if I have to be out any more, but I don't think it will be necessary.

In the first conversation the superintendent was not unfriendly, but he was so preoccupied with the problems of staffing his department that he failed to get information from Tony that was needed in dealing with the situation constructively. In the second interview, the superintendent said very little until Tony had talked about *his* problems. Then the superintendent was in a much better position to take action that would avoid future absences.

Guides for Listening

From studies in clinical psychology and psychiatry, and from over twenty-five years of experience with nondirected interviewing in industry, have come a series of guides for empathetic listening. For a manager the most useful of these guides are:

1) Listen patiently to what the other person has to say, even though you may believe it is wrong or irrelevant. Indicate simple acceptance (not necessarily agreement) by nodding, lighting your pipe, or perhaps interjecting an occasional "Um-hm," or "I see."

2) Try to understand the feeling the person is expressing, as well as the intellectual content. Most of us have difficulty talking clearly about our feelings, so careful attention is required.

3) Restate the person's feeling, briefly but accurately. At this stage, you simply serve as a mirror and encourage the other person to continue talking. Occasionally, make summary responses such as, "You think you're in a dead-end job," or, "You feel the manager is playing favorites"; but in doing so, keep your tone neutral and try not to lead the person to your pet conclusions.

4) Allow time for the discussion to continue without interruption, and try to separate the conversation from more official communication of company plans. That is, do not make the conversation any more "authoritative" than it already is by virtue of your position in the organization.

5) Avoid direct questions and arguments about facts; refrain from saying, "That just is not so," "Hold on a minute, let's look at the facts," or "Prove it." You may want to review evidence later, but a review is irrelevant to how the person feels now.

6) When the other person touches on a point you want to know more about, simply repeat his statement as a question. For instance, if he remarks, "Nobody can break even on his expense account," you can probe by replying, "You say no one breaks even on expenses?" With this encouragement he will probably develop his previous statement.

7) Listen for what is *not* said—evasions of pertinent points or perhaps too-ready agreement with clichés. Such an omission may be a clue to a bothersome fact the person wishes were not true.

8) If the other person appears genuinely to want your viewpoint, be honest in your reply. But in the listening stage, try to limit the expression of your views, for these may condition or repress what he says.

9) Do not get emotionally involved yourself. Try simply to understand first, and defer evaluation until later.

A great deal of practice and self-awareness are needed before most managers can follow these guides for listening. Much of the time, a manager must assume a positive, self-confident role, making decisions and giving orders. Clearly, empathetic listening calls for a sharp change in pace. But unless he can develop the self-discipline and humility to listen respectfully, a manager is likely to lose touch with the reality of others.

When to Use Empathetic Listening

The process of listening we have just described will be effective only under several necessary conditions. One requirement is *time*. The kind of conversation we have considered takes more than a minute or two. An executive must be willing and able to give his subordinate uninterrupted private attention for fifteen minutes, half an hour, or perhaps longer—just for listening. With other demands on his time, an executive must value highly the benefits of listening before he will take such a block of time out of his busy day. Moreover, he must be willing to listen when a subordinate wants to talk.

Another requirement is recognizing the unique qualities of each subordinate. We cannot understand the feelings and problems of another person unless we *respect his individuality.* R. L. Katz has pointed out that each person has his own values, which

stem from his previous experiences (his expectations of how other people behave), his sentiments (the loyalties, prejudices, likes and dislikes which he has built up over a long period of time), his attitudes about himself (what kind of a person he is—or would like to be), the obligations he feels towards others (what he thinks others expect of him), his ideals (the ways he thinks people should behave and how things ought to be done), his objectives and goals (what he is trying to achieve in a given situation), and perhaps many other things.

For empathetic listening to be successful, we do not have to know everything about an individual, but we must be prepared to respect individual differences in personalities.

The *personal discipline* of the executive is a third requirement. All of us are inclined to respond emotionally to what others say. We normally approve, challenge, get angry, or react in other ways. Yet for empathetic listening, we must remain objective, and objectivity calls for practiced self-discipline.

Finally, a passive, nondirected approach by a manager presumes that his *subordinate has feelings or problems he wants to talk about.* Perhaps the subordinate is disturbed by something that has happened, or he may have a strong response to a proposal his boss or some other executive has made. But if the person is content with—or indifferent to—his work, then "Um-hm" tactics by his boss will result in a fruitless conversation indeed.

Empathetic listening is a valuable process, but it should be used only when a manager can devote the necessary time, remain objective, and respect the individuality of the person he is talking to, and when that person apparently has repressed feelings that the manager wants to understand.

MEANINGFUL REQUESTS

Listening provides a flow of information that we as managers need to predict responses to activating requests and to select energizing forces to shift such responses. When combined with other data about reasons for making the request and the urgency of action, listening gives us a workable understanding. But we must send out information as well as receive it. We must have two-way communication.

Sooner or later we will decide to issue an activating request. Such requests for action—perhaps called instructions or orders—must convey our full meaning. As with receiving information, all too often the meaning we intend to transmit is not fully grasped. Fortunately, guides that improve the chances of being understood do exist.

Vital Attributes
of All Requests

An activating request should always be 1) complete, 2) clear, and 3) doable. Yet in a surprising number of instances, why do managers fail to fulfill these simple requirements?

Often a manager states in general what a subordinate should do, but he omits specific information about desired *quantity, quality,* or *time limit* for completion.[2] The sales manager of an air-conditioning equipment company told his branch managers, "We have decided to push the sale of repair parts. They represent a good source of profits, and we expect the full cooperation of every branch manager in this new campaign." Two branch managers appointed a special representative to concentrate on repair parts, and planned visits to all distributors and large dealers in their areas. Other branch managers simply relayed the message to their sales representatives: "Push sales of spare parts."

---

[2] The concept of a complete order is compatible with "management by results." A complete order often stipulates fully the desired results but leaves the *how* to the receiver.

Within a month, the failure of the sales manager to specify how much effort he expected, and how rapidly action should be taken, resulted in wide variation in practice among the different branches.

The matter of completeness can be critical even for minor requests. A research director in a small electronics firm said to one of his section chiefs, "Here is our proposed budget. I'd like your comments on it." He intended that the subordinate merely look over the expenses for his own section and return the budget the same day. The section chief, however, assumed he had been asked to appraise the plans and projected expenses for the entire research department. Unfortunately he had devoted three full days of work to the project before the misunderstanding was discovered.

A manager should also consider the feasibility of an instruction before issuing it. This problem occurred in a company that makes flour-milling machinery. The firm had received complaints from several important customers, and the cause was finally traced back to parts that had not been machined according to specifications. The general manager wrote a note to the plant superintendent stressing the seriousness of the problem and concluding that "parts *must* be kept within standard tolerances." He asked that a copy of his letter be sent to the foreman concerned and to the workers in his shop. The workers were highly indignant because the machinery they operated was so old it would not produce the quality desired. The foreman also felt that the order was unreasonable and feared that already-poor morale would worsen if some of the work were sent to an outside shop. The net effect of the general manager's request, then, was bad morale and little improvement in quality. Here, because of his not knowing about machine tolerances, he activated a request that he mistakenly felt would produce an acceptable response. Had he thought through his request, he undoubtedly would not have made it.

Options for Communicating Requests

In stressing that all activating requests should be clear, complete, and doable, we do not mean that each one will be communicated in the same way. Routine requests should be made quite differently from instructions involving a change. And when change is desired, the manner of communicating will depend on our choice of coercion, compromise, or congruence as an energizing force.

Two features of an established organization greatly simplify the issuing of *routine* requests. First, standing operating procedures and methods may already have established a whole framework for action. In most companies, we could simply tell the personnel office to "transfer Ralph Alexander to a sales trainee spot in the El Paso office at $800 per month," and the instruction would be sufficiently complete. Existing procedures in payroll, accounting, and personnel would spell out the specific actions to be taken.

Second, customs and habits help round out the meaning of many requests. After two persons have worked together on similar problems several times, they develop customary ways of cooperating. A manager with a good secretary need only say, "I'd like to go to Atlanta Tuesday afternoon," and his secretary will be able to arrange a plane flight in accordance with his usual wishes. Or when a credit manager asks his assistant to make a collection call on the Triple-A Corporation, the latter will understand what to do and how much pressure to exert on the customer. A subordinate's knowledge of what his boss wants may come partly from conscious training; but a large part of his behavior will be the result of previous informal guidance and "decision-elaboration" by his superior.

But when a change from past practice is desired or a novel situation arises, terse instructions are not enough. Here a new understanding is required. One alternative is for the manager to give elaborate and detailed instruction, perhaps accompanied by training and explanations of why each move is desired. Or, we may invite subordinates to participate in laying out the action. When several people participate, the doability is checked from several angles, the reasons for each step become known, and commitment is encouraged.

One danger in using participation, or even thorough explanation, is that an extended discussion may not leave a subordinate with a sharp, crisp idea of what is expected of him. So many aspects of a problem have probably been examined, and the pros and cons of so many possible solutions considered, that he and his boss may not conclude with a clear meeting of the minds. If several people are involved in a discussion, the possibility is even greater that at least one person will come away from the meeting with far different understandings and impressions. To avoid this pitfall, someone—normally the senior person—should summarize everyone's agreement on what action is to be taken. This summary, then, is the order.

Consistent Follow-up

A valuable check on the appropriateness and adequacy of instructions is consistent follow-up: Once an order is issued, a manager should either see that it is carried out or he should rescind it.

This simple practice has a salutary effect on both the manager who issues instructions and the person who receives them. Perhaps the more obvious effect is on the subordinate. He knows for sure that an unpleasant task cannot be postponed in the hope that the boss will forget it: Reports due on Monday cannot be slipped in on Thursday; parts that almost fit are not acceptable. When a supervisor consistently means what he says, a subordinate soon learns to discipline himself—and he tries to be sure he understands his instructions.

For the manager, consistent follow-up: 1) brings to light any tendency he may have to make unclear requests; 2) provides opportunities for supporting subordinates' efforts—and thereby build cooperation, as noted in the last chapter; 3) gives feedback on results, which helps get the immediate task done and also builds a basis for predicting future responses.

*Using Rewards and Punishments
to Interpret Requests*

597
CHAPTER 27
Gaining
Understanding

If "actions speak louder than words," rewards and punishments shout. The basis for a bonus, commendation, rebuke, or penalty is carefully noted by the receiver and his peers. And this message is interpreted as "what the boss really wants."

Positive rewards have the great advantage of providing encouragement. But there are times when indifference or willful disregard of requests calls for a reprimand, demotion, temporary layoff, or other exercise of managerial discipline. As noted in Part Five and elsewhere, the primary aim of such reward and punishment is to guide *future* behavior toward desired goals.

For this cogent form of communication to contribute to understanding, a manager must use it consistently. The message about the kind of behavior desired, and that undesired, must be clear. If each time a pilot flies low over his hometown he is grounded, the meaning will be understood by other pilots. And when exceptions are made for special circumstances, they should be labeled as exceptions. Of course, for rewards and punishments to underscore a message, the reasons for the managerial action must be known to those to whom we wish to communicate.

CONCLUSION: COMMUNICATION MATCHED TO ACTIVATING MODE

Gaining a mutual understanding among the people directly involved in activating any plan is essential. Such understanding of the goals and likely behavior of each other 1) enables managers to predict responses and select activating modes, and 2) enables subordinates to carry out plans with as much insight and fervor as they feel is warranted.

Several concepts that we reviewed early in this chapter are helpful in virtually every setting. Recognizing common obstacles to good communication —differences in viewpoints, organizational distance, perfunctory attention, repressed feelings, and inferred meaning—helps us spot sources of misunderstandings. And if we can develop empathy, self-awareness, and objectivity, we will have a viewpoint that is very useful for constructive analysis. These strengths are valuable in all sorts of situations, ranging from coercion to commitment.

In contrast, the ways of communicating described in the second half should be used selectively. Their effectiveness will depend on the setting and on our activating mode and energizing force (outlined in Chapters 25 and 26). For instance, empathetic listening is well suited to cultivating cooperation and to establishing congruence; but it relies on a frankness that is unlikely to occur when we are using coercion (to change an expected response from opposition to ambivalent compliance) or when we are bargaining in an ambivalent-compliance setting.

Similarly, abbreviated requests are fine when an established behavior pattern exists in an aura of compliance or commitment. But if coercion is being used, detailed instruction is usually essential. Participation in elaborating requests is excellent when we are dealing with committed persons or helping to build congruence. Participation may also be helpful when we are introducing a significant change in a setting of indifferent or ambivalent compliance—although here the manager must usually provide more guidance and initiative. In other settings, participation is likely to add more confusion than light.

To cite still another tie between the manner of communication and the activating modes, consistent follow-up—while always a good practice—serves a more vital purpose when relying on compliance than when commitment is present.

These examples of the need to adjust one's communicating methods to the activating process point to a central thesis of Part Six: We must recognize the differences among activating modes if we are to select interpersonal-relations techniques wisely.

FOR CLASS DISCUSSION

1) Is the need for good two-way personal communication likely to be very low when a manager has decided not to seek commitment to an activating request?

2) An expert on communication has suggested that the term "co-perception" would be a better word to describe what is needed to bring about true communication. What do you feel he means by this? Relate your answer to material in Part Two on human needs.

3) "Management's most important job is communication. If a superior can clearly communicate what is expected and explain the facts that make the expectations valid, no reasonable person will fail to accept the expectations and seek to achieve them." Do you agree? What key assumptions are implicit, if not explicit, in this statement? Discuss the validity of each.

4) To what extent should a line manager consider turning to an "expert" to help him forecast the likely responses to an important activating request? Who should be considered as "experts" in such situations?

5) "I have just one question for those who advocate empathy and understanding of subordinates' problems. Whom do I go to for treatment when I get through? Am I supposed to sit and listen to a lot of silly mistakes, alibis, and complaints, and just say, 'Uh-huh—you're late because you resent your mother's domination'? It seems a lot better for their performance and my psychological well-being that, when there is something wrong and I know what to do about it, I come right out and speak my piece." Comment on this statement.

6) "The best way to ensure good communications is to put what you want to ask or say in writing. Oral communications are quick and easy, but invariably they are imprecise." Comment on this statement by the managing partner of a large law firm. When are written communications best?

7) How may the concept of using the law of the situation, described in Chapter 21, aid in improving two-way communication? What pitfalls should one be aware of when using the law of the situation as an aid to communication?

8) In general, participation in planning not only achieves positive responses to activating requests but also contributes, even more, to good two-way personal communication. How may highly participative planning systems occasionally *interfere* with good two-way communication?

Cases

For cases involving issues covered in this chapter, see especially the following. Particularly relevant questions are listed after each case.

Milano Enterprises (p. 124), 16
Petersen Electronics (p. 211), 9, 16
Merchantville School System (p. 217), 18
Atlas Chemical Company (p. 321), 17
Monroe Wire and Cable (p. 436), 20
Southeast Textiles (p. 620), 14
Household Products Company (p. 627), 18, 19

FOR FURTHER READING

Davis, K., ed., *Organizational Behavior: A Book of Readings,* 4th ed. New York: McGraw-Hill Book Company, 1974, Chapter 12.

Recent studies of communications barriers, especially at the first level of supervision.

Dubin, R., *Human Relations in Administration,* 4th ed. Englewood Cliffs, N.J.: Prentice-Hall, Inc., 1974, Chapter 15.

Explores personal communication in an organizational setting.

Hall, J., "Communications Revisited." *California Management Review,* Spring 1973.

Penetrating discussion of person-to-person communication. Argues that each of us can learn to adjust our interpersonal style.

Harriman, B., "Up and Down the Communications Ladder." *Harvard Business Review,* September 1974.

Describes the need for a formal communications system in a large company, and the problems one firm encountered in installing such a system.

Richards, M. D. and W. A. Nielander, eds., *Readings in Management,* 4th ed. Cincinnati: South-Western Publishing Co., 1974, Chapter 4.

Two useful articles on improving personal-communication skills.

28 Activating in a Dynamic Setting

FITTING THE PIECES TOGETHER

The here-and-now character of activating demands sensitivity to the total, local situation. As managers we come, perhaps abruptly, to a time when all our preceding planning must be translated into action. We have to put the pieces—which have been conveniently separated for analysis—back together.

This need for taking prompt action adroitly, especially in a changing setting, can be highlighted by examining a specific case. Such a case analysis—of an urgent action in the Simmons Simulator Corporation—is the core of this chapter. Although the case does not deal with all aspects of activating, it does give the reader an opportunity:

1) to integrate key elements of activating
2) to fit activating to a dynamic setting
3) to note close ties of activating to organizing, planning, and controlling

The vehicle for carrying out this integrating task is a case in which one of the authors was directly involved. Although the names have been changed to protect the "guilty," the basic facts have not been altered. To sharpen your own skills, read the case carefully before going further into this chapter. See if you can forecast what will happen next. Then jot down what you would do if you could replace George Nichols as director. Before the chapter ends, you will have an opportunity to compare your analysis and recommended action with those of the authors and the actual managers.

The Simmons Simulator Corporation was founded in 1942 by Lionel Simmons, an aeronautical engineer, to provide simulator panels for training naval pilots. Since its inception as a single-product war baby, Simmons has grown into a multimillion dollar company with sales and rentals on more than 17 basic simulation systems. These systems range from small, relatively inexpensive devices used for testing depth perception and reflexes, to elaborate systems used in the aircraft, missile, and space industries. The large systems are usually rented at fees that run in excess of several thousand dollars a month.

Since its inception, the Simmons company sought not only to build high-quality equipment but also to ensure its productive use by developing an outstanding service organization. As the company expanded into more and larger systems, Simmons saw even greater importance in guaranteeing major customers immediate service and maintenance. Building a service organization with an intimate knowledge of Simmons's equipment has proven a costly but invaluable step in the company's continuing growth and profit. Several of Simmons's customers commented that, though there are other companies that offers comparable equipment at lower cost, they have stuck with Simmons because of assurance of quick and competent maintenance.

To provide this service, Simmons has developed a highly trained, well-paid group of about 70 service engineers, who operate out of eight district offices. Since the major customers are closely clustered around six of these offices, Simmons normally is able to put a service engineer in a customer's facility in less than an hour after receiving notice of difficulty. Because of the extreme complexity of the systems, however, it may take many hours to determine the cause of the failure. Frequently the diagnostic time equals or exceeds the time for repairs or replacements. Such situations occur most often in the large, complex rented systems. Thus, every hour spent on diagnosis costs Simmons dollars of profit and delays important tasks in the customer's facility.

In an effort to increase the speed and accuracy of diagnostic work, George Nichols, director of service engineering, has worked with a large computer company on a "diagnostic-assistance" program.

The reason for, and mechanics of, this program are given in the following memorandum from Nichols to the eight district managers reporting to him.

Figure 28–1 Reasons for malfunction of electronic gear are rarely obvious.

TO: District SE Managers
FROM: G. W. Nichols
SUBJECT: Diagnostic-Assistance Program
DATE: October 1st

Because of the increasing difficulty in the maintenance and repair of our large rental systems, we have virtually completed plans for installing a diagnostic-assistance program. Please arrange your schedule to make it possible to be in my Houston office on October 20 for a two-day briefing. More detailed plans will be forwarded to you before the 20th, but it may be helpful to give you an overview of the program as it is now envisioned.

With the introduction of the Series G simulator last year, our records indicate a 15-percent increase in average time required to isolate causes of systems failure. Moreover, with the Series FA-2 simulator now being used in the Neptune project in three locations, we have been experiencing increased problems of locating the causes of systems failures. Fortunately, with both systems, we still have had a very low failure rate; but we cannot expect to hold our market without improving the speed and accuracy of diagnostic work. As you know, Sim-Test has been our strongest competitor in both of these markets, and is bragging about its "larger and better-trained" field staff.

I recognize the pressures our service engineers are under and do not want to appear critical of their work on these series. Rather, the diagnostic-assistance program is designed to make their job a lot easier. We have virtually completed a program for our home office computer that will permit extremely rapid and accurate diagnostic assistance. We plan to connect your offices directly to the computer on January 1 of next year for data-processing purposes and will use the same input-output devices to handle diagnostic problems.

In a nutshell, the system will allow your field people, when they encounter a systems failure that is not readily diagnosable, to call your office and provide symptom data that you will send to the control computer in Houston. Based on tests of this system in several computer companies who use it to repair their own equipment, you should get a request for additional data or a diagnostic estimate within 15 seconds.

There are many bugs in the system that we will have to work out, and I will look forward to getting the benefit of your ideas on October 20.

One final point: Until we have completed our review of the project, I would prefer that you do not discuss it with your people. After the recent incident in San Diego, we do not wish further trouble due to misunderstandings—G.W.N.

The San Diego incident referred to by Nichols caused quite a stir in the company. Although hourly workers in Simmons's plants are unionized, the service engineers are not. Three months ago, however, 14 of the 16 service engineers from the San Diego branch office requested the right to hold a representation election to determine whether the service engineers wished to join an international electronics-workers union. The company's director of labor relations, Alex Michak, advised the engineers of their rights under labor relations law, and after several days' discussion, the engineers dropped the matter. Michak reported that the matter had really stemmed from a "misunderstanding of company policy on tuition refunds for technical courses." Michak explained,

> Tom Snow, who has been with the company for 17 years, is one of the top service engineers in the San Diego branch. For more than six months he has been trying to get permission to take a new course in elctronics under the company's tuition-refund program. His district manager, Bart Dunn, had sat on the request because he didn't want Tom tied up in a course when he might be needed for emergency overtime due to problems with the simulator. Besides, Bart told me that the only reason Tom wanted to take the course was to qualify for work on the new Series G simulator.
>
> Bart told me that he didn't really need Tom for Series G work since he had two new men who had the academic background to specialize on Series G maintenance.

When Snow learned that Dunn had not acted on his request, he and several of the older service engineers in the district became quite upset about the way they "get pushed around" and they sought the union election. Snow said,

> I've been with this company a long time, and I like the work because it's always a real challenge. You are your own boss most of the time, with only your skill and experience to tell you what to do. You really have to know the equipment inside-out to maintain and repair it. If something goes wrong, it's a real test to see whether you can figure it out and fix it. We know that the faster we do our work, the more our customers like us and the more revenue for our company; but for most of us the real reward is knowing we figured it out. Well, by now I know the Series FA-2 simulator inside-out, and though there's an occasional tough one to fix on the Neptune project, I can handle that equipment blindfolded. The challenge has gone and I want to get over to the new Series G equipment and see whether I can handle it. In the old days the company would have encouraged us to get into the new work. Now they want us to do what we know best, and they bring in outsiders for the exciting new things.

George Nichols calmed down Snow and the others by assuring them that there was no company policy against high-seniority employees taking courses under the tuition-refund program. He pointed out, however, that the company found it much harder to shift engineers like Snow to the new systems, because they were so good in their present specialties. "Besides," he pointed out, "the pay's the same regardless of what system you work on."

Tom Snow is presently enrolled in the technical course, which meets after working hours, and two other senior service engineers in San Diego have applied for the same course in the next term.

Nichols was quite relieved when things settled down because, as he put it, "Experienced people like Snow are scarce as hen's teeth. Sometimes they act more like primadonnas than repair people, but right now they're in the driver's seat."

Place yourself in George Nichols's position, and answer the following questions—which highlight the approach to activating set forth in the preceding chapters.

1) What is the nature of the present activating issue?
2) What will be the response to a request to use the new diagnostic technique?
3) Is this predicted response acceptable?
4) What energizing force should be used to shift the response?

Our analysis will first follow this framework. Then we will look briefly at the actual results and at a contrasting action taken by another company that faced a similar situation.

THE NATURE OF THE PRESENT ACTIVATING ISSUE

What Triggered This Activating Effort?

Clearly, Nichols's decision to move to a computer-based diagnostic system arises from his belief that it will greatly benefit the company. He feels that such a system will give Simmons Simulator at least a headstart on its competitors. The new system, when it is operational, will dramatically increase the speed and accuracy of diagnosis on the complex systems. Further, it will significantly reduce Nichols's dependence on people who "act more like primadonnas than repair people but [who are] right now . . . in the driver's seat." When Nichols points out that, "Experienced people like Snow are scarce as hen's teeth," he clearly feels that, in the future, the company will also be less vulnerable if he can reduce his dependence on people like Snow.

To Nichols, there is nothing sinister about his objectives. Technological progress and competitive pressure make it necessary to reduce dependency on humans to diagnose failures in complex customer installations. Yet the narrowness of Nichols's perspective eliminates a contingency approach to activating.

What Is the Basis for Existing Commitment?

The clash between Nichols's view and that of engineers like Snow must be understood if we are to select an activating mode wisely. A good way to get at the crux of this situation—and others like it—is to combine means–end diagnosis (described in Chapter 11) with a personal-needs analysis (introduced in Chapter 7). First, Nichols's reasoning, using his perception of company values, is summarized in Figure 28–2. Then we can prepare a similar means–end diagram representing the way service engineers' needs are being met. By comparing these two diagrams, we can 1) spot potential sources of conflict between management and the engineers if the nature of the job is changed, and 2) examine alternative activating approaches to deal with these potential conflicts.

In Figure 28–2 we see that George Nichols's contributions to company goals depend on how well he directs the field-maintenance department. Although good field maintenance is an important means of achieving higher-level company ends (strategies), to Nichols it becomes almost an end in itself. He is responsible for developing the best means ("hows") of producing effective field maintenance. His success with existing technology depends on 1) having the right service people in the right locations with the right equipment (logistics), and, to achieve this, on 2) having people with high skills in repairing systems, and 3) having people who can diagnose systems failures accurately and rapidly. These corollary means, while all important, are not equally difficult to carry out. Apparently, the diagnostic element is the toughest to achieve, but in this activity Simmons Simulator is better than its competition. Up to now the company has pursued "option 1"—"outstanding people"—as a means of meeting diagnostic needs. Clearly, if "option 2"—"diagnosis by computers"—can be introduced effectively, it is a very appealing alternative to option 1. Although the diagnostic computer system will never completely eliminate the need for people with outstanding diagnostic skills, it promises to reduce greatly at least the *number* of outstanding diagnosticians needed and perhaps reduce the level of human skill required.

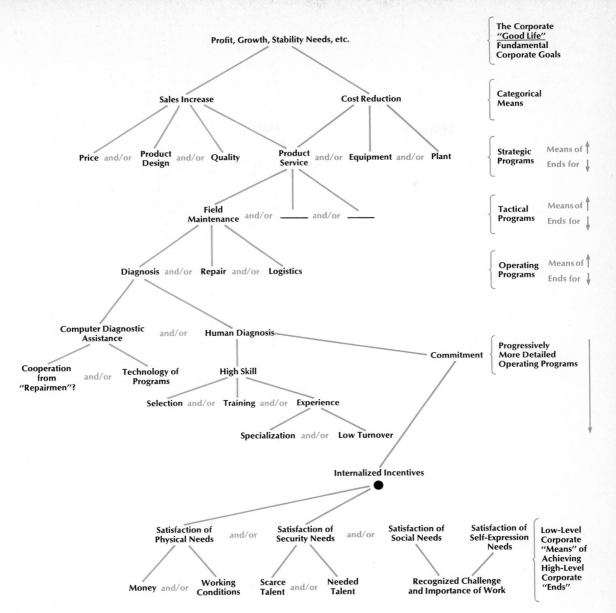

Figure 28–2   Nichols's means–end view of service engineers' work.

In the present operation, to obtain, retain, and motivate good people—as diagnosticians—Nichols has had to be effective in selecting, training, and offering incentives. To a significant extent, many of the 'incentives' are direct outgrowths of the work to be done. Although the company pays these people well and undoubtedly offers good fringe benefits, virtually all remaining incentives come from the work itself. Fortunately, the kind of work that the company wants done also satisfies higher-order needs of the service engineers.

Turning to the viewpoint of the service engineers, Figure 28–3 depicts the means–end relationships in the value structure for people like Tom Snow. The diagram helps us see why congruence and resulting commitment have developed in the existing situation, and also why the proposed method of diagnosis jeopardizes such commitment.

A person like Tom Snow has as his highest-level goals some concept of "The Good Life." Though difficult to define precisely, it serves to guide the means by which he lives. It corresponds to ultimate company objectives such as profit and growth (also difficult to define precisely). Snow, and service engineers like him, pursue this end largely through their jobs. For Snow, his job helps him not only to fulfill physical and security needs, but also to satisfy his social and, especially, his self-expression needs.

For the service engineers like Snow, their job offers 1) high security, 2) status, and 3) opportunity for self-expression. All three points are tied directly to the diagnostic aspects of the job.

Note particularly that the working conditions and results that are attractive to the engineers are almost identical with the means that company management has been using to obtain its goals. Nichols has been depending upon people who combine skill with an ability to work with little supervision and high motivation. The result is *congruence* and *committed* responses to most management requests.

Figure 28–3 Snow's means–end view of his work.

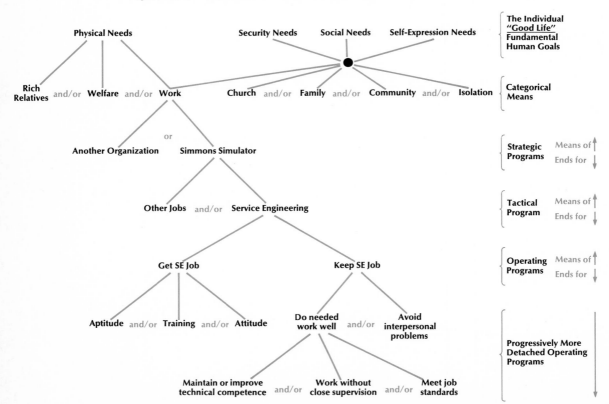

Signs of Trouble

Before the appearance of the diagnostic computer system, the situation in Nichols's department appeared quite good. How much this resulted from conscious management–worker thinking and choice and how much from happy coincidence we do not know. The first cloud on the horizon appeared when Dunn "sat on" Snow's request for a tuition-refund program to prepare him to change to a Series G assignment. Snow saw this change as a new means of making his work retain its ability to meet many of his higher-order needs. To increase his security, status, and sense of growth, he wants to get over to Series G challenges.

Nichols and Dunn apparently feel that Snow's objective is not the best way to achieve their short-term maintenance objectives. When Snow is at school, he won't be available for evening emergencies. When he finishes school, he will want to transfer to Series G assignments. Nichols and Dunn would rather have his specialized skill on FA-2's—even if Snow doesn't find this as challenging. Thus, the goal congruence is being strained.

The new computer-based method of diagnosing machine failures will undercut congruence even more. From the tone of his memo to the district managers, Nichols is clearly anticipating something less than a strong positive response from the service engineers. There are signs, in the case, that two-way personal communication may not be good. Therefore, we may question the accuracy of Nichols's forecasts and subsequent decisions. Nonetheless, Snow's efforts to organize his colleagues and his success (14 of 16 supported the first step to unionizing) have no doubt upset Nichols and increased his desire to reduce his dependence on specialists. Nichols also interprets this as evidence to support his forecast of a negative response from the service engineers. Their threat to unionize is clearly an effort to increase their power to resist coercion by the management and to at least "negotiate" better compromises. Because of the high degree of congruence that has existed in the past, this union threat is a clear sign of potential serious conflict between engineer and management goals.

Response to the
New Diagnostic Program

Very soon Nichols and the district managers will have to request the service engineers to use the new computer-based diagnostic technique. How do you predict the engineers will respond?

The new technique will be a tool that replaces the use of brainpower.

Although the company goals will be met more efficiently and probably create more sales and jobs, the service engineer's job will lose much of its richness. The skills of the engineers will be less vital. This is good for Nichols, but it reduces Snow's safety (security). Recall Nichols' comment, " . . . they act more like primadonnas than repair people, but right now they're in the driver's seat." So, too, will the new system reduce status and self-expression need satisfaction for the engineers.

Consequently, as one executive said in a discussion of this case, the new system will be "as popular as a skunk at a picnic." Nichols also foresees such a reception. Present congruence will be upset and service engineers all over the country will probably resist. At best, compliance will replace commitment; at worst, opposition in some form may arise.

IS THE PREDICTED RESPONSE ACCEPTABLE?

The answer to this question is not so clear. Although in the past commitment has been very helpful, will it be *necessary* when the new system is in operation? In Chapter 25 we pointed out that commitment is not always the most desirable response to an activating request. If a manager considers the costs and benefits of commitment, he may conclude that it is preferable to seek simple compliance.

Commitment by the service engineers was desirable in the past because of the need to retain scarce technical talents and have engineers apply those talents in a highly motivated way, under little direct supervision. Refer back to the four criteria discussed in Chapter 25 for determining whether to seek compliance or commitment—extra results from committed effort, need for creativity, ease of supervision and control, and cost of obtaining commitment. You will probably agree that, without the computer, all four argue for commitment. However, if the computer system can replace much of the rare diagnostic skill, Nichols not only needs the first two elements less but, given the new nature of the work, it will be difficult to retain them. Stated another way, if the diagnostic task can be completed in a quicker way by computer, Nichols neither needs nor can he expect many committed service engineers.

Nichols probably recognizes that some of the "primadonnas" like Snow will leave (or cause trouble and be fired). This prospect is not too disturbing to Nichols, because the kind of service engineers needed under the new technology will be much easier to find. Less-skilled repairmen would welcome the good pay and "easy" work. A few highly skilled people will continue to be necessary to help write future computer programs and to "troubleshoot" unusual maintenance needs. But with seventy service engineers to choose from, these few should be available. Nichols can afford to lose a lot of Tom Snows.

The tough problem lies in the transition—tough for those who must find other outlets for their skills or settle for less rewarding work; and tough for

Nichols. If Nichols were to use our terminology, he would probably conclude the following:

1) After the transition, compliance is more likely, and perhaps more desirable, than commitment—from most of the engineers.

2) But during the transition, the "primadonnas" who are still on the payroll may slow down or even sabotage the new system.

3) Also, they may try to build a union power base to substitute for the power their valuable skills have given them up to now.

4) So, I must either change what I predict will be their response by somehow gaining their support of the system during its introduction. . .

5) Or, I must "debug" the system in secrecy and introduce it in such an advanced form that any insubordinate engineers will have lost most of their bargaining strength; then we can overcome any remaining negative behavior by management strength.

Based on this analysis, the focus shifts to changing the anticipated response during the transition period.

AN ENERGIZING FORCE TO SHIFT THE RESPONSE

Nichols's Proposal

The memorandum Nichols sent to district managers on October 1 clearly indicates that he hopes to keep the new diagnostic system secret as long as possible, and then to rely on coercion to keep the response within the compliance range. He is not indifferent to the plight of his skilled service engineers, and might introduce some limited self-composed compromise later. But he believes the new system must be introduced promptly, to maintain the competitive position of Simmons Simulator, and that the service engineers can no longer be trusted to act in the best interests of their company.

This has two serious dangers. In the short run, *if* the service engineers learn that management is trying to "sneak" the new system around them, the negative reaction will be much stronger and the urgency of taking countermeasures will be enhanced. Also a long-run risk is involved. Even if all goes as Nichols plans and the service engineers find themselves in a weak position, their treatment will become known throughout the company; so future attempts to gain even compliance with unpopular changes will be met with more cynical and better-organized resistance from employees who distrust the management.

Michak's Proposal

Alex Michak, director of labor relations, has his special viewpoint. He is much less concerned about maintenance service than anticompany union behavior. Word of Nichols's memo reached Michak before it reached some of the district managers. He quickly got Nichols's boss to rescind the memo in the hope that the union grapevine was not as good as his own.

Michak felt it would be impossible to keep the new system a secret long enough to test and improve it with only management personnel doing the work. Once the service engineers learned of the system, he was certain they would be strongly opposed. They would believe that Nichols had attempted to "hide" it from them until it was too late. Such a belief was almost certain, in Michak's opinion, to lead to a union or at least to strong resistance to the improved technology.

Predicting this response and wanting compliance, he sought to convince Nichols to 1) tell the service engineers about the system promptly, 2) ask for their help, and 3) use compromise to gain ambivalent or indifferent compliance.

"Tell them," Michak argued, "why the company has to do this to stay in business and assure them that greater efficiency will create more sales, more service engineer jobs, and better money."

There is room for much debate on what might happen under the alternative approaches outlined. Our guess is that Michak was right and that the service engineers would have been less easily coerced and more likely to extract a tougher compromise *if* they found out soon enough. Further, Nichols's approach would certainly impede two-way personal communication and thus hurt chances for knowing how best to achieve compliance now and in the future. Though direct coercion might work, the future costs and risks seem too high.

ACTUAL RESULTS

The reason that we can only speculate on what *might* have happened is that once Nichols, under pressure from his superior, followed Michak's advice, we can only know what *did* happen.

Most of the senior service engineers disliked the new system, and they used far more of their creative talent to discredit it than to improve it. Nonetheless, they did eventually cooperate, but only after extracting salary increases and assurance of "tenure." They also demanded that they do all field testing of the new system. Within a year the computer system was fully implemented and produced great savings. Many of these savings were short-lived, since a few months later Sim-Test introduced similar programs.

Nichols remains convinced that "his way" would have been better. "If they had let me do it my way," he says,

I would have had the system ready for the field in three months—not 11. Then I would have had the leverage [power] to get it implemented fast and well. I wouldn't have had to plead with them and push every move. If they realized I had the power to clobber them, but treated them fairly instead, they would have gone along. Heck, I would have given them the money and job security they wanted; but the difference would have been that *I gave it to them* rather than that they bargained for it. We have just encouraged them to flex their muscles by seeming soft.

Briefly summarizing, all the basic steps in activating are illustrated in this Simmons Simulator case.

1) Nichols *predicted* opposition to his request to use the new diagnostic technique. He recognized that the prevailing commitment of service engineers would be upset by the reduced opportunity to use their skills, initiative, and judgment.

2) The future job requirements for service engineers could not be made very challenging—at least for present engineers, who are unusually well qualified problem-solvers. Except for a few special jobs, compliance rather than commitment is the practical *response to* expect and *seek.* The immediate question for Nichols and his district managers then became how to handle the transition—how to reduce opposition and gain ambivalent compliance.

3) As an *energizing force* in this transition, Nichols favored a mixture of coercion and self-composed compromise. We do know that Michak's counsel prevailed; the transition has been made, but at a substantial cost.

Most of us would like to challenge the wisdom of at least some of the moves made by executives in Simmons Simulator. The main point, however, is that the model developed in Chapters 25, 26, and 27 provides us a powerful tool for dealing with not only the Simmons Simulator situation but also many, many other activating problems.

CONTRASTING APPROACH IN ANOTHER COMPANY

The large computer manufacturer that provides most of the "hardware" (physical equipment) used by Simmons Simulator confronted the same technological change that beset Nichols's department. But its "solution" differs sharply. A quick comparison of these two cases illustrates how activating should be suited to the particular situation.

The computer company—E.D.C.—has installed complex systems in a much wider range of customer industries than Simmons Simulator. It, too, stresses maintenance service and had many service engineers just like Tom Snow. Also, new diagnostic technology was cutting the challenge of its engineering jobs. The chief difference in the external pressures was that E.D.C.'s diversification permitted it to spread its total transition over eighteen months, although in particular industries the change occurred as swiftly as it did in Simmons Simulator.

E.D.C.'s service-engineering management forecast similar negative responses to the new diagnostic techniques, for the same basic reasons. Nevertheless, it chose a very different way of gaining acceptance. It had more options because of some fundamental differences in its methods of managing.

Decision to Seek Commitment

While accepting that the new service-engineer job could not retain its old appeal, E.D.C. managers believed the existing commitment among service engineers was too valuable an asset to lose. Such commitment would be valuable during the transition. It would continue to be needed in troubleshooting and in preparing new diagnostic procedures. And if some of the experienced engineers could be transferred to equally challenging jobs elsewhere in the company, they probably would continue to be very valuable employees.

So the managers of the service engineers sought ways to carry out the transition *and* retain commitment of engineers whose present jobs were being "downgraded." More managerial effort was necessary for this approach than for coercion and compromise. But as one of the E.D.C. managers remarked, "That's why I'm here."

Differences in Way of Managing

Compared with Simmons Simulator, E.D.C. has regularly:

1) designed its organization with serious attention to the needs of its employees (Chapter 7) and to carefully matching jobs with the right individuals (Chapter 10)

2) planned its changes in operations in terms of programs and schedules, including detailed schedules for selection and training of personnel (Chapter 19)

3) cultivated open person-to-person communication among all organization levels, especially in the boss–subordinate relationship (Chapter 27)

Because these management practices were already well established, the engineering-service managers had important resources that Nichols lacked. And when confronted with installing the new diagnostic techniques, Nichols had neither the time nor company-wide influence to reconstruct managerial habits.

Required Effort

The first step the E.D.C. managers took was to find out how *each* of their service engineers felt about future job alternatives. Their established skill in empathetic listening enabled the supervisors to learn several things that eased the transition. First, some engineers actually welcomed the new diagnostic techniques. Mostly, these were people who found the present work a bit "over their heads" and consequently felt insecure with the existing technology. Incidentally, in a bargaining situation these might be the individuals who would protest the most loudly.

A second finding was that not nearly as many engineers as had been anticipated wanted the troubleshooting and design jobs in the new set-up. Although these jobs continue to provide lots of challenge, they also involve a great deal of unanticipated travel. Third, the supervisors identified seven other job categories within the company that at least one of the service engineers—among those who preferred to transfer—felt was as good as or better than his current job.

Armed with this specific personal information, the service-engineering division undertook to transfer 200 very competent people in a period of six to 18 months. The receiving divisions naturally had some fear that they were being sent "losers" instead of "topnotch people who are no longer needed in their present jobs." However, E.D.C.'s long-standing practice of making horizontal transfers reduced this cynicism. And its standing procedures for personnel planning were vital to locating openings and planning specific moves. Experience with careful planning enabled the various managers to work out a schedule that 1) kept the service-engineering division adequately staffed during the transition and 2) provided engineers to the other divisions when they could be absorbed.

Simmons Simulator, in contrast, lacked not only the basic data about jobs, future personnel needs, and similar information necessary to plan such transfers. More importantly, it lacked ability to communicate openly, to organize with human needs as a major consideration, and to make personnel plans a year or two in advance. And without these abilities, maintaining commitment would probably have been impossible even if Nichols had tried to do so.

Failure to Adjust Control Standards

All of E.D.C.'s efforts to introduce its new diagnostic techniques in a way that would encourage committed response almost failed. The stumbling block was its control system. Department managers are measured, rewarded, and penalized largely on how well they meet tangible short-run standards. These controls made no allowance for unexpected transfers. So plant people postponed accepting transferees because they feared that their immediate productivity might suffer. Other departments resisted transfers of an engineer whose salary was higher than one of its own people who could "hold the fort." Only after weeks of discussion with top management was an agreement reached. Hereafter, control "pars" could be modified to recognize and reward those department heads who contributed to the "corporate good" at the expense of short-run, narrow standards. Without such adjustments in the controls, evasion and foot-dragging might have stymied many of the carefully planned moves.

Within 18 months, most of the service engineers who wanted to move were in new positions that appealed to them. And partly because this treatment was known, the less-skilled people who entered the revised jobs in service engineering did so with more enthusiasm. If not committed, these new people are at least high on the scale of indifferent compliance.

So when the next round of activating requests is made, the likely response at E.D.C. will be much more receptive than at Simmons Simulator. We should note, however, that E.D.C.'s management system is comparatively costly; it invests substantial time and money in its entire organizing, planning, controlling, and activating effort.

CONCLUSION

The cases we have just examined are only provocative illustrations of the activating process. To keep them in perspective, two points should be reemphasized.

Each activating situation is unique. Although there are common elements —and useful ways for dealing with these elements—tailoring managerial action to fit the particular circumstances is always necessary. The task to be done, the external pressures and constraints, the personalities of the people involved, the existing social structure with its cumulative history, the management structure and other available resources—all bear on what is wise at the moment. The activating model, or approach, we have set forth in Part Six is intentionally designed to help a manager take these unique factors into account.

The second point so important to perspective is the interdependence of activating with organizing, planning, and controlling. We saw this interdependence in the cases of Simmons Simulator and E.D.C.; in each instance the selected activating mode was highly dependent on the current management structure. For an immediate action a manager—such as Nichols—must work with the existing structure. But when we take time to view managing more broadly, we open up the system. Perhaps the organization or the planning and controlling should be changed to aid a desired activating mode.

Clearly we do not endorse the traditional lore that we should rely on a charismatic leader to get things done. Personal magnetism is a fine asset in developing cooperation and gaining acceptance of company objectives. But charisma is hopelessly inadequate to the task of managing. As important as it is to the quest for excellence, it is like wind without a sail, like precious cargo without a vessel to hold it, and like an inspiring captain with neither crew nor instruments to guide or follow his inspiration. The sail, the vessel, the instruments, and the crew are what we need to manage, and they are resources that can be obtained, organized, planned, controlled, and finally activated.

FOR CLASS DISCUSSION

1) What do you think of Nichols's reference to the incident in San Diego as a "misunderstanding?" Was this an example of how poor communications hurt activating efforts?

2) What might Nichols have done, before writing his memo, to improve his forecast on response to the diagnostic program?

3) Based on what you have read, which activating mode would *you* have sought —ambivalent compliance, indifferent compliance, or commitment?

4) Study Figures 28–1 and 28–2 and review the section in Chapter 26 on "Congruence: Gateway to Commitment." Based on what we know of the situation before the computer, what created the greatest potential for congruence between the company and the service engineers?

5) Most of the discussion of Simmons centers around the predicted vs. desired response of the service engineers. What do you predict will be the long-term impact of this change on the eight district service-engineer managers? What should Nichols do if he shares your forecast?

6) If Michak were more nearly correct in forecasting likely responses to Nichols' approach than Nichols, this would suggest he had better communications channels. Review Chapter 27 and suggest how Michak might have developed more accurate forecasts.

7) What do you feel was the weakest link in Nichols's strategy for activating the diagnostic program?

8) Turning from the Simmons case, consider the following situation. A national sales manager requested all field salespeople to file a lengthy sales report at the end of each month. Most of these reports were late or incomplete for the first six months after the request. Subsequent analysis showed that with slight modification of the company's computerized marketing-information system, all of the vital information could be obtained without this sales report. Upon learning this, the sales manager decided to abandon the field sales report but did not inform his salespeople, thus delaying the abandonment for six months longer than necessary. During that time he put great pressure on the salespeople to get complete reports in on time. What positive and negative results of this action can you foresee? Why do you think the sales manager put off the change in policy?

Cases

For cases involving issues covered in this chapter, see especially the following. Particularly relevant questions are listed after each case.

Petersen Electronics (p. 211), 17, 18
Merchantville School System (p. 217), 19
Monroe Wire and Cable (p. 436), 18
Family Service of Gotham (p. 532), 17
Southeast Textiles (p. 620), 13, 15, 16, 17, 18
Household Products Company (p. 627), 20

FOR FURTHER READING

The following readings deal with the process of making all sorts of changes in organizations, and are not confined to *activating* as the term is used in this book.

Bartlett, A. C. and T. A. Kayser, eds., *Changing Organizational Behavior.* Englewood Cliffs, N.J.: Prentice-Hall, Inc., 1973.

Useful articles by behavioral scientists on introducing changes in organizations.

Brightford, E. G., "How to Introduce Changes in Management Practices: Lessons from Europe." *Management Review,* June 1975.

Argues for a balanced mixture of planning and control, job enrichment, and management by objectives.

French, W. L. and C. H. Bell, *Organization Development: Behavioral Science Interventions for Organization Improvement.* Englewood Cliffs, N.J.: Prentice-Hall, Inc., 1972.

Clear, convenient summary of the "O.D." movement and the techniques gathered together under its wing.

Jun, J. S., ed., "Management by Objectives in the Public Sector." *Public Administration Review,* January 1976.

Difficulties in defining objectives and in obtaining commitment are recurring themes in this symposium. The article by Peter Drucker calls for the least background in public administration, and is applicable to a wide range of not-for-profit organizations.

Tichy, N. M., "Current Trends in Organizational Change." *Columbia Journal of World Business,* Spring 1974.

Focuses on change agents and the techniques they use, and reports on trends in the U.S. and Europe.

Not-for-Profit Note

for Part VI

Activating is likely to be a delicate task for not-for-profit managers. Their use of rewards and punishments is often circumscribed, but this may be offset by greater commitment of subordinates to enterprise goals. Both of these tendencies, however, must be carefully appraised in each situation.

As he starts to convert plans into action, a manager in a not-for-profit enterprise should be aware of how much power he can muster if it is needed. Of course, power to coerce, to bargain, and to induce ambivalent compliance does not disappear just because the goals of an enterprise are other than profit. College football coaches, church sextons, and co-op managers occasionally are fired; some labor unions and some symphony orchestras are run by powerful autocrats. Nevertheless, in a large majority of not-for-profit ventures, *a manager's ability to give bonuses and other rewards for good performance, and to impose penalties for poor performance or insubordination, is quite restricted—* as compared with the pressure available to managers in profit-making firms.

One reason for this restraint on the use of power is the difficulty of evaluating performance. If output is intangible and goals ambiguous—as previous Notes have suggested—a manager lacks a clear-cut basis for giving rewards or punishment. And in the absence of standards that both he and his subordinate understand, rewarding or punishing is apt to appear capricious. So in many not-for-profit enterprises, we find strong traditions against managers making rewards or imposing penalties based on an individual's performance.

Furthermore, in some fields such restraints are formalized. "Tenure" rules are common at all levels of education; "civil service" rules permeate government; "seniority" rules are included in many union contracts; and similar regulations are sponsored by professional groups. These rules originate to prevent abuses of managerial power—to protect academic freedom, to guard against the "political-spoils" system, to stop a boss from favoring only his friends. But in addition to preventing abuses, the rules also sharply restrict managers' power to promote legitimate goals of the enterprise.

Although restraints on the use of managerial power are also found in profit-making ventures, they are more common in the not-for-profit group. Such shackles on managerial power invite insubordination. Obviously, when a manager predicts the likely responses to his activating requests, and when he wishes to overcome a negative response, he must take these restrictions on his power into account.

Fortunately, *commitment to enterprise goals* is often strong among workers in libraries, clinics, child-care centers, and many other not-for-profit enterprises. Activating in such circumstances is eased by this congruence. Even though a manager's power may be limited—for reasons noted above—this impotence is not serious *if* satisfactions from the work itself provide the motivation to accept instructions.

Commitment to service goals, however, is often qualified. Among the factors a not-for-profit manager should be sensitive to are the following:

1) The supervisor who translates broad goals into specific assignments must be accepted as a legitimate spokesman. Professionals such as doctors and professors may resent an intervening executive who is not a qualified member of their own "guild." In fact, workers who feel that their supervisor is incompetent may be even more critical of him when they are concerned about end results than they would be if they were indifferent. Such an "unqualified" supervisor may fail to get a committed response to his requests even though the worker agrees with the overall objective.

2) As an enterprise grows and the work is subdivided—for example, in a large hospital—the persons doing routine tasks may have difficulty relating their task to the lofty service goal. Especially when some elite group of actors, doctors, or curators dominates the planning and the limelight, the lesser folk (stagehands, orderlies, and caretakers) may feel that "commitment to the cause" has a hollow ring.

3) A person's predominant commitment may be to personally performing a service, and he supports the enterprise only as a means of doing his thing. Thus, a devoted teacher who has taught generations of students English grammar may be quite uncommitted to a new educational objective of social adjustment. The very fact that a person is committed—to any goal—means that he is less adaptable to shifts in goals of his employer.

These considerations indicate that managers in not-for-profit enterprises certainly cannot assume that their activating requests will receive a committed response. As we have proposed throughout Part Six, before issuing a request the wise manager will first predict his subordinates' response. If this expected response is less enthusiastic than desired, the manager then considers possible ways of changing the response. At this stage our not-for-profit manager may realize anew that he lacks power to coerce. So he must rely on trying to win commitment through better communication, or on creating either conditions favorable to indifferent compliance or some sort of compromise perhaps in the request itself.

By themselves, these are not usually strong ways of shifting responses. So in vigorous not-for-profit enterprises, we often find that the available energizing forces must be supplemented by charismatic leadership or institutional mystique.

In summarizing these six Notes on managing not-for-profit enterprises, four broad conclusions emerge.

1) The basic processes, concepts, and techniques of management that work well in profit-seeking ventures fit not-for-profit enterprises almost as well.

2) The profit motive itself does not lead us to the chief differences that are likely to exist.

3) Instead, such characteristics are intangible, and multiple objectives, strong employee commitment to professions, intrusion of resource contributors into internal operations, restraints on use of rewards and punishments, and reliance on charismatic leaders—alone or in combination—call for modification of managerial techniques.

4) Since great diversity exists among not-for-profit enterprises, we must look carefully for characteristics like those just listed and then tailor the managerial design to suit each specific situation.

To try to manage either profit or not-for-profit firms without sophisticated use of successful concepts and techniques is to turn one's back on accumulated wisdom. To presume that judicious selection and fitting of these concepts to each situation can be avoided is to court disaster.

Case Studies

---

for Part VI

CASE 6-1
SOUTHEAST TEXTILES

The Southeast Textiles company is a medium-sized manufacturer of heavy-duty clothing. Although 80 percent of its sales come from overalls, work pants, and shirts, and work gloves, the company also sells semifinished heavy-duty fabric to other textile and manufacturing companies for conversion into industrial-packaging material and for camping equipment. As a regional producer of a relatively specialized product line, Southeast has enjoyed more than 35 years of fairly stable profit and growth. In the past five years, however, increased competition both from larger domestic firms and from imports have shrunk Southeast's sales and profit margins; and last year the company suffered its first operating loss in two decades.

In an effort to increase efficiency in the company's major mill in Allison, North Carolina, where 90 percent of its products are produced, an intensive modernization program was undertaken. New equipment was purchased, new procedures were introduced, and the work force was cut from 800 to 690 hourly workers. A team of consultants was used to advise the company's management during the study that produced the program, and one member of the team, Norman Dean, was hired to become staff assistant to the plant manager, Roger Headrick.

Dean works closely with Headrick on the many problems associated with the modernization program, and spends one or two days a week with the company's president, Oliver Hall, and the corporate treasurer, James Davis, advising them on the use of a newly acquired computer system. Hall had been the driving force behind the modernization and had recommended that Headrick hire Dean. Headrick recognized that Dean had a fine background in industrial engineering and was a real "whiz" on computers and modern scientific-management techniques. He had reservations, however, about taking him on as his assistant.

Once we get the new methods and equipment functioning smoothly, [Headrick said], I'm not sure I'll know what to do with him. Despite all of his book knowledge, he still doesn't know many of the tricks of our business, and he has, on more than one occasion, rubbed my people the wrong way by trying to jam his ideas down their throats. Basically he is a pleasant young man, but he is trying hard to justify this program and the faith Hall has in him, and so he can be awfully pushy. But the president has quite a high opinion of him, and right now he is a big help in the transition.

Hall does indeed have a high opinion of Dean.

This is one of the brightest young people I have met. He knows his stuff and he won't be held back by any "We have never done it that way" arguments. Rog Headrick is a first-rate man with a solid background in the practical problems of our business. With Dean to keep him informed about more modern management techniques, we have a first-rate team in the mill.

In addition, Dean is working with Jim Davis and me to get our overall management information-system modernized and to help us use that fancy new computer system we bought to do more than highly specialized clerical work. We had a tough time getting him away from his former firm and had to pay him a very fancy salary, but we think he will earn every penny of it.

One of the areas in which savings were expected from the modernization program was the production-control department. James Rose, manager of production control, has been with the company for 12 years and in his present position for almost five years. He reports to Headrick and is responsible for scheduling the flow of both raw materials and finished product, as well as for actual production planning. He works closely with the plant's purchasing agent and warehouse manager, Everett Sims, and the other members of Headrick's staff (see Exhibit I).

Before the modernization program, Rose had 21 clerks, three expediters, and four supervisors in his department. With the completion of the plan for the new program, Dean recommended that Rose's department be reduced to 12 clerks, two expediters, and two supervisors. This was to be accomplished through new methods and through greater use of the company's computer, located in the administrative offices adjacent to the Allison mill. The shift in production control required not only a reduction in work force but also a change in the nature of most of the scheduling clerks' jobs, requiring somewhat different and higher levels of skills. Rose, after studying the plan, recommended that the company implement it over a six-month period. This would allow him more time to reduce his work force by means of attrition and transfers and more time to retrain the clerks who would remain. Headrick was sympathetic to this approach but agreed with Dean that it would be too slow and costly. The transition was to take place in one month, and on Davis's

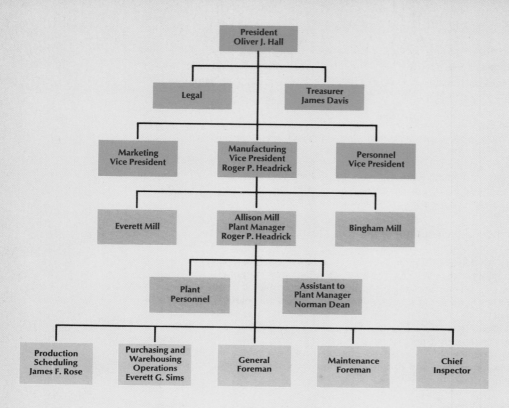

Exhibit I.

recommendation the existing work group was given three weeks' notice and the opportunity to begin retraining on their own.

During this period, eight of the original 21 clerks quit, and four, at their own expense, had begun taking courses offered in a nearby technical institute. Three of the original group of clerks and two supervisors were transferred to other jobs. At the end of the month, ten clerks, including one of the four attending classes, one expediter, and two supervisors, were let go. Nine new clerks and two new supervisors were hired, and the new system was formally introduced. Wage rates for the clerks were increased by eight percent, and for the supervisors, by ten percent.

The next eight weeks were extremely hectic ones throughout the mill, where similar changes were taking place. In production scheduling, two clerks and one supervisor resigned and were replaced. During this period, Rose and Dean were almost constantly in conflict over how to resolve the numerous crises that arose. After several more months, things settled down, the work force stabilized, and it appeared that the program might at last begin to produce the savings that had been promised. At this point, costs are still running higher than Dean had originally estimated but lower than before the new program was instituted. Dean has worked long hours and has supplemented Rose's limited knowledge in certain aspects of the new system. At first he had recommended transferring Rose to another position and replacing him with someone more familiar with the new approach, but Headrick vetoed his proposal.

Because new equipment and layout costs throughout the mill had been high, the president was constantly checking with Headrick and Dean on when the economies would start to show up. Headrick was quick to admit that Rose had been of great help in curbing the presidents desire to see more dramatic and more immediate cost reductions.

The three men who had been in Rose's department before the change-over seemed to adjust to the new system and to the newer employees, and the department's effectiveness increased. Headrick gave Rose much of the credit for the relatively smooth transition within the production-control department because of Rose's skillful handling of his personnel. Many of the other departments had had a much rougher time maintaining morale in the face of the changes. Rumors persist that production workers are being joined by many of the men and women doing technical, clerical, and low-level white-collar tasks in an attempt to bring in a union. So far, no formal request for representation elections have been made.

The president praised Headrick and Dean for their work, but warned them to keep an eye out for union trouble. Hall said:

We have too much invested in this new program to see it thwarted by having to work with a union. One of the reasons I moved the company down here in 1946 was to get away from the fetters a union can place on you. We may have to make a lot more changes before we are through, and I don't want to have to bargain every change in wage rates and work rules with a union. So keep an eye out for trouble and try not to push your people any harder than you have to. Try to recognize and reward the good ones and get rid of the troublemakers.

Although operations continued more or less smoothly, a major problem arose one Friday in the production-scheduling department. As a result of a breakdown in the computer on Thursday afternoon, much of the data required for completion of production schedules for the next two weeks was not available. As a result, at 8:30 Friday morning, Rose suggested to Headrick that they revert to procedures that were followed before the new program to complete the work needed by Monday morning.

Headrick called in Dean, and the three men discussed the problem. Dean listened to Rose's suggestion and said:

No good, Jim! If you go back to those methods with only 12 people, you'll never finish on time, and we'll start the week in a real hole. Most of your men don't even know the old system. I think we had better just wait until they de-bug the "monster" [computer]. If they get it going by eleven o'clock, we can still finish up by giving your people a couple of hours of overtime.

Rose asked:

What happens if they don't get it fixed on time? If I start now, we can get the job finished with the old system even if we need a couple of hours tonight and a half-day on Saturday. The overtime costs will be a fraction of what it will cost us on downtime in the mill if we don't have the schedules by Monday morning.

Dean countered by saying he was sure they would get the computer problem traced in time to avoid the extra cost of bringing the men in on Saturday.

Besides, if worse comes to worst and they don't get us the data we need till this afternoon, then we can bring them in Saturday.

Headrick decided, somewhat reluctantly to go along with Dean. By noon Friday, the problem had been traced to the failure of a component in the computer's central logic system. A replacement was promised by one o'clock. Work was at a standstill in his department, and Rose again requested that he be authorized to get started on the old system. This time, both Dean and Headrick firmly agreed it was probably too late and that with the problem diagnosed they would get the data they needed by two o'clock. Rose was told to ask his people to put in three hours of overtime Friday night and a half-day on Saturday.

Unfortunately, the needed component was not delivered and installed until two o'clock, and when a test was run on the system, a more serious problem was detected. The computer servicemen indicated that now, even working through the night, they could not complete repair and testing in less than 24 hours. When Headrick was informed of the bad news by Dean, he called Rose and told him to get busy with the old system. Rose protested:

Look, Roger, it's almost three o'clock. It's just too late now. When I explained the situation to the boys earlier, I had a tough time getting some of them to agree to stay late tonight and an even tougher time getting them to agree to come in on Saturday if we needed them. Those with families want to get home, and the younger men have dates. I had to pull out all stops and virtually plead with several to come in tomorrow. All but one agreed to come if we needed them, but they were reluctant. How can I go back now and tell them we do need them, when they'll find out, as the oldtimers know, the work simply can't be done even with a full day on Saturday?

Dean's response was:

Plead? For heaven's sake, why should you have to plead? Don't those men have any loyalty to the company? Once in a rare while we really need to have them give a little extra, and you have to plead? Perhaps if you didn't pamper them so, they would recognize that they have an obligation to the firm.

Rose answered angrily:

The firm has an obligation to them, too. If we keep 12 men late tonight and foul up their weekend plans, it should be for a darn good reason. If I get started now, we still won't finish until ten or eleven o'clock on Monday morning even if they work till eight o'clock tonight and all day Saturday. If we start fresh on Monday and I ask them to come in an hour earlier, we'll finish by noon if the computer is fixed this weekend. We are going to lose half a day in the mill on Monday any way we do it now; so I don't see any point in making matters worse by asking my men to ruin their weekends.

Dean was equally adamant and insisted that Rose at least try to get the work done by Saturday. Headrick ended the discussion by saying:

Look, Jim, we've got a bad situation now no matter what we do. If I lose a half-day in the mill at this time of the year, it's not going to be good, and the president won't listen to any excuses blaming the computer. He will want to know why we couldn't work around it. You know how touchy he is about his new brainchild. Get started right now, keep the men until eight o'clock tonight and as long tomorrow as necessary, but get those schedules done.

When Rose left, Dean shook his head and commented:

I don't want to put all the blame on Jim, but if he knew more about the new system he would have been a day and a half earlier in requesting the data we need from the computer. The system was designed to protect against machine failure by giving us a day or so slack at the end of the month. I can't help but feel that this might have been avoided if we had a man in production control who was more familiar with the new system than Jim.

After leaving, Rose announced the decision to his supervisors and then joined them to tell the scheduling clerks. They reluctantly agreed to stay, and the three who had worked under the old system were told to assist Rose in instructing the others.

One of the three, Ken King, asked to speak with Rose privately. He explained that he had planned on asking for the afternoon off so that he and his wife could get to the rehearsal for their son's wedding. The wedding was to be held in a town four hours' drive from their home.

When you asked us to stay late tonight, I almost died [he said]. If I have to stay, I will; but we'll miss the rehearsal and won't get in before midnight for the wedding tomorrow. No matter what you say about this afternoon, I can't come in tomorrow.

Rose thought a moment and then advised King to tell the company nurse that he had a severe headache and wanted to go home immediately.

I'll okay it when she calls me [Rose said]. I'd like to give you the time, but under the kind of pressure we are facing, I can't.

King thanked him, left, and did as Rose suggested. By eight o'clock, it was apparent to Rose that the department could not finish the work on Saturday, and he called Headrick at home to ask what he should do. Headrick indicated that whether they finished or not, he wanted them to try; he insisted that if they worked harder they might still make it. Nine of the 12 clerks reported for work on Saturday and worked until five o'clock, but the schedules were not completed until almost noon on Monday. Because King was one of the three who knew the old system, his absence had slowed things down. But Rose was certain they could not have finished much earlier even with King. He was surprised, in fact, that they had done as well as they had.

The mill worked on certain stock items Monday morning and did not get into the new schedules until amost two o'clock. As a result, a considerable increase over standard costs was anticipated.

On Monday morning, Dean learned informally of what had happened with Ken King. He confronted Headrick with what he had heard and suggested that the time had come to replace Rose.

FOR DISCUSSION AND REPORT-WRITING

Organizing: Structural Design

1) Who is responsible for the general success or failure of the new system for production scheduling? Who is responsible for the failure to complete the schedules by Monday? Relate your answers to the "authority" granted the one(s) responsible.

2) Discuss Dean's participation in dealing with the scheduling problem on Friday as it relates to the role of staff.

Human Factors in Organizing

3) How much attention was given to human factors in redesigning the work of the production-scheduling operations? What may be the long-run effects of the reorganization as implemented under Dean's plan?

4) What power and influence does Dean seem to possess beyond his "formal authority"? What are their sources? Is it good for him to have this power and influence? How would you reduce or increase them?

Planning: Elements of
Rational Decision-Making

5) Define the problem facing Headrick on Monday morning with respect to Rose. Develop and place this problem within the total framework.

6) Can you develop any creative alternatives to the initial problem Friday morning? Try to find ones that solve it directly by getting the scheduling done. Also try to find ones that get "around" it by meeting higher-level goals.

Planning: Decision-Making
in an Enterprise

7) Can you devise any standing plans for dealing with a crisis such as the one that arose on Friday?

8) What do you think of the company's strategy of seeking to make major changes in work, workers, compensation, and working conditions without having to deal with unions? Will it work? What may happen?

9) What benefits and pitfalls might be expanded from having more participation by the schedulers in dealing with a problem such as the one that arose on Friday?

Controlling

627

Case 6–2
Household
Products
Company

10) In what ways will budgetary controls for Headrick's plan reflect and fail to reflect the impact of Friday's crisis and the action you recommend be taken on Monday?

11) How should Hall evaluate the success of his modernization program? Discuss your answer in terms of all elements of a sound control system and its relation to other elements of the process of management.

Activating

12) From the limited information you have, what do you think of Rose as an "activator"?

13) What factors either contributed to or detracted from effective communication between Rose and his superior? Between Rose and Headrick?

14) What will be the longer-run effects of Rose's letting King go home early on the several groups affected? What will determine whether this compromise will facilitate or hinder future compliance or commitment?

15) (Summary Report Question: Part Six) If you were in Headrick's position on Monday morning, what disciplinary action, if any, would you take with Rose and how would you go about it?

16) What responses do you forecast from various company people or groups in reaction to *each* of the several alternative courses of disciplinary action open to Headrick? If the responses you forecast are not what you want, what action would you take to shift the responses to acceptable ones?

Summary Question for Solution of the Case as a Whole

17) Using your answers to questions 16 and 17 above, discuss the several factors you considered, which you placed the most weight on, and why.

CASE 6-2
HOUSEHOLD PRODUCTS COMPANY

HPC: GENERAL INFORMATION

The Household Products Company (HPC) is a leader in the food and hardware industries. For more than 50 years, the company manufactured a wide range of products and distributed them through hardware and department stores. Then in the 1960s, as more of these products were sold through large supermarket chains, HPC diversified into several specialty food markets. With current sales of more than $1 billion, HPC in recent years has matched industry growth, but has had below average profitability.

Eighteen months ago, Henry Norman, who had been president and chairman of HPC for 13 years, announced that he was appointing John Saxon as president and chief operating officer. Although he would retain his position as chairman of the board and his seat on the finance committee, Mr. Norman indicated he would devote most of his time to "issues of interest to the industry" and would not play an active role within the company.

Although all concerned parties deny reports that Norman was pressured to turn the reins over to Saxon, the rumor persists. One industry source said,

The board was not happy with HPC's declining profits and felt the whole organization needed shaking up. Norman had been there too long and it was felt that only a new president could do what had to be done.

JOHN SAXON, PRESIDENT

John Saxon is no newcomer to HPC. He worked in a variety of marketing and finance positions for over 20 years before his promotion to president. At 54, he looks and acts younger, demanding a great deal of himself and his staff. Despite his experience with the company and his reputation for being impulsive, he waited three months before making any significant changes. In the next several weeks, however, "the purge," as it is called in the organization, took place.

One former HPC executive describes this period as follows.

HPC was always regarded as a "family-type" organization. Loyalty and long service were respected and rewarded. It was almost unheard of to fire anyone with more than five years of service. All of the top and middle managers knew each other and understood what was expected of them. Though some people may have gotten a bit complacent, most of us worked hard for HPC and particularly for Mr. Norman. Everyone who knew him loved and respected him.

When Saxon took over, he was probably under pressure from the board to shake things up, and that's just what he did. Over one three-day period, more than 80 managers and senior professionals were either fired or allowed to resign. During the next few weeks another 60 middle managers and three vice-presidents resigned or were fired. I was part of a group that resigned after the purge. It just isn't the same company anymore and we felt we would be happier elsewhere. Many of those who stayed probably would have left if they weren't afraid to start over again somewhere else.

Saxon describes this period of turnover in somewhat different terms.

It was necessary to make some major changes [he says]. Once I knew who had to go and whom I could count on to revitalize the organization, I moved rapidly. There is no easy or pleasant way to make the kinds of changes we had to make. It had to be done quickly and cleanly. We tried to help people find other positions and to make good settlements, but I'm sure some people were hurt. We also lost some people we hadn't planned on removing, but that's probably just as well. My guess is that only the weaker ones left, since they were afraid they would be unable to meet our new standards.

Saxon feels that the shake-up is over and that no major changes will be necessary for some time.

We now have not only a better structure, but also the right people in most of the key jobs. Over the next three or four years I don't see the need for any major changes in structure or personnel. Retirement will take care of the few remaining marginal performers.

For the past year, I have done all I can to reassure people that the shake-up is over, but many are still waiting for "the other shoe to drop." They are still nervous and uncertain. As a result, though I must still press for improvement, I don't want any major changes. I want them to get used to our new organization and to the procedures we have set up to get things done in a more effective way.

CURRENT ORGANIZATION

The "new organization" Saxon speaks of is not a significant departure in structure from the one he inherited. Several staff departments that had reported directly to Norman were consolidated under two newly created positions of vice president of finance and vice president of administration. In addition, two new senior vice presidents' positions were created. Most of the changes that took place were in personnel rather than in structure, and in the procedures by which plans are formulated, integrated, and reviewed.

One senior executive states,

It took us a while to figure out the new system and to determine who really had what "clout." There are still some procedures that need clarifying, but most of us now have a pretty clear notion of who is expected to do what.

Arthur M. Byrnes, one of the two newly appointed senior vice presidents, disagrees with this position.

I am certain, that my title is *senior* vice president to compensate me for the fact that no one knows what I am supposed to do.

Byrnes had been general manager of two of HPC's hardware divisions before his promotion. According to the grapevine, Byrnes had been one of those senior managers whose performance was good but who "didn't fit in." According to one source,

Byrnes had always done a good job but he was set in his ways. Apparently he resisted Saxon's pressure to remove a number of his subordinates and it was only after his promotion that his replacement agreed to these changes.

Officially, Byrnes is one of two senior vice presidents reporting directly to the president. It was announced that they would assist the president in coordinating plans and evaluating the results of the company's 11 operating divisions. Byrnes, whose greatest strength is considered to be in marketing, is supposed to look across the divisions for opportunities to coordinate efforts, reduce expenses, and increase efficiency in marketing. The other senior vice president, Bert Wing, was also a former division general manager with long experience in production and engineering. His responsibility is similar to Byrnes's but directed toward matters of production, engineering, and plant location rather than marketing.

Both of these senior vice presidents and the other five vice presidents reporting to Saxon serve on the operations committee, which formally reviews division plans and results (see Exhibit I). In addition to the operations committee, the finance committee meets to review capital and operating budgets and to set overall financial policy.

The two senior staff vice presidents each have only three people reporting to them—an administrative assistant and two "senior analysts." Saxon states that,

I don't want big staff groups getting in the way of my operating people. Both Byrnes and Wing are very experienced people who can help me pull things together and carry out special projects. They are both frustrated in their new jobs, however. As former general managers they don't like being "advisors," but I can really use their experience. As long as they don't have big staffs, they won't have time to get in trouble trying to outdo the operating people. They will be too busy carrying out my requests.

Exhibit I.

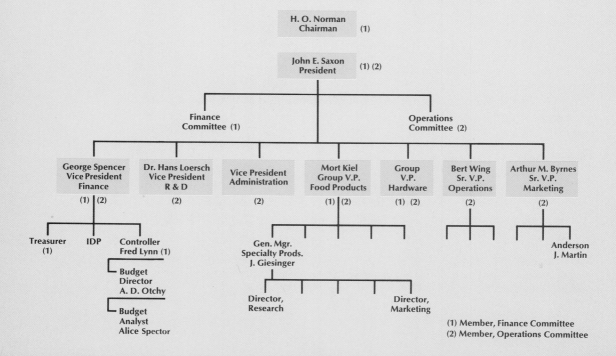

(1) Member, Finance Committee
(2) Member, Operations Committee

One of the requests Saxon recently made of Byrnes and Wing was for each to assign one of their analysts to search for "fat" in division operations. When results for the first six months of this year were below profit forecasts, all divisions were requested to "seek ways of improving efficiency so that end-of-year results will meet original targets." A number of promises have been made to Saxon by his two group vice presidents, and if they are fulfilled, year-end results will exceed targets.

> Though I am pleased with the promises, I remain a bit skeptical [explains Saxon]. Therefore, I asked Byrnes and Wing to see if they might find a few places to save some money.

Byrnes assigned this project to Anderson Martin, one of his two analysts, and warned him to

> Go about your work quickly but without fanfare. We are looking to save some money but not to stir up any trouble.

After three weeks, Martin presented Byrnes with seven recommendations which, if approved, might save over a quarter of a million dollars. According to Martin, not all of these proposals would pan out, but one alone would save $125,000. Byrnes was delighted with Martin's work and the fact that he had completed it before Wing.

He approved five of the seven recommendations and met with the president on a Thursday morning to discuss them. Saxon was extremely busy and reviewed the proposal quickly. He rejected one of the five, giving no explanation, and asked Byrnes to wait on one other until he Saxon had "checked it out." The other three proposals he approved and said,

> Good work, Art. Write up instructions on these three and get them off as soon as possible.

Byrnes relayed this message to Martin, and on Thursday afternoon received Martin's draft memos and issued them over his [Byrnes's] signature. The following Tuesday afternoon Byrnes was called to Saxon's office.

> It looks as though we must have hit a "hot button," Art—namely, this proposal to save $125,000 by eliminating the "Spice Grading." So far, I have gotten five or six phone calls, several memos, and a visit from Mr. Norman on it. Please discuss these memos and my notes with Martin and let me know what you want me to do. I'll back you if you really think it's worth it. It obviously would have been better if I had run this one through channels, but so much for hindsight.

Byrnes returned to his office and read the material the president had given him, along with a memo Byrnes had received from George Spencer, vice president of finance. He then walked to Martin's cubicle.

> Next time you find an easy way to save $125,000, remind me to check. Read what this request has stirred up and give me your thoughts within an hour.

Anderson J. Martin, known as "A. J.," says he felt as though he had been struck in the solar plexus.

This weekend my wife and I celebrated my having saved the company over $100,000. On Thursday my boss had hinted that I could look forward to a sizeable bonus this year as a result of my work on the "spice project." Today [Tuesday], he dumped these memos on my desk and very angrily told me to bring him my recommendations in an hour. I just read through these memos and I can hardly believe what I read. I started out trying to save the company a substantial amount of money, and it looks as though I have succeeded in getting three vice presidents working to have me fired.

"A.J." Martin has worked for HPC for almost three years. After completing a law degree, he spent four years with a major law firm before joining the legal department of HPC. He had begun working for an MBA at night school before joining the company, and completed the requirements for this degree a year ago. At that time, he accepted a job as assistant to Arthur Byrnes, the newly appointed senior vice president.

Although Mr. Byrnes is not the easiest person to work for [said Martin], he seems to like my work, and recently he has given me a number of very interesting and challenging assignments. Though I am not always sure I know what he expects of me, I regard this an an opportunity. He gives me a good bit of latitude and a chance to take the initiative. So far he has backed me when I needed his help. I hope he will this time.

THE SPICE-GRADING PROPOSAL

The "spice-grading proposal" involves the largest single savings from among the three approved by both Byrnes and Saxon. It arose as a result of a conversation between Martin and a budget analyst, Alice Spector (see Exhibit I).

Alice and I attended the same MBA program [Martin explains]. When I told her I was looking for ways of saving some significant money, she quickly suggested I find out about the spice grading, which is carried out by our Specialty Products Division. She had questioned $126,500 allocated to this activity but had been directed by her superior—A.D. Otchy, the budget director—not to question the request.

Upon investigation, Martin learned that for more than 12 years, the Specialty Products Division had employed five people and maintained a small laboratory to test and classify spices and herbs.

This started [Martin said], as a result of a suggestion made by H. O. Norman when he was president that such a classification system would help HPC and later the entire industry. In the beginning the company got a lot of favorable public relations in industry circles for doing this work and making the results available.

I learned that now most of the data we provide can be gotten from the Departments of Agriculture and Commerce and from the Food and Drug Administration. Though its more convenient to get it from us, the industry can pull it together from these sources. What cannot be acquired from public sources, I was told, is of relatively little value; and if it is to be compiled, it should be done by a trade association so that all users share the costs.

Martin checked these assumptions with the directors of research and marketing of the Specialty Products Division. According to Martin both felt this project was of marginal value. Therefore, he found it hard to explain the memos he had been handed by Byrnes.

It is clear from their language and the timing of these memos that something is going on here that goes beyond the spice grading. I guess I can see why Kiel [group vice president, food products] may be a little upset. He and Giesinger [general manager, specialty products] probably feel we showed them up. But how in the world did Spencer [vice president, finance] and Loersch [vice president, R&D] get in the act? I can't imagine what kind of "horse-trading" brought that coalition together.

I have read these memos a dozen times and I am still puzzled (See Exhibits II–VI). I wish I had time to contact my original sources, but I don't; Mr. Byrnes wants answers now.

EXHIBIT II

To: M. A. Kiel
From: A. M. Byrnes
Subject: Cost Reduction Program

I have just completed a review of several proposals to reduce expenditures as part of our effort to improve our profit picture by year-end. Despite the enormous efforts that have been made by all operating departments, the president feels additional efforts will be needed.

It has come to my attention that the internal and public-relations benefits accruing from our "Spice Testing and Grading" work no longer justify expenditures of over $125,000. Noting the magnitude of your operation, it is not surprising that a project this small was not subjected to closer scrutiny. Nonetheless, I am sure you will agree with the conclusions drawn by Anderson J. Martin that in these difficult times such a project cannot be justified.*

I have reviewed Martin's conclusions with the president, and he concurs that the project should be discontinued. Unless you find substantial error in our findings, please take steps to disband this department.

If you have any questions please call me. I tried to reach you today, but I learned you would be away until Monday.

/s/

* Attached was a four-page memo from Martin to Byrnes supporting this recommendation.

EXHIBIT III

To: John Saxon
From: Mort Kiel
Subject: Byrnes's Proposal on Spice Project

This is to follow up on my telephone call yesterday. I have, as you suggested, checked carefully with Jack Giesinger. He in turn has reviewed this proposal with both his research and marketing directors, and they unanimously reject the conclusions drawn by A. J. Martin.

I am told that Martin was clearly informed that this project, initiated years ago by H. O. Norman, continues to have valuable internal and external benefits. My people insist that the data available from government sources is neither timely nor specific enough for our purposes. Though it is impossible to calculate the value of this service to our internal operations or to the good will we generate by showing leadership in our industry, it is clear that these benefits exceed the cost.

Please be assured that if our current profit pressure dictates the need for additional economies, I will take whatever steps are needed to effect them.

I am certain that Art Byrnes will agree that we are in the best position to judge the merits of such projects. I will try to see him tomorrow to answer any questions he may have. As I mentioned on the phone, I feel it is unfortunate that Art should be put in such an awkward position by an overzealous young staffer who apparently did not bother to check his assumptions carefully.

/ s /

EXHIBIT IV

To: J. E. Saxon
From: H. Loersch
Subject: Cost Reduction

Dear John:

As you suggested when I called, I am putting my views on the Byrnes's cost-reduction proposal in writing. I find it unfortunate that he has been led by incomplete data to a false conclusion. My people review all such testing activities on a quarterly basis to provide an independent audit on the quality of such work and its value to the company. Let me assure you that we are in a far better position to judge the merits of such programs than an inexperienced young man whose eagerness to impress has created a potentially embarrassing situation.

Sincerely,

/ s /

EXHIBIT V

To: Arthur Byrnes
From: George Spencer

Dear Art:

I am sure that by now the misunderstanding on the spice-testing business has been cleared up. I received calls Monday night in Cleveland, first from Jack Giesinger and then Mort Kiel. In effect, both asked me whether I was aware of a new procedure for auditing division budgets. Mort read me your note to him and Martin's proposal to you.

For all I know, you may be right, but I must object to the process that was followed. In the future, if you turn up something like this please check with me or Fred Lynn. I'm sure that if there is anything to it, we can follow up and keep you posted on what happens.

I hope you will withdraw your recommendation and let me have Alex Otchy [budget director] look into the issues Martin raised. He certainly is better equipped than Martin to check out a project like this.

If you have any questions, call me when I get back from Cleveland next week.

Sincerely,

/s/

Dictated by phone but not read

EXHIBIT VI

Notes from John Saxon on discussion with H. O. Norman

Dear Art:

I am dictating the following for your information. I spoke with Hank Norman this afternoon. He indicated that he had heard that "some eager beaver was trying to save a few dollars by getting rid of the spice-grading project." I thought at first that he was going to join those asking me to overrule you. He would not tell me how he learned of the proposal, but he chuckled that "the troops must still respect the old man because I still hear from them when they think I'm interested in something." I believe I can summarize his position on this matter with the following four points:

1) The proposal was his idea years ago, and he feels it was well worth the cost at that time.
2) Martin may be correct that this project is no longer worth the expense, and Norman feels he is certainly in no position to judge.
3) If I feel this activity should be dropped, he would not object.

4) If the project is continued, he would like to be assured that it is still justified on the basis of a careful cost-benefit analysis.

Sincerely,

/s/

FOR DISCUSSION AND REPORT-WRITING

Organizing: Structural Design

1) Assume that Wing and Byrnes were given their current positions because Saxon felt that they could be of considerable help to him. Develop job descriptions for each of them that you feel would be consistent with the rest of the organization design.

2) What authority should Byrnes be given by Saxon to facilitate Byrnes's ability to use his marketing expertise to bring about cost reductions?

Human Factors in Organizing

3) How do you feel about the former HPC executive's comment that, "It just isn't the same company anymore."? Is this feeling likely to a) exist and b) persist, if it does exist, among those who remained after the "purge"?

4) Saxon states, "There is no easy or pleasant way to make the kinds of changes we had to make." Assuming changes did have to be made, what do you think of Saxon's approach? If you believe that it was correct, why? If not, how would you have made the necessary changes?

5) How will the apparent residual stress felt by many HPC employees affect performance on the job?

6) What do you think about Saxon's statement that, "We also lost some people we hadn't planned on removing, but that's probably just as well. My guess is only the weaker ones left"?

7) What human characteristics should you look for in people who are to fill positions such as Wing's and Byrnes's?

Planning: Elements of Rational Decision-Making

8) How might Martin have gotten additional data and thus built a stronger case for dropping the spice-grading project? In this connection, how should he have estimated the current benefits of this group's work?

9) How might Martin's recommendation have been "tested" before Byrnes brought it to Saxon? Why do you suppose this was not done?

Planning: Decision-Making
in an Enterprise

637

Case 6–2
Household
Products
Company

10) What role(s) might Byrnes and Wing play in the development of corporate-level strategies and long-range plans?

11) How will your answers to each part of question 10 be affected by your answer to question 2?

12) Martin states, "It is clear from their language and the timing of these memos that something is going on here that goes beyond the spice grading." What do you think about this sentence and the rest of Martin's statement on the memos?

Controlling

13) If in fact the spice-grading project is no longer worthwhile, couldn't conventional controls have spotted this and led to its being reviewed critically by Keil, Spencer, and/or Loersch? How did it gain budgetary approval?

14) How will Saxon evaluate the performance of Byrnes and Wing and be informed of whether they are carrying out their duties satisfactorily? Review your answer to question 1.

Activating

15) How do you explain that an experienced executive like Byrnes did not forecast Kiel's response to Martin's request?

16) Can Byrnes gain compliance from Kiel if he decides to support his original proposal? Is "compliance" by Kiel an acceptable response to this activating request?

17) If Byrnes "backs down" or compromises on his original request, is he likely to increase or decrease his chances of gaining compliance (if not commitment) in his future dealings with the group vice presidents and division general managers?

18) Why did Byrnes press Martin for an immediate response to the memos rather than take charge of the project and speak personally with the people who contacted the president?

19) To what extent were the president and Byrnes to blame for Martin's predicament because of their poor communications?

20) (Summary Report Question: Part Six) a) Should Martin have expected compliance or commitment in the eventual activating of his recommendations? b) Based on your answer, prepare the proper steps for Martin to have followed to develop a proposal that would have gained the desired degree of acceptance.

Summary Question for Solution of the Case as a Whole

21) Based on the facts of the case and *your forecasts* of how various executives will respond, what actions do you recommend Martin take at this time?

Conclusion:

Thinking of management in terms of organizing, planning, controlling, and activating sharpens our analysis; it helps us sort out issues and then concentrate on a particular opportunity for improvement. But like any analytical device, it leaves us with parts. However much we refine these parts of the management process, they become operative only when we fit them back into the total management system. We may be especially pleased with a new scheme for motivating executives or with an operations-research model, but unless our new creation is compatible with the overall management design, it will be of little value. Achieving a *synthesis* of various management parts is the central theme in the following chapter.

In addition to achieving internal synthesis, the manager must keep his management design adjusted to external needs. In Chapter 16 we described master strategy as the evolving formulation of a company's plans for dealing with its environment. Now we shall give specific attention to the interrelationships between that master strategy and the overall management design. In other words, as stressed in Chapter 1, full synthesis involves both internal and external integration.

Two popular concepts are embraced in the kind of synthesis we are discussing. 1) The total *system* of management must be considered. Each phase

Need
for Synthesis

fits in with other phases; working together they provide mutual support. 2) Each company designs a system that should be suited to its particular needs. The specific features of that design are *contingent upon* the company's individual aims and resources.

The following chapter, "Maintaining a Dynamic Management System," suggests that we can build this bridge between a company's individual needs and the management system we design for it by focusing on its technology. The character of the technology—stable, regulated flexibility, adaptive—provides a clue (along with size, complexity, uncertainty, and need for speed) to the most appropriate kind of management instruments.

Complicating this entire meshing of overall management design with company strategy is the unceasing environmental change. A system that performs well today may need revamping tomorrow. So a neatly integrated management design cannot remain static. Managers continually face the issues explored in this chapter.

Management is a great potential social resource. To be fully effective, however, the practice of management demands great skill in fusing many elements into a total design suited to each specific opportunity.

29

Maintaining a Dynamic
Management System

NEED FOR DYNAMIC BALANCE

Two themes have appeared often throughout this book: 1) The phases of managing—organizing, planning, controlling, and activating—interact with each other. Consequently, wherever a change may be initiated, we should consider its possible effect on the *total* management design—or, system. 2) The system selected by a manager should be carefully suited to the situation which that manager faces. Any single managerial setup is either strong or weak, depending on local circumstances and what we wish to accomplish. In this concluding chapter we will reemphasize and illustrate these two central themes.

To keep the managerial system of a dynamic enterprise in balance we must:

1) Grasp the significance of the management *systems* concept.
2) Make sure that *refinements* in any part of our existing system are *integrated* into the total system.
3) Adapt the overall system to *growth.*
4) Suit the system to *new strategy.*
5) Build *compound systems* when necessary.

MANAGEMENT SYSTEMS CONCEPT

The modern "systems" concept applies to a wide range of phenomena. We speak of a water-supply system, political system, transportation system, medical-care system, and ignition system in our car. Every system includes 1) several specialized parts that perform specific activities. These parts are connected so that one part feeds or supports another; thus the output of the system relies on dependable interaction between the parts. And each system has 2) regular ways of responding to environmental stimuli. The systems concept does not add any activities or hardware; it merely focuses on the way parts are fitted together into an integrated arrangement, and on the interaction of the total system to its environment.

641

CHAPTER 29
Maintaining a
Dynamic
Management
System

Company management is such a system. It has parts—planning devices, organizational arrangements, control mechanisms, and activating methods; and these parts must support each other to achieve the purposes of the company. Also, this internal management-system has established ways of keeping watch on the company environment and responding to external opportunities and threats.

The main benefit of thinking of management as a system is the emphasis on interrelations—for example, in the way a change in organization must be tied to corresponding adjustments in controlling and activating. For instance, a French electronics manufacturer is rapidly expanding its production in other Common Market countries. This shift affects not only the production activities; it is also forcing a modification in the close controls traditionally used by central management and a change in the activating modes that senior executives customarily employ. By taking a systems view, the impact of a change on other parts is more easily recognized, and adjustments can be made to bring about a new balance.

In each situation, the areas of management should be synergistic. That is, organization structure should facilitate control; control should stimulate useful data for planning; planning should assist activating; and so forth. As we have stressed repeatedly, these mutually supporting effects are a vital feature of a good management system.

REFINEMENTS AND ADJUSTMENTS

Most changes in a management system are small adjustments in existing patterns of behavior. A new opportunity arises or something is not working quite right, so we add a policy or modify the organization. Such refinements leave the basic system intact. Nevertheless, *reinforcing the adjustments in several parts of the system is often necessary to make the initial change effective.*

A leading university has adopted an "affirmative-action plan" to increase its employment of racial minorities and women at all levels. The first move was to adopt procedures for recruiting and promotion which ensure that persons from underemployed groups are carefully considered. However, the new procedures alone are not adequate. A staff position has been added to the president's office to encourage, advise, and review the way the new procedures operate in each department. Also, yes–no controls on all new appointments have been introduced. Although commitment to the new plan is certainly desired, university officials rely primarily on simple acceptance. Here we can see that planning, organizing, controlling, and activating are all involved; each supports the other in creating a greater change than would occur with any separate move.

Several related changes were also needed by a North Atlantic shipping company when it introduced container ships. The new technology calls for steel containers, the size of a large truck, to be filled by the original shipper and handled as a single, sealed unit all the way to the doorstep of the receiver. Each major port served by the company now has a company branch engaged in overland transportation to dockside. In addition to setting up these new organization units, more authority has been delegated to the local branches; the planning and scheduling procedures have been greatly modified; headquarters control is now confined largely to postaction reports (see Table 24–1); and local commitment to the new way of handling cargo is crucial. To take full advantage of the container ships, the entire management system has had to be revised.

GROWTH AND MANAGEMENT SYSTEMS

Company growth affects the kind of management system that is needed. We have already seen, in Chapter 5, how growth leads to changes in organization. Four stages of development stand out—I. single entrepreneur, II. departmentalized firm, III. multiple-mission company, and IV. conglomerate. But reorganization alone is inadequate. We must likewise recast the planning, controlling, and activating.

When a motel grows from a single to multiple locations (as in the examples cited in Chapter 5), more than a shift from a Stage I to a Stage II organization will be required. Because senior managers are more remote, standing operating procedures for many activities from bookkeeping to bedmaking may be adopted. Departmental targets will also become more explicit and detailed. With the activities thus prescribed by detailed plans, the manager of each location can efficiently direct the day-to-day operations with a consistency of service for guests. Control in the expanded organization will shift to a policy of occasional "audits," to ensure that standing procedures are being followed, to monthly postaction review of departmental results versus targets, and to yes–no controls on capital expenditures, appointment of key supervisors, and increased sales-promotion efforts. Although commitment would be the better activating mode, the prevailing attitude will probably be acceptance of centrally established plans and programs.

This kind of management system suits a medium-size motel chain. But other Stage II companies will need more adaptability in their planning and control—as we shall see in the next section, on the matching of technology and management systems.

Planning and control mechanisms change sharply when a company moves from a Stage II departmentalized to a Stage III multiple-mission organization. In the larger Stage III organization, each of the operating divisions has its own internal management design. So planning in the headquarters focuses on new strategic opportunities and long-run programming. Aside from accounting and perhaps labor relations, where consistency becomes the ruling virtue, there will be few company-wide standing operating procedures. Controlling will be largely concerned with having effective systems within each division, a few warning signals for steering-control, and postaction reviews. In the activating relationships between central executives and division managers, commitment will be a *sine qua non;* decentralization and remoteness is so high in the typical Stage III company that central executives must rely on strongly committed subordinates.

643
CHAPTER 29
Maintaining a
Dynamic
Management
System

A Stage IV conglomerate organization calls for greater reliance on the operating companies to do their own planning and controlling. Except for the board-of-director role of the supervising executive, central managers confine their attention to financial- and market-position objectives and results. Yes–no controls will be used for major decisions. But the prevailing system will be simple: Get a good manager to run each company; if he succeeds reward him, if he fails replace him. The rationale for so little planning and control at headquarters is that, in such a large and heterogeneous concern, executives with the competence to effectively direct a business can use their talents best within an operating company, where the real action takes place.

Just as with smaller changes, when growth forces a company to shift to a new stage, the total management system—not just one part—is subject to redesign.

STRATEGY AND STRUCTURE

A new company strategy can have a more profound effect on the management system than growth. A change in strategy often alters the kind of activities performed, the degree of uncertainty, frequency of change, and other characteristics of company operations. And the management system should be suited to these new characteristics.

But we have no simple process of moving from a new strategy to a system for executing that strategy.

Technology:
The Intervening Variable

The best bridge between strategy and system design is "technology." Here we use technology in a very broad sense to include numerous methods for converting resource inputs into products and services for consumers. The

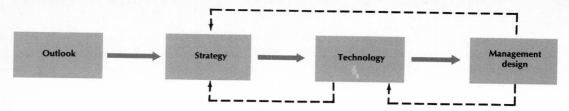

Figure 29–1   A simple flow diagram with technology as an intervening variable.

inputs can be labor, knowledge, and capital, as well as raw materials.[1] Thus an insurance company has its technology for converting money, ideas, and labor into insurance service, just as an oil company has its technology for converting crude oil and other resources into petroleum products. By extending our thinking from strategy to the technology necessary to execute that strategy, we move to *work to be done*. Once we comprehend the work to be done—both managerial and operating work—we are on familiar ground. Most of our management concepts relate directly to getting work done, so preparing a management system to fit a particular task falls within the recognized "state of the art."

The use of technology as an intervening variable produces the arrangement shown in Fig. 29–1. To maintain perspective and to highlight key influences, strategy should focus on only a few basic ideas. Its formulation is by necessity in broad terms. We cannot jump directly from strategy to management design, for we have not yet classified the array of actions necessary to execute the strategy. Thinking of technology helps us to elaborate the implications of the strategy and thereby provides us with the inputs for shaping an effective management system.

Types of Technology

Technology, especially in the broad sense in which we are using the term here, deals with all sorts of situations and methods. For purposes of relating technology to management, however, we can concentrate on only a few characteristics. For instance, the way a technology deals with *change* is very significant for our purpose.

In a company with a given strategy and technology, the need for change will fall somewhere along a continuum of infrequent to frequent. Similarly, the

[1] For an expansion of this concept of technology, see C. Perrow, *Organizational Analysis: A Sociological View* (Belmont, California: Wadsworth Publishing Co., 1970). Other writers have explored the relation between technology and structure, but they have concentrated on the narrower concept of physical conversion of materials. See T. Burns and G. M. Stalker, *The Management of Innovation*, 2nd ed. (London: Tavistock Publications Limited, 1966); J. Woodward, ed., *Industrial Organization: Behavior and Control* (London: Oxford University Press, 1970); A. J. Grimes and S. M. Klein, "The Technological Imperative: The Relative Impact of Task Unit, Model Technology and Hierarchy of Structure," *Academy of Management Journal* (December 1973).

kinds of changes the company typically faces will fall somewhere along another continuum ranging from unprecedented problems to familiar, precedented ones; in the case of the latter, the company will have a well-established pattern for resolving them.

Using these two characteristics of technology, we can set up the matrix shown in Fig. 29–2. Of course, many technologies will fit around the middle of one or both dimensions, but by thinking about technologies toward the ends of the scales, we arrive at three well-known types of businesses.

Enterprises confronted only with familiar problems—and even these not very frequently—are basically *stable*. Paper mills and other firms processing large volumes of raw materials fall into this category. When the need for change moves from infrequent to frequent, and the problems remain precedented, we encounter businesses that display *regulated flexibility*. Job shops—used by management writers since Frederick Taylor to illustrate management concepts—fit this category. But when the need for change is frequent and the

645
CHAPTER 29
Maintaining a
Dynamic
Management
System

Figure 29–2 Viewing businesses in terms of need for, and nature of, change.

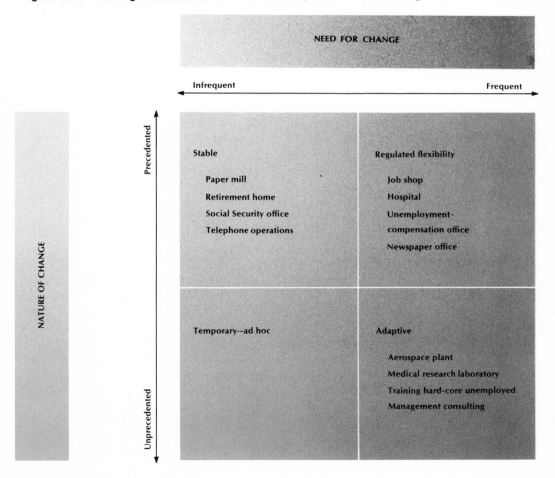

problems are unprecedented, we face a sharply different situation. Here—for instance, in the aerospace industry—technology requires an *adaptive* structure.

As the Figure shows, these three technology types—stable, regulated flexibility, and adaptive—are each found in many lines of endeavor.

In contrast to the first three types, the fourth division in the change matrix does not point to a clear type of technology or management design. Unprecedented problems that arise only infrequently are handled by some temporary arrangement. This *ad hoc* setup does not exist long enough to modify the underlying structure.

From Technology to Management Systems

An intriguing aspect of the first three technology types is that each leads to a well-known management system. The usual relationships between technology and system are presented in Table 29–1. To sharpen the analysis, the four major phases of managing have been subdivided; the features of each phase most likely to be affected by strategy are listed separately in the left column. Then the rest of the table shows, for each of these features, the typical response by a stable technology, a regulated-flexibility technology, and an adaptive technology.

Within each type of technology, the primary features of each system remain substantially the same even though the companies come from different industries. For instance, when the work situation is stable (as it usually is in a paper mill, retirement home, Social-Security office, and telephone exchange), planning tends to be comprehensive and detailed, intermediate goals are sharply defined, decision-making is centralized, and central staff is strong. In addition, we find limited participation and low job commitment. Controls are focused on dependability and efficiency, checks are made frequently, and few mistakes are tolerated. These and other management features indicated in Table 29–1 enable an executive working in a stable situation to convert inputs of various resources into the maximum output of consumer services.

Today regulated flexibility is actually much more common than the stable technology just described. A job shop, hospital, unemployment-compensation office, and newspaper all face a continuing procession of new situations, most of which can be handled by well-developed techniques for resolving such problems. For this kind of technology, the typical management system introduces flexibility by the use of craftsmen and professionals, separate scheduling units, careful programming of workloads, close control of work passing from one stage to the next, prompt information on the status of work at each stage, and so on. The kind of flexibility needed is anticipated, and provisions for dealing with it are built into the system. Each person understands the limits of his discretion, and other conditions are fully planned and controlled so that reliability of the total system is not lost.

Adaptive technology calls for quite a different management system. The research lab, consulting firm, and training project for the hard-core unemployed all face unprecedented problems frequently. Here operating units become smaller, greater reliance is placed on face-to-face contacts, authority is decentralized, planning tends to focus on objectives and broad programs, managers use participation and expect high personal commitment, control checks are less frequent and concern results rather than methods. These and other features listed in Table 29–1 are often called "organic" or sometimes "democratic."

This adaptive type of situation is the dream of many human-relations advocates. It provides ample opportunity for employee participation and self-actualization. However, the fact that only a small portion of all work involves frequent, unprecedented problems explains why a lot of human-relations training has failed to find practical application.

Of course, no company will fit exactly into any one of the technology–management-system types we have described. But the examples do suggest how thoughtful analysis of technology provides a basis for designing a suitable structure.

Related Influences of Strategy on Systems

Although it is fruitful to analyze technology in terms of the frequency and uniqueness of the problems it faces, we should not overlook other influences. For instance, technology will also be affected by complexity and the need for speed. When several interrelated variables affect the work, as in building a communications satellite, more thorough planning and control will be necessary. The need for speedy action usually has an opposite effect. Here the urgency to get prompt action reduces the opportunity for thorough planning and control; quick results now may have a higher value than somewhat improved results that are available a month later.

Uncertainty permeates many activities. Because of an unknown environment or unpredictable responses to our own actions, we are confronted with uncertainty. If time permits we may try to reduce this uncertainty by further tests and experiments; and this will probably add staff to our organization and reduce the permissiveness of the structure. On the other hand, if such attempts are impractical, we may hire people with the best intuitive judgment we can find, get rid of our staff, and decentralize authority to the experts. This latter response to uncertainty, which is favored by the managers of most conglomerates, creates a simple, lean management system.

Management systems, then, must be developed in light of a variety of influences. However, the added dimensions just cited still fit into our basic proposal of moving first from strategy to character of work, then from work to management systems.

647

CHAPTER 29
Maintaining a
Dynamic
Management
System

TABLE 29–1   TYPICAL FEATURES OF MANAGEMENT STRUCTURES
FOR THREE TYPES OF TECHNOLOGY

Primary Features That Distinguish Management Systems [1]	Nature of Technology		
	Stable	Regulated Flexibility	Adaptive
Organizing			
Centralization versus decentralization	Centralized	Mostly centralized	Decentralized
Degree of division of labor	Narrow specialization	Specialized, or crafts	Scope may vary
Size of self-sufficient operating units	Large	Medium	Small, if equipment permits
Mechanisms for coordination	Built-in programmed	Separate planning unit	Face-to-face, within unit
Nature and location of staff	Narrow functions; headquarters	Narrow functions; headquarters and operating unit	Generalists at headquarters; specialists in operating units
Management information system	Heavy upward flow	Flow to headquarters and to operating unit	Flow mostly to, and within, operating unit
Characteristics of key personnel	Strong operators	Functional experts in line and staff	Analytical, adaptive
Planning			
Use of standing plans:			
Comprehensiveness of coverage	Broad coverage	All main areas covered	Mostly "local," self-imposed
Specificity	Detail specified	Detail in interlocking activities	Main points only
Use of single-use plans:			
Comprehensiveness of coverage	Fully planned	Fully planned	Main steps covered
Specificity	Detail specified	Schedules and specs detailed	Adjusted to feedback
Planning horizon	Weekly to quarterly	Weekly to annually	Monthly to three years or more
Intermediate versus final objectives	Intermediate goals sharp	Intermediate goals sharp	Emphasis on objectives
"How" versus results	"How" is specified	Results at each step specified	End results stressed

[1] In any single system only a few of these features will dominate, and others may be insignificant. In addition, for unusual circumstances a feature not listed here may be critical. Nevertheless, careful consideration of the features listed will enable us to comprehend and to deal with the management systems of most enterprises.

649

CHAPTER 29
Maintaining a
Dynamic
Management
System

Primary Features That Distinguish Management Systems	Nature of Technology		
	Stable	Regulated Flexibility	Adaptive
Controlling Performance criteria emphasized	Efficiency, dependability	Quality, punctuality, efficiency	Results, within resource limits
Location of control points	Within process; intermediate stages	Focus on each processing unit	Overall "milestones"
Frequency of checks	Frequent	Frequent	Infrequent
Who initiates corrective action	Often central managers	"Production control" and other staff	Men in operating unit
Stress on reliability versus learning	Reliability stressed	Reliability stressed	Learning stressed
Punitive versus reward motivation	Few mistakes tolerated	Few mistakes tolerated	High reward for success
Activating Resort to coercion	Sometimes	If necessary to maintain system	Rare, undermines congruence
Emphasis on on-the-job satisfactions	Limited scope	Craftsmanship and professionalism encouraged	Opportunity for involvement
Sharing information	Circumspect	Job information shared	Full project information shared
Participation in planning	Very limited	Restricted to own tasks	High participation
Form of bargaining	Often manager-composed compromise	"Horse-trading" on conditions of work	Open confrontation
Commitment	Indifferent compliance, little job commitment	Job commitment, mixed with ambivalence	High congruence and commitment
Permissiveness	Stick to instructions	Variation in own tasks only	High permissiveness, if results o.k.

COMPOUND SYSTEMS
WITHIN A COMPANY

Thus far we have discussed the management system for a whole company. We have assumed that one technology and one system predominates; and for a single-function company this holds true. Most enterprises, however, are more complex. Within the corporate scope, quite different activities may take place. So if we are correct in urging that the management system reflect technology, the concepts should also be applied to the parts of a complex company.

Diverse Technologies of Departments

Consider the Greenfield Company, which has a strategy of performing the complete job of providing new, low-cost housing, from land acquisition to planting shrubbery in the play yard. Separate departments deal with architecture, real estate and finance, component manufacture, and building. The architects are the planners who conceive of types of construction, space utilization, layouts, and specifications that will create good housing at low cost; their work ranges from the highly unique and creative to the painstaking preparation of specifications for actual construction. The real-estate and finance people spend much time negotiating with government agencies and other outsiders; their problems are technical and often unique. In contrast, manufacture of components (standard wall-sections, bathroom and kitchen modules, and the like) is standardized, routinized, and mechanized as much as possible. Actual construction is necessarily "job order" in character, and requires the synchronization of various craftsmen.

In this one company, two of the major departments—architecture and real estate and finance—come close to the adaptive type described in the preceding section. The building department clearly displays regulated flexibility, and the component-manufacturing department is moving as close to the stable type as volume permits.

A university is as heterogeneous as the Greenfield Company. Although the suitability of the same technique for teaching biology, logic, and fine arts is debatable, everyone will agree that the controller's office and the buildings and grounds department are in a different category. Other enterprises may not have as much diversity as the Greenfield Company or a university, but mixed activities are very common.

This diversity has serious implications for management systems. Many executives who have had successful careers in one type of system believe their style of managing should be extended to all parts of the company. We often find that the managerial practices that are well suited to a company's dominant department are automatically applied throughout. Such consistency in managerial methods does have benefits, but the astute manager will at least consider the possibility of using more than one administrative style.

Composite Systems   **651**

CHAPTER 29
Maintaining a
Dynamic
Management
System

Generally, when a department is both large and strategically vital, it should be managed with a system suited to its own activity. In other words, companies embracing diverse technologies should use several different managerial styles. The justification for this mixture of managerial designs lies, of course, in the improved performance of the individual departments.

Such diversity also has its costs:

1) *Cooperation between departments becomes increasingly difficult.* Voluntary cooperation between groups with different values, time orientations, and willingness to take risks is inevitably strained (as we saw in Chapter 9). Divergent management systems add to this "cultural barrier." Because the departments are so different, we may even separate them geographically—remove research labs from the plants, separate mills designed for long production runs from those for short runs, and so on.

    When management systems differ sharply, a special liaison staff or other formal means for coordination is often needed. Having deliberately accentuated the difference between departments, we then add a "diplomatic corps" to serve as a communication link between them.

2) *Companywide services drop in value.* With a composite system, the rotation of key personnel is impeded, budgeting is complicated, training programs fit only parts of the company, capital-allocation procedures must be tailored to different inputs and criteria. In other words, synergy arising from pooled services and the reinforcing features of a management system is lacking for the company as a whole.

3) *The task of central managers is complicated.* Understanding the subtleties of the several management systems, and personally adjusting one's leadership style to each, calls for unusual skill and sophistication. Most managers, often unconsciously, favor departments whose management system they find congenial.

Blended Systems

Because of the drawbacks of a composite system and because dissimilar departments may be too small to support a distinct management structure, we often try to blend two or more systems.

Some types of systems are compatible. For instance, both the stable and the regulated-flexibility systems (used as examples earlier) call for a high degree of central planning, strong staff, limited permissiveness, and control at intermediate points. The chief difference lies in frequent adjustment by the latter to variations in client requirements; nevertheless, these adjustments normally occur within anticipated limits and often follow rules. Consequently, a combined arrangement that accommodates both technologies (for example, the component manufacturer and building construction in the Greenfield Company) can be devised. The blended system is not what each department would do for its own purposes, but the modification can be tolerated.

Another common arrangement is to build one strong structure and then recognize that exception must be made for certain segments. For instance, accounting usually gets special treatment in a research laboratory, just as members of the advertising group are accepted as "oddballs" in a manufacturing firm. If the people in the exceptional spots have enough zeal for their specialty to withstand the normal pressure to conform, the mismatch can function reasonably well.[2]

The fact that many companies need a composite, or blended, management system does not detract from the major theme of this chapter. Coherence in each management system is vital whether the system be simple or complex. The criteria for shaping each system are the size of the company and the character of the work to be managed; the character of the work, in turn, is a function of the company strategy. Diversity of work and the resulting complexity of systems only multiply the components that we must take into account. The combined result, of course, is a completed mosaic of planning instruments, organizational relationships, control mechanisms, and modes of activating.

A final check, after arranging the many parts, involves going back to the master strategy of the enterprise, identifying the key elements to success, and asking whether the management system promises to emphasize these elements. In thinking through the necessary refinements of a system, we are always in danger of losing perspective on the major mission.

CHANGING TO A NEW MANAGEMENT SYSTEM

The introduction of a revised management system involves more than rational choice. The configuration of plans, organization, and control that we have been discussing must be converted into social reality. This is a major, recurring task.

Inevitable Need for Change

Strategy cannot remain fixed. With the swirl of technical, political, social, and economic events, a company's niche is sure to change. We see this clearly in a product's life cycle. When a product is new, the key strategic variables are usually technical and educational. During expansion, market position is crucial; profits can be earned but initial capital investment is high. In maturity, the spotlight shifts to low cost; capital now flows in. Adjustment of strategy to these

---

[2] A variation on making exceptions from the major pattern within the enterprise is to use outsiders for the deviant activity. Thus consultants may be called into a "stable" company to provide creative ideas. Brokerage firms subcontract janitorial and equipment-maintenance work. Dress manufacturers often obtain designs from freelance designers. Although volume of work and flexibility are also factors in such subcontracting, simplification of the management design is a prime benefit.

shifting key variables will typically move a company through all three types of structure that we discussed earlier in this chapter.

653

CHAPTER 29
Maintaining a
Dynamic
Management
System

Success also breeds change. Growth itself leads to system modifications. And as a company's position in the industry improves, its strategy has to be adjusted. Doubling from two to four percent can be achieved with little external reaction, but doubling from fifty to one-hundred percent will precipitate price wars, antitrust suits, and vastly different social responsibilities. Here again the necessary shifts in strategy call for modification in the management system.

Few enterprises offer the identical service over a long period. Success prompts diversification. A decline in demand leads to a search for new opportunities. When the revised strategy pushes the firm into new lines of endeavor, rarely will the old management system be best suited for the new venture. In fact, a very difficult design problem arises when a company is working with several lines in various stages of their development.

Every manager, then, should be prepared to assist in, and adapt himself to, changes in the management system.

What Change in Systems Involves

The process of changing to a new management system is more than an intellectual exercise. Both adjustment of the social structure and modification of personal values are required.

An enterprise is productive as a joint endeavor only when it has its own social structure. To work together effectively, people need to know what to expect of others, what their own role is, where they can get help, who has power, and what sources of information are available—as we have noted especially in Chapters 8 and 15. A revised management system upsets many of these established relationships.

Assume, for example, that you are a branch manager confronted with the following changes:

Bob Brown, whose actions after ten years in the treasurer's spot could be predicted, is now in Los Angeles; a young banker has the title of treasurer, but central budgeting work has been transferred to a new assistant controller. Meanwhile, all scheduling is to be done in regional offices, and data from the computer memory is available to everyone. The general manager has taken "personal charge" of the ailing mobile-home business. Your boss reports that the president has revived his campaign for management-by-results.

You will not know what these changes really mean until you and others have had actual experience with the new relationships, have carefully observed the behavior of new people, and have tested the strength of the central staff. The new social structure—the way of working together—takes time to form.

Individual values and behavior must also change to fit the new system.

When one of the most prestigious New York banks changed its strategy to include active solicitation of small accounts, a host of modifications were made in procedures, branch-office organization, lending authority, and the like. The basic problem, however, was to modify the attitudes of employees toward the blue-collar depositor. Genuine interest in such people had to replace crisp politeness.

Comparable adjustments in attitudes are usually necessary to achieve significant change in activating modes. So difficult are some of these value shifts that a new setup is ineffective until persons compatible with the new way of life are put in key posts. For example, federal programs for aid to local education have been significantly hampered because people administering them could not quickly adjust their personal values regarding local autonomy, desegregation, religious instruction, role of parent groups, importance of professional training, and similar issues.

Time to Absorb the Change

Conversion to a new management system takes time. Social structure and personal beliefs cannot be altered overnight. Managers can assist in the transition, however, by dealing with three psychological factors: learning, anxiety, and confidence (see Fig. 29–3).

Learning new relationships and attitudes—like other learning—is aided by clear explanations, opportunity to try the new way, further questions and explanations, more trials and adjustment, and then practice. If a manager helps everyone involved recognize that this kind of process may be tedious at first but will avoid confusion later, the total transformation will be expedited. But mature and successful people will not always willingly accept the need for learning.

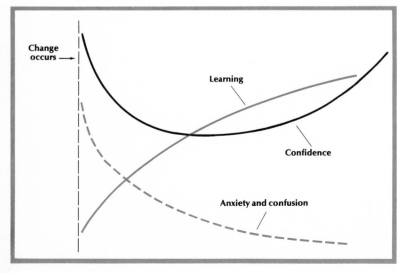

Figure 29–3 Psychological factors involved in a change of systems. Diagram indicates how response to change shifts over time.

655

CHAPTER 29
Maintaining a
Dynamic
Management
System

Any change that alters a person's primary source of satisfaction for his security, social, and self-expression needs is sure to create anxiety. Just the uncertainty about how the new system will affect him personally is unsettling. Such anxiety often causes odd behavior—irritability, resistance, lack of enthusiasm. A manager should do all he can to relieve anxiety during a transition period. Stating facts, explaining future plans, stressing future benefits, having people meet new associates, scotching rumors, showing awareness of a man's personal problems—all help allay anxiety. With rare exceptions, bad news faced promptly is better than extended worry. If answers to specific questions cannot be given, assurance of when and how the information will become available is helpful.[3]

Both learning and relief of anxiety help to rebuild confidence. In addition, a manager can bolster confidence by reinforcing desired behavior. Public recognition and reward to persons who successfully utilize the new design will transfer attention from old ways to the new pattern; and continuing acknowledgment of success will restore a sense of competence that had been placed in doubt when familiar behavior had to be altered.

These personal and social adjustments take time. Experience indicates that major reorganizations require at least a year to digest, even with strenuous efforts to speed the conversion. Because of this required investment in time and energy, we naturally hope that a new system can be used for several years. Like research for a new medicine or tooling-up for a new airplane model, we want a period of stability when we can recoup our investment. Similarly, most people need a spell of stable productivity following a siege of readjustment. Although we anticipate recurring need for change in the management system, the wise manager knows that there are personal and economic tolerance limits to the frequency of change.

CONCLUSION: FROM ANALYSIS TO SYNTHESIS

The study of any complex subject like management must be divided into parts, and each must be examined carefully. We have followed this pattern by devoting separate parts of the book to organizing, planning, controlling, and activating. We considered the nature and importance of each of these processes, discussed the elements of each, covered problems in the field typically confronting a manager, and suggested possible ways of dealing with these problems. This analytical approach is more than a pedagogical device. It can be used directly by managers because they frequently encounter difficulties of the same scope as the subdivisions (chapters) of our discussion.

[3] *Participation* in the formulation of strategy and design of the new structure will speed up learning. On the other hand, participation may extend the period of anxiety, unless the participant sees clearly that he will fare well in any alternative being seriously considered.

Nevertheless, the interdependence of the parts of the book has been frequently stressed. In the first chapter we singled out a manager's role in external and internal integration. The present chapter goes even further. Master strategy, which expresses a firm's attempt to integrate with its environment, has been related to management systems, which express primarily the firm's internal integration. We have focused especially on how a manager can design structures that are internally coherent and also suited to the company's strategy. Thus we have turned from analysis to synthesis.

A manager must be prepared either to redesign his management systems to support new developments, or to regard his existing management system as a limiting factor on growth and in selecting new strategy. Because shifts in the environment occur so rapidly, most managers set their strategy first and then undertake the difficult task of shaping a management system to match it. This kind of synthesis calls for a high order of sophistication and competence.

FOR CLASS DISCUSSION

1) Much of the thrust of this chapter is directed toward maintaining effective management in the face of growth and change. Though this question may sound heretical, why not build a system that resists growth and change, an organization that seeks not to grow and to maintain stability wherever possible?

2) The text emphasizes the importance of recognizing the potential impact of a change in one managerial process (e.g., planning or organizing) on other elements of the process (e.g., leadership or control). Who should be given the responsibility for considering these potential impacts and for seeking a coherent, whole management design?

3) Many corporations are diversifying to the point where the differences in product/market mix within a single firm may be great. Would it be possible for one company to have some divisions that are in the stable category, while others are in the regulated-flexibility and adaptive categories? When would such a situation prove most troublesome to central management?

4) Give an example of how a decision to shift from a centralized functional organization structure to a decentralized profit-center organization would be likely to affect activating modes.

5) Cite one major addition to the control system used to evaluate George Nichols (Chapter 28) that could have led him to pursue *at least* a different strategy for shifting the predicted response of his service engineers and perhaps to choose a different activating mode.

6) To what extent may serious personnel problems arise as a company grows and finds it necessary to shift its strategy from skimming new products and markets to profitably servicing more mature products and markets? How might these problems be dealt with?

7) From the enterprises you encounter in your daily life, pick an example of each of the technology types described in this chapter—stable, regulated flexibility, and adaptive. For each of these examples, check what you know of their management design against Table 29–1. What reasons do you think explain any differences between the features listed there and those in your examples?

657

CHAPTER 29
Maintaining a
Dynamic
Management
System

8) Which of the various courses offered at your university (economics, history, psychology, sociology, anthropology, mathematics, engineering, law, and the like) have the highest potential for providing new ideas which will be useful to future managers? That is, where do you think new, useful ideas are likely to come from? Why?

Cases

For cases involving issues covered in this chapter, see especially the following. Particularly relevant questions are listed after each case.

Milano Enterprises (p. 124), 17, 18
Atlas Chemical Company (p. 321), 18
Graham, Smith, & Bendel, Inc. (p. 445), 21
Monroe Wire and Cable (p. 436), 1
Central Telephone and Electronics (p. 527), 1, 19
Household Products Company (p. 627), 21

FOR FURTHER READING

Greiner, L. E., "Evolution and Revolution as Organizations Grow." *Harvard Business Review,* July 1972.

Discusses the character of management at various stages of company growth, and the need to make sharp changes at transition points.

Heydebrand, W. V., ed., *Comparative Organizations: The Results of Empirical Research.* Englewood Cliffs, N.J.: Prentice-Hall, Inc., 1973.

A collection of 30 empirical studies by organizational sociologists. The array of issues, terms, models, research methodology, and cautious inferences of this recent branch of sociology can be found in this single volume.

Khandwalla, P. N., "Viable and Effective Organizational Designs of Firms." *Academy of Management Journal,* September 1973.

Statistical support for the advantage of a consistent and integrated management design.

Lorsch, J. W. and S. A. Allen, *Managing Diversity and Interdependence.* Boston: Harvard Graduate School of Business Administration, 1973.

Research study of the organization of multidivisional companies. Chapter 9 summarizes broad guides to organizing and controlling companies with varying degrees of diversity in their activities.

Ouchi, W. G. and R. T. Harris, "Structure, Technology and Environment," in G. Strauss, et al., eds., *Organizational Behavior, Research and Issues.* Madison, Wis.: Industrial Relations Research Association, 1974.

Excellent summary of sociological studies of the interaction between organization structure, technology, and environment—written in ordinary English.

Perrow, C., *Organizational Analysis: A Sociological View.* Belmont, Calif.: Wadsworth Publishing Company, 1970.

One of the more readable sociological views of organization structure. Stresses the possibility of modifying organization design, rather than individual behavior, to make an enterprise responsive to external opportunities.

Rumelt, R. P., *Strategy, Structure and Economic Performance in Large American Industrial Corporations.* Boston: Harvard University Press, 1974.

A study of the relationship between diversification strategies and organization designs in over 200 companies, with the unique feature of using profitability to assess the soundness of various combinations of the two variables. Written from a managerial viewpoint.

Index

PICTURE CREDITS